The Young Person's Guide to Wisdom, Power, and Life Success:

Making Smart Choices

Dr. Brian Gahran

San Diego, California

The Young Person's Guide to Wisdom, Power, and Life Success: Making Smart Choices

PAPERBACK ISBN 978-0-9912193-8-4
E-BOOK ISBN 978-0-9912193-7-7
LCCN 2013955843

Cover design by John Susoeff
Artrock77, Los Angeles, California

Pie and author photos by Christopher Gahran
CG&A Photography, Los Angeles, California

Interior design and layout by Robert Goodman
Silvercat™, San Diego, California

Ebook design and coversion by David Wogahn
Sellbox™ San Diego, California

Front cover photography by:
Johnny Grieg/iStock.com
Edyta Pawlowska/123rf.com
Wavebreak Media Ltd/123rf.com

Website (www.YPGBlog.com) by Karl Meimer,
Utterly Creative, Red Rock, Arizona

Printed in the United States of America

Dedication

Thomas A. Crescenzo
Shipmate, colleague, and friend.
You had it right.

Nov, 2019

For Elliot -

Great teachers convey wisdom, build self-esteem, and inspire the imagination. Young persons need not suffer their way to wisdom! Thank you for making a difference.

Keep the faith -

[illegible]

Contents

Disclaimer v
Preface vii
Introduction 9
The Lesson 14

Part 1: Getting the Gist (The Big Picture)

Chapter 1: Who You Are 17
Chapter 2: Defining the Problem 27
Chapter 3: How Your Guide Can Help 33
Chapter 4: The Path to Success 43

Part 2: What's at Stake (An Unpredictable Future)

Chapter 5: The Stakes Are High 61
Chapter 6: Where Risk Comes From 79
Chapter 7: How We Make Mistakes 103

Part 3: Understanding Yourself (The Person in the Glass)

Chapter 8: Confidence Traps 129
Chapter 9: Change Traps 151
Chapter 10: Maturity Traps 179

Part 4: Controllable Decisions (The Hot Breath of Reality)

Chapter 11: Who You Marry 209
Chapter 12: How Many Children 235
Chapter 13: Level of Education 261
Chapter 14: Where You Live 303
Chapter 15: Choice of Lifestyle 331

Part 5: Making Smart Choices (Develop the Power)

Chapter 16: How To Make Better Decisions 367
Chapter 17: Tapping Tribal Elders 395
Chapter 18: Yes You Will! 415

Appendices

A: What Trusted Adults Need to Know 441
B: Generation NeXt Traits 463
C: Decision-Making Tools 465
D: "Wrinkle Wisdom" Cheat Sheets 487
E: Epistemological Underpinnings 507
F: Where to Go For More Info (on-line) 515

Acknowledgements 517
From the Author 519

It's reading that makes us realize we are being lied to.
~ Anna Quindlen, author, journalist

Disclaimer

The *Young Person's Guide to Wisdom, Power, and Life Success: Making Smart Choices* ("*Young Person's Guide*" or "*Guide*") is designed to provide young persons with self-improvement information to help them achieve personal economics success. It is sold or otherwise distributed with the understanding that the publisher and the author are not engaged in rendering legal, financial, psychological, coaching, or other professional services. If expert advice or assistance is required, the services of a competent professional should be sought.

The purpose of the *Young Person's Guide* is to educate and inform. The scope of the book is to complement, amplify, and supplement other sources of information that is otherwise available. It is not a get-rich-quick scheme or a cure-all prescription. As such, the book should only be used as a general guide and not as the ultimate source to achieve personal economics success. Anyone who decides to improve him or her self must expect that there are other factors that might affect one's level of success besides those presented in this book. Readers are cautioned to rely on their own judgment about their individual circumstances and act accordingly.

Every effort has been made to make the *Young Person's Guide* as complete and accurate as possible. Nevertheless, mistakes, both typographical and content, are possible. No representation as to accuracy or fitness for a particular purpose is made for the information contained in this book, nor for any of the references cited. This book contains information and references that may or may not be current as of the printing date.

The author and publisher shall have neither liability nor responsibility to any person or entity with respect to any loss or damage caused, or alleged to have been caused, directly or indirectly, by the information contained in this book. Any perceived slight of specific persons, peoples, or organizations is unintentional. Readers are asked to please contact the author if errors are found so that they can be corrected.

If you do not wish to be bound by the above, you may return this book to the publisher for a full refund.

Preface

Many receive advice, only the wise profit from it.
~ Publilius Syrus, Roman author

On December 26, 2004 a 9.0-magnitude[1] earthquake struck off the coast of Indonesia. Movement of the sea floor created a deadly tsunami that killed more than 157,000 people across southern Asia and 5,300 in Thailand. It was a terrible tragedy—in one day, millions of lives were forever changed.

One tribe, the Moken, lived in villages on islands off the coast of Thailand and Myanmar (Burma). They were situated directly in the path of the tsunami, and although their village was destroyed, the Moken people were saved. How was this? Receiving advanced warning that a tsunami was coming, they sought safety on a hilltop before the first of three huge waves hit the island.

The Moken is a society of fishermen and their lives depend on the sea. For hundreds and perhaps thousands of years, their ancestors studied the ocean and passed their knowledge down from father to son. One thing in particular was carefully taught by Moken elders to the new generations: what to do if the ocean suddenly receded. According to their traditions, when this happens the "Laboon"—a wave that eats people—will arrive soon after.

On that fateful day, tribal elders detected unusual movements in the Bay of Bengal. With a sense of urgency, they warned the villagers to run to high ground. At first, not everyone listened. As one older fisherman related afterwards, "None of the kids believed me. Even my own daughter called me a liar." Still, the elders did not relent until everyone had left the village and climbed to higher ground. The Moken people were fortunate that people of conviction warned them of the Laboon that was to follow. Had they not, they would surely have perished.

Like the old fisherman's clarion call, the *Young Person's Guide* is a warning to you, sons and daughters of the Baby Boom generation. This book is the harbinger not of a physical wave, but a personal economics Laboon—a tsunami in slow motion—that will engulf you if you fail to recognize the signs early. Dither, even for a few years, and you risk a retirement filled with unpleasant circumstances and

1 The Richter scale, named after Charles Richter, was a commonly used measure of the size of earthquakes. In the 1970s, the U.S. Geological Survey shifted to using the Moment Magnitude Scale ("MMS") to estimate intensity magnitudes for all modern large earthquakes (3.5 and up). Even though the formulae are different, the new scale retains the familiar 0–10 continuum defined by the older one. Many in the general public and media continue to erroneously refer to the Richter scale due to their unfamiliarity with the MMS scale.

regret. React while you are young and you dramatically improve the chances that you will be where you want to later in life. The choice is yours.

Ultimately, the *Young Person's Guide* series is about learning how to make smart life-choices, achieve freedom from financial fear, and fulfill your life's dreams. At the end of the day, it is the person looking back in the glass[2] that you have to please. And on that score, do not kid yourself.

> *What message I would give to my own twenty-two-year-old self if I could travel back in time?... I would have to break the bad news: that she knew nothing, really, about anything that mattered. Nothing at all. Not a clue.*
> ~ Anna Quindlen, journalist

2 In the United Kingdom, the archaic term *looking-glass* was considered the "proper" word to use when referring to what we now would call a mirror. Wealthier people would "look in the glass" for personal grooming or to admire themselves. Most Americans encountered this expression in *Through the Looking-Glass, and What Alice Found There* (1871), by English writer and mathematician Charles Lutwidge Dodgson (1832–1898). Better known by his pen name, Lewis Carroll, Dodgson wrote *Through the Looking-Glass* as the sequel to his earlier book, *Alice's Adventures in Wonderland* (1865).

Introduction

The best we can do is to hang out the red flag over the dangerous places; to chart the rocks and shoals, whereon multitudes of vessels, which left the port of youth with flying colors, favoring breezes and every promise of a successful voyage, have been wrecked and lost.

~ Orison Swett Marden, founder, *Success* magazine

The Gist

The Good:

- Centenarians (persons 100 years of age and older) are the fastest-growing segment of our population. One-half of your generation, Generation NeXt, is projected to live to be more than 80 years old. A child born today has a 50-50 chance of living to be 100; many will live to be 120.

You have an excellent chance of being one of them!

The Bad:

- Nearly 70 percent of Generation NeXt workers eligible to participate in a tax-deferred 401(k) retirement plan are not doing so. A large and growing number of young persons will be hard pressed to maintain an adequate standard of living throughout retirement.

You have an excellent chance of being one of them!

The Reality:

- Gen NeXt, you are the first generation where the standard of living is projected to decrease. You and your children will be stuck paying the debt of the Baby Boom generation. It's no fun being old. It's less fun being poor. It is hell being old *and* poor. Your parents and the government will not save you.

You do not want to be one of them!

Success in life is increasingly becoming a performance business. Whether you achieve your aspirations in life, whatever they might be, is not up to your parents, your family, your school, your company, the government, or society as a whole. It depends upon what *you* do. For the vast majority of young persons, success as measured in any terms—financial or non-financial—will be determined by the decisions that you make. And the first rule for making good life decisions is exercising sound judgment and taking responsibility for your own beliefs and behaviors.

Young persons reading this book are smarter and more capable than any previous generation. But your parents' generation has one discriminating advantage over those of you who are in your salad days.[3] That is the perspective of nearly 40 years down the pike. To the extent that they have been scarred by experience, they have wisdom to share with today's youth.

Many Boomers lament that no one explained these lessons to them. High schools assumed that parents talked about these things (they didn't) and colleges assumed these skills were learned at home or in high school (they weren't). The lucky ones got a few basics like "save for a rainy day" and "stay away from that side of the tracks." Many, if not most Boomers learned simply by trial and error. That some survived with their hide intact probably has less to do with their planning prowess and more with being lucky to have avoided any major pitfalls.

Young persons have come of age at a particularly merciless moment. Since your parents' time, the world has become much more competitive and cynical. It's not that previous generations didn't also tend to drift—they did. It's that opportunities today are less forgiving of trifling mistakes. To succeed nowadays, young persons must make smarter choices than did their Boomer parents at the same age.

Jack Palance: *Do you know what the secret of life is? One thing. Just one thing. You stick to that and everything else don't mean shit.*
Bill Crystal: *Yeah, but what's that one thing?*
Jack Palance: *That's what you've got to figure out.*
~ from *City Slickers*, Columbia Pictures

What is the secret of life? The secret is—ahem—there is no secret. There are no quantum revelations, no easy solutions, no top-ten lists to instant success. Las Vegas, Atlantic City, and just about every state lottery flaunt this path, so don't be lured by the siren call to "big bucks." Indeed, the *Young Person's Guide* is not about getting rich, at least not in the traditional sense, and certainly not quickly. The old saw "money does not guarantee happiness" is true. But having insufficient money almost assuredly guarantees a life of want and misery. *You do not want to be one of them.*

Much of what is presented in the *Young Person's Guide* falls under the rubric of common sense. But common sense ain't so common. Guys, there is more to life

3 From Shakespeare's Antony and Cleopatra (1606). Regretting her youthful dalliances with Julius Caesar, Cleopatra laments "My salad days, When I was green in judgment." The phrase has come to mean a period of youthful inexperience, innocence, idealism, or indiscretion.

than finding a fresh lawn to mow. Gals, you would do well to spend more time shaping your future than pining for Mr. Right. This volume looks at some of the critical skills for developing power over an unpredictable future. The secret, if there is one, is making smart life-choices. We'll see how a "gist" way of thinking can improve judgment. We'll examine how bias influences decision-making. We'll learn some methods that can help us make better decisions. And before you interrupt, you are right—this is not an exhaustive list. Many other factors can affect one's personal economic success, such as inheriting wealth.

Ten, fifteen, maybe twenty years from now many among you will find yourself still living paycheck-to-paycheck, not living the life you think you should be living. Sad to say, some of you may need to serve cat food at the dinner table. It's hell to be old and poor. For the rest of you, one day, all of a sudden, you'll realize that you are a little better off than the average Joe or Jane. Some will be significantly so and it's gonna be a great feeling. And for the one in 23 million that hits the lottery and gets their photo on the front page, congratulations in advance. Don't hold your breath though.

Many of you do not face the decisions described in this book at this time. Although it may be five or ten years down the road, it is highly likely that most of you will make them at some point during your life. By reading this *Guide*, and speaking with others in whom you trust, you can make better, more purposeful choices. You will also learn a few things you didn't know, pick up some desirable new habits, and (most important) improve your judgment and decision-making.

This leads us to three fundamental questions:

1. Why does each generation have to "figure it out for themselves?"
2. Is learning learn life's lessons the hard way, the only way?
3. How can young persons make better life-choices?

To answer these questions (and more) let us talk of many things…

Doctor's Prescription (Rx)

It is a pity that, as one gradually gains experience, one loses one's youth.
~ Vincent Van Gogh, painter

At the end of each chapter in the *Young Person's Guide*, the section titled "Doctor's Prescription" offers helpful suggestions for improving yourself. It is marked by the symbol "Rx," which is customarily printed at the top of a medical prescription.[4] Let's try one on for size.

4 The origin of Rx is a subject of debate. The symbol is usually attributed to an abbreviation for the Latin word recipere, which means recipe, and is customarily part of the superscription (heading) of a prescription. Another explanation is that it was derived from the astrological sign for Jupiter, once placed on prescriptions to invoke that god's blessing on the drug to help the patient recover.

Want to pursue a successful life? Your "prescription" is as follows:

1. Find a glass (mirror).
2. Stare at the most beautiful face you will ever see.
3. Say to the person in the glass: "I cut my own slice of the pie."
4. Once a month, repeat steps 1–3.

Who cuts your slice of the pie?
You do!™

Each of us cuts our own slice of the pie in life. Whatever the goals and aspirations we want to fulfill, our ability to reach those goals is largely in our own hands. We are all born with a remarkable potential for achievement, with numerous natural talents and aptitudes. It is up to us to become aware of our innate resources and capabilities, and to fine tune and develop them into practical skills that we can utilize daily to achieve our goals. Individually, each of us cuts our own slice of the pie.

~ Thomas Crescenzo, economist (1987)

The Lesson

I believe the ultimate aim of all human beings is to obtain happiness and a sense of fulfillment. These objectives can be achieved through physical amenities and proper mental development but the dominant and ultimate factor is the mental aspect.

~ Dalai Lama, His Holiness

Indeed, today is already the tomorrow, which was shaped by our decisions of yesterday. As surely as the hen to the egg and the flower to the seed, the long-run consequences of our controllable decisions can be traced back to flaws in our thinking and fallibilities in our beliefs.[5] Thus, the art of personal economic success can be reduced to a single lesson and the lesson can be reduced to a single formula:

To develop power over an unpredictable future, you must understand reality as it exists (not as you want it to be), know your limitations, and form the conscious habit of making smart life-choices.

Reali-tude:™[6]

The present casts its shadow far into the future.

5 Grateful acknowledgement is extended to Henry Hazlitt (1894–1993), economist, journalist, and philosopher. Hazlitt was one of the most influential public intellectuals of the 20th Century. The inspiration for "The Lesson" comes from his *Economics in One Lesson*, perhaps the most popular economics text ever written.

6 Dubbed "reality with an attitude," a Reali-tude™ is a rule of thumb for achieving success. Reali-tudes are not banal platitudes, such as "Think positive!," "Believe and it will come!," or "Just love yourself!" Rather, they are pithy nuggets of wisdom, distilled from real-life experiences and common sense. The author gratefully acknowledges Sheryl Roush, motivational speaker and creator of Sparkle-Tudes®, for the inspiration.

Part 1: Getting the Gist

(The Big Picture)

Chapter 1

Who You Are

I care about our young people, and I wish them great success, because they are our hope for the future, and some day, when my generation retires, they will have to pay us trillions of dollars in Social Security.

~ Dave Barry, Baby Boomer humorist

The Gist

Gen NeXt Demographics:

- Largest consumer group in U.S. history (70 million+)
- Racially and ethnically diverse
- Plugged-in and technologically savvy
- Strikingly family-centric (40–50 percent still live at home)

The Good:

- Optimistic, confident, and full of self-esteem
- Pragmatic, adaptable, and street smart
- Values learning and is big on education
- Socially conscious but dislikes ideology

The Bad:

- Short-term outlook that demands instant gratification
- Limited life experiences often lead to overoptimism
- Two top goals are getting rich and becoming famous
- More skeptical, cynical, and less civil than Baby Boomer parents

The Reality:

- Hard working but really stressed
- Psychologically hardened by the world-wide economic meltdown
- Transition to adulthood is shifting upward to 30 years old
- Women and minorities are still at a comparable disadvantage

Introduction

Parents are the chains around your ankles until you've managed to: (a) run away; (b) obtain a stable job and income; (c) die; (d) turn 18.
~ Amanda, frustrated student

Generations are not defined by formal process. Rather, they are categorized by demographers,[7] the media, popular culture, market researchers, and by members of the generation themselves. Academics formally define a generation to be a "cohort-group whose length approximates the span of a phase of life and whose boundaries are fixed by peer personality." Translated into ordinary English, a generation is basically an age group that shares behaviors and beliefs.

Young adults aged 18 to 30 (give or take) comprise what has been popularly called *Generation* Y, often abbreviated as *Gen* Y. Use of this term has been somewhat controversial—the wedgie is that Generation Y connotes "following Generation X," which was originally coined as a derogatory term. There have been other labels given to this demographic group, and while the range of birth dates varies somewhat, some common ones are:

- Millenials (New Millenials)
- New Adults
- Echo Boomers
- Net Generation
- Boomerang Generation
- Generation Whatever
- Generation.com
- GenMe
- DotNet Generation
- Yeppies

The label "Generation Next" was popularized by Public Broadcasting Service (PBS) in connection with their report of the same name. This descriptor seems to capture the zeitgeist, or cultural spirit of Generation Y, without being condescending. In the *Young Person's Guide* series, we'll use the moniker "NeXt," coined by former Arkansas State University guidance director Mark L. Taylor. We'll refer to the dynamic window of 18 to 30 year olds as "Generation NeXt."

***BRAIN SNACK:** Your parents' generation is called the Baby Boomers. When they were your age, the "establishment" referred to them pejoratively as hippies. Although most young persons looked the part, relatively few actually burned their draft card or high-tailed it to Canada. Slogans that defined the Boomer generation included "Make love, not war," "Put a tiger in your tank," "Never*

7 Demographers study demographics. Demographics are characteristics and/or statistics of a human population, such as size, growth, distribution, birth, marriage, death, etc.

trust anyone over thirty," "Question authority," "Power to the people," and "Give peace a chance." Looking in the rear-view mirror, the irony is the degree to which Boomers now resemble their parents, not just in their waist size and hairline, but in their attitudes as well. During the drug-fueled, anti-establishment 60s, who would've figured that?

In their 2010 study *Millennials: A Portrait of Generation Next*, the Pew Research Center defined the various generations thus:

- *Millennials:* Born after 1980, the first generation to come of age in the new millennium.
- *Generation X:* Born from 1965 through 1980, this name replaced the original "Baby Bust" label.
- *Baby Boomers:* Beginning with the great spike in fertility following World War II (1946), and ending almost as abruptly in 1964 around the time the birth control pill went on the market.
- *Silent Generation:* Born from 1928 through 1945, they were children of the Great Depression and World War II. Their "Silent" label refers to their conformist and civic instincts.
- *Greatest Generation:* Born before 1928, they fought and won World War II.

The Demographics

> *Whooo are you? Who who, who who? Who are you? Who who, who who? I really wanna know.*
>
> ~ The Who, British rock group

If there is something to be observed, you can be sure that somewhere, someone has an interest in studying it. This is how we make sense of our world. Social scientists study the human aspects of who we are and how we relate. For those who examine generational differences, the rule of thumb used to be that 20 years represents a generation. In more recent years, however, this thinking has changed. Many scientists reason that as the pace of change in society accelerates, the time frame that constitutes a generation is getting shorter.

The broadest definition of Generation NeXt is those born between 1977 (some say 1980) and 1994 (some say 1998), a group that represents over 20 percent of today's population. For our purposes, we'll simply bracket Gen NeXt at ages 16 and 30. There are a lot of you out there and your generation is making a huge social and economic impact.

Who are you? Who who, who who? Well, making regnant generalizations about a group is a slippery prospect at best, especially when we are trying to describe one as diverse as Gen NeXt. But if we remember that there is great variation within any group, and if we do not rigidly hold the descriptions as universal stereotypes, we can make some generalizations to help us better understand your generation. Researchers offer the following observations of NeXters as a group:

Size of the herd

- At 75 million, you are the largest consumer group in U.S. history.
- The children of Baby Boomers, Gen NeXt is three times larger than Gen X.
- Your generation is more numerous, more affluent, better educated, and more ethnically diverse.

Herd characteristics

- *Multiculturalism.* Working and interacting with people outside of your own ethnic group is the acceptable norm. One out of three of you is not Caucasian.
- *Working mothers.* One in four of you reside in a single-parent household, and three of four have working mothers. You were raised in a pro-child culture.
- *Connected and tech savvy.* E-mail, cell phone, instant messaging, and the Internet are the principal vehicles for person-to-person communication. Group chats are the first choice as the source for many kinds of information. For NeXters, it's all about customization and self-expression.

Character-shaping events

- *Terrorism:* Virginia Tech, Columbine, September 11th, World Trade Center, Oklahoma City, Olympics bombings, and the invasion of Iraq;
- *Disasters:* Global warming, natural disasters, and AIDS;
- *Culture:* MTV and talk shows, "It Takes A Village," Girls' movement, and the 2000 elections;
- *People:* Princess Diana, Monica Lewinsky, Sammy Sousa, Barrack Obama, and O. J. Simpson;
- *Finance:* Unprecedented bull market followed by an economic meltdown.

Herd values

- Optimistic about the future;
- Close collaboration and bonding with friends;
- Socially communitarian and tolerant of diversity;
- Honesty, caring, and realism garner respect;
- Family, country, and planet are valued over income and status.

There are lots of people interested in knowing the demographics about Generation NeXt, and many (if not most) want to sell you something. *Young person's alert:* researchers perform sophisticated studies in an attempt to get inside your head (nature abhors a vacuum...LOL). They want to learn what makes you tick and these days they are amazingly good at it. Once they figure you out, clever marketers will use these characteristics to make educated predictions about your preferences and behavior.[8]

8 Ivan Pavlov (1849–1936) was a Russian physician who developed the "conditioned reflex." After ringing a bell, Pavlov gave Rover a treat. The dog soon learned to associate the sound of the bell with the

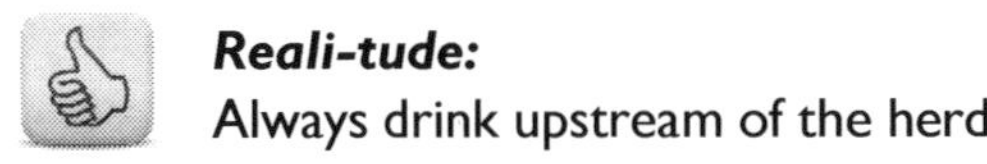

Reali-tude:
Always drink upstream of the herd.

The Good

Just the facts ma'am.
~ Sgt Joe Friday, Detective Sergeant *(Dragnet)*

There is much that is good about Generation NeXt. In 2000, Neil Howe and William Strauss published a book titled *Millennials Rising,* followed in 2003 by *Millennials Go to College.* According to these authors, the Millennials could emerge as the next great generation, harkening back to the "Greatest" generation that won WWII. Strauss and Howe show how today's teens are recasting the image of youth from downbeat and alienated to upbeat and engaged. They reveal that NeXters are held to higher standards than Baby Boomers apply to themselves, and argue that over the next decade you will entirely recast what it means to be young.

> *So many young people (myself included) are trying so hard to prove themselves in spite of unprecedented amounts of cynicism and elders who insist that "today's youth are always the worst"—what we really need is for the general public to realize our potential and help us to cultivate it. I wish all young people today would...feel encouraged that they have the power to make a positive difference in the world.*
> ~ Mandela G. (Seattle, born 1986)

Gen NeXt has experienced a profound cultural change in the structure of the family. In the 1960s, 75 percent of families looked like those on *Leave It to Beaver* and *Father Knows Best*—a working father, a stay-at-home mom, and at least one child. By 1997, only three in a hundred families fit that picture. This is the greatest change in the family structure since the Industrial Revolution, when fathers left the farm to work in industry. Despite the effects of the migration of mothers into the workforce, along with high divorce rates, day-care, and latchkey children, NeXters exhibit some admirable behaviors:

- Adaptive to changing environments, you are not afraid to ask questions;
- Technologically savvy, you are the most plugged-in generation;
- Parallel thinkers and efficient multi-taskers;
- Confident, competitive, and street smart;
- Upbeat, determined, full of self esteem;
- Ambitious and hard working;
- Learning oriented and big on education;
- Anti-ideological, socially conscious, and civic minded.

---

food. Later, at the mere sound of the bell, he began to drool even when no treat was given. Marketers intensely analyze your buying behavior to figure out what makes you drool. Then they sell it to you. Woof!

For many of you, growing up was strikingly family-centric. Parents were hands-on and very involved in your daily lives and decisions. They helped you plan your achievements, took part in your activities, and showed strong beliefs in your worth. The Boomerang generation—young adults who have returned to live with parents—became a prevalent social phenomenon. And research reveals that NeXters continue to be close to their parents:

- More than three-quarters of students chose colleges in their home states.
- 86 percent closely trust their parents (90 percent of teens report being *very* close).
- 73 percent see their parents at least once a week; half see them *daily*.
- 40 percent still live with their parents and expect to retain close bonds after leaving home.[9]
- Most are likely to consult with parents on major decisions, such as co-purchases and work.

When asked to name heroes, NeXters tend to point to people with whom they have personal relationships rather than famous persons (for Boomers, it was the opposite). Parents are seen as role models and are often cited as their heroes. When asked to describe their parents' generation, NeXters used words like "hard-working," "conservative" and "hippie." One reason cited why NeXters often cling to each other is that for many of them, parents and role models are in short supply.

BRAIN SNACK: *Attitudes toward parents were not always so favorable. In 1974, parents were seen as obstacles on the path to true enlightenment. At that time, more than 40 percent of Boomers said they'd be better off without their parents. Once out of high school, many Baby Boomers jettisoned their parents, refused to thank them for their sacrifices, and never looked back. Today, the emerging adult who resides at home is subtly accepted and often encouraged by their Boomer parents. Some parents may view this as an opportunity to re-visit earlier issues and "get it right."*

Reali-tude:
Remember those who care about you. There are very few of them.

The bottom line:

- Generation NeXt is the largest U.S. consumer group ever.
- Gen NeXt is the smartest generation yet.
- The world-view of NeXters was shaped more by events than by parents.
- NeXters are close to their parents and value their advice on major decisions.

9 Adult sons (age 25–29) are about 2.5 times more likely to live with their parents than are adult daughters.

The Bad

True terror is to wake up one morning and discover that your high school class is running the country.
~ Kurt Vonnegut, author, humanist

Generation NeXt is the predictable product of our consumer-driven society. But not everyone sees this as a good thing. One expert on the behavior of young people in the workplace put it this way: NeXters "have been pampered, nurtured and programmed with a slew of activities since they were toddlers, meaning they are both high-performance and high-maintenance." In his article, "Misreading Millennials," Julian Sanchez, editor of *Reason Magazine,* refers to Millennials as "the most doted upon, fussed over, and scheduled generation in living memory." Not surprisingly, researchers have identified a number of less than desirable characteristics of NeXters. Some of the more prominent include:

- Impatient, also called the *microwave generation* ("I want it hot, fast, and now");
- Skeptical, fed up with superficiality, and quick to spot flaws;
- Blunt and expressive, they favor self-expression over self-control;
- Image-driven and making personal statements is important;
- With limited life experiences, many exhibit the *Peter Pan syndrome;*[10]
- Overly optimistic, the top two goals are getting rich and becoming famous;[11]
- Strong sense of entitlement ("We deserve the best and want to start at the top").

Cell phone surgically implanted into their hand. Over ten blogs currently active, over a thousand message boards bookmarked. E-everything: a completely digitized existence. Has never spent more than 3 hours in a natural or wilderness state without experiencing E-withdrawal. More materialistic than their parents, as if that was possible, and overly-prescription medicated since age three. The mutated creatures that Ritalin, soccer practice, and endless gated-community pampering have produced. The generation of whose entire collective behavior will eventually be posted on YouTube for the world to see. Narcissism isn't even an adequate word to hurl at them: they just shrug it off with a "WTF LOL" and continue browsing through their Ipod catalog looking for that dance remix.
~ Garbageman, "the other side of California"

Appendix B offers an insightful, and perhaps somewhat controversial, list of Generation NeXt traits as compiled by social scientists. Check it out!

---

10 The Peter Pan syndrome describes the behavior of an immature person who seeks a "Neverland" as a way to delay becoming an adult and avoid impending responsibilities. Many graduate students, for example, do not have a strong desire to learn. Rather, they want to postpone life in the "real world" for as long as possible.

11 These dreams apparently diminish with age. Only about 14 percent of adults between the ages of 30 and 49 place a high premium on being wealthy. By the time adults reach their 50s, just one in ten place a similarly high priority on riches.

The Reality[12]

The majority (of Generation NeXt) will settle down, buy houses, get steady jobs, get married, and have children just as their parents did.
~ Kate Fox, Director, Social Issues Research Centre

Crapaganda from the media and popular press will have us believe that all Gen NeXters are caught in the grip of what has been termed a "quarter-life crisis." Such prognostications for personal Armageddon are somewhat dubious. Many older persons who interact with young persons daily do not see the frenetic look of impending doom on their faces that others seem to perceive.

Nevertheless, most 18- to 25-year olds do not consider themselves to be adults. Parents attest that many in this generation are having difficulty negotiating, or perhaps more precisely "completing," the transition to adulthood. It is common to see up to a decade of extended emerging adulthood, what political columnist David Brooks calls "odyssey." Odyssey is a period of individual volition when young persons explore different lifestyles, change residence, and experiment with intimate relationships, types of work, and worldviews. As a result of this delay, the trend is toward thirty, rather than the traditional 18 or 21, as the new "official" age for transition to adulthood.

Some researchers see Gen NeXt as an engaged "civic generation" with a deep commitment to community and helping others. Political scientists Morley Winograd and Michael D. Hais, co-authors of *Millennial Makeover: MySpace, YouTube, and the Future of American Politics*, refute the idea that today's young persons are narcissistic, self-indulgent, and apathetic. Others have a different view, however. Education consultant Mark L. Taylor closely studies Gen NeXt students and finds them having increasingly high—in some cases unrealistic—expectations of a comfortable lifestyle. Taylor sees little evidence they are conventional conformists that are "respectful of social norms and institutions, extremely focused on grades and performance, busy with and eager for extracurricular activities and community projects, interested in math and science, and demanding of a secure and regulated environment."

So, are you saints or schnorrers?[13]

It depends. Drawing on eight years of data and more than 500 interviews with young people between 18 and 34, sociologist Richard Settersten and author Barbara Ray counter the myth that this generation is cynical and self-indulgent. They find that many NeXters have not been coddled into laziness; rather, they are working their butt off 20, sometimes 30 hours a week at a job, plus attending classes. Why the widespread belief that you are all slackers? In their book *Not Quite Adults*, Settersen and Ray attribute it to a growing divide between the

12 A takeoff on *The Good, The Bad and The Ugly*, a 1966 movie directed by Sergio Leone Early that starred Clint Eastwood early in his career. The cast featured Clint Eastwood ("The Good"), Lee Van Cleef ("The Bad"), and Eli Wallach ("The Ugly"). Shot in Italy, the film was one of a series of "spaghetti westerns" that helped propel Eastwood to stardom.

13 Sly chiseller, a sponger.

haves and the have-nots, what they call "swimmers" and "treaders." Swimmers often have supportive parents, university degrees, and wider social networks. But most twenty-somethings, they say, are treaders "who simply replicate the lessons of their poorer, less stable, non-voting, and hands-off parents, but to worse effect."

BRAIN SNACK: *If you are a young woman, progress toward pay parity continues to be painfully slow despite women's enormous gains. According to economist Linda Babcock, women are socialized from an early age to accept what they get. "We really teach our girls to be very passive and we teach our boys to go out there and be aggressive," she says. This feeling of diffidence in young women today can keep them from fulfilling their potential. Minorities still get a poke in the eye as well. Despite the perception of progress, gaps in college-going and college completion for minority students are actually wider than they were thirty years ago. "Today, our country not only has less economic mobility[14] (see p. 28) than we did 20 years ago, but we have less than in most other developed countries" says Kati Haycock of The Educational Trust.*

In the final analysis, lacking a singular, defining challenge that demands near universal participation, it is doubtful that NeXters will be called to make the level of personal sacrifice as did the Greatest Generation in WWII. Except for those who are serving in the military and their families, the Iraq and Afghanistan conflicts do not even come close. Nevertheless, it is likely that your generation will in time become more practical, more accommodating, less ideological, and more centrist. You will have a chance to make your mark on history. And horror of horrors, one day you might even end up like your parents. Worse things could happen...

Reali-tude:
You are not entitled to anything.

The bottom line:

- NeXters are often naïve—what you don't know you don't know can hurt you.
- Fear and anxiety about the unknown can lead to isolation and inaction.
- Virtually none of you will become rich and famous.
- Limited life-experiences can skew your thinking, usually in an adverse way.

14 Economic mobility is the degree to which your economic success is independent of the economic success of your parents. A higher level of economic mobility is often interpreted as a sign of greater equality of opportunity in a society. Researchers have found that the effect of high (or low) incomes in one generation lasts for at least two more.

Doctor's Prescription (Rx)

If you can't face it, moon it.
~ Ashley H., student, 16 years old

1. *Who the heck is Gen NeXt?* Pew Research Center for the People & the Press is a well-respected, independent, non-partisan public opinion research organization that studies attitudes toward politics, the press, and public policy issues. A new generation has come of age, shaped by an unprecedented revolution in technology and dramatic events both at home and abroad. Their report *A Portrait of "Generation Next": How Young People View Their Lives, Futures and Politics* takes stock of this new generation and explores their outlook, lifestyle, and politics. Four adult generations, Gen NeXt, Gen X, Baby Boom, and Seniors are compared. Download a copy at: http://people-press.org/report/300/a-portrait-of-generation-next.

2. *I'm OK. Are you OK?* In his book, *Grown Up Digital: How the Net Generation is Changing Your World*, strategist Don Tapscott drew upon a $4.5 million research study of over 11,000 young people. Outlining the demographics of what he calls the "Net Generation," he examines how they are changing the world and its intuitions. The problem, he suspects, is not young persons but befuddled Baby Boomers. Tapscott says parents need to discuss the dark side of the Internet with young persons through honest conversation. Read about the study at: http://www.grownupdigital.com.

3. *Watergate? Is that where Monica Lewinsky lived?* Students entering college in 2008 have lived their whole lives in a digital world, where GPS has always been available, phones have always had caller ID, and tax returns could always be filed on-line. For incoming freshmen in 2010, phones never had cords, the computers they played with as kids are now in museums, and few have ever worn a wristwatch. The Class of 2016 has never lived in a world where Kurt Cobain was alive and is accustomed to seeing women in positions of leadership. These are some of the cultural landmarks on the *Beloit College Mindset List,* an annual compilation that offers a glimpse of the world as seen through the eyes of each incoming class. While entertaining, this disconnect has implications for how Boomers relate to Gen NeXt. Check out their latest at: http://www.beloit.edu/mindset.

4. *Where to go for info?* See Appendix F for additional information relating to this chapter.

Chapter 2

Defining the Problem

The dawn of the 21st century may be considered both the best of times and the worst of times for youth, a time of ominous trends as well as new opportunities.

~ Jeylan T. Mortimer and Reed W. Larson, from *The Changing Adolescent Experience*

The Gist

The Good:

- There is no guarantee in life, but you can definitely improve the odds
- Recognizing the seriousness of the problem is half the battle

The Bad:

- Income and wealth gaps are creating a two-class system
- American men in their 30s are worse off than their father's generation
- Gen NeXt is projected to have a lower standard of living than its parents

The Reality:

- Welcome to the middle-class treadmill
- Life has become a performance business
- The problem (and the solution) lies within you
- Some of you are clueless. No one will save you.

Introduction

We work our jobs, collect our pay. Believe we're gliding down the highway, when in fact we're slip sliding away.
~ Paul Simon, from *Slip Slidin' Away*

The rich and powerful in this country have access to resources and opportunities that regular folks do not. Despite what they say, few of those in control genuinely look out for the everyday Jane and Joe. This is especially true for those too new on the scene to have any effective stake in the system beyond what their consumer dollars will purchase. That would be young adults like you.

America has always been the land of opportunity, and as a group we have always tended to be optimistic about our ability to control our own economic destinies through hard work. We are also less likely to believe that coming from a wealthy family is important to getting ahead. A noble thought were it correct, but it is not. Most studies find that about half of the advantages of having a parent with a high income are passed on to the next generation.[15] Thus, one of the biggest predictors of your future economic success—the identity and characteristics of your parent—is predetermined and outside of your control. What this means is if you don't have a silver spoon in your mouth, you are starting a few steps down the economic ladder from those that do. In this case, you need to auto-debit your ability to move up the ladder.

If you had not already noticed, things are not copasetic for Generation NeXt. Your generation is projected to be the first in the history of this country to have a standard of living below that enjoyed by its parents. And like the Moken people, many of you do not have a clue that you are at serious risk. Worse still, the negative consequences may not only be palpable, but probable. First generation. Ever. Something to think about dude.

Reali-tude:
Heed warnings by tribal elders.

The Good

Don't offer me advice; give me money.
~ Spanish proverb

15 Research finds that at least 45 percent of parent's advantage in income is passed along to their children, and perhaps as much as 60 percent.

Warren Buffett is an outstanding American. Mr. Buffett has built one of America's most respected and successful companies and is one of the world's wealthiest persons. Under his stewardship, Berkshire Hathaway averaged a 25 percent annual return for its shareholders for over 25 years. In 2008, its Class A stock price reached a cool $140,000 per share. Magnanimously, Buffett is transferring the lion's share of his net worth, some $30 billion, to the Gates Foundation. This foundation, administered by Bill and Melinda Gates, is dedicated to bringing innovation in health and education to the global community.

TV's Charlie Rose (formerly of PBS) interviewed Warren Buffett in early 2007 as one of his conversations with important and influential persons. When asked whether the yawning national trade deficit was a forecast of doom for this country, Buffett shared this with viewers:

> *We will not shake the habit of consuming more than we produce. The forecast is for transferring what (the country) owns elsewhere. Your children and grandchildren will be spending some of their time at work to service the debt that you have incurred. It means you will live less well than you would otherwise. We have used up our savings account to consume and are now using our credit card. Our economy will do well over time. I guarantee that your child and grandchild will live better than you.*
>
> ~ Warren Buffett, CEO & Chairman, Berkshire Hathaway

Reflect on Mr. Buffett's statement. Our country is addicted to debt, which will crimp our long-term affluence. Despite this, he remains confident that your children will live better than you and your parents did (to be fair, it remains unclear what the exact definition of "live better" is). Optimists say the U.S. may be on the threshold of a period of remarkable progress, what they call the "New North American Decades." Everything's chim, or soon will be. Or, as George Tenet put it, "It's a slam dunk."[16] How cool is that?

The Bad

> *Today, there are three kinds of people: the haves, the have-nots, and the have-not-paid-for-what-they-haves.*
>
> ~ *Earl Wilson, columnist*

Robert Reich served in three national administrations, most recently as the 22nd Secretary of Labor. He is Professor of Public Policy at the University of California and a recipient of the Vaclev Havel Foundation Prize for pioneering work in economic and social thought. Reich, who writes and lectures extensively on the widening gap in income and wealth between the rich and the poor, says that wages and benefits, adjusted for inflation, have gone nowhere over the past 25 years. Commenting in his blog about his article, "An Introduction to Economic Populism," he writes:

16 George Tenet was Director of Central Intelligence in the G.W. Bush administration.

Inequality is far more worrisome now. The incomes of the bottom 90 percent of Americans have increased about 2 percent in real terms since (a decade ago), while that of the top 1 percent has increased over fifty percent. An expanding economy that benefits only those at the top, while the rest struggle just to stay even, is not a healthy economy. Nor does it promote a just and democratic society.

~ Robert Reich, former U.S. Secretary of Labor

Reflect on Dr. Reich's statement. According to Reich, half of U.S. households own some shares of stock, usually through their IRAs or 401(k)'s, but the vast majority own less than $5,000 worth. Their equity is in their homes, but home values have slumped. The reason the post-Boomer generation is less educated than the Boomers is their families can't afford the cost of college. "Jane and Joe Ordinary American are caught in the squeeze," exhorts Reich. Not cool at all.

There you have it: two heavyweights with two very different perspectives. One is optimistic that a rising tide will lift all butts. The other is upbeat only for those at the top of the income ladder and pessimistic for the rest of us. They can't both be right.

Reali-tude:
Watch your back—no one else will.

The Reality

LA is a great big freeway, put a hundred down and buy a car. In a week maybe two they'll make you a star. Weeks turn into years, how quick they pass. And all those stars, that never were, are parking cars and pumping gas.

~ Dionne Warwick, singer

Credit for breaking the tie went to President George W. Bush. The day after his 2007 *State of the Union* address, Mr. Bush delivered his *State of the Economy* address at Federal Hall in New York. Federal Hall is located in the middle of Wall Street, the capital of capitalism. Mr. Bush acknowledged, "The fact is that income inequality is real. It has been rising for more than 25 years." This observation, while astute, was hardly timely. That income inequality has been widening for nearly three decades in America has not been lost on even the most comatose economist. But the proverbial cat was now "officially" out of the bag.

Amidst the flurry of coverage of the 2008 financial system meltdown, politicians can no longer pretend the problem does not exist. Of course, getting a straight answer from any politician is always a challenge. The truth is the impending Baby Boomer retirement will require major changes in government policy. The most obvious changes, and politically the most difficult, are to increase taxes and/or reduce expenditures, things no politician up for re-election wants to do. A third, more insidious alternative is inflating the currency to reduce the public debt.[17] In reality, the problem is so staggeringly large that a combination of all three is likely. For those at or near the top of the income ladder, inflation will save your bacon. For the ninety-some-odd percent of regular working stiffs, BOHICA—Bend Over, Here It Comes Again. They get the pork, you get the stick. Capisce?

We are feeling distraught that we may never get ahead, but will always be pedaling just to keep up.
~ Vermont couple, mid-30s, college educated, with two young children

Even before the financial crisis, there was a tangible and growing sense of pessimism among the public. Many Americans were increasingly worried whether they would be able to maintain the standard of living they were currently enjoying. Following the meltdown, this feeling has gotten much worse. In increasing numbers, Baby Boomers are coming to realize that they cannot retire in the foreseeable future. They will need to work until they die. For them, this is sobering news indeed.

***BRAIN SNACK:** According to a study by Pew Charitable Trusts, American men in their 30s today are worse off than their fathers' generation, a reversal from just a decade ago. The study suggests that since 2000, the typical American family's income has lagged far behind productivity growth, a departure from most of the post-World War II period. Between 2000 and 2005, productivity rose 16 percent while median income fell 2 percent. This challenges the notion that a rising tide will lift all boats.*

NeXters, welcome to the middle class treadmill—it's time for you to wake up, smell the javelina, and start pedaling. Your biggest challenge is your own questionable beliefs and risky behaviors. You need to begin asking questions *now*, while you are young. Remain ignorant about your situation, or stupidly refuse to do anything about it, and your hiney will be grilled to perfection. Palliative bromides[18] by namby-pamby politicians and profit-minded CEOs will ring hollow when the time comes for you to retire. *Young person's alert:* when it's your time for Botox, it will be too late for you to recover. So, what is a young person to do? Here is your roadmap to success:

1. Develop awareness of yourself and your limitations.
2. Learn the gist of how the real world works.
3. Improve your judgment and make smarter choices.
4. Change your attitudes and behaviors for the better.
5. Be proactive, take responsibility, and stop making excuses.

---

17 Inflation means each dollar has lower purchasing power. Thus, it will take more "dough" tomorrow to buy the same bread today.

18 A bromide is a saying that lacks significance.

Reali-tude:
Wake up and smell the hot breath of reality.

The bottom line:

- Your standard of living is projected to be less than that of your parents.
- Look in the glass: YOU are the problem (and the solution).
- You must take responsibility for your future success.
- Heed the warnings of others—no one will save you.

Chapter 3

How Your Guide Can Help

There is nothing new in the world except the history you do not know.
~ Harry S. Truman, 33rd U.S. President

The Gist

The Good:

- *Economics:* the choice of allocating limited resources to unlimited wants
- *Personal behavioral economics:* how we think influences our economic behavior
- Develop the habit of thinking strategically about your controllable decisions
- To succeed, understand reality as it exists, know yourself, and choose wisely

The Bad:

- The world view of Gen NeXt is more detached and materialistic
- Many of your expectations will ultimately prove unrealistic
- Complex problems are not solved using simplistic solutions
- You must value learning through education, not entertainment

The Reality:

- Gists communicate the essential meaning of your environment
- Wisdom from trusted adults helps compensate for your lack of experience
- Fear is a powerful motivator
- Do something really different—THINK!

Introduction

Whatever you do, make sure to have things your way.
~ Burger King commercial

You can't always get what you want.
~ Mick Jagger, the Rolling Stones

Welcome to *Final Jeopardy*! You are competing against two other brainiacs for the grand prize. Spotlights are hot, palms are sweaty, ticker is clocking. The category is "Most Boring School Subject" and you decide to wager it all. For guts, gold, and glory Alex Tribeck says, "The answer is . . . the dismal science." ♫Doo-doo, doo-doo, doo-doo, doo . . . ♫ Bzzzt! Sorry pork rind. The correct question is not "What is all of them?" It is "What is economics?" Maybe you should have kept awake in class. You can keep the marker pen as a souvenir though.

In school, economics was one of those topics that nobody cared about, let alone tried to understand (civics always seemed condemned to a similar fate). As an elective, economics was often an orphan that was largely ignored, rarely enjoyed, and almost instantly forgotten. Like CIA operatives, no one really knows what economists do for a living, but the government seems to keep an awful lot of 'em busy.

The word itself—economics—conjures up synonyms such as dreary, desolate, and distressing. This is an unfortunate consequence of the 19th century historian Thomas Carlyle, who first described economics as the dismal science.[19] Economics is commonly defined as a social science that studies how people participate in society. At its most basic, it is about decision-making and the study of choice—how individuals and society divvy up limited resources in an effort to satisfy everyone's unlimited wants.[20] Whether the problem involves foreign aid, Halloween candy, or a mother bird feeding her brood, not everyone gets all they want.

In this respect, you can see that economics is really not about money; it is about the choices related to the use of money. In our personal lives, nearly every moment of every day we are faced with choices, many of which demand little thought or effort. Nevertheless, each choice is the act of making up our mind and each decision we make involves costs. And these tradeoffs do not necessarily involve money.

BRAIN SNACK: ***Some aspects of economics are amusing. When American companies expanded globally, there was considerable hubris about retaining the***

19 Carlyle did not base his "dismal" description of economics (political economy as it was then known) on the inherent pessimism of its practitioners. Rather, it was his reaction to economist John Stuart Mill's support of the emancipation of slaves.

20 The "economy" is an aggregate of the choices all of us make as individuals.

names of domestic brands. In China, the name "Coca-Cola" was first rendered as "Ke-kou-ke-la." After thousands of signs had been printed, the company discovered that this phrase meant (depending upon dialect), "Bite the wax tadpole" or "Female horse stuffed with wax." KFC got fried when its signature phrase "Finger-lickin' good" translated into Chinese as "Eat your fingers off." And when General Motors introduced the Chevy Nova in South America, it was apparently unconcerned that "No va" in Spanish means "Won't go." Once the company figured out why it wasn't selling any cars, GM renamed the car "Caribe" in its Spanish markets. Aye-yi-yi!

In the *Young Person's Guide* we are not concerned with the success of GM, KFC, or the government. We are interested in your success, so our focus is on personal economics. Since many people, adults as well as young persons, tend to confuse "personal economics" with "personal finance," it is useful to distinguish between them.

Personal finance. Sometimes called financial management, personal finance is the application of the principles of finance to the money decisions of an individual or a family. Personal finance is primarily concerned with the mechanics of managing your personal wealth; it addresses the ways in which you obtain, budget, save, and spend your monetary resources over time, taking into account various financial risks and future life events. (Btw, the second volume of this series, *Freedom from Fear*, looks at this.)

Personal economics. Junior Achievement, an organization that inspires young people to value free enterprise to improve the quality of their lives, defines personal economics as that part of economics that focuses on "personal skills and interests, career options, and personal and family financial management." Rooted in the discipline of behavioral economics, *personal behavioral economics* more broadly examines how you think influences decision-making and personal economics behavior.[21] In other words, it encompasses the whole enchilada.

As with any of life's endeavors, successful personal economics involves more than simply having "champagne wishes and caviar dreams." It is not sufficient to just talk the talk—you must be aware of your limitations, expand your knowledge, and apply what you learn in a practical manner to your own life. Luck can sometimes be a factor, but relying solely on serendipity to realize your dreams almost always disappoints. The overall goal of the *Young Person's Guide* is to stimulate you to THINK and then DECIDE. Thinking is your first line of defense!

It's even more disheartening when Stanford grads, even some economics majors, can define sunk cost without a second thought, but can't apply it to their everyday lives

21 Behavioral economics is an emerging discipline that represents the confluence, or joining of psychology and economics.

(it shows up more often than you'd expect). What's the point of learning anything if one can't use that information? Or, viewed differently, has one learned anything if one can't use it?

~ Flip Tomato, "soon to be Ph.D. in physics"

The Good

The illiterate of the future will not be the person who cannot read. It will be the person who does not know how to learn.

~ Alvin Toffler, futurist

The good news is the *Young Person's Guide* is written specifically with young persons (and caring others) in mind. Weird math, boring tables, supply and demand curves, and the like are verboten. Research findings are principally focused on the United States and are explained in language that ordinary humans can comprehend. Dollops of common sense are provided so you can learn before you burn. Your *Guide* is not a run-of-the-mill self-help book ("I got rich and you can too"), drive-by Internet post ("Ten tips to lose 15 pounds"), or treacly talk-show bombast ("Stand by for the shocking news, right after the break"). Like the Mississippi River—a mile wide and a foot deep—we cover just enough depth to get your feet wet and stimulate your thinking!

"Why should I care?" you snicker snarkily.

Hmmm...do you also wear a pyramid hat to sharpen your thoughts? Don't be a blivit. Turn off your cell phone, iWhatever, DVD player, TV, or computer and get a clue (for a generation that was fed Ritalin like M&Ms, we realize this is not easy). This is why you need to care: the retirement system for regular folks is principally underwritten by (1) the government, (2) corporate America, and (3) the person looking back at you in the glass. Now, soberly ask yourself whether you trust Uncle Sam and big business to take care of you when you are your parents' age. If you are breathing and conscious, the answer in a New York second had better be "Fuhgedaboudit!!"

Your *Guide* will also help you develop an appreciation for taking the long-view. Yes, the same "ounce of prevention is worth a pound of cure" crapola you heard from your nagging parents—the decisions you make today can haunt you down the road. Why? Years ago, if you got a speeding ticket you simply skipped the court appearance and didn't drive through that town again. Today the world is interconnected and it is increasingly difficult to dodge accountability. Past transgressions, like footprints in concrete, are not easily erased and have a nasty habit of resurfacing at an inopportune time. Just ask a politician!

Still not convinced? Consider this metaphor Consuela. When it comes to car repairs, many people wait until something breaks and then they fix it. This is called corrective maintenance. It is a reactive response that is usually inconvenient and expensive. In contrast, smart cookies practice preventive maintenance.

A proactive response helps you avoid failures before they occur. The same is true with your health, your wealth, and your happiness.

As we shall learn, life works the same way. Leading the wave (being proactive) instead of paddling to catch up to it (being reactive) not only improves control and reduces the risk of costly surprises, it also increases your peace of mind. In short, it's all about taking responsibility to better manage your life. So get with the program—it's so easy a caveman can do it. You can too! Here are the overall objectives of the *Young Person's Guide*:

1. *Think strategically.* Seemingly minor decisions today can hijack your lifestyle tomorrow.
2. *Increase self-awareness.* How you think may lead to questionable beliefs and risky behaviors.
3. *Understand reality.* Identify the facts you have and those you should have, and then get the gist.
4. *Improve judgment.* Absent experience, learn from the mistakes of others.
5. *Make smarter choices.* Acquire wisdom and improve your life.

As a bonus, along the way you will expand your mind and learn some things you didn't know.

Reali-tude:
The best place to find a helping hand is at the end of your arm.

The bottom line:

- Economics is the choice of allocating limited resources to unlimited wants.
- Personal behavioral economics looks at how our thinking influences our economic behavior.
- Preventing a problem is usually much less painful than fixing it.
- Develop the habit of thinking long-term versus short-term.

The Bad

It's hard to do it because you gotta look people in the eye and tell 'em they're irresponsible and lazy. And who's gonna wanna do that?
~ Bill O'Reilly, TV journalist, teacher

By and large, the message here is an uphill battle. Let's not fool ourselves folks. It is being preached to an audience of young adults that are distracted, disinterested, and near tone deaf (metaphorically speaking). To understand why, we invoke a concept that psychologists call *world view*.[22] Our world view describes the overall perspective

22 Sometimes referred to as one's "mental model of reality." For example, a person raised in the Bronx views how the world operates quite differently than someone raised in Osaka; Boomers see

from which we see and interpret the world, and it helps us to define our beliefs and motivations. Researchers determine a generational world view by interviewing people and drawing inferences from the comments they receive. What they tell us about Generation NeXt is your world view is more detached and materialistic than that of your parents' generation. To get the gist, consider some typical NeXter responses:

- "What, me worry? I live for the moment."
- "The system is rigged against us so beating the system is good."
- "Dude, what's in it for me?"
- "Spending is empowering and bling is my thing."
- "I am bored—somebody entertain me!"
- "We deserve to be wealthy and I want to start at the top."
- "Debt is a necessary inconvenience to support my lifestyle."
- "If my savings are not adequate, things will eventually work out."

Of course, these generalizations may or may not accurately describe you as an individual. To be fair, most young persons are mentally acute, fair-minded, and open to learning. But some of you are mental mendicants.[23] Fawned over by doting parents, you strut like western gun slingers, vain gloriously cocksure, and lacking the attention span of a dragonfly. One day you'll discover that your Pollyannaish expectations regarding your degree of control in the real world were completely unrealistic.

> *Although Madonna may have you believing differently, time is going by far too quickly. the pace has picked up and it's not as if it's entirely apparent in the actions themselves, but more so in the peripheral details. more specifically, my increasingly dirty home and my general inability to do anything useful with myself. well, I need advice. who can help me with this? I'm losing my shizz* people (* inclusive of, but not limited to: mind, brain power, hott wordage, mojo, Mojo JoJo, egg salad sandwich.)*
>
> ~ Lividia, Internet blogger

Earth to NeXters: most of you want your information hot, fast, and unvarnished. If it isn't pithy and entertaining, it doesn't get past your firewall, right? But brevity comes at a cost. Simple solutions do not solve thorny problems. Hit a pothole and it is only a distraction. Trigger a *lifebomb*[24] and your future may change for keeps. This is the hard way to learn.

***BRAIN SNACK:** William Ross Ashby was an early pioneer of the science of cybernetics. Cybernetics studies the behavior of complex systems, such as computers, the weather, and human behavior. In 1956, Ashby developed what is now*

---

things differently than NeXters; Republicans vs. Democrats, etc.

23 One who habitually begs for a living, such as Congressional lobbyists.

24 A lifebomb is an undesirable life-choice outcome. Some outcomes, such as a pregnancy, are soon obvious. Others may remain undiscovered (or ignored) until your goose is fully cooked. Misuse of credit, for example, can stealthily undermine your financial security over time.

called Ashby's Law of Requisite Variety. *In a nutshell, the law states that to be successful, the complexity of your response must match the complexity of the problem you are trying to solve (and no more). This is why having a high school diploma does not qualify you to do brain surgery.*

Ashby's concept was applied to human thinking by Nobel laureate (Economics, 1978) Herbert Simon. Simon developed his theory of bounded rationality, which said that humans cannot handle problems when they exceed a certain level of complexity. Once this level is passed, people can no longer understand what is going on or respond in a meaningful manner. What happens then? They wig out and crash.

How does this apply to you? *Controllable decisions* represent complex decision situations that can, and often do, have significant and unintended consequences. This volume looks at five controllable decisions most all young persons will make: who you marry, how many children you have, your level of education, where you live, and your choice of lifestyle. We'll refer to these as life-choices. These kinds of judgments should not be made in the whim of the moment. The problem is not whether you can handle complex judgments—you can. It is choosing not to exert the necessary mental energy until you are forced to do so.

> *So what exactly are we supposed to do about all this? Train yourself to get suspicious every time you see simplicity. Any claim that the root of a problem is simple should be treated the same as a claim that the root of a problem is Bigfoot. Simplicity and Bigfoot are found in the real world with about the same frequency. Problems cannot be solved with clever slogans and oversimplified step-by-step programs (so) DON'T LET ANYBODY simplify it for you. Anyone who tries to paint a picture of the world in basic comic book colors is most likely trying to use you as a pawn.*
>
> ~ David Wong, author, "Inside the Monkeysphere"

Young person's alert: predators lurk outside of the parental bubble and your innocence is their power. Don't let this realization come too late for you. Still looking for a simple solution? Play tic-tac-toe.

Reali-tude:
God forgives, but capitalism does not.

The Reality

> *If you want a guarantee, buy a toaster.*
>
> ~ Clint Eastwood, actor, director

Once they begin making life-choices on their own, many young persons express regret that they have insufficient knowledge and wisdom. On the other hand, they pay little attention to useful information that is not directly relevant to them at the time they receive it. Of course, this is very frustrating to their parents. When experience is limited, understanding the quintessential meaning, or "gist" of a particular situation, even without knowing the details, can help them make smarter choices.[25] As we'll discover in the *Guide*, gist thinking is a valuable element of wisdom.

Navigate the *Guide* according to your own personal style. Remember, self-help books are like car repair manuals—you can read them all day, but doing so doesn't fix a thing unless you put them to use. If you are receptive to learning, read everything. If not, at least read the chapter gists and maybe something will stick. Parents and trusted adults, read Appendix A, "What Trusted Adults Need to Know." Of necessity, much relevant content has to be overlooked or marginalized since the territory is simply too vast and too varied to include more than the most salient landmarks. And when all is said and done, some advice has to be taken on faith rather than on guarantee. Otherwise, we'd all be selling toasters.

The degree

Wizard of Oz: *They have one thing you haven't got: a diploma. Therefore, by virtue of the authority vested in me by the Universitartus Committiartum E Pluribus Unum, I hereby confer upon you the honorary degree of Th.D.*
Scarecrow: *Th.D?*
Wizard of Oz: *That's...Doctor of Thinkology.*[26]

To those who are reading this *Guide*, you are to be commended for your good judgment. Upon completion, you will earn your Th.D. The book is luculent so try to read it several times; discuss aspects with parents, other trusted adults, and friends. Learn to be engaged within as well as without. You will find that what you lack in experience, you can largely compensate for with wisdom. And when opportunities appear, you will find yourself to be a better thinker and much better prepared to succeed.

Regrettably, some of you will continue to learn only through direct personal experience. Keep in mind that the world today is much less forgiving of failure than it was for your parents and it exacts a heavy price for the unprepared. As one unemployed executive lamented, "I don't mind working hard. But it is starting from ground zero, again and again, that gets old."

25 The Germans have a bodacious word for this capability: *fingerspitzengefühl*. Pronounced finger-spits-zen-ga-fuel, this mega-mouthful means to feel something with your fingertips. It describes having a sure instinct or an intuitive understanding about something. Cool beans!

26 After receiving his diploma, Scarecrow impressed his friends by reciting the Pythagorean Theorem. Unfortunately, the formula he stated was incorrect!

That's all folks. The whole kit and caboodle.[27] You will learn much here, but only if you want to learn. And for you popinjays who know-it-all, use the *Guide* to line your bird cage. For the rest, good reading, good thinking, and good luck.

Reali-tude:
Your mind, like a parachute, works best when it is open.

The bottom line:

- Many of your expectations will ultimately prove unrealistic.
- You cannot solve complex problems using simplistic solutions.
- Fear is a powerful motivator.
- Do something different today: THINK!

27 A kit is a set of objects (as in a toolkit), that a soldier would put in his kit-bag. A caboodle is an archaic term meaning group or collection, usually of people. The phrase, whole kit and caboodle has come to mean the "whole ball of wax," or "the whole lot."

Chapter 4

The Path to Success

The purpose of words is to convey ideas. When the idea is grasped the words are forgotten. Where can I find a man who has forgotten the words? He is the one I would like to talk to.

~ Chuang Tzu, Chinese philosopher (4th century B.C.E.)

The Gist

The Good:

- Time is your single greatest advantage—act now!
- Develop prudence and wisdom by learning from the experiences of others

The Bad:

- The passage of time speeds up as you age beyond 17
- Affluenza is a dysfunctional and unhealthy relationship with money
- Narcissism ("It's all about me") is increasingly prevalent

The Reality:

- *Personal economic servitude:* Gain control and become independent
- *Personal economic stability:* Make smart choices and avoid the lifebombs
- *Personal economic security:* Spend less than you earn and manage the difference
- *Personal economic success:* Know what's important and achieve your dreams

Introduction

But time, keeps flowing like a river (on and on), to the sea, to the sea, till it's gone forever, gone forever, gone forevermore.
~ from *Time*, the Alan Parsons Project

At the gut level, most of us agree that time flies. By the end of high school, many young persons sense that every year of life seems to go by faster than the year before. Others may not think about it until it spawns a mid-life crisis or when they return to their old house or school years later. Like Alice in Wonderland, they find them self asking, "Gee, did I really spend a part of my life here? Where did the time go? Were these rooms really this small?" Ask anyone with gray hair and you'll discover that this progression is near universal:

1. In grade school, we measured time in hours or days. Time flowed like frozen molasses. Riding in the car for more than 20 minutes was torture ("Are we there yet?"). Waiting for Halloween, our birthday, or Christmas was nearly unbearable. Summer days went on and on, and each afternoon we whined to our parents about not having enough to do.
2. In high school, we measured time in weeks or months. An afternoon was usually enough time to get things done. The slowest clocks were found in history or economics class and it seemed that we would never get out of "prison." Eventually we tossed our hat in the air and stampeded for the exit. Although many did not realize it then, this was a halcyon time of life.
3. In college, we measured time by the number of semesters under our belt. In the afternoon, we hung out with friends and weekends were for new experiences. The lucky ones had a summer job that paid for wheels or travel. After the first two years we were a little anxious about what we wanted to do after graduation, but not really too worried about it.
4. By our 30s, we measured time in years. Time seemed to pass quickly because we were mentally juggling activities such as work, shopping, cleaning up, having dinner, raising kids, seeing friends, etc. Most afternoons were a blur. After dinner, when we looked back at the first activity of the day, it seems like ages ago.
5. By our 40s and 50s, we measured time in decades. With each passing year, the days and weeks seemed to zip by even more quickly. Is March almost over? Didn't they play the Super Bowl just last week? Wow, the annual insurance premium is due again?

Researcher's findings have generally supported the widespread perception that the passage of time speeds up with age. Ever wonder why? Well, maybe the answer depends on the type of time you are referring to.

Biological time

Ask the young. They know everything.
~ Joseph Jobber, French moralist

Studies of human time perception show that age-related changes in the nervous system alter one's sense of time. Biopsychologists[28] have suspected that the brain contains a special clock to track time intervals that are critical for learning and survival. The key to how this clock works—or fails to work—is *dopamine*, a neurotransmitter produced in the brain (a neurotransmitter is a chemical that carries messages between different nerve cells or between nerve cells and muscles). Drugs can affect our perception of time; for example, cocaine and methamphetamine increase the amount of dopamine and speed up the brain's interval clock. Conversely, marijuana reduces the amount of dopamine and slows the clock down. When a person's life is in danger, dopamine floods the brain and time seems to stand still or move incredibly slow.[29]

In a study by psychologist Peter Mangan, people in different age groups were asked to estimate when three minutes had passed by silently counting one-one-thousand, two-one-thousand, three-one-thousand, and so on. People in their early 20s were accurate within three seconds, and some got it exactly right. People in their 60s estimated that three minutes were up after 3 minutes and 40 seconds had passed. Middle-aged subjects fell in between but, like the older people, all underestimated the passage of time. Researchers hypothesize this may be due to the gradual fall in dopamine levels that begins when people are in their 20s and declines through old age.

Studies have found other factors that influence our perception of time such as working memory loads, time of day, and body temperature. Changes in time perception have also been linked to changes in one's metabolic rate, or the rate at which we use energy at complete rest. According to microbiologist Ramish Zaidi, "When general human metabolism is fast, as in the case of a child, time runs slow. When metabolic rate is relatively slow, as in the case of an adult, time runs relatively faster" (neglecting other factors). The inescapable conclusion: time passes faster in proportion to the expansion rate of the waistline!

---

28 Biopsychology is a branch of psychology that analyzes how the brain and neurotransmitters influence our behaviors, thoughts, and feelings.

29 This phenomenon is called time-dilation. Neuroscientist David Eagleman researched why our perception of time seems to crawl during life-threatening situations. Dropping 23 people 150 feet into a net, every person overestimated the fall time at nearly 4 seconds rather than the actual time of 2.6 seconds. His findings suggest that their brains did not actually perceive time at a slower rate; they just remembered it that way.

Psychological time

Anyone who thinks psychological time is the same as clock time has forgotten childhood; has never convalesced in a hospital; has never flown economy across the Pacific; and certainly has never been hopelessly in love.
~ C. Burrows, senior research fellow

Psychologists tell us that psychological factors influence our perception of the passage of time. Our experience of time is flexible; it depends on attention, motivation, our emotions, and mood. Ever notice how time flies when we are busy with an interesting career, a tour of Europe, or an active social life? Then again, who has not watched the clock drag while waiting for commercials to end or for Windows® to load? Could something other than transient psychological factors be affecting our time perception?

Retired engineer James Kenney thinks so and coined the term *psychochronometry* to mean the psychology of time estimation. According to Kenney's *Logtime* ("logarithmic time") hypothesis, we think about the years of our lives in terms of decades: our teens, twenties, thirties, etc. But there is a problem. While this implicitly assumes that all years are equally long, it does not square with our perceptions as we age. By our middle years, most of us are aware that the years that formerly crawled are now racing by. Why do we now seem so rushed by life? Where are all the things we wanted to accomplish but never seemed to find the time for?

Kenney suggests this is a real scientific phenomenon. It is not just that we've got more to do than we used to, but that our *perception of time* is actually accelerating exponentially. Imagine that you are a six year-old. Relatively speaking, what fraction of your lifetime does one year account for? If we assume awareness at age two, one year out of the remaining four represents 25 percent, or one quarter of your cognitive life. If you are now 27, one year amounts to only four percent of your life. At 40, you perceive one year the way a 6 year-old perceives 5 weeks. For an estimated life expectancy of 80 years, Logtime shows your effective life is half over at age ten, and three quarters over at age thirty. The age at which one year really seems to last one year occurs at 17.2 years says Kenney. This should be a sobering thought for anyone over 17.

Chronological time

Put your hand on a hot stove for a minute, and it seems like an hour. Sit with a pretty girl for an hour, and it seems like a minute. THAT'S relativity.
~ Albert Einstein, physicist

Chronological time is simply clock time. As long as our watches are in good working order, time is the same for everybody. Or is it? In his landmark paper, "Special Theory of Relativity," published in 1905, physicist Albert Einstein (1879–1955) changed the way we view time, matter, and the universe.

According to Einstein, there are two basic ideas of relativity. First, light travels at a constant speed, regardless of the motion of the light emitter or the observer. This is an experimentally proven fact.[30] Second, the laws of physics are the same regardless of the point of view, or "reference frame," from which you observe them.[31] To understand this concept, suppose that you are floating in outer space—in a space suit of course—and another astronaut, a pretty girl, is drifting toward you. Are you moving toward her or is she moving toward you? The answer is yes to both questions! Einstein said it is impossible to say absolutely that her reference frame is "moving" while yours is "standing still," or vice versa. All we can say is that the two frames are in relative motion. Hence all things are relative, including your cousins.

One of Einstein's greatest insights was realizing that time, like motion, is relative. It speeds up or slows down depending on how fast one thing is moving relative to something else. Imagine that you and that pretty girl are moving very, very fast relative to each other (say, 90 percent of the speed of light, or about 167,000 miles per second). Each of you perceives the clock of the other to be running slower than your own. Thus, while you are old and decrepit, she remains young and virile (and looking for a younger boyfriend).[32]

Reali-tude:
In our youth, time seems endless (from 17 on, it's all downhill).

The Good

This time for sure.
~ Bullwinkle Moose

"Tiiiiime, is on your side," croons Mick Jagger, and this gives nubile NeXters some big advantages over balding Boomers. For example, you don't need to inject a poisonous neurotoxin into your face to plump away wrinkles. You are not intimidated by the "*National Geographic*" look of bangles, studs, and plugs poking out of various body parts. Here are some other advantages to being young that you may not have thought about:

- *Fewer resources.* You are unlikely to have much in the way of income or assets so managing finances are a snap. With no dog in the fight, do you really care about all the barking on Wall Street?
- *You are healthy.* Health care is very expensive so many young persons simply opt out, pay the fine, and save the bucks.

30 The speed of light, usually labeled as "c," is nature's speed limit. Light travels approximately 3,000,000 meters (186,000 miles) each second through a vacuum.

31 Physics is the scientific study of matter, energy, force, and motion and the way they relate to each other.

32 Hold the phone Philo—it gets even weirder. As you approach this speed you become about 40 percent shorter in the direction you are traveling and about twice as massive. Although you do not notice anything different about your age and physique, the pretty girl does!

- *Fewer responsibilities.* Not being forced to make difficult financial choices because you have children, a mortgage, sick parents, or a business to run gives you a lot of freedom that isn't available to adults.
- *You can do it.* You can accomplish things that older people won't even attempt. When others say "It can't be done!" you have that power to say, "Yes, it can!"
- *Hiring preference.* Retaining older employees is principally a cost issue. Most of the time this works in your favor, not theirs (unless experience is important).

Being young does not always tilt the board in your favor though. In a weak economy, reverse age discrimination becomes more common, and younger workers find themselves competing with older hires for work. The reason many Baby Boomers sphincter their positions is they failed to adequately plan for retirement and now must continue working to survive. There is a perception by some gray hairs that yours is a generation of slack butts and job hoppers can leave you at a further disadvantage.

> *Because you're young... you have the vitality, you have energy, you have commitment. What happens is, because you're younger, all these older people, who are 20 years older than you are, look at you as some kind of a freak, a miracle. "Ah! A young one! Gee, a young one! They're gonna take over from us! A young one!" And, so, their response to you being energetic is they become energetic. They crawl out of their coffin and say, "What!? You want me to be energetic again? Here I was resting comfortably, with all my prejudices and opinions.*
>
> ~ Lyndon LaRouche, political activist

But the most important economic advantage for NeXters is something you rarely think about. You have one enormous resource at your disposal and yet most young people severely underappreciate it. This resource is time (chronological time, of course). To really succeed, you must become acutely aware of how important it is to make good use of this fantastic resource while you are young. Why, you ask?

- *You'll enjoy your life longer.* If you build a good career for yourself at 25, you will enjoy fifty years of prosperity. Someone who does so at 60 will only get 15 years worth.
- *You'll develop breadth of experience.* Explore yourself and find out what it is that you really like to do.
- *Most quality investments take time.* When they eventually pay off, you are likely to have the opportunities to fully enjoy them.
- *You can fail and start over.* If you lose everything at 20, it's usually not that hard to rebuild. Losing everything at 50 can be devastating, both financially and emotionally.

Reali-tude:
Waste your time, waste your life.

The Bad

The first thing that came into my mind when I signed the grill contract for $137.5 million was, I'm going to make my sisters millionaires. After all these years, they're finally going to be millionaires. And they did become millionaires—with the same old troubles as everybody else.

~ George Foreman, former heavyweight champion of the world

In your effort to achieve personal economic success, you need to be aware of two prickly values that can work against you: affluenza and narcissism. The term *affluenza* is often used by critics of consumerism. This portmanteau word[33], coined by psychotherapist Jessie H. O'Neill, is a contraction of the words "affluence" and "influenza." Although exact definitions vary, a good one is the following:

Affluenza, n. 1. A painful, contagious, socially transmitted condition of waste and indebtedness resulting from efforts to keep up with the Joneses. 2. An epidemic of stress, overwork, and anxiety, caused by the dogged pursuit of more.

Simply put, affluenza is a dysfunctional or unhealthy relationship with money.[34] We tend to want more, and more, and still more. Across all socio-economic levels, people buy into the overriding notion within our culture that money solves all problems. Symptoms of affluenza identified by O'Neill include:

- Low self-esteem;
- Preoccupation with externals;
- Rampant materialism and consumerism;
- Psychological dysfunctions frequently passed from parent to child.

Don't think this applies to you? Think again, Thurgood. Asked about the life goals of those in their age group, most NeXters say their generation's top goals are fortune and fame. Roughly eight-in-ten say people in your generation think getting rich is either the most important, or second most important, goal in their lives. About half of you say becoming famous is valued highly by fellow NeXters. Okay fine, here's some food for thought: since all of you plan to be world renowned, highly paid, and livin' large, who will be left to actually DO the work?

BRAIN SNACK: ***The pay of America's top CEOs has skyrocketed into the stratosphere, according to findings by Associated Press. In 2006, half made more than $8.3 million a year. Of the 386 companies on the AP list, only six reported their CEOs made less than $1 million. The lowest paid was Costco Wholesale Corporation's CEO James Sinegal at $411,000, but shed no tears for him. He***

33 A word formed by merging the sounds and meanings of two different words, such as chortle from "chuckle" and "snort."

34 Affluenza also applies to organizations and was a principle psychological driver behind the 2008 financial system meltdown.

also owned 2.4 million Costco shares, worth about $1.3 billion, with options to buy 1.2 million more shares. In comparison, for Joe Six-pack the first minimum wage increase in 10 years took effect in July 2007, going to $5.85 an hour, up from $5.15. In July, 2009 the base pay for millions of workers was increased to $7.25 an hour. "When adjusted for inflation, the minimum wage is at a 52-year low," says social policy researcher Liana Fox of the Economic Policy Institute.

The assumption that lucre buys happiness is the myth of the new American Dream. In truth, there is more to personal economic success than simply the bottom line. Unfortunately, this does not stop some from continually succumbing to "What's in it for me?" Take a minute to look in the glass and ask yourself whether you secretly harbor affluenza tendencies. Remember: it is not money, but the *love of money*, that is the root of all evil.[35]

The second prickly value is the accelerant that fuels affluenza—*narcissism* (no, this does not refer to DEA agents). Narcissists believe "It's all about me." For them, the world exists for the benefit of numero uno; el supremo; big cheese; numba one; top dawg; big kahuna; top banana; da cat's meow, and all that schlock. "Narcissism is a sense of entitlement," observes counseling director Daniel Jones. "People suffering from narcissism feel they should not have to wait in line at the movies. They feel they should not have to struggle or work their way up the ladder. They feel superior and self-absorbed. There is iTunes, MySpace, YouTube. Everything is I, me, you. The more friends you have, the more status you have" he adds.

Growth of narcissism among young adults has been extensively studied. Psychologists Jean Twenge and W. Keith Campbell examined the responses of more than 16,400 college students nationwide who, between 1982 and 2006, completed an evaluation called the *Narcissistic Personality Inventory* (NPI). The evaluation asked for responses to statements such as "I think I am a special person," and "I can live my life any way I want to." By 2006, two-thirds of the students had above-average scores, 30 percent more than in 1982. In a follow-on study, Twenge found a majority say social networking makes them more narcissistic and they believe their generation is the most narcissistic of all.

Narcissism has some real downsides. According to Twenge's findings, narcissists are more likely to have romantic relationships that are short-lived and lack emotional warmth. Twenge also found that narcissists tend to lack empathy, react aggressively to criticism, and favor self-promotion over helping others. In the work place, people with strong narcissistic tendencies at the lower levels are disruptive to the productivity and the morale of the organization as a whole. Regrettably, America has become a less polite society overall than it once was. At one time, if your phone rang in error, you received a contrite "Sorry, wrong number." Nowadays, all you get is 'Click!' *Young person's alert*: You may think you are the key to the future of mankind, but narcissism is not cool to those who control the money. And don't forget, she probably has caller ID. Click!

---

35 The Bible (1 Timothy 6:10).

I'm not sure which was worse—the university graduate blowing bubbles during the graduation ceremony or bored youngsters asking their parents when they could go home since most of the audience paid little attention to the speeches anyway. That is total disregard for those who prepared and planned the program, to say nothing of being downright rude. Shame on them! Where is our respect for others?
~ Yvonne A., college professor

Reali-tude:
Pigs get fed, hogs get slaughtered.

The bottom line:

- There are significant economic advantages to being young.
- Time is a young person's greatest advantage.
- Wisdom is the exercise of good judgment and prudence.
- Affluenza and narcissism are unhealthy, "me centered" values.

The Reality

What's more important than wealth per se is financial independence. One can be rich and not be financially independent. One can be relatively poor and still be financially independent.
~ Logan Feys, founder, *Individualist Voice*

Today, young persons face difficult challenges. Regardless of your background, it's almost guaranteed that most of you will have little money at this point in your life. Sure, rich kids get good allowances but these often come with all sorts of strings attached. Compounding matters, emotional harassment is more commonly aimed at the young and statistically young persons are much more likely to be victims of violence than adults. Whew—it is tough being young!

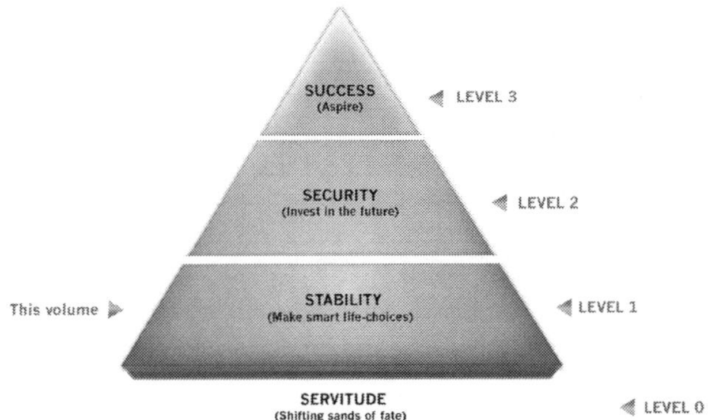

Figure 4.1 Path to personal economic success.

By and large, your redemption will come from the consistent application of sound principles over time. Figure 4.1 shows the model for achieving personal economics success. Basically, it is four fundamental challenges: be self-sufficient, make smart choices, invest in your future, and realize your dreams. Each level builds on the success of those below it. Practiced over a lifetime, the pursuit of personal economic success can be rewarding both monetarily and spiritually.

Level 0: Personal Economic Servitude

Personal economic servitude is the bottom rung of the personal economic ladder and is not where you want to be. At this level, you are not self-sufficient and are unable to meet your basic financial obligations. Put less politely, you are broke. These persons have little to no financial freedom and find themselves dependent upon friends, relatives, or some sort of government program in order to meet their basic needs. Many students find themselves in this condition as the price for entering adulthood and getting out of the house. They reluctantly accept the parental tether because they have few real responsibilities and little earning potential.

Widows (and less commonly widowers) may also find themselves on shaky financial footing due to the death or divorce of a spouse. A particularly egregious example is the military wife who, due to the demands of the service, willingly sacrifices her own career pursuits in support of her husband's. If they later divorce, the woman often finds herself destitute with few sellable skills. Until Congress enacted the *Uniformed Services Former Spouses' Protection Act* (1982), the courts denied her any portion of her ex-husband's retirement. Although the act permits, it does not require state courts to divide a former service member's military retirement upon divorce, legal separation, or annulment.

Personal economic servitude also haunts those who rely on government welfare. Not infrequently, they find themselves psychologically as well as financially dependent, and the negative effects on young persons can be profoundly tragic. Studies have connected welfare dependency to significant reductions in a child's IQ score, and negative effects on the earnings and employment capacity of young men. In these situations, the primary concern is survival and it is very difficult to break this demeaning cycle.

In modern society, money is synonymous with power. Not being self-sufficient means that you have no real control over your life—you are subject to the fickle and often humiliating sands of fate. With the possible exception of the hapless student, it is hard to imagine that this is a condition someone would willingly choose. Fundamentally this is a societal problem that is beyond the scope of the *Young Person's Guide* series to resolve.

Level 1: Personal Economic Stability

Personal economic stability means you are able to meet your near-term obligations without having to depend on regular contributions from friends, relatives, or the government. But paying your bills is not enough. Despite being self-sufficient, many people, young and old, find themselves struggling to get ahead. For them, life is a constant paycheck-to-paycheck treadmill. While short-term, day-to-day basic needs are met, one shift in the status quo, such as loss of a job, death of the breadwinner, or a long-term illness, can result in desperate measures like personal bankruptcy.

BRAIN SNACK: *Harris Interactive, known widely for The Harris Poll, is the 12th largest and fastest-growing market research firm in the world. According to their study conducted for CareerBuilder.com (2012), four in ten U.S. workers are living paycheck to paycheck. And this is not limited to the bottom of the income scale. Of more than 3,800 employees polled nationwide, twelve percent of employees who were earning upwards of $100,000 said they still lived paycheck to paycheck. The survey found that more than a quarter do not save anything each month and women were more likely than men to live on a tight budget.*

To be sure, none of us can predict unexpected catastrophes. But we can take measures to avoid creating our own. Achieving personal economic stability is about making smart choices and avoiding the lifebombs—these are controllable life-decisions that have bad outcomes. Young persons are particularly prone to triggering a lifebomb because they are full of energy, lack experience, and are impatient. While this gives them tremendous drive, it can lead to questionable beliefs and risky behaviors.

The real tragedy is so many young people mentally operate in cruise control, sacrificing long-term goals in pursuit of short-term gains. We'll look at this, along with other errors in our thinking, and try to put a finger on some of the consequences. Many different ways of life are fulfilling and can bring you great happiness if you learn how to make good decisions. Over the long-haul, freedom comes from making smart life-choices, and is the subject of the first volume in the *Young Person's Guide* series.

Level 2: Personal Economic Security

Personal economic security means you are saving and investing for the future while keeping pace with day-to-day basic needs. When you are young, it is important to learn how to assess risk and manage money. Building financial assets allows you to achieve goals that require a lot of money, such as buying a car or real estate, paying for a college education, starting a small business, and providing for a steady stream of income in retirement. And the benefits to being financially independent are many: less economic strain, more financial resiliency, greater education attainment, less marital dissolution, less risk of poverty spanning across generations, and a higher level of healthy living. Sounds good, doesn't it?

So, what does financial independence mean to you? Having tons of bling? Never having to work again? Being able to ignore price tags? Shuttling between your Caribbean yacht and your Aspen chalet? Outside of the uber-rich, being economically independent usually means paying our bills without worry, being free of debt, and having enough in our savings for emergencies, family vacations, retirement, college funds, etc. The bottom line is having money gives you choices—wouldn't it be great to have enough so you don't have to worry?

There isn't a part of our lives that money doesn't touch. It affects our relationships, the way we go about our everyday activities, our ability to make dreams reality, everything. But true financial freedom doesn't depend on how much money you have. You can balance your checkbook until you're blue in the face, you can move money every day between your mutual funds, you can double your life insurance, you can buy lottery tickets, and none of it will do you any good until you get beyond the worry and fear.

~ Suze Orman, personal finance guru

Achieving personal economic security is straightforward: create a plan, maximize the goes-in, minimize the goes-out, manage what's left, provide for the long-term, and protect your nest egg. Over the long-haul, freedom comes from removing the worry and fear about money, and is the subject of the second volume in the *Young Person's Guide* series.

Level 3: Personal Economic Success

Having enough money is only half the battle. Achieving *personal economic success* is about increasing your sense of self-worth and self-satisfaction. Freedom from anxiety about money gives you the empowerment and self-control you need to realize your potential and feel in control of your destiny.[36] Regrettably, however, the trend has been in the opposite direction; young Americans seem to be more anxious today than ever. Psychologist Jean Twenge analyzed 269 studies conducted between 1952 and 1993, all of which had measured the anxiety levels of children or college students. She finds that young persons are becoming increasingly worried and anxious about their future. This is even more disturbing when we realize that Twenge's research was conducted before the financial system meltdown.

Studies reveal that despite being far better off financially than previous generations, we are no happier. Except in the case of an extreme windfall—roughly $1.5 million by some estimates—no amount of wealth will turn an unhappy person into a very happy one. And the odds of you pulling that rabbit out of a hat are slim to none. Guide your life on your consciously chosen values, not on the values of anyone else, and you will feel a tremendous sense of satisfaction from being in control. Over the long-haul, freedom comes from achieving your aspirations and living the life you have always wanted, and is the subject of the third volume in the *Young Person's Guide* series.

Reali-tude:
Learn from the mistakes of others.

36 This is psychologist Abraham Maslow's (1908–1970) *Hierarchy of Human Needs*. Often depicted as a 5-level pyramid, the lower levels are associated with physiological and safety needs; the upper levels are associated with social, self-esteem, and self-actualization needs. Maslow described self-actualization as a person's need to be and do that which the person was "born to do."

The bottom line:

- *Personal economic servitude (Level 0):* Gain control and become self-sufficient.
- *Personal economic stability (Level 1):* Make smart choices and avoid the lifebombs.
- *Personal economic security (Level 2):* Spend less than you earn and manage the difference.
- *Personal economic success (Level 3):* Know what's important and achieve your dreams.

Doctor's Prescription (Rx)

> *Youth cannot know how age thinks and feels. But old men are guilty if they forget what it was to be young.*
>
> ~ J. K. Rowling, author

Face it Fred. Ours is a culture dominated by youth ideals. Everyone wants to be young, act young, or do and buy the things that young people do or buy. It is a great time to be a plastic surgeon because being young is not entirely a time of life—it is a state of mind. No one grows old merely by living a number of years and this keeps the "aesthetics docs" in a new Mercedes each year.

Of course, it cuts both ways. Many of you have encountered situations, particularly in the workplace, where an older person is "put off" when someone younger offers advice. Sometimes they do not respect a young person's idea even if they are intelligent and practical. Regrettably, we tend to judge the knowledge of our advisors based on time and age, not on wisdom. In fact, young people can be superior decision-makers in specific areas where they have high interest, have experienced some tragic event, or suffered from a serious illness early in life. Other than those areas, however, superior decisions are generally made by older than by younger adults.

Your assessments of situations profoundly affect—sometimes negatively, sometimes positively—whether you make a smart choice. *But simply to know is not to be wise.* To be wise is to know how to use knowledge and this implies an understanding of people, of values, and ourselves. Wisdom comes not so much from experience but from reflecting on experience and then assimilating it. This is something that people your parents' age really want to pass on to your generation. You've heard all the lectures . . . but did you listen? Of course not! Your receptivity to ask, listen, reflect, and acquire wisdom from others can help you avoid repeating the same mistakes and painful setbacks of the previous generation.

Reali-tude:
Little things matter.

Talking Points

The cat, having sat upon a hot stove lid, will not sit upon a hot stove lid again. But he won't sit upon a cold stove lid, either.
~ Mark Twain, humorist, author

Chapter 17 describes some tools to help you acquire wisdom by interviewing others. To benefit from these techniques, you need only have access to a parent, educator, or other trusted adult (tribal elder) and a desire to listen and learn. Based on the ideas in this chapter, here are some starters:

1. "I am trying to improve myself. Sometimes young persons have common sense and information, but lack experience and wisdom. This can lead to poor judgment and costly decisions. Reflecting on your experience, or that of someone you know, do you recall a situation where a young person had to learn the hard way how to make a good life-choice?" If they say "Yes" then ask:

   - "Would you tell me the gist about what happened please?"
   - "How did you (they) feel about this at the time?"
   - "What two things did you learn from this that you can share with me?"

2. "I am trying to improve myself. Sometimes young persons do not appreciate the value of time and find themselves procrastinating until it is too late. Reflecting on your experience, or that of someone you know, do you recall a situation where a young person did not act in a timely manner and jeopardized his long-term well-being? If they say "Yes" then ask:

   - "Would you tell me the gist about what happened please?"
   - "How did you (they) feel about this at the time?"
   - "What two things did you learn from this that you can share with me?"

   In either case, if they say "No," simply say "Thank you."

3. "I want to make wise life-choices. Reflecting on your experience, would you have two ideas that I can implement to improve my judgment and decision-making skills?" Be sure to thank them for their response.

Knowledge Nuggets

This world demands the qualities of youth: not a time of life but a state of mind, a temper of the will, a quality of imagination, a predominance of courage over timidity, of the appetite for adventure over the love of ease.
~ Robert Kennedy, former U.S. Attorney General

1. *Are you wise?* Can something as subjective as wisdom be measured like stress or cholesterol? Monica Ardelt, a sociology professor and researcher at the University of Florida, has been trying to do just that. She has developed a questionnaire that attempts to assess not what wisdom is, but how wise a person is. Although the questionnaire was developed for older people, you can gain some valuable insights into the three elements of wisdom. Be wise and check it out at: http://www.nytimes.com/ref/magazine/20070430_WISDOM.html?_r=1&oref=slogin.

2. *Do you suffer from affluenza? Affluenza* is a one-hour PBS television special that looks at the high social and environmental costs of materialism and overconsumption. It also explores the strategies used by marketers to sell products to young people. Do you have affluenza? You might be surprised. In his book *Affluenza*, Oliver James says that we have become absolutely obsessed with measuring ourselves and others through the distorted lens of affluenza values—earnings, possessions, appearances, and celebrity. He lists a series of statements to test your own values. Here are a few:

   - I often compare what I own with what others own.
   - Shopping or thinking about what to buy preoccupies me greatly.
   - I admire people who own expensive homes, cars, and clothes.
   - I like to keep up with fashions in hair and clothing.
   - I would like my name to be known by many people.

   According to James, if you answer "yes" to any of these questions, you have contracted the affluenza virus. The more you answer "yes," the more infected you are and the greater your likelihood of becoming emotionally distressed. See the complete list at: http://peace-and-freedom.blogspot.com/2006_07_14_archive.html. Learn more about this obsessive compulsion and test your Consumption Quotient at: http://www.pbs.org/kcts/affluenza.

3. *Growing old in America.* A *Pew Research Center Social & Demographic Trends* survey on aging found a sizable gap between the expectations that young and middle-aged adults have about old age, and the actual experiences reported by older Americans themselves. The survey examined key aspects of everyday life such as mental acuity, physical dexterity, sexual activity, and financial security. Find out what is in store for you later in life at: http://pewresearch.org/pubs/1269/aging-survey-expectations-versus-reality.

4. *Where to go for info?* See Appendix F for additional information relating to this chapter.

Part 2: What's at Stake

(An Unpredictable Future)

Chapter 5

The Stakes Are High

Seems funny to say it, but I'm glad I lived when I did. These kids coming up, they'll be living on table scraps. We had the meal.
~ Harry Angstrom, from John Updike's *Rabbit is Rich*

The Gist

The Good:

- Half of you will live to be more than 80 years old
- Gen NeXt was fortunate to experience the financial system meltdown

The Bad:

- Resist jumping on the wagon because everyone else is doing it
- Most people's retirement expectations are like Swiss cheese
- Beyond survival, young persons show little interest or urgency in financial affairs

The Reality:

- Today is the golden age of benefits for retirees
- Generation NeXt faces serious personal economics challenges
- Americans and their government are drowning in debt
- To be ignorant is to lack knowledge or education (clueless)
- To be inept is to fail to translate what you know into action (careless)

Introduction

Res tantum valet quantum vendi potest.

~ Latin for "a thing is worth only what someone else will pay for it."

The year: 1634. The place: Amsterdam, Holland. Tulips were introduced to Western Europe from Turkey in the 16th century and were immediately popular for their varied and unpredictable colors. Unknown at the time, the tulips with more exotic patterns were a result of a virus called *mosaic*. These were scarcer, and thus more valuable, than common uninfected bulbs, which already were selling at a premium. Prices were bid early in the year, but the bulbs were not actually delivered until late summer after the growing season. As the bidding progressed, more people started to jump on the bulb wagon and prices started to rise. Over the next two years, the "artisan" class—the early Dutch equivalent of the working class—saw the tulip trade as a sure-fire way to make some quick and easy money.

In late 1636 and early 1637, demand and prices rocketed and lost all connection to reality. In his *Memoirs of Extraordinary Popular Delusions*, historian Charles Mackay recounts how the price of the common bulb, the Witte Croonen, rose by more than 25 times. As the market frenzied, one fancier agreed to pay a deposit of four cows for a quarter pound of bulbs, with an additional cash payment on delivery. Incredibly, houses and land were sometimes part of the deals and the price of a single exotic bulb rose to 5,200 guilders, about 21 years' salary for a carpenter.

Then—with no direct trigger—prices plunged.

In the first week of February, Witte Croonen fell to one-twentieth of its peak price and over the next few months, overall prices had plummeted some 95 percent. Seventeenth century Dutch speculators were right in believing that tulips would catch on, but they were terribly wrong in assuming they could forever make money by investing in them.

This phenomenon is called a "speculative bubble." A bubble exists if the reason the price is high is only because investors believe that the selling price will be higher tomorrow and fundamental factors do not seem to justify such a price. Speculators jump in to make a quick buck (guilder) with little consideration of risk. This rapidly spirals: a continuous sharp rise in the price of a particular asset, leading to further price increases driven by new speculators, who are seeking profits through even higher prices. According to economist Douglas French, "These higher prices are driven by the potential profits to be made through trading, rather than the earning capacity or economic value of the asset."[37] At the peak of the boom, optimists feel their instincts have been justified. The free fall begins as expectations suddenly change and buyers quickly become sellers in mass. Consequences are often disastrous, with the ensuing crash inflicting severe financial pain, massive worker dislocation, and great numbers of bankruptcies.

> **BRAIN SNACK:** *Speculative bubbles have occurred throughout history and there have been some real doozies.[38] In 1720, the South Sea Company sold exclusive trading rights to all trade with Mexico and South America. Dubbed the "Enron of England," stocks that were traded for 1,000 British pounds in 1711 were reduced to nothing by 1720.[39] In Miami, land bought for $800,000 in 1926 could, within a year, be resold for $4 million before it crashed to pre-boom levels. Precipitating the Great Depression, in 1929 the stock market dropped 40 percent from early September to late October. It bottomed out in 1932, down nearly 90 percent from its high. In possibly the greatest speculative bubble in history, in the 1840s share prices in Britain's railways shot up, peaked in 1845, then collapsed. Investment advisor Sandy Nairn, author of* Engines That Move Markets, *says anyone who invested in railways in 1847 would have had to wait until the end of the century to get their money back.*

Can't happen these days? Wrong. When too much fiber-optic cable was laid to support the 1990s telecom boom, an infrastructure bubble was created. Wholesale prices fell at an annual rate of 60 percent and massacred Internet infrastructure companies. This period also saw a major jump in growth of Internet users, seen by companies as potential consumers. Internet startups were funded based on nothing but "vaporware." In March, 2000 the NASDAQ Composite—the index for technology shares traded on Wall Street—peaked at 5,046 points, double the value of where it was the year before. Two and one-half years later, the NASDAQ hit a low of 1,114 points, a whopping 78 percent loss of value. The implosion of the "dot.com" bubble rocked the financial system.

But these were only warm-ups for the main act. Up to 2006, the housing market in the U.S. was flourishing. Government policies made it easy to get a home loan, so more people wanted to buy a house. Increased demand raised prices, and this attracted "flippers" who were looking for fast turnaround and quick profits. The froth created more demand and higher prices, and while some people could not afford it, lending institutions didn't let that get in their way. Riskier adjustable rate and interest only loans were hyped with no down payment or proof of employment

---

37 Interestingly, economists Earl Thompson and Jonathan Treussard don't see this as a speculative bubble. Rather, they see tulip-bulb investors as rationally responding to changes in the rules of tulip investing after the Dutch Legislature converted tulip-bulb futures contracts (an obligation to purchase bulbs at a fixed price) into tulip-bulb options (an *opportunity* to do so).

38 Something that is extraordinary; named after the Duesenberg, a luxury car of the late 1920s and 1930s that was renowned for its quality.

39 Sir Isaac Newton is quoted as stating, "I can calculate the movement of the stars, but not the madness of men." Newton's niece Catherine Conduitt reported that he lost twenty thousand pounds in the company, a fortune at the time (equivalent to about $3.75 million today).

required (remember those annoying TV ads?). Whenever someone experienced difficulty making their mortgage payments, they simply borrowed against the value of their house since—huzzah!—it was now worth more! Wall Street firms rolled up huge numbers of these loans like tobacco leaves in a cigar.[40] Independent rating agencies assessed the riskiness of these mortgage backed "fatties" and pitched them as being "savings account safe." Sliced and diced into marketable chunks, they were sold and re-sold to profit-hungry investors—from individuals to big financial institutions—all over the world. Life was delicious for everybody.

Then, property values stopped going up.

Rising prices had masked the consequences of cheap money. Like a neutron bomb, falling prices triggered a devastating chain reaction. People found themselves overextended and began to default on their mortgages. This increased the number of houses on the market. The oversupply and lack of buyers (due to tightened credit) further depressed prices, causing some people to owe more than their property was worth. This produced more defaults. By the time the Wall Street suits started to panic, it was already too late: Titanic was headed for the bottom. In truth, these securities were so complex that no one knew their real value so the whole system froze in fear. Later, when models used by rating agencies to assess risk were found to be flawed, most of these issues ended up worth less than half their initial value.

The irrational exuberance of the real estate bubble brought the world's financial system to the brink of total collapse. Few managed to dodge the bullet and with the smoke still clearing, households lost $13 trillion of wealth. By early November, 2008 the Standard and Poor's 500, a broad U.S. stock index, was down 45 percent from its 2007 high. Housing prices dropped 20 percent from their 2006 peak and in California they fell 33 percent in one year alone. According to a Spectrem Group report, retirement plans lost nearly a quarter of their value during the crisis. This time when the bubble burst, the blood bath was universal.

How the BLEEP! could this happen? Nobel Laureate Robert Shiller (*Economics*, 2013) reckons that "animal spirits" animated investors during the property boom. But urban economist Edward Glaeser argues that bubble behavior is often consistent with investors' reasonable beliefs about the future. What is the lesson for those of us on Main Street? Perhaps the best advice comes from economist Kenneth Rogoff, co-author of *This Time Is Different: Eight Centuries of Financial Folly*: "It's not a matter of could it happen again; it's a matter of when."[41]

Reali-tude:
Beware the phrase, "It's different this time."

40 This process is called *securitizing* the loans (think of a security as a stock).

41 The enormous level of student debt in higher education is seen by some as the next bubble to burst. Total student debt now exceeds $1 trillion, more than total credit card debt. Critics allege a viciously wasteful circle—the size of the loan pool expands to enable students to pay ever higher fees to schools, whose costs expand because money is coming their way.

The Good

A man has got to know his limitations.
~ Clint Eastwood, actor, director

If you were in school during the 2008 financial meltdown, there is a good chance that you were not directly affected by the turmoil. If you worked through the recovery, however, this wrenching crisis carries a silver lining. Homes are now more affordable if you have good credit. Contributions to your retirement plan bought stocks at cheaper prices than before the crisis. Most of you cut back on discretionary spending and added money to savings.[42] But the single most important benefit is psychological—you now realize that good times are not guaranteed. Life is no bed of roses.

In the midst of the crisis, Congress passed the *Consumer Credit Fairness Act* (2009), designed to protect consumers from abusive practices by credit services companies. As expected, the financial services industry lobbied heavily against passage of the bill. Why? Your fees pay for their bonuses. Some of the protections enacted that affect young persons include:

- *Payment period.* Bills must be sent out 21 days before payment is due. If the due date falls on a holiday or weekend they must accept your payment on the following business day without charging a late fee.
- *Pay highest balance first.* Payments above the minimum amount are applied against the highest-interest balance first rather than against the lowest-rate balance.
- *Banned retroactive rate hikes.* The interest rate you are already charged on any existing balance you carry on the account cannot be increased. New, higher rates apply only to future purchases.
- *No short-lived teasers.* Promotional interest rates must be maintained for at least 6 months and the rate on your card cannot be raised for the first year that you hold an account.
- *Notification time.* Companies must now give you at least 45 days notice before any interest rate, fee, penalty, or finance charges are raised.
- *No card shuffling.* Previously, credit card companies could hike the interest rate charged on your account simply because you made late payments on another card.
- *College students.* With few exceptions, young adults through age 21 must have a parent co-sign on their account and they must request permission for a credit limit increase on their student's card.
- *No bill-pay fees.* Companies can no longer charge cardholders fees to pay their bills on-line by electronic transfer.

42 The U.S. Bureau of Economics tracks a metric known as the personal savings rate; this is the percentage of one's income that's saved rather than spent. In 2005, this was actually negative—more was spent than was earned. In 2008, savings spiked upwards as people were alarmed by the financial crisis, but by the end of 2012 the savings rate was once again precipitously low. Old habits die hard.

Nothing drives change more than bad times and this recession—Generation NeXt's Great Depression—has profoundly transformed the way you live, think, and work. The recession forced NeXters to go head-to-head with older workers for jobs observes business psychologist Debra Condren, author of *Ambition Is Not A Dirty Word*. "What young persons discovered was distinctly old-fashioned. They need to pound the pavement, take less money, and work their way up the ladder, just like the generations before them," she writes. This is a good thing.

BRAIN SNACK: *In their book,* The Fourth Turning, *historians William Strauss and Neil Howe argue that the western world consistently moves in 80-year cycles. Within each cycle are four "turnings." The first turning (*High*) is a heightened sense of community and collective optimism following a period of great crisis, most recently in the U.S. in the mid-1940s through early 60s. The second (*Awakening*) is when society begins to gravitate to more individualistic pursuits and demands that personal interests come first (mid-1960s through early 1980s). The third (*Unraveling*) is a period when individualism, cynicism, and bad manners dominate and institutions are increasingly discredited (mid-1980s through the '90s). Finally, the fourth turning (*Crisis*) is a time of great turmoil, when society's basic institutions are torn down and rebuilt. If their theory is correct, we can look forward to a future first turning period of renewal, collective optimism, and willingness to work together.*

Reali-tude:
Credit services companies make money from your stupidity.

The bottom line:

- You will likely experience several speculative bubbles in your lifetime.
- Once everyone else is "doing it," resist the temptation to join.
- The 2008 financial system meltdown was a valuable life-lesson.
- The stakes are high for Generation NeXt.

The Bad

If we fail to act now to improve economic literacy in this country, our children will be at risk for crippling personal debt, costly decisions at work and at home, and lack competitive skills in a fast-paced global economy.
~ National Council on Economic Education (NCEE)

In an era of intense global competition, being literate about personal economics is very important. Financial writer Helen Myers warns that "An economically literate population is essential to the well-being of our nation. Educating young people in economics and personal finance is one of the smartest things we can do to prepare our next generation of adults." In a report titled *Goodbye to Complacency*, the

Institute for Socio-Financial Studies waves the red flag: "Times have changed and individuals must change too. Today, everyone must wake up to the financial realities, responsibilities, and opportunities that demand their attention. Americans can no longer afford to be complacent about their financial well-being. *The need for financial literacy education in the U.S. is on high alert.*" (Note: Italics by original authors.)

Okay, ladies and gentleman. You've heard the warnings, most of which have gone in one ear and out the other. Why is this? You are prone to two cognitive flaws that are catalysts for failure: ignorance and ineptitude.

Ignorance (lack of knowledge)

> *This ain't no party, this ain't no disco, this ain't no foolin' around.*
> ~ Talking Heads, new wave band

To be ignorant is to lack knowledge or education. We are unaware of certain things we should know. But we are also ignorant if what we know and believe to be true, is actually not true. Regardless of cause, ignorance leaves us with insufficient true information to accurately judge a situation and make a smart decision. In the extreme, ignorance leaves us totally clueless as to the realities of the world and the inherent risks of our actions.

Although Gen NeXters are technologically sophisticated and highly discerning as consumers, they are alarmingly uninformed about the basics of personal finance. Many high school graduates are unable to balance a checkbook and most have no knowledge of the management principles of credit, spending, saving, and investing money. Too many fail in the management of their first consumer credit experience, establish poor financial habits, and stumble through their lives learning by trial and error. Consider that:

- Only 21 percent of students between the ages of 16 and 22 say they have taken a personal finance course through school.
- Only 7 percent of parents say their child understands financial matters well.

What this means is high school and college graduates will be making important life decisions with hardly any experience on which to base their reasoning. Upon graduation, it suddenly hits a young person that he or she must adjust to an entirely new protocol, one for which they have been minimally exposed. With the exception of your parents, there is no safety net once you bid adieu (adios) to your alma mater.

> *I find it interesting that we are taught how to read, write, and communicate in school; how to drive in driver's education; how to shoot and handle a gun in hunter's safety course; and how to have safe sex in gym class, yet most of us have never been taught how to handle money. One of the common patterns ... is that our generation spends money when we have it, and charges it when we don't. What's happening*

is that we are living in a microwave society. Everybody wants it hot, fast, and now. They plan more for a two-week vacation than they do for their retirement.
~ Jason Steinle, UPLOAD EXPERIENCE

The hot breath of reality is not encouraging. In a 2008 nationwide financial literacy survey of 6,856 high school 12th graders in 40 states, Jump$tart Coalition found the average score was a failing 48 percent. While white students scored an average of 52 percent, Hispanics and African-Americans scored significantly lower at 45 and 41 percent respectively. Most alarming was the 50 percent of students who don't plan to attend college, and hence will likely manage their own money sooner. They scored the worst at 35 percent.[43]

This has created a time bomb. The lack of widespread or formal training about personal finance in high schools and colleges contributes to a sense of complacency among students, who are simply not aware of the long-term consequences of their ignorance. Few even recall the subject being covered. Worse yet, young people show little interest in financial matters. Says Monica Kirgan, Vice President of the Principal Financial Group, "[young persons] would rather spend than save, and they're spending like crazy. They view saving for retirement as something old people do."

Young women face even more challenging obstacles. Compared to their male counterparts, many women earn less, change jobs more frequently, and may need to take time away from the workplace to care for their children and parents. Women are more likely to be single parents and outnumber single fathers by more than 5-to-1. And the long-term picture for women is particularly worrisome. Over the next 40 years, the number of women over 85 is expected to at least triple, with 3/4ths of this population single, divorced, or widowed. In retirement, a woman is six times more likely than a man to be single and twice as likely to have an income below the poverty level. Ironically, because they live longer than men, they will have more time to suffer from their mistakes.

Reali-tude:
What you don't know can hurt you.

Ineptitude (lack of care)

All you need in this life is ignorance and confidence, and then success is sure.
~ Mark Twain, humorist, author

To be inept is to be careless. Although we are aware of what we know (or should know), we lack the maturity, skill, or judgment to handle a situation. For a variety

43 The 'rents fare little better. While 63 percent of Americans know the difference between a half-back and a quarterback, only 14 percent can tell the difference between a growth and an income stock. Seventy-eight percent can name a character on a TV sitcom, but only 12 percent know the difference between a load and no-load mutual fund.

of reasons, we fail to make wise controllable decisions and do not take appropriate action to prevent adverse long-term consequences. In the extreme, ineptitude is a result of conscientious stupidity.

Regrettably, there is intense pressure nowadays for young persons to "fit in" through what you own or consume. Consumer values are being applied to many aspects of young adults' lives, and many are approaching most if not all situations asking "What's in it for me?" A study of 18–24 year olds concluded that mainstream young adults are highly influenced by lifestyles portrayed by celebrity role models, many of whom have become famous through no particular talent but the medium of reality TV. This has set a new benchmark for personal style and success, and makes significant wealth seem to be a realistically obtainable goal. It has given rise to the belief that anyone can, and will, become wealthy regardless of their background and a feeling that they "deserve" to do so:

1. I am Gen NeXt and I am good.
2. I am financially illiterate but I am indifferent about it.
3. I want to be wealthy therefore I will be wealthy.
4. I do not see #2 as being an obstacle to #3 because I deserve to be wealthy.

This insouciant attitude was confirmed in a study associated with the PBS documentary, *Generation NeXt*. Although young persons believe they will earn high incomes and live the lifestyle they desire without working in traditional jobs, the evidence does not support it. Sociologist John Reynolds and colleagues found the gap between young persons' goals and their actual achievements had grown over the 25-year period between 1976 and 2000. "Today's teens are both highly ambitious and increasingly unrealistic," says Reynolds. "While some youth clearly benefit from heightened ambition, it can lead to disappointment and discouragement rather than optimism and success." Future tycoons of America, if it is so easy a cave man can do it, why aren't we all happily rich?

The bottom line:

- To be ignorant is to lack knowledge or education (clueless).
- To be inept is to lack competence or motivation (careless).
- Young women and minorities are at particular risk.
- The future is out there . . . somewhere.

Reali-tude:
What you don't do (right) can hurt you.

The Reality

> *This country is in terrible trouble. The nation is on course to go broke in a generation unless budgets can can be accurately balanced. This is about the future of our country, our kids and grandkids.*
>
> ~ David M. Walker, former Comptroller General of the United States

If you are tuned in to what your representatives have been doing in Washington, you know that our country's financial situation is in hot water. In 2007 America's fiscal Cassandra,[44] former Comptroller General of the United States David M. Walker, sounded an early warning that the nation was on course for disaster. In response to the economic slowdown, the federal government passed the *American Recovery and Reinvestment Act* of 2009. This program, known as a Fiscal Stimulus, injected nearly $1 trillion of direct government spending on infrastructure and social welfare into the U.S. economy. In 2010, the Federal Reserve pumped in another $600 billion. We borrow a billion dollars a day just to buy oil, he warns, and have a net debt to the rest of the world of about $3 trillion dollars.[45] Like an IV in reverse, our overall standard of living is being drained away.

"What, me worry?"[46]

> *Retirement is not like buying a cup of coffee. It's not something that you get to do over and over again and learn from your mistakes.*
>
> ~ Joseph E. Stiglitz, Nobel laureate (Economics, 2001)

Yes, you should worry. The bad news was spelt out in *Global Ageing 2010: An Irreversible Truth*, a report released by Standard and Poor's, a rating agency. As the Baby Boomers retire over the next two decades, the burden on the government will rise sharply. This demographic has been coming for some time since many Boomers have not provided enough for their old age retirement and healthcare. *Young person's alert*: their problem will become your problem.

NeXters, to appreciate the fiscal train wreck that is headed your way you need to have a basic idea of how the U.S. retirement system works. Fundamentally, retirement funding involves three tiers. The lowest is Social Security, which provides Americans with bare bones living (the average payment is $12,000 a year). The highest tier, for those who are rich, is private savings. In between, for ordinary folks who do not have a hedge-fund account, there are pensions and 401(k)'s. But most people's retirement expectations are like Swiss cheese—full of holes—and

---

44 One who utters unheeded prophecies. From Greek mythology, Cassandra was the daughter of Priam, the king of Troy. She was endowed with the gift of prophecy but fated by Apollo never to be believed.

45 In October, 2008 the *National Debt Clock* near Times Square ran out of numbers to record the federal government's shortfall (it could only handle a debt count up to $9,999,999,999,999). Since then, two additional digits have been added.

46 Quote by Alfred E. Newman, fictional mascot of *Mad Magazine*, © Warner Bros. Entertainment.

the cracks are already evident. Nearly one in three of today's seniors depend on Social Security for more than 90 percent of their income. For some groups, the statistics are even more ominous: 19 percent of widows and 29 percent of elderly African-Americans fall through Social Security's safety net.

Social Security has promised future generations far more in retirement benefits than its current funding sources will allow it to pay.[47] Worse yet, the country is literally bankrupt because of future Medicare obligations, which are *five times* those of Social Security.[48] "For decades politicians in Washington D.C. have looked up at the size and scale of the fiscal challenges facing our country, particularly in Medicare, and chosen to kick the can down the road" warns House Speaker John Boehner. "We have now run out of road."

But wait—the red ink doesn't stop there! In 2010, the Heritage Foundation found that the average federal employee earns 85 percent more than the average private-sector worker. This means that for every $1 in pay and benefits a private employee earns, a fed worker receives $1.85. Not far behind, reports the *Wall Street Journal*, state and local government workers receive a 45 percent premium in pay and benefits over workers who create wealth in the private economy. And this has created a huge hole in the pension pot for many states. Illinois, for example, is short 241 percent of its annual tax revenues. For Connecticut, the figure is 190 percent. Altogether, unfunded or underfunded government pension and benefit liabilities add up to an incredible 4 trillion dollars. If even close to true, future taxpayers from Hartford to Honolulu (that's you) will be hopelessly in hock to the police, firefighters, city managers, and teachers of the past.

Take New York, for example, where some 3,700 retired public employees earn more than $100,000 a year in pension payments, including a former policeman at the ripe old age of 47. Or California, where more than 20,000 former state or local employees have retirement incomes of over $100 grand a year? How about that fire chief who, at 51, was collecting more than $241,000 in retirement pay? The retired county official who is guaranteed $423,664 a year for the rest of her life (plus cost of living increases)? Or the state worker that accumulated large amounts of comp time and unused vacation, and cashed out with more than $800,000?

The dirty little secret? It is impossible for the government to honor all of its obligations. When Boomers retire en masse and the dam breaks, every city, county, and state will be flooded with a rush of liabilities that could suck your future financial lifeblood out to sea. Finance professors Joshua Rauh and Robert Novy-Marx estimate that seven states will have exhausted their pension assets by 2020, and half will run out of money by 2027.

---

47 The retirement nest egg of an entire generation is stashed away in Parkersburg, PA where $2.5 trillion in paper bonds are stored. These are IOUs payable to the Social Security Administration for payroll taxes that were collected by the federal government but spent over the years on other programs. In 2010, the government began borrowing money to cash in these bonds to pay current benefit recipients.

48 In 2011, federal government liabilities and unfunded obligations totaled an estimated $84 trillion (equivalent to $520,000 *per household*). But this is somewhat misleading, however. Although current debt is hard cash owed, the government has the power to change unfunded programs, either by reducing spending or increasing taxes.

IT MIGHT BE TOO LATE. We all have been told in college and in graduate school that there is nothing left for us... at least not a lot. So we have a different battle to fight. Knowing this, and having been told this over and over, makes me have NO TRUST in the government whatsoever. It might be too late... I am not the expert obviously. We just assume we are going to make enough now and have later. Young people are fierce though. We always think it will work out, no matter what.

~ Justyna S., grad school student

Corporate pensions? Don't bet your bippy Brenda. Most of the nation's private pension plans suffered major losses in 2008 and all together are underfunded by as much as $500 billion, the highest figure since the Second World War. In 2011, the average corporate pension plan had a funding ratio (the proportion of liabilities covered by assets) of just 72 percent. And traditional pensions are disappearing faster than your father's hairline. In 1980, nearly 40 percent of all workers in private industry were covered by employer-funded group pension plans. Today, only 20 percent have that kind of coverage. Yet nearly 65 percent of Gen NeXt workers say they expect to receive a monthly pension payment when they retire. Fat chance Frank. With the proliferation of the 401(k) as the primary savings vehicle for employees' retirement, companies are off the hook. They have shifted most all of the responsibility and the risk from them... to you.

Corporate promises are often not worth the paper they're printed on. Long before today's Americans reach retirement age, policy decisions by Congress favoring corporate and special interests over workers will drive millions of older Americans—a majority of them women—into poverty, push millions more to the brink and turn retirement years into a time of need for everyone but the affluent.

~ *TIME* Magazine investigation

Many NeXters remain blithely unaware of these disquieting trends, although they may acknowledge a fear that they are not accumulating sufficient resources to maintain their lifestyle later in life. Even if workers retire at age 65 and annuitize[49] all their wealth, including receipts from reverse mortgages on their homes, more than 4 out of 10 of you (43 percent) will still be at risk. Many of you face having to work far longer in your old age than you could ever imagine. And while illegal, age discrimination is prevalent. Ask anyone over 40. One day, that be you.

You're young! Why the kerfuffle about retirement? Thought you'd never ask. People are having fewer children, so the younger age groups are much too small to counterbalance the growing number of old people. Also, we are living longer—seniors are living 50 percent longer than they were in the 1930s, when Social Security set 65 as the benchmark retirement age. See those swanky retirement commercials on late night TV featuring preserved movie stars, washed up politicos,

49 To annuitize is to cash out all of your wealth in equal monthly installments over time until there is nothing remaining when you die.

and flabby sports figures? They are pitching to the "Boomer blip"—for the next 20 years, Baby Boomers will swell the ranks of pensioners like water in a sponge. According to the U.S. Census Bureau, those who are 65 and older currently make up 13 percent of the population and this number will double to 88.5 million by 2050. NeXters, you are completely out-gunned; nearly a third of the voting public is 65 or older and they are overwhelmingly more inclined to vote than you are.

The other elephant in the room is health care. Boomers' health will inevitably deteriorate, leaving the country (yes, that's you) struggling with potentially crippling health care costs. The *Affordable Care Act* (2010), commonly called Obamacare, was a watermelon swallowed whole. The good news is health care will improve for low income seniors and the uninsured. The bad news is someone has to pay for it. But the government and the health care industry, from insurers to injectors, have already figured this out. Currently, a retired couple in the U.S. without employer-sponsored health insurance can expect to pay $200,000 for out-of-pocket health care costs like premiums and co-pays. Do your parents have investment savings and home equity? Odds are they will be kissing those assets goodbye. Your parents saved a dollar; you stand to inherit a peso. The wind softly whispers... BOHICA.

> *I am 17 years old, and am working on my communications merit badge for the Boy Scouts of America. I am writing because I am concerned about the economy for the youth. People's homes are being foreclosed on, and education keeps getting its funding cut. If things continue like this, how will the minors today be able to afford houses and make sure that our children get a good education and make ends meet? I sincerely hope that the economy gets better, or the kids will be the ones having to pay the price.*
>
> ~ Garett L., Letters to the Editor

What does the crystal ball show for you? Although half of NeXters are reckoned to live past age 80,[50] a survey by MetLife found that 40 percent of workers ages 21 to 30 had not begun to save for their retirement. Worse yet, many young adults do not have a clue how to begin doing so. Clearly, many young persons remain deluded about their ability to be self-reliant in their golden years. Think of a 900 mile drive across the blazing Sahara. When you get to the 550-mile marker, it suddenly hits you that you only have enough gas for 700 miles. Are you with me cameraman?

Reali-tude:
Do not rely on the government to help you.

The bottom line:

- Thanks to AARP, today is the "golden age" of benefits for retirees.[51]
- Companies have shifted responsibility for retirement funding to you.

---

50 In 2005, the Social Security Administration extended the life expectancy tables up to 119.

51 The American Association of Retired Persons (AARP), a special interest group that represents people age 50 and over.

- There is a fiscal train wreck headed straight for Generation NeXt.
- You need to be worried—it is hell being old and poor.

The End of Disney World

> *When we look at the average graduating class, many of them see money as a lifetime goal. Yet, less than five percent of these graduates will become wealthy. The remaining 95 percent will shape their lives struggling for these values.*
> ~ Richard J. Leider, coach

The economic downturn has been especially bitter for those NeXters who lost their first job because of the recession. They found themselves competing head-to-head with older workers, who by virtue of their greater experience, proved difficult to dislodge. Take Lindsey Rhein, 24, of Placentia, California. Interviewed by journalist Eve Tahmincioglu, Lindsey was out of work for nearly four months after getting laid off as a legal assistant for a construction company. During that time, she applied to over 700 jobs with only seven interviews, all leading nowhere. With a master's degree in forensic psychology and a bachelor's in sociology, she wasn't able to land a sales associate job at Target. Not even a call back from McDonald's, where she had applied for the fast food chain's management training program.

> *It's a very insecure world out there. It was a little shocking to the system.*
> ~ Angela T., age 26, New Jersey

Getting laid-off has been a humbling experience for Gen NeXters who have never experienced real financial hardship or big disappointment. Nancy Molitor, a clinical psychologist, relates that many of her young adult patients feel depressed, devastated, and uneasy about their future. "A lot of these kids grew up thinking they were going to be able to have it all," she says. "They feel frozen just when they should feel excited and hopeful about the future." According to Alexandra Robbins, author of *Conquering Your Quarterlife Crisis*, NeXters were raised to believe they can do and be anything and are finding their high expectations dashed. "Many were raised to believe that the world was their oyster," she said, "and in this kind of economy, that's just not the case."

BRAIN SNACK: *Psychologist E. Tory Higgins developed* Self-Discrepancy Theory *to help determine feelings that arise from differences between our aspirations and our frustrations from goals or desires not being attained. When the actual experience is somewhat less than we think we can achieve—such as achieving a nice body shape—we tend to feel sadness, dissatisfaction, and other dejection-related emotions because there is no positive outcome. When the experience is less that we feel we should achieve—for instance, successfully landing a good job or having to compromise our career choice—we experience fear, worry, and other anxieties. Higgins said this applies not only as we see ourselves, but as others see us as well.*

Many historians, economists, and psychologists say the economic downturn could shape Generation NeXt's values and attitudes in much the same way that the Great Depression shaped those growing up in the 1930s. A 2009 survey of 1,065 Americans age 18 and older (243 were age 18–29) suggests that 60 percent feel Generation NeXt is being dealt an unfair blow because of the recession. "I call it the end of Disney World," says Michael Bradley, an adolescent psychologist in suburban Philadelphia. Unfortunately NeXters, you came on stage at the wrong point in history. But then, you already know this.

Reali-tude:
Gen NeXt, you got screwed.

Doctor's Prescription (Rx)

Kwitchyerbellyakin.
~ Old Irish saying

The *bandwagon effect* can be seen at almost all levels of human interaction.[52] It is the reliance upon the behavior or beliefs of those around—and similar—to you as a guide to what is correct to do or believe. Often pejoratively called "herd behavior," this effect describes how individuals can follow the crowd without examining the merits of the situation. Some examples of the bandwagon effect include speculative bubbles, sporting events, trends and fads, mob violence, persecution of minorities, and political or religious zealotry. Here are some tips to help you base your decisions on your beliefs and values, independent of the herd:

- *Avoid being overly optimistic.* Americans tend to be extremely optimistic about the future and in a bubble people believe prosperity will continue forever. It never does.
- *Everybody else is doing it!* Generally, people believe there is safety in the middle of the herd. After all, isn't everybody recommending and buying it? Without doing independent research, however, people stampede like the buffalo: "Hi ho, hi ho, it's off the cliff we go!"
- *Analyze the situation critically.* Instead of thinking about contingencies, people daydream about their future prosperity. Simply being aware of the larger picture is a good starting point. But unlike the buffalo, you can recognize when you are being stampeded.
- *Beware of "pseudo-professionals."* Talking heads generate froth, but their judgment is little better than yours. True professionals will cash out at your expense—you cannot outsmart them. Talk to a trusted adult if you do not know what you are doing.

52 The phrase "jump on the bandwagon" first appeared in 1848 when Dan Rice, a popular circus clown of the time, used his bandwagon and its music to gain attention for political campaign appearances. As campaigns became more successful, politicians vied for a seat "on the bandwagon." We'll look more closely at this behavior in Chapter 9.

- *Bigger fools?* People pay ridiculous prices for stocks, tulips, etc. because they are sure someone else will pay even more for them. They fail to notice when the price is so high that no one is willing to pay anymore. Once you see the hood start to crumple, it is too late to put on your seat belt!
- *Use common sense.* Avoid knee-jerk reactions. Many of us fear looking foolish if we pass up our one great opportunity in a lifetime to get rich quick.

Then again, not all herd behavior is bad. In his book, *Influence: The Psychology of Persuasion*, Robert Cialdini explains that relying on the behavior of those around us for evidence of what to do in a situation can often be a useful rule. If you are at a dinner party and you don't know what fork to use on the course just served, it's a good idea to look at the other diners for a clue. At best, no one will notice that you followed her example; at worst, there will be at least one other person who looks stupid.

BRAIN SNACK: *Keeping an eye on what the next guy is doing is the secret to survival for many fish. Ichthyologists[53] tell us that schooling is one of the primary ways smaller fishes defend themselves from predators. In a school, each fish near the edge serves as a lookout, helping to protect the rest of the fish.[54] Others inside the school watch their neighbor's "lateral line," a system of specialized receptors along the sides of the body that detect minute changes in water pressure when another nearby fish suddenly changes speed or direction. Thus, all of the fish in a school can virtually react simultaneously to the sudden movement of a potential predator lurking nearby.*

Wall Street professionals mimic this schooling behavior. Without bubbles, Wall Street bankers and their cohorts would starve. Sure they would make solid salaries—as they have historically—but not bonuses in the millions of dollars a year. Since this would doom their species, there is a powerful incentive for Wall Street to push for a continuation of the bubble economy. Lest you become too sanctimonious, however, keep in mind that their greed feeds off yours. Trump that temptation and you are one hoof ahead of the other buffalo, Bill.

Talking Points

Most of the important things that a human being ought to know cannot be comprehended in youth.

~ Robert Hutchins, president, The University of Chicago

Chapter 17 describes some tools to help you acquire wisdom by interviewing others. To benefit from these techniques, you need only have access to a parent,

53 Scientists who study fish (no, they are not sushi chefs).

54 Researchers have determined that these animals are not benevolently working to protect the group. The *Selfish-Herd Theory* states that each organism is looking to put one of its weaker or slower fellows between itself and a predator.

educator, or other trusted adult (tribal elder) and a desire to listen and learn. Based on the ideas in this chapter, here are some starters:

1. "I am trying to improve myself. Sometimes young persons fail to comprehend personal finance (saving, budgeting, investing, etc.). Reflecting on your experience, or that of someone you know, do you recall a situation where financially illiteracy lead a young person to make poor judgments about money and jeopardized his long-term well-being? If they say "Yes" then ask:

   - "Would you tell me the gist about what happened please?"
   - "How did you (they) feel about this at the time?"
   - "What two things did you learn from this that you can share with me?"

2. "I am trying to improve myself. Sometimes young people lack the judgment and real-world experience necessary to resist speculative bubbles (such as the dot. com and real estate collapses). Reflecting on your experience, or that of someone you know, do you recall a situation where a young person "jumped on the bandwagon" and jeopardized his long-term well-being? If they say "Yes" then ask:

   - "Would you tell me the gist about what happened please?"
   - "How did you (they) feel about this at the time?"
   - "What two things did you learn from this that you can share with me?"

   In either case, if they say "No," simply say "Thank you."

3. "I want to make wise life-choices. Reflecting on your experience, would you have two ideas that I can implement to improve my judgment and decision-making skills? Be sure to thank them for their response.

Knowledge Nuggets

> *You can bail out a bank, but you can't bail out a generation.*
> ~ Dean Kamen, Segway inventor

1. *Learn before you burn?* John Kenneth Galbraith (1908–2006) was one of the most widely read and influential economists of modern times. In his pithy book, *A Short History of Financial Euphoria* Galbraith offers a guided tour of get-rich-quick movements, from tulip mania to the 1987 stock crash, which he accurately predicted. More importantly, he examines the foolish thinking behind such phenomena. According to Galbraith, the "mass escape from sanity by people in pursuit of profit," which he always viewed as the cause, is never blamed. Read the reviews at: http://www.amazon.com.

2. *Sleepwalking toward impoverishment?* A 401(k) is a *defined contribution* (DC) savings plan for retirement—you put in money from your paycheck and you take

the risk. Public pensions are *defined benefit* (DB) plans—the government pays a retirement based on your pay and length of service and it assumes the risk. Startlingly, an employee who pays into a DC scheme for 40 years may only get half the retirement income he could have expected under a DB scheme. See why at: http://www.cfo.com/article.cfm/11560487/c_11560671.

3. *Is the American Dream alive and well?* Economic opportunity and upward mobility are the foundation of the American Dream. *Economic mobility* is the ability to climb up or fall down the economic ladder within a lifetime or across generations and varies widely from place to place. It is highest in integrated places with good schools, strong families, lots of community spirit, and smaller income gaps within the broad middle class. Over the last generation, however, economic growth has slowed and income inequality has widened without evidence of an offsetting increase in relative mobility. Sadly, African Americans and women more often experience downward mobility. Find out the facts at: http://www.economicmobility.org.

4. *Where to go for info?* See Appendix F for additional information relating to this chapter.

Chapter 6

Where Risk Comes From

Risk comes from not knowing what you're doing.
~ Warren Buffett, investment entrepreneur

The Gist

The Good:

- Rules of thumb can simplify decision-making
- Risk relates the probability of occurrence and the downside consequences

The Bad:

- YOU are your single greatest source of risk
- Your perception does not necessarily represent reality
- Not recognizing risk does not mean it does not exist
- No one can protect you from yourself

The Reality:

- Social class depends largely on education, personal income, and job role
- There is a 97–99 percent probability you will be middle class or below
- For the last 30 years, the middle class has steadily lost ground
- Education is the single most important factor to a high standard of living

Introduction

Prediction is very difficult, especially about the future.
~ Niels Bohr, Danish physicist

As you cruise through life, you'll make many decisions. Most will be trivial. Relatively few will be truly significant. Regardless of importance, however, each time you make a decision you close off alternatives. These alternatives represent your "coulda-beens." For instance, a decision to go out for Peking Quack tonight means you'll need to pass on the Tuscany Tortellini. A decision to buy a new car may mean you cannot take a vacation. Deciding to marry Carlos means you'll have to ditch stud puppet Derek.

As Saint Thomas Aquinas said, every choice is a renunciation; to choose one thing is to reject others.[55] In making a choice you give up an "opportunity cost," a cost that is not always measured in dollars. The trade-off might refer to the income you forego by attending school rather than working. It can be the time that you spend shopping around to compare brands for a major purchase. Perhaps it is the loss of satisfaction in having selected a poor restaurant for your anniversary, or regret for having lived a meaningless life. In any decision, this opportunity cost represents the risk—the risk of not making the optimal choice.

The mere act of deciding invokes risk. It may be economic risks, risks to health and safety, environmental risks, risks of inconvenience or embarrassment, to name a few. Most of the time we simply accept these risks intuitively. If you ride in a car, it may crash; if you choose to walk, a truck may hit you; if you stay at home, you may get blasted by a meteorite. But, what exactly is risk? Well, a good place to start is to consider what risk is not. Risk is not the same as danger. Walking downstairs carries a definite degree of risk. In fact, it is one of the most common causes of accidents in the home, but most of us would hardly call it dangerous. Nor does risk mean uncertainty. Uncertainty is when we have more than one possible outcome and we don't know which one will happen. Risk enters the picture when some of those possibilities involve a loss, catastrophe, or other undesirable outcome.

To complicate matters, human psychology is a major influence on our perception of risk. Attitudes toward risk are shaped by our perceptions, observational learning, and experience. And since attitudes are a choice, they can be modified to better manage or avoid risky situations. Like beauty, risk is in the eye of the beholder and each of us assesses risk differently. As a young person, what comes to mind when you think about risk?

55 Saint Thomas Aquinas (1225–1274 A.D.) was an Italian Catholic priest in the Dominican Order, and is considered by many faithful to be the Catholic Church's greatest theologian and philosopher.

- Waiting until the night before the mid-term to open the book?
- Cruising through a red light at 2 am?
- Unprotected sex?
- Wearing your "El Rushbo" button to a Young Democrats rally?
- Dropping off friends in the handicapped zone?
- Getting up in the morning?

Age makes a huge difference in our perception of risk. When it comes to risk, young persons tend to be quick with opinions and short on experience. In comparison, older people are usually not so quick on the draw. Some of the risks that keep your parents awake at night include:

- Smoking
- Driving
- Sex and pregnancy
- Suicide
- Marijuana use
- Crime
- Drinking
- Dropping out of school

Generally, in any decision risk represents a trade-off between the value of something to us and our assessment of two variables: (1) *consequence*, which asks "What is the worst thing that can happen?" and (2) *probability*, which asks "What is the likelihood it will occur?" In this sense, the nature of risk is universal, regardless of context. Whether we are talking about investment, legal, credit, love, parachuting, or any other risk domains, all risks share a common denominator: the chance that a decision outcome may be undesirable.

Reali-tude:
Risk is a four-letter word.

The Good

We're gonna come around at twelve with some Puerto Rican girls that are just dyin' to meet you.
~ from *Miss You* by The Rolling Stones

Relative to most animals, humans receive a massive amount of incoming sensory data—terabytes worth.[56] According to *PC Magazine*, "the volume of information that crossed our brains in one week at the end of the 20th Century is more than a person received in a lifetime at the beginning of it." As a result of this accelerating rate of change, our ability to evaluate and mitigate all of the risks we encounter before we make a decision is increasingly being outpaced.

56 The prefix *tera* comes from the Greek word meaning "monster." A single 500GB hard drive is a half-terabyte drive. The books in the U.S. Library of Congress contain a total of approximately 20 terabytes of text, about the same base storage of 20 new iMacs.

Faced with data overload, we compensate by using *heuristics*.[57] A heuristic is a mental shortcut, or "rule-of-thumb" that helps to make our decision-making easier. In action, we calculate an approximate value or we recall something from our own experience or that we have learned from others. In many cases, heuristics simply represent the application of common sense. While not as accurate or reliable as if we were to take time to fully figure things out, a rule of thumb generally yields a better estimate than a "wag" (wild-assed guess). In fact, they are so handy in simplifying everyday tasks that we often are not aware we are using them.

For example, the "Rule of 72" is a useful rule of thumb to approximate how long it will take for your hard-earned savings to double at a specified interest rate. The rule says "Divide the number 72 by the interest rate." If the interest rate is say, 8 percent, it will take about 9 years (72/8) for your stash-o-cash to double in size. Some other rules of thumb are "Whatever Barry estimates to do the job, be sure to double it"; "The math teacher never gives a quiz on Fridays"; and "Add one spoonful for each cup, plus one for the pot."

"Aha" (hissed the sly dude as he finagled her bra), "there's a catch!" Heuristics are quick 'n dirty and in everyday situations are good enough for government work. Yet most are not foolproof and this can cause problems. For instance, when measuring the distance of an object we take into account the sharpness of the image. The clearer an object appears, the closer we judge it to be. This simple mental shortcut helps us to make the continuous stream of distance judgments needed as we drive along the freeway. But this heuristic does not work when it is raining or foggy. In these situations, our eyes tend to trick our minds into thinking that the car in front of us is more distant than it actually is. This flaw in sensory perception is one reason why accident reports go up under such conditions. Likewise, we exhibit a whole series of perceptual fallibilities in the way we think. Many of these can be difficult to notice because they are so widespread and natural in our usage.

BRAIN SNACK: *Surgeons in ancient Greece and Rome dealt with hemorrhaging from severe war wounds by the technique of tying off, or ligating, blood vessels during surgery (as is done today).*[58] *Unfortunately for the hapless soldiers, this effective technique was forgotten for the next thousand years. During this period, physicians cauterized blood vessels by dipping the amputated limbs in boiling oil. While this definitely stopped the bleeding, it also deep fried healthy tissue. As a result, many wounds later became infected and survival rates were very low.*

In the 16th century, French physician Ambroise Paré faithfully followed this method on the battlefield. There were so many casualties, however, that he ran out of oil and was forced to apply a wound dressing made from eggs, oil of roses, and turpentine. To his great surprise, those treated with his "digestive medicine" felt little pain and their wounds healed without inflammation. In contrast, the ones he treated with boiling oil were in great pain and feverish with infection.

---

57 Pronounced hyu-RIS-tik, from the Greek *heuriskein* meaning "to find or discover."

58 The most famous ancient physicans are Hippocrates of Greece (*ca.* 460–370 B.C.E.) and Galen of Rome (*ca.* 129–216 A.D.). Today, the Hippocratic Oath, "Above all, do no harm" is traditionally taken by newly minted physicians.

Thus, a heuristic that solves one problem (stop the bleeding) may create a worse one (kills the patient).

Decisions that are heuristics-based tend to make us feel good and they are intuitively satisfying regardless of their correctness. But they can also lead to errors in reasoning called *biases*. Marilyn vos Savant[59] describes bias, sometimes referred to as prejudice, as a "learned or emotional predisposition to believe a certain way, regardless of the facts." Everyday examples are rife: "White guys can't jump"; "Don't trust anyone over thirty"; "Democrats always vote for tax and spend"; and "All Latinas are hotties." Psychologists say that a bias exists if one's views are subjective rather than neutral or objective.

Indeed, people can become obstinately or intolerantly devoted to their biases. Young persons like to think they have less prejudice than their parents, but in fact they are simply bigoted about different things. Many are down on fat people, smokers, and people who drive Humvees, for example, rather than blacks or homosexuals. What is important to recognize is that even the most cognitively skilled individual displays considerable bias, often unknowingly.[60]

When used in a purposeful manner, a bias can be useful. Indeed, a certain amount is essential in today's world in order to extract meaning from new information. What makes some biases so risky, however, is their invisibility. Hardwired into our thinking process, we fail to recognize their presence even as we exhibit them. They insidiously trap our thinking and sabotage our judgment. Many young persons underestimate how easily these prejudices can create risk and set them up for failure.

Reali-tude:
You don't see things as they are. You see them as you are.

The bottom line:

- Risk varies from person to person.
- The use of heuristics simplifies decision-making.
- Bias increases the risk of an adverse outcome.
- Rules of thumb do not always work.

The Bad

There are 3 kinds of people: The ones that learn by reading, the few who learn by observation, and the rest of them who have to touch the fire to see for themselves if it's really hot.

~ Anonymous

59 Marilyn vos Savant is listed in *Guinness Book of Records* under "Highest IQ." Her IQ has been assessed at approximately 225, with a rarity of 1 in 26 million.

60 Scientists have attempted to calculate the cost of hidden bias. Students about to graduate were found to unknowingly be willing to pay a 22 percent reduction, or tax, on their starting salary in order to have a male boss. This was true whether the student was male or female.

Using the two criteria from our definition of risk (probability and consequence), we can classify four broad categories of decisions according to their level of risk. One simple but useful method of illustrating these categories is through the use of a "two-by-two" (2x2) assessment matrix[61] shown in Figure 6.1.

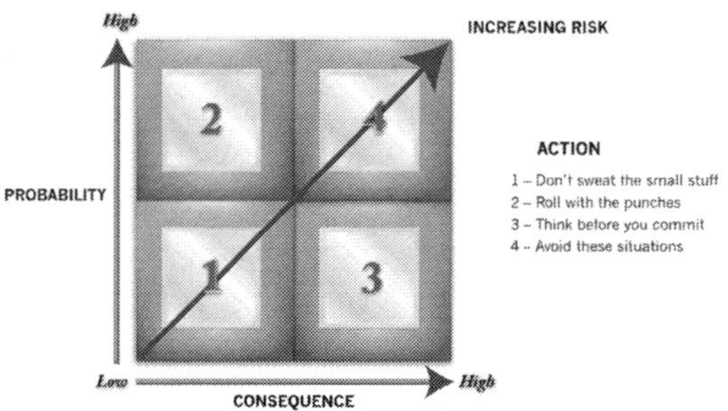

Figure 6.1 Decision risk.

All of our decisions are seduced to some degree by our biases. In making a decision, we mentally assess the outcome probability and consequences, each of which varies from low to high. For most routine decisions, this assessment is automatic and subliminal. Looking at the figure, we can see that Type 1 and Type 2 decisions have a low risk of adverse consequences. If we are making a Type 3 or a Type 4 decision, however, the odds of screwing up our life substantially increase.

Type 1 decisions (low risk). The outcomes of these decisions are unlikely to occur, but if they do, they have very little downside. Basically, these are minor annoyances. Yakking on your cell phone and, oops... missed the freeway exit? No biggie—take the next one. *Doctor's prescription:* Life is too short. Don't sweat the small stuff.

Type 2 decisions (low to medium risk). These outcomes are more likely to occur, but also have little downside. Think of them as pesky potholes on the road of life. Blew off returning those library books because you scored a hot date with Cheryl? Sometimes a guy's gotta do what a guy's gotta do. *Doctor's prescription:* Roll with the punches.

Now things begin to get a little dicey...

Type 3 decisions (medium to high risk). Although these outcomes are not very likely, if they do occur the effects can be nasty. Welcome to lifebomb country! Inclined to ride bareback? Odds are, Romeo, that you will contract a gift that keeps on giving. *Doctor's prescription:* Pause to consider the downside gist before you commit.

Type 4 decisions (high risk). These outcomes are severe and highly likely. You don't need to be Ansel Adams to get the picture—poor judgment will bring you a boatload of regret. Are you a smoker? Fascinated by Russian roulette? Although they differ in efficiency, both virtually guarantee you will die early. *Doctor's prescription:* Avoid these situations. Your long-term well-being depends on it!

---

61 The assessment matrix is based on the *Ansoff Matrix* developed by management theorist H. Igor Ansoff (1957).

BRAIN SNACK: *More complicated assessment matrices such as "five-by-fives" are often used in industry to portray risk. Scales of these matrices are often not quantitative (that is, they have descriptions rather than numbers), and varying degrees of risk are color coded. Project engineers, for example, use these types of matrices to assess the failure risk associated with structures in a nuclear plant or an oil platform. Insurance companies find them useful in determining your auto policy rates. This is one reason why you pay more for the same coverage than grandpa does.*

Increased probability means it is more likely that a lifebomb (bad outcome) will be triggered. Increased consequence means its effects are more likely to be painful.[62] Interestingly, Type 3 situations are decision wildcards. They have the greatest upside potential since we can apply prophylactic countermeasures (such as a condom) to reduce the probability of a less that satisfying outcome (pun intended). In Type 4 territory, your decision-making process has failed you. Barring divine intervention, your life is almost certainly poised to change for the worse. At this point, the only practical advice is, "Good luck with damage control dude."

Reali-tude:
There is no substitute for sound judgment.

The bottom line:

- A bad Type 1 or Type 2 decision is an irritant.
- A bad Type 3 decision gambles your future.
- A bad Type 4 decision can ruin your life.
- Risk rises with increasing probability and consequence.

Your greatest source of risk

We have met the enemy, and it is us.
~ Pogo

Anytime we are forced to make a decision we do so without perfect knowledge of what the outcome will be. This introduces risk, and our perception of that risk shapes our attitude toward dealing with it. Sometimes we see the risk immediately, like the not-so-happy policewoman in our rear-view mirror. Sometimes we don't realize there was any risk until years later, say, after dropping out of school or marrying the wrong person. In a few circumstances, the risk might not be evident until decades hence, such as running out of money in retirement.

Where is risk created? From happenstance, bad luck, punishment from outer space aliens, or maybe a vast hot-wing conspiracy? It is human nature to blame the consequences of our flawed decisions on external factors. If we accept responsibility for our actions, however, we can see that the real problem lies within us. Risk

62 Researchers tell us experts stress the probability component when asked about their risk judgments, while lay people tend to stress the consequences.

arises more from what we do, rather than what the world does to us. This leads to the stark revelation that the single greatest threat to personal economic success is the person looking back in the glass: YOU.

In making a controllable decision, risk arises from two mental shortcomings: ignorance (lack of knowledge), and ineptitude (lack of care). Also called *cognitive flaws*, these shortcomings influence how we think about and process information. As a result, we develop *questionable beliefs* that "trap" our better judgment and trigger risky attitudes and behaviors. Think of a flaw as something we have, a trap as something we believe, and risk as something we perceive. Where people go astray is they tend to think these terms are the same thing. As shown in Figure 6.2, they are not.

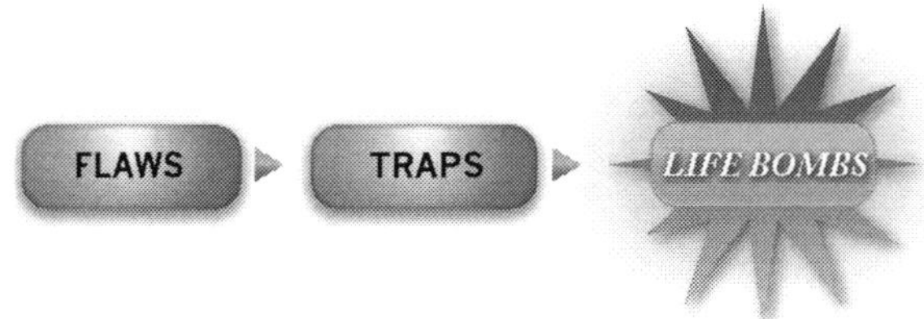

Figure 6.2 Self-generated risk.

- *Flaws* distort our perceptions of how the world works and how we view ourselves. Young persons often underestimate the degree to which these shortcomings can affect their assessment of reality and risk.[63]
- *Traps* are questionable beliefs (mental fallibilities) that promote errors in judgment. Young persons fail to recognize that trap thinking often trumps mature judgment and common sense.
- *Lifebombs* are trap thinking, put into action. Lifebombs can lead to unintended consequences you will later regret. Young persons often under-appreciate the degree to which today's life-choices can adversely affect tomorrow's well-being.

Ultimately you are the one responsible for how your life turns out—not the government, your company, your school, not your family. And by and large, the efficacy of your thinking process will determine whether you will benefit or suffer from the decisions you make today.

Reali-tude:
You cut your own slice of the pie.

63 Young people tend to assess dangers as being lower than older people do, and as a result, take more risk. There is a biological difference too—women inherently perceive more risk than men do. One's level of education is also a factor.

The bottom line:

- Ignorance and ineptitude are mental weaknesses that set cognitive traps.
- Cognitive traps are questionable beliefs (mental fallibilities).
- Immature judgment leads to bad decisions, risky behaviors, and unintended consequences.
- Lifebombs are trap thinking, put into action.

Dealing with risk

> *Depend on the rabbit's foot if you will, but remember, it didn't work for the rabbit.*
> ~ R.E. Shay, humorist

Dealing with risk is both a reality and a feeling, and they are not the same. At its core, assessing risk is mathematical and is based on the probability that a particular loss will occur. The purpose of risk assessment is to provide the decision-maker with the best possible information about various loss probabilities. For instance, with some basic personal data such as your age, health condition, driving habits, etc., an insurance company can statistically determine whether you represent an acceptable risk to be issued a policy. Do they call it right every time? No. Reality is far too complex to ever model exactly. Do they call it right most of the time? You bet they do. For them, it all boils down to the numbers.

At the individual level, however, there is a problem with this approach—people are not numbers.

In everyday life, few of us evaluate risk trade-offs mathematically by calculating the probabilities of different events. There is no "risk-o-meter" that alerts us to impending danger. Instead, we react to risk psychologically as an emotional feeling. We do this by using heuristics—those handy rules of thumb, stereotypes, and biases that we discussed earlier—to weigh the likelihood of perceived benefits (say, personal enjoyment or social respect) and costs (such as level of effort or future health risks). Subjectively we assess the situation and conclude the likelihood of an outcome. Often we express the chances to ourselves in discrete, quantized terms like "improbable," "better than even," "highly likely," and so on.

Our perception of risk represents intuitive judgment and is important because it shapes our attitudes and behavior. But perceptions are not reality and like heuristics, they are not foolproof. Think of it as the difference between terrain that is represented by a map and the terrain itself. People selectively interpret what they see on the basis of their interests, background, experience, and attitudes. In our daily lives, we frequently encounter situations where "what we see" is not necessarily "what we get," such as:

- "Results are not typical" (diet infomercials);
- "Some settling may have occurred" (cereal boxes);
- "Mileage ratings under controlled conditions" (auto ads);
- "You've never seen me without my makeup" (a whisper in the dark).

The fact is, people frequently have only a vague idea of the risks they face. We downplay risks that are not discussed, along with risks that are long-term, diffuse, or that evolve slowly over time. This is especially true of young persons for whom confidence often exceeds knowledge. Lack of experience or education can limit our imagination to even consider risk, or cause us to overlook information that is necessary to anticipate its effects. As a result, many of us tend to rely on misleading perceptions and transient emotions to resolve uncertainties. This can be downright dangerous because most of the big questions in life have no simple answers.

In addition, many young persons worry about the wrong things. They pay too much attention to minor risks and not enough attention to major ones. They also incorrectly assess the magnitude of risks. In a study of adolescents, nearly three-quarters (73 percent) of them estimated they would have a 4-year college degree by age 30. The actual figure was less than one-third (30 percent). When asked how many of them would die in the next year from any cause (crime, illness, accident, and so on), they estimated 19 percent. This represents 5 to 6 young persons out of every 100. The actual expiration rate is 0.08 percent, or less than 1 in 1,000.

BRAIN SNACK: *Counter to what many Boomers believe, studies have shown that adolescents actually overestimate their risk of suffering negative effects from risky activities, according to Human Development Professor Valerie Reyna of Cornell. A study at the University of California, San Francisco found teenagers were more likely than adults to overestimate risks for every outcome studied, from low-probability events like contracting H.I.V., to higher-probability ones such as acquiring more common sexually transmitted diseases or becoming pregnant from a single act of unprotected sex. In reality, "The risk of pregnancy from a single act of unprotected sex is quite small, perhaps one chance in 12," explains Reyna, "and the risk of contracting H.I.V., about one in 500, is very much smaller than that."*

Fundamentally though, our perceptions *are* our reality and when cognitive traps skew our perceptions, we make risky decisions that may result in unpleasant outcomes. Consider the nineteen-year-old who decided it would be fun to jump the fence after closing to take a dip with Binky the polar bear. Gee…Binky Bear is sooo cute! What could be more stimulating than a midnight swim with a warm, cuddly ball of fur? Wrong—anthropomorphism works only at Disneyland. The bear enjoyed home delivery of a delicious thigh sandwich. Care for a pickle on the side Binky?

Reali-tude:
Risk exists, independent of your (mis)perceptions.

The bottom line:

- People often have only a vague idea of the risks they face.
- Emotions and rules of thumb are frequently used to assess risk.

- Your perception of risk does not necessarily represent reality.
- No one can protect you from yourself.

The Reality

Both men and women are fallible. The difference is, women know it.
~ Eleanor Bron, actress

Life is a numbers game. There are no guarantees, only risks and probabilities. All of us deal with uncertainty and make predictions of future events while having only limited knowledge. When responding to uncertainty, however, it is important to realize that *possibility* does not mean *probability*. Possibility is an either/or condition; something is possible or it is not; either 100 percent or 0 percent; you win the lottery, or you don't.[64] On the other hand, probability reflects everything between absolute certainty and impossibility. Probabilities help us make educated appraisals of the future—such as getting that raise—and better decisions based upon those appraisals.

BRAIN SNACK: *Probabilities help us illuminate reality as it exists, not as we want it to be. Every young and talented basketball player dreams of one day playing in the NBA. So, what is the probability they will make it to the top? Educator Jawanza Kunjufu and colleagues at Tufts University calculated the odds: of 1,000,000 boys and girls that wish to be in the NBA, 400,000 make their high school basketball team, 4,000 play in college, 35 make it to the NBA, and of those only seven are starters. This works out to less than 1 out of every 10,000 high school hoopsters and less than 1 in every 100 college players that will make the big leagues. And for that crème-de-la-crème who prevails, the average NBA career is four years. Best to keep those textbooks dusted.*

A hard life-lesson is learning that superior talent and hard work alone are not sufficient to propel you to the ranks of the rich and famous. The world is awash with talented detritus. The odds of attaining extraordinary income or great wealth are so slim for Gen NeXters that your concern would be more fruitfully turned to the risks of not even being part of the middle class. And here is where we see some disturbing trends.

Reali-tude:
The ultimate risk is regret for what might have been.

Social class in the U.S.

64 You are twice as likely to be killed in a car accident on your way to buying a lottery ticket than you are to win the lottery.

> *The income gap between the rich and the rest of the U.S. population has become so wide, and is growing so fast, that it might eventually threaten the stability of democratic capitalism itself.*
> ~ Alan Greenspan, former Chairman, Federal Reserve

The term "social pecking order" does not refer to the items on a KFC menu. Rather, it is a distribution or a list of social classes. At the Joe Six-pack level, most Americans believe in a three-class social model: the rich, middle class, and the poor. Among sociologists, however, there is considerable controversy regarding how best to define a social class. Some sociologists consider only numerical measures such as wealth or income. Others take into account qualitative factors, such as education, occupation, culture, and social status. Still others consider American society to be so sociologically and economically fragmented that no clear class distinctions can be made. As always, opinions are like bung-holes—everybody has one!

> *It is impossible to understand people's behavior...without the concept of social stratification, because class position has a pervasive influence on almost everything... the clothes we wear...the television shows we watch...the colors we paint our homes in and the names we give our pets. Our position in the social hierarchy affects our health, happiness, and even how long we will live.*
> ~ William Thompson and Joseph Hickey, sociologists

For people age 25 or older, personal income, educational attainment, and the job role itself are frequently used to establish one's social class. According to sociologist Dennis Gilbert, "People in similar positions grow similar in their thinking and lifestyle...they form a pattern, and this pattern creates social class." Figure 6.3 shows a widely cited (and still useful) paradigm[65] proposed by sociologists William Thompson and Joseph Hickey (2005).[66]

Class	Typical characteristics
Upper class (1%)	Top-level executives, celebrities, heirs: income of $500,000+ common. Ivy league education common.
Upper middle class (15%)	Highly educated (often with graduate degrees) professionals with household incomes from high 5-figure range to commonly above $100,000 (sometimes referred to as the "professional class")
Lower middle class (32%)	Semi-professionals and craftsman with some work autonomy; household incomes commonly range from $35,000 to $75,000. Typically, some college education.
Working class (32%)	Clerical, pink and blue collar workers with often low job security; common household incomes range from $16,000 to $30,000. High school education.

65 A paradigm is a model for something, especially one that forms the basis of a methodology or theory.

66 From: Thompson, W. and Hickey, J. (2005). *Society in Focus.* Boston, MA: Pearson, Allyn & Bacon.

Lower class (14%–20%)	Those who occupy poorly-paid positions or rely on government assistance. Some high school education.

Figure 6.3 Social Classes in the United States

In the United States, Thompson and Hickey show an upper class consisting of the rich and powerful, an upper middle class of highly educated and well-paid professionals and managers, a lower middle class consisting of semi-professionals, a working class constituted by clerical as well as blue collar employees whose work is highly routinized, and a lower class of those with limited participation in the labor force. Since social classes lack distinct boundaries and commonly overlap, it is difficult to state any definitive income thresholds. Nevertheless, the demarcations cited have largely remained stable.

To gauge the pulse of real Americans (not that sociologists aren't real or American), a 2007 *New York Times* survey asked people to self-identify their social class. The results showed only 1 percent of those surveyed considered themselves to be upper class, 67 percent were middle or upper-middle class, 35 percent were working class, and 7 percent saw themselves as lower class. Additional insight comes from the National Opinion Research Center (NORC) at the University of Chicago. Beginning in 1972, NORC has periodically surveyed people as to their social class. Their 2010 cumulative survey data indicated that 3.2 percent of the population considered themselves to be upper class, with the dividing line between middle and upper class at just over $200,000. The takeaway from these surveys is the overwhelming majority of Americans feel they are part of the greater middle class.

The rich are different

Fitzgerald: *The rich are different from you and me.*
Hemingway: *Yes, they have more money.*

How do government and industry calculate the odds that you will become rich? They use a statistics tool called a "frequency distribution," which assigns probabilities (many of us were introduced to statistics in school and forgot what little we learned, often within seconds of the final exam). The best known of these is the *normal distribution*, often referred to as the "bell curve" because of its shape. Many human characteristics such as IQ, weight, blood pressure, cholesterol count, hockey skills, and exam test scores of a large number of students follow this pattern. The normal curve is characterized by the majority of observations showing up in the middle and gradually tapering off on the left and right side. An intuitive example is human height—a few blokes are really short, a few are really tall, and in between stands everybody else (incidentally, the "height hump" for U.S. adults is 67–73").[67]

Personal income is certainly a human characteristic, but unlike height and hockey skills it is *not* normally distributed. In this case, the *Pareto distribution*,

67 Many natural phenomena are approximately normally distributed. For example, errors in machined parts, star luminosity, behavior of huge numbers of atoms, width of stripes on a zebra, and the daily returns of the S&P stock index to name a few.

named after the French-Italian economist Vilfredo Pareto (1848–1923) is more useful.[68] Sometimes referred to as a *fat-tailed* distribution, the Pareto curve neatly describes many real-world situations that involve "the small to the large," as well as near-equilibrium situations that have rare but large scale departures from the past (called "punctuations"). Examples of phenomena that are sometimes seen as being approximately Pareto-distributed include:

- Size of human settlements (a few cities plus many hamlets/villages);
- Value of oil reserves in oil fields (a few large fields and many more small fields);
- Number of web site visitors (1 percent of sites capture more than half of total web volume);
- U.S. public policy making (continuous year-to-year, but occasionally dramatically changed);
- Biological evolution (large stable populations, with rare but rapid new species development).

As mentioned, the distributions of personal wealth and income are fat-tailed. Translated from math-speak into practical jargon, what this means is a small number of extremely wealthy people earn and hold the lion's share of the riches. It explains why, though the worldwide median net worth is a little over $2,000, we also see a number of bazillionaires. Brian Hayes, senior writer for *American Scientist*, explains the comparison this way "If height had the same distribution as wealth, there would be people two million meters tall."

> ***BRAIN SNACK**: "On the whole, people have normally distributed attributes, talents, and motivations. Yet we finish up with wealth distributions that are much more unequal than that," says economist Robin Marris. In the past decade or so, a syncretic field called Econophysics has emerged from physics and economics. Analyzing data from the Internal Revenue Service, physicists have confirmed that incomes among the super-wealthy—about 3 per cent of the population—follow Pareto's law, while incomes for the remaining 97 percent of us follow a normal distribution. Surprisingly, this appears to be a universal pattern. It exists irrespective of many differences in culture, history, social structure, indicators of relative prosperity, and, to some extent the economic policies followed in different countries.*

The pendulum has swung so far that some econophysicists suggest that we now have only two economic classes. This bifurcation is not caused by some devilish conspiracy of the rich, but as a consequence that naturally emerges from our economics network. And these inequalities are significant. The income gap between the richest and poorest Americans has grown to its largest margin ever. From 1979 to 2007 the top one percent of households saw their after-tax income grow by 275 percent

68 The Pareto distribution was popularized by management consultant Joseph Juran as the 80/20 rule: 80 percent of the problems come from 20 percent of the causes. Interestingly, this nonlinearity makes problems in the 20 percent group 16 times (not 4 times) as important as those in the 80 percent group.

according to a 2011 Congressional Budget Office study. Meanwhile, income for the 60 percent of households that make up the middle of the income scale increased by slightly less than 40 percent. In his book *Conscience of a Liberal*, Nobel laureate Paul Krugman (Economics, 2008) recounts that we fail to appreciate just how rich today's rich are. The top 1 percent of the population earned a fifth of the total income in 2012, and the top 10 percent pocketed almost half of all the money earned in the country. This is the highest percentage recorded since 1917.[69]

In his book, *Richistan*, Robert Frank of the *Wall Street Journal* opines that "The rich weren't just getting richer; they were becoming financial foreigners, creating their own country within a country, their own society within a society, and their own economy within an economy." And the rich are governed by a different set of rules from the vast majority of Americans, according to social psychologists Joris Lammers and Adam Galinsky. "People with power think that they are justified to break the rules not only because they can get away with it, but also because they feel at some intuitive level that they are entitled to take what they want," they argue. *The Economist* is more blunt in its assessment: "The rich *are* different: they are more selfish and ruthless."

Research seems to back up these claims. A series of experiments at the University of California, Berkeley suggests that people who are socially and financially better-off are more likely to lie, cheat, and otherwise behave unethically compared to individuals who occupy lower rungs of the socioeconomic ladder. "Elevated wealth status seems to make you want even more, and that increased want leads you to bend the rules or break the rules to serve your self-interest," says psychologist Paul Piff. In a study based on unpublished Internal Revenue Service data, the rich were found to hide more of their income. Taxpayers whose true income was between $500,000 and $1 million a year were estimated to have understated their adjusted gross incomes by 21 percent overall. Yet, underreporting was only 8 percent for Americans earning $50,000 to $100,000, and even lower rates were found for those earning less. "The aura of power surrounding you makes you feel immune from consequences" says psychologist David Schmarch. "There's a sense, 'I won't get caught.'" Or, as billionaire "Queen of Mean" Leona Helmsley snarkily quipped, "We don't pay taxes. Only the little people pay taxes."[70]

Of course, lightning fries the wealthy as well as the middle class. High-net-worth individuals got whacked in the financial crisis because they own a disproportionately large share of stocks and property. As a result, many shifted from conspicuous consumption to "bling on a budget" during the recovery.

---

69 In his 2011 *Dear Taxpayer* report, U.S. Senator (OK) Tom Coburn exposes how the federal government's spending and tax policies are fleecing the taxpayer and rewarding the rich. "What it reveals is sheer Washington stupidity with government policies pampering the wealthy costing taxpayers billions of dollars every year. All and all, over $9.5 billion in government benefits have been paid to millionaires since 2003," he reports.

70 Warren Buffett decried the inequity of his secretary's having paid a larger percentage of her income in taxes than he did (and was soundly criticized for doing so). President Obama referred to this as the "Buffett Rule" in calling for wealthy Americans earning over $1 million a year to pay at least the same tax rate as middle-class earners.

> *The rich are tightening their belts, too. Even if it is still a Gucci. The cutbacks by the wealthy are clearly different from the grocery-aisle economizing so many Americans have begun making... the rich typically don't trade down to lower-priced brands and stores. Instead of six pairs of Manolo Blahnik shoes at $700 each, they will buy two—not browse the shoe department at J.C. Penny or shop at Nine West.*
> ~ Anne D'Innocenzio, Associated Press

But for Jane and Joe Ordinary American, worried about their monthly car or mortgage payment, this is a Pyrrhic victory.[71] Census data shows the wealth gap between younger and older Americans has stretched to the highest ever, even pre-dating government records. The typical household headed by a person age 65 or older has a net-worth 47 times greater than a household headed by someone younger than 35.[72] This wealth gap is now more than double what it was in 2005, and nearly five times the 10-to-1 disparity a quarter century ago (inflation adjusted). In reality, very few young persons will realize an upper-class income regardless of your level of talent, dedication, or cleverness.

Does this mean you should not pursue your dreams? Of course it doesn't. It does mean you must think about setting goals that are commensurate with your aspirations and capabilities. It also means that making smart choices early in the game can help you avoid disappointments later in life.

Reali-tude:
The rich *are* different.

The bottom line:

- Social class depends largely on your education, personal income, and job role.
- Statistics answers the question, "How likely is it that I will...?
- Possibility does not mean not probability.
- The rich are governed by a different set of rules from most Americans.

Who are the middle class?

> *The most perfect political community is one in which the middle class is in control, and outnumbers both of the other classes.*
> ~ Aristotle

In many respects, what constitutes the American middle class still remains largely ambiguous. As we saw in Figure 6.3 (page 90), contemporary sociologists generally

71 Any victory that comes at such staggering cost as to be meaningless. The expression alludes to the Greek King Pyrrhus who, after defeating the Romans in battle in 279 B.C.E., stated "One more such victory and we shall be undone."

72 Net worth includes the value of a person's home, possessions, and savings accumulated over the years, including stocks, bank accounts, real estate, cars, boats, or other property, minus any debt such as mortgages, college loans, and credit card bills. Older Americans tend to have higher net worth because they are more likely to have paid off their mortgages and built up more savings over time.

divide the middle class into two sub-groups. About 15 percent of all households are in the upper or professional middle class, consisting of highly educated, salaried professionals and managers. About twice as many (one third of all households) constitute the lower middle class, consisting mostly of semi-professionals, skilled craftsmen, and lower level management. Pew Research Center sees the middle class as four groups, each differing in its attitudes, outlook, and financial circumstance:

1. *Top of the Class.* Predominantly male and disproportionately well-educated;
2. *Anxious Middle.* Enjoys some of the Top's economic advantages but has many of the same worries as those who are struggling;
3. *Struggling Middle.* Disproportionately composed of women and minorities;
4. *Satisfied Middle.* Disproportionately old and young, has everything but money.

Most researchers agree that one prominent indicator of middle class status is having a college education. Not surprisingly, education significantly enhances one's earnings potential. For example, those with graduate degrees have an average per capita income that exceeds the median household income of married couple families among the general population. Another prominent indicator of middle class status is income. In 2008, the median U.S. household income, most frequently cited for measurements of income inequality, was $52,285. But yardsticks vary considerably due to varying number of earners per household and the effects of later marriages, fewer children, and divorce.[73] Often it is easier to simply consider one's lifestyle as the defining characteristic:

> *Lower class: one who rents and cannot afford to own; takes the bus, rides a bike, or walks and barely has enough to feed and clothe their family. Middle class: one who owns their home and a car, eats prime steak every other week, and has a plasma large screen TV in the living room. Upper class: one who owns their primary home and several vacation homes, eats out at fine restaurants all the time, has a plasma large screen TV as part of their home theatre system in the living room of their yacht, which is docked behind their vacation home.*
>
> ~ FlaRiptide2, Internet blogger

> *Middle class should be defined as a standard of living and not an income. It is enough money to buy a three bedroom house, have two cars, two kids. Be able to pay for at least half their education. Take some sort of weeklong vacation once a year. It does not contemplate a five bedroom house, endless lessons for the kids, $40,000 cars.*
>
> ~ Willman, Internet blogger

73 Defining income is not straightforward. Money income includes income from earnings, interest and dividends, Social Security, and other forms of social insurance. It does not include the value of non-money benefits such as food stamps, housing subsidies, or capital gains. Economist Brian Domitrouic points out that pre-tax income is a terrible measure of income inequality. When taxes are high, inequality is lower, in part because the rich find ways not to have large incomes, he says.

We should base it on gas. If you can afford $5/gallon, you're middle class.
~ fundfund, Internet blogger

So, how do we sum up the middle class? Perhaps it is best described as those folks who typically have a comfortable standard of living, significant economic security, considerable work autonomy, and rely on their expertise to sustain themselves. They encompass the majority of voters and they pay billions in taxes. America's strength comes from her middle class—these are the people who drive the economy, teach the children, police the streets, and fight the wars.

The "new economics"

Now, here, you see, it takes all the running you can do, to keep in the same place. If you want to get somewhere else, you must run at least twice as fast as that.
~ Lewis Carroll (in *Through the Looking-Glass*)

The term "economic inequality" refers to disparities in the distribution of economic assets and income.[74] Social scientists speak of the *middle class squeeze*—the "squeeze" occurs when increases in wages fail to keep up with price increases (inflation) for middle income earners, without having a similar impact on the top wage earners. In *Who Stole the American Dream* (2012), Pulitzer Prize winning journalist Hedrick Smith makes a well-documented case how events and policies since the 1970s have destroyed the "virtuous circle of growth" that created the broad prosperity of America's middle class and led to a concentration of wealth and income at the top. *New York Times* columnist David Brooks predicts the rise of a new social class—"the formerly middle class."[75]

Income inequality has left America's middle class "too unstable financially to fuel demand for goods and services as in the past," argues former U.S. Labor Secretary Robert Reich in *Aftershock: The Next Economy and America's Future.* Eighty-five (85) percent of middle class Americans say it's tougher now than a decade ago to maintain their standard of living and "fewer Americans now than at any time in the past half century believe they are moving forward in life," concludes *The Lost Decade of the Middle Class,* a 2012 Pew Research Center study. Testifying before the Senate Finance Committee on what she calls the new economics of the middle class, former Consumer Financial Protection Bureau Director Elizabeth Warren warns:

74 The classic tool for measuring income inequality is the *Gini coefficient,* which ranges from 0 (everyone has the same income) to 1.0 (one person has all the income). Thus, a higher Gini means that the wealthier are getting wealthier, or the poor are falling behind, or both. Since the 1980s, the U.S. coefficient rose from 0.34 to 0.48 in 2011, says economist Tim Worstall. This finding is disputed by economist Lee Ohanian, who points out that the Gini coefficient ignores the panoply of government benefits and transfer payments such as Medicaid, nutrition assistance, earned income tax credits, etc.

75 Concerned about the growing gap between productivity and middle-class incomes, the dramatic rise in economic inequality, and the challenge of balancing work and family responsibilities, the Obama Administration issued its first *Annual Report of the White House Task Force on the Middle Class* in 2010.

Middle class families have undergone a powerful economic transformation in the last generation that is quietly reshaping the face of America. The typical man working full-time today, after adjusting for inflation, earns about $800 less than his father earned back in the early 1970s. After decades of rising incomes earlier in the 20th Century, about thirty years ago wages for middle class men flat-lined. When wages quit increasing, how did family incomes rise? The answer is all around us. Mothers of minor children went back to work in record numbers, and many increased the hours they worked. In the early 1970s, the median family lived on one paycheck. Today the family in the middle brings home two paychecks. The shift from one income to two has had seismic implications for families across America. It means that all the growth in family income came from adding a second earner. The economic rules have changed and millions of hard-working, play-by-the-rules families find themselves in a battle for economic survival.[76]

~ Elizabeth Warren, U.S. Senator (MA)

On the other hand, not everyone sees the sky falling. Prominent researchers argue that measurements of income inequality are misleading. They point to *relative income*, that is keeping up with the Joneses and staying ahead of the Smiths, as an important determinant of happiness. And in this respect, their findings show that the quality of lives across the income scale is becoming more similar, not less. Nobel laureate William R. Fogel (Economics, 1993) notes that "In every measure that we have bearing on the standard of living... the gains of the lower classes have been far greater than those experienced by the population as a whole."

Political scientist Gregg Easterbrook agrees, and asserts this is a perceptual problem caused by relentlessly negative impressions of American life presented by the media. Author of *The Progress Paradox: How Life Gets Better While People Feel Worse*, Easterbrook describes what he terms the two odd realities of life in the United States today: the way we are and the way we think we are.

...paycheck stress is on everybody's mind today, but you can't factor out of the equation that what that money is buying is a higher quality of life. There isn't any doubt that stress on the middle class constantly rises and it takes more money to achieve things, but remember your outcome is also better; let's not lose sight of that. Families today that aspire to put their children into white collar positions are aspiring to a fundamentally better life. You could still have the lifestyle of the 50s at a much lower price, but we would all say it's not sufficient.

~ Gregg Easterbrook, journalist

And that's not all. Nobel laureate Gary Becker (Economics, 1992) has thought a lot about income inequality. In an interview with National Public Radio he comments, "It's not always a bad thing. I strongly believe that inequality in earnings has been mainly the good kind. Good inequality gives more rewards to people with

76 In 1978, CEOs at the largest U.S. companies earned 35 times as much as the average worker. In 2010, that figure was more than 300:1.

more education, more skills, and a greater ability to create value in the world. If you're in an environment where knowledge counts for so much, then if you don't have much knowledge, you're going to be a loser," he says. "Poor people are learning that to get ahead, they need more skills, and the more skilled the workforce is, the better the overall society does. The rich are getting richer and the poor are falling further behind, mostly because the better off have more education" explains Becker. "That's good, even if some people are left behind."

Reali-tude:
Don't get left behind.

The bottom line:

- There is a 97–99 percent probability you will be middle class or below.
- Growth in middle class family income came from adding a second earner.
- The middle class is getting squeezed.
- Education is the single most important factor to improving earnings.

It's up to you dude

> *[W]e cannot protect every single person against every single threat at every moment and in every place... Given finite resources and personnel, we have to focus ourselves on those priorities which most demand our attention...*
>
> ~ Michael Chertoff, former Secretary, Department of Homeland Security

You are at risk for a more worrisome future than your parents faced at your age. In their retirement, however, don't count on them for more than sympathy and a hot meal. Why? The Great Recession hemorrhaged their life-blood. In the meltdown, $2 trillion in home equity was erased. Household balance sheets shed almost $3 trillion in the third quarter of 2008 alone, thanks in large part to a decline in stock prices. More that $5 trillion from pensions and savings evaporated as parents watched their 401(k)'s shrink to 201(k)'s. In total, the economic crisis resulted in the disappearance of $13 trillion in American household wealth between mid-2007 and March 2009, say economists Barry Bosworth and Rosanna Smart. Sure the economy is clawing back, but Boomers are over the hill. Count on your parents conserving what remains of their wealth to supplement their retirement and health care costs.

And don't turn to Uncle Sam with your palm up. Regardless of bleating promises, the government will only provide you with only a token supplement—politicians have maxed out the country's credit card and the social safety net is broke by any rational accounting standard (except the government's that is). There are prescriptions a-plenty, but in the end dear NeXters, watch what they do, not what they say. *Young person's alert*: It is no fun being old. It is no fun being poor. It is hell to be old and poor.

Reali-tude:
To control risk, control yourself.

Doctor's Prescription (Rx)

Ministering to people who are dying is not what saddens me. It is listening to so many broken dreams.
~ Clergyman

What's it all about, Alfie? Is it just for... the moment... you live? Um no. Not if you value the future as you *want* it to be, not as you *hope* it will be. The penalties for ignoring risk are too great for you to be a spectator in this sport. But anticipating risks that you have not encountered before can be difficult. Although you cannot protect yourself from every single threat at every moment and in every situation, you can reduce your exposure. Here are some tips:

- *Acknowledge your fallibilities.* The place to start is being honest with yourself about your shortcomings. This opens the possibility that poor habits can be improved.
- *There are no instant results.* While expedient, "Top Ten" lists and "one solution fits all" prescriptions generally do not alter aberrant behavior over the long-haul. If success was this easy, your first diet (of the last six) would have worked.
- *Consider the negative consequences.* Ponder potential downsides that could result from your controllable decisions. Act on your rational beliefs, not your emotions.
- *Be wary of help from friends.* Birds of a feather flock together and many suffer from the same biases that you do. It is difficult for friends to be truly objective—many will tell you what they think you want to hear, not what you need to hear.
- *Get a second opinion.* Chat with a trusted adult. Adults can be great sources of wisdom regarding risk because they have the hindsight (and the scars) that young persons lack. Explain your thoughts and have them challenge your reasoning.
- *Curb impulsiveness.* Once you have made up your mind, wait one day before acting. It is better to be careful a hundred times than to be killed once.
- *Use your toolkit.* To develop power over an unpredictable future:
    - § Understand reality as it exists (not as you want it to be);
    - § Know your limitations (develop self-awareness);
    - § Form the conscientious habit of making smart choices (become a mature decider).

Talking Points

I not only use all the brains that I have, but all that I can borrow.
~ Woodrow Wilson, 28th U.S. President

Chapter 17 describes some tools to help you acquire wisdom by interviewing others. To benefit from these techniques, you need only have access to a parent, educator, or other trusted adult (tribal elder) and a desire to listen and learn. Based on the ideas in this chapter, here are some starters:

1. "I am trying to improve myself. Sometimes young persons fail to comprehend how bias can negatively influence their judgment. Reflecting on your experience, or that of someone you know, do you recall a situation where personal bias distorted a young person's view of reality and jeopardized his long-term well-being?" If they say "Yes" then ask:

    - "Would you tell me the gist of what happened please?"
    - "How did you (they) feel about this at the time?"
    - "What two things did you learn from this that you can share with me?"

2. "I am trying to improve myself. Sometimes young persons fail to comprehend how minor decisions today can have major consequences tomorrow. Reflecting on your experience, or that of someone you know, do you recall a decision situation where a young person's failure to assess the long-term consequences jeopardized her long-term well-being? If they say "Yes" then ask:

    - "Would you tell me the gist of what happened please?"
    - "How did you (they) feel about this at the time?"
    - "What two things did you learn from this that you can share with me?"

    In either case, if they say "No," simply say "Thank you."

3. "I want to make wise life-choices. Reflecting on your experience, would you have two ideas that I can implement to improve my judgment and decision-making skills? Be sure to thank them for their response.

Knowledge Nuggets

You've got to know when to hold 'em, know when to fold 'em.
~ Kenny Rogers, singer

1. *Why is risky behavior so common among teenagers?* Could it be they think they are immortal, invulnerable, or immune to the hazards that adults see so clearly? Or maybe they simply do not appreciate the risks inherent in activities like driving too fast, driving drunk, having unprotected sex, experimenting with drugs, binge drinking, jumping into unknown waters, or failing to save early for retirement? Wrong on all counts Woodstock. A study titled "Risk and Rationality in Adolescent Decision Making" by Valerie Reyna and Frank Farley asked why teenagers do stupid and dangerous things. Their conclusions may surprise you—adolescents are actually, in some ways, more rational than adults. For a report of their findings, see: http://www.newsweek.com/id/44701 or http://www.medicalnewstoday.com/articles/56613.php.

2. *Those slippery statistics!* You should always be skeptical about statistics, including the ones in this book, because it's so easy to misinterpret numbers. "There is terror in numbers," writes Darrell Huff in *How to Lie and Cheat with Statistics*, the most popular book on statistics ever sold (first published in 1954). "The secret language of statistics, so appealing in a fact-minded culture, is employed to sensationalize, inflate, confuse, and oversimplify," warns Huff. "It's not the statistics which are in question—it's how they're used." Here are some questions to ask when you see stats:

    - *Who did the study?* The phrase "numbers don't lie" is true; what you need to examine is who is publishing the numbers and what are they trying to prove with them. Every statistic has an agenda behind it. Be sure the numbers come from reliable sources and you understand the context.
    - *What are the statistics measuring?* Make sure that the findings reported are actually what were measured (and that all of the data has been reported).
    - *Have the data been interpreted correctly?* Do not confuse *correlation* (when two things vary in sync, such as ice cream sales and frequency of shark attack) with *causation* (when one thing causes another, for example the sun rises and the cock crows). Just because two things change simultaneously, does not mean that one caused the other.
    - *Which average?* There is not one, not two, but three different definitions of "average" in statistics:
        - § *Mean*: sum all the numbers and divide by how many there are (outliers can significantly affect this);
        - § Median: the number or value that is in the middle of a list (the 50 percent point), where half are greater and half are less (typically a more useful indicator);
        - § Mode: the number or value that occurs most frequently in a series.

    Find out what the stats are really saying at: http://faculty.washington.edu/chudler/stat3.html.

3. *Middle class progress?* Is the typical middle class family doing better today than they were 25 years ago? The answer is no, according to new measures of economic well-being developed by senior economist Christian E. Weller. "The combination of stagnant incomes and staggering cost increases for important middle class items—housing, health care, education, and transportation—have left families with less money to save and spend. They are working longer to achieve the same results." See why the middle class is nervous about its future: http://www.americanprogress.org/issues/2005/10/b1119025.html.

4. *What's in your wallet?* Educator David Chandler offers a unique (if somewhat political) perspective of the fat-tailed distribution of income in the U.S. Consider the population as the length of the football field, arranged in order of income.

Now, picture your annual family income as a stack of $100 bills. The median (the family at the 50-yard line), at a little less than $50,000, is a stack of $100 bills about 2 inches high. Does your family make $100,000? You are on the 95-yard line and your stack is 4 inches high. At the 99-yard line, your income is about $300,000, a stack about a foot high. The curve reaches $1 million (a 40-inch high stack of $100 bills) one foot from the goal line. For Bill Gates, his stack reached about 30 miles. Income distribution is not a bell-shaped curve—it is an "L-shaped" curve! Check it out at: http://www.youtube.com/watch?v=woIkIph5xcU or http://www.lcurve.org.

5. *What is your attitude toward risk?* Knowing your attitude toward risk is important. According to Humanmetrics, a firm that specializes in Internet on-line personality testing, your success in life depends to a large extent on whether your activities suit your character and your personality. Their Risk Attitudes Profiler assesses the strength of expression of mutually opposed psychological qualities, such as aspirations for emotional order, peace, and safety on one hand and aspirations for "kicks" activity and risk on the other. The proportion of these varying qualities helps determine a person's character and the style of one's behavior in life. Discover your attitude toward risk at: http://www.humanmetrics.com/rot/riskguide.htm.

6. *Where to go for info?* See Appendix F for additional information relating to this chapter.

Chapter 7

How We Make Mistakes

There are two causes of human fallibility—ignorance and ineptitude.
~ Atul Gawande, Indian-American General Surgeon, journalist

The Gist

The Good:

- Memes propagate from brain-to-brain and constitute human culture
- Understanding memes helps us to identify our cognitive biases

The Bad:

- *Ignorance:* not knowing things we should know (lack of knowledge)
- *Ineptitude:* misapplying things we know (lack of care)
- Ignorance and ineptitude distort our perception of reality
- Our biggest risk is from things we know that aren't true

The Reality:

- Attitudes are influenced by our parents, peers, perceptions, and experiences
- People are often unaware that they have an attitude
- Young persons resemble their times more than they resemble their parents
- If you change your attitude, you can change your life

Introduction

Wisdom is keeping a sense of fallibility of all our views and opinions.
~ Gerald Brenan, British author

There is no one category of people who make mistakes. It happens to all of us: the well- and not so well-educated, the skilled and not so-skilled, the young and not so-young. We say the wrong thing, choose the wrong friends, or pass gas in a crowded elevator. Human beings are inherently not foolproof; to err is to be human. This likelihood of making errors is called *fallibility* and is a key characteristic of human behavior. Throughout history, fallibility has represented "lack of perfection."

Perhaps the greatest tale of human fallibility is that of the Trojan Horse. The Horse was first mentioned by the Greek poet Homer (not Simpson) in his epic poem, the *Odyssey* (ca. 850–800 B.C.E.).[78] Historian Barbara Tuchman describes the story of the Trojan Horse as "the most famous of the western world, the prototype of all tales of human conflict, the epic that belongs to all people and all times since—and even before—literacy began. It has endured deep in our minds and memories for twenty-eight centuries because it speaks to us of ourselves." That's powerful stuff.

Scholars tell us the "Trojan Horse" refers to the strategy that was used by the ancient Spartans to breach the walled city of Troy during the Trojan War. One of the most important events in Greek mythology, the war was dated by the Greek mathematician Eratosthenes to 1194–1184 B.C.E. This roughly corresponds with modern archaeological evidence of the burning of the city.[79]

The war was waged after Paris (not Hilton) of Troy abducted the beautiful Helen of Sparta. Sparta was a powerful Greek city-state and "hot lips" Helen was the main squeeze of Menelaus, Sparta's king. Following a fruitless 10-year siege of Troy, the Greeks got smart and built a huge wooden horse in which a select force of men hid (usually cited as 20 to 50 men). One morning at dawn, Trojan scouts discovered that the enemy had vanished, leaving only the strange and awesome wooden figure at the city gates. On it, the Greeks inscribed a dedication to Athena, goddess of heroic endeavor, asking for her aid to ensure their safe return

78 The most detailed and familiar version of the story is in *The Aeneid*, written by the classical Roman poet Virgil (70–19 B.C.E.). By Virgil's time, the tale incorporated the accumulated versions of more than a thousand years.

79 Ancient cities were often rebuilt on the ruins of older cities. The city identified as the Troy of Homer (Troy VIIa) is located on the western coast of modern day Turkey and shows clear evidence of catastrophic burning. A new city called Ilium was founded on the site in the reign of the Roman Emperor Augustus.

home. Sensing nothing amiss, the Trojans triumphantly pulled the Horse into their city as a victory trophy.

According to Homer, the wily Greeks only pretended to sail away. In actuality, they had stealthily sailed back under cover of darkness. Later that night the Greek contingent crept out of the Horse and opened the gates for the rest of the Greek forces. The Greek army swarmed in like locusts and destroyed the city, thus decisively ending the war. Hence the phrase, "Beware of Greeks bearing gifts."

Why did the Trojans fall for the ruse? Homer tells us the horse was held sacred in the Trojan culture and they were intrigued by the strange offering. Priam, the Trojan King, was flummoxed and sought counsel on what he should do with it. Ignorant of the danger, some of his advisors accepted the Greek inscription at face value. Capys the Elder, the voice of reason, cautioned that they should open the figure or burn it while it was still outside the city walls, a warning echoed by Priam's daughter Cassandra. She perceived the Greek's treachery and told the king to destroy the Horse. Despite clear warnings (and the clang of arms within), Priam carelessly ordered the Trojans to pull the Horse into the city and celebrate the victory. This they did, "heedless and blind with frenzy."

Although it speaks to us across nearly three millennia, the episode of the Horse is still relevant today. The story exemplifies how our questionable beliefs, despite clear and convincing evidence to the contrary, can be detrimental to our self-interest. And the rest, they say, is history and hors d'oeuvres. Anyone for a toasted Trojan on the half-shield?

Reali-tude:
Skepticism does not sell well.

The Good

Think about how stupid the average person is; now realize half of them are dumber than that.

~ George Carlin, comedian

Prior to Homer committing the *Odyssey* to writing in the 8th century B.C.E., ancient Greeks acquired knowledge via word-of-mouth. Learned poets, later called "bards," remembered and retold society's myths and legends and imparted important information to younger persons.[80] This reliance on memory led to considerable variance in stories because they were repeatedly altered over the course of many generations. Ancient people also learned by imitating behavior—for example, a person unskilled in the making of pottery observed the actions of a skilled potter in order to understand the trade. Since children commonly inherited the trade

80 A bard is a person who composes and recites epic or heroic poems. William Shakespeare is often referred to as a bard.

of their parents, imitation was a commonly used method to transmit important trade knowledge and skills.

With the advent of writing, knowledge no longer perished with the minds of those who could understand it. Experience could now be codified so that future generations might benefit. Following Homer, ancient Greeks extensively recorded scientific discoveries, philosophical thinking, government edicts and laws, literary works, and historical facts. Writing improved the *fidelity*, or accuracy of copied information, which meant that government edicts were less likely to undergo change as they spread. With the invention of the movable-type printing press by Johann Gutenberg (15th century A.D.), written works were mass-produced at relatively little cost and in relatively little time. This led to a quantum improvement in the *fecundity*, or the rate that information was copied, as well as the *longevity* with which the information stuck around so that it could be replicated again.

In his book *The Selfish Gene*, science writer Richard Dawkins labels the information that gets copied the "replicator" and points out that the most familiar information replicator is the gene. In classical (Darwinian) evolutionary theory, genes control the inheritable traits of organisms, such as blue eyes and big feet. Fundamentally, genes are simply a form of information—instructions for building proteins that are written in our DNA. They evolve by natural selection through the processes of variation, mutation, and inheritance. Over the course of many generations, genes that give their bearers a survival advantage and favor production of many offspring tend to proliferate at the expense of others. Those genes that are most proficient at being replicated, that is, passed to the next generation, gradually prosper. Those that are not proficient will, like the dodo, become extinct.

Cultural overload

> *We live in the Postmodern world, where everything is possible and almost nothing is certain.*
>
> ~ Vaclav Havel, former president of the Czech Republic

Now for the cool part. Dawkins extended the principles of natural selection to explain the spread of ideas and cultural phenomena. To emphasize the commonality with genes, Dawkins coined the term *meme* (pronounced "meem"), derived from the Greek word *mimema*, which means "something imitated." According to the Oxford English Dictionary, a meme is "an element of culture that may be considered to be passed on by non-genetic means, especially imitation." Examples of memes include ideas, tunes, habits, jokes, trends, fashions, fads, and inventions. Memes also represent ways of doing things that we copy from person to person such as rules of thumb, standards of social behavior, and holiday rituals. *Memetics*, the study of memes, helps us understand a number of things that genetics has difficulty explaining—why we have exceptionally large brains, why we alone compose symphonies, drive cars, eat spaghetti with a fork, do the Harlem Shake, and wonder about the origins of the universe. It also explains the development of grammatical language, marketing campaigns, and behaviors relating to cults, ideologies, and drug use.

> *"My boyfriend just told me about memes, the theory of which apparently involves looking at ideas as viruses that invade the human brain. Strong memes replicate, causing the ideas to spread from person to person, and you wind up with things like religion and professional sports. Please... what's the story on this?"*
> ~ Susan P., Internet blogger

According to Dawkins, the meme is to culture what the gene is to biology. Just as genes propagate themselves in the gene pool by leaping from body to body via sperm or eggs, so memes propagate themselves in the meme pool by leaping from brain to brain via imitation. Since the person who transmitted the meme will continue to carry it, the process can be interpreted as a replication—a copy of the meme is made in the memory of another individual, thereby making him or her into a carrier of the meme. It is this process of self-reproduction, spreading over a group of individuals, which defines the meme as a true replicator. In this sense, memes are similar to parasites or infections.

Like genes, memes are in a Darwinian survival contest, struggling to out-compete rival memes for our attention. Think about all the ideas that you have in your head right now. They are all memes, and they all came from somewhere.[81] Some came from friends, some from television or the Internet, and all are competing to get themselves copied into other people's minds. Every time you utter a curse word or display a "hang loose" sign you are facilitating the spread of those memes. Each time you sport a schnoz stud you are helping that fashion idea enter other people's minds. Some memes are powerful—for example, if we compare the relative number of cats and dogs killed on the streets to the number of children with similar fatal encounters, we see the value of the "look-both-ways-before-you-cross" meme. Other memes are trivial such as, "Can you hear me now?" and "I'm lovin' it." Evolving cumulatively over time, in the aggregate memes constitute human culture, which many scientists believe is the primary factor that gives humans a competitive advantage over other animals.[82]

How big are memes? Like a bra, only as large as needed to do the job. A memetic "unit" can be considered to be the smallest pattern of information that copies itself completely while remaining intact. For example, the first four notes of Beethoven's Fifth Symphony is a meme, but the first three is not; the fourth note is always included. The entire symphony can also be regarded as a single meme. This begs the question, "Are all mental contents memes?" No, because not all of them were copied from someone else. If all your memes were removed, you would

---

81 Sometimes referred to as white knowledge. the constant stream of communication in which people live helps us learn things without being conscious that we're learning them. For example, cultural incidences, slang words, and texting acronyms are white knowledge.

82 Outside of humans, memetic copying in the animal world is rare. Examples include birdsongs, dolphin tail-walking, and fish nesting sites. Also, certain primate techniques for hunting or using tools are memes that are passed from parents or the social group to the youngsters.

still have many perceptions, emotions, imaginings, and learned skills that are yours alone, that you did not acquire from anyone else, and can never share with another. Only your hairdresser (or body piercer) knows for sure!

Where do we find memes? Besides being recorded in the neural structure of a person's brain, philosopher Brent Silby identifies four other repositories, or encoding mediums for memes: (1) musical notation (such as a page of sheet music), (2) written text, (3) visible or vocal action, and (4) electronic data. Memes that are good at replicating tend to leave more copies of themselves in these repositories. If a story replicates by getting told or read (like the *Odyssey*), then it will survive. Successful replication has made *Guinness World Records* the best-selling copyrighted series of all-time and *Apple* the most successful world brand. Memes that are not so good at replicating tend to become dormant or extinct. Libraries are full of memetic fossils in the form of books with ideas that are never looked at.[83]

Word of mouth, referred to as a "parentally-transmitted" meme, tends to be an imperfect replicator because errors are easily introduced. We may embellish a story, forget a word of the song, or modify an idea, leading to what marketing guru Seth Godin calls "meme decay and extinction." Technology provides a quantum leap in efficiency, spreading memes horizontally like a virus between people who do not know each other. These are called "culturally-transmitted memes."[84] The term "going viral" is a neologism used to describe a catchphrase or concept that spreads quickly from person to person via the Internet, much like an inside joke. Within minutes, it can be multiplied to thousands, if not millions of recipients (high fecundity) without information degradation (high fidelity). Many of these Internet memes originated on "crowd psychology" websites like 4chan, LOLcats, and others that enable content to quickly be passed on to large numbers of viewers. If sufficiently attractive, the meme might become a cultural classic (longevity), such as "If you knew that visiting your grandparents could change the world, would you do it?" or "Let's do the time warp again!"

Beyond curiosity, do memes really matter?[85] Yes, they do. Many memes are learned in school and provide the mind-tools that we need to be competent in life. With the digital revolution, however, the trend has been for conservative, parentally-transmitted memes to lose ground to more radical culturally-transmitted memes. The latter experience more intense competition than do the former and spread at a much faster rate. As a result, culturally-transmitted memes are rushing headlong toward the future and have no need for the past. And as we shall

---

83 In a huge loss for humanity, the burning of the ancient Library at Alexandria destroyed the world's largest repository of recorded scientific memes. The library contained works in mathematics, astronomy, physics, natural sciences, and other subjects. Two millennia later, "herbologists" Tommy Chong and Cheech Marin lamented that all the good stuff had gone "up in smoke."

84 Neuroscientist Susan Blackmore introduced a special category of memes called temes. Temes reside in technological artifacts instead of the human mind.

85 Unlike physical genes, the vagueness of memes make them difficult to study scientifically. Thus, while theoretically interesting, they are of limited scientific value. Semiologist (one who studies signs and symbols) Paul Bouissac notes, "Some thirty years after the publication of Dawkins' landmark book... it is still debatable whether this notion is a fanciful fad on the wane or has some serious scientific legitimacy."

see, this has implications regarding what you know, what you don't know, and ultimately how you behave.

Reali-tude:
Always consider the sources of your information.

The bottom line:

- We often hold questionable beliefs despite clear evidence they might be harmful.
- A meme is cultural information that replicates in the mind like genes in the body.
- Technology vastly multiplies the reach and potency of memes.
- Memes influence what we know and how we behave.

The Bad

All we are saying, is give memes a chance.
~ John Lennon, musician (misquoted)

The accelerating number of memes we receive has made our social environment less stable and predictable. We are bombarded by memes from newspapers, the Internet, advertising, television, and so forth. To cope with this avalanche, we have developed cognitive biases, or mental shortcuts that help us navigate complexity, make choices, and adapt. According to philosopher Matt Gers, these shortcuts help us discriminate which memes to "bank" in our knowledge inventory, which ones to ignore or discard, and which get expressed in our behavior. But there is a problem. Like a computer virus, certain memes may infect us with what cognitive scientist Dan Dennett calls "toxic ideas." These emotional bits of programming, if strong enough, can completely mute our sense of logic and cause us to do some very self-destructive things.

Memes develop characteristics that make it more likely for them to be replicated (thus increasing their chances of survival)... The fatal mistake (people make), however, is just because a meme is emotionally appealing doesn't make it actually beneficial to the host.
~ Trendem, Super Moderator, *Online Debate Network*

Where mistakes originate

Nothing in the world is more dangerous than a sincere ignorance and conscientious stupidity.
~ Martin Luther King, Jr., clergyman, activist

Bad decision outcomes do not happen from a generalized tendency to screw everything up. Rather, they stem from fallibilities in the way we think. In recognizing these fallibilities, or mental traps, we stand a better chance of avoiding poor life-choices and living happier lives. What causes our fallibilities? In their 1975 essay *Toward a Theory of Medical Fallibility*, philosophers Samuel Gorovitz and Alasdair MacIntyre explored the nature of errors made by medical practitioners. They found two principal mental weaknesses, or "cognitive flaws" why people are prone to fail: ignorance and ineptitude.[86] Expanding their descriptions in the context of young persons:

1. *Ignorance is failing to know:* To be ignorant is to be clueless. We lack the knowledge or education to reasonably assess a situation, act with sound judgment, and make a smart choice. In other words, we have insufficient true information about how the world really works and the realities of risk. For example, ignorance on the part of "Shotgun" Willie Nelson as to what his accountants were up to earned him a fat $16.7 million tax bill from the IRS. Investor ignorance (and greed) allowed convicted financier Bernie Madoff to bilk them out of $50 billion.

2. *Ineptitude is failing to know better:* To be inept is to be careless. We lack the self-awareness, skills, or judgment to make a smart choice. This may be due to apathy, faulty reasoning, lack of objectivity, complacency, negligence, shortsightedness, arrogance, or even fear. In the extreme, ineptitude may simply be conscientious stupidity. Who has not heard of competent medical practitioners that operated on the wrong limb, left surgical tools behind in the rib cage, or injected the wrong vial? The blue dress that visited the Oval Office? Or Binky the Bear's midnight playmate?

These flaws in our thinking—ignorance (lack of knowledge) and ineptitude (lack of care)—are the seeds from which our fallibilities germinate and knowledge is their common underpinning. Knowledge that is specific information about something is referred to as "knows-that." Wouldn't studying be a breeze if we knew the questions on the final exam? Knowledge in terms of the practical use of information is called "knows-how." This is expertise and skills that are acquired through experience or education. In his book *Personal Knowledge*, polymath Michael Polanyi uses the example of riding a bicycle to emphasize that knowing the theory of balance (knows-that) cannot substitute for the practical knowledge of how to ride (knows-how).

The difficulty with acquiring knowledge is the world plays hard to get. Instead of providing us with clear and accurate information that would allow us to better "know," it presents us with a messy mosaic of random, incomplete, unrepresentative, ambiguous, inconsistent, unpalatable, and secondhand data. "We must recognize the inherent fallibility of human thought," writes philosopher Karl Popper. "Knowledge must always be seen as tentative and subject to correction." In his book *The Age of Fallibility: Consequences of the War on Terror*, bazillionaire George Soros argues that Popper did not go far enough—the divergence between

86 These cognitive errors were introduced in Chapter 6.

reality and the participant's perception of reality ensures that we are bound to be wrong, he points out.

It is estimated that around 60 percent of aircraft accidents are caused or partially caused by human fallibility. Similarly, a high percentage of patients that are treated in hospitals (around 15 percent) are there because of the fallibility of medical staff. Having said this, there are accidents which are simply a consequence of human stupidity. For example, an air crash in Russia was caused by the pilot allowing his son to play with the controls on an aircraft in flight.
~ Ian Sommerville, professor of software engineering

How can this be? *Zut alors*—are we not the masters of our fate; the captains of our soul? Pinnacles of perfection? Far from it Snerdly. What we know and what we do not know in large part determine our success for picking winners and avoiding losers in life. In Figure 7.1 the circle represents our personal "knowledge space." It is the sum total of all of the memes in our environment (all copyable or learnable behaviors and semantic knowledge) plus any "non-meme" derived knowledge that we may acquire. This total space can be partitioned into what we have already learned (things we know) and everything else (things we do not know). Each of us has our own uniquely defined knowledge space.[87]

Figure 7.1 Personal knowledge space.

That really annoying person you know, the one who's always spouting bullshit, the person who always thinks they're right? Well, the odds are that for somebody else, you're that person. So take the amount you think you know, reduce it by 99.999%, and then you'll have an idea how much you actually know regarding things outside your Monkeysphere.
~ David Wong, author, "Inside the Monkeysphere"

Reali-tude:
Believing something is true does not make it so.

87 Epistemology, or theory of knowledge, is the branch of philosophy concerned with the nature and limitations of knowledge—it is the study of how we know what we know. Epistemological modesty is the knowledge of how little we know and can know.

The bottom line:

- Mistakes originate from ignorance and ineptitude (our mental weaknesses).
- "Knows-that" represents specific information about something.
- "Knows-how" represents practical expertise and skills.
- All of us might, at any time, be wrong.

Cognitive flaw #1: Ignorance

> *The recipe for perpetual ignorance is a very simple and effective one: be satisfied with your opinions and content with your knowledge*
> ~ Elbert Hubbard, author, philosopher

Ignorance—*what we do not know*— is a lack of knowledge or education. As shown in Figure 7.2, ignorance has two uncertainties: our "unknown-unknowns" and our "unknown-knowns." The "unknown-unknowns" are *what we don't know we don't know*. In other words, we are unaware of things we should know. If you were ever admonished by a traffic court judge that "ignorance of the law is no excuse," you learned this lesson the hard way. What we do not know also includes our "unknown-knowns," which is *what we know that just ain't so*. In other words, things that we know and believe to be true, which are in fact *not* true. Let's briefly look at each of these forms.

Figure 7.2 What we do not know (ignorance).

☞ *What we don't know we don't know (our "unknown-unknowns")*

"Unknown-unknowns" are things we don't realize we do not know, but should. Charlatans grow fat off your ignorance and not being savvy about what is going down can leave you standing on the sloped deck of the Titanic without a life-jacket. When it comes to making smart life-choices, the thinking young person should pause and reflect, "Is there anything important I have not considered?" Sure, ignorance is bliss... that is, until the music stops, the lights go out, and your feet get wet.

***BRAIN SNACK:** What you don't know you don't know is staggering. In their 2008 "Founders' Letter," Google's Sergey Brin and Larry Page reported on the growing amount of researchable information. Every minute, 15 hours worth of video are uploaded to YouTube (which Google acquired in 2006), the equiva-*

lent of 86,000 new full-length movies every week. With Gmail, some Googlers have more than 25 gigabytes of email going back nearly 10 years. Google Book Search makes possible to search the full text of almost 10 million books. Not written in your lingo? No problemo! Google Translate supports automatic machine translation between 1,640 language pairs. And a few clicks on Google Earth places you at your front door. While guarded in their predictions, Messieurs Brin and Page expect computers to be 100 times faster still and storage to be 100 times cheaper in the coming decade, with artificial intelligence becoming accepted as standard computational capabilities. Sick!

The lesson of Google is we are awash up to our nostrils in information. But wait! As our sphere of knowledge increases, so does its contact with the unknown, what psychologist Peter Standen calls the *zone of ignorance*. So, in the final analysis all we can really say with absolute certainty is, "I think therefore I am."[88] And even that isn't good enough. The human mind is easily fooled from without, which is how magicians and pick-pockets make a good living. But the mind is also easily fooled from within. The pain felt by the brain in an amputated limb, for example, makes no logical sense but hurts just as bad as if the limb were still present.

Reali-tude:
Absence of evidence is not evidence of absence.

☞ *What we know that just ain't so (our "unknown-knowns")*

The old saw says, "It isn't what you know that will get you in trouble. It's what you know that just ain't so." What things have you believed in that turned out not to be true? And why did you believe in them? Here are a few that come to mind:

- Santa Claus
- Loch Ness Monster
- Y2K non-event
- UFOs and alien abductions
- Weapons of mass destruction
- O. J. Simpson
- Rising real estate prices
- The daVinci code

"Unknown-knowns," or things we know that just ain't so, are insidious because they operate below the truth detection radar.[89] Although we think or assume these things to be true, in fact they are not true. As such, they may create a false sense of security, self-importance, or self-righteousness. What is the difference between a person who genuinely knows, as opposed to merely believing or having an opinion? The answer is hard evidence and a clear perception of reality.

88 This quote is from *Principles of Philosophy* by French mathematician René Descartes. Descartes laid out four rules of thought to ensure that our knowledge rests upon a firm foundation: (1) accept nothing that is not clear and distinct; (2) divide difficult subjects into many small parts; (3) start with the simplest problems; and (4) be comprehensive.

89 One beneficial variant of what you don't know you know is intuition. We'll taker a closer look at this in Chapter 16.

We're at the end of the age. Planet Earth is about to be recycled. Your only chance to survive or evacuate is to leave with us. I'm here to offer you... an opportunity to know the truth so that you can connect with it, at any level, then you might survive the re-spading or recycling that is about to occur.
~ Marshall Applewhite, founder of Heaven's Gate[90]

Being in tune with what is happening "within" is just as important as knowing what is happening "without." As we shall discover, ignorance can lead us to be overly confident in our judgment, misinterpret the context of change, and underestimate the long-term consequences of our controllable decisions. We can overcome ignorance by improving our education, thinking critically, and effectively using intuition and common sense.

The discipline of reality: personal economics success depends upon our understanding reality as it exists, not as we want it to be!

Reali-tude:
Reality is an objective absolute.

Cognitive flaw #2: Ineptitude

Briggs was right. You guys don't have enough experience.
~ Clint Eastwood, actor, as Dirty Harry in *Magnum Force*

In the myth of the Trojan Horse, the Greeks cleverly exploited the Trojan's mental rather than their military vulnerabilities. King Priam was not ignorant of the danger, nor was he necessarily stupid. Questionable beliefs often exist in spite of the evidence, for experienced and less informed people alike. For Priam, it was not fate but free choice that took the Horse within the walls. The feasible alternative—that of destroying the Horse—was always open. Priam had all the info he needed to make the right choice but misapplied what he knew. The disinclination to value reliable sources of information and objectively examine one's own fallibilities trapped his judgment. And this has implications for us today.

Like the hapless Trojans, it is in our nature to be complacent and careless. But negligence is only one form of ineptitude. We are also shortsighted. Despite knowing we need to take action, we niggly avoid doing that which is in our long-term interest. Take the woman who knows the importance of periodic mammograms, yet for whatever reason never bothers to get screened. It may be that she is too busy, too lazy, or willfully ignorant for fear of the results or the cost. Later, when she is diagnosed with breast cancer, she is angry with herself and feels guilty for hurting her family.

90 Applewhite and 38 of his followers committed mass suicide on March 26, 1997. Their deaths were timed to coincide with the passage of the Hale-Bopp comet, which Applewhite believed contained a spacecraft that would whisk them away. A tragic example of what he knew that just wasn't so.

We also fall prey to "wooden-headedness," or the inclination to believe what we want to believe regardless of the facts. In *The March of Folly*, historian Barbara Tuchman describes wooden-headedness as the "assessment of a situation in terms of preconceived fixed notions, while ignoring or rejecting any contrary signs." Tuchman says this stubborn, "I've made up my mind, don't confuse me with the facts" mentality is present in all human affairs and is a major problem in today's society. We see this in the partisan discourse that masquerades as political debate among government officials and on talk radio and TV.

Finally, we are susceptible to what historian Richard Shenkman calls "bone-headedness." This broad category basically points to our gullibility to meaningless phrases and stereotypes. We fall prey to irrational biases and are receptive to simplistic diagnoses and solutions that play on our hopes and fears. Our inability to apply some basic common sense about what we are told allows others to easily take advantage of us. In his book, *Just How Stupid Are We?*, Shenkman describes these manifestations as "defining characteristics of stupidity."

> *"In a way that's different from all of human history, ineptitude has become as much our difficulty as ignorance. Go back 60 years; the major reason that people didn't live to 80 like the average person does now was because of ignorance. We didn't know how to treat heart disease and didn't know how to prevent it; we didn't know how to take care of high blood pressure, stop strokes, or treat many infectious diseases. But look where we are today: we have 6,600 different drugs, thousands of surgical treatments, and hundreds of ways to make diagnoses. We have this vast edifice of scientific knowledge and the challenge is there's a gap between what we know and what we actually do. Our struggle is ineptitude, or the nice way to put it is "performance."*
> ~ Atul Gawande, professor of surgery, Harvard Medical School

Thus, we are the products not of irrationality, but of flawed rationality. We are, in the words of sociologist Robert Merton, "irresistible products of our own experience."[91] And lacking the wisdom that comes from experience, attempts to cope with the complexities of modern life too often lay bare the shortcomings of youth. No rational young person marries with the prior intent to get divorced or abuses credit just so he can file for bankruptcy. As we learned from the story of the Trojan Horse, smart people do dumb-ass things (too).

☞ *What we know (our "known-knowns" and "known-unknowns")*

Looking at see Figure 7.3 (page 116), we see that *things we know* has two certainties: our "known-knowns" and our "known-unknowns." The "known-knowns" are things we are consciously aware we know. For example, we know that wearing seat belts saves lives. Things we know also includes the "known-unknowns." These are

91 Merton, an American sociologist, also coined the phrases "self-fulfilling prophecy," "role model," and "unintended consequences."

things we are consciously aware we don't know.[92] For example, when buying a new car we know we need info on prices and features so that we can make an informed decision as to the right model for us.

Figure 7.3 What we know (ineptitude).

No one is completely immune from error. Even an experienced writer cannot write a few pages of text without making a grammatical mistake. A programmer faces the same problem—no matter how good you are; on average you'll make a number of mistakes per N lines of code. To be sure, the more careful you are, the fewer mistakes you will make. If you are diligent, you will do this anyway. But no matter what the effort there will always be mistakes, and to one degree or another, we seem to compound these unavoidable errors. Philosophers Gorovitz and MacIntyre label these "necessary fallibilities."[93] Let's face it, doo-doo happens.

Then there are avoidable errors. Doesn't everybody know there are all sorts of indulgences that are delightful at the moment but disastrous at the end? Doesn't every little boy know that if he eats enough candy he will get sick? Doesn't the smoker understand she will one day be wheezing with an oxygen bottle? The dipsomaniac that he is ruining his liver and shortening his life? The Don Juan that he is letting himself in for every sort of risk, from blackmail to disease? Don't the idler and the spendthrift know, even in the midst of their glorious flings, that they are headed for a future of debt and poverty? Like, /obvious dude. Or is it?

> *Every scar has a story. Scarred is an intense look at some of the most gruesome scars from across the country. These aren't actors. There are no special effects or makeup department. These are real people, experiencing real pain and winding up with real scars. These real-life risk takers share their stomach-turning "Scar Stories" about how even simple stunts can go horribly wrong.*
>
> ~ Scarred, mtv.com

As with ignorance, being in tune with what is happening "within" is just as important as knowing what is happening "without." As we shall discover, ineptitude

92 "Schrödinger's Cat" was a thought experiment used by physicist Edwin Schrödinger to illustrate the bizarreness of quantum mechanics. If we place a cat in a box, the known-known is that he is in the box (because we put him inside). The known-unknown is whether he is alive or dead (because he is very quiet). Unlike the everyday world, at the atomic level the "cat" exists in a state that is simultaneously both alive and dead. We cannot know for sure until we open the box and clear the ambiguity, hopefully in the cat's favor!

93 According to Gorovitz and MacIntyre, as we move from predicting how things behave in general to predicting how a certain thing will behave, skill and experience can only go so far. Despite our best care, errors in judgment will persist due to faulty data, flawed reasoning, incomplete knowledge, limitations of human processing, and inherent biases.

can lead us to be overly confident in our abilities, slow to change, and favor immediate gratification of our emotional self-interests. We can overcome ineptitude by taking time to self-reflect, seeking other points of view, and acquiring wisdom from trustworthy sources.

The discipline of awareness: personal economics success depends upon knowing our limitations as they exist, not as we want them to be!

Reali-tude:
Lack of care is as big a risk as lack of knowledge.

The bottom line

- *Ignorance:* not knowing things we should know (lack of knowledge).
- *Ineptitude:* misapplying things we know (lack of care).
- Cognitive flaws are destructive because they lead to self-deceptions.
- Things we know that just ain't so are the most troublesome unknowns.

The Reality

The greatest discovery of my generation is that human beings can alter their lives by altering their attitudes of mind.
~ William James, psychologist

Although sometimes used interchangeably, values, biases, and attitudes are different. Values are abstract ideals—global beliefs and feelings—that guide our lifelong thinking and behavior. Values, such as living one's life according to the Golden Rule, are fairly well set by teens and tend to be consistent over time and related situations. Bias is a preference toward a particular point of view. It distorts our perception of reality and inhibits impartial, unprejudiced, or objective judgments. For example, believing that things will always work out in the end is a bias. Attitudes are particularly important, so they are worth a closer look.

Attitudes

Ooh ooh, ooh ooh, oooohhh, I gotta new attitude...
~ Dr. Laura Schlesinger, talk show host

The concept of attitude seems to cause confusion. Psychologists Alice Eagly and Shelly Chaiken define attitude as "a psychological tendency that is expressed by evaluating a particular entity with some degree of favor or disfavor." In other words, attitude is a like or dislike that we direct toward a specific thing, person, or event. Parents, friends, and peer groups are very influential in shaping attitudes.

Our perceptions, direct life experiences, and even our genetics also play a part in forming our attitudes.

All attitudes fall between two extremes, or bipolar dimensions, such as like/dislike, good/bad, love/hate, warm/cold.[94] Attitudes may be positive ("Go Chargers!"), negative ("Neil is a dweeb"), or neutral ("Either Pepsi or Coke is okay"). We may also harbor more than one of these feelings toward something. When we simultaneously like and dislike something, such as "I am attracted to the power and responsibility that comes with a high-powered corporate job, but I worry that my commitment to this career will compromise my chance of raising a family," we say that our attitude is ambivalent.

BRAIN SNACK: *In the early 1980s, computer geeks began to make heavy use of dial-up bulletin board systems or BBSs (named after the cork bulletin boards often found in entrances of supermarkets, schools, Laundromats, or other public areas). Once logged in, a user could download or upload software and data, read news, and exchange messages with other users through electronic mail. With the proliferation of BBSs (and later, email), the vast majority of people communicating did not know each other well, if at all. Minus the facial expressions and verbal inflections that face-to-face communication affords, misinterpretation of one's attitudes and intentions was all too easy.*

Computer scientist Scott Fahlman is generally credited with solving this shortcoming by using the smile and frown icons to convey one's emotions. In a 1982 post to a Carnegie Mellon University message board, Fahlman suggested the use of ":-)" to show one's pleasure (or to indicate a joke) and ":-(" to show displeasure. These caught on and evolved into small pieces of graphic art called emoticons, a portmanteau of the English words "emotion" (or "emote") and "icon." Today, emoticons have become an important part of on-line lingo by visually expressing one's attitudes, emotions, and moods.[95] *:-)*

Attitudes are important because they are woven into the fabric of daily life. Research shows that we register an immediate and automatic reaction of "good" or "bad" toward everything we encounter in less than a second, even before we are aware of forming an attitude. Once we have established an attitude, it then becomes closely linked to the representation of the object. Usually our behaviors reflect our established beliefs and attitudes, but not always. Just because you yell, "You can take this job and shove it maggot!" to yourself does not necessarily mean that you intend to quit your job.

---

94 Attitudes are typically measured using a Likert scale, named after its inventor, psychologist Rensis Likert. Respondents indicate their level of agreement to a questionnaire statement such as, "Pre-marital sex is okay if you are in love." One commonly used scale is: Strongly Disagree; Disagree; Neither Agree or Disagree; Agree; Strongly Agree.

95 The Japanese use ideograms and pictographs called "emoji" (from "picture" (e) + "letter" (moji)) in their electronic messages and Web pages. The characters are used much like emoticons elsewhere, but a wider range is provided and the icons are standardized into the hardware. In 2013, *Emoji Dick* became the first emoji novel accepted into the Library of Congress.

Unlike personality, attitudes are malleable and we often don't realize when they change. For example, your attitude toward global warming might be, "I think global warming is just a long-term cyclical trend that has nothing to do with humans." When your belief changes after watching Al Gore's documentary, *An Inconvenient Truth*, you are unlikely to be aware what changed your mind. At other times, however, we are keenly aware of our change in attitude. Most of us have seen the stark reaction of the panel on *American Idol* when a less physically attractive person reveals a one-in-a-million singing voice!

Reali-tude:
To know a person's attitude, read his bumper sticker.

The generational divide

> *When I was young, we were taught to be discreet and respectful of elders, but the present youth are exceedingly disrespectful and impatient of restraint.*
> ~ Hesiod, Greek poet, 8th century B.C.E.

> *God but I can't wait until the ultra-conservative stubborn uncooperative ancient mentality of our elders is wiped away from america, so we can be progressive and do things right.*
> ~ Shiney, Internet blogger

The basic characteristics of Generation NeXt—motivated by a search for new experiences and treated with suspicion by its elders—are not new. Just about every generation has been described in exactly the same way and this often creates friction. The most significant (and to some, the only) reason is age. People have different priorities and operate in different ways because of their stage in life. For example, freedom from commitments makes a young person's attitude toward leisure activities considerably different from that of her parents. A second divisor is the current economic, social, and political conditions. People are products of their times, and these act upon people of different ages in different ways. Witness the overwhelming youth vote for Obama over McCain (68 to 30 percent) in the 2008 Presidential election.

Experiences that occur during our formative years help to define and shape differences between generations. Baby Boomers' attitudes were influenced by the advent of the television, rock and roll, the Cold War, the Vietnam War, free love, and the threat of nuclear annihilation. Gen NeXters were shaped by the Internet, cable TV, globalization, September 11th, environmentalism, and (until 2008) a growing economy. Of course, not every individual fits their generation's personality profile exactly. Some embody it, and some spend a lifetime trying to live it down.

BRAIN SNACK: *The Baby Boomer generation includes those who were born during the Post-World War II baby boom between 1946 and 1964. Boomers* *number 80 million strong and have been called the "pig in the python"—by sheer numbers, they are a demographic bulge that has remodeled society as it passed through it. The youngest Baby Boomers are only 45 or so now and have another 20 years before they even start retirement. As a result, Boomers will continue to be the dominant economic powerhouse in the United States for some time. NeXters with an attitude, take note!*

The 2008 world-wide economic meltdown touched a generational raw nerve. Many young persons hocked a loogie at the chicanery of financial services moguls, who they saw as nitro-fueled on greed. They were also po'd at what they considered to be Homer Simpson-type government regulators who were caught dozing at the switch. As evidenced by the Occupy Wall Street demonstrations, many NeXters are outraged by what they view as a sellout of their financial future (along with the effects of global climate change) by the older generation. And Baby Boomers were often clueless regarding the role played by their rampant consumerism in helping create the debacle. Following a lifetime of work they were shell-shocked to see their nest-eggs vaporized and retirements delayed (or denied). As evidenced below, attitudes expressed by members of these two generations can be very different.

☞ *NeXters (as seen by NeXters):*

- "I must say I was ignorant of the fact that we Millennials were in for such hard times. It's true though, we will not be as blessed as our parents in America. It is also hitting me how much I will owe with student loans if I graduate without a heart attack from anxiety."
- "Many Millennials work very hard to earn their own money and pay their own bills. Many care deeply about the state of society and take action to improve it. How can anyone of the Baby Boomer generation pretend to be surprised at how the Millennial generation has turned out when they raised it?"
- "I have been working for half a decade and am still in debt from college. A nice chunk of my salary each month goes to Social Security/Medicare and subsidizing (Boomer's) costly insurance premiums. The Boomer generation doesn't have the balls to discuss the problem; any politician who might mention it is immediately attacked by the AARP."
- "I rarely see an older worker wanting to really communicate with a younger one. They don't trust them because they dye their hair an odd color or have a pierced eyebrow. We can accomplish a lot more than the older generation thinks, if they will only pay attention."

☞ *NeXters (as seen by Boomers):*

- "I teach in a university and see Millennials daily. They are the most educated, competitive, and technologically savvy generation of all. Their economic concerns are modest compared to the generation that has built a benefit structure for itself that is unsustainable."

- "A lot of my students who post questionable content on-line feel entitled to act like idiots AND get jobs. Before we start trumpeting how Gen (NeXt) "gets it" we ought to take a very serious look at the things they are NOT getting:

  Myth: I don't want to work for the kind of employer who would judge me based on my exhibitionist videos.
  Fact: Employers regard questionable behavior as a risk. Their question is not one of morality but pragmatism: "How can I trust you with responsibility for my clients and our accounts when you clearly do not possess sound judgment?"
  Myth: I am a different/creative/interesting individual and can get away with things others cannot.
  Fact: In addition to your outlandish behavior, you'd better have some very special insights, experience, or talent to support your value to an employer. Being simply interesting, cool, or fun means zero to an employer who is hiring you to DO A JOB."

- "It's great that the new iPhone-toting generation is more connected, Internet savvy, and digital oriented, but they'll need to learn other skills if they're to advance and grow professionally. In other words, just what the rest of us did."
- "People are still people, and as the (NeXters) get more responsibilities (family, mortgage, aging parents, saving for college and retirement, etc.) they will be no different than other middle aged folks. Boomers were idealistic in the 1960s and 1970s; now they are the establishment."

☞ *Boomers (as seen by NeXters):*

- "Boomer mentality = NO SAVINGS + ME FIRST + OVER STRETCHED CREDIT + NO LONG TERM DECISION MAKING + BOTOX"
- "Feel sorry for Boomers? No way. Feel sorry instead for those who are young teens now. They will be stuck with having to pay huge taxes to pay for Boomer entitlements and the federal deficit. Look to a future election that is not split Red/Blue, but Gray/Not Gray."
- "Most of my friends have parents with multiple divorces, insatiable appetites for stuff they cannot afford, and little to no retirement. My parents (no longer married) squandered tons of money trying to 'out do' the Joneses and declared bankruptcy three times."
- "How many 21–25 year olds will end up using their college degrees to work at Wal-Mart because some old farts didn't plan for their retirement and can't vacate their positions?"
- "The Boomer generation is no different than government. Both spend way beyond their means, and want children and grandchildren to pay for it."

☞ *Boomers (as seen by Boomers):*

- "A lot of Boomers WILL go broke and I don't feel sorry for them! I have been in the financial services industry for 38 years and have been preaching saving that entire time, mostly to deaf ears. Spend-spend-spend! That's the mantra of these people. Vacations, huge houses, credit cards to the max. Save? Buy insurance? Invest? Not a chance. No, I don't feel sorry at all. But I DO feel sorry for my son and his son... their generation will be stuck with paying the debts of ours."
- "As a Baby Boomer, so many of my friends are realizing retirement is not an option due to the need to support their kids and parents, and wanting to stay alive and connected."
- "People in their 50s have difficulty finding work that actually pays for a living. Don't tell me to go back to school. I went back 10 years ago and added an MBA and a CPA to my credentials, now I'm told repeatedly that I'm overqualified. People in the 20- to 30-year range have no idea what it's like trying to find a decent job when your only disqualification is your age."
- "A substantial number of Boomers have prepared well for retirement. Being prepared is not the result of some sudden flight of fancy and fortune. It began 40+ years ago with career choices, education, discipline, sobriety (for the most part) and planning."

Reali-tude:
People are often unaware they have an attitude.

The bottom line

- An attitude is a like or a dislike directed toward a specific thing.
- Attitudes are influenced by memes, other people, and direct life experiences.
- People often fail to realize that their attitude has changed.
- Young persons resemble their times more than they resemble their parents.

Doctor's Prescription (Rx)

There are three things extremely hard; steel, a diamond, and to know one's self.
~ Ben Franklin, in *Poor Richards Almanack*

Memes are at the base of the information food chain. They are packets that we receive from our environment, and if successful, are added to our knowledge inventory. To navigate the bombardment of memes, we have developed a variety of cognitive biases. These biases are used to identify data that we perceive to be relevant, but they may also affect our judgment. Here are some tips:

To develop meme awareness:

- *Think in new ways.* Dubbed "information packets with an attitude," memes are a different way to look at the world. When you allow for alternative explanations for the way the world works, you are more receptive to other perspectives and less likely to judge in haste. This helps you to be tolerant of other people who are infected by memes you might disagree with.
- *Spot mental viruses.* There are zillions of ideas in the ideaosphere and their hosts have evolved clever ways to sneak them into your mind unnoticed. Like weeds in your garden, they take root and before you know it, they take over. Knowing how ideas can "take on a life of their own," you can be more adept at mentally quarantining idea viruses.
- *Immunize yourself.* Familiarity with memes provides the best immunity from dangerous information-contagions like emotional stampedes, asset bubbles, fads, and political hype. Let common sense, not emotions be your guide. Understand that your biases affect your judgment. Think, do a fact check, then work out the implications.
- *Challenge assumptions.* Avoid memes that ask you to "act immediately." A meme that instructs you to forward it right away is a mind virus trying to reproduce. Memes don't go viral without people power, so look for reputable communities working for change rather than blindly replicating ideas.
- *Be skeptical.* Question sources, especially those on-line. Examine memes for hidden agendas in the context of the larger picture. Look to actual authorities and tribal elders to validate rumors. Refrain from forwarding anything whose origin you don't know. When in doubt, throw it out!

To counter ignorance and ineptitude:

- *Get educated.* Education is the key to not getting duped. Understand the extent to which there are things you do not know, but should. Culture acquires information that is useful to you at a much faster rate than you are able to absorb it. Don't re-invent the wheel.
- *Increase your awareness.* Developing a sense of self-awareness is a critical skill. Make it a habit to periodically review your beliefs, motivations, attitudes, and biases. If in doubt, examine your behaviors (what you do) then make inferences.
- *Improve your attitude.* Stop whining and criticizing others. In the end, only your mother will put up with your complaints. Focus your energy on dealing with problems effectively.
- *Learn from others.* "Knows-how" is as important as "knows-what" and having too little knowledge is risky. Compensate for your short-comings by seeking advice from an educator, trusted adult, or a qualified professional. Knowing what did not work for them is also beneficial.
- *Stop and think.* Before you jump into the lake, think. If you are still not sure, ask. If you are still not sure, provide for a life-line and then get wet.

Talking Points

To achieve, you need thought. You have to know what you are doing and that's real power.
~ Ayn Rand, author, philosopher

Chapter 17 describes some tools to help you acquire wisdom by interviewing others. To benefit from these techniques, you need only have access to a parent, educator, or other trusted adult (tribal elder) and a desire to listen and learn. Based on the ideas in this chapter, here are some starters:

1. "I am trying to improve myself. Sometimes young persons accept things they hear as true when they actually aren't. Reflecting on your experience, or that of someone you know, do you recall a situation where a young person's "tunnel vision" jeopardized his long-term well-being?" If they say "Yes" then ask:

    - "Would you tell me the gist of what happened please?"
    - "How did you (they) feel about this at the time?"
    - "What two things did you learn from this that you can share with me?"

2. "I am trying to improve myself. Sometimes young persons fail to comprehend that attitudes are a big deal to older generations. Reflecting on your experience, or that of someone you know, do you recall a decision situation where a young person's attitude jeopardized her long-term well-being? If they say "Yes" then ask:

    - "Would you tell me the gist of what happened please?"
    - "How did you (they) feel about this at the time?"
    - "What two things did you learn from this that you can share with me?"

    In either case, if they say "No," simply say "Thank you."

3. "I want to make wise life-choices. Reflecting on your experience, would you have two ideas that I can implement to improve my judgment and decision-making skills? Be sure to thank them for their response.

Knowledge Nuggets

Knowledge is like teenage sex. Everyone says that they are using it, but few actually are, and very few are using it well.
~ Luke Naismith, strategy manager

1. *Feeling anxious about a decision?* When we believe something about ourselves and then do something against that belief, an uncomfortable feeling called *cognitive dissonance* arises. Say you consider yourself to be an honest person. If you then rip off someone, you're likely to find yourself in a state of cognitive dissonance.

Feelings of anxiety, guilt, shame, anger, embarrassment, stress, foolishness, and so on reflect dissonance in action. After a bad decision, we often reduce negative feelings by rationalization or by invoking denial. We may also search for information to confirm our pre-conceptions or use cognitive biases to defend our ego. Cognitive dissonance theory is one of the most influential and extensively studied theories in social psychology. Soothe your ego at: http://en.wikipedia.org/wiki/Cognitive_dissonance.

2. *How large is your Facebook network?* Coined by anthropologist Robin Dunbar, *Dunbar's Number* is the theorized number of other humans that we can possibly cram into our brains as social contacts. These are relationships in which an individual knows who each person is and how each person relates to every other person (for humans, the number is about 150). David Wong redubbed Dunbar's Number the *monkeysphere*. Once above a certain number of friends, family, and individuals that we interact with on a regular basis, people are far less real to us because they are outside the monkeysphere. "The death of one man is a tragedy, the death of millions is a statistic" not because the majority of humans don't care about other people; it's because we cannot empathize with them the way we would a neighbor, friend, or family member. Outside the monkeysphere many built-in constraints against bad behavior simply vanish, which explains why we are so much less moral when dealing with people we do not know. Wong's article is a hoot at: http://www.cracked.com/article_14990_what-monkeysphere.html.

3. *Don't know what you don't know?* The *Johari Window* relates "what you don't know you don't know" to the realm of human interactions. The "unknown" region of the Johari Window identifies positive personality traits that are not known to either you or others. For an insightful interactive exercise with your friends, visit: http://en.wikipedia.org/wiki/Johari_window and http://kevan.org/johari.

4. *Do memes matter?* TEDTalks (TED stands for *Technology, Entertainment, Design*) is an on-line knowledge forum that features 15-minute talks by the world's most inspired thinkers. According to TED, "We believe passionately in the power of ideas to change attitudes, lives and ultimately, the world." In his talk, philosopher/cognitive scientist Dan Dennett starts with the simple tale of an ant and then unleashes a salvo of ideas regarding the existence of memes. He warns that toxic memes, particularly in the areas of education and technology, threaten to wipe out whole cultures. Meme your mind at: http://www.ted.com/index.php/talks/dan_dennett_on_dangerous_memes.html.

5. *Where to go for info?* See Appendix F for additional information relating to this chapter.

Part 3: Understanding Yourself

(The Person in the Glass)

Chapter 8

Confidence Traps

The only things worth learning are the things you learn after you know it all.

~ Harry S. Truman, 33rd U.S. President

The Gist

The Good:

- Positive thinking accentuates the positive
- Confidence and optimism are beneficial when grounded in reality

The Bad:

- *Optimism trap*: a tendency to see overly rosy futures
- *Superiority trap*: a tendency to think you are better than average
- People believe that bad things only happen to other people
- You are not money-savvy because you know how to spend the stuff
- Young persons rarely recognize their susceptibility to these traps

The Reality:

- You are not as unique as you (or your parents) think you are
- Boomers have set many young persons up for failure in the real world
- Young persons are increasingly anxiety-ridden

Introduction

Before you attempt to beat the odds, be sure you could survive the odds beating you.

~ Larry Kersten, sociologist

"Sherman, set the WABAC machine for 480 B.C.E. We are going back to the Battle of Salamis!"[96] We first rewind the reel to a decade earlier when King Darius the Great of Persia (modern-day Iran) was hell-bent to bring Greece under his thumb. But, as sometimes happens in love and war, things did not go quite as planned. In 490 B.C.E., the Persians made their move but had their clock cleaned by the Greeks at the Battle of Marathon. The battlefield count was staggeringly lopsided: 6,400 Persian dead versus 192 Athenians and 420 of their Plataean allies. The chastened Persian army withdrew to fight another day.

Unfortunately (for King Darius), he died four years later. So the empire, along with the unfinished business of dealing with those pesky Greeks, was left to his son Xerxes.[97] Eager to win one for the Gipper, in 480 B.C.E. Xerxes decided to mount another, more massive expedition against Greece. According to general consensus, he drafted an army of about 200,000 men (roughly the population of Richmond, Virginia) from 46 nations. Suitably outfitted, he marched his army through what is now Turkey, and in a brilliant feat of engineering, bridged the Dardanelles. Bearing down upon the Greek homeland, Xerxes kept his hungry land force supplied via a huge navy of several thousand ships that hop-scotched along the coast.

Of course, the Greeks did not take this lying down. Their hackles up, a force of 300 Spartans under King Leonidas of Sparta, in cahoots with about 3,000 other Greeks, positioned themselves in a narrow mountain pass near Thermopylae in northern Greece. For three days the Greeks checked the mighty Persian army's advance through the geographical bottleneck. Unfortunately, they were turned into Greek salad after one of their own, a turncoat named Ephialtes, betrayed them by showing the Persians a back way through the mountains.[98]

Having the green light, the Persians proceeded to sack and burn every Greek city that refused to knuckle under. No match for the invading horde, the Athenians beat feet from their beautiful city one day before the Persians strode into town. Their wily commander Themistocles understood that Xerxes' umbilical cord was his navy. Without his supply ships, the Persian king would be unable to feed and support his huge army from resource-poor Greece. By some clever intrigue,

96 *From Peabody's Improbable History,* Jay Ward, © Bullwinkle Studios.

97 Pronounced "Zerk-zees."

98 The film *300* by Warner Bros. (2007) recounts this heroic battle.

Themistocles managed to entice the entire Persian navy of more than 1,200 warships into the narrow strait near the island of Salamis. With an average of 200 men aboard each ship, the Persian naval force was enormous.[99] Against their massive fleet, the Greeks had but 378 ships. But Themistocles had a clever plan: he would let the Persian commanders defeat themselves.

Among the Persian top brass, there was one dissenter, Artemisia, a queen from Asia Minor and a close ally to Xerxes. After Thermopylae, she reasoned, Athens had been captured and the Athenians and Spartans driven back to their last lines of defense. Since his navy dwarfed that of the Greeks, all Xerxes had to do was hang loose and wait them out until they surrendered. Unfortunately (for him), Xerxes ignored her advice. So confident was he of victory, that he had a golden throne installed on the nearby slopes of Mount Aegaleo. Here he could watch the grand spectacle in comfort, style, and surround-sound.

As it turned out, it was an instant replay of Thermopylae except in water. Once again, the battle proved to be a complete bust for the overconfident Persians. In order to fit into the straits, the Persian fleet had to narrow its formation to such an extent that it lost the advantage of both numbers and tactics. The geography and prevailing winds of the gulf at Salamis provided little room for Xerxes' triremes to maneuver, allowing the Greek ships to easily flank and destroy them. By day's end, the Greeks had eaten Xerxes' lunch—lock, stock, and salami. In a cruel twist of fate, Artemisia was the only Persian general who showed any productive bravery by ramming nine Athenian ships. This prompted Xerxes to lament, "My men have become women, and my women men." Way to go ladies!

The battle of Salamis has been described by many historians as the single most consequential battle in human history. The decisive defeat of the Persian navy dramatically shifted the war in Greece's favor and was instrumental in thwarting Persia's plan to conquer the known world. Ultimately, Themistocles' victory helped preserve Athenian democracy, the concept of individual rights, relative freedom of the person, and its contributions to philosophy, art, and architecture. In doing so, it laid the foundation for the flowering of Western civilization. Not to mention, the gyros sandwich!

Xerxes' blunder was allowing pride and overconfidence to interfere with common sense. Although he was a brilliant land strategist, he had never before commanded a naval battle (of course, anyone who mentioned that got a haircut at the shoulders). When it came time to fish or cut bait, Xerxes failed as an armchair admiral. After his stunning defeat, he rolled up his rug, withdrew from the Peloponnese, and headed back to Persia. The following year the contingent he left behind was wiped slick by the Greeks. The Persians never returned... except on tourist visas.

Reali-tude:
Overconfidence breeds carelessness.

---

99 Most of what we know about the Greco-Persian Wars is from the Greek writer Herodotus, known as the father of history. This figure was provided by Herodotus and confirmed by others who were at the battle, and did not include the numerous auxiliary vessels. Some modern scholars dispute this and peg it at no more than 600 ships.

The Good

Optimism is the faith that leads to achievement. Nothing can be done without hope and confidence.
~ Helen Keller, blind and deaf American author and educator

Before World War II, a major focus in psychology was social dysfunction. Referred to as *negative psychology*, the idea was figuring out how to fix what was wrong with people. Following the war, researchers shifted their focus 180 degrees to finding the best dimensions of human nature, what they termed *positive psychology*. Positive psychology seeks to enhance and improve productivity in people's lives and nurture exceptional human potential. Psychologist Martin E. P. Seligman is credited with bringing widespread awareness to the field.

Two key traits of positive psychology, thinking positively and being optimistic, can help develop confidence. These three terms are often used interchangeably, but in theory they are not the same. Let's take a closer look.

1. *Positive thinking.* Positive thinking is "the practice or result of concentrating one's mind affirmatively on what is constructive and good, thereby eliminating negative or destructive thoughts and emotions." You name it—business, family, or health, the most fulfilled and successful individuals practice positive thinking. While positive thinkers know that bad things happen, they focus on the things in their external and internal environments that can help them accomplish their purpose. Oprah Winfrey's *O Magazine* advises its readers to "Look at yourself in a full-length mirror. Now compliment yourself. Yes, you can do it."

Psychologists and self-help gurus have long touted positive thinking as the key to success and happiness, and there's plenty of evidence to back up their claim. Studies have shown that positive thinking can reduce tension, enhance emotional well-being and cardiovascular health, promote resilience in the face of difficulties, lead to healthier lifestyle habits, and help us cope with stress more easily. In recent years, evidence has accumulated that the power of positive thinking may have more direct health benefits by promoting a stronger immune response and enhancing the effectiveness of painkillers. Those who believe they can control their own destiny tend to achieve more, make more money, and are less vulnerable to being manipulated.[100] If you believe that things are beyond your control, they probably will be. Believe that you can do it, and maybe you will.

But research also suggests that positive thinking works only for the 20 percent of the population who already are emotionally positive with high self-esteem. These people have always been accomplished, excelling in sports, or academics, or business from the start. For the 80 percent of the population that got C's in school, sat on the bench during ballgames, and had little or no success in business, positive thinking doesn't help. Worse yet, it appears that positive self-statements may

100 Researched in more than 1,000 studies, a feeling of self-control is commonly referred to as one's *internal locus of control.*

actually backfire for the very people who need them most. Findings by psychologist Joanne Wood suggest that positive self-statements cause negative moods in people with low self-esteem because they conflict with those people's views of themselves. When positive self-statements strongly conflict with self-perception, she argues, there is not more resistance but a reinforcing of self-perceptions.

BRAIN SNACK: *The market for self-improvement products—books, audiotapes, life-makeover seminars and regimens of all kinds—keeps growing. In* Self-Help, Inc.: Makeover Culture in American Life, *sociologist Micki McGee shows that for Americans today, working on themselves has become a central requirement of their professional lives. "They are retraining and reschooling for new types of work, maintaining their appearance as youthful and vigorous, and searching for their "true calling," she says. Ironically, the less predictable and controllable the life course has become, the more gurus urge us to chart our own course and "master" our destinies.*

2. *Optimism.* Optimism is what is visible on the outside as a result of positive thinking on the inside (which is why your dog wags his tail). What does it mean to be optimistic? In his book, *Learned Optimism*, psychologist Martin Seligman describes optimism as viewing the positive side of a situation. As optimists, Seligman says, we have a general tendency to expect a good outcome. That is, no matter how dismal a dilemma we face, there is a "sense of hope" that we can always find a way to make it work. When we believe that goals are attainable, we feel better, work more efficiently, and are not encumbered by negative emotions. Optimists tend to practice preferable health routines, experience better immune systems, incur fewer infectious diseases, and have a life span that is normally longer than a pessimist's. In contrast, reports Seligman, pessimists tend to have higher blood pressure, greater difficulty dealing with anxiety and stress, and not surprisingly, being chronic party poopers they have more interpersonal difficulties.

There are also personal economic benefits to being optimistic. Behavioral finance researchers Manju Puri and David Robinson find overwhelming support that optimism affects one's work, career, retirement, portfolio, and marital choices. For young persons, the main advantages may be found when you set yourself to pursue a goal—optimism is likely to increase effort, commitment, and persistence in the struggle of competitive activities such as sports, completing college, or finding a mate.

3. *Confidence.* Thinking positively and being optimistic help you develop confidence, which is a byproduct of having high self-esteem. At its core, confidence is how much you value yourself. When you feel confident, the future looks promising. You have positive beliefs about yourself and what you can reach. You are in tune with personal power to make things happen in your life. You believe the world is able to meet your needs and desires. You strut your stuff and the curb fairly rises to your feet.

Although people seem to have an intuitive understanding of what confidence is, its meaning is rarely explained (we, of course, shall not fall into that trap). Behavioral scientists describe confidence as "the subjective probability or degree of belief in the correctness of a judgment or decision." For most of us, confidence seems to be a feeling of assurance or certainty, with the strength of this feeling being our level of confidence. In everyday life, we typically associate confidence with how certain we are in the correctness of our perceptions, judgments, or decisions.

Confident people are often admired and envied in American society. All of us enjoy perceiving ourselves as superior, gifted, generous, attractive, etc. and we tend to cultivate these perceptions. Confidence has been linked to increased enthusiasm and tenacity, which can lead us to undertake more challenging tasks and ultimately, greater success. To counter the inevitable down times, who has not had a parent, teacher, friend, or colleague provide false positive reinforcements to boost our confidence? These can help improve our future performance and may speed a faster recovery from life's disappointments.

Reali-tude:
Optimism and confidence are good in moderation.

The bottom line:

- The way you think influences your level of confidence.
- Positive thinking eliminates negative thoughts and emotions.
- Optimism is a positive attitude that hopes for the best.
- Confidence is how much you value yourself.

The Bad

No problem in judgment and decision making is more prevalent and more potentially catastrophic than overconfidence.
~ Scott Plous, educator

Confidence is like wine. A little can be beneficial. Too much can be a real headache. Overconfidence is the expensive and often disastrous tendency to put too much trust in one's own judgment, predictions, or abilities. The overconfident person tends to inflate the chances of his future success, underestimate the associated risks, and overestimate the rightness of his own thinking. A widely documented trait in human decision-making, overconfidence has repeatedly been shown to occur in many different samples of the population. Researchers cite members of the armed forces, CIA analysts, clinical psychologists, bankers, executives, negotiators, lawyers, civil engineers, and of course, students to name a few.[101]

101 This is not to say that overconfidence is always bad. Overconfidence can be a major advantage in military situations where unwarranted belief in one's abilities may lead to higher motivation, better performance of leaders and warriors, and ultimately victory.

Subjective perceptions about how well someone is performing, will perform, or did perform are often characterized by widespread overconfidence and excessive optimism. But confidence and optimism have been shown by objective measures to be poor predictors of performance. Many young persons do not realize how little they know and how much additional information they still need. Faith and conviction do not make something true, and the power of positive thinking can be made impotent in the real world of hard facts.

> *People believe that they will be able to solve problems when they won't; they are highly confident that they are on the verge of producing the correct answer when they are, in fact, about to produce a mistake; they think they have solved problems when they haven't; they think they know the answers to information questions when they don't; they think they have the answer on the tip of their tongue when there is no answer; they think they produced the correct answer when they didn't, and furthermore, they say they knew it all along; they believe they have mastered learning material when they haven't; they think they have understood, even though demonstrably they are still in the dark.*
>
> ~ Janet Metcalfe, psychologist

If confidence and accuracy do not correspond to each other, then a confidence bias is said to be present. Psychologists have found two systematic drivers of overconfidence bias. The first, and most dramatic, is the *optimism trap* (also called "Pollyanna Effect"). People tend to overestimate the likelihood that one's personally favored outcome will occur. They underestimate the negative effects of random chance and events that are beyond their control. In this respect, overconfidence is not only a common bias but is likely near universal.[102]

A second form of overconfidence comes from superiority bias. The *superiority trap* (also called the "Lake Wobegon" or "Better-Than-Average" effect) arises because people consider themselves better than average in most things they do. Feelings of superiority, fostered by doting Boomer parents, can reduce a young person's objectivity when evaluating him- or herself. These feelings encourage them to overestimate their knowledge, ability, or level of command. Not all NeXters exhibit this, but many of you do.

In general, *confidence traps* reflect a cocksure attitude—we are eager to seek evidence that supports our perceptions and beliefs, and we are averse to look for evidence that might contradict them. We also overemphasize our ability to control the outcomes of our decisions. As shown in Table 8.1 (page 136), our thinking can become "trapped" by questionable confidence beliefs that distort how we perceive ourselves, our circumstances, and those around us. Since our judgments are based on perceptions—which may not reflect reality as it exists—we increase the risk that we will make a dumb life-choice. And the outcomes of some of these choices may haunt us down the road.

102 Note that people can also exhibit underconfidence bias.

Cognitive Flaws	Confidence Traps	Questionable Beliefs
Ignorance (lack of knowledge)	**Optimism Trap** (overconfident in our judgment)	1. Overestimate the likelihood that the outcomes we want will occur 2. Underestimate the impact of random chance and uncontrollable events
Ineptitude (lack of care)	**Superiority Trap** (overconfident in our abilities)	1. Exaggerate the extent of our knowledge, ability, or memory 2. Overemphasize our sense of self-control over events

Table 8.1 Confidence traps.

Here is the gist: psychologists have determined that most people are unreasonably optimistic about their future and overconfident about their own relative abilities with respect to a variety of situations and challenges. Ignorance can lead us to overestimate the adequacy and certainty of what we know. Ineptitude can lead us to overestimate our knowledge, capabilities, or memories. Although we see these cognitive biases in others, it is much more difficult seeing them in operation within ourselves.[103] This self-denial reduces our ability to control events rather than have events control us. Avoiding these traps will help us to better function as healthy economic adults.

***BRAIN SNACK:** Researchers find these two traps to be closely related. Individuals who believe they are better than average are also more likely to be overconfident. And the higher one's assessment of ability relative to others, the more likely one is to be overconfident when making judgments related to that domain. NeXters, many of you were anointed the "Chosen One" by your parents. As a result, some of you paragons of human perfection grossly overestimate your capabilities and will undertake activities that are clearly beyond your reach. Over time, you will find yourself getting into difficulties, undermining your credibility, and suffering needless failures. The lug nuts among you won't have a clue what happened.*

As the day follows the night and the years accumulate, young persons almost always come to discover why their parents are the way they are. So, to all of you mavericks out there who feel you have a unique ability to see what those who have labored long and hard to raise you over the years cannot...try to keep an open mind about why they may have a different perspective. Instead, consider a truly novel idea: *you might be wrong.*

Reali-tude:
Failing to recognize confidence traps prevents you from working to correct them.

103 The tendency not to compensate for one's own cognitive bias is referred to as the *bias blind spot.*

Confidence Trap #1: Optimism Trap

> *"Ignorance more frequently begets confidence than does knowledge."*
> ~ Charles Darwin, English naturalist

Psychologists have found most people panglossian, which is to say they systematically overestimate their odds of success. To succeed in a Darwinian, "dog eat dog" world, knowing what you know is not sufficient; not knowing what you do not know, but should have, is just as likely to get you into hot water. Ask anyone who has contracted a sexually transmitted disease (STD). For them, optimism was a poor substitute for wearing a raincoat. Common sense dude.

☞ *Optimism trap trigger: "Things will always work out in the end."*

Sorry poopsie, but only a laxative is guaranteed to work out in the end. The *optimism trap* is perhaps the best documented of all psychological errors and young persons systematically tend to have more confidence in the accuracy of their judgments than is reasonable. Around 96 percent of 18–29 year olds agree with the statement, "I am certain that someday I will get to where I want to be." They believe they are more likely to experience positive events and less likely to experience negative events than the average person.

Think you are immune to this trap? Think again, Thelma. Optimism bias applies to professionals and laypeople alike. More than 100 published healthcare studies have demonstrated that people believe "bad things happen to other people." But any medical practitioner will tell you that this belief is nonsense. In their article "When Predictions Fail: The Dilemma of Unrealistic Optimism," researchers David Armor and Shelley Taylor cite many examples where optimism bias was found to be a significant factor in adversely affecting judgment. Here are a few:

- Between 85 and 90 percent of respondents claim that their future will be better—more pleasant and less painful—than the future of an average peer.
- Students expect to receive higher scores on exams, at least when those exams are still some time away, then they actually receive.
- Most people expect they have a better than average chance of living long, healthy lives, having a gifted child, being successfully employed and happily married, and avoiding a variety of unwanted experiences such as being robbed and assaulted, injured in an automobile accident, or having health problems.
- Most smokers believe they are less at risk of developing smoking-related diseases than others who smoke.
- Second-year MBA students were found to overestimate the number of job offers they would receive, the magnitude of their starting salary, and how early they would receive their first offer.

- People expect to complete personal projects in less time than it actually takes to complete them.[104]
- Vacationers anticipate greater enjoyment during upcoming trips than they actually expressed during their vacations.
- Newlyweds almost uniformly expect that their marriages will endure a lifetime, an expectation that is unrealistic in view of divorce rates that are 50 percent and higher.

And so it goes, from auto accidents, to promotions, to unwanted pregnancies. What is behind this pervasive reliance on one's sunny disposition to succeed? Toothy television minister Joel Osteen? Prosperity prognosticator Bob Proctor? Attraction articulator Rhonda Byrne? Not really. The source of the problem looks back at you in the glass. To understand the origins of this belief, let's look at some of the ways the *optimism trap* can be triggered.

1. *Everything's coming up roses.* People who refuse to take off their rose-colored glasses put their emotional, physical, and financial health at risk. Many young persons tend to be casually optimistic about their future, no matter what. Thanks to overindulgent parents they have a sense of security, feel empowered, and expect things to be given to them. According to psychologist David Armor, "Optimism bias is clearly not an unnoticed accident. People want to be so biased." Holy guacamole.

> *Beauty is a former South African prostitute whose immune system has collapsed due to AIDS. Prior to contracting the disease, Beauty came each month to a clinic that had muffins and hot tea at the ready. Researchers tested her for HIV and gave her free condoms, extensive AIDS counseling, and a modest stipend. Yet when one of her regular customers—a truck driver who paid about $35 per visit, four times the going rate—insisted on not using condoms, she chose to risk contracting a lethal disease. "I heard about it, but I didn't think it would happen," she said. "Your heart just tells you, you won't get it."*
> ~ Tim Timberg, journalist

In her book *Bright-sided: How the Relentless Promotion of Positive Thinking Has Undermined America*, social activist Barbara Ehrenreich lambasts what she sees as a widespread insistence that a positive outlook itself is the solution to people's problems. Ehrenreich warns that denying reality has "infiltrated the large career-counseling industry that serves the unemployed; the Ivy League, where positive psychology has nested in the curriculum; the best-seller list, where *The Secret* has taken up residence; mega-churches run by evangelists; and conferences for motivational speakers."

104 This is known as *Hofstadter's Law* (after its author Douglas Hofstadter). The law states: "It always takes longer than you expect, even when you take Hofstadter's Law into account."

2. *Wet behind the ears.* Lack of experience can lead young persons to overemphasize the degree of control they have over outcomes and underestimate the impact of random chance on their lives. They are overconfident they can estimate risk with great precision and avoid it. Or, if risk does occur, that they can control it. Not unlike the bloke who falls off a ten-story building and as he passes each floor calls out, "So far, so good!" Research also suggests that overconfidence may be a coping mechanism. When confronted with evidence that contradicts closely held beliefs, people tend to cling even more tightly to their convictions. According to Patrick Leman, a psychologist who specializes in conspiracy theories, people tend to be terrified by the fact that a few bad apples can profoundly alter the course of history. For those convinced that we live in a stable world where major events have understandable causes, a belief that the 9/11 event was an "inside job" helps them sleep at night. Keep this in mind when your brother-in-law insists that the twin towers were felled by explosives placed there by the FBI.

3. *Queen of Denial.* Some people reduce anxiety by simply denying that uncertainty exists. This is done through selective perceptions and faulty memory. Many young persons see less risk for themselves because they believe that warnings apply only to other people. They rationalize by saying "I know the risk but it won't happen to me." Social psychologist Robert Cialdini explains that optimism can trump logic since "It's simply easier to put on blinders and believe everything will work out than to confront the complexities of modern life."

> *We all tend to be optimistic about the future. On the first day of my MBA class on decision-making at the University of Chicago, every single student expects to get an above-the-median grade yet half are inevitably disappointed.*[105] *This optimism will induce me to predict that economics will become more like I want it to be.*
>
> ~ Richard H. Thaler, behavioral economist

The word *ostrichism* sums up this vulnerability rather nicely. This nifty word describes the tendency to avoid unpleasant situations by simply refusing to acknowledge that they exist. In other words, out of sight, out of mind. To keep *your* head out of the sand, expand your horizons, think positively, and apply some horse sense!

Reali-tude:
"I don't know" is an acceptable admission.

---

105 "Median" is useful because it divides the class into two equal groups, from which we learn two related facts: the grade itself and that half of the students earned that high or more (and half earned that high or less). In contrast, "average" provides only one fact: the sum of the grades divided by the number of students. This leaves us wondering how many students earned that figure. All of them? Half? None?

Confidence Trap #2: Superiority Trap

Conceit is when people have an excessively favorable impression of them self. In a society that loves self-esteem, some folks overdose on it.
~ Marilyn vos Savant, world's highest IQ

On the radio program A *Prairie Home Companion*, host Garrison Keillor describes life in fictional Lake Wobegon, Minnesota, with the palliative words: "Welcome to Lake Wobegon, where all the women are strong, all the men are good-looking, and all the children are above average." This phrase has spawned a line of psychology research called the "Lake Wobegon Effect," also known as superiority bias. It refers to the human propensity to believe that one is above average in relation to others.

☞ *Superiority trap trigger: "Believing you are above average."*

Most of us have a tendency to view our selves favorably, particularly when judgments are more subjective than objective, or when we are in a private versus a public setting. Typically we show our self-serving face when we compare our self to others or affirm our goodness. This has some distinct benefits: seeing ourselves in an overly positive light may help us avoid anxiety or depression, become motivated, or maintain our self-esteem.

But snobbery has a downside. "The general finding has been that people with high regard for themselves have equally low regard for others" says family psychologist John Rosemond. "Yes, they feel really good about themselves, but they tend to be seriously lacking in sensitivity to anyone else." This *superiority trap* occurs because we systematically prefer to be better than others on a given ability, not worse.[106] This often appears in the form of unrealistically high appraisals of our own abilities and achievements, including unwarranted feelings of fairness, virtuosity, and luck. And researchers tell us snobbery is getting worse. In 1950, a personality test asked teenagers if they considered themselves an important person. Twelve percent said yes. By the late 1980s, 80 percent said yes.

Generation Me has never known a world that put duty before self, and believes that the needs of the individual should come first. This is not the same thing as being selfish—it is captured, instead, in the phrases we so often hear: "Be yourself;" "Believe in yourself;" "You must love yourself before you can love someone else." These are some of our culture's most deeply entrenched beliefs.
~ Jean Twenge, author, *Generation Me*

Think you are immune to this trap? Think again, Theodore. In fact, young persons are particularly vulnerable. In their article "The Better-Than-Average Effect," researchers

106 People can and do exhibit worse-than-average beliefs. New theories have associated these perceptions to situations involving uncommon or rare abilities, or hard tasks.

Mark Alicke and Olesya Govorun cite a number of studies that found superiority bias to be a significant factor affecting their judgment. Here are some examples:

- A college entrance examination board survey of 829,000 high school seniors asked students to rate their abilities against their peers. Seventy percent placed themselves above the median in leadership ability, 60 percent above in athletic ability and 85 percent rated themselves above in their ability to get along well with others (amazingly, one-fourth rated themselves in the top one percent on this characteristic). Less than one percent of the students rated themselves as below average.
- Ninety-five percent of the faculty at a major university considered themselves above average in teaching ability and 68 percent placed their teaching abilities in the top 25 percent.
- A famous early study found 88 percent of American college students and 77 percent of Swedish college students considered themselves above the 50th percentile (the top half) on driving safety.
- University students were given four objectively marked tests and then asked to evaluate their own performance compared to their peers. In all four tests the worst-performing quarter (the bottom 25 percent) showed an enormous superiority bias, having rated themselves in the top 50 percent.
- Students rate themselves as much less likely than their peers to experience negative life events such as developing a drinking problem, having a heart attack, being fired from a job, divorcing a few years after getting married, being sterile, or attempting suicide.
- Most university students regard themselves as well above the 50th percentile in the degree to which they exhibit sought-after attributes such as social grace, humor, athletic prowess, leadership ability, having a mentally gifted child, living past 80, getting a good job after graduation, and other positive outcomes.

The *superiority trap* is not limited to students. A large majority of the greater population claim to be above average, and this includes many professionals. This phenomenon has been observed among vehicle drivers, CEOs, stock market analysts, police officers, and state education officials, among many others. Hundreds of studies have repeatedly shown the human tendency to be more confident in one's behaviors, attributes, and physical characteristics than one ought to be. Taken to extreme, superiority bias may lead to excessive self-admiration and narcissism.[107] To misquote Elizabeth Barrett Browning, young persons seem to be asking, "How do I love me? Let me count the ways."

> *Of course, the Lake Wobegon Effect is no surprise to anyone who has taught freshmen or non-majors, dealt with incompetent (but invariably "experienced") teachers or administrators, argued with intelligent design "experts," or read a newspaper*

107 Narcissism is often used as a pejorative to denote vanity, conceit, egotism, or selfishness. The word comes from the Greek myth of Narcissus, a handsome Greek youth who rejected the desperate advances of the nymph Echo. As punishment, he was doomed to fall in love with his own reflection in a pool of water. Unable to consummate his love, Narcissus changed into the flower that bears his name, the narcissus.

in the last five years. The hardest thing for many people to learn, especially in a subject that they've never seriously encountered before, is that they don't know what's going on, that their opinions are not facts, that their intuition is not proof. It's almost impossible to actually learn anything if you don't realize that you have something to learn. The first step, as they say, is to admit that you have a problem.
~ Bora Zivkovic, Public Library of Science

Additionally, the *superiority trap* jades not only how we perceive individuals, but groups as well. We tend to treat all members of a group as above average, particularly with respect to numerical values such as test scores or executive salaries. One survey of educational departments reported the statistically impossible finding that all 50 states claimed average student test scores above the national norm. And so it goes, from attractiveness, to intelligence, to weight, to football teams. What is behind this propensity to believe we walk on water? Hello? To understand, let's look at a few of the ways this trap can be triggered.

1. *Dumb as a rock.* Psychology researchers Justin Kruger and David Dunning, authors of *Unskilled and Unaware of It…*, tell us "People tend to hold overly favorable views of their abilities in many social and intellectual domains. This overestimation occurs, in part, because people who are unskilled in these domains suffer a dual burden. Not only do they reach erroneous conclusions and make unfortunate choices, but their incompetence robs them of the ability to realize it." IOW, they are ignorant and inept.

BRAIN SNACK: ***The mission of the American Savings Education Council (ASEC) is to make saving and retirement planning a priority for all Americans. In a poll of 1,000 students regarding their attitudes and behavior toward money, ASEC found that young people often consider themselves money-savvy simply because they know how to spend the stuff. Says ASEC President Don Blandin, "There seems to be a sense of false confidence…that they know more about money management than they actually do, based on their behavior. Of the 16- to 22-year-olds who have credit cards, 28 percent are already rolling over that debt every month. At that young age, that's a very bad habit to get into."***

2. *Style over substance.* Many of us interpret subjective criteria to our best advantage in order to artificially inflate our perceived level of accuracy or importance. But some people are excessive. Our image-related behaviors read like a laundry list: an exaggerated positive opinion of our worth and abilities, unrealistically high expectations for ourself and others, vanity, extravagant style in dressing, excessive need for competition, pride, sentimentalism, snobbishness, a tendency to discredit other's opinions as less important or weak, and many others. These behaviors are calculated to favorably impress other people and protect our self-esteem.

Regarding online dating…the reported weights of the women were substantially less than national averages and about 30 percent were blonde. Online men always

lie about their height. I keep dating men who are 5'8" online and shrink to shorter than my 5'4" when we meet. :)
~ Anonymous blogger

3. *Delusional thinking.* According to sociobiologist Robert Trivers, in a world of "walking lie detectors" one of the easiest ways of fooling others is by self-deception. If we don't consciously know that we are lying, we are more likely to fool those who are seeking to assess such motivations. Effectively, we lie to ourselves in order to avoid detection. If you don't believe this, tactfully ask a woman her weight (the average American female weighs 163 pounds) or a man his flaccid penis length (at 3.5 inches on average, it barely edges out a gherkin).

How do we manage to think of ourselves as great drivers, talented lovers and brilliant chefs when the facts of our lives include a pathetic parade of dented cars, disappointed partners and deflated soufflés? The answer is simple: We cook the facts. What gets us through life is just the right amount of delusion, enough to fool us into feeling relatively good about ourselves.
~ Daniel Gilbert, psychologist, from *Stumbling on Happiness*

4. *Lack of objectivity.* Additionally, people sometimes reduce internal conflict by choosing to totally disregard information that adversely evaluates their ability. Feedback that is inconsistent with our initial perceptions is not as readily assimilated as that which is consistent. As a result, people's descriptions of their behavior (not to mention their penis length) are often unreliable and reflect a lack of objectivity. In other words studly, you see what you want to see...

Reali-tude:
Believing you are above average does not mean you are.

The bottom line:

- *Confidence traps:* ways of thinking that reflect a cocksure attitude.
- *Optimism trap:* a tendency to see overly rosy futures (they aren't).
- *Superiority trap:* a tendency to see yourself as better than average (half of you aren't).
- People rarely recognize their susceptibility to these traps.

The Reality

Always remember that you are unique. Just like everyone else.
~ Anonymous

You are a child of the universe, winner of trophies, a legend in your own mind. If people would just get with the program and stop sweating the small stuff, they would immediately comprehend your startling insights! Um, sure. Many people believe they are unique and expect that their experience in love, career, and life will be different from the rest. Sorry to rain on your parade but you are not unique Dominique. And if you are, it is only in the eyes of your mother. But even a crocodile can make that claim.

Charles Sykes is the author of *50 Rules Kids Won't Learn in School: Real World Antidotes to Feel-Good Education*. His book talks about how the feel good, politically correct philosophy has created a generation of kids with no concept of reality. Sykes provides a list of 50 things that high school and college graduates did not learn in school, three of which are listed below:

- The world won't care as much as your school does about your self-esteem. It will expect you to accomplish something before you feel good about yourself.
- Sorry, but you will not make 60 thousand dollars a year right out of high school. And you won't be a vice president or have a company car.
- You are not entitled, period.

When it comes to knowing who we are, most of us are not very good at it. In fact, we do not know ourselves well enough to know that we do not know ourselves! As a result, many of us blissfully spin through life, completely oblivious to our elevated view of our own abilities. Fundamentally, we lack a sufficient level of maturity to examine out thinking and temper our behavior. Ah, but let's say that you are the rare bird who has his act together—you eschew hubris and exude humility. Remember that clever book, *Where's Waldo?* This was the first title in a series of books created by British illustrator Martin Handford. Dressed in a red and white striped shirt and shellfish hat, the bespectacled Waldo travels to everyday places like the beach, the ski slopes, and the zoo. The challenge for the reader is to find Waldo in a busy picture jam-packed with people.

Now, replace Waldo with yourself (figuratively that is). This will give you an idea of your visibility in today's large, modern organizations. Most are complex, convoluted, impersonal, and sometimes demeaning environments. Their structures, systems, and processes are created for the benefit of the organization, not necessarily for you. A cast of thousands and you, an Army of One, in there... somewhere.

> *The process floundered because you had a few people who believed they were the smartest on the planet and they alone knew the right way to do things, and nearly seven years later here we are.... I think the results show what happens when you combine excessive arrogance with excessive ignorance.*
>
> ~ COL Morris D. Davis, Chief Prosecutor, Guantanamo Bay

Yes, one person can and should make a difference. Nevertheless, you need to be honest with the person in the glass and ask, "To what degree do I stand out from all the rest?" Most of the time the sober response is "Very little." By and large, along life's journey most of us will influence no more than the immediate circle in which we live, work, pray, and play. And Gen NeXters, brace yourself by for a real shockeroo—the majority of you will eventually settle down, get steady jobs, marry someone, buy a house, and have children. Just like your parents did. Not to mention one day have wrinkles. *Young person's alert:* most all of you are not as unique as you think you are.

The trends

Based on data drawn from the last three decades, young adults are increasingly anxiety-ridden says Jean Twenge, a psychology research professor at San Diego State University. According to Twenge, this can be attributed to two main factors: a decrease in the strength of bonds with loved ones, friends, neighbors, and organizational members, and perceived threats to a young person's well-being such as the crime rate, fear of nuclear war, and AIDS.

Increased anxiety, she argues, can be linked to a feeling of powerlessness whereby today's problems seem beyond the control of the individual or the community. As a result, young persons find themselves saying, "What I do doesn't matter." This can lead to an attitude of ambivalence, or worse. In a survey of 20,000 students, a surprising number of teenagers—nearly 15 percent—think they will die before the age of 35. Such feelings of doom lead many to drug use, suicide attempts, and other unsafe behavior.[108] A cornered rat takes no prisoners.

In a 2008 Associated Press-mtvU poll, the vast majority of college students reported feeling stressed. At 40 U.S. colleges, 85 percent of the students surveyed reported feeling stress in their daily lives in recent months. Worries about grades, school work, money, and relationships were the big culprits. At the same time, 42 percent said they had felt down, depressed or hopeless several days during the past two weeks and 13 percent showed signs of being at risk for at least mild depression.

College admissions expert Anna Ivey concurs. "Gen Y (NeXt) is under a lot of pressure to achieve and excel, and is really, really stressed out. Up until 1966, college students sought counseling because of problems in relationships. Today the most common problem is anxiety," she says. To throw gas on the fire, Gen NeXt has taken multitasking to new extremes, leading to a new term called "constant partial attention"—the need to scan electronic and digital environments to ensure that they are not missing out on something important. According to a Nokia study, the urge to check a mobile phone hits, on average, every 6 minutes based on a 16-hour waking day. Young persons don't want to be left out of the loop. As a result, they suffer from anxiety and stress, isolation and loneliness, and the feeling of being overwhelmed.

Reali-tude:
Life is not fair. Get used to it.

---

108 A national survey by the Substance Abuse And Mental Health Services Administration revealed that one in 5 adults in the U.S. had a mental illness in 2010. People in the 50-plus age bracket had the lowest incidence of any mental illness at 14 percent: those ages 18 to 25 had the highest at 30 percent.

The bottom line:

- You are not as unique as you (or your parents) think you are.
- Make sure your level of confidence is based on objective evidence.
- Many Gen NeXters are worried about their future (but don't want to admit it).
- Generation NeXt is really, really stressed out.

Doctor's Prescription (Rx)

The future is not something we enter. The future is something we create.
~ Leonard Sweet, author, clergyman

Beware the shoals of overconfidence. Not knowing what you do not know may lead you to overestimate the adequacy and certainty of what you do know. Not being objective in evaluating yourself can easily result in you grossly overestimating your knowledge and capabilities. While lack of confidence can be a hindrance to progress, being too cocksure will almost certainly be your downfall. You need to strike a balance.

To avoid triggering the optimism and superiority traps:

- *Ask where you might be wrong.* Suppress all of the favorable reasons for a decision and state one good reason why you think your judgment might be wrong.
- *Construct a dialectic.*[109] Perhaps the most effective debiasing technique to combat overconfidence is to consider the opposite. Making a case for an alternative outcome forces you to consider contradictory information and exposes weaknesses in your arguments.
- *Plan for the worst.* By deliberately engaging in disaster scenarios and then creating "predict and prevent plans" we lessen the chances of being blindsided by a lifebomb.
- *Get a second opinion.* Compare your assessment with a trusted adult. Adults can be good sources of wisdom because many have the benefit (and scars) of hindsight. Explain your thoughts and have them challenge your reasoning as a devil's advocate.[110]
- *Ease back on the throttle.* Fantasies that are less positive—that question whether an ideal future can be achieved and depict obstacles, problems, and setbacks—are seen as more beneficial for mustering the energy needed to attain actual success.

---

109 Dialectic is a method of argument where an alternative choice is developed, contradictory facts are weighed, and the best ideas combined into a coherent decision. The invention of dialectic is attributed to the ancient Greek philosopher Zeno (early 5th century B.C.E.). Zeno lived in Elea, a Greek colony in Campania, Italy.

110 Derived from a tradition in the Roman Catholic Church, in which a person would act as an advocate for the devil and argue against the canonization of someone as a saint. This would ensure the canonization was undertaken in good faith and that the candidate truly was a saint. A modern day devil's advocate is someone who argues against you for the sake of argument, rather than out of actual opposition. The process can stimulate discussion and identify weak points in an argument that need to be addressed.

- *Be optimistic when appropriate.* Limit the use of optimism to situations that (1) involve achievement; (2) are concerned about how you are feeling; (3) involve a prolonged situation and physical health is an issue; or (4) if you want to lead and inspire others. "If the cost of failure is high, or if you are planning for a risky and uncertain future, optimism is the wrong strategy and will not pay" says Martin Seligman.
- *Examine your credibility.* Make sure that your level of confidence is based on objective evidence. In dealing with others, credibility, or the degree to which others believe that you are truthful and authentic, is earned over an extended period time. Screw up and it can be lost in a heartbeat.
- *After making a life-choice.* Try to get immediate feedback from others about the accuracy of your decision. Adjustments or compensations are best made sooner than later.

You should take a disciplined approach to making forecasts and judging probabilities. On the other hand, don't over-analyze your self-confidence to the point where you can't make a decision. Any human who is truly objective is also truly dead. Realistic and honest self-confidence, derived from objective evidence rather than emotions, can help you make the smart choice in any change situation.

Reali-tude:
Handle routine matters in a routine manner.

Talking Points

Respect your efforts, respect yourself. Self-respect leads to self-discipline. When you have both firmly under your belt, that's real power.
~ Clint Eastwood, actor, director

Chapter 17 describes some tools to help you acquire wisdom by interviewing others. To benefit from these techniques, you need only have access to a parent, educator, or other trusted adult (tribal elder) and a desire to listen and learn. Based on the ideas in this chapter, here are some starters:

1. "I am trying to improve myself. Sometimes young persons fail to comprehend that overoptimism can negatively influence their judgment. Reflecting on your experience, or that of someone you know, do you recall a situation where a young person's overoptimism jeopardized his long-term well-being?" If they say "Yes" then ask:

    - "Would you tell me the gist of what happened please?"
    - "How did you (they) feel about this at the time?"
    - "What two things did you learn from this that you can share with me?"

2. "I am trying to improve myself. Sometimes young persons exaggerate their capabilities and their ability to control events. Reflecting on your experience,

or that of someone you know, do you recall a situation where a young person's overconfidence jeopardized her long-term well-being?" If they say "Yes" then ask:

- "Would you tell me the gist of what happened please?"
- "How did you (they) feel about this at the time?"
- "What two things did you learn from this that you can share with me?"

In either case, if they say "No," simply say "Thank you."

3. "I want to make wise life-choices. Reflecting on your experience, would you have two ideas that I can implement to improve my judgment and decision-making skills? Be sure to thank them for their response.

4. Research suggests that we are persuaded more strongly when we make an argument ourselves, even if it isn't in line with our own viewpoint. For example, you are more apt to avoid being cocksure when you deliver a message on the risks of overconfidence than if you passively receive it. The explanation seems to be that we are very good at convincing ourselves because we know just what sorts of arguments will sway us to improve. Pick a *confidence trap* that you think describes you and generate your own arguments. Then share them with a tribal elder. You may be surprised at the results!

Knowledge Nuggets

Know thyself.
~ Plato

1. *Does thinking positive help?* "One-third of all Americans wake up depressed every day," says Father John Powell in *Happiness Is an Inside Job*. Professionals estimate that only 10 to 15 percent of Americans think of themselves as truly happy. Norman Vincent Peale is arguably the most renowned expert of positive thinking and how it affects happiness in modern living. Nearly every American achiever has been impacted at some time in their life by his wisdom. Peale authored 46 inspirational books including *The Power of Positive Thinking*, printed in 41 different languages. To learn more about his contributions see: http://en.wikipedia.org/wiki/Norman_Vincent_Peale.

2. *How do I know if I am happy?* We could all do with a little more happiness in our lives and that is what Happier.com is all about. This site is associated with psychologist Martin Seligman, a leading researcher on positive psychology. Here you can take self-assessments on happiness, optimism, character strengths, life satisfaction, life balance, and the emotions. Exercises aim to help increase your happiness by controlling negative thoughts, increasing gratitude, letting go of grudges, and others. For an ego boost, check it out: http://www.happier.com.

3. *How important is common sense?* Never underestimate some people's ability to make stupid decisions. Named in honor of Charles Darwin, the father of evolution, the Darwin Awards highlight those who improve the gene pool by eliminating themselves from the human race through a lack of common sense. Consider the man who used household current to electrocute fish in a pond, then waded in to collect his catch without removing the wire. How about the "Einstein" who peeked inside a gas can with a cigarette lighter? Read more ironic tales of fatal misadventure at: http://www.darwinawards.com.

4. *Who are you... really?* Personality can be defined as the sum total of a person's qualities and traits that make them a unique individual.[111] Do you remember the Sorting Hat at Hogwarts School of Witchcraft and Wizardry? Each arriving student was called, one by one, to put on the hat. The hat listened to each student's thoughts for a few moments before announcing one of the four houses at Hogwarts that best matched the student's personality. Modern personality theories function like a Sorting Hat by providing useful models of how we approach life. The Keirsey Temperament Sorter (and a congruent test called the Myers-Briggs Indicator) can help you determine your personality type based on a combination of four elements:

   - What energizes or stimulates you;
   - How you process information;
   - How you make decisions;
   - How you tend to live your life.

   According to Keirsey, "people tend to feel very proud of their own type once they have gained some insight and understanding." For a real hoot, have your main squeeze complete it too. Take the test at: http://www.personalityzone.com or http://www.keirsey.com/aboutkts2.aspx.

5. *Where to go for info?* See Appendix F for additional information relating to this chapter.

111 Theories about personality date back to ancient Greece when Hippocrates (400 B.C.E.) tried to relate personality temperaments, what he called humors, to an excess of one of four bodily fluids (no guys, that was not one of them).

Chapter 9

Change Traps

The future has a way of arriving unannounced.
~ George Will, journalist

The Gist

The Good:

- Globalization and technology development are major change drivers
- Change requires you to learn, adapt, and renew

The Bad:

- *Framing trap:* misunderstanding the context of a change situation
- *Inertia trap:* unwillingness to change from the status quo
- Framing is done by outside parties and within ourselves
- Inertia comes from delaying tactics and peer group effects
- Young persons rarely recognize their susceptibility to these traps

The Reality:

- Change affects choice, connectedness, convenience, and contentment
- Reacting to change brings benefits, headaches, and costs
- The rate of change is accelerating

Introduction

We live in a moment of history where change is so speeded up that we begin to see the present only when it is disappearing.
~ R.D. Laing, Scottish psychiatrist

Many, if not most of us, suffer from "too much information, too much choice, and too much technology." Point the fickle finger at computers, email, the Internet, globalization, mobile devices, whatever you like—the 21st century is a maelstrom of change. The result is 24/7 access to goods and services, multitasking, microwave meals in minutes, stock trades in seconds, eye shadow applied at 70 mph, video on demand, and everybody wants everything tomorrow (if not sooner).

As Bob Dylan crooned, "The times, they are a'changing." But, what is change anyway? What comes to mind when you think of the word change? Ripe underwear? Flat things that feed parking meters? Time to dump the boyfriend? Robert wants to become Roberta? The effects of global warming? Ron Paul?

Change was certainly on the mind of Heraclitus of Ephesus (ca. 535–475 B.C.E.).[112] Known for his doctrine that change was central to the universe, Heraclitus's philosophy has been described as more fundamental in the formation of the European mind than any other thinker in European history. Before he came on scene, ancient philosophers perceived the essence of the natural world as everlasting and unchangeable. Heraclitus upset the olive cart with his axiom of *panta rhei*—literally, "all things are in constant flux"—where reality is merely a succession of transitory states and "Nothing endures but change." Heraclitus became famous for the metaphor, "You cannot step into the same river twice, for other waters are ever flowing in upon you." This simple sentence expresses the gist of his philosophy that nothing is the same now as it was before, and nothing that is now will be the same tomorrow. The river constantly changes... and so do you!

We'll get our feet wet with a more contemporary look. Today, all manner of technological, cultural, social, geo-political, and economic change influences who we are, how we think, and what we do. As our environment becomes increasingly less stable and less predictable, we seem to continually be transforming or transitioning to something new. One insightful description of this sense of change comes from strategic management theorist H. Igor Ansoff.[113] Ansoff described the concept of *environmental turbulence*, a quantitative measure of the degree of changeability and predictability in

112 A city of ancient Ionia, which today is modern Turkey.

113 Strategic management is a systematic approach to managing a firm's relationship to its environment in a way that will assure its continued success and make it secure from surprises. Ansoff is widely regarded as the father of strategic management.

an organization's operating environment. Generalizing Ansoff's concept, we see that change in our environment can be described using four characteristics:

I. Changeability Factors:

1. *Complexity of our world.* Globalization and the explosion of technology-related choices have significantly increased the degree of complexity. We see nations like Japan and Germany matching American production and consumption of technology. Developing countries like China and India are investing in the infrastructure to join the new economy. The world is being flattened, asserts journalist Thomas Friedman, and young persons must be comfortable functioning within a world economy that is an interdependent system of people, products, and ideas.
2. *Relative novelty of change.* New technologies obsolete existing ones. One example is the migration of music from vinyl records to 8-track tapes, cassettes, compact disks, computers, MP3 players, and iPods. Each technology represents a novel improvement over the previous generation and requires new equipment, new protocols, and new learning. The advent of cell phones, the Internet, and e-commerce have reshaped how we live our lives. To succeed, young persons must embrace a future that rewards continuous renewal.

II. Predictability Factors:

1. *Rapidity of change.* Increasingly, challenges or opportunities are evolving faster than our ability to avoid or capitalize on them. The term *global village* refers to the "shrinking" of time and space as air travel and electronic media have made it faster and easier for people to communicate. Young persons must prepare themselves for more job changes than their parents experienced. One negative to this constant churn is anxiety and burnout—long-term emotional, mental, and physical exhaustion along with diminished interest, especially in one's career.
2. *Visibility of the future.* Opportunities favor those who respond decisively, but our view of the future is becoming increasingly fuzzy. Thus, young persons find themselves having to plan for a future that is already happening, with implications that are not clearly understood. To reduce risk, they need to be skillful in making smart choices using imperfect or untimely information. They must also learn how to self-examine their present actions to ensure they are consistent with their long-term goals. Forewarned is forearmed.

In the Charles Dickens classic *Great Expectations*, wealthy spinster Miss Havisham stopped the clocks in her house at twenty minutes to nine.[114] This was the time of her abandonment by her betrothed on the day that she was to be married. For the rest of her long life she remained in the same room, frozen in time, still wearing her white wedding dress and bridal veil, complete with dusty, dried flowers and stomach-churning wedding cake (not to mention the b.o.). The world, for Miss Havisham, was stable, unchanging, and completely predictable. You don't have this luxury Chumly!

114 *Great Expectations* was a novel by British author Charles Dickens, serialized from December 1860 to August 1861.

Reali-tude:
Today is the tomorrow you worried about yesterday.

The Good

It is not necessary to change. Survival is not mandatory.
~ W. Edwards Deming, statistician

Two main processes are driving change in the world economy. The first is globalization. Today our lives have been transformed by the increasing movement of goods, people, and capital across borders. But it was not always this way. Boomers saw the world outside of their hometown by thumbing through *National Geographic* magazine. In those grainy b&w photos, Orientals all looked the same—buck teeth with coke-bottle eyeglasses. China was located somewhere near the moon and was discovered by some dude in a polo shirt. Sub-continent Indians charmed their snakes and snaked their charms. Africans kept a firm clutch on their spears, undoubtedly to fend off those pesky photographers. Arabs mounted their camels and enjoyed eating their dates. Throughout the world, women knew their place and it was definitely not where they wanted to be. Oy vey—we've come a long way baby!

Or have we? Nowadays, the world is upside down. Everyone else seems to be calling the shots. Competition is global and fierce. New dynamos like India and China threaten American dominance thanks to their cheap labor and manipulated currencies. Everything is made abroad, forcing American manufacturing to decline and our economy to go to hell in a hand basket.

Or has it? Economist Robert Reich defends the global economy as a good thing. "Globalization was understood as a competition between foreign companies and American companies. But it was nothing of the sort," he relates in his book *Supercapitalism*. "The rising tide will lift us regardless of where the headquarters of the global company is," says Reich. "I was getting my hips replaced when I started thinking about where my hips are from. I found out that my hips were fabricated in Germany and designed in France—I have French designer hips," he muses. The reality is almost every company doing business and producing is doing it all over the world. These days, business is all about "competing with everyone from everywhere for everything," write the authors of *Globality*, a book by the Boston Consulting Group (BCG).[115]

Globalization... is the object of intense criticism from those who see only the destructive side of creative destruction. Yet all the credible evidence indicates that the benefits of globalization far exceed its costs, even beyond the realm of economics. The Beatles did well in Britain, but they did spectacularly well when they gained access to the

115 After growing for decades, cross-border trade is slowing and is a harbinger of a manufacturing revival in the U.S.

world market and reaped the benefits of vast audiences and record sales far beyond what was available to them at home. Nobody complained about globalization.
~ Alan Greenspan, former Chairman, Federal Reserve Bank

As important as globalization is, however, it is not the primary force behind economic change. By far, technological progress and automation is the bigger elephant driving the bus. "Our economy is evolving in ways that favor skilled workers" says economist Charles Wheelan, author of the book *Naked Economics*. "Technology makes smart workers more productive while making low-skilled workers redundant. ATMs replaced bank tellers; self-serve pumps replaced gas station attendants; automated assembly lines replaced workers doing mindless, repetitive tasks." In his book *The Road Ahead*, Bill Gates takes an optimistic view about the fruits of technology, where new work will be discovered and new careers developed. X-Prize Foundation[116] Chairman Peter Diamandis and journalist Steven Kotler make the case in *Abundance: The Future Is Better Than You Think* that the world is on the cusp of a succession of abundance-producing breakthroughs.

Technology advancement is fueled by the growth of knowledge. Science journalist Joel Garreau has traced the growth of knowledge in human evolution, what he labels *the Curve*. The Curve is the untamable force of exponential growth that propels technological progress, says Garreau, who calls it "compound interest on human ingenuity." Futurist Ray Kurzweil calls this exponential pattern of technological progress *The Law of Accelerating Returns*. By 2029, he predicts, the human brain will be reverse-engineered, leading to an exponential expansion in human capacity through non-biological intelligence. Kurzweil refers to the point where humans transcend our biology as the *Singularity*. Sardonically referred to as the "Nerd Rapture," it will be a time when technological change, propelled by the explosive growth of artificial intelligence, accelerates past the point of current human comprehension. "Mankind will become the first species capable of deliberately directing its own evolution!" exclaims Kurzweil.[117]

An analysis of the history of technology shows that technological change is exponential, contrary to the common-sense "intuitive linear" view. To express this another way, we will not experience 100 years of progress in the 21st century; rather we will witness on the order of 20,000 years of progress (at today's rate).[118]

---

116 The X PRIZE Foundation awards large incentive prizes to drive radical breakthroughs for the benefit of humanity. It is best known for the $10 million Ansari X PRIZE for private spaceflight and the $10 million Progressive Automotive X PRIZE for 100 mile-per-gallon equivalent cars.

117 Kurzweil is no kook. A pioneering inventor, Kurzweil was awarded the National Medal of Technology by President Clinton in 1999, the nation's highest honor in technology. In 2001 he received the $500,000 Lemelson-MIT Prize, the nation's largest award in invention and innovation. Kurzweil has been awarded 12 honorary doctorate degrees and was inducted into the National Inventors Hall of Fame in 2002.

118 Moore's law is used as a metaphor for the exponential rate of growth of technology. The "law" refers to a prediction made in 1965 by Gordon Moore, co-founder of Intel. Moore said that the number of components on a computer chip with the smallest manufacturing costs per component will double roughly every 12 months (later revised to 24 months).

Within a few decades, machine intelligence will surpass human intelligence, and given time, will overcome most, if not all, human illnesses and limitations.
~ Ray Kurzweil, inventor and futurist

Others dismiss these predictions as technological optimism, or worse yet, little more than self-serving hokum. Research funded by Templeton Research Lectures (TRL) at Arizona State University places people before technology when it comes to improving the human condition.[119] Believing the actual human future will be far more gradual and less dramatic, they call for more critical thinking and research agendas that emerge not from the intellectual momentum of science, but from the needs and goals of society. Regardless of cause or outcome, however, we must all come to terms with accelerating change and a future that is more complex and novel. And the lead time to understand the effects of these changes before they impact our lives is dramatically shrinking.

Adaptability—the ability to think through new situations, continuously learn, and rapidly adapt—is increasingly critical to personal economic success. Being adaptive allows you to be flexible when change occurs in your personal life or career. These skills allow you to react to unexpected events by refocusing your mind in new directions and making smarter choices based on your desired outcomes. "An adaptive individual is open to change, knowing it is the set of the sail that matters, not the direction of the wind" advises professional life success coach Steve Brunkhorst. *Young person's alert:* get with the program before you become "dated merchandise" and your opportunities evaporate faster than water droplets on a hot griddle.

The bottom line:

- Change is the product of instability and is ubiquitous.
- "Changeability" is how different and complex the future is from today.
- "Predictability" is the speed of change and how clear the future is.
- Globalization and technology advancement are the primary drivers of change.

Reali-tude:
Life is change, growth is optional. Learn to adapt.

The Bad

Inflections change us far less in the short term than we expect, but have a far greater impact in the long term than we realize.
~ Robert X. Cringely, Cringely's Law (modified)[120]

119 TRL was founded by investment fund billionaire Sir John Templeton to promote research between the domains of science and theological philosophy. Templeton attributed much of his success to his ability to maintain an elevated mood, avoid anxiety, and stay disciplined. He drove his own car and never flew first class.

120 Robert X. Cringely is the pen name used by technology journalist Mark Stephens. The quotation, "We tend to overestimate the effect of a technology in the short run and underestimate the effect in

The way things change was on the mind of two really smart dudes, German mathematician Gottfried Wilhelm Leibniz (1646–1716) and English scientist Sir Isaac Newton (1643–1727). In the 1680s they independently developed a higher form of mathematics called Calculus (no, not the crud on your teeth).[121] Calculus is useful for solving complex problems that regular mathematics cannot complete. One of the two branches of Calculus, called *differentiation*, helps us determine how fast something changes.

To understand the concept of "rate-of-change," let's hop on an imaginary roller coaster. As we roll along the track, our car cycles up and down (for simplicity we'll ignore any left or right turns). We notice that the steepness of the curves varies; the steeper the downward drop, the faster our speed increases; the steeper the upward slope, the quicker our speed drops. The important thing to observe is that each cycle begins with a momentary change of direction—at the peak of the climb before dropping down (where we regret having gotten on), or in the trough of the dip before heading up (where we regret having eaten that second hot dog). Calculus labels these spots where the direction of movement is about to change *inflection points*. In mathematics parlance, it is where the curvature changes sign.

***BRAIN SNACK:** The concept of an inflection point marking where something is about to change was adapted from Calculus to the business world by Andrew Grove. Grove was CEO of Intel Corporation and ultimately played a key leadership role in its success. He is credited with having transformed Intel from a manufacturer of memory chips into one of the world's dominant producers of microprocessors. In his 1996 book* Only the Paranoid Survive, *Grove describes a "strategic inflection point" as a time in the life of a business when the fundamentals of how it conducts business are about to change.*

Grove points out that a strategic inflection point can be deadly when unattended to. "Let's not mince words. Companies that begin a decline as a result of its changes rarely recover their previous greatness," he said, adding "We live in an age in which the pace of technological change is pulsating ever faster, causing waves that spread outward toward all industries. This increased rate of change will have an impact on you, no matter what you do for a living. We can't stop these changes. We can't hide from them. Instead, we must focus on getting ready for them."

As Ansoff and Grove warn, the accelerating pace of change is inescapable. For Baby Boomer parents, the effects of change in the last 20 years are nothing short of breath-taking. Instantaneous results have become the expected norm. Technological skills are rapidly outdated and shortcomings more readily exposed. Time management is now a critical success factor and missed opportunities carry substantial cost. In today's rapidly changing world, maintaining the status quo risks becoming just another oil stain on the Infobahn.

---

the long run," paraphrased by Cringely from Roy Amara, is sometimes known as *Amara's Law*. Amara was a researcher, scientist and past president of the Institute for the Future.

121 The word "Calculus" is Latin for stone. The ancient Romans used stones for counting and arithmetic.

Grove's concept of strategic inflection can be applied to personal behavioral economics. We can think of a strategic inflection as a point when a young person's chances of achieving long-term success are about to change. Our focus is not on a sudden surge to new heights; it is easy to ride the wave of success when things change for the better. Rather, we are interested in situations where our long-term prospects for happiness nose-dive. These inflection points can be triggered by *change traps*, which are ways of thinking about change that create risk.

Two *change traps* lurk below the radar. The first is the *framing trap*, where we misinterpret the context of a situation. In social theory, framing is the way that information we use in making a decision is presented, worded, formulated, described, called, categorized, or pictured. Think of frames as our individual collection of stereotypes that we rely on to understand and respond to change. Cognitive psychologists Amos Tversky and Daniel Kahneman,[122] who discovered and extensively studied the framing bias, identify two types of frames: (1) the way that others interpret their message for us, and (2) how we interpret the world around us. They suggest that the way a decision is presented or "framed" clouds our mind, traps our thinking, and affects the choice we make.[123] Why is framing important? As rational "choosers," most all of us believe that we always strive to make the most rational choices possible. The problem is we don't.

The second fallibility is the *inertia trap*. This cognitive trap principally arises from mental laziness and our persistent desire to procrastinate (in extreme cases, we may overtly deny there is even a problem). It is also manifest when we are unduly influenced by our friends and peers. Often referred to as the herd instinct, this questionable belief represents a compelling inclination to conform to the norms of the group rather than independently evaluate our own actions. Who has not heard the siren call, "Are you in?"

Cognitive Flaws	Change Traps	Questionable Beliefs
Ignorance (lack of knowledge)	**Framing Trap** (misinterpret the context of change)	1. Underappreciate how others shape our opinions and desires 2. Tunnel vision regarding other possible outcomes and contingencies
Ineptitude (lack of care)	**Inertia Trap** (unwilling to change the status quo)	1. Procrastinate or deny the need to take action 2. Overly influenced by our peers (the "herd instinct")

Table 9.1 Change traps.

In general, *change traps* reflect our preference to "not rock the boat." Rather, we tend to favor inaction until we are prompted by crisis (think of the frog that refused to jump out of the pot as the water warmed). As shown in Table 9.1, our thinking

122 Kahneman was awarded the 2002 Nobel Prize in Economics. Tversky would have no doubt have shared the prize had he been alive.

123 Other related cognitive biases within the framing trap include representativeness bias, in which simplified stereotypes are taken as models and availability bias, where the first perception or interpretation is what jumps into your mind.

can become "trapped" by questionable beliefs about change that distort how we perceive ourselves, our circumstances, and those around us. Since our judgments are based on perceptions—which may not reflect reality as it exists—we increase the risk that we will make a risky life-choice. And the outcomes of some of these choices may haunt us down the road.

Here is the gist: psychologists have determined that people tend to resist changing their established behavior unless the incentive to change is compelling. Ignorance can lead us to underappreciate the "big picture" and exposes us to manipulation by others. It limits our recognition of other decision choices and outcome possibilities. Ineptitude can lead us to procrastinate or be overly influenced by our friends and peers. Although we see these cognitive biases in others, it is much more difficult seeing them in operation within ourselves. This self-denial reduces our ability to control events rather than have events control us. Avoiding these traps will help us to better function as healthy economic adults.

Reali-tude:
Failing to recognize change traps prevents you from working to correct them.

Change Trap #1: Framing Trap

There's a sucker born every minute.
~ attributed to P.T. Barnum, American showman[124]

The framing bias originates from two distinct sources. The first is intentional spin from outside parties that feed the decider (that's you) with information. The media, advertisers, organizations, and the government all disseminate their own picture of things. Framing is also done by the decider herself. This is because we act based on the "pictures inside our heads," rather than objective reality. In other words, we create our own mental picture from our perceptions and representations of reality. This jades how we react to an issue and influences the choices we make.

☞ *Framing trap trigger: "The enemy without."*

Outside parties attempt to shape the way you view reality by influencing or controlling the informational content that you receive. Framing an issue reflects judgments made by message creators or "framers"—they decide what to include, what to leave out, and what to emphasize.[125] Here are some framers and the messages they frame:

---

124 Despite popular attribution, there is no evidence that Barnum actually said this. What he did say was, "No man can be dishonest without soon being found out and when his lack of principle is discovered, nearly every avenue of success is closed to him forever."

125 In George Orwell's dystopian novel *Nineteen Eighty-Four* (1949) the government attempts to control the thoughts of its subjects. Disapproved thoughts were labeled "thoughtcrimes," and were punishable by the "Thought Police."

- Lobbyists shape political issues
- Clergymen win over sinners
- Diplomats influence foreign opinion
- Advertisers persuade consumers
- Politicians frame policies
- Companies mold public image
- Doctors set patient's expectations
- Lawyers manipulate juries
- Parents and teachers shape attitudes
- Surveys (un)wittingly sway results
- Activists create social movement agendas
- Salespersons sell sizzle

Framing is an unavoidable part of human communication and understanding how information is biased by it is a valuable skill. A primo example of framing comes from producers of consumer products. Advertisers use framing to separate you from your dollar and they possess an arsenal of incredibly effective psychological and manipulative techniques that are very difficult to resist. To them, you are nothing more than a digital Pringle to be chopped, formed, shaped, and sold. Tune in to the TV or Internet for 10 minutes. What do you see? Happy people having fun, buff models, and satisfied customers being satiated. Kinda makes you wanna whip out the old Visa card, doesn't it? "What's in your wallet?" is the phrase that pays—them—and your ignorance is their bonanza.[126]

Estimates of the number of advertising messages that you are exposed to daily range from 250 to 3,000 and each is hell-bent on getting what's in *your* pocketbook into *theirs*. Baaaa—stand by to get fleeced sheeple! Nor is the shearing process limited to individuals. Meatier mutton also succumb to framing for everything from bathroom fixtures to bombers.

> *For much of my career, the defense contracting industry has been a sucker's bet for the taxpayer. There were two rules of the game: (1) the answer is always "Yes!" and (2) promise 100 percent and deliver 80. As contractors, we were savvier at spinning the solicitation process to our advantage than the government was at detecting it. Then, once it was a done deal, we brought up issues that the Program Manager had overlooked. We reframed the project as a personal risk, that is, the possibility that he would not be promoted if something went awry. After some hard-sell, the contract ceiling was invariably raised 20 percent to cover contingencies. The Program Manager got his star, we got the gravy, and the taxpayer got the bill.*
>
> ~ Peter K., defense contractor

Perhaps nowhere has the art and science of framing become more evident than in politics. Political campaigns hire legions of image makers to help frame the issues and sway public opinion. These "spin doctors" shape their message by casting information as positive or negative, subtly rephrasing terms, and engaging in creative storytelling (usually at the 6th grade level). According to the *New York*

126 In his 1957 classic *The Hidden Persuaders*, Vance Packard revealed the psychological tricks that the advertising industry uses to make Americans want stuff. *Brandwashed: Tricks Companies Use to Manipulate Our Minds and Persuade Us to Buy* by Martin Lindstrom (Crown Business, 2011) is an updated version of Packard's original book.

Times, framing goes far beyond merely shaping perceptions of the issues; it can be a tool to set agendas, control discussion, and limit debate.

Both major political parties utilize weasel words so extensively that framing has become a new political buzzword. In a private memo (widely reported by Democrats) titled, "The 14 Words Never to Use," political consultant Frank Luntz advised conservatives to restrict themselves to phrases from what he calls the *New American Lexicon*. In Luntz's view, a smart politician never advocates "drilling for oil"—he prefers "exploring for energy." He should not criticize "the government," which cleans our streets and pays our firemen; instead, he should attack "Washington," with its ceaseless thirst for taxes and regulations. Another prominent voice regarding the effects of framing on politics is George Lakoff, a leading scholar on cognitive linguistics. In his book *Thinking Points*, Lakoff describes what he calls "deep frames" that underlie our political understanding of the world. For example, the use of tax "relief" suggests that taxes put a strain on the citizen and the "war on terror" indicates that America only fights good wars, he says.[127]

BRAIN SNACK: *Ever wonder why those inane political ads are repeated again and again? Repetition is one of the easiest and most widespread methods of persuasion. In what psychologists call the illusion of truth effect, familiar things require less effort to process and that feeling of ease unconsciously signals truth. As every politician knows, there's not much difference between actual truth and the illusion of truth. Since illusions are often easier to produce, why bother with the truth? Conversely, if something is hard to think about then people tend to believe it less. This is bad news when trying to persuade young persons that a complex world requires more than simplistic responses. Mature deciders recognize the importance of dealing with reality as it exists, not as they want it to be.*

Ultimately, you are being fed a seemingly endless diet of half-truths and lies designed to persuade you to change, whether it is to buy their product, vote for their candidate, or support their cause. As a result, "there is an interest in authenticity or *realness*," reports futurist Richard Watson. "People want to know where things (or people) are from and whether they can trust them." Don't be a marionette—resist the tendency to blindly accept information without questioning the judgments and motives of the message framers. John Lennon had it right: "Everybody's got something to hide except for me and my monkey." In other words, everybody's got an angle and your job is to expose their monkey.

Reali-tude:
Watch what they do, not what they say.

---

127 A reason cited for The Association of Trial Lawyers of America renaming itself The American Association of Justice was the negative political connotations of the words "trial lawyers" and the positive connotations associated with the word "justice."

☞ *Framing trap trigger: "The enemy within."*

Neither a wise man nor a brave man lies down on the tracks of history to wait for the train of the future to run over him.
~ Dwight D. Eisenhower, 34th President

Most everyone is trying to change your mind and lifestyle for their benefit. It is not enough that you be "en garde." It is also important to ask, "Am I helping them to succeed?" To find out, turn the telescope around and look through the other end. Do you see situations as they truly exist…or how you think they ought to be? Framing bias affects the importance you assign to information that you obtain from long-term memory and the environment. Assigning saliency based strictly on your emotions can limit you to the one choice that is most apparent or that fits your narrow beliefs. Additionally, how you frame your attitude and behavior influences the response of others. Have you seen what your monkey is up to lately?

A Jesuit and a Franciscan were seeking permission from their superiors to be allowed to smoke while they prayed. The Franciscan asked whether it was acceptable for him to smoke while he prayed. His request was denied. The Franciscan asked the question a different way: "In moments of human weakness when I smoke, may I also pray?" His request was approved.
~ Edward Russo and Paul Shoemaker, behavioral scientists

The first step in making any controllable decision is one of the most dangerous. Why? Because choices are not always about reality! Rather, they are about what you believe. According to cognitive psychologists Amos Tversky and Daniel Kahneman, "framing is the decision maker's internal conception of the acts, outcomes, and contingencies associated with a particular choice." In practice, we frame an issue by blanking out all parts of the universe that are outside the frame. But these blinders can lead us to make choices that are based on incomplete information, reasoning errors, logical fallacies, confusions, or false knowledge. Inattention can deliberately narrow our thinking and we may ignore subtleties or important details. Usually, this happens because we are lazy.

What we end up with is a selective and simplistic picture of reality called *tunnel vision* (also called "cognitive myopia"). Tunnel vision has been defined as a "phenomenon that can render an individual unaware of impending or existing danger." This comes from focusing attention only on what you know, without thinking about what you should know. As a result, you may find yourself considering only choices that are too narrow, selective, or flat out wrong.

Think you are immune to this trap? Think again, Theone. Many young persons fall victim to this trap because of their limited life experience and maturity. "These are not parlor-game demonstrations of human stupidity," Kahneman cautions us. "The ease with which framing effects can be demonstrated reveals a fundamental limitation of the human mind." And this can put your future happiness at risk. Three types of framing that you need to be aware of are:

1. *Attribute framing*: The simplest form of framing. People tend to evaluate something more positively when it is presented in positive terms than in negative terms. This is a favorite marketing ploy! Here are some examples:

- Prices set one cent below the nearest dollar value are more appealing.
- Three dollars a day seems less costly than 1,095 dollars a year.
- Cash back offers are much more attractive than similar or greater discounts.
- Ground beef is evaluated more favorably when labeled as "75 percent lean" rather than "25 percent fat."
- Ice cream makers offer "33 percent extra free" rather than "25 percent off" the cost of the regular size, even though these are arithmetically the same thing.
- Saying there is a "50 percent chance of success" instead of a "50 percent chance to fail" can influence the outcomes.

2. *Risky choice framing*: People prefer to take risks when there is something to lose but tend not to take risks when there is something to gain. This behavior is called "loss aversion," and is experienced even by well-educated, sensible people. Loss aversion is often encountered in gambling or in those "Once in a life-time, act now!" type solicitations. "Everyone has a knee jerk reaction to what they think will work for a persuasive message," says Yale psychologist Peter Salovey. "But their intuitions are usually not right."

3. *Goal framing*: Somewhat counter-intuitively, people fear the loss of health, money, prestige, etc. more than they value the benefits of the gain. In other words, people tend to be persuaded to change their behavior more strongly by information that is framed in negative terms than by information framed in positive terms (although they claim otherwise). Some examples include:

- Women are more apt to engage in breast self-examination (BSE) when presented with information stressing the negative consequences of not engaging in BSE than when presented with information stressing the positive consequences.
- People are more willing to forego credit card bonuses than to accept credit card surcharges.
- People are more likely to buy mouthwash when shown pictures of "bad" mouths than when shown pictures of "good" mouths.

BRAIN SNACK: *A few years ago, an anti-smoking campaign called Truth was launched, with ads paid from a national $206 billion lawsuit settled against four tobacco companies. One of the ads, a 30-second spot called "Body Bags," stood out. Here is the scene: Vans pull up outside the corporate offices of an unnamed tobacco company. Teenagers pile out, dragging body bags and dumping them on the sidewalk in front of the offices (1,200, the ad tells us). One teen shouts into a loudspeaker: "Do you know how many people tobacco kills every day?" The camera catches a curious corporate suit peering out the window to the kids below. "You know what?" the teen says*

> ***looking up, "We're going to leave these here for you, so you can see what 1,200 people actually look like." Cut to an overhead shot of the body bags covering two city blocks. Sound of wind blowing and fade to black.***

Around the same time that this commercial aired, Philip Morris decided to launch its own series of anti-smoking ads geared to youth. Their ads, which featured clean-cut, dutiful looking teens, gave a simple and clear message: "Think. Don't Smoke." Research published in the *American Journal of Public Health* showed that teens who saw the *Truth* commercials were 66 percent *less* inclined to smoke. Incredibly, those who saw the "Think. Don't Smoke" campaign were 36 percent *more* inclined to smoke.

While fear of future pain can be a strong motivator, there are no body bags in the world of personal economics. There are, however, many tales of woeful regret from tribal elders. Young persons are fortunate because their future is still malleable. You have the power to change your destiny! To do so effectively, you must be cognizant of sources of framing from within as well as without. Above all, you need to be honest with the person in the glass—(s)he is the most trusted confidante you will ever have.

Reali-tude:
Understand reality as it exists, not as you want it to be.

The bottom line:

- *Change traps:* ways of thinking that reflect our preference to not "rock the boat."
- *Framing trap:* a failure to correctly interpret the context of a situation.
- Our perceptions are our realities.
- The rate of change is accelerating.

Change Trap #2: Inertia Trap

> *Everyone thinks of changing the world, but no one thinks of changing himself.*
>
> ~ Leo Tolstoy, Russian novelist

Sir Isaac Newton did not invent the fig cookie. Despite this shortcoming, he is famous for inventing three laws of motion that fundamentally changed our understanding of the physical universe. Newton's first law, known as the *Law of Inertia*, states that a body continues in a state of rest or of uniform motion unless acted upon by an external unbalanced force. In everyday usage, we often hear it expressed as "a body in motion tends to stay in motion." One need not be a physicist to understand the implications. Inertia is what makes stopping a fullback who is carrying the ball up-field a risky thing to do (unless you happen to be another fullback, that is).

Cognitively, people exhibit "mental inertia" in responding to life's ups and downs. Mental inertia is a rather common human tendency in which we prefer to avoid having to change our way of doing things. "It's the way we've always done things around here" is characteristic not only of individuals, but also for groups, businesses, institutions, and even populations, countries, and civilizations. Mental inertia is a product of the status quo bias, which is a tendency to resist change as a result of habit, mental laziness, neglect, etc. It can also stem from the herd instinct, where we do something because everyone else seems to be doing it. Young persons in particular may find themselves blithely following the crowd without examining the merits of what it is they are following. These biases can trigger the *inertia trap*, an unwillingness to change.

☞ *Inertia trap trigger: "What, me worry?"*

Faced with new circumstances, most of us prefer to avoid any change of opinion, decision, behavior, or other habit that we have used in the past. Status quo bias leads us to prefer that things remain the same, or if they absolutely must be altered, that things change as little as possible. The effects of status quo play a role in many areas of society including economics, political science, sociology, and psychology.

At its root, psychologists tell us that the source of status quo is our desire to protect our egos from damage. Not surprisingly, we naturally look for reasons to do nothing because this represents the safer course and puts us at less psychological risk. Of course, this may not always be the best action—our strong desire to keep things the same can sometimes stifle more appropriate choices. We may even prefer something that is bad but well known and practiced, to something that is good but less familiar. For example, why do you persist in keeping your deposits at your current bank when you are offered a better interest rate at another financial institution that is essentially identical in all other respects? What chains are holding your feet? Physical? Emotional? Habitual? Need a little fire Scarecrow?

***BRAIN SNACK:** Many experiments by behavioral economists have shown the magnetic attraction of the status quo. In a classic experiment, economist Jack Knetsch administered a questionnaire to two different groups of undergraduate students. As a reward, participants in the first group received a mug bearing the university logo; those in the second group were given a chocolate bar. After students received their remuneration, they were given the option to trade for the other reward. Almost 90 percent of them preferred to keep the gift they had initially received. People seem to prefer their current state of affairs because they fear the pain of giving it up. This may explain our reluctance to change our current phone, health insurance, or 401(k) plan, even when presented with more attractive alternatives.*

Status quo can also play a role in our daily routines. Without variation, many of us eat the same thing for breakfast day after day, walk to work along the same route, think in exactly the same patterns. Same boring job, same boring girl(boy) friend, same boring life. We have, as Pink Floyd put it eloquently, become "comfortably numb." This inability to be flexible can cause us to become stressed when a situation forces us to take a definitive stand and make a choice.

It may also close our eyes to potential opportunities. And, as with many cognitive biases, this bias can be insidiously subtle making it harder for us to break out of set patterns. By being aware of the role that status quo plays in our own lives, we can take steps to reduce its influence on our decision making. As one of the characters in Giuseppe di Lampedusa's novel, *The Leopard* observed, "if we want things to stay as they are, things will have to change."

Reali-tude:
Tomorrow is another day. But what about the day after tomorrow?

Delaying tactics

> *Time goes by so slowly, time goes by so slowly, time goes by so slowly, I don't know what to do.*
> ~ Madonna, entertainer

Status quo bias shows up through the use of delaying tactics and a conscious practice of postponing decisions or actions. The aim is to "gain time" before doing something that we are not really ready or happy to do. Not that this is always a bad thing. In some situations, it may be advantageous to "wait and see" since there is often an initial period of doubt about what action we should take (this may also result from a lack of anticipation or preparation). Deciding too fast can also lead to feelings of regret, fear, depression, or anxiety. On the flip side, delaying a decision that must be made can have nasty consequences. Common reasons why people resist change in favor of maintaining the status quo are:

- Comfort with the familiar (i.e., poorly adapted to change);
- Apathy, laziness, or stubbornness (change requires effort);
- Avoidance of something that is difficult or unpleasant;
- Overconfidence, which may underestimate the associated risks;
- Underconfidence, which may lead to self-doubt or false hope.

Worse yet, some people shift from delaying to total inaction. They freeze like a "deer in the headlights," regardless of circumstances. One reason why is a denial of reality. Denial is a defense mechanism, in which a person is faced with a fact that is too uncomfortable to accept. Instead, he rejects it, insisting that it is not true despite what may be overwhelming evidence. Another reason is fear, which may lead to panic and paralysis. Others may simply have a strong inhibition or aversion to making any firm decision. Change can turn these people into venison jerky.

BRAIN SNACK: *Buridan's donkey is a figurative description of a man of indecision. It refers to a paradoxical situation wherein a donkey, placed exactly in the middle between two stacks of hay of equal size and quality, will starve to death*

since it cannot make any rational decision to start eating one rather than the other. First mentioned in another context by Aristotle, the paradox is named after the 14th century French priest and philosopher Jean Buridan.[128]

Hands down, the most commonly encountered delaying tactic is procrastination. Virtually all of us dither from time to time, but some have perfected it into a way of life. Who are the champion procrastinators? Bingo! College students, say psychologists. According to social scientist Piers Steel, an estimated 80–95 percent of college students engage in procrastination, approximately 75 percent consider themselves procrastinators, and almost 50 percent procrastinate consistently and problematically.[129] Students report that procrastination typically occupies over one third of their daily activities (and rising), often enacted through sleeping, playing, or TV watching. Adults are not far behind with some 15–20 percent self-identifying as "chronic procrastinators." Ironically, over 95 percent of procrastinators wish to reduce it!

The tendency to procrastinate is a measure of the lack of self-regulation that can have debilitating influences on motivational, affective, social, and behavioral outcomes over the course of a student's first term, and ultimately may affect academic achievement.
~ Gary J. Kennedy, Ph.D., from his dissertation on procrastination

No matter what we say or do, human beings are prone to making excuses. Like hunger and sex, procrastination just seems to be a part of our psyche's "firmware." We put off doing unpleasant tasks, even though this can be costly. We stress out in mid-April because we put off completing our taxes. We dine on cat food when we are old because we delay planning for retirement. We die young because we procrastinate in quitting smoking, starting a diet, or scheduling a medical check-up. Our slothfulness affects others too. "In personal relationships, if you say you'll do something and you don't do it, people begin not to trust you," says clinical psychologist Linda Sapadin. "If they can't trust you to do what you say you'll do . . . it creates a lot of disturbance in relationships." In the extreme, relationships are ruined, spouses feel betrayed, and bosses are disgusted. You become dirt dude.

I'm so lazy that I would rather wait until the water and electricity have been turned off before I pay the bill. I make other people do things for me because I am too lazy to do it myself. My slothfulness has a lot to do with procrastination and my amazing ability to not really give a shit about things. I just want people to get along! And this is why I'm on a fast track to Hell: my desire for ease in life is at the

128 Jean Buridan (ca. 1295–1358) was a French priest who sowed the seeds of the Copernican revolution in Europe. One of the most famous and influential philosophers of the late Middle Ages, he is today among the least well known. Buridan developed the concept of impetus, the first step toward the modern concept of inertia that was described by Newton 300 years later.

129 Curiously, graduate students are more likely than undergraduates to procrastinate, in spite of being statistically superior students.

expense of righteous behavior. So, if being slothful is wrong, I don't wanna be right. Oh, and could you bring me another Margarita? It seems I'm too lazy to get up.
~ Alisa W., Internet blogger

I think that life would suddenly seem wonderful to us if we were threatened to die. Just think of how many projects, travels, love affairs, studies, it—our life—hides from us, made invisible by our laziness, which, certain of a future, delays us incessantly.
~ Marcel Proust, French novelist

Why do we procrastinate in completing tasks? Generally, excuse making appears to have positive benefits for "procrastibators." Being a lard butt makes us feel better, but laziness is not the only reason. Some psychologists think people delay because they have low confidence they will succeed in the task. It may be that procrastinators are perfectionists. Perhaps they are impulsive and lack self-control, or they are simply depressed. It is no great surprise that people defer tasks that are unappealing, difficult, or expensive.

On the other hand (a favorite phrase of economists),[130] not all procrastination is bad and not all procrastinators are deficient performers. Procrastinating may have value as a winnowing process. As President Calvin ("Silent Cal") Coolidge wryly commented, "If you see ten troubles coming down the road, you can be sure that nine will run into the ditch before they reach you." Research by management professor Brian Gunia shows that slowing down our decision-making versus making a snap decision makes us five times more likely to do the right thing.

Another perceived payoff of delay may be a sharpened degree of focus and commitment. Creative people of all stripes often pull all-nighters, claiming that it enhances their creativity. "When you are faced with a hard project," says Adam Savage of Discovery Channel's *MythBusters*, "I've learned that a deadline is a potent tool for problem-solving. Deadlines refine the mind...and the closer the deadline, the more likely you'll start thinking out of the box." Possibly the peculiar genius that is born out of desperation at 4 a.m. is worth the cost. It certainly makes for an exciting life!

The more important are a person's goals, the more ambitious are her plans. But the more ambitious are her plans—i.e., the higher is the effort she intends to incur—the more likely she is to procrastinate in executing those plans. Investing for retirement is perhaps the single most important economic decision that people (should) make. In spite of—or perhaps because of—its immense importance, many people never get around to carefully planning their investment for retirement.
~ Edward O'Donoghue and Matthew Rabin, behavioral economists

What is a procrastinator's busiest day? Tomorrow. So the real questions ditherers should ask themselves are, "If I delay tackling this problem, will it grow worse if I ignore it?" and "Can I catch up with the train after it has left the station?" In other

130 President Harry Truman lamented, "Give me a one-handed economist! All my economists say, On the one hand...on the other hand..."

words, "Can lost time be recovered?" To answer these, check with the person in the glass. Keep in mind that Lady Gaga and Simon Cowell do not have to worry about funding a comfortable retirement. But you do.

Reali-tude:
Manage delay like you manage everything else.

☞ *Inertia trap trigger: "I herd it through the grapevine."*

American society has changed dramatically in recent decades. Accentuating the traditional American emphasis on individuality, we tend to see a greater interest today in choice, freedom, mobility, and new horizons. Prompted by the disintegration of the nuclear family, adolescents are increasingly relying on peer groups to provide emotional and informational support that used to come from the family. Peer group members tend to share a similar age, culture, religion, or educational status, and conformity to "the group" is an important aspect of youth culture.[131] Conformity is the process by which an individual's attitudes, beliefs, and behaviors are influenced by other people. Any unwillingness to conform carries with it the very real risk of social rejection, so in this respect, conformity can also be seen as a means to achieve a sense of security as well as a source of information.

Conformity has a downside though, in that it can lead you to be overly influenced by your peers. Although direct and overt social pressure is sometimes involved, it may also result from subtle, even unconscious influences. Commonly referred to as the herd instinct, or *bandwagon effect*, people often do and believe things because many other people do and believe the same things. Conduct and beliefs spread as memes among people in a group, and the probability of any individual adopting it increases with the proportion that have already done so. As more people believe in something, others tend to hop on the bandwagon regardless of the underlying evidence. For instance, everyone is "going green"—including multi-billion dollar corporations looking for some good PR—and therefore you should too. It doesn't matter if the cause is good or not. Companies use bandwagon appeals so you'll feel that you want to be a part of the majority.

BRAIN SNACK: *In a survey of 29,760 high school students by The Josephson Institute, a Los Angeles-based ethics institute, overall 30 percent of students acknowledged stealing from a store and 64 percent having cheated on a test that within the last year. Despite such responses, 93 percent of all students said they were satisfied with their personal ethics and character. President Michael Josephson commented, "In a society drenched with cynicism, young people can look at it and say, "Why shouldn't we? Everyone else does it."*

131 Peer influence is highly related to parenting practices. Researchers say young adults are more like their parents than they appear during adolescence. They are more likely to choose peers whose behaviors are similar to theirs than to be influenced by peers' behavior.

Young person's alert: a belief that is widely held is not necessarily a guarantee that the belief is correct. If the belief of any individual can be wrong, then the belief held by multiple persons can also be wrong. Shades of the *inertia trap!* When you forgo independently evaluating your beliefs and behaviors, concluding that something is true because many or all of your friends believe or do it, you are a goose that is just waiting to be plucked. This is known as an *argumentum ad populum*, a red herring that alleges, "If many believe it is so, then it is so."[132]

Think you are immune to this trap? Think again, Thurston. Our desire to be approved by others can be a strong motivator to jump on the bandwagon. Many young persons feel it's better to be "normal" than to go against the crowd and they invent rational motives to justify their inaction. Political hacks and advertising sharks understand this "go with the flow" tendency of young persons. Many of their clever slogans are geared to take advantage of your susceptibility to this questionable belief. Here are some examples of the herd instinct:

- Nine out of 10 people opposed the Wall Street bailout; therefore it is a bad idea.
- All of my friends voted for Barack Obama so I did too.
- Fifty million Elvis fans can't be wrong.
- Sony. Ask anyone.
- Since 88 percent of the people polled believed in UFOs, they must exist.
- Millions of people have downloaded songs so there is nothing wrong with it.
- "But officer, I don't deserve a ticket. Everyone goes this speed!"

Clearly, not all peer pressure is bad. Positive peer relationships contribute to the development of skills such as social self-confidence, empathy, communications, and so on. But one must exercise a degree of independent judgment apart from the crowd. "With every day that passes," warns transhumanist Pierre Teilhard de Chardin, "it becomes a little more impossible for us to act or think otherwise than collectively." And for all you young fashionistas, remember that eyebrow rings and tongue studs are herd statements that Baby Boomers find less than appealing. Before you show up for that job interview, keep in mind it is Boomer buffaloes, not nubile NeXters, that control most of corporate America (but your turn is coming).

Reali-tude:
You can't roller skate in a buffalo herd.

The bottom line:

- *Inertia trap:* an unwillingness to change.
- Mental inertia avoids having to change one's way of doing things.
- Procrastination is a common delaying tactic that makes us feel better.
- Herd instinct alleges, "If many believe it is so, then it is so."

132 Argumentum ad populum is Latin for "popular appeal or appeal to the majority." A *red herring* is something that draws attention away from the central issue. The name of a smoked fish in 19th century Britain, a red herring pulled across the trail of a fox could divert the hounds onto a false path. Thus, by analogy the phrase came to be used to describe any false trail.

The Reality

Summing it up, it is clear the future holds great opportunities. It also holds pitfalls. The trick is to avoid the pitfalls, seize the opportunities, and get back home by six o'clock
~ Woody Allen, film director

The realities of globalization and the speed of technological change have had profound implications on our environment, our relationships, and indeed on us. For young persons, change can bring tremendous opportunities. Like the proverbial dual-edged sword though, for every benefit there is an associated cost. Some areas where the realities of continuous change are good, as well as not-so-good, are listed in the "4 C's" below.

I. Choice.

The good:

- Lower prices;
- Customization ("I want it my way or no way");
- Increased diversity and selection in products and services;
- Easier access to the rare and unique (say, tracing one's genealogy).

The not-so-good:

- Too much choice (do we really need 26 types of Colgate toothpaste?);
- Too much information fosters *paralysis by analysis*;
- Too much technology ("You mean I have to learn *another* new system?");
- Things have become too complex and too complicated.

II. Connectedness.

The good:

- Six degrees of separation from anyone on the planet;[133]
- Many more "touch points" for personal growth;
- Increased transparency for reviewing claims made by others;
- Better access to the "wisdom of the crowds."[134]

The not-so-good:

- Evaporation of trust ("I know who you are... I think");
- Loss of personal privacy and anonymity;

---

133 "Six degrees of separation" refers to the idea that, if a person is one step away from each person they know, and two steps away from each person who is known by one of the people they know, then everyone is an average of six "steps" away from each person on Earth. A study of 30 billion e-conversations among 180 million people from around the world pegged the figure at 6.6. Thus, in theory any 2 people could be linked by a string of 7 or fewer acquaintances. In 2011, Facebook analyzed the 731 million users and found that an average of 4.7 hops could link any two of them via mutual friends.

134 Large groups of people are smarter than an elite few, concludes business columnist James Surowiecki, no matter how brilliant. "Under the right circumstances, groups are remarkably intelligent, and are often smarter than the smartest people in them," he says in his book, *The Wisdom of Crowds*. "They are better at solving problems, fostering innovation, coming to wise decisions, and predicting the future."

- Continuous partial attention limits critical thinking;
- The insecurity of being disconnected from 7/24 connectivity.

III. Convenience.

The good:

- Mobility;
- Immediate gratification ("I want my pizza hot, fresh, and NOW");
- Convergence of technologies increases flexibility;
- Movement toward standards reduces technology frustration.

The not-so-good:

- Keeping up with changing technology ("You must upgrade to access this file...");
- The trend toward "sound bites" limits information richness and detail;
- Always responding to what's urgent rather than what's important;
- Cascading loss of functionality when complex technology breaks.

IV. Contentment.

The good:

- Increased individualism and self-reliance ("I can do it myself!");
- Expanded opportunities for finding a meaningful career;
- Exposure to new cultures and points of view;
- Locating others of like mind and interests.

The not-so-good:

- More anxiety and stress regarding work/life balance;
- Pessimism about one's ability to influence change and achieve happiness;
- Shallower relationships and loss of cultural identity;
- Increased isolationism and escapism (fake is the new real).

Reali-tude:
Change comes at a cost.

Doctor's Prescription (Rx)

Procrastination is the greatest killer of success.
~ Phil Laut, money management coach

Hard work often pays off in the future, but laziness always pays off now.
~ Anonymous

Not knowing what we do not know exposes us to manipulation by ourselves as well as others. Lack of objectivity can lead us to persistently procrastinate on our commitments and be overly influenced by our peers. Worse yet, we stubbornly cling to our views even when our flaws are exposed. When someone has the impudence to suggest that we change our ways, we maintain our saint-like feelings and regard them with unadulterated bafflement. It's an interesting three-way dynamic:

1. First, we think the other person is confused. They are misinformed and don't know what they are talking about. They have us mixed up with someone who truly does need to change, but we are not that person.
2. Second, as it dawns on us that maybe the other party is not confused—maybe their information about our perceived shortcomings is accurate—we go into denial mode. The criticism does not apply to us, because no one knows us better than our self.
3. Finally, when all else fails, we attack the other party and discredit the messenger. "Meh," we think, "why is a smart person like me listening to a loser like you?"[135]

These are heady defense mechanisms to overcome. After all, no one likes to be told that they are biased. Calling attention to it is irritating to anyone, young or old. And, persuading you to be mindful by invoking an endgame that doesn't matter to you at this point in your life is very hard to do. Here are some trap avoidance tips:

To avoid triggering the framing trap:

- *Accurately define the problem.* A poorly framed problem can undermine even the best-considered decision whether (or not) to change. The most critical step is to ask yourself whether you have truly defined the real problem that you need to address.
- *Question "givens."* Do not automatically accept the initial frame, whether it was formulated by you or by someone else. When others recommend something that will affect your long-term future, examine the way they framed the situation. Ask them to provide a rationale for their choice and look for distortions in information and reasoning. If you focus on the essence of the data provided rather than how it is presented, you will be less likely to make a judgment based on prior convictions.
- *Consider other perspectives.* Examine the problem and the issues through another person's eyes. For instance, if you are thinking to "pop the question" and you are a spendthrift, reverse the context and consider how you would accept this if you were your betrothed.
- *Cast your net wide.* Choose a frame that captures everything that is important in the decision. For example, ask, "What is the total cost of ownership?" not "What is the price?" Ask, "What qualities does he have that will bring me happiness?" rather than "Is he a hunk?"
- *Use your gray matter.* Asking "What if?" type questions throughout the decision-making process will attenuate or eliminate the framing bias. Ask "What if?" type questions. Just before making a final decision, provide a rationale for your choice and ask how your thinking might change if the framing changed.

---

135 Adapted from Marshall Goldsmith and Mark Reiter, *What Got You Here Won't Get You There,* Hyperion Books: New York (2007).

- *Be honest with yourself.* Simply acknowledging "I don't know," combined with taking steps to find out if needed information is available, increases the likelihood that important uncertainties are identified and dealt with. Check with a tribal elder.

To avoid triggering the inertia trap:

- *Step out of the comfort zone.* In any controllable decision, maintaining the status quo may indeed be the best choice, but do not choose it just because it is comfortable. To lessen the pull of the status quo trap, always remind yourself of your long-term objectives and see whether elements of your current situation are acting as barriers to achieving your goals.
- *Other choices exist.* The status quo is never your only alternative! Learn to look at your life as constantly in play. Seek out and identify new alternatives as counter-balances and carefully evaluate the pluses and minuses. If you are stumped, ask a tribal elder.
- *Clean the slate.* Ask yourself whether you would choose your current situation as an option if it wasn't already the status quo. If not, use today as a baseline to begin a plan for change.
- *Look at the long-term.* Over time, a change becomes the status quo and its desirability may diminish. In comparing alternatives, always evaluate them in terms of the future as well as the present. Remember, Romeos and Juliets, over time faces wrinkle, tummies sag, tools dull…
- *Don't dither.* If you have several alternatives that are superior to your current situation, avoid defaulting to the status quo just because you are having a hard time picking the best alternative. Force yourself to choose.
- *Beware of the herd.* If you give in and do something that is contrary to your character or core values, it will cause you distress. Later, you will feel regret. Doing the right thing is always rewarding. Always be true to yourself.
- *Defeat procrastination.* Some tips to help get your rear in gear include:
    - § Create concrete "to do" lists and use self-imposed deadlines.
    - § Imagine the good feelings when you finish (or bad feelings if you don't).
    - § Do your second-most important job while procrastinating over the most important one.
    - § Actually do the items on your list and take the time to go back over it.
    - § Divide complex, longer tasks into short, manageable tasks.
    - § To stick to a task, keep the ultimate goal in mind when carrying it out.
    - § Learn to persist and work through and around interruptions.
    - § Do not blame yourself for not finishing an item or items.
    - § Watch being a perfectionist.
    - § Start somewhere…anywhere. The rest will tend to follow![136]

136 Known as the *Zeigarnik Effect*, named after the Russian psychologist Bluma Zeigarnik. This says, "Don't start with the hardest part; try something easy first. If you can just get underway with doing something, however trivial, you are much more likely to complete the task."

Talking Points

Change is inevitable—except from a vending machine.
~ Robert C. Gallagher, author

Chapter 17 describes some tools to help you acquire wisdom by interviewing others. To benefit from these techniques, you need only have access to a parent, educator, or other trusted adult (tribal elder) and a desire to listen and learn. Based on the ideas in this chapter, here are some starters:

1. "I am trying to improve myself. Sometimes young persons underappreciate that the context of a situation can negatively influence their judgment. Reflecting on your experience, or that of someone you know, do you recall a decision where a young person "saw only what she wanted to see" and jeopardized her long-term well-being?" If they say "Yes" then ask:

    - "Would you tell me the gist of what happened please?"
    - "How did you (they) feel about this at the time?"
    - "What two things did you learn from this that you can share with me?"

2. "I am trying to improve myself. Sometimes young persons fail to comprehend how strongly their peers can influence their judgment. Reflecting on your experience, or that of someone you know, do you recall a situation where "going with the herd" resulted in a young person jeopardizing his long-term well-being?" If they say "Yes" then ask:

    - "Would you tell me the gist of what happened please?"
    - "How did you (they) feel about this at the time?"
    - "What two things did you learn from this that you can share with me?"

    In either case, if they say "No," simply say "Thank you."

3. "I want to make wise life-choices. Reflecting on your experience, would you have two ideas that I can implement to improve my judgment and decision-making skills? Be sure to thank them for their response.

4. Research suggests that we are persuaded more strongly when we make an argument ourselves, even if it isn't in line with our own viewpoint. For example, you are more apt to resist peer pressure when you deliver a message on the value of independent thinking than if you passively receive it. The explanation seems to be that we are very good at convincing ourselves because we know just what sorts of arguments will sway us to improve. Pick a *change trap* that you think describes you and generate your own arguments. Then share them with a tribal elder. You may be surprised at the results!

Knowledge Nuggets

> *It is not the strongest of the species that survives, nor the most intelligent, but the one most responsive to change.*
> ~ Charles Darwin, English naturalist

1. *Is change in your future?* Futurists, or futurologists, are those who speculate about the future. Below are a few respected organizations that prognosticate about the future. These sources (and others like them) can be an adjunct when scoping out promising career areas:

    - *World Future Society (WFS).* WFS offers futures-related research and reporting by experts in a wide range of fields such as business, creativity, education, economics, environment and resources, values, and more. According to WFS, they take no stand on what the future will or should be like and strive to serve as a neutral clearinghouse of ideas. Read the tea leaves at: http://www.wfs.org/futurist.htm.
    - *What's NeXt. What's NeXt*, written and produced by British futurist Richard Watson, is a report that offers clear, concise, and non-sensationalist commentary on trends in society, business, science and technology, government, and the environment. His annual *10 Trends: Predictions and Provocations* report, *Innovation Timeline*, and *Trend Blend Map* are particularly enlightening at: http://www.nowandnext.com.
    - *Acceleration Studies Foundation (ASF).* ASF is an educational organization engaged in outreach, education, research, and selective advocacy with respect to issues of accelerating change. ASF promotes understanding of change processes to better economic, political, social, professional, and personal development. Look into their crystal ball at: http://www.accelerating.org/slides.html.
    - *Futurologists.* Lists of contemporary experts with interesting perspectives on the future can be found at: http://en.wikipedia.org/wiki/List_of_futurologists and http://accelerating.org/community.html. Check out futurologists Michio Kaku (*Physics of the Impossible*), Ray Kurzweil (*The Singularity Is Near: When Humans Transcend Biology*), John Naisbitt (*Mind Set! Reset Your Thinking and See the Future*), and Alvin and Heidi Toffler (*Revolutionary Wealth*).

2. *What, me biased?* Young people, who have mostly not faced discrimination themselves, generally believe that this world is a meritocracy and that prejudice based on race, religion, and gender have long ago disappeared. In reality, most well meaning people still harbor abundant prejudices. Project Implicit, a virtual laboratory for the social and behavioral sciences, blends research and education where visitors can examine their own hidden attitudes, biases, and stereotypes. Since 1998, visitors have completed more than 15 million demonstration tests on bias. Some observational findings include:

- Implicit biases are pervasive;
- People are often unaware of their implicit biases;
- Implicit biases predict behavior;
- People differ in levels of implicit bias.

Spend a few minutes to explore your inner self at: http://www.projectimplicit.net and https://implicit.harvard.edu/implicit.

3. *Framing fun.* The well-known Asian Disease Problem from cognitive psychologists Kahneman and Tversky demonstrates that framing affects decision outcomes. Imagine that the U.S. is preparing for the outbreak of an unusual Asian disease that is expected to kill 600 people. Two alternative plans to combat the disease have been proposed. Each plan has two programs available, and the scientific estimates of the consequences are described below. For each plan, select the one program that you most favor:

   Plan 1: For this plan, if Program A is adopted, 200 people will be saved. If Program B is adopted, there is a one-third probability that 600 people will be saved and a two-thirds probability that no people will be saved. Which of these two programs do you favor?

   Plan 2: For this plan, if Program C is adopted, 400 people will die. If Program D is adopted, there is a one-third probability that nobody will die and a two-thirds probability that 600 people will die. Which of these two programs do you favor?

   After choosing one program for each plan, check out how your selections compare to those in the study (see *Framing Exercise* on the next page).

4. *Where to go for info?* See Appendix F for additional information relating to this chapter.

Framing exercise: The Asian Disease Problem (from previous page).

Framing effects are valid only if the information given in the different frames (i.e., choices) is exactly the same. This is called "information equivalence." *The Asian Flu Problem* from Kahneman and Tversky demonstrates systematic reversals of preference when the same problem is presented in different ways. In reality, the two questions posed in each plan are logically identical as to outcome. But this is not how people perceive them.

Research reveals that when people are presented with Plan 1, 72 percent preferred Program A. When presented with Plan 2, 78 percent preferred Program D. The preferred outcome depended upon whether the decider's "frame" constituted a choice among gains (that is, the number of people who would be saved) or losses (the number of people who would die). Logically, this is inconsistent. But then, so is anyone who has ever been in love! See why at: http://www.nationmaster.com/encyclopedia/Framing-(economics).

Chapter 10

Maturity Traps

Ah, but I was so much older then, I'm younger than that now.
~ Bob Dylan, poet, musician

The Gist

The Good:

- Long-view thinkers self-examine their present actions
- For young persons, mature judgment is a work in progress

The Bad:

- *Projection trap*: underestimating the long-term consequences
- *Self-control trap*: immediate satisfaction of emotional self-interests
- Impulsive lack of self-control is the hardest behavior to avoid
- Most of us cannot imagine a future that is radically different from today
- Young persons rarely recognize their susceptibility to these traps

The Reality:

- Gen NeXters and their parents see the world very differently
- Baby Boomer aging and retirement issues will affect Gen NeXt
- Parents are worried they will outlive their money

Introduction

Maturity of the mind is the capacity to endure uncertainty.
~ John Finley, editor, The *New York Times*

In the 5th century B.C.E., the Athenians were the greatest shipbuilders of their era, and successfully applied their superior carpentry skills to working with stone in constructing the famous Acropolis at Athens.[137] Despite primitive technologies, the Greek builders demonstrated an astonishing degree of architectural maturity, matched only by our most modern capabilities.[138] "A popular misconception exists that the (ancient) builders...were somehow less intelligent than we are" write Peter James and Nick Thorpe in their book *Ancient Inventions*. "There is simply no evidence that this is true," they note.

The foundations of math, science, logic, and reasoning established by the Greeks are still used by modern day scientists, philosophers, mathematicians, and engineers. Many of today's government buildings are built to aesthetic standards, designs, and specifications developed by the Greeks. Examples include the Lincoln Memorial and the Supreme Court buildings in Washington D.C., the U.S. Stock Exchange building in New York, and the replica of the Parthenon in Memphis, Tennessee. The original Parthenon in Athens, built during the Golden Age of Greece (ca. 432 B.C.E.), is one of the most beautiful buildings ever constructed. Nineteenth century French engineer Auguste Choisy commented that the Parthenon represents "the supreme effort of genius in pursuit of beauty."

One of the difficulties in constructing any large building is that optical illusions distort the look of the structure. Even though they are absolutely straight, long horizontal lines appear as if they sag toward the center and tall columns tend to look narrower in the middle. To counter these illusions in the Parthenon, ancient builders used an architectural design technique called *entasis*, which applies a convex curve to a surface for aesthetic purposes. Using this technique, they intentionally raised the center of the base and upper portions of the structure approximately 4 inches on the sides, and 2-1/2 inches on the ends. On the columns, they refined the look by giving the shafts a 4.65 centimeter (slightly less than 2 inches) "bulge" along the diameter and tilting them outwards slightly to counter a natural tendency to view tall objects as tilting inward. The effect of

137 The Greek word *acropolis* means "city on the extremity." It is a citadel or fortified part of an ancient Greek city, typically built on a hill. The *Acropolis at Athens* refers to the ancient citadel at Athens, containing the Parthenon and other notable buildings.

138 Incredibly, the Parthenon was built in only 8 to 9 years. Some estimates put the cost of the Parthenon's construction at $300 million in today's dollars. Greek building techniques and tools were used by the Romans and the great cathedral builders of Europe almost 2,000 years later.

these intentional departures from true made the Parthenon appear to be perfect in shape to a worshipper on the ground.

One key to the Greek architects achieving perfection in stone was their mastery of the *art of the long-view*, or the ability to consider the inter-dependencies of the whole rather than each action in isolation. They were mature planners, who took time to anticipate the effects that everyday decisions would have on the long-term visual appeal and structural integrity of the building. Adjustments were made before the building was "set in stone," not after. Philosophically, all of us build a personal "temple," or ways of thinking that drive our behavior. Those who master the art of the long-view see value in practicing mature judgment rather than reacting with impulsive immediacy. They self-examine their present actions to ensure they are consistent with long-term goals, and make adjustments if needed along the way. Long-view thinkers are "life-architects" who take responsibility for the end-game from the start.

Reali-tude:
Maturity is the art of the long-view.

The Good

> *Never trust anything that can think for itself if you can't see where it keeps its brain.*
>
> ~ J. K. Rowling, from *Harry Potter and The Chamber of* Secrets

Why do so many young persons not develop the art of the long-view? The answer lies between your ears (space, the final frontier...). To illuminate, we look to the field of neuroscience, which is devoted to the scientific study of the nervous system, the brain, and the mind. Of particular interest is a subset of this field called *neuroeconomics*, a relatively nascent approach to economics that focuses on personal choices and decisions. Economists and psychologists have teamed to look into the "black box" of our brain to figure out how decisions are made. This field promises to put economics on a firmer footprint by describing people as they really are, not as some oversimplified mathematical model would have them be. This has implications for young persons.

In 1952, physician Paul D. MacLean proposed a model of the human brain to explain the functional traces of evolution that exist in the brain's structure. While this early concept has since been superseded, it has stuck in the popular imagination. MacLean's model, dubbed the "triune brain," segregated the brain into three separate but interconnected parts. These parts are nested together like *Matryosha* dolls;[139] each has its own special intelligence, subjectivity, sense of time and space, and memory. It's nature's triple-header!

139 Matryosha is a set of Russian dolls of decreasing size placed one inside the other.

The first part of the brain is the oldest. Referred to as the stem or *reptilian brain*, it processes our most basic survival instincts and is entirely "me" centered (a common neurologists' joke defines these as the four F's of reptile brain behavior: feeding, fighting, fleeing, and reproduction). The reptile brain controls an animal's muscles and balance, along with autonomic functions such as breathing and heartbeat. Think of this as the "housekeeping brain." It is what we find in the noggin of a snake or a lizard.

Next on the evolutionary scale is the limbic system or *mammalian brain*. More advanced than the brain stem, the limbic system girdles the reptilian brain like the flesh of a peach around the pit. It provides us with emotion and motivation capabilities and is involved in the formation of memory. We share this brain with earlier mammals such as dogs, cats, horses, and mice.

Finally, we have the most recently evolved (and also the largest) portion of the brain: the *primate brain*. This part envelops our reptile and mammalian brains and is the wrinkly, sausage-like tissue that most of us associate with the human brain. The primate brain is responsible for our higher order thinking and reasoning. It is what allows us to perform sophisticated mental tasks like playing Halo, figuring out why men are from Mars, or finding the cheapest set of tires. Called the neocortex, it is nature's "pièce de résistance."[140]

One of the most important things a living creature uses its brain for is assessing and reacting to risk. After all, having smarts is what seats you *at* the dinner table, rather than *on* it! Scientists have traced this critical function to a very primitive part of the reptilian brain called the *amygdala* (pronounced ah-MIG-dal-ah), which in humans is an almond-shaped structure about one inch long.[141] The name, rather appropriately, is derived from the Greek word for almond. Researchers tell us they seem to play a pivotal role in selecting memories for long-term storage.

Amygdalae have a very important primary function: they are an organism's "911 circuit." When an animal—a lizard, a bird, a mammal, or you—sees, hears, or feels something that is a potential danger, the amygdalae are what trigger the "fight-or-flight" response. They are your source of gut feelings, responsible for processing base emotions that arise from sensory inputs such as anger, avoidance, defensiveness, and fear. Neurosciences professor Robert Sapolsky calls them "ground zero" for fear in the brain because in times of stress they cause adrenaline and other hormones to be pumped into your bloodstream. Have you ever experienced stage fright? You can thank your amygdalae for those sweaty palms, racing heartbeat, and puckered sphincter.

BRAIN SNACK: *Here is a fun way to observe your amygdalae in action. There is a direct neurochemical connection between the amygdala and the olfactory nerves (your sense of smell). First, locate something foul smelling—some raunchy sneakers or your roommate's beer fart will do nicely. Now, take a good whiff.*

---

140 Love comes from the neocortex, but lust, or "animal instincts," comes from the limbic system.

141 Humans actually have two *amygdalae*, one in each hemisphere, located deep within the brain inboard of your ears.

When you instinctively draw back from the source of the smell, your amygdalae are largely responsible for your feeling of repugnance. Repeat this test with a fragrant rose. What happens? A feeling of delightful pleasure washes over you. Once again, your amygdalae have done their job!

Big deal. Sure, the amygdala works great for the lounging lizard who wishes to avoid becoming lunch. For him it is all about surviving another day. The human brain, however, is more complex. To understand how we react to risk, we also need to spotlight the neocortex, the part of our brain that is responsible for adopting the long-view.

Unlike most animals, humans have a dual sensory input system. Along the first path, inputs from the eyes, ears, and other sense organs go directly to the amygdalae. They impulsively trigger a physiological response called the *startle circuit* that prepares the body for reaction to the stimulus. But wait! These inputs also travel via a separate neural path to the neocortex. Although the amygdalae immediately react with "Shoot first, ask questions later," the more logical and staid neocortex analyzes the stimulus in detail using information from many parts of the brain. This double wiring affords humans a unique capability for reacting to risk—a primitive system and a more intelligent and analytic system—and they operate in parallel. Thus, we have an evolutionary advantage: the ability to quell the knee-jerk response while we work out a more sophisticated analysis of the situation and assess our options for dealing with it. But override can be a challenge. Once an emotion has been turned on by the primitive system, it is difficult for the neocortex to turn it off. Figure that out and dealing with the mother-in-law is a no-brainer.

Groovy! Well...not quite. At least, not for some millennia to come. This is because, evolutionarily speaking, the neocortex currently has some rough edges.

The brain is a beautifully engineered get-out-of-the-way machine that constantly scans the environment for things out of whose way it should right now get. That's what brains did for several hundred million years. And then, just a few million years ago, the mammalian brain learned a new trick: to predict the timing and location of dangers before they actually happened. Our ability to duck that which is not yet coming is one of the brain's most stunning innovations; we wouldn't have dental floss or 401(k) plans without it. But this innovation is in the early stages of development. The application that allows us to respond to visible baseballs is ancient and reliable, but the add-on utility that allows us to respond to threats that loom in an unseen future is still in beta testing.

~ Daniel Gilbert, psychologist

In addition to coping with this evolutionary short circuit, young persons have to contend with another sticky wicket on the road to maturity. As anyone who survived them knows, the adolescent years are a time of impulsivity, immediate gratification, sensation seeking, and indifference to risky behaviors. Although brain structures involved in anticipating future reward mature at a younger age, writes neuroscientist Jay Giedd, the reasoning and judgment areas of the neocortex that inhibit many emotional impulses are still developing until age 25. As a result, young persons are constantly grabbing for whatever they want, consequences-be-damned.

Why is this? According to the National Institute for Health, young adults represent "craniums under construction" while a massive reorganization of the neural connections takes place. This "pruning" resembles an extensive network and wiring upgrade that adapts their brain to the life skills they are going to use. Scientists tell us their brains have not yet matured to the point where the fear of risk can outweigh the hope of reward.

BRAIN SNACK: *According to psychiatrist Gary Small, author of the book* iBrain: Surviving the Technological Alteration of the Modern Mind, *daily exposure to digital technologies such as the Internet and smart phones can alter how the brain works. Today's wired world is all about speed—gathering a lot of superficial information fast—and people often develop a jumping pattern of thinking called multitasking.*[142] *Contrary to what young persons believe, when the brain switches back and forth between tasks it becomes more difficult to filter out irrelevant information and our ability to do any one task is degraded, says psychologist Russell Poldrack. Furthermore, when the brain spends more time on technology related tasks and less time exposed to other people, it drifts away from fundamental social skills like reading facial expressions during conversation. Small observes that the effect is strongest in so-called digital natives, people in their teens and 20s who have been "digitally hard-wired since toddlerhood." That be you, Gen NeXt.*

Science now offers some insight into the maturing process. Why do young persons prefer the company of those their own age more than ever before? Peers offer far more novelty than do familiar family slugs, and young persons are looking to invest in the future rather than the past. But, says *National Geographic*'s David Dobbs, sometimes they recognize "that the parent can offer kernels of wisdom, knowledge valued not because it comes from parental authority but because it comes from the parent's own struggles to learn how the world turns." And that's a good thing.

Reali-tude:
To curb impulsiveness—think twice, act once.

The bottom line:

- Mature decision-makers are prone to long-range thinking.
- To master the art of the long-view, supplant emotions with facts and reason.
- Impulsive behavior might not be your fault (but you still own the consequences).
- Reasoning and judgment capabilities are "works-in-progress" through age 25.

142 Some experts say multitasking is more properly described as "task switching" or "time slicing." Notes computer scientist Nikki Reynolds, "A few seconds of attention to the phone, now switch to the homework, now the TV, now back to the phone. This means it takes them longer to complete any one task, such as their homework and also appears to affect the quality of their work."

The Bad

You've got the brain of a four-year old, and I'll bet he was glad to get rid of it.
~ Groucho Marx, comedian

Most of us have been conditioned to believe that one's rational intelligence quotient, or "IQ" for short, is the best measure of human potential. Not so fast Frankenfurter. Researchers have found this is not necessarily the case! Psychologists John Mayer and Peter Salovey think that your emotional intelligence quotient, or "EQ," might be a greater predictor of success. They define EQ as "the ability to monitor one's own and other's feelings, to discriminate among them, and to use this information to guide one's thinking and actions." Psychologist Daniel Goleman popularized the concept of EQ in his book *Emotional Intelligence: Why It Can Matter More Than IQ?*. According to Goleman, IQ contributes about 20 percent to the factors that determine success in life, with other extraneous factors such as luck and the characteristics of EQ constituting the other 80 percent.[143]

People with high EQ are prone to be long-range thinkers, says Goleman. They spend more time defining problems and strategizing than blindly jumping in. They control their impulsivity better by overriding it with the logical, thinking brain. They know when to wait and when to act. These qualities are representative of one who exhibits psychological maturity. Think of EQ as your amygdalae override!

The concepts of EQ can be usefully applied to personal economics. In making a life-choice, a young person is said to demonstrate personal economic maturity if he or she responds in a manner that appropriately balances the long-term payoff with the near-term gain. Failure to do so is often caused by "maturity myopia," that is, a lack of foresight or self-control. One systematic source of myopia is the *projection trap*. This trap occurs when we try to project our current emotional or physical state into the future, what psychologists call "mis-predicting future preferences." A second, and more dramatic source, is the *self-control trap*. Most of us value a dollar now versus two dollars later, even when we clearly know that we will regret it in the long run. Age does not have an exclusive on these traps; many people act as though they are far less economically mature than their chronological age would suggest.

Maturity traps distort our preferences toward the near- versus the long-term, and overall, they are the most risky of all cognitive traps. Lacking self-control and emotional maturity, we favor impulsive reactions and preferences. As shown in Table 10.1 (page 186), our thinking can become "trapped" by questionable maturity beliefs that distort how we perceive ourselves, our circumstances, and those around us. Since our judgments are based on perceptions—which may not reflect reality as it exists—we increase the risk that we will make a risky life-choice. And the outcomes of some of these choices may haunt us down the road.

---

143 There is far from universal agreement as to the efficacy of EQ.

Cognitive Flaws	Maturity Traps	Questionable Beliefs
Ignorance (lack of knowledge)	**Projection Trap** (underestimate long-term consequences)	1. Underappreciate how different tomorrow's preferences will be from today's 2. Focus our attention solely on the immediate situation at hand
Ineptitude (lack of care)	**Self-Control Trap** (inability to control our emotional impulses)	1. Sacrifice our long-term interests for short-term rewards and pleasures 2. Fail to follow through on our intentions

Table 10.1 Maturity Traps.

Here is the gist: psychologists have determined that many people act in an immature manner when predicting their future behavior and fulfilling their intentions. Ignorance can lead us to overlook key inter-relationships that link our present actions to adverse future consequences. Ineptitude can foster impatience and impulsiveness, rendering us unable to overcome the desire for immediate gratification. Although we see these cognitive biases in others, it is much more difficult seeing them in operation within ourselves. This self-denial reduces our ability to control events rather than have events control us. Avoiding this trap will help us to better function as healthy economic adults.

Reali-tude:
Failing to recognize maturity traps prevents you from working to correct them.

Projection Trap

The great source of both the misery and disorders of human life, seems to arise from over-rating the difference between one permanent situation and another.

~ Adam Smith, Scottish philosopher

Entire industries are based on the belief that we aren't getting everything we can out of life. Self-improvement and dieting products are replete with claims they will increase our happiness. Yes sir, yes ma'am, success can be yours if only you make the right decision (i.e., buy their product). Okay, fine. Then why is it we don't make choices that will maximize our long-term happiness? Behavioral economists have begun to examine why people are not always able to choose what is in their best interest.

Outcomes often fall short of expectations because we inaccurately predict how we will feel in the future. And somewhat surprisingly, predicting our "future self" is not something we tend to be very good at. Decision researchers have identified the projection bias as a contributing factor in our failure to choose wisely. Those who exhibit projection bias tend to underappreciate the effects of changes in their emotional or physical states. Hence, they tend to exaggerate the degree to which their future preferences or tastes will resemble their current ones.[144] There is strong support for the assumption that people suffer from the projection trap and triggering it can lead to choices they will later regret.

The only trouble was the heat. The heat was tremendous and nowhere in Rome was hotter than Laura's apartment. She had been so eager to get back into her own place that she had forgotten how hot it would be. Heat is like that. In the course of winter unbearable heat cools in memory and becomes attractive, desirable. Now it was terribly hot.

~ Geoff Dyer, British author, from *Out of Sheer Rage*

☞ *Projection trap trigger: "Through a glass darkly."*

The roots of projection bias are deceptively simple: most of us are short-sighted. We simply cannot imagine a future that is radically different from the present and fail to understand that consequences may unfold gradually. As a result, what you predict you will experience in the future may be a horse of a different color from what you actually experience when that time arrives. Psychologists call these "visceral states." When you make a prediction you are in a *predictor* state of mind, and when you experience the prediction you are in an *experiencer* state of mind. And these can be radically different. For instance, as a predictor you might be rested, full, or sexually not aroused. Later, as an experiencer, you might find yourself feeling tired, hungry, or horny. Psychologists have experimentally confirmed this cognitive pretzel.

***BRAIN SNACK:** In* **Why We Under Prepare for Hazards,** *marketing professor Robert J. Meyer analyzes the psychology behind the Hurricane Katrina disaster. New Orleans decision makers knew they were living in risk-prone areas. They also knew what steps to take to mitigate losses, and in many cases, could afford to undertake them. In the face of Hurricane Ivan in 2004, Mayor Ray Nagin ordered a general evacuation of the city. Fortuitously the city was spared (although Florida was not so lucky), but major flaws were identified in the city's evacuation system. After Ivan, officials made inadequate investments in public safety and failed to predict the future consequences of these flawed policies. One year later, Mayor Nagin did not evacuate New Orleans for Hurricane Katrina and the city experienced $100 billion in losses and 1,300 dead.*

An excellent example of the projection phenomenon is underappreciating the effects of hunger. Shopping on an empty stomach, we act as if our future taste for

144 Projection bias is why it is difficult for someone who has not been in combat, given birth, or won the lottery to truly appreciate the mental and physical experience of a person who has. It is also why we unconsciously assume that others share the same or similar thoughts, beliefs, values, or positions. Another interesting variant of projection bias is *anthropomorphism*, the attribution of a human form, characteristics, or behavior to nonhuman things. Mickey Mouse and Binky the Bear are splendid examples.

food will reflect such hunger. This inclines us to buy too much. Picture yourself going to the supermarket on your way home after work. You skipped lunch and are starved out of your gourd. Worse yet, you have no shopping list. Somewhere between the pasta and the broccoli, a giant-size bag of cheese snacks leaps off the rack and into your cart! Of course, you know these are not good for you, and as a savvy predictor you decide to scarf down only a handful on your way home. By the time you pull into the driveway, however, the contents have mysteriously shrunk by a third and your fingers are bright orange. Now, as a satiated experiencer, you can no longer stand the taste of cheese munchies and swear off eating them forever. Until next time that is.

We often succumb to the *projection trap* when dining out. Ordering food at the beginning of a meal, we must predict how hungry we will be at the end of the meal. Yet, many of us order too much food. Restaurants take advantage of this by offering all-you-can-eat meals to hungry diners who underestimate how quickly they will become full. Why should this be? The reason is that in the moment, when you are hungry at the supermarket or the restaurant, you are out of touch with your future emotional self. This occurs despite the fact that we have plenty of experience regarding the problem's undesirable consequences. The same experience holds for people who are currently satiated and do not expect to be hungry later on. A classic case of man versus food!

Why would a person's future lifestyle preferences differ from her present ones? Habit formation, day-to-day mood fluctuations, social influences, or simply maturing are common bends in the road. Differences may also arise from adapting to changes in one's life circumstances, such as moving to a different climate or changing occupations. The basic pattern of the *projection trap* is we qualitatively understand the direction that hunger (or other preference) will change, but we systematically underappreciate the magnitude of the changes.

Think you are immune to this trap? Think again, Theresa. Young persons routinely deviate from rationality in their decision making processes. They repeatedly fail to behave in their own best interests and for the most part remain agnostic (noncommittal) about what those interests are. The evidence indicates that projection bias operates across a broad array of domains including sexual arousal, pain, thirst, fear, drug addiction, test-driving a new car, and even the influence of the weather at the time people make catalog purchase decisions.[145] Here are some illustrative examples:

- Office workers were told they could have a free snack in a week's time and were asked to choose between a healthy snack (an apple) or an unhealthy snack (a Mars bar). When they thought their future self would not be hungry, only 26 percent predicted they would choose the unhealthy snack. At the actual time of choosing, however, 70 percent chose the unhealthy snack.

145 Danger, Will Robinson! Inappropriate displays of behavior on the Internet such as boob flashing, mooning, or worse can have unexpected and undesirable consequences. Reputation still counts and potential employers (and future beaus) DO check.

- People plan to attend health spas, golf clubs, vacation time shares, or season ski passes because they frequently project their current enthusiasm into the future. They then decide not to attend in the future when their enthusiasm has waned.
- When making summer vacation plans during the cold of winter, projection bias may cause people to choose overly warm destinations. They may also plan long vacations, believing that the ninth day lying on the beach will be nearly as enjoyable as the first. It never is.
- People who had won a lottery within the last year were found to be no happier than non-lottery winners.
- A stressed student who underappreciates the addictiveness of cigarettes may start smoking with the plan to quit upon graduation, only to continue after graduation once she becomes addicted.
- Respondents were asked whether they would accept a grueling course of chemotherapy if it would extend their lives by three months. While only 10 percent of healthy people said that they would accept the chemo treatment, 42 percent of current cancer patients said they would.
- Many consumers pay insufficient attention to contractual arrangements for ceasing service at the time they sign up, since they may not anticipate their tastes changing.
- People spend too much time and energy generating wealth and too little time on leisure activities. Thus they enjoy the increases in their material consumption less than they think they will.

Nor is the *projection trap* limited to short-term decisions. Behavioral economists George Loewenstein, Ted O'Donoghue, and Matthew Rabin note that important long-term life-decisions such as marriage, divorce, fertility, and indeed even suicide all display a pattern consistent with projection bias. For example, projection bias might lead people to make proposals of marriage that are costly to rescind. In the thralls of love (or fit of rage) they may say things they later wish they had not. Or they may fail to use birth control or follow safe sex practices in the heat of passion. Projection bias can also lead people to underappreciate the long-term effects that result from adapting to a shifting standard of living. Many Baby Boomers found this out the hard way after the 2008 financial meltdown evaporated their retirement nest eggs.

Are young persons more susceptible to projection bias than adults? According to Loewenstein et al., the answer is almost certainly "Yes." Psychologists believe that while young persons are similar to adults in terms of their ability to carry out the decision-making process, they have considerable difficulties associated with projection bias. Why is this? In order to evaluate the long-term consequences of many risky behaviors, young persons must be able to accurately predict how they will feel as adults. But how do you know what it is like to live in France if you have never left Flagstaff? Since they cannot adequately project themselves into the future, they imagine that their current preferences will remain constant.

Invariably, they won't. For example, high school seniors considering dropping out from school may not appreciate the fact that when they are older they will care about the quality of their job. To these students, all jobs seem equally unappealing, so they decide that none are worth the effort. In failing to take the long-view, they underestimate the value to them of having a high school degree in life and increase the chance that they will drop out from school today. How about the young man who joins the military and then intentionally screws up to get out of his enlistment? At the time, he is solely focused on getting out and does not fully comprehend the negative effect that a dishonorable discharge will have on his future job prospects.

> *When I wuz thirty, I woulda bet one million dollars I wouldn't be here today.*
> ~ Ozzie Osborne, rock star, on his 60th birthday

In addition, many young persons make plans they end up not carrying out. For example, as time passes and a young professional habituates to higher income and consumption levels, he is prone to consume even more than he had anticipated. Folk wisdom tells us that spending nearly always rises to meet, or exceed one's paycheck, causing long-term saving to fall short of intentions. As predictors, they fail to account for changes in their behaviors.

Young persons also underappreciate the intrinsic costs they face. Nearly half of Gen NeXters still live with parents, either because they are still in school or from financial necessity due to the high cost of independent living. While you are in school (and increasingly after you are out), parents often subsidize your living expenses. This may include food, shelter, clothes, insurance, tuition, laundry, transportation, and taxes. Yes, you do pick up the tab for the lattes. *Young person's alert:* accurately projecting your present lifestyle into the future is contingent upon continuing or replacing these subsidies, a nettlesome detail that is often forgotten by would-be rebels.

> *Vera is upbeat about her plans after graduating from the Harvard Divinity School in June, even though she has no job prospects, no savings and $20,000 in graduate school loans. Her parents pay her rent, though she isn't pleased about needing their help at the age of 24. "It's been on my mind: I should be saving. I should be saving. But I've never done it," Vera said. "It's very horrifying." But, she added, "I always think anything is possible. When I look ahead, I don't see a gloomy, hopeless situation.*
> ~ Roxana Popescu, journalist

Finally, in not mastering the art of the long-view, we may "compartmentalize" our decisions. Focused solely on the situation at hand, we make our choices in isolation of the overall effect on our life. Thus, key inter-dependencies and implications may be overlooked and lead us to be overly optimistic about the certainty of our judgments. For example, turning off the patient's dialysis machine to conserve electricity certainly achieves the objective. But it also eliminates the need for the machine.

Reali-tude:
Be careful what you wish for because you just might get it.

The bottom line:

- *Maturity traps:* ways of thinking about time that can adversely influence choice.
- *Projection trap:* a failure to accurately predict one's future preferences.
- Youth are more susceptible to the *projection trap* than adults.
- Compartmentalizing isolates decisions, blinding us to key inter-dependencies.

Self-Control Trap

Adams: *"You still refuse to face the truth."*
Morbius: *"What truth?"*
Adams: *"Morbius, that thing out there. It's you."*
Morbius: *"My evil self is at that door and... I have no power to stop him!"*
~ Dr. Edward Morbius, expedition scientist[146]

Do you save as much as you'd like to? Always live within your means? Never had a problem sticking to a diet? Brush your teeth after every meal? Homework assignments always turned in on time? Never carried away by the moment and had unprotected sex? Hmmm? Well, if you don't get straight As, don't feel too bad. No one else does, either. Having trouble with self-control is part of the human condition: while we would "like" to behave in one manner, instead we "choose" to behave in another. We seem unable on a moment-by-moment basis to behave in ways that further our long-run best interest.

Of all traps, self-control is the most important to appreciate and the most difficult to avoid. Self-control problems influence how much we (under)save, why we (over)eat, whether we get addicted to cigarettes, alcohol or other drugs, fail to practice safe sex, and whether we finish tasks punctually or we procrastinate. When we decide about the distant future, we are roughly as rational as economic textbooks assume, and we mean it! In the near-term, however, we can be as impulsive as chimps. "When faced with the choice between new shoes now or a better funded retirement in 20, 30, or 40 years, the reflexive system wins every time," says Jason Zweig, an investing consultant. "The prospect of a better retirement in the distant future just doesn't have the same emotional wallop as a new pair of shoes today."

☞ *Self-control trap trigger: "If I knew then what I know now, I would not have fill-in-the-blank."*

In varying degrees, all of us make decisions in a manner that fails to balance near- versus long-term payoffs. At any age, impulsiveness and the desire for immediate gratification are two behaviors that are very difficult to control. But youths are more impatient than adults and immediate gratification is the rule, not the exception. They lack a "rear-view mirror" in their mind's eye—that is, they do not have the life experience to reflect on, which can encourage them to

146 Dr. Morbius is a character in the sci-fi movie *Forbidden Planet* (Metro-Goldwyn-Mayer, 1956).

make smarter choices about their future. Mastering the art of the long-view can help mitigate this natural immaturity. As Dr. Morbius learned, the problem, as well as the solution, lies within *you*.

Lack of self-control

It is always thus, impelled by a state of mind which is destined not to last, that we make our irrevocable decisions.
~ Marcel Proust, French novelist

It is not enough to accurately predict one's future preferences and experiences. We also need to *act* on our predictions. Yet many young persons do not always do this in a rational manner. Rather than choose what they predict will generate the greatest overall long-term happiness, say, saving for higher education, they fail to reach an optimal balance between impulsivity and self-control. Instead of education, they blow their wad on a hot new car and assume they can learn what is needed when then actually need it.

We can think of control behaviors as two ends of a continuum. At one end, we exhibit self-control and forgo small, immediate gains in favor of waiting for large gains in the future. Since these large outcomes might be delayed or uncertain, we mentally assess their value on the basis of their proximity, or nearness to the present, and our guesstimate of the likelihood they will occur. At the other end of the continuum is impulsiveness. Here we ignore future possibilities in favor of whatever we can get today. We fail to follow through with what we *need* to do versus what we *want* to do. In varying degrees we are all somewhere in between.

What might explain our lack of self-control? Psychologists describe this type of behavior as being *bounded*. While we try to exercise (diet, quit smoking, follow through on New Year's resolutions, pull it out in time,[147] etc.), too often we prove to be limited in our capacity or desire to implement our intentions. Bounding can have many causes such as ignorance, impatience, laziness, fantasy, anxiety, or poor long-term planning skills. We procrastinate, knowing that it will undermine our long-term well-being, because we simply lack the willpower.

***BRAIN SNACK:** Retirement planner Robert Recchia of California Corporate Benefits points out that 401(k) plans not only let workers save and invest for retirement, in many cases they are a bonanza of free money. "Many firms will match employees' contributions to such plans. In this case, each dollar an employee invests automatically becomes two dollars, an instant 100 percent return! It is the equivalent of finding $100 bills on the sidewalk," Recchia emphasizes. Wow! Any rational person would snap up this golden opportunity for free money, right?*

Wrong. They plan to enroll soon, year after year, but don't do it. Typically, a new employee takes a median time of two to three years to enroll, observes

147 This is the world's second-most broken promise (the first is, "We won't go all the way."). Ladies take note.

economist David Laibson. "Since Americans change jobs frequently—say, every five years—this delay could mean losing half of one's career opportunity for these retirement savings." Although he walks employees through the calculations, showing them what they are doing wrong, "Almost all of them still don't invest," Laibson laments. "They are happier with the idea of doing it tomorrow."

It turns out that most of our behaviors are not purposeful, thought-out choices, although this is an illusion we have about others. Our behaviors are driven more by the seductive "now-moment"—all of the things going on in our environment in real time. The extent to which the present looms large in our mind was measured in a field study of adults, aged 20 to 81 years old, all relatively highly educated and in good health. Participants rated how frequently (almost never to many times a day) they thought about five different time periods: tomorrow, the next few weeks, this year, the year after this, and 10 years from now. Adults of all ages reported that their thoughts were concentrated only on the next few months.

Thinking excessively about our present circumstances and preferences disproportionately influences our decisions. Behavioral scientists call this focus *temporal myopia*, or the present bias.[148] Like visual myopia, temporal myopia causes clarity to decrease with distance, but it applies to our perception of the future rather than of our sense of sight. Often our short-term inclination of what to do—watch TV rather than study—does not accord with our assessment of what is in our long-term best interests—studying rather than watching TV. The point is not that watching TV is necessarily a worse way to spend our time than studying quantum mechanics. Rather, the point is that we may wish we would study rather than watch TV, yet we still watch TV.

Reali-tude:
Self-discipline is doing what you have to do, whether you feel like it or not.

Discounting the future

I'll gladly pay you Tuesday for a hamburger today.
~ J. Wellington Wimpy (Popeye's friend)

In almost every decision that we make, we have to make a judgment in advance of the outcome. Otherwise, we are just reacting like jellyfish. This is where the issue of discounting comes in. If we can receive an apple in 100 days and two apples in 101 days, most of us will wait the extra day for another apple. But when the decision shifts to the present, our patience wears thin and we think "I'd rather have an apple today than wait for two tomorrow." Economists call this behavior *hyperbolic*

148 A lack of self-control in humans has been linked with having lower intelligence. Scientists have found a biological basis for it in the brain's circuitry associated with reward and pleasure. Gents take note.

discounting. People who are "hyperbolic discounters" tend to place a lower value on future benefits and overvalue the present.[149]

Why is this? In general, humans prefer large-to-small, immediate-to-delayed, and guaranteed-to-uncertain gains. After all, future outcomes are more uncertain; they may be delayed, or worse, not happen at all. Physiologically, scientists tell us our brains evolved for immediate gratification. On the African savannah, when our ancestors could not be sure where their next meal was coming from, they didn't ask themselves, "Should I let this antelope live now in the hope that a fatter one will come along tomorrow?" In those days, it was eat or be eaten, and to a large extent our brains still function this way. As the delay before delivery of a larger reward increases, or the chances that we will get the larger reward drop, we mentally *discount* or reduce its subjective value. Or as they say in Texas, "An armadillo in the hand is worth two in the Bush."

Think you are immune to this trap? Think again, Thaddeus. "People act irrationally in that they overly discount the future," says economist Max Bazerman, who studies decision-making at Harvard Business School. "We do worse in life because we spend too much for what we want now at the expense of goodies we want in the future. For example, people buy things they can't afford on a credit card, and as a result they get to buy less over the course of their lifetimes." Broadly speaking, consequences tend to have a lot less bearing on our choices the more distantly they fall in the future . . . even when one's life is at stake. Consider these examples:

- A survey of 10,000 employees at a single firm found that 68 percent of participants said their retirement savings rate was "too low." When queried, they reported that they should be saving 14 percent of average earnings, whereas in fact, they were only saving about 6 percent. While one third of those planned to raise their savings rate, four months later almost none had done so.
- According to Edward Miller, dean of the medical school at Johns Hopkins University, over 1-1/2 million people undergo coronary-artery bypass graft surgery every year in the U.S. "If you look at people after bypass grafting two years later, 90 percent of them have not changed their lifestyle," Miller says. They decide to forego the necessary lifestyle changes to prevent future surgeries and premature death in favor of the short-term pleasures of unhealthy foods and laziness.
- Which would you prefer: $100 today or $150 one year from today? Many studies over the past 20 years asked this type of question, varying the amounts and periods. The predominant finding was the discounting of future gains averaged 20–25 percent. People were willing to give up nearly one quarter of the value of a future reward in order to have it immediately.

149 "Discount" refers to what we are willing to give up to enjoy something today rather than wait until tomorrow. It is often expressed as a rate, e.g., 10 percent. "Hyperbolic" refers to the reversal of preference from the larger, later reward to the smaller, sooner reward as the delay time between the two gains gets shorter. Interestingly, experiments have shown that animals also exhibit this preference reversal.

- After the Gulf War in the early 1990s, the military enticed soldiers into retirement. Soldiers were given a choice between a one-time, lump-sum payment (on the order of $20,000) and an annuity, or guaranteed monthly payment worth around $40,000 in present value. Fifty percent of 11,000 officers and more than 90 percent of 55,000 enlisted men chose the lump sum. This saved the U.S. Government $1.7 billion but was not in the soldiers' best interest. If they really wanted the money immediately, they could have taken out a loan for even more (say $25,000), used the annuity income to pay it back, and still come out ahead.
- An estimated 450,000 Type 1 diabetic women in the United States—one-third of the total—have skipped or shortchanged their insulin to lose weight in a condition called *diabulimia*. In trade for short-term weight loss, they risk long-term organ damage, coma, and early death.
- Discounting causes us to overcommit our future schedules. Research has found that most people will make commitments long in advance that they would never make if the commitment required immediate action.

From the perspective of behavioral economists, these examples clearly demonstrate that people have trouble acting in their own long-term best interests. And this discounting of the future can lead to a more insidious problem: the habitual desire for immediate gratification.

Immediate Gratification

I can resist everything except temptation.
~ Oscar Wilde, playwright, from *Lady Windermere's Fan*

Psychologist Margot Prior argues that the lives of families in western societies are increasingly influenced by three major cultural changes over the last few decades. First, the high value placed on the culture of self-realization; that is, individual wealth and pleasure rather than collective or community good. Second is narcissism, or excessive love and pampering of one's self. The third influence is the higher level of disposable income in the family and the need for instant pleasure with little patience for any delay of gratification. Robert Manning, director of the Center for Consumer Financial Service, agrees. "The problem of immediate gratification is ruining large portions of society," he says. "This focus on instant gratification and the cognitive denial of long-term consequences shifts the view of responsible spending from living within a budget to more quickly acquiring the material accouterments associated with professional success."

BRAIN SNACK: *In the 1960s, Stanford psychologist Walter Mischel researched the ability to delay gratification and exert self-control in the face of strong and emotional temptations. In his study, he placed marshmallows in front of hungry four-year-old children. He told them they could have one marshmallow now, or if they could wait several minutes, they could have two. Some* *children quickly grabbed the treat. Some lasted a few minutes before succumbing. Still others were determined to wait, covering their eyes or singing in order to cope.*[150]

Mischel followed the group and years later found that the "grabbers" suffered low self-esteem. Teachers and parents saw them as stubborn, easily frustrated, and prone to envy. In contrast, the "wait-for-two-fers" exhibited better coping skills. They were more socially competent, optimistic, self-assertive, dependable, and trustworthy. Two-fers also scored about 210 points higher on their SATs, got into better colleges, and had, on average, better adult outcomes. This suggests that a key factor for long-term success is not merely hard work or superior intelligence, but the ability to delay gratification.[151]

Technology has accelerated this trend toward immediate gratification. In his book, *Generation Text: Raising Well-Adjusted Kids in an Age of Instant Everything*, Michael Osit writes that the time and space between a desire for a commodity and access to it has shrunk to the vanishing point—all we need is a credit card, a cellular phone, and Federal Express. "The world economy now works on the related principles of immediate gratification and convenience," says Osit. Parents have inadvertently enabled their children to expect immediate gratification, spawning what he calls "Generation Text"—the technology-enhanced, push button, "get what you want, when you want it" culture.

It's not that NeXters are lazy or against hard work. It is just that most of you see very little perceived value in delaying gratification. This confounds traditional economists, who see this type of behavior as irrational. There again, what we most value often has little to do with the rationality of economics wonks and everything to do with humanity. Should we maximize our lifespan by leading lives of pure asceticism, never enjoying an occasional greasy pizza or ice cream cone? Do economists feel generous only when there is quid pro quo? Have they never been inspired by art? Or fallen in love? Or gotten drunk?

So for me, whilst I sit here and eat some fattening chips WITH dip and drink my cherry coke, and when I step outside to smoke my Marlboro, I will know that temporal myopia has won. I will be 100% certain that my id beats the ego without fail damn near every single time and, really, I will be okay with this. Different strokes for different folks, carpe diem and all that jazz... You really never know when your number is up, why deny yourself the things that make life good?

~ everythingzen, Internet blogger

---

150 The most successful youngsters were those who controlled their impulsivity by distracting themselves. Scientists have observed that chimpanzees will also exhibit self-restraint if they can distract themselves with magazines and toys while waiting.

151 According to psychologist Sigmund Freud, our drive for immediate gratification originates with the "id." Present at birth, the id is the part of the human psyche that is responsible for our basic drives such as food, water, sex, and basic impulses. The id is completely illogical and is focused strictly on instant self-gratification. It will not take "no" for an answer. Sound familiar?

Whether immediate gratification is logically correct or not depends greatly on circumstances. Not everyone meticulously plans out their tomorrows or follows through with whatever plans they've managed. It is visceral factors like uncertainty, impatience, fear, or envy that make our preferences and risk assessments largely subjective. And just because someone makes a decision that is not the best one in one sense does not mean their decision was not the best one overall for them. Take, for example, the man with heart disease who continues his detrimental behaviors (eating fatty foods, laziness, etc.) solely because he enjoys them for their present benefits without care whether he lives longer without these risks. His actions are not irrational. Focusing on the present only becomes irrational when one is also focused on a future benefit or benefits. Thus, the man who wants to live longer, stay in shape, and remain handsome without the problems associated with heart disease—yet still eats greasy foods and does not exercise—is irrational.

BRAIN SNACK: *In Greek mythology, Odysseus is the legendary Greek king of Ithaca and the hero of Homer's epic poem, the* Odyssey *(he was the brains behind the Trojan Horse). On his return voyage, the goddess Circe warns Odysseus that his ship will soon pass the island of the Sirens, whose irresistible singing lures sailors to their death on the rocks. The Sirens are a marvelous metaphor for human craving, both in its seductions and its pitfalls. Circe advises Odysseus to plug his crew's ears with beeswax so they cannot hear the Sirens' songs. She tells him that he alone may hear their sweet voices if he commands his sailors to lash him to the mast and ignore his pleas for release. As they pass the island, the Sirens began to sing beautifully, promising Odysseus wisdom and knowledge of past and future. Enchanted by their song, he struggles to break free but his men refuse to release him until they have safely passed the danger.*

Odysseus resisted the perils of craving by pre-committing himself. We still do this today through the use of commitment "tricks." Finance researchers Olivia Mitchell and Stephen Utkus say these help impose a degree of discipline on our wayward behavior through rules about what we can and cannot do. Assigning a designated driver for a sorority party or allowing a 3 to 7-day cooling off period for certain purchases such as credit repair, weight reduction, health clubs, or timeshares help protect us from ourselves. And increasingly, we are turning to technology to control our impulses. Car ignition locks, bank card spending cutoffs, and Internet-blocking programs help us to counteract lapses in personal willpower.

In the final analysis, life is not cut and dried. If you do not care how your future pans out, hey, party like its 1999 dude. If you want something to show besides crow's feet in your later years, you need to figure out a way to resist the temptation(s) of the moment. And the moment can be very tempting.

The bottom line:

- *Self-control trap:* a failure to control one's impatience and impulsiveness.
- "Discounting" means things in front of us now are worth more than things far away in time.
- We buy more, eat more, and save less tomorrow than we wish our tomorrow selves to do.
- Use commitment devices to resist immediate gratification.

Reali-tude:
The ability to delay gratification is a key factor for success.

The Reality

Financial planners today tell us that the biggest difference between Baby Boomers and their parents is that Boomers are more concerned about outliving their money than about leaving a massive estate.
~ Jay MacDonald, Bankrate.com

The reality is many young persons are frustrated by what they perceive as wanton indulgence by Baby Boomers. They already have a sneaky suspicion that the problems created by the Boomer generation will end up screwing their own financial future. Count on one thing NeXters: you will inherit their problems. Stand by to receive.

Generational dynamics

Christmas is a time when kids tell Santa what they want and adults pay for it. Deficits are when adults tell the government what they want and their kids pay for it.
~ Richard Lamm, former Governor of Colorado

A "megatrend" is a widespread, but slowly formed, social, economic, political, environmental, or technological change. This term was first made popular by John Naisbitt in his bestseller *Megatrends: Ten New Directions Transforming Our Lives*. Once in place, a megatrend influences a wide range of government/societal activities and perceptions, possibly for decades. And two megatrends are particularly worrisome for Generation NeXt: population aging and Boomers' retirement.

The first megatrend, aging of the U.S. population, is a demographic shift "with no parallel in the history of humanity," say historians Richard Jackson and Neil Howe. In *Baby Boomers, Generation X and Social Cycles: North American Long-waves*, demographer Edward Cheung says the "long-wave" of Baby Boomer retirement has begun and the number of people over 65 years old has started to grow at an increasing rate. In 2005 the National Centers for Disease Control and Prevention found that 12 percent of the population was over 65. By 2050, more than a quarter of the developed world's population is projected to be over 65. Geezers rule!

The second megatrend, an economic dynamic, involves several Boomer-related retirement issues that will directly affect Gen NeXt. First is the continuing rise in the general level of prices of goods and services over time. Economists call this *inflation.*[152] Inflation hurts retirees most of all, since many live on a fixed income (albeit many receive cost of living increases). But the biggest inflation worry by far is the increasing cost of health care. Findings by the Employee Benefit Research Institute show that individuals age 55 who live to age 90 would need to accumulate $210,000 by age 65 to pay for insurance to supplement Medicare and out-of-pocket medical expenses in retirement—far more than all but about 10 percent of workers currently have saved for all retirement expenses. Medicare is the federally-funded medical plan available for all Americans when they turn 65 and covers medical expenses such as doctor's visits, hospital stays, drugs, and other treatments. Already in the red on a cash basis, Medicare is not sustainable as currently implemented and has been a vexing problem for federal legislators.[153]

Uh-oh. There is another pachyderm in the aisle. Social Security (SS) is a mandated supplemental retirement system (plus other benefits) set up to ensure that no one falls through the cracks. The program provides a minimum subsistence level of income to any worker who had paid into the program. Benefits are paid based on a sliding scale depending on your income, how long you work, and at what age you retire. In 2008, SS paid about $1,150/month for a single retiree or $1,900/month for a retired couple. This is not a lot to live on. Unlike the financial crisis facing Medicare, current estimates are that Social Security will remain solvent for several decades.

So, here's the rub. Technically, Medicare and Social Security are not funds, but "pay-as-you-go" programs. Both are funded out of payroll taxes; that is, a certain percentage of your paycheck goes directly into the respective programs to provide benefits to current recipients.[154] But the number of old coots (that's Boomers) drawing benefits is going up, while the number of young coots (that's you) paying for those benefits is going down. As a result of this imbalance, government benefits for retirees (mainly Social Security and Medicare) are estimated to rise from 9 percent of national income in 2005 to 21 percent by 2050. And future benefits will also be strained by immigration trends. The Pew Hispanic Center estimates that by 2050, the population may exceed 430 million, up from about 300 million now. About four-fifths of the increase will reflect immigrants, their children, and their grandchildren.

Like lambs to the slaughter

> *Stein's Law: Things that can't go on forever don't.*
>
> ~ Herbert Stein, economist

---

152 Many economists are concerned that the huge amount of money injected into the economy by the government from December, 2008 to March, 2010 ($1.5 trillion) may lead to runaway inflation. In November, 2010 the Federal Reserve injected another $600 Billion. This spawned the joke, "Why does my *Big Mac* keep going up in price? Because the government is eating your lunch."

153 The long-term costs associated with the *Health Care and Education Reconciliation Act of 2010* signed into law by President Obama in March, 2010 are still unclear.

154 When you get your first "real" job, look for the hefty chunk of change labeled *FICA/Medicare* on the deductions side of your pay stub. Thank you for your donation.

For NeXters, this could be the ultimate rocky horror show. Longer living parents will be competing with younger and poorer immigrants—heavily Hispanic—for government social services and benefits. In order to pay for these goodies, Uncle Sam will need to renegotiate some of the promises it has made to its citizens. This is "political-speak" for raising taxes and lowering benefits, and this has spawned a political firestorm. Gentle ladies and men of Generation NeXt, you need to pay attention and begin asking questions like "Will there be enough money to pay for a secure retirement for me?"; "To keep the system solvent, how much will my benefits be lowered?"; "What will be the minimum age for me to begin drawing my benefits? 74? 76? 78?"; and "Can I afford cat food in bulk?" Financial adviser Dan White sums it up succinctly: "There's only so many dollars to go around."

> *This is an unfair burden for future generations. You'd think young people would be riled up over this issue, since they're the ones who will foot the bill when they're out in the working world. But students take more interest in issues like the Iraq war and gay marriage than the federal government's finances. It's not something that can fire people up.*
>
> ~ Emma V., University of Texas Young Democrats

The plot thickens. In the old days, people worked for one employer their entire career and were assured of pension and health benefits at retirement. Nowadays, under the guise of efficiency, more companies are figuring out ways to "scrape off" employee obligations. In 1980, about 40 percent of the jobs in the private sector offered pensions. Today, only 18 percent do. Worse yet, some of these plans have been underfunded (but not the CEO's salary). With its customary good use of taxpayer dollars, the federal government set up an independent agency called the Pension Board Guarantee Corporation (PBGC) to pay benefits that companies had promised, but failed to deliver. PBGC operated as an industry funded insurance plan and this worked... for a while. Without government backing, however, payments were not guaranteed and as more and more pension plans came up short, so did the PBGC till. This prompted the Government Accountability Office (GAO) to warn, "PBGC's accumulated deficit is too big, and plans simply do not have enough money in the system to back up the long-term promises many employers have made to their workers." In other words, they ain't got the dough to pay. This means trouble for some pensioners. It could be your parents.

The follow-on act is the ubiquitous 401(k).[155] This plan, also called a *defined contribution plan*, is the universal replacement to the pension. In the world of 401(k)'s, the burden for retirement funding has largely shifted from the firm to the employee. This was a good deal for corporations, but not for you. In their book, *Working Longer: The Solution to the Retirement Income Challenge*, Alicia Munnell

155 Named after a section of the Internal Revenue Code that took effect in January, 1980. A 401K is an individual retirement account funded by employee tax-free contributions into various investment options, usually a range of mutual funds. Taxes are paid later when these funds are withdrawn. Within two years, almost half of large firms were either offering a 401(k) plan or considering doing so. Can you guess why?

and Steven Sass of the Center for Retirement Research argue that savings through defined contribution 401(k) plans will not be sufficient for future retirees. Matters were made much worse with the financial industry meltdown, which nuked as much as $2 trillion—or about 20 percent overall—of Americans' retirement plans. "Unlike Wall Street executives, America's families don't have a golden parachute to fall back on," says Rep. George Miller (CA), chairman of the House Education and Labor Committee. "It's clear that their retirement security may be one of the greatest casualties of this financial crisis." Although many plans have since recovered, those dollars have reduced purchasing power due to inflation.

What is a Boomer to do? Most likely, opt to delay retirement and continue working. But older workers cost companies more than younger ones and have been shed like winter coats in a July heat wave. Knowing this, displaced Boomers are willing to settle for less and work only part-time in order to have a job. This increases competition for lower paying positions that would have gone to younger persons.

But even this may prove to be a pipedream. According to global human capital consultant Ingrid Selene, most people in the 45–64 age group leave full-time work for reasons beyond their control. Two in three men withdraw from full-time work prior to pension age, but not by choice. They lose their job and can't get another one or they have health problems (poor health is by far the biggest factor causing unplanned early retirement). For women, one in three are forced to leave work before they wished to for reasons similar to those for men. Since many Boomers waited until their peak earning years to save, this suggests that a fair proportion of them will come up short in their retirement. The Center for Retirement Research estimates that a large percentage of households—43 percent, and higher for late Boomers—is at risk of having inadequate retirement income. NeXters, these are your parents.

All in the family

> *Parent: (n.) A member of the family, who takes first priority in trying to make your life miserable.*
>
> ~ firedemonhiei, Internet blogger

Counting on a large inheritance? Scale down those expectations Sonya. Many Boomers are consuming their home equity and 401(k) assets just to make ends meet. Reverse mortgages allow home owners to siphon out the equity, or value, in their home while they live in it. From 2001 to 2007 these types of mortgages increased by a factor of 12 and the trend has been younger borrowers. Borrowing from 401(k) retirement plans has also surged, from 11 percent of workers in 2006 to nearly one in four workers in 2010. Loans against long-term assets just to pay the bills are not healthy signs there will be anything left for you but the toothbrush.

Finally, in a reversal of fortunes, Gen NeXters may find themselves having to not only provide for themselves and their children, but also for their retired parents. Few kids will refuse to help his/her parent(s) in their old age. "People tend to assume they're going to die earlier than they actually do," says Mark Iwry, a senior fellow at the Brookings Institution. "They have a 50 percent chance that they'll outlive their average life expectancy." And don't bet your life on that long-term care insurance policy. Insurers underestimated how fast medical costs would rise and how many seniors would actually use those benefits. Double-digit rate increases are squeezing existing policyholders tighter than a python and many face having their coverage dropped.

And in a classic case of the *projection trap,* young persons underestimate when they too will begin to experience age-related problems. A Pew Research Center survey on aging asked respondents about aspects of negative benchmarks often associated with aging such as illness, memory loss, an inability to drive, an end to sexual activity, a struggle with loneliness and depression, and difficulty paying bills. In every instance, older adults report experiencing these "markers" of old age at lower levels, often far lower, than younger adults report expecting to encounter them when they grow old.

NeXters, follow the bouncing ball: costs of living are rising; Social Security and Medicare benefits are thinning out; pensions are going the way of the Dodo; Boomers are consuming their assets; white hairs will work until they drop dead; parents may be moving in with you; your own aging problems will start earlier than you think. Hopefully, this ignites a fire under a tender area!

Reali-tude:
Don't get bitter, get busy.

The bottom line:

- Two worrisome megatrends are an aging population and the impending Baby Boomer retirement.
- The federal government will need to renegotiate the social promises it has made.
- Many Boomers are worried about outliving their money in retirement.
- You may have to provide for your parents in their golden years.

Doctor's Prescription (Rx)

No sensible decision can be made without taking into account not only the world as it is, but also the world as it will be.
~ Isaac Asimov, author

We overlook the future consequences of our present actions by failing to use "mental time travel" to project alternative outcomes. Lacking self-control, we are unable on a moment-by-moment basis to resist impatience, impulsiveness, and a desire for immediate gratification. Insulate yourself from strategic inflections by becoming a mature decider. Your future self will congratulate you on your wisdom! Here are some things you can do to help master the art of the long-view:

To avoid triggering the projection trap:

- *Be a "Second Hand Rose."* For major leisure-time purchases that require future attendance to recover your investment (e.g., health, golf, and travel memberships, vacation time shares, season sports passes, etc.), check out the secondary (resale) market before you buy.
- *Develop emotional maturity.* Emotional maturity involves self-examination. Asking yourself, "How do I feel about my feelings?" when making a decision can help you develop greater confidence. Consider writing out your feelings and sharing them with a tribal elder. You'll almost always feel better.
- *Don't assume.* The future will not be the same as right now. Don't assume it will be. And don't assume that others have the same knowledge, opinions, and views as you do. Assume they do *not* unless they clearly prove otherwise.
- *Avoid imitating others.* Many people imitate the decisions of others or follow social norms. This works only if their decisions and norms are rational. Many are not. What is right for your friends may not be right for you. Ask "WWWWWW?" (Why We Want What We Want) and be clear on your values, the principles that guide your actions.
- *Maximize happiness.* In making a choice, avoid overestimating the quantitative aspects (often, but not always, this is money) to the detriment of the qualitative aspects. People underestimate their ability to adapt to changes in life circumstances. Every challenging situation brings a chance to grow wiser and more skillful.

To avoid triggering the self-control trap:

- *Self-commit.* Making a positive self-commitment can be of value when your long-term intent and your short-term actions diverge. Think of what is really important to achieving your plan. Sharing with a trusted adult can help you resolve conflicts, adjust deadlines, and reinforce your determination.
- *Chillax dude.* During periods of stress, we focus more on the present than on the past or the future. This exacerbates our desire for immediate gratification. Conversely, we tend to be more future-oriented if we have experienced positive events in our immediate past. Concentrate on and mentally rehearse an upcoming positive life change.
- *Use "auto-pilot" devices.* If you are unable to set your own rules and follow through on them, use commitment devices such as automatic payroll deductions that force you to save. If you still cannot restrain your spending, consider having someone else help manage your money.
- *Walk a mile in their shoes.* Learning is not just acquiring and manipulating information; it is also influenced by our emotions and feelings. Get a feel for the frustrations of retirement living by attempting to live on, say, two-thirds of your income for a month. Experiencing their situation firsthand can be a real motivator.
- *Develop "long-view" habits.* Bolster your resistance to temptation by thinking about the goal you want to obtain. Thinking "why" versus "how" at the moment of decision can significantly increase self-control and help you make the right choice.

Reali-tude:
If you do not control events, events will control you.

Talking Points

You don't make a pickle by squirting vinegar on a cucumber. It has to soak awhile before you get what you want.
~ Author unknown

Chapter 17 describes some tools to help you acquire wisdom by interviewing others. To benefit from these techniques, you need only have access to a parent, educator, or other trusted adult (tribal elder) and a desire to listen and learn. Based on the ideas in this chapter, here are some starters:

1. "I am trying to improve myself. Sometimes young persons fail to comprehend how much their preferences will change with time. Reflecting on your experience, or that of someone you know, do you recall a situation where lack of mature judgment resulted in a young person jeopardizing his long-term well-being?" If they say "Yes" then ask:

    - "Would you tell me the gist of what happened please?"
    - "How did you (they) feel about this at the time?"
    - "What two things did you learn from this that you can share with me?"

2. "I am trying to improve myself. Sometimes young persons fail to comprehend that lack of self-control can negatively influence their judgment. Reflecting on your experience, or that of someone you know, do you recall a decision situation where a young person's impulsive desire for immediate gratification jeopardized her long-term well-being? If they say "Yes" then ask:

    - "Would you tell me the gist of what happened please?"
    - "How did you (they) feel about this at the time?"
    - "What two things did you learn from this that you can share with me?"

    In either case, if they say "No," simply say "Thank you."

3. "I want to make wise life-choices. Reflecting on your experience, would you have two ideas that I can implement to improve my judgment and decision-making skills? Be sure to thank them for their response.

4. Research suggests that we are persuaded more strongly when we make an argument ourselves, even if it isn't in line with our own viewpoint. For example, you are more apt to resist temptation when you deliver a message on the value of delayed gratification than if you passively receive it. The explanation seems to be that we are very good at convincing ourselves because we know just what

sorts of arguments will sway us to improve. Pick a *maturity trap* that you think describes you and generate your own arguments. Then share them with a tribal elder. You may be surprised at the results!

Knowledge Nuggets

You should never underestimate the predictability of stupidity.
~ Bullet Tooth Tony

1. *My country 'tis of thee?* Everyone likes to look their best. This is the reason lipstick sells, companies inflate their stock prices, and the federal government manipulates its data. In an interview titled, "Shadowing Reality," economist John Williams explains how the government manipulates not only the methods it uses to calculate its "official" statistics (e.g., cost of living, unemployment, and inflation figures), but fudges some of the data to produce the desired results. Why the spin? Transfer payments (such as Social Security) are indexed to the figures, so lower stats mean lower payments to recipients. In 2006, Williams accurately predicted the 2008 financial meltdown. For a real eye-opener see: http://www.weedenco.com/welling/Downloads/2006/0804welling022106.pdf.

2. *What about my parents?* According to the Center for Retirement Research (CRR) at Boston College, ensuring retirement security for an aging population is one of the most significant challenges facing the nation. They have some gloomy predictions for retiring Baby Boomers: longer retirements and lower retirement incomes. Because many Americans appear unaware of these disquieting trends, CRR has developed the National Retirement Risk Index to measure the share of working-age households who are at risk of being unable to maintain their pre-retirement standard of living in retirement. The situation is not hopeless though. Share some of these insights with your parents at: http://crr.bc.edu/briefs/a_new_national_retirement_risk_index.html.

3. *What is my emotional intelligence?* Much emphasis has been put on certain aspects of intelligence such as logical reasoning, math skills, spatial skills, understanding analogies, verbal skills etc. New research has found that the skills for success in college and beyond have less to do with smarts than with ordinary personality traits, like an ability to stay focused, control impulses, and persist. Accounting for other factors, people with high Emotional Intelligence Quotient, or "EIQ," tend to be more successful in life than those with lower, even if their classical IQ is average. Take the challenge to evaluate your own emotional intelligence, and discover suggestions on how to improve it at: http://www.queendom.com/tests/access_page/index.htm?idRegTest=1121.

4. *Where to go for info?* See Appendix F for additional information relating to this chapter.

Part 4: Your Controllable Decisions

(The Hot Breath of Reality)

Chapter 11

Who You Marry

Almost everything in life is easier to get into than out of.
~ Agnes' Law

The Gist

The Good:

- Nine out of ten people will eventually get married
- Married people tend to be wealthier, happier, healthier, and have better sex

The Bad:

- Young persons often marry for the wrong reasons
- Marriage is a financial as well as a romantic union
- Divorce can leave severe emotional scars and financial wreckage

The Reality:

- Women are increasingly less dependent upon men and marriage
- For men without a college degree, the pool of eligible women is shrinking
- Most starter marriages do not work out
- Cohabitation is becoming more prevalent and socially acceptable
- Nearly two-thirds of married couples fail to talk about finances before the wedding

Introduction

No one will ever win the battle of the sexes; there's too much fraternizing with the enemy.

~ Henry Kissinger, former U. S. Secretary of State

In the U.S. Supreme Court's white marble courtroom, the nine sitting justices are not the only presiding presence. High above the justices' mahogany bench, the 18 great lawgivers of history are depicted in marble friezes that commemorate written law as a force for stability in human affairs. One of them is Hammurabi (1795–1750 B.C.E.).

Reigning in Babylon, the world's first metropolis, Hammurabi produced the first surviving set of laws. The *Code of Hammurabi* is a compilation of 282 legal procedures and penalties that dealt primarily with business matters, crime, and family relationships. We know about the Code because just after the turn of the 20th century, French explorers unearthed a black granite stele[155] that proclaimed the laws to the greater public (think of it as an early billboard ad). Today, it is on display in Paris at the Louvre. The inscriptions on the eight-foot tall column are in 3,600 lines of Cuneiform, an ancient written language that looks like chicken tracks.

In Hammy's day, the law regarding marriage was simple. Considered a form of purchase, the marriage of young people was typically arranged between relatives, accompanied by the usual dickering about the dowry and such. Should plans not work out, divorce was allowed but only as an option "du jour" for the man. If the woman had been a bad wife, the Code allowed him to send her away while he kept the children and her dowry. Or, he could demote her to the position of slave in his house and provide her with food and clothing in return for fringe benefits. Or, he could simply drown her. You've come a long way baby!

Today the law traditionally views marriage as a legally recognized relationship, established by a civil or religious ceremony, between two people who intend to live together as domestic and sexual partners. But the institution of marriage is not cast in stone, though many people define it that way (or believe that God has defined it that way). There are different marriage laws in all the states and different definitions of marriage in every religious tradition. Other far less common forms of marriage exist that are accepted in other societies, for example polygamy (one dude, many dudettes) and polyandry (one dudette, many dudes).

155 An upright stone or slab with an inscribed or sculptured surface that was used as a monument or commemorative tablet.

To muddy the holy water a bit more, it is important to realize the distinction between civil marriage, those performed in accordance with state law, and religious marriage, those performed in accordance with canon law or religious decree. These different institutions are often confused with each other because states typically recognize the religious marriage for civil purposes.

A civil marriage is one where a government or civil official (such as a judge or ship's captain) performs the ceremony, and it takes place without any religious affiliation. Civil definitions of marriage do not usually mention childbearing, sexual relations, living arrangements, and religious beliefs or observance. It exists to meet the legal requirements of the locale and can be as simple as a visit to your neighborhood wedding chapel.[156] When clergy or congregations marry couples, however, it is a religious rite not a civil ceremony. Clergy and congregations may be more restrictive than the state; for instance, they may reject interfaith marriages or refuse remarriages after divorce. Some faiths may have a broader definition, such as blessing the unions of same-gender couples.

But civil and religious marriages are not the only way to get the proverbial ring through the schnoz. Marriage may also be created by legal operation alone. Termed common-law marriage, the law recognizes that two people who have been living as domestic partners are entitled to the effects of marriage. Each state has varied requirements for proving the establishment of a common law marriage. Once established, however, a common law marriage can only be ended by court decree. *Young person's alert:* this could be an issue when distributing jointly owned assets acquired in a domestic partnership should you later decide to separate.

Marriage is not a prerequisite to cohabitate. Cohabitation is an emotionally and physically intimate relationship that includes a common living place and exists without legal or religious sanction. Your grandparents called this "living in sin." Boomer parents called it "shacking up." For many of today's inseparables, *cohabitosis* is seen as an acceptable way to go for a trial spin, share expenses, and satisfy the "in-and-out" urge.

Finally, marriage is the only family relationship in the United States today that people generally enter by choice. We cannot choose our parents, our siblings, our grandparents, and so forth. But, we do choose our marriage partner. And your choice of marriage partner is likely to influence the entire course of your life in terms of where you live, whether you will have children, how your children will be raised, your occupation, your financial situation, and your general level of happiness. In terms of lifebombs, this one's a biggie.

---

156 Don't want people to know that you are married? Go west, young lovers! On the books since 1878, a little known "only-in-California" concoction is *confidential marriage*. A favorite of Hollywood celebrities, confidential marriage is in most respects the same as any old legal marriage—solemnized and binding. But unlike public marriages, the record is sealed. Nobody knows except you, your spouse, the official tying the knot, and Master Card (whatever).

The Good

Women want to find one Mr. Right, and men want to find all the dream girls they can get their hands on.
~ Bill O'Reilly, TV journalist, teacher

The inclination to marry is pervasive. While most Gen NeXters are not yet married (85 percent have yet to take the plunge) the vast majority hopes to marry some day. Among the unmarried, only 12 percent of you say you probably or definitely don't want to get married. When 25 year olds were surveyed as to where they saw themselves in 5 or 10 years' time, or what they saw as their next important "life-change," almost all talked about marriage. And for young Casanovas, studies show that roughly nine-in-ten adults in this country will eventually succumb and marry. Why is this? Underlying this desire to be married is a deep-seated need for security and stability.

Today's young persons appear to be more idealistic, hold higher expectations, and tend to be choosier in the hope of finding the perfect partner. Contrary to popular folklore, most successful romances are not a case of opposites attracting. In real life, we get married to people who share our goals: a family, a home, and a secure future enjoying each other's company. A *Money Magazine* poll found that while couples may not know it, they are remarkably in sync about what really matters to them. For example, chances are you and your mate will share the same priorities (e.g., saving for retirement and emergencies), worries (Will one of us lose our job? Can we pay off our debts?) and values (um, two kids or three?). On the whole, NeXters are not naïve about the seriousness of this commitment, with nearly two thirds of 18–25 year-olds saying that it is hard to have a good marriage.

I think all men should wait to get married. At least until 30. Women should wait until they know they have the right man and that can be at any age, but hopefully after 24. Then people can make a wise decision and not a rushed one. In my experience, the happiest people are the ones that feel good about the choices they have made.
~ Finesse Mitchell, writer

The good news is that national divorce rates have been declining. Well, slightly that is. Partially this is because the proportion of married people, especially among younger age groups, has been declining for decades. Between 1950 and 2000, the share of women 15-to-24 who were married plummeted from 42 to 16 percent. Of those who do marry, the divorce rate actually dropped slightly in the 1990s, from a high of more than 50 percent of new marriages ending in divorce to about 43 percent more recently. Although headed in the right direction, most experts consider these numbers to still be unacceptably high.

The effects of the financial meltdown have also held the divorce rate in check. In tough times, many people find it is cheaper to stay together even if they cannot stand each other's guts. Another contributor is more people are opting to cohabitate rather than formally tie the knot. Cohabs argue that any steady, long-term relationship is bound to increase happiness, promote good behavior, and allow for a better sex life. "Try before you buy" is seen as an attractive alternative to marriage—better to find out early that your "Prince Charming" won the Oscar for Best Actor, or your "Fairest of the Fair" is a latent Bridezilla so as to manage a relatively unencumbered exit.

For couples who decide to divorce, another positive trend is they are demonstrating increased realism and civility. Divorce lawyer Lee Rosen observes that many couples are seeking mediation as they split and arrange for joint legal custody of their children. "People are coexisting more peacefully, whether they stay together or come apart," Rosen says. "They are more contemplative and serious about their relationships, and I see people stay together who once would have allowed the marriage to unravel."

Finally, there is ample evidence that marriage provides considerable benefits. The U.S. Government Accounting Office has identified 1,138 direct benefits of marriage bestowed by the federal government, ranging from family leave, health care decision-making, and parenthood involving taxes, property rights, and inheritance. Barbara Whitehead and David Popenoe, who run the National Marriage Project at Rutgers University, have called marriage a "wealth-generating institution." On average, those who stay married end up four times richer than those who never marry, they say. In a 15-year study of 9,000 people, of those who married and stayed married—even when all other factors such as income and education were held constant—just the fact that they were married contributed to a 4 percent annual rise in these couples' wealth.[157] Compounded over a lifetime, this is a whole lotta dough.

Married couples are also much more likely to accumulate sufficient assets to maintain their standard of living throughout retirement, while unmarried individuals are far less likely to do so. Economist Isabel Sawhill links as much as half of the income inequality in the U.S. to changes in family composition. Single-parent families (mostly those with a high school degree or less) are getting poorer while married couples (those with education and dual incomes) are increasingly well-off. "This is a striking gap that is not well understood by the public," she says.

In addition to financial benefits, researchers tell us that married people are happier, healthier, and having better sex. They tend to take fewer risks, have better health habits, and have kids that seem better socialized for success. Most married women gain about ½ hour of leisure each weekday when compared to single women (husbands break even), and married men live longer than unmarried men (wives break even). But marriage historian Stephanie Coontz caveats that it isn't the mere fact of being married. "It is the relationship, not the institution that is key," she reminds us.

Reali-tude:
Marriage is a financial as well as a romantic union.

157 Economist Audrey Light examined the effect of marriage and of cohabitation and found that both of these institutions confer sizable—and identical—financial benefits on women, while men break even.

The bottom line:

- A civil marriage is one performed by an official (mayor, judge, peace officer, etc.).
- States allow religious marriage ceremonies to double as civil marriages.
- The national divorce rate has declined slightly but is still unacceptably high.
- The marriage advantage: those in good marriages tend to have a better quality of life.

The Bad

Guys are like roses—watch out for the pricks.
~ Anonymous

For better or for worse, your spouse or significant other will likely affect almost every aspect of your life. Even if you are merely taking a test drive with your main squeeze, you significantly heighten the risk to your long-term personal economic success if you screw it up. Intelligence or social class have nothing to do with it; one glance at the shenanigans of the super smart, the rich, and the powerful tells you that these people are often poster couples for what not to do. When it comes to marriage, questionable beliefs can trap your thinking and jeopardize your long-term well-being. Learn about some of the lifebombs and you'll stand a better chance of making a smart choice.

Cognitive Flaw: Ignorance

Ah, yes, divorce... from the Latin word meaning "to rip a man's heart out through his wallet."
~ Robin Williams, comedian, actor

Clueless about the implications of saying "I do?" Well, you'll definitely increase the risk that unexpected consequences will electrify your relationship! Let's look at how failing to be objectively informed when making this important life-choice can put your future happiness at risk.

☞ *Lifebomb #1: "Marriage could be a taxing proposition."*

First comes love, then comes marriage, then comes Uncle Sam with his hand out. If the couple is in good financial shape, a second income is usually beneficial because it means more money (that's good). When a couple marries and both spouses work, however, they are likely to go into a higher tax bracket on April 15th because they've joined their two incomes together. This often triggers steeply higher taxes when the tax return is filed jointly, rather than if each had remained single (that's not good).

This is Uncle Sam's so-called "marriage penalty," a raw deal that affects over 40 percent of married couples and disproportionally affects the working poor.

The marriage penalty refers to the higher taxes levied on married couples where spouses make approximately the same taxable income and they file one combined tax return (as "married, filing jointly"). The source of this increase in taxes has its roots in the progressive tax-rate structure in the income-tax laws, whereby a higher income pays a higher *rate* of tax.

Too in love to care? Research bears this out *(projection-2 trap)*. The initial decision to cohabit or marry is only slightly affected by the income tax consequences of one form of union versus the other. But if you are currently a cohabitating couple and you decide to get married, stand by to get fleeced. Since more and more households are two-income families, the transition will have significant tax consequences. In certain cases the penalty can be so large that accountants urge some clients planning to get married to consider delaying the ceremony until the following year. This allows each taxpayer to file two separate tax returns (as "single") for another year and use the tax savings to pay for an expensive honeymoon!

Married couples get screwed on their taxes in other ways too. Under the *Health Care Overhaul Law* (2010) some married couples may see health insurance coverage costing significantly more compared to unmarried couples living together. Fewer married couples can convert a traditional IRA to one of the new Roth or Education IRAs (savings plans for retirement and education purposes) and many stand to lose out on the education tax credit because their combined adjusted gross income is too high. To rub salt in the wound, the total deduction for investment losses is halved the moment you marry. With the U.S. Supreme Court's recognition of gay marriage in June, 2013, experts say many two-earner, same-sex married couples will likely see an annual federal income-tax increase of hundreds or thousands of dollars. To all nubile newlyweds, welcome to the club!

Reali-tude:
Make sure that your best man is not the tax man.

☞ *Lifebomb #2: "Cohabs— easier to slide in than out."*

Cohabitation is increasingly accepted as a dress-rehearsal for 20-somethings to achieve some of the benefits of marriage and avoid the downside of divorce. This appears to be a new norm among younger adults; in a survey of teenagers by the University of Michigan, 64 percent of boys and 57 percent of girls agreed that "it is usually a good idea for a couple to live together before getting married in order to find out whether they really get along." And there is evidence that cohabitation pays off for some. According to sociologist Daniel Lichter, the odds of divorce among women who married their *only* cohabitating partner were 28 percent lower than among women who never cohabitated before marriage.

On the face of it, cohabitation looks attractive. Couples who live together can share their expenses, assets, and labor. They can also share emotional and sexual intimacy and discover whether their partner has what it takes to be married. Should things not work out, they can amicably part ways and not have to seek legal or religious permission to dissolve their union. With traditional weddings costing $25,000 to $100,000 for a one-day performance (and the average price of a honeymoon at $4,466), cohabitation avoids siphoning the financial life-force out of a family.

Cool. Or is it? Is cohabitation really risk free? Maybe not. Since no explicit commitment is made, it is easier to drift into living together than it is to drift into a marriage. Once a couple starts living together, one partner may see this as a prelude to marriage. The other—usually the man—may see it as something more temporary but convenient. "They basically stay together because of inertia," says Scott Stanley of the Center for Marital and Family Studies. It's like signing up for a credit card with zero percent interest. At the end of 12 months when the interest goes up to 23 percent you feel stuck because your balance is too high to pay off. Cohabitation can be exactly like that.[158] "What happens is "many of these men end up married to women they would not have married if they hadn't been living together," says Stanley *(inertia-1 trap)*.

Women can suffer emotional, psychological, and financial costs by cohabiting. Divorce rates for women who cohabit with more than one man are more than twice as high as for women who cohabited only with their eventual husbands (thus mirroring the overall divorce rate). And once a woman has a child, she invariably doesn't want to hear "Hasta la vista baby" from a partner who suddenly decides he isn't ready to be a parent. Even if they eventually marry, she and her little one may still become trapped in a situation in which they are not really happy. According to *The Economist*, two-thirds of children born to cohabiting parents who later marry will see their parents split up by the time they are ten. In contrast, those born within wedlock face only half that risk. Many young persons find this surprising.

> *There seems to be some confusion about this issue (amongst women), so let me clarify this: women of the world, men want to screw you. Likely, the women want to screw men too, but in our society it's very much, men = chasers, women = chasees. Shocking revelation, I know. So ladies, here's a heuristic you should use to judge the man's intentions. Your intentions may be crystal clear and completely platonic in your head, but the guy* is likely just trying to score some nookie. All of those fun little things you do, all the meets over coffee, all the sailing, all the dancing, wining, movieing, and dining? Those are all social tactics used by the guy to get in your pants. Just remember: when in doubt, he wants to whip it out. (*By guy here, I mean the person who likes to screw persons of your gender. So, if the chasee is female, then gay males don't count, but gay females do.)*
>
> ~ Chris M. (*Pearls of Wisdom*)

Many see no problems associated with cohabitating. Understandably, most of these people are young *(optimism-2 trap)*. It is important, however, to recognize that there are legal ramifications beyond the superficial. Perhaps the most significant

158 In behavioral economics, this is called *consumer lock-in*. Lock-in is the decreased likelihood to search for, or change to, another option once an investment in something has been made. The greater the setup costs, the less likely we are to move to another, even better, situation, especially when faced with switching costs or the time, money, and effort it requires to make a change.

disadvantage of a non-martial relationship is how to deal with the question, "What will happen if we break up?" Those who marry do not have to wrestle with this. Marriage is a legal, social, and religious institution with a set of formal and informal rules that stretch back some 5,000 years. Historically, marriage has been a legally binding agreement that clearly spells out what happens when the relationship ends, whether by death or by divorce.

In comparison, cohabitation law is messy and affords people more limited rights than in divorce. In most states, the law is much looser and usually does not recognize or give such individuals or life partners many—if any—legal rights. And assessing whether financial outcomes are "fair" can be highly complex and subjective. For instance, being part of an unwed couple may give you no specific right to inherit property from your partner. Additionally, partners may not have a say in each other's medical care, work benefits, and financial affairs unless those wishes are spelled out in advance. This has been an especially vexing issue for same-sex marriage proponents. "That's the single most frequent complaint we hear on our web site—that they can't get benefits," says Nicky Grist, executive director of the Alternatives to Marriage Project.

Reali-tude:
If you cohabitate, avoid joint ownership of assets.

☞ *Lifebomb #3: "'Til divorce do us part."*

You and your beau have decided to throw in the towel and call it quits? Join the stampede dude! Divorce was made much easier by the implementation of "no-fault" divorce. Beginning with Oklahoma in 1953, by 1985 every state had adopted some form of no-fault divorce. No-fault describes any divorce where the spouse asking for a divorce does not have to prove that the other spouse did something wrong. To get a no fault divorce, one spouse must simply state a reason for the divorce that is recognized by the state. In most states, it's enough to simply declare that the couple cannot get along, citing terms like incompatibility, irreconcilable differences, or irremediable breakdown of the marriage. In some states, however, the couple must live apart for a period of months or years before they can obtain a no-fault divorce. Let's look at some of the ramifications.

1. *The demographics of divorce.* Although divorce rates can be calculated in several ways, there is general agreement that between 40 and 50 percent of all U.S. marriages today end in divorce.[159] And most of these go kaput within the first few years of marriage. Another 20 percent of couples seriously considered divorce,

159 The government divorce rate calculation is derived by comparing the annual marriage rate per 1,000 people compared with the annual divorce rate. The method preferred by social scientists is to calculate how many people who have ever married subsequently divorced. While a few Liz Taylors will skew the figures by jumping in and out of marriages like cheap shoes, "about half is still a very sensible statement" say divorce researchers.

but for various reasons they decided to stay married. Sadly, more than one million children are affected by the million-plus divorces each year.

Age at marriage is probably one of the best predictors of marital outcome. Generally, the probability of divorce increases as the number of years of marriage decreases. If you are a young couple in love, the odds are that one or both of you will change in a manner that will require some relationship accommodations. And these can be difficult to visualize and accept *(framing-2 trap)(projection-1 trap):*

- The divorce rate for brides who marry between 20–22 years of age is double that of those women who wait until they are between 22–24 years old to marry.
- When both husband and wife are teenagers at marriage, more than two-thirds of these relationships end in divorce.

Divorce most often occurs during the second and third years of marriage, reports a *TIME/CNN* poll, in which 45 percent of respondents say that couples do not take marriage seriously. A study of several hundred newlywed couples reveals a troubling reality: 63 percent had serious problems related to their finances, 51 percent had serious doubts about their marriage lasting, 49 percent had significant marital problems, 45 percent were not satisfied with their sexual relationship, 41 percent found marriage harder than they had expected, and 35 percent stated their partner was often critical of them. Hardly encouraging news.

2. *The soft costs.* Therapist-author Michele Weiner Davis notes, "The decision to divorce or remain together to work things out is one of the most important decisions you will ever make. It is crucial for those considering divorce to anticipate what lies ahead in order to make informed decisions *(projection-2 trap).* Too often the fallout from divorce is far more devastating than many people realize when contemplating the move."

> *I am continuously amazed at the number of people I meet in their 20s who have been divorced once and even twice. The highest rate for divorce exists in the Quarterlife generation, those of us who married in our late teens and early 20s.*
> ~ Jason C. Steinle, author, *Upload Experience*

There is no question there are legitimate reasons for divorce. Experts estimate that nearly one-third of the divorces in the U.S. involve marital relationships with a high degree of conflict. Couples who divorce often need the help and support of family, friends, neighbors, and religious leaders, particularly when children are involved. According to syndicated columnist Katherine Heine, the emotional trauma divorce inflicts on families takes years to heal. Divorce counselors that she has interviewed have likened divorce to open-heart surgery; it takes about a year of healing for every four years of marriage, they say.

BRAIN SNACK: *E. Mavis Hetherington has been a major trailblazing figure in the research and scientific study of the effects of divorce. After studying almost*

1,400 families and more than 2,500 children, some of them for three decades, Hetherington found that women tend to come out of divorce better than men, despite the financial dilemmas many experience. Women "turned out to be more competent, able people than if they had stayed in unhappy family situations," she concluded.

Most people who divorce end up marrying a second and sometimes a third time. Approximately two-thirds of second marriages end in divorce, and about three-quarters of third marriages bite the dust.[160] Not a good track record. A major source of friction is these couples bring assets and emotional baggage from former relationships, which complicates the issue of what is his, hers, and theirs. Also, couples who have been married before tend to be more suspicious of each other and are more likely to draft prenuptial agreements that spell out who gets what in case of divorce.

Once people have made the decision to divorce, how do they later feel about the choice? Family science professor Brent Barlow estimates that about one-third of the couples who divorce felt they made the right decision. Another one-third were uncertain or have mixed feelings about their divorce and about one-third of divorced couples eventually regretted the decision within five years.

3. *The hard costs.* If matters of the heart seem complicated, they are nothing in comparison with the fiscal (money-related) aspects involved with the legal dissolution of a marriage. These can be both complex and multiple, and have a variety of lasting consequences for both parties involved.[161]

How often is money an issue in divorces? More often than you think, Mable. In a study by the Financial Planning Association, nearly 40 percent of financial planners who have worked with divorcing couples say it's frequently a "key factor" in a couple's decision to split up. Spouses are simply unable to agree on spending styles, earning capacities, and priorities for spending their money. One of the greatest misunderstandings about divorce is the seemingly universal concept that all will be over quickly and that the two parties can get on with their lives as if it never happened *(superiority-2 trap)*. Many also naively believe that each party will receive half of what was shared.

Au contraire, Pierre. Divorce can take longer and cost more money than you could ever imagine. According to iVillage (Pregnancy & Parenting), the average divorce process requires one to two years and varies in cost from several hundred on up to several thousand dollars. Worse still, the longer you are married the more marriage-specific capital you accumulate, the more emotional the divorce, and the greater the cost. Bankruptcy, which is a legal judgment, and even the IRS can't touch certain assets such as money in retirement plans. But nothing is safe from

160 According to *Guinness Book of Records*, the world's "most married" woman has been married 23 times (and is looking forward to #24).

161 National burdens of the high divorce rate include higher crime rates, higher poverty rates, more welfare, less education, and more public health care.

the divorce attorneys, and like sharks they go for blood. As country singer Jerry Reed lamented, "She got the gold mine, I got the shaft."

Wake up and smell the java young lovebirds. Divorce is big business in the United States. According to Americans for Divorce Reform, divorce is about a $30 billion-a-year industry. The divorce system is bred to be adversarial and encourages partners to morph into pit bulls. Too many couples have wanted to settle their divorce with limited hassle and then the attorneys con them into World War III *(framing-1 trap)*. Lawyers who make their livings off litigating contested divorces are as thorough as watchmakers and as speedy as tortoises. Besides, lawyers make lousy therapists; at $200–$300 per hour, it is not about fairness and compromise. It's all about "billable time."

Beyond the immediate costs associated with divorce, such as housing, moving expenses, transportation, legal fees, etc., there are other costs as well. For example, spouses do not necessarily earn the same amount of money or possess the same potential to earn money in the future. In many cases couples are extended financially beyond their combined means, let alone singularly. A present or former spouse may default on a loan, commit fraud, file bankruptcy, or become disabled. Additionally, some transactions performed in conjunction with a divorce such as alimony, child support, or a home sale, may, in the eyes of the Internal Revenue Service be considered a taxable event. This is tax-speak for "cough up more dough" on April 15th. In the extreme, couples suffer their own *Nightmare on Elm Street*, where they cannot stand living together yet cannot divorce because of financial obligations.

Since your spouse is no longer helping you financially, often the bigger issue for young persons is dealing with a drastic reduction of income. Failing to appreciate how different your life will be after divorce can be a killer *(projection-1 trap)*. Research has shown that after separation, it is common for both the man and the women to be worse off financially, if only from the loss of economies of scale and the costs of moving to separate households. Without the contributions of your ex-spouse, it is virtually impossible to maintain your previous standard of living since some of your expenses just cannot be proportionally reduced. Here are a few examples:

- Two auto policies will be more expensive than one with a two-car discount;
- Both of you will need some type of homeowner's or renter's insurance;
- Utilities (water, phone, electric) will need to be paid on both residences;
- Don't forget changes in costs for medical and life insurance coverage.

Finally, two "facts of life" can make your ex-partner very happy and you totally pissed off. Did you support your partner through college? If so and you split, your partner has just won the lottery. Are you likely to inherit a sizeable chunk of money or property? If that comes through before the divorce, your partner passes "Go" and collects half. Cha-ching! Sorry about that Chief.

Reali-tude:

Divorce has significant short-term and long-term consequences.

Cognitive Flaw: Ineptitude

> *The trouble with some women is that they get all excited over nothing, and then they go and marry him.*
> ~ Cher, entertainer (in *Rolling Stone*)

Careless about the implications of saying "I do?" There is no question that young persons are far more impatient than adults and the desire for immediate gratification is typically the default *(self-control-1 trap)*. Jumping into marriage is no exception. Let's look at how failing to think seriously when making this important life-choice can put your future happiness at risk.

☞ *Lifebomb #4: ♫ I got the wedding bell blues… ♫*

Young persons are sometimes motivated to be haltered[162] for the wrong reasons:

Pressure:	Psychological squeeze from friends, family, society, or yourself *(inertia-2 trap)*.
Avoid growing up:	I want to be "taken care of" (surprisingly, this is gender independent).
Avoid your own life:	My life will never be fulfilled unless I am with fill-in-the-blank.
The great escape:	Once I get away from the parentals' clutches, I will be an adult.
Ease loneliness:	I have a need for somebody. Hello? Anybody? Are you out there?
Fantabulous sex:	Deal me in that poker game (always a big hit with the guys).
Money:	I pray for a sugar-daddy that will last and last.
Immigration:	Abracadabra—you just hit the jackpot!
Pregnancy:	Oops…

With the possible exception of marrying for money, most of the reasons cited above have a high probability of producing a lemon instead of a marriage. And, marrying for money can be tricky to maintain over the long-haul, unless you manage to secure a meaty prenuptial before you consummate the deal.

BRAIN SNACK: *A study reported in the* Proceedings of the National Academy of Sciences *found humans were similar to most other mammals in that they follow Darwin's principle of choosey females and competitive males. Participants were first asked to identify the qualities that were important to them in looking for a mate and then took part in a speed dating exercise. When it was time*

162 An arrangement of straps put over the head of an animal and used to lead it. Also, a rope with a noose used to hang somebody.

to make a choice, the men appeared to base their decisions principally on the woman's physical attractiveness, regardless of their stated preferences. Women were much more discriminating about their selection. They were aware of the importance of their attractiveness to men and adjusted their expectations to select the more desirable guys. The study confirmed what women already know: despite what they say, most guys go for looks.

Love is eternal and all that good stuff but personal economics makes no moral judgments. Chubby babies, who float around like dandelion seeds and shoot arrows into people, have no place in the equation. Reality check for guys: good looks fade and one day your Princess Precious will morph into a nagging dugong. Reality check for gals: your stud puppet will eventually sport a thinning thatch and will lose the battle of the bulge.[163] Chill out everyone—it's a DNA thing. Look beyond the superficial and reflect on what your relationship might be like in 20 years *(projection-1 trap)*.

Reali-tude:
Don't get married because you want to get out of a bad situation.

☞ *Lifebomb #5: "And in this corner, wearing the red trunks..."*

Who manages the family finances? The power of the purse is a huge advantage and according to Pew Research, in the typical American family it's the woman who wears the pantsuit. In households where the husband earns more, women are just as likely to make the final decisions regarding household finances. Where the wife earns more, she is more than twice as likely to do so. Sorry guys. Regardless who wears the financial pants, however, money and matrimony remain a very incendiary combination.

Why is this? The reason money causes so many arguments is what money represents. Money has always conspired to antagonize couples because at a deep emotional level "it's about power, control, freedom, success, security, acceptance, status and love," explains author Syble Solomon, an educator/motivational speaker who encourages couples to talk about money. "It's the No. 1 taboo topic. People will tell you about their intimate sexual lives before they'll tell you about their money," she says.[164]

In a poll by *Money Magazine*, almost all of the respondents (84 percent) admitted that money is a cause of tension in their marriage. Money causes more fights than sex or even in-laws, with 7 in 10 polled owning up to arguing about it. "Couples can't even agree on how much debt, income, and assets they have," reports social research scientist Jay Zagorsky. "People don't want to admit they're doing terrible," he says.

163 Newton's Law of Universal Gravitation: R = GAW (Reality = Gravity • Always • Wins).

164 Our hesitancy to talk about money has spawned anonymous money management forums, such as the website *Wesabe.com*, where spouses looking for help bare their souls.

In truth, men and women often have dramatically different ideas about who does what with the family finances and what their partners really care about. Worse still, many lie about it. A survey by *Redbook Magazine* and *lawyer.com* found that roughly a third of couples have been dishonest about spending habits, and many married couples suggest that figure might be somewhat low. Common secrets were clothes, hobby-related items, and gambling. And financial deception can be an indication of other types of deception. Although spouses are trained to look for the proverbial lipstick on the collar, most fail to periodically check to make sure their spouse has not cashed out the 401(k) on Internet gambling. *Young person's alert:* if you have a gut feeling about your partner, you are probably right.

Differences in spending habits can have a huge negative impact on a couple's finances. A couple's efforts to gain control of household finances can actually be counterproductive, with each partner tugging and pushing like two dogs fighting over a slipper. Despite good intentions, they fail to follow through and stem the red ink *(self-control-2 trap)*. And households where both adults work can create a vicious cycle of stress. "Affluenza" makes us crave more and more stuff, which creates more spending, which causes people to work harder, which causes more stress. As health care costs escalate and employers cut pensions, thus shifting the burden of retirement saving onto employees, couples face increasing pressure to work even harder and longer.

"The most common reason for divorce is money," says certified financial planner Judy Martindale. And the numbers are disturbing—of the marriages that wind up on the rocks, 8 out of 10 cite money matters as the reason for the separation. But it isn't necessarily the amount of money a couple has that tends to trip them up, says divorce attorney John Thyden. "It's the differences in their spending habits and especially their lack of communication." While findings show that more than 70 percent of couples talk about money on a weekly basis, "The problem is most don't know how to talk about money," points out Mary Claire Allvine, a certified financial planner and co-author of *The Family CFO: The Couple's Business Plan for Love and Money*. "People tend to be emotional and reactive about money, not strategic," she says.

Plan to avoid bickering with your honey about money by waiting to tie the knot? Um, maybe not. Along with their photo albums, people tend to bring more assets and debt into later marriages. What you get is two very strong opinions about managing money, with each partner having managed his or her own money for years. "If you wait until 30 to get married, you've been in a series of jobs, accumulated benefits such as 401(k) assets, and you might even have a house," says Sheryl Garrett, editor of *On the Road: Getting Married*. "It makes things more complicated."

Reali-tude:
Objectively discuss money management *before* matrimony.

☞ *Lifebomb #6: "Marry a millionaire!"*

This year thousands will marry wealthy. Marla Maples did it. Joan Kroc and Anna Nicole Smith did it. Roxanne Pulitzer did it and so did Tom Arnold. All of them went from first base direct to home plate, taking the shortcut to easy street. Say—you're good lookin' too—why not you? Well, you have no shortage of people to help. A rash of dating gurus are promoting guidebooks on how to land a high net worth partner, that is, one with $750,000 or more in cash or assets. They outline simple steps to locate and reel in a trophy hunk (babe) with a bulging wallet (Gucci bag). Are you interested in spring boarding from hoi polloi to highbrow? Here are some tips from the pros for snagging your very own Sugar Daddy (Momma):

- Hang out where the wealthy do (you can't troll for tuna in a koi pond);
- Live where the rich live (although you might have to live in a cardboard box);
- Take a part-time job where the elite play (say, retrieving golf balls from the water traps);
- Volunteer where the hi-brow coalesce (charity events are "in" places to see and be seen);
- Don't sleep with your quarry right away (hold out until he or she drools);
- Avoid signing a prenuptial agreement (if you can pull this off, you win an Oscar).[165]

Thankfully for most Joes and Janes, not everyone is convinced that money is the brass ring to ultimate happiness. "It is good fortune if the person you love—male or female—happens to have money," says Kim Gandy, president of the National Organization for Women. "It's a wonderful thing, and it can certainly make life better and open opportunities for you and your children. But it is a real mistake to think that money can buy love or happiness. It can't."

Whassat? You just got back from a Tony Robbins seminar where you walked over hot coals? Planning to pimp your way to the good life through your obvious wit, charm, and good looks *(superiority-1 trap)*? Well, wannabe gold digger, you first have to locate where the gold is. According to Thomas Stanley and William Danko, authors of "*The Millionaire Next Door*," the average millionaire may not be recognizable, nor at all what you expect. Before donning your stalking gear, consider the following representative profile of your quarry:

The good:

- Self-employed;
- Average annual income: $247,000;
- Homeowner;
- Invests about 20 percent of taxable income each year.

165 Sugar spouses are not stupid. They will be looking to protect their financial security and most in this league will look at your starry-eyed love as a business transaction that also holds the potential promise of future love and devotion.

The bad:

- Involved in fairly dull business;
- Works 45–55 hours per week;
- Has conservative spending habits;
- Dresses inexpensively.

The reality:

- He is a 57 year old man (sorry guys).
- He is married (sorry gals).
- He has three children.

Holding out for the REALLY big bling? Merrill Lynch describes ultra-high net worth individuals as having $30 million or more in financial assets. The good news is some 62 of these financial leviathans marry each year in America, according to futurist J. R. Mooneyham. The bad news is that's 62 out of approximately two million marriages annually. Potential gold diggers, do not be vainglorious *(optimism-1 trap)*. Sure it worked for Joan Croc, but get real—you are one set of buns out of millions served. And for you guys who were smart enough to achieve some manner of wealth, why on Earth would you be dumb enough to fall for this?

Reali-tude:
Don't waste your time, energy, and reputation marrying for money.

The bottom line:

- The #1 reason cited for a failed marriage is problems with money.
- Getting married may have significant tax implications.
- There may be legal ramifications if you cohabitate and break up.
- Many young persons fail to appreciate the trauma of divorce.

The Reality

> *That was sort of an eye-opener to me, that marriage is hard. But going into it, no one tells you that. They just tell you, "Do you love him? What does the dress look like?"*
>
> ~ Michelle Obama, First Lady

The most frequently occurring form of marriage unites a man and a woman as husband and wife. In 1996, President Clinton signed into law the *Defense of Marriage Act* (DOMA), which for purposes of federal law, defined marriage to be the union of one man and one woman. The intent of Congress was to specify what official state documents other states have to recognize, so that no state would be forced to recognize a same-sex marriage license issued in another state.

Since then, public attitudes toward gay rights have been changing, and rapidly. Beginning in 2001, civil marriage expanded to include same-sex marriage in some jurisdictions. In 2012, President Barack Obama announced his support for same-sex marriage, saying he believes it's important to "treat others the way you would want to be treated." A 2013 ABC News-*Washington Post* poll showed that 58 percent of American voters support the freedom of same-sex couples to marry. And the number is 81 percent for those under 30. By the close of 2013, eighteen states and the District of Columbia had legalized same-sex marriage.

On June 26, 2013 the U.S. Supreme Court struck down DOMA as unconstitutional, which until then had denied federal benefits to gay couples married under state law.[166] With the Court's ruling, the more than 1,100 federal rights and benefits that were formerly bestowed only on heterosexual marriages now apply to all legally married couples, regardless of sexual orientation. Tens of thousands of married gay couples stand to benefit when it comes to federal taxes, estate planning, bankruptcy, student aid, Social Security, child-care rights, and other matters. One of the biggest changes is equal tax treatment of health insurance premiums. Prior to the ruling, the value of a gay spouse's benefits coverage was treated as taxable income because he or she wasn't considered a spouse or dependent under federal law. Gay spouses are now automatically considered beneficiaries for 401(k) retirement plans and pensions, unless the couple agrees otherwise. Noncitizens who are married to American same-sex partners will likely qualify for permanent resident status. And the Pentagon has moved quickly to extend benefits given to opposite-sex servicemember spouses to same-sex couples, including medical, dental and housing allowances, and the transfer of G.I. Bill benefits.

Not all is settled though. The ruling left intact a separate DOMA provision that states need not recognize same-sex marriages performed by other states. Yet to be resolved is how to treat lawfully married same-sex couples who live in states that don't recognize same-sex marriages. There are roughly 114,000 legally married same-sex couples in the U.S., with about two-thirds of those couples living in states where their marriages are recognized. The rest will be in legal limbo while the lower courts navigate through the mess, and this will take years.

An institution in flux

Marriage, traditionally a key marker of the transition to adulthood, is being postponed these days. Many young persons now feel under less pressure to get married or "settle down" with a long-term partner while still in their twenties. As a result, the median marriage age for first marriage is rising. In 2011, for females it was about 26 and for males nearly 29. The "never married" includes 46 percent of young adults age 25–34, the first time the share of never-married young adults exceeded those who married, 45 percent (the rest being divorced or widowed). Young persons are increasingly choosing to delay marriage as they struggle to find work, sociologists say.

In his book, *The Social Animal*, political columnist David Brooks defines adulthood by four accomplishments: moving away from home, getting married, starting

166 The Court also let stand a ruling that a California initiative ending same-sex marriage is unconstitutional, making no judgment on the merits. California has since resumed issuing marriage licenses to same-sex couples.

a family, and becoming financially independent. In 1960, 7 out of 10 American 30-year olds had accomplished those things. By 2000, fewer than 4 out of 10 had done the same and the larger trend is unmistakable. "There is no going back to a world where we can assume that marriage is the main institution that organizes people's lives," warns Stephanie Coontz, co-chair for the Council on Contemporary Families, a not-for-profit research group. But the declining marriage rate doesn't tell the whole story about what's going on with marriage even among straight couples. "People are not giving up on marriage," Coontz says. "They are simply waiting longer to tie the knot." *Young person's alert:* in an increasingly single society, your best defense is to be self-reliant.

No mano, no problemo!

These days, more women than ever are saying, "I don't." In 2005, 51 percent of women said they were living without a spouse, up from 49 percent in 2000 and 35 percent in 1950. According to demographer William Frey, the shift represents a clear tipping point. "For better or worse," Frey says, "women are less dependent on men or the institution of marriage. Younger women understand this better, and are preparing to live longer parts of their lives alone or with non-married partners." After a divorce, women are more likely than men to delay remarriage and are living longer as widows later in life.

BRAIN SNACK: *U.S. Census Bureau numbers (2010) showed 36 percent of men in their early 30s had never been married, compared with 27 percent of women, and the decline in marriage for men was most pronounced among those with less education. Many men without college degrees are not marrying because the pool of women in their social circles—those without college degrees—has shrunk. Why? Many women with limited education have turned theirs sights on "marrying up," that is choosing men who may be older, more established, and more educated. "It's a mistake to think of this as just happening to the underclass at the bottom," says sociologist Christopher Jencks. "It is also happening to people with high school diplomas or even some college." No woman, no pride.*

In addition, the divorce rate among college-educated women has plummeted (the divorce rates for couples with college degrees are only a third as high as those with a high school degree). Women with college degrees also have very few children born out of wedlock, only 4 percent today. But climbing the corporate ladder comes at a price. In a *Forbes* report, *Why You Shouldn't Marry Career Women*, women's work hours consistently increase divorce whereas increases in men's work hours often have no statistical effect. Studies have found that professional women are more likely to cheat, less likely to have children, and, if they do have kids, they are more likely to be unhappy about it.

Finally, women are commanding more power. Studies suggest that the greater a woman's education level and earning potential, the more bargaining power she tends to have in household decisions—including financial ones—according to research by economists Jennifer Ward-Batts and Shelly Lundberg. And increasingly women don't need to rely on men. More than 7 out of 10 women ages 25 to 54 are working today, up from about half of such women 30 years ago. Working wives now contribute more than a third of the typical family's income, and in a third of married households, they are the bigger breadwinner.

Reali-tude:
Try to marry within one academic degree.

"Starter" marriages

The view that one should not settle for a less-than-perfect relationship seems to be widely accepted among Generation NeXt *(superiority-1 trap)*. Today, young persons are prepared to experiment, to "try on" a number of relationships until they find the one that is right for them. Increasingly common among those in their early twenties is the tacit acceptance of what has been termed the *starter marriage*. These are marriages that are almost expected to fail, allowing the young partners to "move on" and try again.

In her book *The Starter Marriage and the Future of Matrimony*, journalist Pamela Paul defines a starter marriage as one "that is a childless union between people under 35 lasting less than five years." While these marriages are entered into with the best of intentions, many are doomed from the start due to unrealistic expectations of marriage and relaxed attitudes toward divorce. "They are often superficial, immature, or weak and fizzle out within five years, always ending before children begin," says Paul. Sadly, reflects mediator Anju D. Jessani, clients from starter marriages are often among the most devastated at the loss of their marriage and their dreams for the future *(projection-1 trap)*. In terminating a starter marriage, here are some potholes you may encounter:

- Most couples intend to file for divorce under irreconcilable differences, but in some states you must first obtain a legal separation and wait a period of time.
- Many young persons lease their cars. These are difficult to amend or transfer, and extremely expensive to terminate.
- It is not unusual to see credit card debt exceeding $20,000 for these marriages.
- With no children to fight over, pets become a good substitute.
- For Catholics to remarry you must first obtain an annulment. Couples with children very rarely do.

To cavalierly attribute the failure of your marriage to circumstances beyond your control is to shirk personal responsibility. Real life is not what you see on TV. Unless you are svelte, wealthy, and bored it makes no sense to consider your marriage as nothing more than a "junior varsity" experience on your way to the big leagues. Perhaps the best that can be said is it hopefully teaches you how to get married again for a lifetime. Save your money, time, and emotions. Before you take the plunge, check with a tribal elder.

Reali-tude:
Marriage is not for the fickle.

Cohabitation is increasingly prevalent

According to a 2010 Pew Research Center study, about 4 out of 10 Americans believe that marriage is becoming obsolete. Younger adults attach far less moral stigma than do their elders to out-of-wedlock births and cohabitation without marriage. Living together before the actual wedding ceremony now precedes 6 out of 10 of all first marriages. Census data shows that over 60 percent of American women giving birth to a child while in their early 20s are not married, tying the trend to lower income levels. And young persons are engaging in these behaviors at unprecedented rates. According to Census figures, there were 6.8 million unmarried couples living together in 2010. Roughly, only one in eleven of these households are unmarried same-sex partners (rulings by various states that have legalized same-sex marriage will likely change this figure over time).

> *What's never changed is that people have a deep, abiding need to be loved, to love, to have a companion, to be really intimate and close, to feel safe, to feel that warmth and the joy you were all talking about. That has never changed. That will never change.*
> ~ Dr. Laura Schlesinger, radio talk show host

By about a 2 to 1 margin, those who have ever lived with a partner reject the notion that their cohabitation was (or is) a trial marriage. In the view of many young persons, it is simply "friends with benefits." So, do these unions last? And do they lead to marriage? In 4 out of 10 cases, the answer is yes, says *First Premarital Cohabitation in the United States,* a report by the Centers for Disease Control and Prevention, which studies male-female relationships. The study found that 40 percent of women living with significant others for the first time between 2006 and 2010 transitioned to marriage within three years, 32 percent of those relationships remained the same, and 27 percent dissolved. The odds of transitioning bump up about 10 percent for those who live together after making plans to marry or getting engaged, notes Scott Stanley, co-director of the Center for Marital and Family Studies. "The nature of commitment at the time of cohabitation is what's important," he says.

Reali-tude:
Cohabitation can work if you are serious about marriage.

Alternatives to WWIII

If we approach a black hole, our speed increases exponentially.[167] This means that over time, we travel faster and faster toward our doom. In similar fashion, the legal

167 A mathematical function where the slope of a line gets steeper and steeper with time. Think of an ant crawling down the side of a melon.

costs associated with a divorce can escalate faster and faster toward the black hole of bankruptcy. And the more dysfunctional the relationship, the more expensive the divorce. Divorce lawyers make a lot of their money by babysitting the couple who can't even have a conversation with each other about the most minor things.

Thankfully, there are alternatives available to help keep the lid on sky-high legal costs associated with a divorce. Mediation is growing in popularity. Here, couples meet with an impartial lay person who helps them determine the terms of their divorce. The mediator then presents the lawyers with the mediation agreement, which the lawyers take before the court. Once it is entered in court as a judgment, the agreement becomes legally binding. Another method is termed "collaborative law." Similar to mediation, the goal of collaborative law is to keep the divorce from escalating to a court case. It differs from mediation in that the meetings involve the lawyers representing each of the partners versus an independent mediator. Divorces through mediation and collaborative law cost thousands of dollars less than the average contested divorce, according to DivorceNet, the Internet's largest divorce resource.

Pardon the pun, but no law says you have to hire an attorney. Many couples do not realize they can complete a divorce without the assistance of a lawyer or the hassle of court hearings. If you feel that you and your spouse can rationally come to an agreement on who will get what, purchase a divorce kit and settle things over a latte or two. It is perfect for the young couple who has nothing to dispute and no children. "Each state is different," says Ginita Wall of San Diego, a Certified Public Accountant who specializes in divorce. "They all have different legal forms so use caution and get the divorce kit that is particular to your state."

> *I divorced after 14 years, the wife and I separated first, agreed to our own terms, wrote our own separation agreement, had my attorney make it legal, and had it incorporated into the divorce decree. The divorce and its terms were not contested, we each held our own lawyers in check and it was easy.*
>
> ~ Rapier, Internet blogger

Reali-tude:
If you are not compatible, fold your tent as early as possible.

The bottom line:

- Women are becoming less dependent upon men or the institution of marriage.
- For blue collar men, the pool of available women for marriage is shrinking.
- Starter marriages encourage a lack of commitment and responsibility to the relationship.
- Cohabitation pays off for women who cohabited only with their eventual husbands.

Doctor's Prescription (Rx)

The mind can calculate, but the spirit yearns, and the heart knows what the heart knows.

~ Stephen King, author

New York Times personal finance reporter Tara Siegel Bernard says that the key to wedded bliss just might be marrying someone who shares your attitudes about money. But often this is not the case. Although much research finds that "birds of a feather flock together," ironically surveys of married adults suggest that opposites attract when it comes to emotional reactions toward spending. That is, the data show "tightwads," who generally spend less than they would ideally like to spend, and "spendthrifts," who generally spend more than they would ideally like to spend, tend to marry each other. Social scientists Scott I. Rick and colleagues found that this complementary attraction is not the result of a deliberate search for dissimilar mates. If anything, the attraction occurs in spite of people's tendency to seek mates with similar emotional reactions toward spending. Such a marriage starts out well, but it is with purchases that really matter, such as cars and houses, that tensions rise. While such marriages "might be refreshing at first... they (can) then become maddening" as couples bicker over spending issues. This often leads to full-fledged trench warfare.

Many young persons buy into the simplistic belief that love conquers all. Because they tend to gloss over a partner's potential flaws when dating, they may be surprised once married to find that their views on money do not match those of their one-and-only. The problem is individual money habits are notoriously difficult to change. A *USA TODAY/CNN/Gallup* poll found nearly two-thirds of responding married couples said they talked little or not at all before the wedding about how to combine their finances. Before you walk down the aisle, here are some tips to consider.

Openness:

- *Communication is key.* Both partners are typically involved in the family's financial future so it's important that you share your financial situation and expectations. If you cannot talk openly about finances now, it probably won't be any better once you marry.
- *Pay attention to red flags.* If your partner enters the relationship with excess debt from past spending habits, expects you to help pay down their debt, or doesn't respect your financial decisions, it's time to ask yourself important questions about who your partner is and what your future might look like.
- *Is there middle ground?* If you are a strict saver and your partner is a free-wheeling spender, are you willing to honestly compromise on your behaviors? If not, consider delaying marriage to see if your partner can sustain the changes that you feel are necessary.
- *Trust is paramount.* Hiding money, having private accounts, or having debt that your partner doesn't know about is a breach of trust in the relationship.

Compatibility:

- *Y'all on the same page?* Make sure you and your partner have discussed ideals, goals, habits, and views when it comes to money before you walk down the aisle. As a couple, hammer out your long-term financial goals in advance. Do you want to save for a house? Do you plan to have kids? What are your views on investing and retirement?
- *Know about your partner's debt.* One of the worst ways to start a marriage is with debt. Generally, student loan debt incurred before a marriage is considered separate property but still should be weighed carefully if it is in the tens of thousands of dollars. If your partner is on shaky financial ground, consider waiting to marry to see if they are willing to improve their financial situation.
- *How will joint finances be handled?* Before marriage, it is wise to agree on who will handle the day-to-day as well as the long-term financial decisions. Handling them together is best but doesn't work for all couples. Will you combine your moneys or keep separate accounts? Many couples keep some level of independence by maintaining separate allowance accounts for each.
- *Monthly financial planning.* You have heard it before—every healthy relationship starts with a budget. Budgets are simply a plan that you and your partner agree on for handling your income and paying bills. Saving takes self-discipline and if you don't save, you won't be prepared for your future. Having a "rainy-day fund" reduces the chance of financial disasters.
- *Get help if you need it.* If you need help, talk to a financial planner. If you are shy, ask a tribal elder to be an interlocutor or ask for a referral where you bank.

Prenup?

- Do you need a prenuptial agreement? Probably not if you both are young and have not accumulated any real assets. For those with established careers before marriage, a "prenup" is used to protect what both partners have earned before the marriage such as assets, an inheritance, or a business. It may also shield against a debt.[168]
- Kids not included. A prenuptial agreement does not apply to issues relating to children who were not born at the time of the agreement.

Timing:

- *When you marry.* By delaying the walk down the aisle for a few years, you can potentially save a decade (or more) worth of frustration. Before making the commitment, set a goal to become financially independent, carry little or no debt; and establish your investments. Once you have these three things in place, your odds of success are drastically improved.

---

168 A 2010 Harris poll found that only 3 percent of people with a spouse or fiancé have a prenuptial agreement.

Doesn't sound romantic? It isn't, but neither is divorce. Now do the right thing.

Talking Points

> *By all means, marry. If you get a good wife, you'll become happy; if you get a bad one, you'll become a philosopher.*
> ~ Socrates

Chapter 17 describes some tools to help you acquire wisdom by interviewing others. To benefit from these techniques, you need only have access to a parent, educator, or other trusted adult (tribal elder) and a desire to listen and learn. Based on the ideas in this chapter, here are some starters:

1. "I am trying to improve myself. Who you marry may be critical to your personal financial success or failure. Reflecting on your experience, or that of someone you know, do you recall a situation where a couple's differing views on managing money either significantly benefited or hindered their long-term well-being?" If they say "Yes" then ask:

    - "Would you tell me the gist about what happened please?"
    - "How did you (they) feel about this at the time?"
    - "What two things did you learn from this that you can share with me?"

2. "I am trying to improve myself. Today, many young persons believe it is a good idea for a couple to live together (cohabitate) before getting married in order to find out whether they really get along. Reflecting on your experience, or that of someone you know, do you recall a situation where cohabitation either significantly benefited or hindered a couple's long-term well-being?" If they say "Yes" then ask:

    - "Would you tell me the gist about what happened please?"
    - "How did you (they) feel about this at the time?"
    - "What two things did you learn from this that you can share with me?"

    In either case, if they say "No," simply say "Thank you."

3. Getting married is an inflection point in a young person's life. Reflecting on your experience, or that of someone you know, what two suggestions would you have for a young person that is contemplating this decision?

4. "I want to make wise life-choices. Reflecting on your experience, would you have two ideas that I can implement to improve my judgment and decision-making skills? Be sure to thank them for their response.

Knowledge Nuggets

When marrying, ask yourself this question: Do you believe that you will be able to converse well with this person into your old age? Everything else in marriage is transitory.

~ Friedrich Nietzsche, German philosopher

1. *How important is money to marriage?* Marriage and financial counselors advise couples to observe each other's money habits and spend significant time talking about money as soon as they begin to think seriously about marriage. After you are married, watch for habits or attitudes that may irritate or concern you and discuss them openly. Discussing money may seem intimidating in the atmosphere of developing a love and life relationship, but it is a prelude to developing a dialogue about money that lasts the rest of your lives. You'll find an excellent discussion of the importance of marriage and money at: http://www.usaaedfoundation.org/financial/pf04.asp.

2. *What are the trends?* The National Marriage Project is a nonpartisan, nonsectarian initiative located at the University of Virginia and provides research and analysis on the state of marriage in America. The project annually publishes *The State of Our Unions*, an index of the health of marriage and marital relationships in America, including trends regarding marriage, divorce, and cohabitation. You can view their latest report at: http://nationalmarriageproject.org. Another source of information on marriage and cohabitation trends is found in two U.S. government reports: Households and Families 2010 at http://www.census.gov/prod/cen2010/briefs/c2010br-14.pdf and First Premarital Cohabitation in the United States: 2006–2010 National Survey of Family Growth at http://www.cdc.gov/nchs/data/nhsr/nhsr064.pdf.

3. *Are you and your intended financially compatible?* Compatibility means a lot more than liking the same movies or flavor of ice cream. It also means being able to successfully talk about and manage your finances. Like many other resources, The *360 Degrees of Financial Literacy* Website offers general information for managing personal finances. Their Couples Quiz: What's Your Financial Compatibility? can be of particular value to young persons who are thinking of getting married. Find out how prepared you and your mate are as a financial team at: http://www.360financialliteracy.org/Life+Stages/Couples+and+Marriage.

4. *Where to go for info?* See Appendix F for additional information relating to this chapter.

Chapter 12

How Many Children

Anyone who wants to have children has got to be crazy!
~ Bill Cosby, entertainer

The Gist

The Good:

- Raising children is the defining purpose in life for many people
- More companies are accommodating working mothers

The Bad:

- The cost to raise a child to age 17 is $¼ million (not including college)
- Parenting is one of the most difficult jobs today
- You don't get to push the reset button if you screw it up

The Reality:

- Parenting has significant personal and opportunity costs
- Your life will never be the same once you have a child
- Love, sex, money, and kids—don't count on having it all
- The number of single-parent, one-child, and childless families is increasing
- The main purpose of marriage is now seen as happiness and fulfillment, not child raising

Introduction

Before you was born dude, when life was great. You are the burden of my generation, I sure do love you—let's get that straight.
~ Paul Simon to his son from *That was your mother*

In The Bible, God created male and female, and commanded them to "be fruitful, and multiply, and replenish the earth" (Genesis 1:28). In those days, a large family was considered a blessing from God. The book of Genesis also contains one of the oldest references to birth control in the account of Judah and his sons, Er and Onan. In the story, Er was a wicked man so the Lord put him to death. This left his wife Tamar with no husband or children. In accordance with their belief, it was Onan's duty as Tamara's brother-in-law to step in and give her offspring. This practice, where the brother of the deceased would provide offspring to the childless widow to preserve the family line, was later referred to as a *Levirate marriage.*[169] Levirate marriage has been practiced by societies with a strong clan structure where exogamous marriage (i.e., outside the clan) is forbidden.

But Onan was in the game only for bush benefits, not for producing more rug rats. Disregarding God's command to be fruitful, he withdrew before climax and thus "spilled his seed (semen) on the ground." While this avoided having more mouths to feed, his act greatly offended the Lord. So, like his brother, Onan was bumped off. Since then, this method of contraception has been called *Onanism* or *coitus interruptus*, more commonly referred to as the "withdrawal" method.[170] According to Planned Parenthood, of every 100 women whose partners use withdrawal, 4 will become pregnant each year if they always do it correctly. And if they don't, the pregnancy rate rises to 27 out of 100 each year. As grandma said, the only sure-fire prevention is to keep your knees touching!

Fast forward a few millennia. In 1960, the combined oral contraceptive pill, often referred to as the birth-control pill or simply "the Pill," was first approved to prevent pregnancy in the U.S. When taken by mouth every day, the Pill does a bang up job of inhibiting female fertility. Considered safe and effective by the government, medical establishment, and public, this method of birth control has had an enormous social impact. The Pill is currently used by more than 100 million women worldwide and by almost 12 million women in the U.S. *TIME Magazine* placed it on its cover in April, 1967.

Far more effective than withdrawal (and most other reversible methods of birth control), the Pill gives women unprecedented control over their fertility without

169 The term is a derivative of the Latin word *levir*, meaning "husband's brother."

170 The TV analog is the commercial break.

sacrificing sexual relationships. The choice to take the Pill is a private one and there are no special preparations at the time of sexual activity that might interfere with the "magic of the moment." Use of the Pill heightened a moral debate and the Roman Catholic Church continues to teach that artificial contraception distorts the nature and purpose of sex. From a personal economics point of view, economist Claudia Goldin points out that this new contraceptive technology allows women to pursue careers through higher education and has sharply increased their college attendance and graduation rates.

Reali-tude:
Pregnancy is like an omelet: the chicken is involved but the ham is committed.

The Good

You really shouldn't say 'I love you' unless you mean it. But if you mean it, you should say it a lot. People forget.
~ Jessica, student, age 8

Many couples find themselves trying to decide whether or not to have children. Young persons with a yearnin' for younguns invariably choose not merely to have a child but to become a parent. Polls find that 8-in-10 men always wanted to be fathers, or think they'd like to be one someday (about 7-in-10 moms do). Like choosing an occupation, becoming a parent represents an opportunity to develop their own life along with that of their little Boboli. Done correctly, raising a child can be one of life's most rewarding experiences.

The good news is kids are a hoot! "In the short term, if you look at the dollar value you lose... but at the same time, it's like an ongoing, lifelong investment in happiness," says Clark Derry-Williams, research director for Northwest Environmental Watch. This investment has positive spillovers to parents and their children that cannot be captured by purely dollars and cents. For example, how do you value the crayon artwork that little snookums made you for Mother's (Father's) Day? Or the tug at the heartstrings when your rug rat starts school? It is these personal, qualitative benefits that usually compel parents to incur the high costs of having children. Below are some of the intangible benefits of having kids:

Emotional bonds:	A commitment to selfless devotion and unconditional love.
Enjoyment:	Children are entertaining and fun; you get to be a kid again.[171]

171 In each show of *House Party*, on CBS day television from 1952 to 1969, Art Linkletter interviewed five children between the ages of 5 and 10. He sat at eye level with his little subjects and, time and

Sense of purpose:	Procreation enriches your life and gives it meaning.
Support in old age:	Reduced uncertainty and anxiety later in life.
Sense of pride:	Shaping the life of another human being makes you a hero.
Maturity:	Being ultimately responsible for an infant's survival.
Legacy:	Kids are extensions of us; through them, our memory lives on.
Personal development:	Increased self-esteem, understanding, and compassion.[172]

Many parents derive great happiness from their investments in children, and while children themselves are the primary beneficiaries, other adults also indirectly benefit. In her book *Valuing Children, Rethinking the Economics of the Family*, economist Nancy Folbre notes that successful parenting cultivates children's feelings of concern for others. This contributes to the emotional well-being of adults and makes for safer, more respectful relationships. In other words, the reason your roommate did not make off with your girl along with your car may have been an earlier shellacking he had gotten from his old man.

> *Having children is the best thing I have EVER done in my life or ever expect to. It is amazing to take part in the first miracle and then watch as their personalities unfold. It is a ton of work. But it was always worth it. I've never looked back. And I rarely got enough sleep.*
>
> ~ Susan, Internet blogger

Your fecundity also benefits society. In addition to the happiness we hope they will provide us, children grow up to become the workers, caregivers, and taxpayers on whom our economy depends. What would the IRS do if no one had kids? Baby Boomer parents have an economic stake in the productive capabilities of Generation NeXt because their government retirement benefits, such as Social Security and Medicare, are funded from taxes paid by NeXter workers (thank you very much). Childless couples make out like bandits because they enjoy these retirement benefits without having paid the cost of the resources devoted to raising them.

There is more good news. Support for working moms is on the rise. A Pew Research Center study found 6 out of 10 working mothers now say part-time work is their ideal rather than full-time, compared to 48 percent a decade ago. But wanting is not getting. Writing in *USA Today*, Candice Choi notes that this

---

time again, their responses made their parents wish television had never been invented. Mr. Linkletter assembled their humorous quips in his book, *Kids Say the Darndest Things!*

172 It seems that having kids is good for your health. In a study of 21,276 couples, medical doctor Esben Agerbo estimates that the women who ended up without children experienced an annual rate of death four times greater than those in his sample who did give birth. For childless men, the death rate was twice that suffered by fathers. Psychologist Sonja Lyubomirsky suggests that parenthood, and fatherhood in particular, really are blessings. Examining data on 6,906 Americans, she found that parents had higher happiness, satisfaction, and meaning-of-life scores than non-parents. This enhanced enjoyment came from activities which involved children rather than those that did not.

emerging preference for part-time work is at odds with reality, as three-quarters of today's working mothers have full-time jobs.

Fortunately, some companies have gotten the message. Once regarded as a career setback, taking extended time off work to care for children is no longer a liability. In hopes of preventing an exodus of talent, a growing number of companies offer ways for new mothers to balance family and work. These include discounts and reimbursements for childcare, emergency backup childcare, telecommuting and work at home options, flexible hours, and part-time scheduling. Other company programs go even farther, providing personal time far beyond the 12 weeks of unpaid maternity leave guaranteed to most women under federal law. In the case of IBM, some working moms can take up to a three-year leave of absence then transition back to full time.

Ellen Galinsky, president of the Families and Work Institute, points out that those programs mean women no longer have to pick between their career or their family. But make sure to read the fine print. Transition programs are often tighter than a corset. Many are intended for new mothers from among what the company considers "key talent," reserved for a smaller subset of women in top managerial or executive positions. Good luck if you are a line worker or if you already have kids. Whether you will qualify boils down to your job description, time in the saddle, and perceived value to the company. For many young women, being a mother will still be a 24/7 job in addition to another 40-plus hours outside the home.

Reali-tude:
Kids are bad investments with big returns.

The bottom line:

- Once you have a child, your life will never be the same.
- Children bring many positive intangible benefits.
- Smart companies are increasingly accommodating working mothers.
- Society derives significant benefits from parents' investments in their children.

The Bad

If you bungle raising your children, I don't think whatever else you do well matters very much.

~ Jacqueline Kennedy Onassis, former First Lady

In many ways, having a child is the first irrevocable decision that most of us make. If you are young when a kid squirts out, you will find that you need to grow up fast. If you are very young, kiss your childhood goodbye—while other young persons look forward to graduation day, you'll be pushing a perambulator and watching your friends move on. Unless you have actually raised a child, you cannot imagine the degree of commitment it takes to be successful at it (babysitting doesn't count). When it comes to children, questionable beliefs can trap your thinking and jeopardize your long-term well-being. Learn about some of the lifebombs and you'll stand a better chance of making a smart choice.

Cognitive Flaw: Ignorance

> *The family you come from isn't as important as the family you're going to have.*
>
> ~ Ring Lardner, humorist

Clueless about the implications of having a child? Many things about early child-rearing come naturally, such as tending to a crying infant or feeding a baby. Infants quickly teach adults how to meet their needs and most of these require no special thought or training. But being a mother (or a father) is not the same as being a parent. "Mothering came easy; it's parenting that I'm having difficulty with" relates one frustrated mother. Remember, you don't get a "reset button" with kids. Let's look at how failing to be objectively informed when making this important life-choice can put your future happiness at risk.

☞ *Lifebomb #1: "That's what parents do... isn't it?"*

It used to be that people planned for such important things as marriage, child-bearing, child-rearing, finances, and living arrangements. For many young persons today, however, it seems that these important milestones and responsibilities take a back seat to impulsive behavior and immediate gratification *(self-control-1 trap)*. But unlike picking a vacation hotspot, choosing to become a parent will change your life forever. From that moment on, the focus needs to shift from "me" (my career) to "us" (my family).

> *I have been stunned at the growing number of callers who marry without consideration for religion, finances, extended family problems, lifestyle, goals, and even personality differences... many couples will marry before either one of them is in the position to support a family, yet they start making babies and then the fights begin, over not having enough money or time to have any freedom, fun, or opportunities.*
>
> ~ Dr. Laura, talk radio host

> *My husband and I often laugh at our friends who are so eager to have children, yet, have no idea about planning childcare or even the basic physical demands of having a child. And surprise, a few weeks/months later they are miserable, with a laundry list of things that make them feel trapped, poor, and stupid that indirectly stem from their new baby.*
>
> ~ Future Mocha Mom, Internet blogger

Are good parents born or are they brewed? To find the answer, demographers Lixia Qu and Ruth Weston of the Australian Institute of Family Studies analyzed a survey of 5,000 Australian parents ages 18 to 55. Asked whether parenting skills are something you are born with, the youngest mothers said that they were twice as confident in their innate abilities—that parenting comes "naturally"—as the oldest moms. Fathers were slightly more confident than mothers about their abilities. But confidence does not equate to competence *(optimism-1 trap)*. "Young mothers may underestimate the importance of experience" cautions Weston. Family writer Lisa Belkin adds, "Whether they actually DO what they intend, once they have mortgages and teenagers, remains to be seen *(superiority-2 trap)*."

Children are selfish by nature and expect their own needs to be taken care of above all else. What makes this so difficult for a young parent is that you are just venturing into the real world and trying to understand your own needs. Think about it. In the midst of figuring out "Who am I?"; "What is my purpose?"; and "What is the meaning of life?" you are also caring for another human being whose very survival depends on you. This conflict may overwhelm NeXters who do not understand their roles and responsibilities as parents:

1. *Roles*. A role is the characteristic and expected social behavior of an individual. Parenting and gender roles are culturally defined and represent a shared belief in what constitutes a "good" parent.

- *Motherhood:* The traditional view emphasizes mothering as a woman's highest achievement and fulfillment in life. It sees a good mother as enjoying all of her mothering duties such as child rearing and housework. If she does not, it implies something is wrong, which can instill guilt in some women. A mother's employment is often blamed for children's problems.
- *Fatherhood:* Traditionally, the father is the breadwinner and the authority figure in the family. In her book *The Second Shift*, public sociologist[173] Arlie Russell Hochschild suggests that this older ideal has partly given way to the "nurturant father," who bonds with his child but still pays some bills. When moms are employed, dads are an important source of care for young children.

2. *Responsibilities*. Kids are not pets, fed at one end and cleaned at the other. Nor can they be traded in for a new model. As a parent, you have a legal duty to care for your children whether you are feeling happy about them or not. You are responsible for providing them with basic needs such as adequate nutritious food, a safe and secure shelter, clothing, and medical care. You must protect your kids from psychological and physical threats and harm. You are also expected to provide guidance in cognitive, educational, physical, sexual, social, moral, cultural, and spiritual development. You need to set limits, provide information and support, and model appropriate behaviors. You may be held financially liable for damage to property or injury of another person caused by your child. In short, you are a jack-of-all-trades for at least 18 years, maybe more. There is no return to a carefree life.

173 Public sociologists seek to transcend "academic-speak" and engage a wider audience on the scientific study of human society.

Happily, most young parents acquire the skills they need to fulfill their responsibilities along the journey. What happens if you don't? In cases of severe abuse, neglect, abandonment, or long-term substance abuse, the state will intervene. In the extreme, a judge may issue an order that terminates your parental rights. Overall, it seems that the best determining factor for having children is whether you're emotionally ready. More than money or how old you are, the most important question is "Are you ready to devote yourself to raising a child?" One last thing. Do not wait until you are financially ready because you never will be.

Reali-tude:
You cannot walk away from your obligations because they are now inconvenient.

☞ *Lifebomb #2: "It takes a village—no one else can afford them!"*

It is almost certain that most young prospective parents do not correctly estimate how much children will cost them over a lifetime *(superiority-1 trap)*. The expense of raising a child means more than baby clothes and the cost of Jose's summer camp. Parents must also weigh the effect a child will have on their careers and free time, as well as their bank account. Generally, child bearing expenses fall into three categories:

1. *Direct costs:* $$$ shelled out for food, clothing, housing and transportation, school-related expenses, disposable income for social activities, medical care, gummy bears, etc.
2. *Personal costs:* Just as parents require a certain amount of food they also require a minimum level of sleep, personal care, and leisure time.
3. *Opportunity costs:* There is a large "hidden" cost, particularly for women. Women today (especially those with a college education) forgo important career options to raise a child.

Economic conditions also affect the ease and affordability of raising kids, and the cost will depend on a person's or couple's unique circumstances. Some factors that affect parental expenditures include the parent's occupation and income, the health of the child, geographic location, family support, married or single-parent status, and age.

BRAIN SNACK: *The U.S. Bureau of Labor Statistics (BLS) began administering consumer spending surveys around 1900, partly in response to trade union efforts to define a "living wage." In their classic* The Money Value of a Man, *published in 1946, Louis Dublin and Alfred Lotka used this data to develop an estimate of family spending on an average child up to age eighteen. Since 1966, the U.S. Department of Agriculture (USDA) has used the BLS Survey of Consumer Expenditures (CE) to provide regular estimates of expenditures on the*

cost of raising children in two-parent and one-parent families in urban areas.*[174] *This survey also provides the basis for updating the Consumer Price Index, or CPI, which is used to adjust incomes for the effects of inflation.

Here is a revelation for young minimum-wage earners everywhere: children are expensive—REALLY expensive. Got an urge to merge? Stand by for sticker shock...

The USDA estimates direct costs on children in much the same way it does the costs of raising apple trees or cattle to maturity. And children are an expensive crop. The 2010 survey cites that a typical middle-income, husband-wife family, with an average 2009 pre-tax income of $76,250, will spend about $12,000 a year or $222,360 total to raise a child to the age of 17. Yes, you read it right folks: more than $222 thousand smackeroos. Housing costs accounted for almost one-third of the total, followed by child care, education, and food. With a modest (and likely) annual inflation of 2.8 percent, the total you are likely to shell out is $286,050—more than a quarter-million dollars. Are you a higher income family? They spend more on their children, so bump this up to roughly $367,000. Remember NeXters—this is for ONE (1) kid.[175]

One of the largest changes in the USDA report over time has been the increase in costs related to care for young children. In the first year alone, you can easily spend $4,000–$6,000 for diapers, formula, clothing, baby furniture and gear, etc. According to MarketWatch writer Ruth Mantell, a 2009 report by the National Association of Child Care Resource & Referral Agencies found the average annual cost of full-time child center care for a four-year-old started at a low of about $4,000 in Mississippi and ran to a high of more than $13,000 in Massachusetts. "Monthly child-care fees for two children at any age exceeded the median monthly rent cost, and were nearly as high, or even higher than, the average monthly mortgage payment in every state," she reports. "The high costs of child care can lead to lifestyle adjustments," adds *USA Today*'s Stephanie Armour. "Working parents are basing major decisions about where they work so that they can afford child care costs."

You decide to have children because you love them and want them. Not because you can afford them. I have three and if I could have at least one more I would, no matter the cost.

~ Parent's response to the cost of children

---

174 The 2009 CE survey interviewed 11,800 husband-wife households and 3,350 single-parent households. Detailed questions were asked regarding their income and expenditures in seven areas: housing, food, transportation, clothing, health care, child care and education, and miscellaneous good and services. While not perfect, the CE survey provides an indispensable source of information on how people spend their money.

175 Families in the urban Northeast face the highest expenses and those in the urban South and rural areas have the lowest.

Keep your calculator turned on because the USDA estimates do not take into account all the expenses for some families. If your child is enrolled in private school, the cost-o-meter jumps. If your child has medical problems or special needs, chalk up even more. College costs? Cha-ching—not included! That alone will set you back another $30,000 to $300,000 per child, depending on where he or she goes to college and for how long. Also, the figures do not offer any cost estimates if your child remains in your home as a dependent after the age of 18.

Among parents who said they don't plan to have additional kids, nearly three-quarters cite they are concerned about the cost of raising them, according to Pew Research. "Young persons gain a new appreciation of their parents (as well as some apprehension about becoming parents in the near future) when they learn that two-parent families with two children devote, on average, about 40 percent of their annual expenditures to those children until they reach 18," says economist Nancy Folbre.

On the plus side, there are some bulk discounts as the number of children you have grows. Some things such as housing and transportation can be shared, resulting in a 20–30 percent savings per additional child. But no one who wants three rug rats is going to be deterred from having that many anyway. And many people who really wanted to hold the line at two kids have three, and sometimes more, by what is euphemistically[176] called an "accident." A half century after the Food and Drug Administration approved the sale of birth control pills, nearly half of parents who had another child said "There wasn't a reason; it just happened" *(self-control-2 trap)*. This is among the most expensive mistakes you can make.[177]

Reali-tude:
Each child costs the equivalent of a house to raise.

Cognitive Flaw: Ineptitude

Moderator: *And how do you like children Mr. Fields?"*
W. C. Fields: *Well done.*

Careless about the implications of having children? No one forces you to have them. If you elect to bring children into the world, you cannot walk away from your obligations to them merely because the obligations now feel inconvenient. As psychologist Nathaniel Branden admonishes, when children are involved—especially young children—self-responsible adults act slowly, thoughtfully, and

176 A euphemism is the substitution of an inoffensive expression for one that is considered offensive or harsh, such as "passed away" for died. Salespeople ("pre-owned car") and politicians ("undocumented workers" and "enhanced interrogation techniques") are particularly adept at using euphemisms.

177 If a couple chose not to raise another child, reallocated those funds to investments enjoying an average 5 percent annual rate of return, and left that nest egg untouched until they retired, say twenty years later, they would have accumulated more than $1 million. Now you know why your childless friends seem to have so much more money than you do!

non-impulsively. Your thinking does not stop at, "Don't I have a right to my self-interest?" Let's look at how failing to think seriously about this important life-choice can put your future happiness at risk.

☞ *Lifebomb #3: "All joy and no fun."*

Parenting is one of the most difficult jobs anywhere and today's parents face more challenges than ever before. Learning how to raise a child is like learning to do your taxes—you really don't think about it until you know that you have to *(inertia-1 trap)*. Then you pay attention! Baby gurus know this and they make beaucoup bucks selling "what to expect during parenthood" books and CDs to expectant parents. The problem is these rulebooks never tell the whole story. Here are some of the personal challenges that no one tells you about:

1. *Your lifestyle ist kaput!* Once baby makes his debut, the days of wine and roses become the days of whine and rashes. Romance? Not a chance; the privacy you once enjoyed is ancient history. Dinner for two becomes supper for three. Getaways to Cancun and Vail are now vacations at Sea World and Disneyland. You will feel increasingly isolated from friends and family members who are single or childless, many of whom do not understand how much extra work, time, and stress is involved in raising a child. Since child-rearing duties fall mainly on the mother, she bears the brunt of this adjustment, as women always have.

They're a huge source of joy, but they turn every other source of joy to shit.
~ Psychologist, when he finally got around to having a child

2. *No time and no life.* You cannot believe how little time you will have, especially moms. New mothers lose an average of 700 hours of sleep the first year. There is no way to begin to measure the hidden costs of loss of sleep, sanity, and solitude. How do you account for having to feed a newborn every two hours, or getting up at 3 a.m. to do a load of laundry with more vomit on it than a frat house floor? How about cooking dinner with a screaming baby in your arms, a toddler doing cartwheels off the couch, and the phone ringing? Life becomes measured in minutes and seconds, such as "If his nap lasts another 10 minutes, maybe I can get in and out of the shower."

Seven-of-10 of today's married mothers say they crave more time for themselves, as do almost 6 out of 10 married fathers. As a result of the stress, marital stability and satisfaction drops 70 percent due to role conflicts and restrictions on freedom. According to *Changing Rhythms of American Family Life*, compiled by sociologist Suzanne Bianchi and colleagues, husbands and wives spent less than 10 percent of their home time alone together. And do you think they were saying, "Gee honey, you look lovely. I just wanted to pick up on that fascinating conversation we were having earlier..." Nope. They were exhausted and staring at the television.

Parenting is incredibly hard. Harder than anyone imagines it will be before having kids. It's so hard I can't hold it in mind. I keep forgetting how difficult it is, and remembering only the joys. Whenever friends of mine are wondering whether or not they should have kids, I always advise them not to if they think they could possibly be happy without children, especially if they are concerned about how much work raising kids will be. You're scared of the work? It is that much work. It is more work than that.

~ Sierra, Internet blogger

3. *The treadmill.* "A trap that many families fall into is building a lifestyle dependent on their entire income prior to children," cautions financial planner Brandon Corso *(projection-1 trap)*. "If you are living a lifestyle before children that is tight financially, watch out when the kids come. Expenses go way up," he warns. For instance, think of the cost to go to a movie when you are also paying for a babysitter. The "new" economy has forced many young parents to work double shifts or alternate work schedules in order to save on childcare expenses. Finding a job with a schedule flexible enough to let them meet family responsibilities is a problem cited by about one half of mothers and their need for time off may cause their job performance to suffer.

4. *Totally s-t-r-e-s-s-e-d.* We lead overscheduled and harried lives. In the "good old days" parents were not carting their kids around to soccer practice, dance lessons, tae kwon do championships, math tutoring, and elaborate birthday parties.[178] Then there is the worry. You worry that they'll stop breathing in their crib and obsess about getting the car seat in correctly. Then you'll worry about them falling down the stairs or choking on an Atomic Fireball. Later, you'll lose sleep over school bullies, driving, and dating (a big hurdle for dads). Along the way, you'll wear out the worry beads providing for food, health insurance, and college.

5. *Collateral damage.* Older kids face a different set of problems. A study by the Pew Social Trends Staff reports that the biggest challenge in raising children today is dealing with the outside influences of society. Societal factors—including drugs and alcohol, peer pressure, and the impact of television and other media—are the top concern for nearly four-in-ten Americans. Other perceived challenges in raising children include teaching morals and values, handling the financial aspects of childrearing, and dealing with the educational system.

Reali-tude:
Children don't come with a manual.

178 Researchers tell us that all parents, including mothers, spend more time today with their children than they did in 1975. Yet 85 percent of all parents still think they don't spend enough time with their children.

☞ *Lifebomb #4: "Time for Teletubbies!"*[179]

It is interesting that babies hold an almost universal appeal for adults, regardless of culture. There's just something about their big shining eyes and button noses that draws us in, creates a smile, and stirs our most tender feelings. Because babies are cute, there is a widespread belief that children bring happiness. When people are asked to think about parenthood—either imagining future offspring or thinking about their current ones—they tend to conjure up pictures of healthy babies, handsome boys, and gorgeous-looking girls who are flawless in every way.

> ***BRAIN SNACK:** Adults seem to respond favorably to the typical infant facial structure of disproportionately large heads and eyes, small noses, and chubby cheeks.[180] Brain imaging has hinted at a biological basis for this by revealing a region of the brain that is stimulated in response to pictures of babies but not in response to shots of adults. Why do almost all humans find this particular set of features so appealing? According to biological anthropologist Jeffrey Kurland, the answer lies in evolution. Over many generations, mothers and fathers prefer cuter infants, although whether babies merely look better or are better (i.e., better adapted to survive) remains in contention. In reality, they all look like Winston Churchill!*

There is no question that children provide unrivaled moments of joy. But they also provide unrivaled moments of frustration, tedium, anxiety, and heartbreak. Yet, even when the prospective parents know that raising a child will be painstakingly difficult, they tend to think quite happily about parenthood. Eventually most of them will leap into it, many without adequate thought, and this rosy view about parenthood can trigger unintended consequences. Some of the reasons why young persons want the to stork visit their homes include:

- They have not figured out what to do with their life (their children will be their success).
- Their kid will make a positive difference in the world (behold their child, the savior!).
- Society expects them to have children *(framing-1 trap)*.
- Beat the biological "expiration date" (as Elvis crooned, "It's now or never.")
- Continue the family name (no one cares except you anyway).
- Gee, everyone else is having them *(inertia-2 trap)*.

---

179 *Teletubbies* was a BBC children's television series produced from 1997 to 2001. Although the program is aimed at children between the ages of one and four, it has a substantial cult following with older generations, especially university and college students.

180 Konrad Lorenz (1903–1989) was an Austrian zoologist who shared the Nobel Prize for Physiology/Medicine in 1973. Lorenz introduced the concept of "cuteness," later replaced by the clinical term, *neoteny*. Neoteny describes an evolutionary adaptation where some animals retain child-like facial features into adulthood, thus eliciting the same affection that infants enjoy.

For most of human history it was horniness that led to babies, not necessarily a burning desire to raise children. "The desire to have children, however natural, is not explicitly embedded in our genes," says economist Nancy Folbre. Although many people assume that having children will make them happier, research conducted over the past four decades reveals otherwise. In a 2004 study, Nobel laureate Daniel Kahneman (Economics, 2002) surveyed working Texas women and found that child care ranked *sixteenth* in pleasurability out of nineteen activities. Endeavors they preferred included preparing food, watching TV, exercising, talking on the phone, napping, shopping, and housework. Economist Nattavudh Powdthavee finds evidence that, in aggregate, parents often report lower levels of happiness, life satisfaction, marital satisfaction, and mental well-being compared with non-parents. "As a rule," writes Jennifer Senior, author of *All Joy and No Fun, Why parents hate parenting*, "most studies show that mothers are less happy than fathers, that single parents are less happy still, that babies and toddlers are the hardest, and that each successive child produces diminishing returns."

We all have visions of how picturesque our family will become. Understandably, most who become parents express the hope that they will form an enduring relationship with their offspring *(optimism-1 trap)*. But our hopes are often disappointed. For moms, disciplining children is a problem and one in five named this as the most difficult part of being a mother. Dads say they feel guilty that they don't see their kids enough. "They don't want to be stick figures in their children's lives," says Ellen Galinsky, president of the Families and Work Institute. And no matter how hard you try, some negative influences are beyond your control *(optimism-2 trap)*. The gap between the ideal and reality can lead to disappointment when your kids don't turn out the way you wanted and you are replaced with an electronic device *(framing-2 trap)*.

> *I think a lot of parental unhappiness has to do with parental expectations. So many people have children thinking they are going to get the 'perfect' baby or child, who will have a sweet, even-keeled temperament; who will be attractive and smart but not too needy; who will provide them with boundless unconditional love; who will not disappoint them in their choice of education, mate, profession, etc.; and who will spend unlimited time caring for them in the parents' old age. The reality is that no one knows what kind of child they will get. Kids can be difficult, contrary, stubborn, defiant, lazy, mean and disappointing. If you get them to age 18 and they still want to have periodic contact with you that is not entirely about money or about what a crappy parent you were, count yourself lucky. But I would not trade the experience of being a parent for anything.*
>
> ~ Amy, Internet blogger

So, sports fans, this begs the question: why does anyone have children in the first place? One explanation for all those baby showers is we may be "deluding" ourselves when choosing parenthood *(projection-2 trap)*. According to Powdthavee, we may be focusing more of our attention on the good things of being a parent (the coos and chubby cheeks)—and less on the bad things about being a parent (the mess that comes out of each end)—because of our belief that children bring happiness.[181] Then, when reality kicks in later, our well-being drops considerably. *Young person's alert:* more than 25 separate studies have established that marital quality drops, often quite steeply, after the transition to parenthood.

Yet, receiving little pleasure from child rearing is not the same as regretting having undertaken it. About twenty years ago psychologist Tom Gilovich made a striking contribution to the field of psychology, showing that people are far more apt to regret things they haven't done than things they have. In a follow-up study of high-IQ students who were singled out for a life of greatness, not one told him of regretting having children, but ten told him they regretted not having a family.

How can this be? There is a distinction between what behavioral economist Daniel Kahneman calls your *experiencing-self*, who lives for the present and takes pleasure or pain as events unfold, and your *remembering-self*, who looks back on your life and judges whether you are satisfied or not. "When you pause to think what children mean to you, of course they make you feel good," says psychologist Daniel Gilbert. "The problem is, 95 percent of the time, you are not thinking about what they mean to you. You are thinking that you have to take them to piano lessons." What makes your remembering-self fulfilled about raising children? Significant moments and how they end up. In other words, happiness is about the journey not the destination. Grab yours as it unfolds!

Reali-tude:
Loving one's children and loving parenting are not the same thing.

☞ *Lifebomb #5: "Oops—can I have my childhood back?"*

Among Western industrialized nations, the U.S. has the highest rate of teenage pregnancy, roughly four times higher than in several European nations. A sexually active girl not using contraceptives has a 90 percent chance of pregnancy within a year, according to the Guttmacher Institute, which studies unplanned pregnancy. Yet, in a 2012 CDC survey report of thousands of teenage mothers who had unintended pregnancies, about one-third who didn't use birth control said the reason was they didn't believe they could get pregnant. The good news is teen birth rates in the U.S. are at an all-time low. In 2010, there were 34 births per 1,000 women aged 15–19, down 44 percent from a peak in 1991.

I had two children very young. Not recommended, wait til you're 30 and your figure is shot to hell anyway.
~ Mouse, Internet blogger

---

181 This is captured in the maxim "Nothing in life is quite as important as you think it is while you are thinking about it." Behavioral economist Daniel Kahneman and organizational psychologist David Schkade refer to this as the *focusing illusion*.

Too many febrile teens underestimate the huge impact that a random pregnancy will have on their lives *(optimism-2 trap)*. In their book *Our Sexuality*, authors Robert L. Crooks and Karla Baur describe the human suffering that is associated with teenage pregnancies, and the wreckage is chilling. A pregnant teenager is more likely to have physical complications than a woman in her 20s. These include anemia, toxemia, hypertension, hemorrhage, miscarriage, and even death. Children of teenage mothers are also at greater risk of having physical, cognitive, and emotional problems than are children of adult mothers.

Furthermore, young persons are especially vulnerable to the gift that keeps on giving: STDs. The numbers are stunning: three million teenagers—one in four in the U.S.—contracts one or more STDs every year. A girl's single unprotected sexual encounter with an infected partner runs a 1 percent risk of HIV, a 30 percent risk of genital herpes, and a 50 percent risk of gonorrhea. While "gent tents" are the best protection against both STD and pregnancy, in the heat of the moment these are not always used *(self-control-2 trap)*. Many pregnant teenagers cease to use them because they are no longer needed to prevent pregnancy (research finds less than 30 percent and perhaps as few as 8 percent of sexually active pregnant adolescent women use condoms consistently during intercourse). This is worrisome because contracting an STD during pregnancy can have negative health consequences for both the youthful mother and her baby.

Additionally, an unintended pregnancy and the decision to keep her child often have serious adverse effects on a young woman's education and on her financial resources. About 7 out of 10 teen mothers drop out of high school and many do not return. Only 2 percent will graduate from college. Lacking maturity and a means of self-support, they become dependent upon social service agencies. Low education levels and limited employment skills often thwart the efforts of these young mothers to obtain economic independence as they move beyond teenage years. For a decade or more, they will feel like they are swimming the English Channel wearing a fur coat.

Why such a big deal? After all, TV actress Jamie Lynn Spears, Britney's unmarried kid sister, gave birth to a son at 17. The hit movie *Juno* featured a spunky heroine who remains at high school while pregnant and recruits a married couple to adopt the baby. The 17-year-old daughter of Republican vice presidential nominee Sarah Palin got pregnant then married her boyfriend. Hell, if they can pull it off... why not you?

Here's why. How many teenager moms do you know that come from supportive and financially stable families? Which ones have an array of future opportunities that a more typical teen mom might not have? What are the odds they will be performing on *Dancing with the Stars*? Evelyn Rodriguez, 34, a New Yorker from a low-income background who gave birth to a son at 15 shared her story with social issues author David Crary. Now, after more than a decade of juggling jobs and classes, she is on the verge of earning a college degree. "It's been glorified all over the place," says Rodriguez. "People who don't have the money and great support, they say, 'Oh, wow, they're doing it. It's cool," she says, referring to Spears and Palin. "But it's not cool. I've been through it. It's a job. I don't appreciate what's going on out there making it seem so beautiful, when it's not." *Young person's alert:* no guy wants to take out a 16-year-old girl who has a baby.[182]

Reali-tude:
Don't trade a few hours of fun for a lifetime of regret.

☞ *Lifebomb #6: "I can have it all!"*

Though we devote considerable resources to raising them, children are not investments. We usually think of an investment as some sort of property we acquire for future financial return or benefit. But investments can be ignored or jettisoned if they do not perform. Instead, children should be considered as a personal commitment. Raising a child remains binding even if an expected "rate of return" fails to materialize because each child is unpredictably unique. The reality is children are a crapshoot. Kids can be born disabled, develop a debilitating disease, or wind up in jail. To misquote Forest Gump, "Kids are like a box of chocolates. You never know what you're gonna get."

Furthermore, the direct cost of having babies fails to account for the reduction in earnings over an entire lifetime, what economists term "opportunity cost." Clearly, mothers pay a price for interrupting their careers—even briefly—to have children. There is the loss of income while they are absent, compounded by the fact that it may take years for them to reenter the workforce. And when they do, they may have to enter at a lower level or in a different profession than when they left. They may also face subtle forms of discrimination on the job and have to turn down promotions that they think could interfere with family responsibilities.

> *Who can afford children anymore? It does not look like I will have my own student loans paid off until I am old enough to be a grandparent, so how can I ever afford to raise and educate a child?*
>
> ~ Kristin, Internet blogger

Contrary to popular belief, it is the women with high-skills who tend to have the hardest time maintaining their wages after child-birth. In their 2010 study *The Career Cost of Family*, economists Claudia Goldin and Lawrence Katz found a large "mommy penalty" for mothers with advance degrees. According to economist Elizabeth Wilde, head of The Mommy Track Divides, these women tend to earn as much as one-third less over the lifetime of their careers than their childless peers. Lower skilled women tend to see their incomes drop by less than 15 percent, says Wilde. Despite the difficulties of modern living, however, young persons do not

182 *National Campaign to Prevent Teen and Unwanted Pregnancy*, a 2011 government report, showed fewer teens and young adults are having sex. Based on interviews of 5,300 young persons ages 15 to 24, the study found that the proportion in that age group who said they'd never had oral, vaginal, or anal sex rose in the past decade from 22 percent to about 28 percent. Possibly they are more cautious due to increased awareness of sexually transmitted diseases, or the emphasis on abstinence has had some influence, or they are simply too busy.

want to turn back the clock. Among those under age 30, 84 percent disagree with the idea that women should go back to a more traditional role.

So, can women "have it all?" Not likely, Nadine. Helen Gurley Brown's trifecta[183] of "love, sex, and money" can be very difficult to attain if kids are in the picture *(framing-1 trap)*.[184] Often motherhood is foregone as women pursue careers that are fulfilling but also highly demanding of time and energy. Family appears to be one of the key reasons that many women do not break through the "glass ceiling" to the top ranks of management, which may be why more women are opting out. Unfairly, women who do not have children may still be viewed as "potential mothers" by employers, who may give them fewer professional opportunities as a result.

Reali-tude:
What is the point of having kids if you cannot engage them?

The bottom line:

- The best determining factor for having children is whether you are emotionally ready.
- Having too many children too soon is the #1 reason most people will never have any money.
- There are huge direct, personal, and opportunity costs to having children.
- No matter how hard you try, your children may disappoint you.

The Reality

I'm sorry, it's true. Having children really changes your view on these things. We're born, we live for a brief instant, and we die. It's been happening for a long time. Technology is not changing it much—if at all.
~ Steve Jobs, founder of Apple

Since the 1960s, the easy availability of reliable contraception has helped to spur a revolution in sexual mores. Better opportunities for women have opened up in the workplace, giving them an incentive to delay child-bearing without sacrificing sex. The balance of power has changed within marriage as wives have become less economically dependent on their husbands and more empowered to walk out of unhappy or abusive relationships. Here are some of today's trends:

---

183 In horse racing terminology, a *trifecta* is when your bet correctly calls which horses will finish first, second, and third in exact order. It is also used in sports to describe scoring three points at one time or succeeding at anything three times in three consecutive attempts.

184 Helen Gurley Brown wrote *Sex and the Single Girl* (1962), a national best seller that changed single women's attitudes toward their own lives. As editor-in-chief of *Cosmopolitan*, she transformed it into a top-selling international magazine for young women (glamorous, fashion-focused women are sometimes called "Cosmo Girls"). Brown, who had no children, claimed that women could have it all: love, sex, and money.

- The percentage of women in their mid-40s who have never had a child doubled in the last 30 years.
- In 2010, a record 41 percent of births were to unmarried women.
- 64 percent of women said they couldn't afford to have a baby now because of the economy.
- About one-half of all pregnancies are unplanned and about one-half of these end in abortion.
- One-quarter of Gen NeXters have children of their own. Among those who do not have kids, a large majority (86 percent) say they would like to some day.
- Young moms are busy as bees: two-thirds of women with children ages 17 or younger work. Of these, three-quarters work full-time and one-quarter work part-time.

Single-parenting

A single-parent is one who cares for one or more children without the physical assistance of the other parent in the home. Single-parenthood may come about by choice such as divorce, adoption, or artificial insemination. It may also occur by unforeseen circumstances such as death, child abuse or neglect, or abandonment by biological parents. The social stigma[185] around single motherhood, which was intense before the 1960s, has faded and the number of single-parent families has increased dramatically. In 2012, the U.S. Census Bureau cited an estimated 12 million single-parents, with more than eight-in-ten of these families headed by a single mother.[186] For college-educated women, it is usually because they have not yet got round to marrying the man they are living with.

A feature *Economist* article titled "Briefing: Marriage in America, The frayed knot" notes that children in single-parent homes are more than five times as likely to be poor as those who live with two biological parents (26 percent versus 5 percent). Also, children who do not live with both biological parents are roughly twice as likely to drop out of high school and to have behavioral or psychological problems. While co-habiting couples have the same number of hands as married couples, reports *The Economist*, on average their children do worse by nearly every measure. One reason often cited is that such relationships are less stable than marriages.

Children whose father was never around face the toughest problems and this is rampant in the African-American community. In 2011, 68 percent of African-American women who gave birth were unmarried, down from 72 percent in 2008. Many of these mothers shoulder the full responsibility for the care of their children with little or no financial assistance from deadbeat dads.[187] This is a huge problem and has prompted some to question whether the African-American family is dying.

---

185 The word *stigma* goes back to the ancient Greeks. It referred to bodily marks or brands, usually carved or burned into an individual's skin to signify infamy or disgrace. A person thus marked was perceived to pose a risk to society.

186 Only a small proportion of single-parent households are headed by a male. Compared to single-parent mothers, single-parent fathers have a higher level of education and are more likely to hold full-time professional or higher-level jobs.

187 Child support is largely determined by which state you live in. The percentage of parents receiving the full amount they are due ranges from 14 percent in California to 30 percent in Wisconsin (2008).

BRAIN SNACK: *What is the price of a passport? $311,491 in back child support payments for a U.S. businessman now living in China; $46,000 for a musician seeking to perform overseas; and $45,849 for a man planning a Dominican Republic vacation. The State Department is now denying passports to deadbeat parents who owe more than $2,500 in child support. Once deadbeats make good on their debts, they can reapply for passports and the money collected is forwarded to the parent to whom it is owed. In addition, child support enforcement agencies in most states can also suspend not only your driver's license, but also any professional, occupational, or recreational license.*

For kids whose parents split up, the picture is more nuanced. Mary Parke, a policy analyst at the Center for Law and Social Policy, notes that coming from a disrupted family does not necessarily doom a child to later chronic unhappiness or academic or personal failure. Most children in single-parent homes "grow up without serious problems," she says. "If parents detest each other and quarrel bitterly, their kids may actually benefit from a divorce." Sociologist Paul Amato has found that 40 percent of divorces leave the children better (or at least, no worse) off than the turbulent marriages that preceded them. Indeed, many resilient children from disrupted families not only finish high school, but go on to college and have successful careers, marriages, and families. Psychologist E. Mavis Hetherington, a trailblazing researcher into the effects of divorce, writes that the vast majority of children within two years of their parents' divorce "are beginning to function reasonably well again."

Of course that leaves 60 percent of divorces where what is good for the parents may harm the children. Some of these divorces lead to devastating physical, emotional, and financial effects. Rather than bouncing back after the initial pain of their parents' split, these children often continue to suffer well into adulthood, notes psychologist Judith Wallerstein and colleagues. The largest study on divorce, *The Unexpected Legacy of Divorce: A Twenty-Five Year Landmark Study*, found that children's pain plays out in their relationships, their work lives, and their confidence about parenting themselves.

When I was in my early 20s, my friends were all obsessed with getting married and having kids and now in their late 20s and early thirties, they are all miserable, divorced or both.

~ JUL7Y7NYC, Internet blogger

Then there are the grandparents. According to Pew Research, about four-in-ten of those children who live with a grandparent (or grandparents) are also being raised primarily by that grandparent. Often it is triggered by a single parent who becomes overwhelmed with financial problems, is incarcerated, succumbs to illness or substance abuse, or dies. High rates of divorce and teen pregnancies fuel the phenomenon, as do long overseas deployments that confront some parents in the military. These children tend to arrive with pre-existing problems, prompting The

American Academy of Child and Adolescent Psychiatry to warn: "Many grandparents in this caretaking role underestimate or are unaware of the added burdens their new role as 'parents' will place upon them." They struggle with modern schoolwork (math is a special trial), contemporary morals, and sheer exhaustion.

Reali-tude:
Fertility is a joint decision. Copulate carefully.

Having only one child

When the mandate to be fruitful and multiply was first chiseled in stone, it was elementary; the more you bred, the more likely your line was to survive. Large families were social networks and insurance policies and more kids meant more helping hands, more productivity, and more comfort. Nowadays, friends and relatives always seem to urge parents of only children to have another baby, but not for the same reasons as the ancients. They think it will be better for the child they already have since single children are perceived as spoiled, selfish, solitary misfits.

BRAIN SNACK: *Legitimizing the stereotype of the "lonely only" was the work of psychologist Granville Stanley Hall. Hall established one of the first American psychology research labs and was a leader of the child-study movement. He supervised the 1896 study* Of Peculiar and Exceptional Children, *which described a series of only-child oddballs as permanent misfits. "Being an only child is a disease in itself," he concluded. For decades, practitioners disseminated his conclusion that an only child could not be expected to go through life with the same capacity for adjustment that children with siblings possessed.*

Of course we have all heard this, but since the 1970s personality research of only children has debunked the idea. Reviewing more than 35 years of research, psychologist Toni Falbo says there is no truth to the stereotype of the only child as lonely, selfish, and maladjusted. Only children are highly indulged and protected with "no dilution of resources" between siblings. No matter their income or occupation, parents of only children have more time, energy, and money to invest in their kid. Only children tend to higher self-esteem, higher SAT scores, do better in school, and get more education—college, medical or law degrees—than other kids, she writes.

And the child is not the only beneficiary. The single child offers the experience of parenting but with leftover energy for sex, conversation, reading, and so on. Notwithstanding, demographer Samuel Preston finds that many parents fall so madly in love with their first child, they want a second. According to a 2010 Pew survey on American motherhood, a plurality of adults (46 percent) say two children is the ideal number. Only 3 percent said one child was ideal—the same number that said zero. As the acceptability of one-child families increases over time, the number of "onlies" will continue to ascend.

Reali-tude:
Kids are imperfect choices with uncertain outcomes.

Childlessness

Modern society is in transition. Refusal of parenthood in favor of focusing on education and career, longer periods of searching for the ideal mate, and a more flexible and pleasure-seeking life are changing our views on having children. In a feature article "The Only Child: Debunking the Myths" in *TIME Magazine*, journalist Lauren Sandler notes that at a rate of 3 to 1, people believe the main purpose of marriage is the "mutual happiness and fulfillment" of adults rather than the "bearing and raising of children." Children have fallen to eighth out of nine on a list of factors that people associate with successful marriages, well behind sharing household chores, good housing, adequate income, a happy sexual relationship, and faithfulness.

> *I have never wanted children and so never had them. I consider myself to be happy with my lot. Am I any happier than my friends with children? I don't know. What I do know is that my friends often tell me that they envy my vacations, my evenings out, etc. I, on the other hand, do not envy their lives.*
> ~ Laura, Internet blogger

Today, nearly one-in-five American women ends her childbearing years without having borne a child, compared with one-in-ten in the 1970s. Couples who delay parenting are more likely to be white, highly educated, work in professional occupations, and earn high incomes. Over the past decade, childless[188] rates have also risen more rapidly for black, Hispanic, and Asian women as well. Given that the chance of a successful pregnancy declines with age, some women who hope to have children never will, despite the rise in fertility treatments that facilitate pregnancy.

In the U.S., the number of babies born per 1,000 women of childbearing age (called the "general" fertility rate) fell to 63 in the 12 months that ended in June, 2012, leveling off in 2013. This is the lowest since 1920, the earliest year with reliable records. The main reasons cited are the economy and a decline in the number of immigrant women, particularly the champion breeders among us, Hispanic women, who now give birth to 1 in 4 babies. Why does this matter to Gen NeXt? This challenges the long-held assumptions that births to immigrants will help maintain the U.S. population and provide the taxpaying work force needed to support future generations in retirement.

Reali-tude:
Never do three things mindlessly: get married, have children, get divorced.

188 Some people prefer the term "childfree" to childless.

The bottom line:

- Couples are waiting longer to have children and more women are opting out.
- The number of single-parent, one child, and childless families is increasing.
- The main purpose of marriage is now seen as happiness and fulfillment, not child raising.
- No matter how strong your marriage, you must be prepared to raise the child by yourself.

Doctor's Prescription (Rx)

Children are completely egoistic; they feel their needs intensely and strive ruthlessly to satisfy them.

~ Sigmund Freud, psychiatrist

Having a child, either by birth or by adoption, can be one of the most rewarding experiences you can have. At the same time, the financial and legal implications of having a child can be substantial. Here are a few tips for new parents to consider before or shortly after your new bundle of joy arrives:

Financial aspects:

- *Health insurance.* There are medical costs associated with having a baby, and as your baby grows, for the child. If there are any medical complications, those costs can be enormous. Make sure you know what is covered by your insurance and don't forget to add your newborn to your health insurance plan immediately. Failing to do this within 30 days of their birth means you will have to wait for the next open enrollment period, which only happens once a year.
- *Life insurance.* If something happens to you, your spouse or partner will need some resources to help raise your child. And if both parents should die, you don't want to leave the guardian in the lurch. Consider 20-year level term insurance that will last until your child is grown.
- *Disability insurance.* Look into disability insurance, which provides income if you become disabled and cannot work. A 24 year old has a 44 percent likelihood of being disabled for three months or longer prior to age 65. Very few people can endure such a financial blow.
- *Budget.* Going from dual income, no kids status to one income plus another mouth to feed will change your lifestyle dramatically. Prior to delivery, look at what will need to be cut back and then adjust your budget. You will have a lot of new expenses to track so be flexible the first few months.
- *Income.* Are you staying home? Switching to a job with more flexibility? Your expenses will climb at a time when your income may drop and it can catch you off guard if you aren't ready for it.

- *Taxes.* If you're going back to work, consider adjusting your W-4 withholding now that you have another dependant to take care of. Don't forget to take the child tax credit on April 15th.
- *College vs. retirement.* Saving for college is often the first thing new parents want to do but it is wise to provide for your own retirement first. The earlier you can start saving for both, the better.[189]

Legal aspects:

- *Sign a will.* Set up a will and identify a guardian for your child should both you and your spouse die unexpectedly. When selecting a guardian consider financial ability, age, religious beliefs, values, and morals. Would you rather name the person(s) who will raise your child or would you prefer that some drone in the probate court make this decision after y'all have checked out?
- *Update records.* Review the beneficiaries on all of your financial accounts and insurance policies. Be sure to include your 401(k) plan if your employer offers one and any pension plan or trusts. Updating estate plan documents goes overlooked time and time again, so don't procrastinate.

Other aspects:

- *Request a Social Security number.* An SSN identifies your child for federal taxation/benefits purposes, and your health insurance provider will want this number soon after it's issued. Without a Social Security number for Bambino, you cannot claim your child as a dependent on your individual tax return.
- *Employee benefits.* The *Family and Medical Leave Act*[190] allows eligible workers to take 12 weeks of unpaid leave during a 12-month period after the birth or adoption of a child or after the placement of a foster child into your home. Some companies offer maternity (mom) and paternity (dad) leave, but not all, and those that do might not pay for all of the time away from work. Ask about work arrangements such as flex time or job sharing that will make things a little easier.
- *Consider moving.* Your home may feel cramped. If so, save up so that you can afford to move but make sure you are happy with the schools at your next location.

Addressing all these items won't take an excessive amount of time and will help ensure your family's future financial health. Don't rush into a big mistake. *Young person's alert:* there are no bad kids, just ignorant or inept parents. The more you know, the smarter your decisions (and the lower your stress) will be!

---

189 Consider opening a *529 Savings Plan* or *Coverdell ESA* for your child's college expenses. These are college savings plans that offer tax advantages when the money is withdrawn for qualified educational expenses when it comes time for your little critter to go off to college.

190 *The Family and Medical Leave Act of 1993* (FMLA) is a federal law, signed by President Clinton, that requires covered employers to provide employees job-protected and unpaid leave for qualified medical and family reasons. These include (among others) pregnancy, adoption, or the foster care placement of a child.

Talking Points

And as he hung up the phone it occurred to me, He'd grown up just like me;
My boy was just like me.
~ Harry Chapin, from *Cat's in the Cradle*

Chapter 17 describes some tools to help you acquire wisdom by interviewing others. To benefit from these techniques, you need only have access to a parent, educator, or other trusted adult (tribal elder) and a desire to listen and learn. Based on the ideas in this chapter, here are some starters:

1. "I am trying to improve myself. Being emotionally ready is the key factor in successfully raising a child. Reflecting on your experience, or that of someone you know, do you recall a situation where lack of emotional maturity resulted in a young person jeopardizing his or her long-term well-being?" If they say "Yes" then ask:

   - "Would you tell me the gist about what happened please?"
   - "How did you (they) feel about this at the time?"
   - "What two things did you learn from this that you can share with me?"

2. "I am trying to improve myself. It is very expensive to successfully raise a child. In addition to money there is also lost personal time and forgone professional opportunities. Reflecting on your experience, or that of someone you know, can you recall how raising children benefited or hindered a young person's long-term well-being?" If they say "Yes" then ask:

   - "Would you tell me the gist about what happened please?"
   - "How did you (they) feel about this at the time?"
   - "What two things did you learn from this that you can share with me?"

   In either case, if they say "No," simply say "Thank you."

3. Having a child is an inflection point in a young person's life. Reflecting on your experience, or that of someone you know, what two suggestions would you have for a young person that is contemplating this decision?

4. "I want to make wise life-choices. Reflecting on your experience, would you have two ideas that I can implement to improve my judgment and decision-making skills? Be sure to thank them for their response.

Knowledge Nuggets

We never know the love of our parents for us till we become parents.
~ Henry Ward Beecher, minister

1. *Is your workplace "mother friendly?"* For 25 years *Working Mother* magazine has been challenging companies to understand the demands that come with being working mothers. The magazine publishes an annual "Working Mother 100 Best Companies" list and hundreds of companies with at least 500 employees vie for a spot on the list. The application process includes more than 600 questions to prove they truly are working-mother-friendly. In order to make the list, companies must excel in areas including work-life programs, child care, flexibility, and elder care resources. See whether your firm made the list at: http://www.workingmother.com/BestCompanies/2010/08/2010-working-mother-100-best-companies.

2. *How much is that baby in the window?* How much of your family's yearly income is spent on the children? The University of Minnesota Extension walks you through estimating the cost of raising children of several ages in both two-parent and one-parent families. The guidelines are organized into seven areas: housing, food, transportation, clothing, health care, child care and education, and miscellaneous good and services. This is useful if you want to see what adding a child to the family would cost or if you are a parent contemplating divorce. Crunch your own figures at: http://www.extension.umn.edu/distribution/familydevelopment/00178.html.

3. *Are you money wise?* Dr. Moneywise offers savvy financial advice for young persons. His story of the typical divorce is as follows: couple gets married young; they begin having children right away; they have three kids in 4 years; he comes home to crying and complaints; he finds someone else at work where there is less stress; daddy and mommy get a divorce, and now his income has to support two families. If money is tight, which family is going to get less money? Or nothing? His advice for women: Don't have any more children than you can afford to raise through college on one income—your OWN. For more sage advice, visit: http://drmoneywise.com/AboutDrMoneywise.html.

4. *Where to go for info?* See Appendix F for additional information relating to this chapter.

Chapter 13

Level of Education

In a global economy where the most valuable skill you can sell is your knowledge, a good education is no longer just a pathway to opportunity—it is the prerequisite.

~ President Barack Obama

The Gist

The Good:

- On average, college grads will earn up to $1 million more than high school grads
- CTE (VocEd) offers rewarding careers, good-paying jobs, and college opportunities
- Blue collar workers also benefit from a year of college

The Bad:

- If you want a good job, you must continue beyond high school
- Getting an informal education is as important as getting your degree
- Paying tuition does not guarantee you a job
- The world of education is not the real world

The Reality:

- Only one-quarter of young persons between 25 and 34 have a bachelor's degree
- Many young persons are not academically prepared for college
- More women are earning undergraduate degrees than men
- Colleges have boosted fees, raised class sizes, and furloughed faculty
- 75 percent say college is too expensive for most Americans to afford

Introduction

Education is the best provision for old age.
~ Aristotle

If there existed a "Renaissance Man" before the advent of the Renaissance, it was Greece's Aristotle (384–322 B.C.E.). Twenty years a student of Plato (who in turn had studied under Socrates), Aristotle remains one of the most universal thinkers and influential philosophers of all time. He was a prolific writer and polymath, and made contributions in natural science to mathematics, logic, physics, astronomy, anatomy, physiology, biology, zoology, botany, agriculture, and medicine.[191] In philosophy, Aristotle wrote extensively on ethics, metaphysics, psychology, theology, politics, history, economics, rhetoric, aesthetics, sports, dance, and theater. According to contemporary philosopher Bryan Magee, "It is doubtful whether any human being has ever known as much as he did."

Aristotle was summoned by King Phillip of Macedonia to tutor his thirteen-year-old son, later known as Alexander the Great.[192] When Phillip was bumped off, which happened a lot in those days, Alexander ascended to the throne. At the ripe age of 22, he set off to conquer most of the known world. Preferring the staid life of an educator, Aristotle demurred and moved to Athens where he founded his own gymnasium-school called the *Lyceum*. There, Aristotle challenged his students to think great thoughts rather than, as was fashionable at the time, simply kill each other off.[193] A respectful Alexander supported the Lyceum for the next dozen years, sending back booty and bug specimens from lands afar. The school remained in operation until Athens was sacked by the Romans in 86 B.C.E. (sans Aristotle and Alexander, of course).

While lasting almost two millennia, Aristotelian theories came under criticism during the Middle Ages with the creation of a new think tank, the "university." The word university is derived from the Latin *universitas magistrorum et scholarium*, a mega-mouthful that roughly means "community of teachers and scholars." In practice, the term refers to an institution of higher learning that awards degrees. Universities evolved from much older Christian schools since religious men were,

191 Aristotle's work became the basis of classical deductive logic. He perfected the *syllogism*, an argument pattern consisting of two premises, or statements of fact, followed by a conclusion. One classic syllogism is "All men are mortal; Socrates is a man; therefore Socrates is mortal."

192 The Macedonians were a tribe in the northeastern part of the Greek peninsula.

193 Aristotle was referred to as a "peripatetic" lecturer because he reputedly walked about as he taught (from the Greek word *peripatetikos*, which refers to the act of walking). The actual location of the Lyceum complex, lost for centuries, was rediscovered in 1996 under a parking lot during excavations for the new Museum of Modern Art in Athens.

by and large, the only ones who could read and write. The oldest continually operating university is the University of Bologna, founded in Italy in 1088.

Today, there are more than 4,300 institutions of higher learning in the United States, including two-year colleges, four-year colleges, and universities. Admission is normally competitive, based on a number of factors such as high school courses taken, grade point average (GPA), class ranking, and standardized test scores such as the Scholastic Aptitude Test (SAT) or the American College Test (ACT). Subjective factors such as extracurricular activities, a personal essay, and an interview may also be required. A taste for Greek olives is not a requirement.

The modern business of higher learning is abstruse and byzantine. Two-year colleges (often, but not always community colleges) offer associate degrees and four-year colleges and universities offer bachelor's degrees.[194] Enrollment agreements often allow for seamless transition of academic credits earned at another learning institution so many students earn an associate's degree at a two-year institution before transferring to a four-year college or university to complete their bachelor's degree. Broadly, schools are either public or private. Public schools may be state-sponsored, such as University of Hawaii, or federally-sponsored, as with the military service academies. Private schools receive no public funding and may be not-for-profit, such as Harvard and Stanford, or for-profit, such as University of Phoenix. To further fog the issue, private schools may be secular (i.e., offers religious education) or non-secular.[195]

Once admitted, students engage in undergraduate study to satisfy their bachelor's degree requirements in a particular field (called a "major"). Some students choose to continue on to graduate school to earn a master's, doctoral, or professional degree. Earning a master's degree requires an additional two years of specialized study. Earning a doctorate can take considerably longer, depending upon your area of research and how finicky your dissertation chairperson is. Professional degrees are primarily for those who plan to be practitioners instead of academics and also require a serious commitment beyond the bachelor's degree. For example, law school is a three-year program and graduates must take the bar exam to legally practice law in nearly all states. Medical, dental, psychology, pharmacy, and veterinary schools are four-year programs, with formal residencies and internships following graduation before one is considered fully trained. Aristotle would be proud.

Reali-tude:
Education is your passport to opportunity.

194 While not universal, *college* typically refers to an institution that offers a collection of degrees in one specific area, such as the College of Engineering or Liberal Arts. A *university* is a research-oriented collection of colleges that provides both undergraduate and graduate education.

195 A college with a church-related word in its name (such as Wesleyan, Baptist, Christian, or Lutheran) does not necessarily mean that it is a Christian institution. Conversely, the names of many Christian colleges and universities give no obvious indication of their faith orientation.

The Good

The uneducated man is always placed at a great disadvantage. No matter how much natural ability one may have, if he is ignorant, he is discounted. It is not enough to possess ability; it must be made available by mental discipline.
~ Orison Swett Marden, founder of *Success* magazine

For most young persons, your level of education is the largest single influence on the positive side of the personal economics ledger and the scope of this chapter is commensurate with the importance of higher education to your future success. As Ben Franklin advised, "If a man empties his purse into his head, no one can take it from him. An investment in knowledge always pays the highest return." Pay attention class.

Learn and earn

Dig this Dorene: higher education pays off. "A bachelor's degree, whether from a public, a not-for-profit, or a for-profit institution, pays a handsome net financial reward in comparison to a high school diploma," say Jorge Klor de Alva and Mark Schneider, who study the value of a degree at the Nexus Research and Policy Center. Called the "college wage premium," this is the amount by which the average earnings of a person with a bachelor's degree exceed those of a person with only a high school diploma.

Research shows workers' earnings improved by 7 to 10 percent per year of community college and 5 to 10 percent per year across four-year colleges. A study by Georgetown University's Center on Education and the Workforce (CEWF) finds that people with a bachelor's degree make 84 percent more money over a lifetime than high school graduates. According to the study, on average a college graduate will earn $2.3 million over a lifetime compared to $1.3 million for those with a high school diploma. That's a big chunk of change Charlie—what could you do with a cool million more? For those who continue their higher education, a doctorate degree-holder can rake in $3.3 million and physicians nearly $6 million over a lifetime.[196] Cha-ching!

Majors matter. Some undergraduate majors pay a lot more than others, and the difference in earnings potential between one major and another can be more than 300 percent. "It's not so much the degree anymore, it's what you take," says Anthony Carnevale, CEWF's Director. For example, the last several decades have been a real-life version of *Revenge of the Nerds* as the supply of skilled technical workers failed to keep pace with demand. For tech-types, the income improvement was 14 percent per year of education for men and 29 percent for women, a huge

196 Estimates of the college wage premium vary. The Nexus Research and Policy Center estimates career-long salaries for bachelor's degree recipients range from $230,000 to $552,000 more than without the degree. The Organization for Economic Co-operation and Development (OECD) estimates that, on average, male graduates will earn nearly $370,000 more than non-graduates, and females an extra $229,000. Critics point out that gap estimates do not take into account deductions from income taxes, breaks in employment, student debt loads, or declining wages for high school graduates. Regardless of quibbling, all estimates comfortably repay the pricey investment in a university education.

monetary advantage. "With college growing ever more expensive," cautions educator Glenn Reynolds, "a degree that won't add to your earnings potential isn't an investment, but an expensive consumer item. The difference is nobody's encouraging 18-year-olds to take on six-figure debt to buy a Ferrari," he says.

While this is great news for nerds, what if you are not cut out to be a rocket scientist? In considering your career track, it is natural to wonder what various degrees are worth. One measure of the value of a degree is the average salary offered new graduates (another is the risk of unemployment). In its annual *Salary Survey*, the National Association of Colleges and Employers (NACE) tracks starting salaries of new graduates. Below are average starting salaries for the Class of 2013 for selected majors.[197]

2013 Starting Offers (Bachelor's Degree):

Petroleum Engineering	$93,500
Computer Science	$64,800
Business Administration	$54,234
History	$41,200
English	$39,800
Psychology	$39,300

Another way to compare the value of a degree is the payback time for college loans. *Bankrate.com* studied 2013 median pay for some fields and calculated how long it would take to pay off a typical student loan at 6 percent interest, assuming 10 percent of wages go toward repayment. The best fields: advertising, with a median salary of $107,950, takes about 6 years; an economist ($91,860) about 7 years; and a civil engineer ($79,340) about 8.5 years. Professionals take considerably longer: a physician ($179,020) about 11 years and a lawyer ($113,530) about 13 years. And for some majors, the day they repay their education expenses may not arrive until they're about to become grandparents: a teacher ($43,400) about 22 years; a veterinarian ($84,460) about 28 years; and a journalist ($37,090) about 32 years.

Conclusion? Degrees matter, across the board. Hiring managers say they're hiring more employees with college degrees for positions traditionally held by high-school graduates. When college grads lose jobs, they tend to find work more quickly than others and since their wages are higher, they typically have enough savings to survive between jobs. For example, the 2010 unemployment rate for high school graduates was 10.8 percent; the rate for college graduates was less than half that at 4.9 percent. College graduates "have a privileged position in the labor market," notes Lawrence Mishel, president of the Economic Policy Institute. Finally, an educated workforce benefits society. Students from low-income families who earn college degrees will pay far more in taxes over their lifetimes (to the tune

197 *Salary Survey* is a quarterly report of starting salary offers to new college graduates in 70 disciplines at the bachelor's degree level. NACE compiles this data from college and university career services offices nationwide. Find it at: http://www.naceweb.org/home.aspx.

of more than $50,000 per graduate) than they would have without the college degree, even after subtracting the public funds that helped to pay for their studies.

> *You MUST HAVE a high school diploma these days to get any job. I own a convenience store and won't even hire a flunky to work there if they don't finish high school. Dropping out just shows you're not responsible!*
>
> ~ chefjames, Internet blogger

"The evidence for the individual economic benefits of college is overwhelming," says economist Sandy Baum. And despite complaints about the price tag, the public gets it. In a recent Pew Research survey, an overwhelming majority of college graduates—86 percent—say that college has been a good investment for them personally. Nearly everyone surveyed said they expected their child to get a college education.

Other bennies of college

These days, blue-collar workers benefit nearly as much as white-collar workers from a year of post-secondary education (i.e., beyond high school). The high levels of reading, math, and science literacy needed to graduate from college are also needed for high-paying blue-collar jobs. Welders, for example, need strong trigonometry skills, and machine tool and die makers are often the same kind of top math students that go into the tech sector. Going to college can make you a better plumber than you would have been otherwise. Why? You will often need to interact with customers and clients who are themselves college-educated. And, surprising to many, the most important aspects of a college degree may be non-monetary. Consider some of the spin-off benefits of going to college:

- Helps you discover yourself, a key to making better decisions about your future.
- Widens your base of knowledge and prepares you to cope with life's complexities.
- Broadens your horizons by introducing you to people of different cultures and new ways of thinking.
- Additionally, graduates tend to:
    - § Be more tolerant and understanding of others and more satisfied with their jobs.
    - § Create more exciting life styles and make better spouses and parents.
    - § Enjoy better mental and physical health, have lower blood pressure, and live longer.[198]
    - § Do more volunteer work, vote more often, and participate in political and civic organizations.[199]

198 The life expectancy of the college educated is seven years more than non-college educated (82 versus 75 years).

199 Of Americans who join large public-interest advocacy groups such as the Sierra Club, at least three-quarters are college graduates.

I have gained non-financial benefits such as confidence, analytical skills, access to interesting social circles, a lifelong addiction to reading and exploring ideas. Friends who have avoided going to college—amongst them several who are more highly remunerated for their work than me—carry a lifelong chip on their shoulders. If I were to put a monetary value on my "smugness," I'd say it would be an above average IRR with duration of at least 50 years.
~ Balanced Eduardo, Internet blogger

"A college education produces trained minds who know when somebody is speaking rot," advises humanitarian Sanford Pinsker. And recognizing a Rottweiler when he speaks is a very useful life-skill!

Reali-tude:
Yes, it still pays to get a college degree.

The bottom line:

- Higher education is a wise investment for most young persons.
- Yesterday's high school diploma is today's bachelor's degree.
- College can help you find yourself, earn more, and live better.
- Having a degree can lower your car insurance premiums.

The Bad

Mr. Braddock: Ben, what are you doing?
Benjamin: Well, I would say that I'm just drifting. Here in the pool.
Mr. Braddock: Would you mind telling me then what those four years of college were for? What was the point of all that hard work?"
Benjamin: You got me.
~ from the film, *The Graduate* (1968)

How much you receive for your labor depends on how valuable it is. If you have no skills, you'll be paid minimum wage or a little better if you're lucky. So, getting a formal education in a field where you can think critically and help solve real world problems is very important. When it comes to education, questionable beliefs can trap your thinking and jeopardize your long-term well-being. Learn about some of the lifebombs and you'll stand a better chance of making a smart choice.

Cognitive Flaw: Ignorance

There's never a day goes by that I don't miss having graduated and gone to college.
~ B. B. King, musician

Clueless about the implications of higher education? Perhaps the single most influential factor in determining your lifetime earnings potential is matching your level of education to your capabilities. Yet many young persons simply float through school on the promise that there will be a good job and a sweet life for them at the other end. Look at it this way: they will be buying the used car that you trade in. Let's look at how failing to be objectively informed when making this important life-choice can put your future happiness at risk.

☞ *Lifebomb #1: "Un-college is un-cool."*

It is clear that in most areas of human endeavor, ability is not uniformly distributed. Some people can run faster, shoot hoops better, or quaff more beer 'n oysters than others. Same with academic ability. Not every student has the intellectual capacity or the desire to cope with the rigors of a four-year college program. "A bachelor's degree is not a smart investment for every student in every circumstance," caution Isabel V. Sawhill and Stephanie Owen, researchers at the Brookings Institution. It doesn't mean they're stupid. It's just who they are. What it does mean is college, like the military, is not for everybody.

Unfortunately, many who hit the college trail should not. "Of freshmen at four-year colleges who graduated in the bottom 40 percent of their high-school class, two-thirds won't graduate even if given eight and a half years," says career counselor Marty Nemko. "Even if such students defy the odds, they will likely graduate with a low GPA and a major in low demand by employers." For these students and others, career and technical education (CTE) is often a good option. Labor economist Stephen J. Rose predicts that in 2018, more than six-in-ten of all jobs will require some form of postsecondary education, and CTE fits the bill. *Young person's alert:* you can be successful in life without a college education but you WILL need to go beyond high school in order to achieve it.

> *Not everyone needs to go to college. But everyone needs a postsecondary education. Indeed, we have seen ample evidence that some form of postsecondary instruction is increasingly vital to an individual's economic security. Yet too many Americans just aren't getting the education that they need and that they deserve.*
>
> ~ U.S. Department of Education, from "A Test of Leadership, Charting the Future of U.S. Higher Education"

Reali-tude:
Some form of postsecondary education is a must.

CTE is a great alternative

Career and technical education (also called *vocational-technical education*, or VTE) is postsecondary education at the community college level that focuses on practical career preparation rather than academics.[200] It provides students with knowledge

200 VTE began with *The Vocational Education Act of 1917*, also known as the Smith-Hughes Act. The act provided federal assistance to states to promote vocational education in the areas of agriculture,

and skills that are relevant for the job market and offers the possibility of rewarding careers, good-paying jobs, and college opportunities. CTE professors don't do research—they are there to teach—and they provide training in many challenging fields such as agriculture, trade and industrial, business and marketing, family and consumer sciences, health occupations, public safety and security, and technology.

Employment prospects after graduation are excellent for CTE graduates! The Council of Economic Advisers projects "faster-growing demand for those with a two-year technical-college degree, or specific training, than for those with a full university degree." By 2018, projects the Center on Education and the Workforce, the U.S. will need 22 million new postsecondary degrees and will fall short by about 3 million. We will also need nearly 5 million workers with postsecondary certificates, which require fewer courses than a degree and can be obtained through vocational schools. Are we loving it yet?

Myths and mistakes about CTE

People sometimes dismiss CTE programs as poor substitutes for a "real" four-year college education. This line of thinking is bupkis and is perpetuated by several misconceptions:

- *College for all?* "College is what every parent wants for their child," says Martin Scaglione, president of ACT.[201] Kids are told there's one path to success—go to college to earn a bachelor's degree *(framing-2 trap.)*. Eighty-five (85) percent of parents see college as an investment in the future. Yet, while 70 percent of high-school graduates will follow that path (up from 40 percent in 1970), only about 30 percent will earn a degree ten years later.[202] Parents, pay attention: college is not for all.
- *You lack the smarts to get into college.* Many students don't do well in a typical college environment because they don't see the relevance of what they're being taught to the real world. Everything a student learns in CTE is relevant to applying for and getting a job, and being successful in a career that interests them. They just forgo the fluff.
- *Poised for success.* Young persons often believe that if they get grades of B or C in the college-prep track, they are well prepared for college. Such confidence is often exaggerated *(superiority-1 trap)*. An estimated 43 percent of community college students require remediation, as do 29 percent of students at public four-year universities. "These students come out of high school really misled" says former Colorado governor Roy Romer, chair of a group that issued the report, *Diploma to Nowhere*. "They think they're prepared. They got a 3.0 and got through the curriculum they needed to get admitted, but they find what they learned wasn't adequate."

---

trades and industry, and home economics.

201 ACT is the not-for-profit organization best known for its national college admission and placement (SAT) exam.

202 The enrollment rate for female high school completers enrolling in college in the fall of 2010 (74 percent) was higher than the rate for males (66 percent).

- *You can't get a degree from vocational schools.* Many CTE programs offer two-year associates degrees, with courses that can be credited toward four-year college degrees. Students can earn their associates degree, enter the work force, and complete a four-year degree in the future if they wish.
- *You need a college degree to get a well-paying job.* Wrong again Waldo. Only two out of three college graduates find employment in their field of study. Many technical training programs have better placement outcomes than college degrees and the pay for skilled technical workers can be very competitive.

Regrettably, CTE seems to uniquely draw disdain. Many perceive it only for low functioning students and not leading to a desirable career. Parents do not want their kids setting out on "blue collar" career paths they think will quash opportunity. Academically successful students may consider peers who do not go to college as "less" of a person, and what kid would dare say she wants to be a cabinetmaker or a farmer? *(inertia-2 trap)*. Corporate America doesn't help either. With many graduates to choose from, employers increasing turn their noses up at anyone who does not sport a degree, no matter what the job's requirements. The real tragedy is that many graduates of four-year colleges come to community colleges after graduation for training in an actual field.

One of the largest groups of incoming students at the technical college where I taught consisted of disgruntled academic college graduates who couldn't find a job in a field related to their degree, or just didn't like it. I had numerous students from health care backgrounds (nurses, radiology techs, etc.), engineers (up to and including nuclear engineers), liberal arts, mathematics, English and computer science majors, etc. All had spent huge chunks of their lives and lots of financial aid obtaining the documentation required for their degree and they were begging for a change.
~ old hvac teacher

One of my best high school friends is making $70,000, and has his own truck and health benefits. The honest truth is, I feel weird being a college student and having no money.
~ Mr. Daniels, student

Andrew Grove, the former CEO of Intel, conducted an informal survey of philanthropic higher education initiatives in the San Francisco Bay area. Grove's withering conclusion: "Every single program... emphasizes a four-year college degree. We have, collectively, a well-intentioned push toward a one-size-fits-all program of education. Students... are pushed, kicked, enticed, encouraged, and shamed into going on to a four-year college education *(framing-1 trap)*. The consequence of that is a failure to increase the effectiveness of our workforce; that determines the effectiveness of our economy, and most importantly, what it does is destroy the ladder to the middle class," he adds.

Reali-tude:
A four-year college degree is not for everyone.

☞ *Lifebomb #2: "Gimme a break."*

There is no such thing as a typical college student these days. Gone are the days of the "traditional" college student who is 18 to 24 and attends one institution full-time for four years. Nearly a third of undergraduate college students now are 25 or older and almost as many have dependent children. Most that enroll say they plan to get a four-year degree eventually...but few actually do *(self-control-2 trap).*

"Looking back, I wish I had gotten that degree. Four years seemed like a thousand years then. But I wish I would have just put in my four years."
~ Andy B., college dropout

Forty-three. That's the percentage of college freshmen who will drop out of school before getting a bachelor's degree. Community colleges? Even worse. About seven-in-ten community college students will drop out before receiving a credential. That means only 57 percent of college freshmen—and a mere 31 percent of first-year students in community college—will earn the degree they sought.[203] And even these figures may be too rosy. Averages can be misleading, warns editor Evan Sparks of The Philanthropy Roundtable. "Elite universities such as Harvard and Yale have near-perfect graduation rates. Much lower rates persist among the campuses frequented by the students most at risk of dropping out: low-income young people, ethnic minorities, and first-generation college students."[204] Sadly, more than 70 institutions routinely graduate fewer than 20 percent of their freshman within six years.

***BRAIN SNACK:** A 2010 study by the University of Central Florida's Institute for Diversity and Ethics in Sport ranked University of California, Berkeley (UCB) Men's Basketball 64th out of the 65 teams when it came to graduating its players. The overall men's basketball graduation rate at UCB was just 20 percent, eclipsed only by the University of Maryland's eight percent. UCB graduated zero out of seven African-American players and zero of two white basketball players. Two of UCB's three international basketball players managed to graduate, which raised the overall team's graduation rate to 20 percent. "If you can't graduate two out of five of your student-athletes," commented U.S. Secretary of Education Arne Duncan, "how serious are you about the academic part of your mission?" Ouch.*

---

203 The official graduation rate, reported to the government as a condition for receiving federal student aid, is calculated as the percentage of first-year, full-time students who graduate within 150 percent of the time normally required. The U.S. Department of Education is looking to broaden how student success is measured in higher education, taking into account students who transfer, part-time students, and students who are not attending college for the first time. Community colleges have complained for years that the federal data reporting system doesn't accurately reflect the reality on their campuses.

204 As of 2010, 49 percent of Hispanic students, 60 percent of African Americans, and 60 percent of Native American first-time, full-time students failed to complete a bachelor's degree within six years.

Research conducted by Clifford Adelman at the U.S. Department of Education confirms that the best odds for degree attainment are when four years in high school are followed immediately by four years of full-time attendance in a four-year college. "When you look at who succeeds in college," says Kati Haycock, president of The Education Trust, "you realize that any departure from the traditional path... has huge consequences to the likelihood of students succeeding." Once students take a break—a euphemism for drop out—family and work can make a return to school seem even harder than finishing it in the first place. Like Amelia Earhart and cheap gas, they never come back.[205]

This has a huge cost. First, there are the financial and emotional consequences for the individual. The institution also suffers since the resources required to accommodate these "Klingons" might be better spent elsewhere. It also takes an expensive toll on the public purse. In 2010, more than $13 billion in taxpayer grant money (e.g., Pell Grants) was given toward degrees that will never be awarded. By any measure, everybody loses.

So, what is wrong? "We've been so focused on access, people don't really understand that we have a problem with completion" says Hilary Pennington, director of postsecondary success at the Bill & Melinda Gates Foundation. With underwriting from the foundation, researchers at Public Agenda surveyed more than 600 young Americans, ages 22 to 30, who dropped out of college. They examined why young people are motivated enough to start college, somehow find sufficient resources to enroll, but do not complete their degree. Their report, titled *With Their Whole Lives Ahead of Them*, reveals that for many students the decision was dictated by four realities *(optimism-2 trap)*:

- *Work/school balance.* Balancing work and school was by far the hardest challenge, said respondents. Full-time jobs, commutes and children, or parents who need care often get in the way. Seventy-four percent work part-time during the academic year. Among adults ages 18 to 34 who are not in school and do not have a bachelor's degree, two-thirds said a major reason for not continuing their education is the need to support a family.
- *Financial problems.* Some dropped out because their family's income had cratered owing to layoffs or they were unable to borrow the money needed to cover college costs. Some were frozen out by tuition and fee increases. Other students who depended on part-time jobs to make ends meet saw those opportunities disappear. About seven-in-ten dropouts said they had no scholarship or loan aid.
- *Poor preparation.* Finishing high school without being ready for college was another major reason why students drop out. Researchers at the Bridgespan Group have concluded that "Academic preparation is the most effective means of increasing the odds that students will graduate from high school ready for college, matriculate, and eventually receive their degrees."

205 Research by educator George D. Kuh finds that students with two or more of the following characteristics are more likely to drop out of college: being academically underprepared for college, not entering directly after high school, attending part time, being a single parent, being financially independent, caring for children at home, working more than 30 hours per week, or being a first generation college student.

- *Not getting it.* Students may not fully recognize the impact that dropping out without a diploma will have on their future personal economic success *(projection-1 trap).* If this describes you, re-read this chapter.

The study revealed that the vast majority of young people who made the decision to drop out support two proposals that they believe would make college graduation feasible. First, make it possible for part-time students to be eligible for more financial aid and second, offer more courses in the evening and on weekends so that they could continue working while taking classes. Eight-in-ten said these changes would help "a lot."

Reali-tude:
Don't let college be where your dreams are put on hold!

☞ *Lifebomb #3: "The school of hard knocks."*

Most people confuse intelligence with having a formal education. This is not true. The world is awash with educated derelicts and they have their "badges" (diplomas) to prove it![206] Highly educated and supremely cocksure, they proceed to screw up their lives—and those of others around them—by exercising immature judgment and making lousy life-choices.

Getting an informal education

Don't let your schooling interfere with your education.
~ Mark Twain, humorist, author

Defined broadly, an informal education is what we learn outside of the classroom. It is the daily storing of valuable information for use later in life and the constant effort to improve our self that is of inestimable value. We acquire it by reading books and publications, talking to successful people in the field we are interested in, paying attention to what is happening in the world, and asking more experienced people like parents, mentors, and other tribal elders for advice. In short, it is learning what works and what doesn't.

One of the best ways to self-learn is to read lots of books, particularly ones that teach you practical skills about career and life. "Why read books when I can just teach myself from the Web," you ask? Sure, nearly everything is available on-line, but there is a lacuna in relying on the Internet. First, it is a tool that is used with impatience—it is too easy to interrupt to check out Facebook or that new music site. Second, we tend to concentrate on things that we like and skip over the parts that we don't. This introduces bias and skews judgment. Finally, it is difficult to

206 In the classic western *Treasure of the Sierra Madre* (1948), Gold Hat, the Mexican bandit leader, tries to convince gold prospector Fred C. Dobbs that he and his company are the *federales*, or Federal Police. "If you're the police where are your badges?" Dobbs queries. Indignant, Gold Hat sneers, "Badges? We ain't got no badges. We don't need no badges! I don't have to show you any stinkin' badges!"

assess the larger framework of a topic from the Web in a way that a book can provide. Of course, you must be motivated to actually read the books and not just the dust jackets *(self-control-2 trap)*.

We also learn from our own experiences. The "school of hard knocks" is an idiomatic phrase[207] that means "the education one gets from life's (usually negative) experiences." Hard knocks also describes the wisdom you acquire by working from the bottom up. Mohamed, for example, started out 20 years ago washing dishes and hauling trash in a restaurant. Without a formal education, he worked hard, accepted more responsibility, and ultimately bought the business. Would having a degree have helped him become as successful a restaurateur?

How about you? Will a degree get your foot in the door or is work experience a better bet? Thinking like an economist, it all depends. No single recipe can cover all the potential situations of job seekers, potential employers, and career success. The case for experience seems straightforward. An employer wants someone who has done the job, or one like it, before. This gives them more assurance that you will be successful than simply hearing the right answers to interview questions. "Experience absolutely matters," says human resources consultant John Farner. "There's just no way around it." Some arguments in favor of experience include:

- Time in the trenches provides understanding and skills you cannot get in the classroom.
- Lack of a degree does not necessarily indicate lack of ability.
- Many jobs that ask for a degree do not require one to be adequately performed.
- College does not train you to do a job. Employers do *(superiority-2 trap)*.
- Getting a degree does not mean you will get a great paying job, or any job for that matter.

There again, merely holding a job for four years does not guarantee that you have the basic level of knowledge, intelligence, and literacy they need. The bachelor's degree is what economist Bryan Caplan calls a "signaling game." "Courses teach students few useful job skills," says Caplan. "Their main function is to signal to employers that students are smart, hard-working, and conformist. Advanced degrees are what demonstrate that you know something." Some reasons to get your degree include:

- A degree has become a discriminating factor for many jobs.[208]
- In the trenches you learn the "what" and the "how." In college, you learn the "why."
- Freshly-minted graduates come without "bad habits" that the company has to undo.

---

207 An idiom is an expression, word, or phrase with a figurative meaning that is separate from the literal meaning or definition of the words of which it is made. For example, in the expression "to kick the bucket," a listener knowing only the meanings of "kick" and "bucket" would be unable to deduce the expression's true meaning (that is, to die). Idioms sometimes leave foreign students "in the dark." Nyuk, nyuk.

208 Fail to enter the right "badge" in the education block of a job application and your resume is often electronically deleted before anyone sees it.

- Employers associate a degree with being motivated, disciplined, and accepting of responsibility.
- The higher you go on the organization chart, the more you will need a degree.

In the end, the relative value of experience versus a degree depends on the skill sets in question. Investopedia contributor Claire Bradley notes some careers where experience trumps education, and vice versa. In a field like sales, results are what matter most, regardless of the fancy piece of paper on the wall behind your desk. Many construction careers also value experience over education. And do you really think a degree in Asian women's studies will make you a better C++ programmer? In the real world, your chosen career field will dictate how education and experience stack up against each other.

Reali-tude:
Intelligence is not determined by level of education.

The bottom line:

- Four years in high school, followed by four-years full-time in college is your best bet.
- "Do you have a degree or not?" does not measure if you have the skills required.
- CTE offers rewarding careers, good-paying jobs, and college opportunities.
- Only one-quarter of young persons between 25 and 34 have a bachelor's degree.

Cognitive Flaw: Ineptitude

> *WARNING: Study in this university is known to cause thinking, occasionally deep thinking. Typical side effects include mild temporary anxiety followed by profound long-term satisfaction.*
>
> ~ Cover of the student prospectus for University of Chicago

Careless about the implications of higher education? Many young persons are not sure what job they want when it comes time to go to college. College is a great place to discover yourself but failing to objectively identify a viable career path by graduation time can be costly. Let's look at how failing to think seriously when making this important life-choice can put your future happiness at risk.

☞ *Lifebomb #4: "I paid my tuition—where's my job?"*

The ancient Greeks did not design their lyceums for the masses. Rather, they were made for the elite, that is, the well-endowed, prosperous citizen. Higher education continued to be exclusionary until WWII, after which the G.I. Bill funded millions of "non-elite" veterans to attend college before returning to the workforce. One effect of opening higher education to the masses was a change in focus from "discovering truth" to the acquisition of marketable skills for industry jobs.

A college should not aim to teach its students vocations, because an educational institution cannot do a good job of vocational training. In general the way to learn how to do anything is to do it; and industry is the place in which the young should learn how to work in industry. If we allow them to believe that education will get them better jobs and encourage them to get educated with this end in view, they are entitled to a sense of frustration if, when they have got the education, they do not get the jobs.
~ Robert M. Hutchins, former Chancellor, the University of Chicago

What is the purpose of a college education today? The debate continues. College administrators admit that the focus is on jobs. Jim Clifton, CEO of Gallup, states in *The Coming Jobs War* that having a good job is the No. 1 social value for everyone. It outranks having a family, peace, freedom, religion and democracy and numerous other societal goods, he says. In a 2012 cover story, "Is College a Lousy Investment?," Megan McArdle of *Newsweek* criticizes higher education. "Promotional literature for colleges and student loans often speaks of debt as an 'investment in yourself,'" she writes. "But an investment is supposed to generate income to pay off the loans." Marketing consultant Benjamin Edwards points to lifelong learning, mentorship, and the ability to think in multiple ways as the outcomes that students and parents are looking for. And young persons—what do you think? In a nationwide survey conducted by the University of California, Los Angeles (UCLA), 88 percent of more than 122,000 students said that getting a job was a "very important" reason to attend college. It was the highest percentage in the history of the survey and was the first time that students placed career prospects ahead of gaining a general education and appreciation for ideas. Look in the glass. Then decide for yourself.

Here is fee. Get me degree. And job too.

Securing a good job is a powerful motivator to get a formal education and a 2011 poll found nine-in-ten students expect to find a job in their field. Their ultimate goal is not being a "learned" person but merely acquiring a piece of paper to get a job. And they are often quite confident on this point, believing that with a four-year degree they will have a nice, professional job by the time they are 30 years old *(optimism-1 trap)*. Many students suffer from the delusion that they are entitled to a job because they paid their tuition year after year. They expect to leave school, be immediately recognized as a person of genius, and by their sixth month on the job start to climb the corporate ladder *(superiority-1 trap)*.

Unfortunately their expected leap from the classroom to the executive suite was interrupted by the economy, which hit young persons especially hard. In 2010, 32 percent of college- and university-educated young persons were working in low-skill jobs. By 2012, a weak labor market left half of all young college grads either jobless or underemployed in positions that don't fully utilize their skills and knowledge. Labor economist Andrew Sum describes the lack of job growth in professional fields as creating a vicious cycle for young adults. "Every job they take, they take away from the group beneath them," he says. "It's a depression for young people; it's the only way to describe it." Many students decide to attend graduate or professional school after college because an undergraduate degree might not be enough to get them a job. Staying in school buys time for the economy to improve and defers repayment of student loans, but adds living costs and debt.

> *And I'd like to believe what a professor recently told me, as I sat in his office appealing for more financial aid: My master's degree will ensure that I'll get a well-paying job and my loans will pay for themselves. But that's not looking likely, especially in my chosen field. There's no certainty that I or my classmates will get jobs, especially well-paying ones.*
> ~ Emily Hutchins, journalist

> *Why now that I've my degree where is my most excellent paying job and cushy lifestyle? The utopia your school promised you is a lie. Work and life are hard.*
> ~ SnottyNoseBratt, Internet blogger

In the end, your degree will give you a better probability of getting a higher paying job if your field of study is in demand. But do not expect that it entitles you to a job—the purpose of college is not to raise mean salaries among its graduates. It is to teach you how to learn, think critically, and make good decisions. This is the difference between becoming educated and simply getting a degree. To paraphrase Albert Jay Nock,[209] a person trained in a job can only do the job for which they are trained; but an educated person can train themselves to do any job. That is the real return on investment (ROI) of any university degree.

> *How smart do you want 'em? just barely smart enough... not smart enough to see, for example, that, just as an education is not a job, educational institutions are not employment agencies... not smart enough to see that jobs are the problem, not the solution.*
> ~ dubet, Internet blogger

Dang! Who ate my job?

Many graduates have difficulty entering the workforce because of a disconnect between the skills they need to be successful at work and what they think they need to be successful. Adecco, a global human resources consulting company, found that 66 percent of hiring managers say they don't think college graduates of the class of 2013 are prepared for the workplace. If you want a job, you need to ascertain the personal attributes, skills, and abilities that employers and customers value and want. With ever fewer entry-level jobs in many industries, internships have become a critical first step into employment.[210] Internships force you to apply relevant knowledge to "real world" situations, understand the pressure of aggressive deadlines, and fail

209 Albert J. Nock (1870–1945) was an influential United States libertarian author and social critic.

210 A Monster survey of 3,400 persons revealed that 87 percent of students expect to fulfill at least one internship during college.

under controlled conditions. They provide opportunities to interact at a professional level, where reality is often different from the promise and mystique in the classroom. Companies often use internships to test potential recruits.

BRAIN SNACK: *Organizations in the U.S. save $2 billion a year by not paying interns a minimum wage, writes Ross Perlin in* Intern Nation: How to Earn Nothing and Learn Little in the Brave New Economy. *Perlin, an intern activist, views internships among college kids, jobless grads, and high schoolers as not only absurd but legally questionable. Interns often fill roles once held by full-time employees and Perlin estimates that one-third to one-half of all internships at for-profit companies are unpaid. Worse yet, some employers require not only that their charges work for free, but that they also obtain academic credit. This usually means paying tuition fees to work. "Young people and their parents are subsidizing labor for Fortune 500 companies in their highly competitive race to the bottom of the corporate ladder and nobody's paying attention," he says.*[211]

Schools also tout job placement rates as a selling point to attract new students. But learning institutions are unique and information is not always comparable. Placement rates vary because of differences in location and local economic conditions, student characteristics, abilities and preparation, variety and quality of academic programs, and missions of the institutions and their career services offices. Some schools, particularly for-profit career-colleges (if you watch late night TV, you've seen their ads), were found to have systematically overstated job placement rates, in some cases claiming as high as 97 percent. Does a paralegal job count for a law school graduate? Does working as a Starbucks barista count for a culinary institute Chef? Some former students are successfully suing for-profit schools to get their money back, saying they were misled about their job prospects after graduation. New regulations issued by the U.S. Department of Education aim to fix abuses and address whether students actually improve their earning potential upon graduation.

Reali-tude:
Payment of tuition does not guarantee you a job.

☞ *Lifebomb #5: "Daddy wants me to be a lawyer (doctor)."*

Harvard's 2011 *Pathways to Prosperity* project found that nearly every parent surveyed (94 percent) expects their child to attend college. According to economist Alison Wolf, young persons are optimistic about their abilities and they, and their parents, want to keep the option of high future salaries open as long as possible.

---

211 This trend has not gone unnoticed by regulators. In 2010, the Labor Department notified employers that internships in the for-profit private sector will most often be viewed as "employment" unless they meet a six-factor test. In 2013, the U.S. District Court for the Southern District of New York found some internships to be illegal, raising the possibility that unpaid internships may become a high-liability for employers.

The problem is parents don't know a Ph.D. from an STD, but want nothing but the best for their child. Students get pumped with aspirations of high pay; they do not see a doctor or lawyer as a means to help others or improve the world. Instead, they see big $$$ associated with the title, and this can set off intense fulminations. "The parents are hideous" say former admissions counselors Dick Teresi and Janet Macfadyen. "They're worse. They're hysterical." Complains frustrated dad Howard Smiley, "The pressure, it comes from parents, it comes from peers, where the kids almost have to say, 'I'm applying to Harvard.' A lot of kids, I think they'd be happy in another environment *(framing-1 trap)*."

First, kill all the lawyers

Young lawyers in their third to fifth year in the business are walking away from their $200,000-a-year positions in record numbers—at times without another job in view—says attorney Anna Ivey, author of *The Ivey Guide to Law School Admissions.* The reason? They are unhappy with their Blackberry lifestyle, being tethered to the job 24/7, and having to rush back to the office at a moment's notice when e-mail orders pop up on the ubiquitous PDA. According to a survey by the National Association of Law Placement (NALP), over a third of associates leave large firms within the first three years. And close to four-fifths bail before they come up for partner and get the big bucks.

Ivey relates that the worst partners view the dramatic drop-off as part of the "testing" of associates. "By their logic, if you can survive the years of misery when 8 out of 10 of your friends are fleeing like the building is on fire, then you are the sort of person fit for partnership at the firm," she opines. The overworked newbie lawyer mutters, "I will never treat people this way when I'm in charge." Later, when that person controls the work assignments, he has already suffered through a divorce, a receding hairline, and an ulcer. So what does he do? He screws them, just like he got screwed *(self-control-2 trap)*.

"Many applicants have no idea what law school is like, what legal practice is like, whether it's something they'll enjoy, whether Big Law is a good move for them, or what they want to do after their time 'inside'" relates Ivey. "Yet thousands and thousands of young persons go jumping on that very expensive, very time-consuming bandwagon year after year, usually because they lack the courage, are too lazy to think hard about other options, or are being pushed into it by their parents," she says.

Attorney Susan Estrich counsels, "If the primary reason you're applying to law school is because you want one of those big bucks jobs, forget it. A few years ago, law used to be a sure shot to making a very, very good income. Not anymore." The national median starting salary for the Class of 2011 was $63,000, which means half accepted jobs paying less. Barely half of those who graduated from law school that year found full-time jobs as lawyers within nine months of graduation. And they are doing so with a huge debt—an average of $125,000 for graduates of private schools.

Nowadays, students are doing the math. As of January, 2013, applications for law school dropped by more than 20 percent from the same time the previous year, and 38 percent from the year before. Students are realizing that it makes no sense to pile up hundreds of thousands of dollars in debt in order to join the legion of unemployed lawyers.[212] "But hustlers can still hit pay dirt," says law firm hiring partner Mark Greiner. For top graduates, the profession is still "an embarrassment of riches," but he adds that just a notch below them, "even good students are having a tough time."[213]

Is there a doctor in the house?

If not the law, howza 'bout medicine? They make big bucks and few professions can match the satisfaction that comes from a career spent saving and improving lives. Fortuitously, opportunity knocks! A 2012 study published in *The Annals of Family Medicine* pegs today's deficit at 52,000 primary care doctors. Within the next 15 years, the United States will experience a shortage of between 90,000 to 200,000 physicians, predicts Phillip Miller, an author of *Will the Last Physician in America Please Turn off the Lights*.

Why is this? One reason is doctors are overloaded. Currently the average physician is responsible for 2,300 patients, more than twice the recommended number. Another reason is the impending doctor shortage due to growth in the aging population. Hear that rumble in the distance? That is the Baby Boomers—your dads and moms—who are now retiring at the rate of 10,000 *per day*. The avalanche was triggered on January 1st, 2011 when the first Baby Boomers turned 65. And millions upon millions of 'em have been promised that the rest of you will take care of their medical needs. Treating these aging gods/goddesses will take an army of new doctors. But wait—doctors are growing old too, with about a third of them set to reach retirement age in the next 10 years. Holy scalpel Batman!

Pardon the pun future podiatrists, but something smelly is afoot. For many sawbones, the real rewards of medicine are harder and harder to come by. They are eaten away by resentful nurses, suspicious and hostile patients, administrators pushing 10 minute office visits, insurance company drones second-guessing their medical judgment and paying 20 percent of billed fees at 180 days, the increasing cost of medical malpractice coverage, and mountains of CYA paperwork. As one exasperated doctor sighed, "We are no longer treated like a profession; we are a public utility to be regulated."

As if a decade of long, arduous training wasn't enough, you still have to pay for it. These days the average medical school debt, according to the Association of

212 Although many Americans feel they are "over-lawyered," economist Clifford Winston says the number of lawyers has been kept artificially low for decades. The shortage is due to most states requiring that you graduate from law school and pass the bar exam to practice law. Also, only lawyers are allowed to manage or invest in law firms. These constraints are reckoned to have boosted the total amount spent on lawyers by more than a third.

213 From 1978 to 2003 the legal business grew four times faster than the economy. Then, in 2009 and 2010, the 250 biggest firms shed more than 9,500 lawyers, nearly 8 percent of the total. Why the spasm? Clients are more cost-conscious, work is being outsourced overseas, and software performs the search and discovery tasks electronically. Ultimately, lawyering is becoming more of a business than a profession.

American Medical Colleges, is $156,456. At 2.8 percent interest, this saddles you with an estimated monthly payment of about $1,800 at the end of residency. No wonder a survey found 57 percent of 1,175 doctors questioned would not recommend the field to their children.

Like Mary Poppins, the weather vane is shifting. Unlike their dollar-dazed parents, many of today's students aren't blindly pursuing the highest paying careers. "I think students today gravitate toward majors they think will be personally satisfying," relates undergraduate programs director Tom Dalton. Katharine Brooks, author of *You Majored in What? Mapping your Path from Chaos to Career*, agrees. "You have to evaluate your strengths and where you excel," she advises. "It is most important to study what you are interested in, because then you will perform better and be more engaged."

Reali-tude:
Follow your heart, not the money.

☞ *Lifebomb #6: "Tell me I'm wonderful and give me an 'A'."*

Sixty-six percent of students agreed with this statement: "If I have explained to my professor that I am trying hard I think he/she should give me some consideration with respect to my course grade." Earth to student! If hard work alone is what gets rewarded, sharecroppers would all be rich.

Concern about getting an "A" and graduating with their degree on time have made students less concerned about the value of the education they are receiving and more worried if their transcript will look good. According to educator Mark Shapiro, almost 70 percent of freshmen at private universities received "A" averages in high school, as did more than half of the freshmen at public universities. Students believe they are entitled to all those A's despite substandard work *(superiority-1 trap)*, he says, and this has led to an erosion of the value of grades and degrees for the brightest. "'Tell me what I need to know to get an A in this class' has become a familiar refrain," Shapiro laments.

BRAIN SNACK: *Judging by their SAT scores, the kids are smarter than ever. Not. Actually, they are dumber say college admissions counselors Dick Teresi and Janet Macfadyen.*[214] *In 1995, as scores were dropping, the College Board "re-centered" the scoring. This is a euphemism for giving every kid who takes the test an extra 100 points, spread out over the two segments, verbal (add 75 points) and math (add 25 points). Boomers, to see how you would fare in today's market, add 100 points to your SAT totals. The problem with this Lake Wobegon*

---

214 Enhancing SAT scores is now a $100 million business, dominated by two competing companies, Princeton Review and Kaplan. These test-prep services are not cheap. For example, the Princeton Review's "Ultimate Classroom" course costs $1,199 in New York City. A 2009 report by the National Association for College Admission Counseling concludes that these courses have minimal impact in improving SAT scores, about 10–20 points on average in mathematics and 5–10 points in critical reading.

scheme, where the bar is lowered until "average" matches the population in the schools, is it devalues the exceptionally smart kids.

Nowadays, pressure for grade inflation is overwhelming. Professors are faced with teaching 200+ students per class—most of whom are apathetic—that arise from the dead at semester end to "grade-grub" (i.e., whine for a better grade). And if that special snowflake did not receive his or her "A," they throw a hissy-fit in the professor's office. This has generated a fear of negative evaluations in some faculty. Acknowledged one adjunct, "To keep this job, I live and die by student evaluations. I've become an 'edu-tainer'."

Limbo lower now...

"The reason so many students are falling short of their intellectual potential," say psychologists Angela Duckworth and Martin Seligman, "is not inadequate teachers, boring textbooks and large class sizes but their failure to exercise self-discipline." Sociologists Richard Arum and Josipa Roksa concur. In their book, *Academically Adrift: Limited Learning on College Campuses*, they write "It requires academic rigor... you can't just get it through osmosis at these institutions." Sadly, hard work on the part of students is no longer seen as a key factor in academic success, what software architect Mike Arguello labels the "American Idol" problem. "If you've ever seen the reaction of contestants when Simon Cowell tells them they have no talent, they look at him in disbelief," he says.

> *Too many kids are at college wasting their time. With no passion for their subjects, they waltz into class with glazed eyes and dance out with a degree. Most never check out a book from the library. Spark-notes are their best friend. Some of them can not even write at a middle school level, much less a college level. They are not happy with their studies, not happy with the debt they are piling on their heads, but they are happy with the football team and their plans for the weekend.*
> ~ daronmsavor, Internet blogger

"Gen NeXt may be the most academically disengaged college students with all-time low measures for time spent studying and all-time high measures for boredom and tardiness," writes educational consultant Mark L. Taylor. In survey after survey since 2000, college students are alarmingly candid that they are simply not studying very much at all. Labor economists Philip Babcock and Mindy Marks find that "the average student at a four-year college in 1961 studied about 24 hours a week. Today's average student hits the books for just 14 hours." These denizens of AnyU approach college life like a 9 to 5 job. Really darling, why study if you can still get that 4.0 anyway?

And it is not just the students. Educational institutions are doing their part in the race to the bottom. In 2010, Loyola Law School Los Angeles retroactively inflated its grades one step for every letter-based grade recorded since 2004. That brought an A- to an A, and an A to an A+, for example. In recent years at least 10 law schools, including New York University, Georgetown, and Tulane University have deliberately changed their grading systems to make them more lenient. Retired professor Stuart Rojstaczer, who has written extensively about grade inflation being a real problem, says these changes can open more job opportunities for students. "There are employers that have GPA cutoffs, and by inflating grades, you increase the number of students who meet those GPA cutoffs," he laments.[215] Of course, it also boosts a school's placement ratings in *U.S. News and World Report.*

Girls rule, boys drool

In a survey of 90,000 students at 530 institutions, male and female students alike agreed that the slackers in their midst were mostly male and that the go-getters were mostly female. "The men don't seem to hustle as much," says one female respondent. "I think it's a male entitlement thing. They think they can sit back and relax and when they graduate, they'll still get a good job *(optimism-1 trap)*." The survey, titled the *National Survey of Student Engagement*, shows that men were significantly more likely than women to say they spent at least 11 hours a week relaxing or socializing, while women were more likely to say they spent at least that much time preparing for class. More men also said they frequently came to class unprepared.[216]

Education professor Linda Sax found similar gender differences in her study of 17,000 men and women at 204 co-ed colleges and universities. She found that men were more likely than women to skip classes, not complete their homework, or turn it in on time *(self-control-1 trap)*. "Women do spend more time studying and their grades are better," says Sax, "but their grades are better even more than the extra studying time would account for." Guys, next time you are in the cafeteria do a 360. Look at the gender mix. You are in the minority.

> *The big thing, for guys, is to give the appearance of not doing much work, trying to excel at sports and shine socially. It's like some cultural A.D.D. for boys, I think—like Bart Simpson. For men, it's just not cool to study. Women see the long-term benefits, they take their classes seriously, and they're actively learning. Guys don't have their life planned for the next 10 minutes. They study enough for a C.*
> ~ student comment on the gender divide

Of course, not all students are slack-butts. As more and more non-traditional students fill course rosters, many attend despite extreme hardship—working, often full-time, young children at home, various partial disabilities, lack of sleep, financial difficulties, and OBTW, the usual panoply of personal problems such as a

215 According to a study published in *Educational Researcher* by Evangeleen Pattison et al., the relationship between earning high grades and doing better after college (landing prestigious jobs and higher salaries) has remained unchanged. Thus, they say that the "value" of grades can be presumed to have held its ground, not eroded by inflation.

216 Today's 25- to 34-year-olds are part of the first generation where women are measurably better educated than men, and this trend is predicted to continue. In 2016–2017, the National Center for Education Statistics projects that women will earn 64 percent of Associate's degrees, 60 percent of Bachelor's degrees, 63 percent of Master's degrees, and 56 percent of Doctorates.

sibling in Afghanistan, a sick parent, or an unplanned pregnancy. These students are professional jugglers who make a Cirque du Soleil show look like a barn dance. You are to be respected and admired—keep it up.

Also, an increasing number of military veterans are showing up in the classroom. With enactment of the *Post-9/11 Veteran Educational Act of 2008* (also known as the Post-9/11 G.I. Bill), many veterans are taking advantage of their education benefits once they complete their service commitment. The American Council on Education predicts that college campuses are on the cusp of having to serve over 2 million contemporary student veterans. Professors regard veterans as model students since they tend to be more pragmatic, mature, and responsible. *TIME Magazine* calls them the "New Greatest Generation."

Reali-tude:
If we are all Super Heroes then no one is super.

The bottom line:

- A college education is what you make of it.
- In the school of hard knocks they give the test first, then the lesson.
- Overall, the bar has been lowered regarding academic rigor.
- Women and veterans are changing the college landscape.

The Reality

Higher education is a uniquely hidebound industry whose economics largely defy rational explanation.
~ Robert Reich, former U.S. Secretary of Labor

Sure, all of us can put a finger on an individual who never went to college but earned more than some of those who did. But like white crocodiles, these are rare exceptions. Although college is not a guaranteed investment, statistically it is the best indicator of your likely level of success. In *Does Education Matter?*, economist Alison Wolf notes that beyond concrete skills, employers use higher education as a proxy, or indicator, of abilities like intelligence, motivation, or the mastery of a particular body of knowledge. Students who are under-skilled and under-educated will have a hard time finding life-sustaining wages and satisfying employment.

Many NeXters not ready for prime time

Send us better prepared students and we'll give you more and better graduates.
~ College admissions director

If you didn't think these students could succeed, why the heck did you admit them?
~ High school principal

"Is our students learning?" George W. Bush once asked, and for millions of freshman students the answer is no. Even if you have a high school diploma, you may not be ready for college.[217] Although not as well known as the SAT, the ACT exams are taken by more than a million high school seniors each year. This exam tests English, math, reading, and science, with an optional writing test. According to ACT's 2008 *College Readiness Report*, almost eight-in-ten U.S. high school graduates that year did not meet readiness benchmark levels for one or more entry-level college courses in mathematics, science, reading, and English.

The reality is worse that you think. A 2013 study by the National Center on Education and the Economy found "disturbingly low standards among community college instructors." The study concludes that these schools likely are reacting to the inadequate academic preparation of incoming students, and the stats are shocking. Four-in-five Oklahoma community college students needed remedial coursework because they were illiterate, innumerate, or both. At Long Beach City College (LBCC), a whopping 95 percent of students needed remedial English and math coursework in 2008, reports *USA TODAY*. Says LBCC President Eloy Oakley, "It's the number one issue to the entire California community college system, easily. I don't believe that the public in general really understands the magnitude of the problem," he warns. "To cope with this reality," says long-time teacher Mark Shapiro, "the textbook writers have been 'dumbing down' their offerings for a number of years." This cheats students.

> *We're moving into a more demanding cognitive age. In order to thrive, people are compelled to become better at absorbing, processing, and combining information. Information can now travel 15,000 miles in an instant. But the most important part of information's journey is the last few inches—the space between a person's eyes or ears and the various regions of the brain. Does the individual have the capacity to understand the information? Does he or she have the training to exploit it?*
>
> ~ David Brooks, from *The Social Animal*

Nor are math and English the only areas of weakness. Political scientist Jon Miller found that only 20 to 25 percent of Americans are "scientifically savvy and alert," reports science writer Cornelia Dean. Most of the rest "don't have a clue." At a time when science permeates debates on everything from global warming to stem cell research, people's inability to understand basic scientific concepts undermines their ability to make sense of issues like acid rain, nuclear power,

217 Public education K-12 students are "ill prepared to compete with their global peers" concludes the Independent Task Force on U.S. Education Reform and National Security (2012), chaired by Joel Klein, former head of New York City public schools and Condoleezza Rice, former U.S. Secretary of State. As of 2010, U.S. students rank 14th in reading, 25th in math, and 17th in science compared to students in other industrialized countries, putting the country's "future economic prosperity, global position, and physical safety at risk." Warns Microsoft Chairman Bill Gates: "When I compare our high schools to what I see when I'm traveling abroad, I'm terrified for our workforce of tomorrow. Our high schools, even when they're working exactly as designed, cannot teach our kids what they need to know today."

infectious diseases, and the like. "If you don't know a little science it is hard to follow these debates," says Miller."

The squeeze is on

Without a job, it makes good sense to go back to school and learn some new skills for when the economy picks up. As a result, in recent years college enrollment rates have been at an all-time high. According to a Pew Research Center analysis, 40 percent of all young adults ages 18 to 24 were enrolled in either a two- or four-year college in 2008, with the biggest surge taking place at the community colleges.[218] The downside is the number of new jobs requiring a college degree is now less than the number of young adults graduating from universities, so more and more graduates are filling jobs for which they are academically overqualified. Just as too many people stand up at concerts, too many students are going to college. "Employers seeing a surplus of college graduates and looking to fill jobs are just tacking on that requirement" says economist Richard Vedder who heads the Center for College Affordability and Productivity. "De facto, a college degree becomes a job requirement for becoming a bartender."

More applicants means revved up competition. In 2010, college applicants faced one of the toughest years ever to gain admission to the nation's public colleges and universities. Why has the race to get in become so competitive? Here are some reasons:

- *Schools have become picky*. In 2007, UCLA turned down 38,000 applicants. Ohio State rejected 44 percent of its applicants. At top schools, a perfect 4.0 GPA or even a perfect SAT score no longer guarantees admission. Princeton turned down more than 4,200 kids with 4.0's.
- *Tight money*. With deep budget cuts and endowment losses, some schools are shunning students like they had the plague. For example, California State University, a public university system with 23 campuses, reduced enrollment by 20,000 students in 2011. Why? Because it lost $564 million, about 20 percent of its state funding.
- *Blame the Boomers*. Their kids number 800,000 more high school graduates than a decade ago, and the applicants are more talented. Students now apply to as many as 15 colleges, adding to the competition for a limited number of slots.
- *Fewer dropouts*. The share of young adults who are high school dropouts is at a record low—9 percent in 2008, less than half the 20 percent in 1967. More students finishing high school means more are eligible to go to college.
- *Invasive species*. Some cash-strapped schools are admitting more out-of-state students since they pay higher fees. They crowd out seats for in-state students.[219]

218 Community colleges are home to about 40 percent of college students.

219 Some schools are bucking the trend. In North Dakota, colleges hope to draw in young adults by charging low tuition and fees. It's part of a broader trend in which many slow-growing rural states are extending tuition breaks to out-of-state residents who typically are charged more.

In their book *The Shape of the River*, William G. Bowen and Derek Bok, former presidents of Princeton and Harvard respectively, argue that this may be a perceptual problem. "College per se is not all that hard to get into," they write. "Many people are unaware of how few colleges and universities have enough applicants to be able to pick and choose among them. Only 20 to 30 percent of all four-year colleges and universities attract enough applicants to be able to discriminate." And demographics appear to be accelerating this trend. The annual number of high school graduates in the U.S. peaked at 3.4 million in 2010–2011, after a 15-year climb. As this number declines, most universities expect this to translate into fewer applications and less selectivity for acceptance. "For the high school graduate, this becomes a buyers' market," says Daniel M. Fogel, president of the University of Vermont. Nevertheless, the struggle to win entry to the most prestigious universities is likely to continue. "The ones that have the strongest brand identification are still going to be awash in applications, but 99 percent of us are going to see declines," predicts Robert J. Massa, vice president for enrollment at Dickinson College. At private schools, the squeeze has already begun.

Cost of college: To infinity... and beyond!

> *Universities share one characteristic with compulsive gamblers and exiled royalty: there is never enough money to satisfy their desires.*
> ~ Derek Bok, former president, Harvard University

> *This is a bit hard on compulsive gamblers and exiled royals.*
> ~ The Economist

For decades, college fees have risen faster than middle class families' ability to pay them.[220] Tuition increases have exceeded the inflation rate for over 20 consecutive years, including years of large increases in state and federal funding. "There is no law of gravity in higher education pricing," points out Kevin Carey of Education Sector, a think-tank. "What goes up never comes down." Since 1985, college and university tuition and fees have been rising some three times faster than median family income (adjusted for inflation). Costs are up a whopping 538 percent, concludes a 2013 Bloomberg Report. Medical inflation (286 percent) and consumer price index (121 percent) look modest by comparison.

Attention school shoppers! At in-state four-year public institutions, the average tuition for 2010-2011 rose 7.9 percent to $7,605 according to the 2010 College Board's annual *Trends in College Pricing* report. At private colleges a year of coursework rose an average of 4.5 percent to $27,293.[221] How about 2011–2012?

220 According to *Forbes*, a decade ago a year of college cost 18 percent of a typical family's annual income. It has now hit 25 percent and rising.

221 Keep in mind that "average" figures hide wide variations. Public college students in California, Florida, New York, and Washington have seen double-digit percentage increases, while in 2009 the University of Maryland used federal stimulus funds to freeze tuition. At UCLA, a public school, out-of-state students now fork over $50,000/year. That's a whole lotta cheddah, Chestah.

Tuition rose an additional 8.3 percent and 4.5 percent respectively. In comparison, the overall inflation rate was a mere 1.6 percent in 2010 and 3.2 percent in 2011. In addition to spiraling tuition costs and fees, don't forget to throw in as much as $8,000 on housing, $1,100 smackers for books and supplies, and an additional $3,000 on transportation and other living costs per year. This is horrible news for middle class students who pay full price.

"Romeo, Romeo. Wherefore hath my hard earned dough gone, Romeo?" Um, to most everything but teaching. Economists Ronald G. Ehrenberg (*Tuition Rising: Why College Costs So Much*) and Richard Vedder (*Going Broke by Degree: Why college costs too much respectively*) examined the factors influencing the spiraling costs of college. Root causes they point out include increased compensation for faculty, vastly expanded non-instructional staff, and building luxurious country club-like facilities and research labs in order to attract the best and brightest students. "None of these factors contributes to a higher quality education" says educator L. Troy Niskey, author of *The Critical State of College Access and Affordability in the United States*. Here is some of what your hard earned dough is paying for:

- *Lecturing on the cheap*. The average pay for full professors rose to $108,749 in 2008—09 but since they are rewarded almost entirely for research, little of that money goes toward teaching. Sociologist Andrew Hacker and journalist Claudia Dreifus found that "the bulk of the undergraduate teaching at our nation's colleges and universities is performed by part-timers." Gen NeXt observer Anya Kamenetz adds, "Over half of the classroom time at major universities is now logged by... graduate teaching assistants—known as TAs—and adjuncts. At community colleges, part-timers make up 60 percent of the faculties." Why? These teachers cost about 25 percent of a tenured professor.
- *Administrative bloat*. Staffed by casts of thousands, universities have vastly expanded the resources devoted to administration. Social critic Michael Barone notes that from 1975 to 2008, the number of faculty in the California State University system rose by 3 percent, to 12,019 positions. In that time the number of administrators rose 221 percent, to 12,183. "That's right folks; there are more administrators than teachers at Cal State now," laments Barone.
- *Academic excess*. At the top, 36 college presidents received more than $1 million in pay and benefits in 2010, reports a Chronicle of Higher Education survey. But that's not all. A 2011 report titled *Academic Excess* points out that Harvard University alone had 11 employees in excess of $1 million in pay and benefits. In 2010–2011, Shirley Ann Jackson of Rensselaer Polytechnic Institute took top honors at $2.3 million in total compensation. Graham Spanier, the former head of Pennsylvania State University who lost his job amid a sex abuse scandal, cashed out with $2.9 million for 2011–2012.
- *Facilities*. Trade publication *College Planning & Management* shows many campuses are investing in an "arms race" of student amenities to attract students and their parents. Author Greg Beato takes them to task: "Cornell brags about its remarkable 4,800-square-foot climbing wall as the largest indoor natural rock climbing wall in North America. Rutgers, Carnegie Mellon, and many other

universities have all invested in eSuds, an innovative on-line laundry system that allows students to see if their socks are dry without leaving their dorm room. And a legendary Jacuzzi at Washington State University reportedly has room for 53 students." Schools are also investing heavily in new lab space to draw star scientists and research-grant money, but these are mostly for the benefit of faculty members and their graduate students, not for undergraduates.

- *Books (how quaint).* Book editions often come bundled with workbooks, study guides, and CD-ROMs, which sometimes are of questionable value to the student. These "special" editions and supplements often prevent students from buying used textbooks, and force them to pay double or even triple the price of the used book. Since the publisher and authors do not earn any money from the sale of used books, firms raise book prices and produce new editions of standard texts at a rapid rate to compensate.

The effect of rising costs is forcing students to shift to second and third choices. "There are more students who will end up at two-year institutions, not because it's the best fit for them, but because it's all they can afford," says Faith Sandler, executive director of the Scholarship Foundation of St. Louis. "Some may end up skipping college altogether." For those who stay the course, it's creating a mass of young persons sagging under monstrous debt burdens. "They are unable to buy a house, much less start a business. If failure to pay back student loans ruins their credit rating, they can't borrow anything," warns journalist Froma Harrop.

Reali-tude:
If you think education is expensive, try ignorance.

The bottom line:

- Many young persons are not academically prepared for college.
- Since 1982, the cost of attending college has risen 3X faster than average family income.
- More than half of all students don't end up in a career directly related to their major.
- Employers are looking for experience as well as education.

Paying the piper

Trends in College Pricing, published annually since 1998 by the College Board, describes the increases in published college prices and how much students actually pay after considering increases in available grant aid. Their survey of about 3,500 postsecondary institutions across the country determines two prices:

1. *Published price.* About one-third of full-time students pay the full published tuition price with no grant assistance, although some may receive federal tax credits and deductions. In thinking about what is required to pay for college, it is critical to consider the total price for all years of study. Many students require

more than two years of study to earn an associate degree or more than four years of study to earn a bachelor's degree. The largest component of the cost may be the loss of income from not working in their field while they go to school.

2. *Net price.* Although it is generally the published prices that make headlines, it is the net prices paid by individual students that matter most for college access and affordability. Net price is the average price paid by all full-time students, including those who do and do not receive student aid, after subtracting grant aid from all sources in addition to federal tax credits and deductions. And some of the most elite institutions often have the most generous financial aid programs. Think of it as the "sticker price" versus the "sales price" on a new car.

Watch out Wanda—even the "average" net price can be misleading. Different students pay different prices within the same institution. For each student who pays $1,000 less due to grant aid, athletic scholarship, etc., another (on average) pays $1,000 more. One of the problems many students face is how to make sense of all the options and complex pricing structures. Thanks to a 2011 federal mandate, colleges are obliged to feature a new tool to help students and families pin down an answer to "How much is a college actually going to cost?" Each school in the U.S. now offers an on-line calculator on their website so you can estimate what you can expect to pay to attend. Enrollment consultant Kathy Kurz cautions that the calculator may not be accurate since it is based on historical rather than current data and because it is driven by averages. An effort by the Education Department to create a standardized "shopping sheet" has had only modest success at clarifying costs.

If you thought your search for a college or university was challenging, sorting through the maze of how you will pay for it can be daunting. The school you select determines how much moolah you will need to go there. This is your *Cost of Attendance* or COA for that school. COA is the sum total of what it costs to attend for one year: tuition and fees, room and board (living expenses), books and supplies, transportation, personal expenses, and possibly some other expenses such as studying abroad.

Now things start to get murky. In an attempt to make college affordable for everyone, financial aid exists to subsidize some or all of a student's out-of-pocket expense. Nearly every student is eligible for some form of financial aid—the question is how much and in what form. All students interested in financial aid for college start by completing the *Free Application for Federal Student Aid* (FAFSA) on-line. Despite the federal pedigree, the FAFSA application is the gateway to be considered for most all student financial aid programs.[222] The form consists of a set of questions regarding a student's (and their family's) assets, income, expenses, their dependency status, and any special circumstances.

These inputs go into a magic formula that produces a number: the *Expected Family Contribution* (EFC). EFC represents the amount that your family can be

222 The federal government is the biggest player in student financial assistance, accounting for some 70 percent of all expenditures on student aid.

reasonably expected, based on its current financial situation, to contribute toward your college costs. If you are low income, the amount your family would be asked to pay may be as little as a few hundred dollars per year. If your family is higher income, or has considerable assets such as a second home or a large investment portfolio, your part of the tab could be upwards of $50,000 per year. Typically, the lower the EFC, the more financial aid you will receive. Subtracting the EFC (what your family will pay) from the COA (the total cost for attending that school) yields your "Need"—the additional amount that you must cough up to go there. For example, if your EFC calculates out at $2,500 and your COA is, say $23,517, your Need (what you owe the school) is $21,017.

Not wanting to pay full boat, we next look for sources of financial aid to fill the Need. First are the goodies, including federal, state, and private scholarships and grants. These are free money and so research them carefully and apply for as many as you can. Many scholarships and grants have qualifications (such as a minimum GPA level or ethnicity) and are generally based on need. Historically, the federal government's principle vehicle for providing college access to low-income students has been the Pell Grant (in 2012, $5,550 per year for 12 semesters max). The new Post-9/11 GI Bill provides education benefits for servicemembers who have served on active duty for 90 or more days since Sept. 10, 2001, including current and previously activated National Guard and Reserve members. The program covers the full cost of in-state tuition and fees at a state school for up to 36 months, a stipend for housing and books, and is transferrable to your spouse and children. If you can handle military service (for full benefits, at least three years), this is a fabulous deal.

BRAIN SNACK: *Expectations can differ sharply from the realities of college athletics. Excluding glamour sports of football and basketball, the average N.C.A.A. athletic scholarship amounts to $8,707; in sports like baseball or track and field, the number is routinely as low as $2,000. And with N.C.A.A. institutions costing $20,000 and $50,000 a year, athletes often come up short. "You know, maybe if you're a scholarship football player at Oklahoma, everything is taken care of for you," says Tim Poydenis, a scholarship baseball player at Villanova. "But most of us are nonrevenue-sport athletes who have to do our own fund-raising just to pay for basics like sweat pants and batting gloves." What families do not know, coaches say, is that there is a lot more money available outside athletics in the form of grants, loans, and other institutional aid. Study after study has shown that almost all college athletics programs lose money—almost 90 percent.*

In addition to government moolah, schools provide what they euphemistically call "institutional aid." These are incentives offered by the school, such as a merit scholarship or transfer grant, to entice you to enroll. The strategy is to give up say $2,500 now, and then bleed you of $40,000 in the long haul. What they fail to mention during the enrollment management process is that a typical "financial aid" package—even for the neediest of students—includes a large loan component in addition to whatever aid the learning institution provides. "Admissions directors do not speak truth" says college counselor Helen Britt. "It is their business to lie."

> *Many colleges have gone 'need blind,' to level the playing field for rich and poor. Not. It's money that matters. Do you really believe that admissions don't know the difference between Brownsville and Bronxville? That they don't know the significance of a 90210 ZIP code? That they can't tell a kid's background from his essay? They know who needs financial aid and who doesn't.*
>
> ~ Dick Teresi and Janet Macfadyen, college admissions counselors

If you are really poor, you can obtain Perkins Loans, federal money that is lent directly by the school. But the lion's share of government money for student loans by far comes from two other programs, the Stafford Loan Program (for students) and the Parent Loan Program for Undergraduate Students or PLUS (for parents). Students who qualify based on need may obtain *subsidized* loans—no payment is made until six months after graduation or six months after ceasing to be at least a half-time student. In the interim, Uncle Sam pays their interest. Need-based students may also qualify for federal-funded work study, typically 15–20 hours per week. Enough for gas, chips, and beer.

The picture is very different if you are not poor. Nearly half of graduates say their parents or other family members are footing some, or all, of the bill. As costs have risen, so too has the amount of money that families with moderate incomes are expected to contribute. A family with an income of $40,000 to $60,000, for example, might be asked to pitch in $6,000 a year. These students must obtain *unsubsidized* loans to fulfill their Need, which means loan payments begin immediately after graduation.

Private loans should be the last option for financing your college expenses. In his *Irreverent Commentary on the State of Education in America Today*, educator Mark Shapiro (a.k.a. "The Irascible Professor") compares the private student loan industry to an octopus. "Its tentacles were designed to squeeze every last dime out of students who have been forced to go into outrageous debt to cover their college costs. Interest rates for non-subsidized student loans were high, and any drop in a person's credit rating following graduation often leads to increases in rates. A missed payment brings late fees and penalties that give usury a bad name. And, regardless of a person's financial misfortunes, bankruptcy cannot be used to discharge these debts," Shapiro says. Surveying college students, Jen Mishory, Deputy Director of the Young Invincibles, finds that "Two-thirds of students did not know the difference between a federal loan and a private loan." Make sure you know before you sign!

Debt slave zombies

> *It's actually worse than a bad mortgage . . . you have to get rid of the future you wanted to pay off all the debt from the fancy school that was supposed to give you that future.*
>
> ~ Peter Thiel, co-founder of PayPal

Attention class! Have you identified the common denominator? If your family is poor, the government will pay for your education. If you are from a wealthy family, your parents will pay (they can afford it). If you are from a middle class family, you will go into hock up to your eyeballs. And this is where the friction occurs.

> *"As a group, these (middle class) students are unable to rely on family income or savings to pay for college, so they shoulder large debt loads. Policy tradeoffs pit low-income students, eligible for grants, against moderate-income students who must rely on loans, leaving both groups scrambling to try to find a way to pay for the college educations they need."*
>
> ~ Elizabeth Warren, consumer advocate, testifying before Congress

Undergraduate college student borrowing has risen dramatically in recent years, with student debt stretching to a record number of households—nearly 1-in-5. A study by the New York Federal Reserve finds that 43 percent of twenty-five-year olds are now carrying student debt, up from 25 percent in 2003. Mark Kantrowitz, publisher of *Finaid.org* and *Fastweb.com*, now estimates total student debt at about $1.2 trillion, more than the nation's total credit-card debt.[223] And the trends are harrowing:

- More college students are borrowing, says the Pew Research Center. On average, about two-thirds of bachelor's degree recipients borrow money.
- College students are borrowing more. Compared to their counterparts in 1996, 2008 graduates who received a bachelor's degree borrowed 50 percent more (in inflation-adjusted dollars); those who earned an associate's degree or undergraduate certificate borrowed more than twice as much.[224]
- According to The Project on Student Debt, 2011 graduates carried an average of $26,600 in debt, the highest level ever.[225]

Of course, this is just one part of the debt story. Students are also carrying credit cards to meet other expenses. In 2008–09, 84 percent of undergraduates had at least one credit card, and half of all college students had four or more cards. The average outstanding balance on a graduate student's credit card is sitting at about $8,000.

Here is the bottom line: a record share of students is leaving college with a substantial debt burden and this has lasting effects. Among those, about half say that paying off that debt made it harder to pay other bills; a quarter say it has made it harder to buy a home; and about a quarter say it has had an impact

223 The mushrooming debt has direct implications for taxpayers, because 8 out of 10 of these loans are government issued or guaranteed. What does that mean? When students default on their loans, Uncle Sugar picks up the tab.

224 Starting with Princeton in 1998, a number of exclusive schools (Harvard, Yale, UPenn, Copper Union, etc.) no longer require undergraduates to take out loans. All you have to do is get in. Princeton received 27,189 applications and accepted only 8.4 percent (2,282) for the Class of 2015. Tuition free does not mean a free experience, however; you'll still need to pay for room, board, and beer.

225 Student debt data are rife with possible inaccuracies and these figures may be low. Surveys are voluntary, almost half of all colleges and universities don't participate at all, and costly for-profit institutions are under-represented. In addition, colleges may not be aware of all of their students' private loans, loans taken out by parents on their children's behalf, or loans from previous schools attended by transfer students. In reality, no one really knows how much, on average, students borrow at every institution to attend college.

on their career choices. In 2012, the average credit score for 30-year old non-borrowers was 24 points above that for student borrowers. Based on data from five of the nation's largest student-loan agencies, the Institute for Higher Education Policy found that only 37 percent of student borrowers who started repaying their loans in 2005 were able to fully pay them back on time. *Young person's alert:* don't default on your student loans. Harsh penalties and few options face borrowers who do.

Reali-tude:
Heavy debt and no degree = disaster.

How do you spell relief? O-B-A-M-A?

Portraying it as a triumph over an "army of lobbyists," Mr. Obama signed legislation to overhaul the federal student loan program on March 29, 2010. During his State of the Union address that year, the President called it "one of the most significant investments in higher education since the G.I. Bill" and set a goal for 60 percent of Americans between the ages of 25 and 34 to have earned college degrees by 2020. "Education is the economic issue of our time," he added, "No one should go broke because they chose to go to college."[226]

Students who qualify will be allowed to cap repayments at 10 percent of income above a basic living allowance. Plus, the plan forgives loans—no matter what the remaining balance—after 5 years for those working in government or not-for-profit jobs. Working at a public school or teaching at a public university would qualify, as would agencies that provide a public service such as libraries, public health, or safety. Those working in the private sector would have their loans forgiven after 10 years.[227] Not everyone agrees, however, including Sallie Mae, one of the nation's largest providers of student loans.[228] In response to the signing of legislation, the corporation laid off 2,500 employees. For students though, it was a godsend. *Young person's alert:* income-based repayment and loan forgiveness is not available for loans taken out by your parents on your behalf or for private loans.

Rise of the non-traditionals

There has been rapid growth in recent years in the for-profit sector of higher education (the industry prefers the term "career colleges" or "proprietary schools"). For-profit higher education, which ranges from beauty schools to institutions that resemble traditional universities, is one of the greatest success stories in American

226 In addition, the legislation increased the number of Pell Grant awards and boosted the amount to $5,550, created the *American Opportunity Tax Credit* (up to $2,500 per year for 4 years to apply against tuition, fees, and textbook expenses), and simplified the student aid application.

227 One snag: when your debt gets forgiven, the IRS will treat the forgiven principle as income and tax you on it.

228 SLM Corporation (commonly known as Sallie Mae) was originally named the Student Loan Marketing Association. The government founded Sallie Mae in 1972 to increase the supply and lower the cost of student loans. Later, Sallie Mae was completely privatized.

business. In the academic year 2008–09, U.S. for-profit colleges enrolled 3.2 million students, 23 percent more than the year before and 59 percent more than in 2004–05.

University of Phoenix is the largest with an enrollment over 450,000 nationwide. Other large for-profit institutions include Devry and Kaplan University. All tolled, in 2008 for-profits enrolled 12 percent of undergrad students and awarded 5 percent of all bachelor's degrees and 17 percent of all associate's degrees. Tuition at for-profits, which averages around $14,000 a year, runs about twice that of in-state tuition at public colleges and substantially more than two-year public colleges, which cost roughly $2,700 a year.

Free-enterprise, for-profit education seems like a good idea... until you find out that these institutions receive up to 90 percent of their revenue not from students, but from federal financial aid in the form of loans, Pell Grants, etc. "For-profit institutions of higher learning have gotten plenty of criticism lately," writes *Forbes* leadership editor Susan Adams. Congressional hearings, lawsuits, and a 2010 critical documentary by PBS *Frontline* exposed numerous abuses. The 2011 report, *Condition of Education*, issued by the Department of Education (DOE) cited some striking statistics:

- On average, for-profit schools spent $2,659 per student on instructional costs compared with $9,418 per student at public universities, and $15,289 per student at private not-for-profit colleges (2008-09).
- Graduation rates for four-year degree programs were markedly lower at for-profit colleges—22 percent compared to 65 percent at private not-for-profit colleges and 55 percent at public schools.[229]
- For almost every field of study at every level, students at private for-profit schools are more likely to borrow, and tend to borrow more than double the amount, than students at public and private not-for-profit schools.
- On average, just 44 percent of students at for-profit schools are able to repay their loans.

The federal government has been investigating. "The for-profit colleges are rife with misleading recruitment practices, they are expensive to attend, they have huge profits, and have atrocious withdrawal rates," railed Senator Tom Harkin, committee Chairman of a Senate inquiry. For some for-profits, the inquiry revealed as little as a third of their revenue goes into education; the rest goes to marketing, corporate compensation, and overhead. Others have extraordinarily high student withdrawal rates—in one case, over 84 percent of students who signed up for an associate's degree program and 63 percent seeking bachelor's degrees dropped out within the first year. As a result of new legislation, new-student enrollments at for-profits plunged in 2011, in some cases by more than 45 percent, writes journalist Melissa Korn of the *Wall Street Journal*.

229 In 2009 University of Phoenix reported that 23 percent of its students completed an associate's degree within three years of enrolling, and for bachelor's degree students, its six-year completion rate was 34 percent.

It's a business predicated on volume, not quality. How many students can you get to sign on the dotted line? It's a debt that takes over their financial life.
~ Vice President, higher education policy

Who referees whether a college is delivering a quality education? Institutions of higher learning have developed independent accreditation organizations to vouch for the quality of the degrees they offer. Accreditation agencies periodically visit universities and colleges and rate them on the quality of their academic programs. Think of accreditation as a sort of third-party "seal of approval" designed to protect consumers and taxpayers from diploma mills. Accreditation is important to colleges because the U.S. Department of Education relies on it to determine which schools receive federal student aid. It is important to students because it signals that the academic training has met certain standards, which helps them transfer credits from one college to another.[230]

University of Phoenix spokesperson Manny Rivera defends the for-profit industry as serving a key role in educating students. For-profits tend to lead in new innovations and improvements, such as flexible schedules and an on-line focus. Students, especially adult learners, can more easily find and tailor programs that fit their needs, he says. Many prefer for-profit schools because their curriculum often provides greater focus on job-specific programs. In addition, for-profit institutions have been more likely to serve lower income, minority, veteran, and first-generation college students. Deflecting criticisms, Rivera points out students participate in entrance loan counseling and "at some point... have got to take responsibility."

Many for-profit schools offer Internet certificates or degrees, and a growing number of elite universities, think-tanks, governments, and international organizations are putting first-rate material online. One college student in 10 already studies exclusively online and 1-in-4 does so at least some of the time. New start-ups such as Udacity, Coursera, and edX offer "massive open on-line courses" or MOOCS, which are delivered at scale[231] (UniversityNow offers a unique "all you can take for $199/month" approach). MOOCS are seen as real-life lectures where the student can pause, rewind (or fast-forward), and learn at her own pace.

Experts differ whether these forces will influence education, for the better or for the worse. "Students who are motivated and have self-discipline can do well in on-line learning" says journalism professor Tony Rogers. These are typically older, more mature students. "But many younger students do not yet have the time-management skills required for completing on-line courses and are not able to prioritize them as they would for regular classes," says computer science major Tara Meikelle, 23. Those who get discouraged or who need supportive feedback may drop out. Other concerns include the ease of cheating and plagiarism,

230 Accreditation is granted for a period of time, for example, 10 years. In a development that has captured the interest of the U.S. Department of Education, a growing number of for-profits have taken a shortcut to regional accreditation by buying an already accredited not-for-profit college.

231 A Udacity course on machine learning, taught by Peter Norvig, Google's Director of Research, attracted 160,000 students.

technological issues (especially important when it comes to deadlines), and the lack of course accreditation.

The stigma associated with taking classes over the Internet may also be a concern for those about to invest significant time and money to advance their careers. Many hiring managers distinguish between on-line certificates and degrees and do not take the latter seriously. Nevertheless, about half of HR professionals that responded to a Society for Human Resource Management survey said on-line degrees are just as credible as traditional degrees. "It may not be as big a concern if your on-line degree is from a traditional college," reports journalist Candice Choi. "This is a highly subjective area and schooling is just one factor that employers look at."

Going for broke?

When it comes to higher education, most Americans say they simply aren't getting enough bang for their buck. In a 2011 Pew research survey of 2,142 Americans, ages 18 and older, a majority of Americans—57 percent—say the higher education system in the United States fails to provide students with good value for the money they and their families spend. An even larger majority—75 percent—says college is too expensive for most Americans to afford and they are losing trust in higher education leadership. Students agree. More first-year college students have concerns about their ability to finance college than at any time since 1971, according to the 2009 *CIRP Freshman Survey*, UCLA's annual survey of the nation's entering students at four-year colleges and universities.

> *"Even with these high prices, you're still finding a high return for individuals who are bright and motivated. On the other hand, if you're not college ready, then the answer is no, it's not worth it."*
>
> ~ James Heckman, Nobel laureate (Economics, 2000)

While college presidents bleat that their institutions need more resources if they are to continue their mission, recent national opinion survey findings suggest that the majority of the public does not buy this argument. In his 2013 *State of the Union* speech, President Obama re-emphasized that colleges were "on notice" to either control rising costs or lose federal money. A substantial minority—four-in-ten—of college presidents now say the system of higher education in this country is headed in the wrong direction.[232] It looks like those at the top are finally getting the message.

Reali-tude:
Make sure your degree is worth the cost.

232 Their loyalty is not to you though. In a 2012 *Inside Higher Education* survey of over one thousand college presidents, more than 80 percent said that potential cuts to federal student aid programs topped their list of concerns.

The bottom line:

- Community colleges offer equivalent quality education at a fraction of the cost.
- Be sure to earn your degree from an established, fully accredited institution.
- Take time to research the right choice when picking a four-year college.
- Non-traditional schools offer accessibility and convenience, but are not for everyone.

Doctor's Prescription (Rx)

In America, people succeed because of the quality of their character, not the fame of their college. What you do in college is a better predictor of future success and happiness than where you go to college.

~ Tina Moncada, educator

Which college is right for me?

The big school: pros

- Wide variety of academic programs and courses;
- Well-resourced libraries, facilities, and well-funded sports programs;
- Variety of housing and social opportunities;
- Distinguished or famous faculty.

The big school: cons

- Larger class sizes;
- Professors focus on research; many courses taught by teaching assistants;
- Students must take the initiative to cut through the "red tape";
- Potential of getting lost in the crowd.

The small school: pros

- Smaller class sizes;
- Professors, not graduate students, teach most courses;
- Advisors know students very well;
- Strong sense of community.

The small school: cons

- Fewer majors to choose from;
- Limited housing and social opportunities;
- Smaller libraries, fewer physical resources;
- Less emphasis on sports programs.

Talking Points

> *If you want to have the skills to build a career, or the resources to raise a family, you need a two-year or four-year degree.*
> ~ Bill Gates, founder of Microsoft

While knowledge and effort do not guarantee success, ignorance and indolent complacency almost always lead to failure. The demand for educated labor is being reconfigured by automation, globalization, and deregulation. Education, hard work, and responsibility are what will give you the best chance to compete.

Reali-tude:
A university degree no longer confers financial security.

Chapter 17 describes some tools to help you acquire wisdom by interviewing others. To benefit from these techniques, you need only have access to a parent, educator, or other trusted adult (tribal elder) and a desire to listen and learn. Based on the ideas in this chapter, here are some starters:

1. "I am trying to improve myself. Today, having a college education is a requirement to secure a good paying job. Reflecting on your experience, or that of someone you know, do you recall a situation where not having a degree significantly hindered (or benefited) their long-term personal well-being?" If they say "Yes" then ask:

    - "Would you tell me the gist about what happened please?"
    - "How did you (they) feel about this at the time?"
    - "What two things did you learn from this that you can share with me?"

2. "I am trying to improve myself. While many young persons aspire to obtain a degree for financial reasons, college also provides non-financial benefits. Reflecting on your experience, or that of someone you know, can you recall some of these benefits and whether they made going to college worth the cost?" If they say "Yes" then ask:

    - "Would you tell me the gist about what happened please?"
    - "How did you (they) feel about this at the time?"
    - "What two things did you learn from this that you can share with me?"

    In either case, if they say "No," simply say "Thank you."

3. Pursuing higher education is an inflection point in a young person's life. Reflecting on your experience, or that of someone you know, what two suggestions would you have for a young person that is contemplating this decision?

4. "I want to make wise life-choices. Reflecting on your experience, would you have two ideas that I can implement to improve my judgment and decision-making skills? Be sure to thank them for their response.

Knowledge Nuggets

> *A university is a series of individual faculty entrepreneurs held together by a common grievance grievance over parking.*
> ~ Clark Kerr, president, University of California

1. *Will higher ed bubble over?* Peter Thiel, co-founder of PayPal, believes that higher education fills all the criteria for a bubble: tuition costs are too high, debt loads are too onerous, and there is mounting evidence that the rewards are over-rated. Says Thiel, "The education bubble whispers a seductive promise: do this and you will be safe—you will always make more money if you are college educated." Thiel offered 20 students $100,000 scholarships to leave school and start a company rather than enter college. Read two views at: http://techcrunch.com/2011/04/10/peter-thiel-were-in-a-bubble-and-its-not-the-internet-its-higher-education and http://techcrunch.com/2011/04/12/friends-don%E2%80%99t-let-friends-take-education-advice-from-peter-thiel.

2. *Up, up, and away!* In the 1930s, the average GPA at U.S. colleges and universities was about 2.35, says grade inflation czar Stuart Rojstaczer. Over the last 50 years, GPAs have increased by roughly 0.1 to 0.2 per decade at four year schools (at community colleges, grades have actually dropped). As a rule of thumb, the average GPA of a school today can be estimated by the rejection percentage of its applicant pool: GPA = 2.8 + Rejection Percentage/200 + 0.2 (if the school is private). Figure yours at: http://www.gradeinflation.com.

3. *Is college worth it?* A sobering report comes from a 2011 Pew Research Center survey of 2,142 adults ages 18 and older and 1,055 college and university presidents. Hard economic times, sharply rising college costs, changing demands on the nation's workforce, rising global competition, and the ambitious goal set by President Obama for the United States to lead the world by 2020 in the share of young adults who have a college degree are influencing the debate about the value and mission of higher education. Attitudes of those at the top versus rank-and-file Americans may surprise you at: http://pewsocialtrends.org/2011/05/15/is-college-worth-it.

4. *Obsessed over rankings? U.S. News and World Report* has published its list of Americas Best Colleges for the past three decades. Contrary to widespread perceptions, the vast majority of students attend college within three hours of home so national rankings have little meaning. A survey of 576 college admissions officers by Inside Higher Education found 91 percent believe other colleges falsely reported standardized test scores and other admissions data,

thus skewing their institution in a favorable light to serve prestige, rank, and status, not educational values. Some highly regarded schools, having been caught, acknowledge having done so. Reduce your obsession at: http://www.uscollegesearch.org/blog/category/industry-news.

5. *Where to go for info?* See Appendix F for additional information relating to this chapter.

Chapter 14

Where You Live

Toto, I've a feeling we are not in Kansas anymore.
~ Dorothy, in *The Wizard of Oz*

The Gist

The Good:

- Cities and regions are competing to attract creative talent
- Finding that special someone is as important to us as what we choose to do

The Bad:

- Living independently is expensive
- Before you move, match your personality to that of the region
- Telecommuting is not a birthright

The Reality:

- Americans are becoming sorted by the kind of work they do
- Creative class jobs are clustering geographically
- Young persons are the most mobile of all age groups
- Many elements of a happy life are in large part determined by where you live

Introduction

> *Never before in the history of the planet have so many people—on their own—had the ability to find so much information about so many things and about so many other people.*
>
> ~ Thomas Friedman, journalist

The 1980 film *The Gods Must Be Crazy* tells of a Kalahari Bushman named Xi who retrieves a Coca-Cola bottle that had been tossed from an airplane. Xi's band of Bushmen had no knowledge of the world beyond and possession of the bottle exposes them to a hitherto unknown phenomenon: property. They soon found themselves experiencing things they never had before—jealousy, envy, anger, hatred, even violence. Xi thinks the Coke bottle has evil powers so he decides to travel to the "edge of the world" to dispose of it. He eventually finds himself at the top of a cliff with a solid layer of low-lying clouds obscuring the landscape below. Convinced that he has reached the edge, he throws the bottle off the cliff. Mission complete, Xi returns to his band and receives a warm welcome.

The belief that the Earth has an edge was typical of ancient cosmologies.[233] Early Egyptians and Mesopotamians conceived of the world as a flat disk floating in the ocean. Northeastern Native Americans shared a legend that the world was an island on the back of a giant sea turtle. But Greek-geek Aristotle had a more scientific eye. He noted that travelers going south see southern constellations rise higher above the horizon. He also knew that sailors see lights from greater distances at sea if their sources are elevated. And during lunar eclipses, he observed that the border of the shadow of Earth on the Moon is always circular no matter how high the Moon is over the horizon. Through observational evidence and inductive reasoning, he discarded the flat-Earth model as so much hokus-pokus.[234]

Today, virtually no one believes that the Earth is physically flat.[235] But the world in which we live and work has become "virtually flat" says Pulitzer Prize winning journalist Thomas L. Friedman. The title of his book, *The World*

---

233 A cosmology is a field of study that brings together the natural sciences, especially astronomy and physics, in an effort to understand the physical universe as a unified whole.

234 Deductive reasoning can be described as reasoning of the form "If A then B." It starts out with a general statement ("If the dog is hungry"), followed by a possibile outcome ("then he will salivate"). The scientific method uses deduction to test hypotheses and theories. Inductive reasoning is essentially the opposite. It involves trying to create general principles by starting with many specific instances, for example, "That dog has bitten 3 people, so he is not a good pet for children."

235 The notion that people thought the Earth was flat in the time of Columbus is a modern misconception. By the early Middle Ages, it was widespread knowledge throughout Europe that the Earth was indeed a sphere. Islamic astronomers were able to calculate the size of the Earth to within a fraction of one percent.

Is Flat: A Brief History of the Twenty-First Century, is a metaphor for viewing the world as a level playing field in terms of commerce. That is, all competitors have an equal opportunity. In his analysis, Friedman defines ten "flatteners" that have leveled the global playing field. Open sourcing, workflow innovation, Netscape's web browser, and outsourcing are examples of Friedman's flatteners.

Flat-world economists believe that telecommuting, instant messaging, e-mailing, videoconferencing, and offshore outsourcing put all creative individuals, from Boston to Bangladesh, not just on a level playing field but a flattened one. Where you physically are in the world doesn't matter because access to the same tools, technology, and information is the great equalizer. Friedman concludes that it matters less where we live for our economic opportunities than any time in human history. To succeed in the new millennium, he asserts, we must "innovate without having to emigrate." If true, this has major implications for young adults in the work force.

Increasingly complex tasks are being outsourced, and in a flat world any commercial activity that digitizes a part of the value chain will be moved overseas. A 2008 Harvard Business School study found that up to 42 percent of U.S. jobs—more than fifty million of them—are vulnerable to being sent offshore. India offers an illustrative example of this trend. In 2003, some 25,000 U.S. tax returns were done by Indian CPAs making $100 per month. In 2005, this jumped to an estimated 400,000. IBM's head count in India grew by over 1,000 percent from 9,000 in 2003 to nearly 74,000 in 2007, and the company now employs more people there than in the United States. General Electric's health-care arm built a swanky research center in Bangalore, its biggest anywhere in the world. In 2010, Microsoft began outsourcing its general legal work to India. You can even rent-a-tutor in New Delhi to teach math to your bambino in Buffalo. And China? It's on the same trajectory as India.

This flat-world phenomenon has caught many asleep. Described as the greatest reorganization of the world since the Industrial Revolution, it is happening so quickly that many Americans are not yet prepared for what it means for them. "Globalization is changing the United States faster than any other society," observes economist Lester Thurow. But Americans scarcely notice that fact because they have tenaciously held to the belief that the global economy will simply be an enlarged version of the U.S. economy. Although many young persons assume that the United States has an unbeatable edge, our position may be more tenuous than commonly thought.

Others are the fervently "anti-flatulent." Business analysts Ronald Aronica and Mtetwa Ramdoo argue that the world isn't flat—it's networked. "Yes, we are interconnected on a truly astonishing scale" says Lawrence Prusak, former executive director of the Institute for Knowledge Management. "But brute connectivity will not level the playing field, giving that twenty-something in Shanghai the ability to compete head-to-head with anyone, anywhere in the world. For the most part, what we've built is a vast global IT infrastructure that is very good at moving information, but not knowledge, from one place to another." Although the cost of obtaining, storing, and moving information has plummeted, Prusak stresses that "knowledge remains time-consuming and expensive to develop, retain, and transfer."

Global strategist Pankaj Ghemawat sees many indicators of global integration as surprisingly low. In his book *World 3.0*, he writes that only 2 percent of students are at universities outside their home countries and only 3 percent of people live outside their country of birth. Ghemawat argues that we tend to overestimate the extent of globalization and the distance-destroying quality of technology. "The sober view," he chides, "is this is a bunch of globaloney." Urban economist Edward Glaeser, author of *Triumph of the City: How Our Greatest Invention Makes Us Richer, Smarter, Greener, Healthier, and Happier*, agrees. "If the world is so flat," he asks, "then why are cities growing so quickly?"[236] He points out that the striking declines in the costs of shipping goods and communicating knowledge across space should have led to a great dispersal of population. "Yet," he says, "the share of the world living in urbanized areas increased from 41 percent in 1985 to more than 50 percent today." Demographers predict that three-quarters of humanity could be city-dwelling by 2050.

Urban studies expert Richard Florida unabashedly refutes what he calls the "hype" that globalization and telecommuting have flattened the world and made place irrelevant.[237] Relying on 20 years of research, Florida sees place as more important to the global economy and personal happiness than ever before. In his book *Who's Your City?* he asserts that place has a "profound impact on the jobs we have access to, our career path, our social network, and lifestyle choice." "Ultimately," says Florida, where we live "affects the wealth we accumulate, our overall happiness, and is the single most important decision we make."

In a way, they are all right.

Reali-tude:
While you were sleeping, the world has changed.

The Good

Where the boys are . . . someone waits for me.
~ Connie Francis, singer

If geography matters, what is the big attraction to place for young persons? Job growth? Low cost of living? Maybe the culture or sunny weather? Nope. When *Forbes* asked young singles of both genders what matters most in the places they live, the majority of single people surveyed said "The number of other singles." Just behind in importance was "great career prospects" and much further behind

236 Glaeser is no lighweight. Nobel laureate George Akerlof (Economics, 2001) has praised Glaeser as a "genius."

237 Richard Florida of the Martin Prosperity Institute is best known for his work in developing the concept of the "creative class" and its ramifications in urban regeneration. His contribution to the material used in this chapter is substantial and gratefully acknowledged.

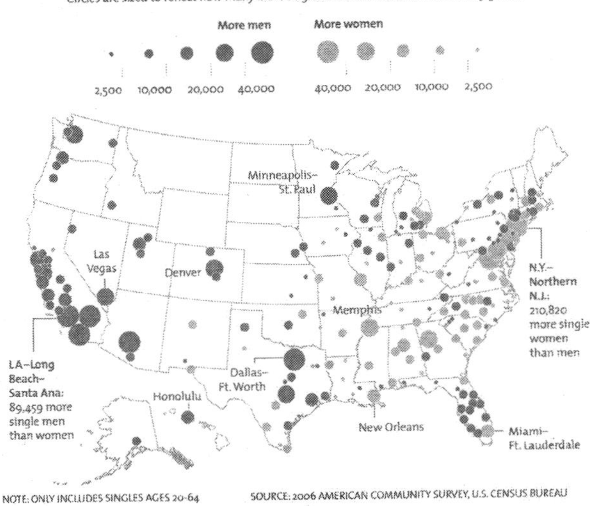

Figure 14.1 Where the singles are.

ranked "wild nightlife" and "low cost of living." Similarly, after interviewing close to 28,000 people over two years, Gallup found the quality that most binds people to place is opportunities for socializing, such as entertainment venues and places to meet. It was the top factor in 21 of 26 communities. This confirms our gut feeling that finding that special someone is as important, if not more important, than what we choose to do for a living.

More than half of all adults are single. In 2008, *The Boston Globe* published a singles map of the United States, inspired by an earlier map published in *National Geographic* (Figure 14.1).[238] What the map suggests is your odds of meeting that special someone appear to vary dramatically across the country. While these "big picture" maps obscure the details, and this can reduce their usefulness, gross trends are still instructional.

Certain locations have far more single people, along with more amenities and activities that bring single people together. And the divergence of personalities in these urban "mating markets" means that any one person will find many more attractive single people than in others. By far the best places for single men, argues Florida in *Who's Your City?*, are the large city areas of the East Coast and Midwest. In greater New York, single women outnumber single men by more than 210,000; in the Philadelphia and Washington, D.C. areas, single women outnumber single men by 50,000. Lookin' for love ladies? Consider heading West or Southwest to trawl for Mr. Right. In metro Los Angeles, for example, there are 90,000 more single men than women. In Phoenix and the San Francisco Bay area, single men outnumber single women by roughly 65,000, and there are considerably more single men than women in San Diego, Dallas, and Seattle too.[239]

238 From: Richard Florida, *Who's Your City?*, New York: Basic Books (2008) and http://www.creative-class.com/_v3/whos_your_city/maps/#The_Singles_Map.

239 An unusually large number of singles of one gender added or subtracted in a particular location can skew the male/female ratio. For example, the high numbers of incarcerated African-American men

Richard Florida fails to take into account the hotness factor. Men move where there are hot women. Women who live on the east coast are not hot, therefore, men move to Southern California to be near hot (though unattainable) women. This leaves the unattractive women to languish on the east coast and men single. Fairly simple explanation really.
~ PM, Internet blogger

As a single female that lives in DC, between the surplus of single females and gay men, I'm doomed.
~ ET, Internet blogger

Where you live can also be a hedge against the downsides of love, though few of us look at a place that way. Let's face it, hearts get broken and relationships flame out all the time. After getting dumped, it is easier to get back on your feet when your location has lots of eligible single people in your age range to date. Perhaps this is so obvious that people overlook it.

More good news: if you have creative talent, cities are competing for you! According to urbanist Jane Jacobs, virtually all economic development since the dawn of time has been generated in cities.[240] If this is true, what gives urbanites the edge over their country cousins? It is the concentration of talent, what economists call *human capital*, explains economist Deirdre McCloskey. "By packing together so many people from different backgrounds, and with a great variety of skills, cities are hothouses for creativity, collaboration, and efficiency. Think of the fusion foods, the cultural inventions, the technological marvels, and the cornucopia of new goods that dynamic cities regularly produce," she says.

But being packed together like hens at the egg farm is not sufficient. "Successful cities must also be diverse" adds McCloskey. Political scientist Scott Page concurs. In his book *The Difference*, he sees diversity not necessarily as ethnicity, race, or religion but "a range of perspectives and skill sets." These intersect to create what he calls "superadditivity"—that is, two plus two equals five. "Your mental garden buds, blooms, and proliferates when cross-pollinated with the many other flowers and fruits crowding the urban jungle," quips *Generation Debt* author Anya Kamenetz. As they say, variety is the spice of life.

BRAIN SNACK: ***City-states are autonomous, self-governing states led by a city.[241] In Medieval Europe, the city-state of Florence was one of the most prosperous and***

in eastern cities like Detroit and Washington, D.C.; gay couples in San Francisco and Minneapolis-St. Paul; older, widowed women in Rust Belt and eastern "Snow Bird" cities like Miami; young men where there is a large military presence as in San Diego; and male immigrant laborers in construction in Sun Belt cities like Phoenix.

240 Jane Jacobs (1916–2006) was an urban writer and activist for over 40 years. Her 1961 treatise, *The Death and Life of Great American Cities*, is arguably the most influential American text about the inner workings and failings of cities.

241 In ancient Greece, city-states numbered in the hundreds. There are very few contemporary city-states: Monaco, Singapore, and Vatican City. (The Vatican, with a population of less than 1,000, is by far the smallest sovereign country in the world.)

respected financial centers. Controlled by the Medici family, Florence established banking houses in important cities such as London, Geneva, and Bruges (Belgium). Its coin, the gold florin, was the standard coinage throughout Europe. The invention of double-entry book-keeping, along with improvements in the management of credit by the Medici Bank, permitted trust and cooperation between strangers. Use of these financial tools expanded world trade and established the framework for modern capitalism. Five centuries later, it was capital markets, rooted in the goldsmiths of Florence, that funded Silicon Valley venture capitalists during the tech boom of the 1980s. From the stockholders of Intel, Google, and Apple, "Grazie Florence!"

For every generation after WWII until now, notes journalist Leigh Gallagher in *The End of the Suburbs*, population flowed from the city to the suburbs. But that tide, which long seemed inexorable, has begun to reverse. Despite the higher financial and stress-related costs of urban life, more than 90 percent of all economic output is produced in metropolitan regions. Why? For every doubling in city size, there's a 14 to 27 percent increase in productivity per worker, making them far more productive than they would be living out in the sticks. Rural America now accounts for just 16 percent of the nation's population, the lowest ever.

Of course this is just dandy so long as growing cities can manage to get the workers they need. But this is becoming a problem. The U.S. is moving from a thirty-year era of rapid labor force growth to a period of much slower growth. As a result, some labor categories may be in short supply over the next two decades and access to talented workers will increasingly be at a premium. Locations with a substantial pool of talented young creative workers, and which are attractive destinations for them to relocate, will do well. Other places will not.

Cities are trying hard to figure out how to attract and root talented young persons. Like the City of London in *Dick Whittington and His Cat*, future-oriented metropolitan areas are tolling their bells to woo Gen NeXters.[242] What's needed to successfully compete for young, creative talent are "constructed amenities" says sociologist Terry Clark. These include a good job market, cultural, social and intellectual institutions (such as restaurants, arts, parks, universities, etc.), appealing aesthetics, safe neighborhoods, and what he calls "pulsating energy." In short, communities are looking to offer a better quality of life. Attention young and restless: one of those great jobs—in a location that rings *your* bell—has your name on it!

Reali-tude:
Place affects all aspects of your life.

242 Sir Richard Whittington (ca. 1354–1423) was a real-life medieval merchant and politician. In the myth, Whittington went to London as a poor country boy to seek his fortune. Failing to succeed, he decided to leave when the bells of the city seemed to say, "Turn again, Whittington, thrice Lord Mayor of London." Returning to London, he became wealthy and was elected Lord Mayor three times. Whittington bequeathed his fortune to form a charity, which nearly 600 years later, continues to assist people in need.

The bottom line:

- Where you live matters.
- Areas with large numbers of singles attract other singles.
- NeXters want to live where they can best "be themselves."
- Urban areas offer the best opportunities for young persons.

The Bad

Love the life you live. Live the life you love.
~ Bob Marley, Jamaican singer-songwriter, musician

The place you live will affect everything from your finances and job options to your friends, your potential mate, and your children's future. Some places offer great career opportunities; others do a better job of providing a high quality of life. No one location offers everything. The key is to decide on a place that fits you—one that makes you happy and enables you to achieve your life-goals. When it comes to choosing where to live, questionable beliefs can trap your thinking and jeopardize your long-term well-being. Learn about some of the lifebombs and you'll stand a better chance of making a smart choice.

Cognitive Flaw: Ignorance

Youth of today are split between two groups: the knowledgeable/arrogant and the optimistic/ignorant.
~ Internet blogger

Clueless about the implications of where you live? Baby Boomers were fledged when they were 18 to 20 years old. In their day, most could not wait to get out of the house. Today, it is not uncommon for parents to carry the freight for their kids for as much as a decade beyond this age. As a result of continued cradling, many young persons underestimate the challenges associated with living independently as well as their ability to afford it *(projection-1 trap)*. Let's look at how failing to be objectively informed when making this important life-choice can put your future happiness at risk.

☞ *Lifebomb #1: "I didn't realize it would cost THAT much!"*

To be truly independent, you need to move out of your parents' house. Many NeXters, saddled with debt to their eyeballs for college, delay their departure because of financial reasons. Some stay because their parents are divorced, widowed, or disabled. "Adhesive" parents actively encourage their kids to remain at home, while others cannot wait to shoehorn the little !@#$! brats out the door. Regardless of exit strategy, young persons will ultimately develop their own life style and yearn for a place of their own. It's nature's way.

***BRAIN SNACK:** How much does it cost to own a dog? More than you think. Veterinarians Race Foster and Marty Smith say that most pet owners calculate the price of the food, add it to the cost of the dog, and figure they can afford it regardless of their budget. In reality, very few people have any idea how much owning a dog really costs and thus grossly underestimate it. Foster and Smith peg the cheapest total lifetime cost of a 14 year old, 50-pound "Heinz-57" mutt in the Midwest at $4,242. If you live in the city, count on little Fifi taking a $12,468 bite out of your purse. And in places like New York, Los Angeles, Miami, and Dallas, it is not uncommon to see some of these doggone numbers double or triple to a high-end lifetime cost of $38,905, they say. Woof!*

Unless you plan to live like Henry David Thoreau or John "Ted" Kaczynski, modern living comes with a hefty price.[243] And not knowing the true costs can get you into trouble. Cost of living includes consolidated expenses for your apartment rent and rental insurance, electricity, cell phone, cable TV, laundry, food and groceries, auto loan, and insurance. Oh, don't forget to budget for entertainment, lifestyle choices, and your good intention to sock away more than the minimum in your 401(k). When faced with these realities, many of you will need to have a roommate in order to make things affordable. *Young person's alert:* a poor choice of roommate is like a bad case of athlete's foot. Once established it is hard to get rid of.

Where you live makes a BIG difference on the bottom line. All states Houdini your wallet—now you see it, now you don't—with varying formulas for taxing income, sales, property, fuel, alcohol, and tobacco. And these differences can be extreme. For example, Ted Taxpayer, who free ranges in the least-taxed state of Wyoming, pays about $7 out of every $100 to the governor. Debbie Deduction, living on the other end of the scale in New Jersey, forks out $12. New Hampshire has high property taxes but no income tax, so you make out nicely if you are a renter. Expecting to win the lottery? You'll keep more of your winnings in Rhode Island, which keeps 22 cents on the dollar than you will in West Virginia, with a 61-cent tax. And so on.[244]

The city where you live also makes a HUGE difference. New York tops the list as the country's most expensive city. The culprit? High rent: $3,400 a month on average for a two-bedroom, unfurnished luxury apartment. In a study conducted by Mercer, a human resources consulting company, New York's housing costs are almost double that of second-place Los Angeles. And it's not just housing costs you have to worry about. In a *Forbes* report, "America's Costliest Cities," grocery items, housing, utilities, transportation, health care, and miscellaneous goods and

243 Thoreau was an American author (1817–1862) best known for his book *Walden*, a reflection upon simple living in natural surroundings. Kaczynski, known as the *Unabomber*, lived in a remote cabin and engaged in a mail bombing spree that killed three people and injured 23 others. He is serving a life sentence without the possibility of parole. Both were highly educated, lived Spartan lifestyles, and hated paying taxes.

244 Under Obamacare, where you live dramatically affects your cost of health insurance. Premiums vary from state-to-state based in part on the number of insurance companies competing in the state and the cost of healthcare services in your area.

services were also considered. According to their analysis, the five costliest cities in the U.S. are (in descending order): New York, San Francisco, San Jose, Los Angeles, and Washington DC.

"Aha, but it's likely that I'll be paid more," you astutely ascertain *(optimism-1 trap)*. Sure, in theory a higher salary in a high-cost city may be expected to provide you with the same quality of life that you could expect in the same position in a less expensive city. Nice try, but no banana Brenda—the increased cost of living often far exceeds those gains due to the effect of taxes and local inflation rate gains. New York is a clear example. To afford a lifestyle that $100,000 can buy you in lower cost cities, says Mercer, you'd need to earn well over $200 grand in the Big Apple. Unless you are a Wall Street magnate-in-the-making, or enjoy sleeping in Central Park, this is a lot to ask for the privilege of a zip code!

Own a vehicle?[245] In urban areas you'll pay higher car insurance premiums. Drive a gas hog? You'll get stiffed at the pump by gas taxes (as of 2010, Alaska was your best bet at 26 cents per gallon; living in California will drain you 65 cents on every gallon). Then there are those pesky metro parking fees you forgot about. The median monthly parking fee in Chicago will set you back more than 3 C-notes per month. New York? Be prepared to cough up almost 600 smackers per month.

Plan to save moolah by commuting from the burbs? Forty-five minutes used to be the threshold that most commuters were willing to drive one way to work. Not any more. The U.S. Census Bureau reports that 11 million people, or just over 8 percent of workers, commute an hour or more to work each way. Amazingly, about 600,000 Americans endure a daily mega-commute of three hours or more each day. The biggest headaches are in San Francisco, Washington D.C., and New York City, where drivers are stuck in traffic over 40 percent of their time on the road. Hapless drivers in Los Angeles win the Oscar for suffering the most—in 2007 the average driver in the City of Angels spent 70 hours inching along streets and freeways. No wonder they answer their email while driving...

Even if we ignore wasted time, commuting may still not be worth it. Analyzing 337 metro areas covering 161,000 neighborhoods and 80 percent of the U.S. population, think tank CNT found that transportation costs can range from 15 to over 28 percent of household income, depending upon where you live. Their overwhelming conclusion: it's cheaper, or just as cheap, to live in cities when transportation is factored in.[246]

Reali-tude:
Living on your own costs more than you think.

245 The Federal Highway Administration reports that, as of 2010, more than a quarter (26 percent) of NeXters age 17 to 32 do not have a driver's license. A Deloitte study found almost half (46 percent) of 18- to 24-year-olds would choose Internet access over owning a car.

246 The closer you are to centers of work or shopping activity, the higher the rent, what economists call *rent gradient*. People are willing to pay more because it cuts down on commuting costs.

☞ *Lifebomb #2: "Location, location, location."*

Few NeXters appreciate how much it matters where we choose to work. Why does it matter? High-paying industries are clustering. According to business strategist Michael Porter, the economic map of the United States has been re-shaped around geographical clusters. Examples include the insurance industry in Hartford, Connecticut; amusements and casinos in Las Vegas; investment banking in New York; entertainment in Los Angeles; biotechnology in San Diego; software in Silicon Valley, Seattle, and Route 128 in Massachusetts; household furniture in High Point, North Carolina; advanced imaging in Rochester; office furniture in Grand Rapids; and golf equipment in Carlsbad, California.

Why do companies agglomerate?[247] Because it's better for business. Close proximity to suppliers, users, and customers creates high levels of productivity, innovation, and efficiency. Economist Benjamin Jones finds that it takes ever more people to produce new research, a trend he attributes to the increasing "burden of knowledge" associated with rising technological complexity. Proximity allows for easier recruitment of skilled labor and rapid exchanges of information through informal channels. These factors are especially beneficial to smaller firms. The economic power that results from these clusters has more than offset mounting pressures for companies to relocate abroad. That is good news for young persons!

Are all jobs clustering? No. Many lower-skill, low-wage, routine service workers such as haircutters, retail salespeople, dental hygienists, home health aides, food service workers, manicurists, landscapers and the like are ubiquitous. Hey, Wal-Mart is Wal-Mart wherever you go. Increasingly, however, young persons who are artistic, scientific, and economically creative are migrating to these specialized innovation areas. Everyone wants to be where everyone is, and it's tough for anyone to go somewhere else, because somewhere else is where people aren't. In other words, birds of a feather flock together. Consider that:

- Three-quarters of our entertainers and performers work in Los Angeles, as do 25 percent of agents.
- Washington D.C. is home to 78 percent of all political scientists, as well as a huge share of economists, mathematicians, and astronomers.
- More than half of all fashion designers work in New York.
- More than a third of all petroleum engineering jobs are in Houston.
- Nearly a third of all gaming supervisors work in Las Vegas.

Where will the hot new jobs be? Estimates of where job growth will occur are difficult to analyze because circumstances may unduly influence a particular region. Government stimulus monies, unemployment rates, proximity to critical

247 The concept of agglomeration was developed by economist Alfred Marshall (1842–1924), who studied the effects that arise from simple *propinquity*, or closeness of firms. Proximity, he said, "creates something in the air" that furthers new ideas. Today's more open trade and improved transport make this less certain, however.

military installations, petroleum and health care prices, or even construction of a large prison nearby are all factors that can skew trends. *Young person's alert:* when you see a jobs rankings list, check the selection criteria carefully. "Good job growth" does not necessarily connote "growth of good jobs."[248]

Rankings by so-called experts vary considerably. For example, job-search site *Juju.com* ranked the best cities to find a job by comparing the number of job seekers to job openings. Their top picks were Washington, D.C., San Jose, New York, Baltimore, and Hartford. *Collegegrad.com* ranked the top cities for jobs according to the number of jobs posted at their site. Their top picks were New York, Houston, Los Angeles, Boston, and Philadelphia. *Forbes* ranked large metropolitan areas based on various growth indicators and trends. Their top picks were Austin, Houston, San Antonio, Ft. Worth, and Dallas. There you have it folks. Three reputable sources, three different prognostications. We report, you decide.

Reali-tude:
Check the selection criteria behind those "Top 10" rankings.

☞ *Lifebomb #3: "When in Rome..."*

Personality captures the characteristic patterns of thoughts, feelings, and behaviors that make a person unique. It is what makes you, YOU! Personality matters because differences between individuals can affect important life outcomes such as academic/occupational success, marital stability, social connectedness, and physical health. Think about your own personality. Do you tend to be reserved and introverted? Or, does gregarious and extroverted better describe you? (For a more objective assessment, ask your Mom or your roommate.)

Decades of research involving hundreds of thousands of individuals have revealed five broad dimensions, or factors of personality. The *Big Five* factors—Openness, Conscientiousness, Extroversion, Agreeableness, and Neuroticism—provide a basic model for describing and measuring personality traits, and is considered the most scientific of the personality tests. Knowing your placement on the five factors can provide useful insights for self-improvement and how well your personality matches that of the place where you live.[249]

Like people, places have distinct personalities. Many people who travel develop an intuitive feel for this. For example, although both are in Texas, Austin has a very different personality than Dallas. Austin

248 Willie Sutton (1901–1980) robbed roughly 100 banks from the late 1920s to his final arrest in 1952. When asked, "Why do you rob banks?" Sutton reportedly said, "Because that's where the money is." (Sutton himself claimed that he never uttered this quote.) Be sure you know where "the money is" before you make your move!

249 Big Five factors vary on a percentage scale. For example, you might be in the 90th percentile for Openness but only in the 50th percentile for Conscientiousness. Professionals tell us factor values tend to remain stable over a 45-year period beginning in young adulthood, which probably explains why Rodger is the same dork at your 20th reunion as he was in senior year. There is evidence that the factors are culturally universal and are, at least in part, genetic in origin.

is weird (and proud of it), while Dallas is more conservative. Ever wonder why New York is full of neurotics and LA attracts laid-back surfer-types? Why no one who lives in Sun City seems to be in a hurry to do anything?[250] Ever reflect on the personality of your own hometown or region?

> *Each city has its own personality, after all. Los Angeles is not Vienna. London is not Moscow. Chicago is not Paris. Each city is a collection of lives and buildings and has its own personality.*
>
> ~ Neil Gaiman, from the *Sandman Series* (1993)

> *Comparing New York and San Francisco... I see San Francisco as being kind of the doped up version of New York, more peaceful and colorful, and without the grown-up quality that New York has... as if SF is New York's little brother. Seattle's kind of the sophisticated older sister, LA is the corrupted cousin that no one talks about... oh i could go on and on.*
>
> ~ Libra, Internet blogger

Analyzing data from over three-quarters of a million on-line surveys, psychologists Jason Rentfrow and Sam Gosling examined the geographic clustering of basic personality traits. In their report, *The New Geography of Personality*, they found that personalities are not randomly distributed but are clustered into distinct geographic patterns. According to their research, residents of the Mid-Atlantic and New England states are "relatively stressed, irritable, and depressed," whereas West Coast residents are more "emotionally stable, relaxed, and calm." Traits associated with intellect, such as creativity, imagination, and openness are higher in the Northeast and West Coast than in the Central and Southern states. "Compared with the rest of the country, residents of the Central and Southern states are more neighborly, friendly, and generous," they found.

Should you base your move solely on these findings? Of course not. But the distribution of personality types does have implications for regional economic development and this can affect you. In conjunction with Rentfrow, urbanist Richard Florida and statistician Kevin Stolarick constructed five personality maps of the United States. For example, people with "neurotic" personality traits—those who are nervous, high-strung, insecure, and prone to worry—are highly concentrated in the Northeastern U.S., particularly around New York City. Secondary neurotic clusters reside in the rust belt sector of the Midwest and in Kansas-Oklahoma. Openness (or open-mindedness) is found most heavily in the Northeast and the West Coast, with pockets in Colorado, Texas, and southern Florida. Figure 14.2 (page 316) shows two examples of these personality maps.[251]

Keep in mind that urban spin-meisters develop clever identities to convince young persons to live and work in their city *(framing-1 trap)*. But branding is not

250 In 1960, Sun City, Arizona was constructed by developer Del Webb as the first planned retirement community.

251 From: Richard Florida, *Who's Your City?*, http://www.creativeclass.com/_v3/whos_your_city/maps/#Personality_Maps.

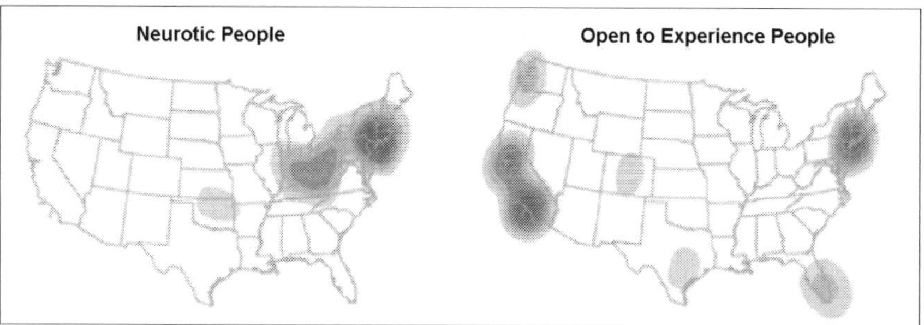

Figure 14.2 Personality Maps.

a universal magic wand. "The brand has to be based on what is already there in a city or else it is just like giving someone a nice haircut," says Marcus Mitchell, a branding strategist. "It might look good for a while, but it doesn't give you a new personality." Individually, each of us needs to look past the haircut. Identify whether the jobs and career prospects that you are interested in are concentrating in particular locations. Then, before you settle on a place, see how its personality matches up with yours and choose the place that best fits you.

Reali-tude:
Places, like people, have personalities.

The bottom line:

- Where you live makes a big difference on the bottom line.
- Areas that pay high salaries often have lower quality of life.
- High paying industries are clustering worldwide.
- People are happier when their personality matches that of the region they live.

Cognitive Flaw: Ineptitude

And I love, love, l-l-love... love those blip-blip-blip-blipverts!
~ Max Headroom, fictional artificial intelligence character

Careless about the implications of where you live? In the early 1990's, a young man from Youngstown, Ohio called the Rush Limbaugh radio show. Youngstown was where his father and grandfather had raised families and where he had hoped to raise his own. Upset that the steel mills had closed years earlier, the young man saw no opportunity for him in his hometown. Limbaugh's advice was simple and direct: "Move!" Today's job hunters are competing in the toughest job market in decades so if you can't find the job you're looking for where you are, maybe it's time to think about moving. Let's look at how failing to think seriously when making this important life-choice can put your future happiness at risk.

☞ *Lifebomb #4: "Like, what's my motivation?"*

When it comes to place, as with most other important things in life, you can't have it all. There are real trade-offs to be made. Young persons who move for their careers give up the joy of being near family and lifelong friends. Those who choose to stay close to family and friends may forego economic opportunity. Wisely picking a location to live requires you to balance many competing factors before making a decision to hit the road or stay rooted. Here are some questionable beliefs to watch out for:

- *Superiority.* Jobs don't just come to you dude. More often, you have to go to the job. Too many young persons resist that truth and instead wait for their dream jobs to fall at their feet like Newton's apple. They treat the idea of living in a certain city or state as an entitlement that they're not willing to surrender *(superiority-1 trap)*. The realities of the labor market usually adjust this attitude fairly quickly.
- *Fear.* According to psychologist Marie-Jeanne Kruger, moving is one of life's most stressful events. "Although a new job and a new home can be exciting," Kruger says, "it can also make us feel unsettled. It takes courage and determination to start from scratch in a new city, moving away from everything that is familiar: your hometown, family, and childhood friends" *(inertia-1 trap)*. Many experience homesickness, alienation, and anxiety, which can lead to another tough choice: whether or not to move back. At a time like this, the support of a tribal elder can be helpful.
- *Escape.* Many of us get restless with our lives and think that a major change, such as a move, will solve whatever situation we might be in. Often we are less concerned about where we are moving to than what we are moving away from *(projection-2 trap)*. If you are unhappy with your current job or relationship, ask yourself if this would be solved by changing employers or simply ending the relationship. If you answer "Yes," most of these changes can be done without packing a single box.
- *Whim.* Numerous studies have found that young people pick where they want to live first and then search for a job in those places. A survey of 4,000 recent college graduates reported in the *Wall Street Journal* found that three-quarters of them identified location as more important than the availability of a job when selecting a place to live. Libido is often the primary focus, not any concern for their future *(self-control-1 trap)*. It is ironic that we spend days trying to find the right apartment to rent or months trying to find the right home to buy, but we often choose where to live on a whim.

It wasn't that I was searching for the right city. I was just looking for something different from what I knew... everything gets so routine. I was doing things I didn't want to do because I didn't have other options. When I moved, it was a fresh start. I could do whatever I wanted.

~ Brian (from *Upload Experience*)

If you have determined your priorities and are honest about the practical aspects and tradeoffs, then you're probably as prepared as you can be to make a final decision. The key to deciding where to live is to reflect on what is most important to you, while being open to new possibilities in your life. Interviewing young persons who took the plunge, authors Alexandra Robbins and Abbey Wilner (*Quarterlife Crisis: The Unique Challenges of Life in Your Twenties*) found that most never regretted moving even though they initially went through some difficult times. They often found other decisions somehow easier to make, perhaps due to a newfound self-confidence that they can do things entirely on their own, after all.

Reali-tude:
Find a place that is the right fit for you.

☞ *Lifebomb #5: "I am connected, therefore I exist."*

Forged by Cyrus the Great, the Persian Empire was the largest geographical empire in ancient times. At the height of its power, Persia spanned three continents: Asia, Africa, and Europe. To facilitate rapid communication across the empire, King Darius I (ca. 500 B.C.E.) built the *Persian Royal Road*. Mounted couriers could travel the road's 1,677 mile (2,699 km) length in only seven days, which in its time, was an incredible technological achievement.[252] The success of the Persian road system inspired construction of *Via Appia* ("The Apian Way") of the Roman Republic, parts of which are still in use today.

Fast forward 2,500 years. Consider the benefits of the telegraph and telephone, the railroad, the automobile, and the airplane. Each invention, it has been argued, has improved communication and eroded the economic significance of physical location. With the rise of the personal computer and the Internet, *The Economist* proclaimed "Death of Distance" on its cover in 1995. Four years later the same publication heralded the "Conquest of Location" as a result of the wireless revolution. Place is no longer relevant it said—"distance will soon be no object."

The great leveler, we've been led to believe, is telecommuting. Also called teleworking, an employee "commutes" by telephone or home computer from an off-site location for part (or all) of the work week. In a report titled *Workshifting Benefits: The Bottom Line* compiled for Citrix Online, telecommuting is a growing trend as companies profit from more productivity, cheaper office costs, less absenteeism, and reduced staff turnover.

Analyses of Best Buy, British Telecom, Dow Chemical, and many other employers have found that teleworkers are 35 to 45 percent more productive. American Express determined that its teleworkers produced 43 percent more than their office-based counterparts.

Workers love it too. They enjoy flexible hours, increased job satisfaction, less commute time, and less out of pocket expense. Figures from Telework Research Network indicate that more than 3 million people, not including the self-employed

---

252 Greek historian Herodotus wrote of the Persian messengers, "Neither snow, nor rain, nor heat, nor darkness of night prevents these couriers from completing their designated stages with utmost speed." His praise was the inspiration for the unofficial motto of the U. S. Postal Service.

or unpaid volunteers, considered home to be their primary place of work in 2011. That is up 73 percent from 1.8 million full-time telecommuters in 2005. An estimated 16 million employees work at home at least one day per month.

But hold the phone Phineas—telecommuting also has drawbacks. Many managers feel that flexible schedule employees are not as productive because they have less oversight. Part of their anxiety is a feeling that they may not be able to reach you when they need to. Indeed, lots of bosses think that if you're not sitting in a cubicle near their office, you are goofing off. It can also paint a bulls-eye on your forehead for layoff—out of sight, out of mind—and that means out of a job. Telecommuters may also generate information security risks because of a need to access corporate networks, systems, and proprietary or customer data from off-site.

There is a cheery optimism among young digerati that teleworking is their birth right *(optimism-1 trap)*. It is not. Social network researcher Duncan Watts and economist Edward Glaeser show that on-line networking tools tend to be complements to—or representations of—your *real-world* network, rather than substitutes for it. Sure, simple tasks with clear instructions and clear outcomes can be worked from afar. But as tasks become more complicated, whether meeting with clients, launching a new product, or conducting a personnel review, face-to-face trumps communicating in bits and bytes. "That's one reason why we still have to congregate in geographically clustered areas," relates Watts. Remote working has also been shown to be ineffective for spreading corporate culture and this has hit home with at least one tech giant. In 2013, Yahoo, Inc. ended its telecommuting program, largely seen as a necessary move to revive the company's struggling fortunes. If you are thinking you deserve to land a job where you can telecommute, here are some reality checks:

- It is extremely rare to find a job that starts out as a telecommuting job. It's much more common to convert an existing job into a telecommuting arrangement by presenting a comprehensive proposal to your supervisor *(superiority-2 trap)*.
- Most telecommuters work from home part-time. Two days per week is the national average among teleworkers, reports the International Telework Association. The rest of the time they work at the company site.
- Working from home is a privilege. As a newbie to the company, you are the last to be considered.

Reali-tude:
The death of distance has been greatly exaggerated.

☞ *Lifebomb #6: "Is geography my health destiny?"*

When you were young, you lived wherever your parents chose to live. You didn't give any thought to whether they had chosen a place that was conducive to your overall wellness. Chances are your parents didn't give it much thought either. Not until recently have people begun to consider that where they live can affect their health. Indeed, where you live could be killing you, according to a four-part PBS series called *Unnatural Causes: Is Inequality Making Us Sick?* Dr. Tony Iton, Alameda County's public health director, reports that this phenomenon has nothing to do with whether you have health insurance or not. Nor is it about individual behavior, such as smoking or drug use. "It goes deeper" says Iton, "to what your neighborhood is like." And some neighborhoods are gawd-awful:

- *Pollution.* The water you drink, the homes we live in, and the cars we drive all have the potential for unhealthy contaminants. The worst is the air we breathe. Some 58 per cent of people in the U.S. live in counties with recorded unhealthy levels of ozone air pollution.[253] If you are black and were born and raised in West Oakland, you are likely to die of diabetes, heart disease, and cancer 15 years sooner than a white person who was born and raised in the Oakland hills. Why? From breathing diesel fumes from the 10,000 trucks that pass through the city on their way to the port each day. The American Lung Association cites California's Los Angeles, Long Beach, Riverside, and Bakersfield-Delano as the most polluted cities in the country (2013).[254]
- *Crime.* Crime is where it finds you, but living in an urban area increases the odds that you will be involved in a violent crime. Some cities are more dangerous than others and young persons need to consider the crime stats before they decide to move *(optimism-2 trap).*

> ***BRAIN SNACK:*** ***In March 2008, Kwame Kilpatrick, 38, was charged with eight felonies, including perjury and obstruction of justice. In August, he violated his bail agreement and was thrown in jail. But Kilpatrick was no average Joe—he was the mayor of Detroit. According to*** **America's Most Dangerous Cities,** ***a list compiled from the FBI's violent crime statistics, the Motor City remains the worst offender. In 2013, it had a staggering rate of 2,137 violent crimes (e.g., murder, non-negligent manslaughter, forcible rape, robbery, aggravated assault) committed per 100,000 people. St. Louis and Oakland, with 1,857 and 1,683 violent crimes per 100,000 people respectively, rounded out the top three most dangerous cities in the country.***

- *Cultural norms.* Widespread acceptance of the abuse of alcohol, tobacco, food, or drugs in a region can be problematic. For example, 2008 data from the Centers for Disease Control and Prevention showed that only one of the nation's 177 metropolitan areas could claim that less than half its population is overweight. That's Boulder, Colorado. Every place else is heavier, and it is getting worse. According to the Trust for America's Health, adult obesity rates have risen in 23 states. In

253 Ozone is the most widespread form of air pollution and is formed when heat and sunshine react with gases emitted from vehicle tailpipes or smokestacks. When inhaled, ozone irritates the lungs causing wheezing, coughing, and asthma attacks.

254 Four cities were cited by the American Lung Association as "cleanest U.S. cities" in 2013: Bismarck, ND; Cape Coral-Fort Myers, FL; Palm Bay-Melbourne-Titusville, FL; and Rapid City, SD.

four southern states, more than 30 percent of adults are medically obese. We are fast becoming a nation of *oblate spheroids*.[255]

- *Other factors*. Are there more liquor stores and fast food restaurants in your neighborhood than in others? Do you have fewer places to enjoy recreational activities? Does your area of town have lower high-school graduation rates? More smoking and higher alcohol consumption? Do you detect a higher level of distrust among residents? These conditions signal u-n-h-e-a-l-t-h-y neighborhoods!

Finally, the accumulation of common but persistent stresses from daily frustrations adversely affects our physical and mental health. And where we choose to live can create a lot of them. Today's technology affords us the ability to communicate with each other from anywhere, at any time in a matter of seconds. Yet, in a crowded city environment we wait a half hour for an open table at a restaurant. Need the ATM? Get in line bubba. Movie? Sorry, it's sold out. A visit to the doctor's office can find us in a waiting room full of germs for hours. To reach a destination only ten miles away, we spend a full hour in heavy traffic.

This crowding brings out the worst in us. Those who are not stress resilient often find themselves becoming impatient, selfish, and callous. In his book, *Designing Healthy Communities*, medical doctor Richard Jackson highlights that where we live makes a difference in our well-being. "Where we live affects how we live," he says, and "young people are very worried about the world we are handing them."

Reali-tude:
You are where you live.

The bottom line:

- Don't be afraid to move where the opportunities are.
- Balance competing factors before deciding which city is the best fit.
- There is much more to telecommuting than just being connected.
- Where you choose to live can have adverse long-term health effects.

The Reality

Location still matters. The more things are mobile, the more decisive location becomes.

~ Michael Porter, competitive strategy expert

Where we live affects how we grow up, how we spend our free time, the educational opportunities available to us, and the people we meet. Knowing about the mega-trends regarding place can help you find a location that makes you happy

255 A spherical-shape, wider than it is tall (think of the Captain's physique in *WALL-E*, © 2008, Walt Disney/Pixar).

and motivates you to pursue your life goals. Stay rooted in place because you want to, not because you have to. Remember: It is no fun being old. It is no fun being poor. It is hell to be old, poor, and stuck.

Giant sorting sound

In *Who's Your City*, urbanist Richard Florida describes ten mega-regions within the U.S. that generate the bulk of our economic output. The largest is the Boston-New York-Washington corridor, stretching some 500 miles down the east coast. Home to some 54 million people, it generates $2.2 trillion in output. Another surrounds the San Francisco Bay area, home to 13 million people and producing a beefy $470 billion in output. The eight other mega-regions are: Southern California, Phoenix-Tucson, Denver-Boulder, Dallas-Austin, Houston-New Orleans, Chicago-Pittsburgh, Charleston-Atlanta, and Southern Florida. By 2025, Florida (the man) projects, output will be considerably more concentrated around these mega-regions than it is today.

Why is this? Nobel laureate Robert Lucas (Economics, 1995) identifies the clustering of people and productivity as the underlying power of economic growth. The principle is simple—when talented and creative people come together, ideas flow more freely and we are more productive than we would be as individual contributors. In other words: 2 + 2 = 5.[256] Likewise, clustering magnifies the collective creativity and economic wealth output of the place that we inhabit. Urbanites consume less but produce more, what Florida refers to as the "clustering force."

The effect of clustering increasingly divides the labor force. Journalist Bill Bishop calls this the "Big Sort," where we are becoming sorted by income, by social and economic status, and by the kind of work we do. As individuals become more affluent, better educated, and freer to make their own personal choices, they acquire the means to live in the kind of community they want to. Highly skilled people understand that the pursuit of economic opportunity often requires them to move when careers require them to do so.[257]

But clustering doesn't benefit everyone. People with low- and moderate-incomes may be trapped in communities where options are limited and the means to get out and move up are ever sparser. And this isn't just laid off factory workers. People remain rooted because of their mortgage, professional licenses, health insurance, family obligations, and so on. Increasingly it also includes college-educated classes entering the global job market with no job prospects and high debt. A 2009 survey by the Pew Research Center found that roughly half (46 percent) of the public would rather live in a different type of community from the one they're living in

256 Unlike biological organisms, all of which slow down as they grow larger, cities become wealthier and more creative the bigger they get. Researchers call this phenomenon *superlinear scaling*.

257 In the 1970s, IBM workers joked that their company name stood for "I've Been Moved." These days most moves are voluntary. According to U.S. Census Bureau data, just over half of all people who move do so for housing-related reasons, such as renters wanting to own, young couples wanting to upgrade, and retirees looking to downsize. Another quarter say they move for family related reasons, such as getting married or divorced, having children, combining families, etc. Less than 1-in-6 say that the main reason for moving is work related, they say.

now, a sentiment that is most prevalent among city dwellers. As evidenced by the bankruptcy of Detroit, long the manufacturing and cultural hub of the U.S. auto industry, clusters can and do fail.

Of course, not everyone is stuck because of economic circumstance. Some are satisfied with the lives that they lead. Great for them. But many *are* stuck and they do not get to choose the cool cities in which to live. You don't want to be one of them.

The geographic sorting of people by economic potential on this scale is unprecedented, notes Florida. Economist Joseph Gyourko agrees, and predicts it "will affect the nature of America as much as the rural-urban migration of the late nineteenth century did." Generation NeXt, in today's highly mobile and interconnected society, your chances for personal economic success are significantly enhanced by your ability to move and relocate.

Where are the jobs?

In his book, *The Rise of the Creative Class*, Florida describes two general classes of workers. One group, the "non-creative class," includes service workers and the blue collar working class. The other group, the "creative class," is comprised of what he calls "core" creative people and creative professionals. Economist Edward Learner dubs these two groups "grunts and geeks." Job opportunities for these classes vary by location and Florida's projections out to 2018 have profound implications for young persons:

- *What and where service jobs will be.* Some 60 million Americans, or more than 45 percent of the workforce, perform low-skill, routine service work such as food service workers, hair stylists, retail sales clerks, and the like. Service class jobs compose the biggest share of all jobs but are mainly low paying (the average worker makes less than $27,000 annually). The good news is that service jobs are projected to account for roughly a little more than half of all new jobs in coming years. The not-so-good news is most of this growth will be in resort towns and tourist destinations that pay crap. Places like Ocean City, MD, Atlantic City, NJ, and Myrtle Beach, FL are expected to have nearly two-thirds of their work force employed in service class work.
- *What and where blue-collar jobs will be.* Blue-collar, working class jobs primarily make use of physical skill or manual labor. These include factory and production work, construction, transportation, installation, and the like. Blue collar workers currently account for 23 percent of all U.S. employment. The good news is that these relatively high-paying working class jobs will continue to be created. The not-so-good news is the number is increasing slowly, with the slowest growth in traditional manufacturing and industrial communities. Places like Elkhart, IN, Dalton, GA and Morristown, TN are projected to have 40–50 percent of their workforce doing blue-collar work.
- *What and where creative jobs will be.* The creative class comprises 40 million workers—roughly one-third of the U.S. workforce. One group, the "creative core,"

represents about 12 percent of all jobs and includes occupations such as science, engineering, education, computer programming, and research (a small subset includes the arts, entertainment, design, and media workers[258]). The primary function of these jobs is to create and innovate. The other group, "creative professionals," is classic knowledge-based occupations requiring a college degree. These solve specific problems by drawing on complex bodies of knowledge and include health care, business, finance, law, high tech, management, and education. The creative class represents high-wage, high-skill jobs and will add roughly half of all projected new jobs, about 6.8 million, by 2018.[259] These will be clustered geographically, with cities like Gainesville, FL, Richmond, VA, Greater Washington, D.C., and Morgantown, WV experiencing a 17 percent or greater increase in these types of jobs.

Reali-tude:
High paying jobs are clustering.

The young and the restless

There are a two periods of life when relocating is more common. First, during one's twenties and then as an empty-nester later in life. Youth is a time of freedom of movement and single men, single women, and young couples trying out newfound independence from parents may find themselves relocating frequently. The reasons vary: going away to school or getting that first job, changing roommates or jobs, getting married, having children, upward movements in the career path, or just wanting to explore the world and find yourself as an adult. Later, as we age, we begin building attachments that root us to place—friends, routines, a network of associates, a mortgage, a family—and we move much less frequently. Some characteristics of today's mobile youth include:

- Young persons with college degrees are the most likely to move of any demographic group and tend to move the greatest distance. The likelihood that one will move peaks at around age twenty-five, declines steeply until forty-five, then trails off into retirement and old age.
- The odds of moving increase with one's level of education. According to the *National Longitudinal Survey of Young Adults*, 45 percent of people with advanced degrees end up leaving their home state, compared with only 37 percent of people with a bachelor's degree and just 19 percent of those with a high school degree.
- Residents of the East and West Coasts tend to relocate more frequently than those in the Midwest or central area of the country. Studies show that residents on the coasts will move an average of every 3 to 5 years throughout their lifetimes

258 Called *Bohemians*, or *Bohos*, these are people with artistic or literary interests who disregard conventional standards of behavior.

259 Not all of these jobs require a college degree. Though nearly three-quarters of college graduates go on to do this kind of work, four-in-ten creative class workers don't hold college degrees.

and, by about two-to-one, they prefer to live in a hot-weather place over a cold-weather place.[260]

- Many NeXters are not driven by a desire to maximize income but seek to find a community that best fits their personality. Highly educated, young adults place a higher priority on quality of life factors, such as amenities, consumption opportunities, and community, social, and family considerations than did their Boomer parents.
- A substantial number of young persons do not realize their intention to move and often do so unexpectedly. To steal a line from Nike, many "Just do it." While flexibility is good, the tradeoff is more instability in your life.
- Young persons are increasingly considering moving abroad for work. In a study of willingness to relocate, 37 percent of workers surveyed said they would consider going anywhere in the world.[261]

One big draw for recent college grads is the classic college town. This clustering of college-educated young persons is fueling prosperity in places like Austin, Charlotte, Atlanta, Portland, and Phoenix. A decisive economic advantage of places like these increasingly derives from the kinds of public and private amenities they provide. And the growing concentration of talented young people makes those places even more attractive, creating a positive pull that attracts other young persons. "Being near smart people matters" says economist Enrico Moretti, who found that people's wages typically rise by about 8 percent as the share of their fellow urbanites with college degrees goes up by 10 percentage points. This is particularly valuable in dense cities, where contact is more common.

A bigger trend among young grads is the lure of the central city, where many young singles gravitate toward downtown areas. Economist Joe Cortright and urban expert Carol Colletta conducted a comprehensive study of where singles live and why. According to their findings, young singles between the ages of twenty-five and thirty-four are 33 percent more likely to live in a close-in neighborhood (within 3 miles of the city center). These young creative types, labeled "urban independents," cluster in places like New York's East Village, D.C.'s Adams Morgan and U Street corridor, Chicago's Wicker Park, Los Angeles' West Hollywood, and San Diego's Gaslamp district. Companies are trying hard to meet the needs of NeXters who choose to live in cities.

BRAIN SNACK: *Social psychologist Stanley Milgram theorizes that the way we behave in cities or busy urban areas is a natural response to information overload. In the city our senses are continually assaulted—there are too many sights, sounds, and other people for us to process properly. City dwellers, therefore, tend to only have superficial interactions with each other, encouraged by*

260 The absolute number of people moving has tumbled to historic lows, despite a rise in the nation's population" notes William Frey, a demographer at the Brookings Institution. Mobility rates have dropped most for young workers, largely due to a more uniform mix of jobs offered in different locations and the plummeting cost of information.

261 The power of the Internet and the hunger of emerging-market economies are driving many brain-intensive jobs overseas.

frowning or looking angry all the time. They keep moving, transact business as quickly as possible, and skip social niceties like apologizing for jostling. In the city the norm is anonymity, says Milgram, and the unwritten rule is "I'll pretend you don't exist if you pretend I don't exist." While city personalities may be brusque, city dwellers aren't bad people. They're just trying to conserve their psychological energy and cope.

In a contrarian report titled *Retrofitting the Dream* by urban development professor and "uber-geographer" Joel Kotkin, analysis of longer-term demographic trends and consumer preferences suggests that the classic American dream of suburban home ownership remains relevant. Generational survey research finds that 43 percent of Millennials describe suburbs as their "ideal place to live, and only 17 percent... identify the urban core as where they want to live," cites Kotkin.[262]

In the final analysis, whether we reside in a city center, a suburb, or a rural area, what we as individuals value about our communities is remarkably similar across the board. Public policy researcher Irene Tinagli says finding a place that makes us happy encourages us to engage in more creative activities than we otherwise would and derive happiness from ourselves by cultivating our individuality. Once we determine that a place fits us, we have something to which we can belong, providing us with a sense of pride and attachment.

Reali-tude:
Experience the world while you are young.

What really counts about place?

Most definitions of happiness describe it as a state of mind or a feeling characterized by pleasure, satisfaction, or joy. True well-being in our daily life basically comes down to balancing two things: having meaningful relationships and enjoying what we do. Although we say it in different ways and live it out using different means, in some fashion it all comes down to love and work. And many elements of a happy life, such as how much we make, how much we learn, how healthy we are, how stressful we feel, the job opportunities we have, and the people we meet are in large part determined by where we live.

Yes, happiness is associated with income—but only up to a point. Beyond an income of $75,000, the effect of money and material goods on happiness levels off and higher levels of income do not necessarily translate into higher levels of happiness. Although they are more satisfied with their lives overall, say researchers Daniel Kahneman and economist Angus Deaton, people earning above this threshold are no happier day-to-day. Why is this? It's because money is relative. You'll never really feel secure in where you live if you don't earn as much as your

262 Recent evidence bears this out. Fourteen of the nation's biggest cities saw their growth slow or their populations fall outright in 2012–2013 compared with 2011–2012. Suburb growth accelerated during the same period, possibly due to a thawing economy.

friends and neighbors around you earn. And if you earn the most in your neighborhood, you'll probably feel like you are pretty well off.

The other thing that makes us genuinely happy is the quality of our personal bonds. That is, doing things we enjoy with people we like. In a PBS interview, sociologist and happiness expert Christine Carter says, "If we've learned anything in the last hundred years of research on happiness it's that a person's happiness is best predicted by the strength of their ties to other people." And the value of these social ties on our life satisfaction has been quantified in the emerging science of *happiness economics*. According to the research of economist Nattavudh Powdthavee, if you relocate from a city where you regularly see your family and friends to one where you would not, you would need to earn $125,000 just to make up for the lack of happiness you feel from being far from these people.[263] Create happiness in your life by cultivating and maintaining intimate, reliable relationships. Live where your friends and loved ones live and the other issues won't matter so much.

Reali-tude:
Live where you want to, not where you have to.

The bottom line:

- Americans are increasingly divided by income and the kind of work they do.
- Creative class jobs are clustering geographically.
- Youth have greater mobility than any other age group.
- Happiness comes from having relative wealth and meaningful relationships.

Doctor's Prescription (Rx)

Where you live should not determine whether you live, or whether you die.
~ Bono, singer-songwriter, activist

People have different motivations for relocating. It may be for more money, a safer neighborhood, better climate or lifestyle, career opportunities, changes in family, and so on. Does anyone really think that the wilds of Papua, New Guinea offer education, employment, and romance possibilities that are competitive with those in Albany, New York? Ah, no. But before you pull up stakes for the wilds of Albany, it is usually a good idea to think through your decision and ask yourself some questions:

Career:

- Will you be earning more money and getting better benefits?
- Does your new location offer more opportunities in your field?
- Are there opportunities for professional development and networking?
- Will you be earning at least the median income for your neighborhood?

263 Powdthavee pegs the worth of a marriage at $300,000 a year. That's definitely worth the effort!

Lifestyle:

- What is the climate and weather like?
- Is the city size right for you and does it suit your lifestyle?
- Does your personality and life stage match the culture of the region?
- What social, entertainment, sports, and leisure activities are there?
- Is there a tolerance for newcomers and do you like the people you have met?

Family:

- How much will you miss your family, friends, and community?
- How often could you afford to return home for visits?
- Is this a place where you would want to raise your own family?

Area:

- How does the cost of living compare to your current city or town?
- What are the crime statistics for the new area and is it safe?
- Are there good educational institutions and healthcare facilities nearby?

Practical:

- Is this a good time of year to find a job?
- How much will it cost to move and can you afford it right now?
- Is transportation adequate and will you have a stable place to stay there?
- Are you able to handle the stress and changes that a move brings?

Talking Points

> *Two roads diverged in a wood and I—, I took the one less traveled by, And that has made all the difference.*
>
> ~ Robert Frost, American poet

The stakes are significant, and yet when faced with the decision of where to call home, most of us do not prepare to make an informed choice. If you ask most people how they got to the place they live now, the common response is they just ended up there—they stayed close to family or friends, got a job there, or simply followed an old flame. Some did not see there was a choice to be made at all. Don't be one of them!

Reali-tude:
If you don't like the neighbors (or the job), move!

Chapter 17 describes some tools to help you acquire wisdom by interviewing others. To benefit from these techniques, you need only have access to a parent, educator, or other trusted adult (tribal elder) and a desire to listen and learn. Based on the ideas in this chapter, here are some starters:

1. "I am trying to improve myself. Today, where you live may be critical to getting a good paying job and achieving success. Reflecting on your experience, or that of someone you know, do you recall a situation where the place they lived either significantly benefited or hindered their long-term well-being?" If they say "Yes" then ask:

    - "Would you tell me the gist about what happened please?"
    - "How did you (they) feel about this at the time?"
    - "What two things did you learn from this that you can share with me?"

2. "I am trying to improve myself. Today, many young persons believe that technology has made where you work irrelevant. Reflecting on your experience, or that of someone you know, do you recall a situation where telecommuting either significantly benefited or hindered their long-term financial well-being?" If they say "Yes" then ask:

    - "Would you tell me the gist about what happened please?"
    - "How did you (they) feel about this at the time?"
    - "What two things did you learn from this that you can share with me?"

    In either case, if they say "No," simply say "Thank you."

3. Moving away from one's home town is an inflection point in a young person's life. Reflecting on your experience, or that of someone you know, what two suggestions would you have for a young person that is contemplating this decision?

4. "I want to make wise life-choices. Reflecting on your experience, would you have two ideas that I can implement to improve my judgment and decision-making skills? Be sure to thank them for their response.

Knowledge Nuggets

If you come to a fork in the road, take it.
~ Yogi Berra, Baseball Hall of Famer

1. *What factors should you weigh before you move?* According to Richard Florida, you need to weigh five factors to find the best place to live. How will the place affect your job and career prospects? How important it is to have close friends and family nearby and what will you give up if you move far away? Are you honest about whether the place suits your lifestyle? Does your choice of the place match your personality and age group? Are you aware of the tradeoffs involved? Follow his ten-step process to decide on your new home at: http://www.creativeclass.com/whos_your_city/place_finder/place_yourself.php.

2. *How healthy is your county?* Where we live matters to our health. The health of a community depends on many different factors such as individual health behaviors, education and jobs, quality of health care, the environment, etc. The Robert Wood Johnson Foundation, in collaboration with the University of Wisconsin Population Health Institute, has developed a collection of 50 reports—one per state—ranking the more than 3,000 counties according to multiple factors that determine a county's health. See how your county rates at: http://www.countyhealthrankings.org.

3. *Are you happy with your place?* Economist Irene Tinagli identifies three clusters of factors as key to our being happy in our communities: (1) things that make a community smart and vibrant, for example, the arts, culture, universities, colleges, nightlife, job opportunities, singles, entrepreneurs, artists, scientists, etc; (2) aesthetics and livability, such as parks, open space, climate, physical beauty, air quality, etc; and (3) equity, or an equitable balance of affordable housing, manageable traffic, good for the seniors and the poor, etc. Check out her complete list at: http://thismakesmehappy.wordpress.com/2009/07/06/.

4. *Where to go for info?* See Appendix F for additional information relating to this chapter.

Chapter 15

Choice of Lifestyle

Human identity is no longer defined by what he does, but what he owns.
~ Jimmy Carter, 39th U.S. President

The Gist

The Good:

- Smart lifestyle choices will help you live healthier and longer
- Centenarians are the fastest growing segment of the population

The Bad:

- Many NeXters feel entitled to the lifestyle they think they deserve
- Consumers are chum for marketing piranhas
- You know the risks, but you do it anyway
- Facebook consumes an enormous amount of time and energy

The Reality:

- For Gen NeXt, online and face-to-face worlds meld together
- People care about online privacy but post too much info for public view
- User sensitivities about privacy have been ill-served by technology companies
- 70–80 percent of our lifespan depends upon how we take care of ourselves
- Education and good habits help you make healthy lifestyle choices

Introduction

There are no lobbyists for the American Dream.
~ Arianna Huffington, author and columnist

What constitutes an American? Not your color, race, or religion. It isn't where you were born, the pedigree of your family, or your social status. Nor is it the size of your bank account or what you do for a living. Rather, being an American citizen is a matter of spirit. We are united by a love of liberty, respect for the freedom of others, and an insistence on our own rights as set forth in the *Declaration of Independence.* These principles are indelibly written in the hearts of all true Americans. Truth, justice, and all that good stuff!

Early on, Europeans noticed America's uniqueness. One who was enthralled by the nine months he spent here was Alexis de Tocqueville (1805—1859), a French political thinker and social scientist. In 1831, Tocqueville traveled widely in the United States and admired the vitality and entrepreneurial spirit of the American people. He took extensive notes about his observations, and after returning to Europe wrote two fat volumes about the country titled *Democracy in America* (1835 and 1840). The French aristocrat proudly declared himself to be "half Yankee."

Tocqueville believed that inequality was an incentive for the poor to improve themselves. The lower classes in Europe, he felt, had no hope of gaining more than minimal wealth. In the United States, however, he saw an optimistic "Yes we will" society where individual achievement and money-making were dominant work ethics. Through hard work and perseverance, Tocqueville concluded, everyday Americans dream that they too will one day have the means to enjoy an aristocratic lifestyle. Americans look to the future and a better tomorrow.

The "American Dream"—the idea that in this country anyone can rise from humble beginnings and succeed—is an aspiration that is deeply woven into our national psyche.[263] Historian James Truslow Adams popularized the phrase "American Dream" in his 1931 book *Epic of America*: "Life should be better and richer and fuller for everyone, with opportunity for each according to ability or achievement." In his 2006 memoir, *The Audacity of Hope: Thoughts on Reclaiming the American Dream*, this same interpretation of the ideals of the American Dream helped establish then U.S. Senator Barack Obama's reputation. Speaking at the 2012 Republican National Convention, Condoleezza Rice recounted how a little girl who grew up in segregated "Jim Crow" Birmingham went on to become the

263 Historically the American Dream originated in the New World mystique regarding frontier life. In 1774 the Royal governor of Virginia noted that Americans "for ever imagine the Lands further off are still better than those upon which they are already settled."

U.S. Secretary of State. Millions of Americans share this hopeful philosophy. The Dream has been credited with helping to build a cohesive American experience.

Today, the influence of the media, sports, and a consumer-oriented culture is shaping a new ethos of the Dream, says Historian Ted Ownby. Rooted in material happiness and overinflated expectations, Ownby sees the emergence of four American Dreams: (1) the *Dream of Abundance*, that offers a cornucopia of material goods; (2) the *Dream of a Democracy of Goods*, whereby everyone has access to the same products; (3) the *Dream of Novelty*, in which ever-changing fashions and unexpected new products broaden the consumer experience; and (4) the *Dream of Freedom of Choice*, so that people can fashion their own particular life style. According to Ownby, the desire to enjoy a modern, consumer lifestyle has radiated out from the major cities, penetrating even the most isolated rural areas.

Although the collective shift toward consumerism has distinct drawbacks, the development of new, abundantly available lifestyle options has nurtured a positive personal economic good—people are living healthier and longer.[264] Since the mid-1970s, there has been a growing recognition that these new lifestyle choices can significantly improve our long-term well-being, in many cases adding quality years to our life. "Increased life spans represent one of humanity's greatest achievements," says Tom Kirkwood, Director of The Institute for Ageing and Health at Newcastle University, "and continues to make an enormously positive contribution to our economy." That's good for everybody!

Reali-tude:
Keep your dreams lubricated.

The Good

May you live a hundred years.
~ Hindu blessing

The word longevity, or having a long individual life, comes from the Latin word longaevitäs (longus: long and aevum: age). It refers to the average number of years that a single person is expected to live under ideal conditions. The goal of longevity is to strive for one's maximum potential age.[265] Although sometimes used as synonyms, longevity is not the same as *life expectancy*. Life expectancy is a calculation performed by life insurance and pension plan companies. It refers to the number of years that the average person is expected to live in the "real

264 An economic good is something that someone desires or values.

265 The maximum human lifespan, which has remained more or less the same for thousands of years, is validated using modern standards by the Gerontology Research Group. The longest unambiguously documented human lifespan is that of Jeanne Calment of France, who died in 1997 at age 122 years, 164 days. She rode a bicycle to the age of 100 and met Vincent Van Gogh in her father's painting shop when she was 12 or 13. The oldest documented male is Dane Christian Mortensen, who lived for 115 years, 252 days. The oldest verifiable living organism is Methuselah, a 4,800-year-old bristlecone pine in the White Mountains of California.

world" of car accidents and cancer. To calculate life expectancy, actuaries imagine a large group of people—say, 100,000—born in a particular year, such as 2010. They statistically project when these people are expected to croak: a few will die as infants, a few as children, a few as young adults, some in middle age, most in old age, and a few in extreme old age. They then take the average age of death of all 100,000 people and that is the group's life expectancy.

But averages can be misleading. According to the National Center for Health Statistics, life expectancy for men in the United States in 1907 was 46 years. By 2010, it had inched up to a new high of 78 years. Does this mean that men in 1907 were dropping like flies at age 46? No, they weren't. But infants, whose mortality was 10 percent, were. Their high death rates skewed the life expectancy calculation dramatically downward and created the mistaken impression that earlier generations died at a young age.[266] Today, infant mortality has declined to less than 1 percent, significantly improving the average. Increases in life expectancy now are largely due to declines in the leading causes of death such as heart disease, cancer, influenza, and stroke.

***BRAIN SNACK:** There's no doubt that many ancient people kicked the bucket early. Young women frequently succumbed to complications of childbirth. In military service, young men were ground up like mincemeat, or if they survived, contracted fatal blood poisoning from battle injuries. Not to mention other early killers such as bacteria, predators, accidents, extremes in weather, and the lack of a reliable food source. Just staying alive was tough. Despite the fact that most ancient people led short, brutal existences, records suggest that reaching the age of 100 was not unheard of. Historians Mirko Grmek and Danielle Gourevitch speculate that during the Classical Greek Period (400 B.C.E.), anyone who made it past the age of five years—surviving all the common childhood illness of that day—had a reasonable chance of becoming a geezer. Ancient doxographers[267] tell us that philosophers Democritus and Isocrates lived to over 100 years and age 98 respectively. Xenophanes, Pyrrho, and Eratosthenes are credibly thought to have lived beyond the age of 90. Egypt's Pharaoh King Ramses the Great lived into his 90th year.*

All this is good news for NeXters, who may one day be shopping for their Beemers and Botox as healthy centenarians. A centenarian is a person who has attained the age of 100 years or more (much rarer are super-centenarians, who have lived to 110 or more). In 2010, the United States had 70,490 centenarians.[268] This number is predicted to more than quadruple by 2030 and may top one million by 2050. For 2100, the U.S. Census Bureau's high projection puts the number at a jaw dropping

266 This is an example of what management-scientist Sam Savage calls the "Flaw of Averages." The Flaw of Averages contends that plans based on the assumption that average conditions will occur are usually wrong. He recounts the tale of the statistician who drowns crossing a river with an average depth of three feet. The problem is that although the stream is shallow near the shore, it's 12 feet deep in the middle.

267 Doxographers collect, compile, and comment on extracts from classical Greek philosophers.

268 U.S. centenarians traditionally receive a letter from the President upon reaching their 100th birthday, congratulating them for their longevity.

5 million.[269] "Centenarians are the fastest-growing segment of our population," say Richard Hodes and Robert Butler, Directors of the National Institute on Aging. *Wal-Mart alert:* That's a lot of senior discounts!

Reali-tude:
If you are young, in time you will be old. Those who are old were once young.

The bottom line:

- For many, the American Dream has shifted toward material happiness.
- Life expectancy is a group statistical average; half of you will live longer.
- Longevity—how long you will actually live—is what counts.
- The number of centenarians in the U.S. is dramatically increasing.

The Bad

Californians invented the concept of lifestyle. This alone warrants their doom
~ Don DeLillo, author, from *White Noise*

To develop power over an unpredictable future and achieve the American Dream you need to make good lifestyle choices. But sound decision-making can be tricky. Seemingly innocuous circumstances today may lead to unanticipated financial, emotional, or physical consequences tomorrow. When it comes to choosing a lifestyle, questionable beliefs can trap your thinking and jeopardize your long-term well-being. Learn about some of the lifebombs and you'll stand a better chance of making a smart choice.

Cognitive Flaw: Ignorance

I wanna be rich. With BBQ sauce.
~ Overheard in an auto parts department

Clueless about the implications of your lifestyle? One of the most influential factors that determine your lifestyle choices is the degree to which your behavior is manipulated by others. Most of us have been so thoroughly brainwashed into overconsuming that it has become part of our identities. What we own has become more important than who we are, and this can have profound effects on our long-term well-being. Let's look at how failing to be objectively informed when making this important life-choice can put your future happiness at risk.

269 Being extremely old doesn't necessarily mean being extremely disabled. About 15 percent of people have no signs of age-related disease at 100 years and 43 percent have no signs of disease until 80. "It's not the older you get, the sicker you get," says medical professor Thomas Perls. "What we see is that the older you get, the healthier you've been," he says.

☞ *Lifebomb #1: "Champagne wishes and caviar dreams."*

Lifestyles of the Rich and Famous is a television series that aired in syndication from 1984 to 1995. Hosted by Robin Leach for the majority of its run, the show featured the extravagant lifestyles of wealthy entertainers, athletes, and business moguls. Leach ended each episode with a twangy wish for his viewers that became his signature phrase: "Champagne wishes and caviar dreams." *Lifestyles* was largely intended to be an insight into the opulent residences and the glamorous lifestyles of those it profiled. Describing it as the first "nice reality show," Leach interviewed wealthy people to learn the reasons for their success. Later spinoffs such as MTV's *Cribs* and VH1's *The Fabulous Life Of*... toured celebrity homes and looked at the places, things, and services that wealthy people enjoy. WealthTV's *Social* let viewers live vicariously by becoming a socialite with the rich and famous for an evening.

But television has the capacity to manipulate, cautions social psychologist John Condry in *The Psychology of Television*. By shaping our attitudes, beliefs, and judgments, says Condry, the images TV places in our minds will inevitably mold and distort our reality into one we believe is true. And research supports this. In their book *The New Elite: Inside the Minds of the Truly Wealthy*, marketing consultant Jim Taylor and colleagues found that the wealthy are poorly understood by the average American *(framing-2 trap)*.[270] Unlike the misbehaving celebrities we see on TV, the vast majority of people who drive our economy are not Ivy-league educated, luxury seeking socialites. They are—surprise!—hard working, small-business owners with middle class values. Some counter-intuitive characteristics of America's wealthy they identified are:

- More than 90 percent come from poor or middle class backgrounds. Most attain their wealth after years of hard work and low compensation. Many consider themselves lucky.
- Approximately 90 percent are college graduates (about half attended public colleges and half private).
- About 80 percent shop at Target and Best Buy and make use of sales and coupons. Around half consider luxury items to be a waste of money.
- Roughly 95 percent describe themselves as very happy.[271]
- The vast majority don't want people to know that they're wealthy.

And that's not all Noel. In their classic, *The Millionaire Next Door: The Surprising Secrets of America's Wealthy*, affluence authorities Thomas Stanley and

270 "Wealthy" is defined as at least $5 million in net worth (excluding their primary home) or having at least $500,000 in annual discretionary income. Using these criteria, there are 750,000 such households in the U.S. In 2008 the top 1 percent of Americans (about 1 million households) owned 34 percent of the country's wealth; the top 5 percent (about 6 million households) owned 60 percent.
271 Numerous studies have found that once your basic needs are met, having more money doesn't make you happier. The authors of *The New Elite* contest this, however, pointing out that the majority of these studies had essentially no participants with an annual income above $250,000.

William Danko compiled twenty years of research and interviews with wealthy families of America. They argue that the rich and famous we see in the media are not representative of the wealthy households of this country and how they live. The majority of them, they say, don't live that way at all. What *Next Door* reveals is millionaires are often the least likely people you would suspect. "You aren't what you drive," admonish the authors. Their findings closely parallel those of *The New Elite*:

- Half of the millionaires interviewed lived in average neighborhoods in average houses.
- They lead frugal lifestyles, live below their means, and shop for bargains.
- They're self-employed or own their own businesses and feel very passionate about their work.
- The majority received no family money and do not plan to leave a lot to their children. They want them to succeed the same way they did—on their own.

Today, many young persons feel certain of the success they expect and deserve *(superiority-1 trap)*. But feelings of entitlement regarding financial gain, appearance, and social popularity are unwise. Planning to be the next Teresa Giudice? You're gonna have a problem. It is not enough for you to simply have faith that you will be rich, beautiful, and popular; you must be motivated to discover what means, actions, or conditions are required to achieve these goals! *Young person's alert:* wealthy people become wealthy by driving in the front seat, not by watching the scenery from the back seat. They accept responsibility for their own success in all facets of their life and work hard to achieve them.

> *There is a great segment of society that now resents luxury and success and achievement by others. You have to have incentive. You have to have reward for hard work. I think that the spirit of America is still very much one of where people want to work hard... they want to be entrepreneurs. (Otherwise) there would be no* Lifestyles of the Rich and Famous. *It would be* Lifestyles of the Broke and Boring.
> ~ Robin Leach, entertainment celebrity

So, what does this mean for NeXters eager to make big bucks? Essentially, there are two ways that you can make a million dollars: the easy way and the harder way.

1. The easiest (but least likely) way to become a millionaire:

    - If you are lucky, be born (or marry) into a wealthy family.
    - If you're incredibly lucky, win the lottery or be the next pop star on *American Idol* or *The X Factor*.
    - If you have extreme athletic talent, you stand a slim chance of making millions as a professional athlete.

2. The harder (but much more likely) way to become a millionaire:

    - Decide what you are good at, love what you do, be disciplined in thought and deed, have integrity, tenaciously persevere, and have a smidgeon of luck.
    - Run a profitable small business, create a big enterprise, be at the top of a lucrative occupation, or manage a major company.

Take a closer look at the lifestyle of your neighbor in the apartment next door. College grad? Older car? Wal-Mart shopper? She just might be well on her way to being a future millionaire! (Single guys take note.)

Reali-tude:
Keys to success: become educated and work hard.

☞ *Lifebomb #2: "We control the horizontal. We control the vertical."*[272]

Unlike the frugal millionaires next door, millions of young Americans have been brainwashed in a culture to overconsume. They have been conditioned to see "stuff" as an important social self-identity marker. For example, driving a certain type of car, wearing particular designer labels, or owning the latest iWhatever all support a particular lifestyle image. Many Gen NeXters spend a significant amount of time and treasure on "competitive consumption," continually comparing their own lifestyle to people whose incomes are two, three, or more times their own. They are confident that their ship of fortune is just around the river bend *(optimism-1 trap).*

In her book, *The Overspent American*, sociologist Juliet Schor calls this national culture of upscale spending the "new consumerism." For millions of us, our values, attitudes, habits, and practices reflect this culture of addiction. "What we want grows into what we need," she writes, and "we live with high levels of psychological denial about the connection between our buying habits and the social statements they make." Increasingly, she emphasizes, what constitutes "the good life" focuses far more on material goods and luxuries than a happy marriage, one or more children, and an interesting job that contributes to the welfare of society.

BRAIN SNACK: *The film* The Queen of Versailles *is the true story of the collapse of billionaire David Siegel, a time-share apartment mogul who lost his shirt in the financial crisis. Siegel's dreams included a trophy wife and the largest house in America, a 90,000 sq. ft. Versailles-themed Florida home complete with tennis courts, bowling alley, and baseball field. Asked why he wanted to build*

272 The *Outer Limits* is a cult classic science fiction series that originally aired on television from 1963 to 1965. At the beginning of each episode, a voice announced: "There is nothing wrong with your television set. Do not attempt to adjust the picture. We will control the horizontal. We will control the vertical. For the next hour, sit quietly and we will control all that you see and hear."

such an ostentatious monstrosity, Siegel said, "Because I can. If you don't want to feel rich, you're probably dead."

To feed this beast, we are producing and consuming products at rates unseen in history. Communications expert Robert McChesney, named one of *Utne Reader* magazine's "50 Visionaries Who Are Changing the World" (2008), labels this effect "hyper-commercialism." Fueled by mass media advertising, manufacturers have shifted from product marketing to lifestyle marketing. They pitch upscale items from luxurious lattes to sexy shower heads at rich and non-rich alike. Through the magic of plastic, anyone can buy designer anything, at the trendiest retail shop. Or at outlet prices. And for many young persons, the siren call "You can have whatever you want, whenever you want it" is very hard to resist.[273]

Stand by to get fleeced (again!)

Media—films, television shows, magazines, and more recently, the Internet—are the main sources of lifestyle influence around the world, cites media critic Douglas Kellner. Media shapes how people think and behave, and provides "materials out of which we forge our very identities," he cautions. Much of our mass "culture to consume" economy is shaped by media advertising, and they are dead serious about getting you to say "Yes."

> *Over the years I have been more and more inundated with images of desirability and the subtle message that I'm not hip enough, or whatever. I literally cannot go anywhere or be connected to anything outside my home and not be constantly confronted by marketers telling me what I want or what I want to be. TV has become nothing but a marketing machine. So have shopping malls. Ditto for "urban centers" and "town centers." Ditto. Ditto. Ditto. And in my own measly way, I try and build myself up, knowing I'm as fake as everyone else. Authentic? I don't even know what that means anymore.*
>
> ~ klwi3329, Internet blogger

Unquestionably, advertisers contribute to the betterment of society by making us aware of products and services that can improve our lives. Okay corporate America, we get the upside. The downside is consumers are bombarded with more choices than a bird in a locust swarm. Researchers tell us the average person sees between 1,500 and 4,000 advertising message *per day*. Roughly 5 percent of these messages actually register with us, which means 75 to 200 daily connections. This makes marketeers drool. Let's consider a few examples:

- Consumer researchers have determined that the more you watch TV, the more materialistic you are and the more you want stuff (which they will sell you). This is in spite of your belief that you aren't affected by commercials.

273 See Chapter 4 for a description of the phenomenon called "affluenza."

- Compare a copy of a 20-year old magazine with a current issue of the same publication. Ever wonder why the subscription price is cheaper today? Notice the huge increase in advertisements? See how the ads look like the articles? Of some 20,000 periodicals carrying advertisements in 2011, the total income secured from subscriptions for all these publications was less than the amount paid for the advertising pages.
- At its core, Google was once a search engine, focused on producing relevant search results. Then they figured out how to sell things. At Web 2.0 Expo (2011), the company's chief economist Hal Varian estimated Google's value to advertisers and publishers at $54 billion. What Microsoft derisively calls "Scroogled," Google calls "Cha-ching!"
- Two brothers from a New York City suburb have an advertising concept that's on a roll—a roll of toilet paper that is. Bryan and Jordan Silverman are creators of *Star Toilet Paper*, toilet tissue printed with ads and coupon codes that can be read by cell phones. They anticipate cleaning up.

With so many messages peppering our daily lives, advertisers use highly crafted persuasion techniques to reach their target consumer in the right place, at the right time (it doesn't get more personalized than when you are sitting on the can). It's not the product that receives close attention—it's predicting consumer behavior and generating "buzz." Many businesses are now using gaming tricks, or "gamification," to try to get you hooked on their products and services. Earn points, badges, and leader boards, all for the privilege of forking over your dough. Interactive computing professor Ian Bogost has a one-word response for this trend: "Bull****!" Calling the practice *exploitationware*, the very point, says Bogost, "is to make the sale as easy as possible."

We tolerate this mass sell-job because we assume that we tune most of it out. Right? Wrong. Things are not so rosy, Riveter. Marketing professors Melanie Dempsey and Andrew Mitchell say we usually assume that advertising functions mostly to tell us about the properties of a product. Ads do that, but they also do other, more sneaky things. Their research suggests the most powerful effect of advertising is simply to create a good feeling by surrounding the product with other things that you like. In other words, we are seduced more by the giggling baby in the ad than whether the product actually heals her diaper rash. Or, we identify with the macho man shown buying a drink for the sexy lady, rather than the taste of the rotgut inside the bottle.

Why do we choose things just because we feel good about them? In large part it's because we lead busy lives. We simply have limited time to objectively research the facts. Rather than make a rational, informed decision, when its time to make a choice we are likely to go with the option that feels good *(framing-1 trap)*. Just like chimps. Clever marketing magnates know this. Care for a banana?

***BRAIN SNACK:** Inundated with advertising, today's young persons have become more cynical about marketing and less responsive to entreaties to buy. "Consumers are like roaches," say advertising executives Jonathan Bond and*

Richard Kirshenbaum in their book* Under the Radar—Talking to Today's Cynical Consumer. *"We spray them with marketing, and for a time it works. Then, inevitably, they develop an immunity, a resistance." And some of the most cynical consumers, say the authors, are the young. Nearly half of all American college students have taken marketing courses and "know the enemy." For them, "shooting down advertising has become a kind of sport."

Now for the real irony. Advertisers target people with money to burn, but the lifestyles most often portrayed are well beyond the means of all but a very small percentage of young persons. So who's buying all that high-street stuff? A 2011 *Wall Street Journal* article headlined, "Who's Buying All That Luxury? Not the Rich," revealed that most spending on luxury goods is now done by the young and less affluent.

Marketing researchers Susan Fournier and Michael Guiry found that more than one-quarter of respondents to their survey said they "dream about things they do not own" very frequently. Lexus automobile? Can't leave home without it. Hilton Hawaiian vacation? Yep, I deserve that. Rolex? Nothing less than the best. Next big thing? Count me in! "We see attractive lifestyles represented to us," remarks psychologist David M. Carter, "but in attempting to realize our aspirations we borrow heavily." Constantly seeking that which will make us feel fulfilled, we ramp-up our acquisitive lifestyles, often unaware of the vicious cycle. "It just never seems to happen though" says Carter. "We feel poorly about ourselves because, regardless of our income, we just can't seem to get there." Look in the glass. Are you one of them?

Attention sheeple! Do not attempt to adjust your lifestyle. We will control the horizontal. We will control the vertical. Sit quietly and we will control all that you see and desire. Operators are standing by. Please have your credit card handy. "Baaaa!"

Reali-tude:
Want to be less materialistic? Turn off the TV.

☞ *Lifebomb #3: "I make it, I spend it."*

Why do you need your savings to last to age 100 if your average lifespan is much shorter, you wonder? "Many fail to understand the potential consequences of living beyond their own planned life expectancy," say researchers at the Society of Actuaries (SOA)." *Longevity risk* is the risk that, on average, people will live longer than expected. "When people are told they will live to an age such as 80 or 85, they don't realize this means there is a 50 percent chance they could live longer than that age." *Money Magazine* senior editor Walter Updegrave concurs: "Using your average life span to estimate how long your savings will have to last in retirement could leave you in the unpleasant position of having no savings but a whole lotta living to go" *(projection-2 trap).* "Unless you have serious health problems or a family history of dying young, plan on living into your early or mid-nineties" advises Updegrave. "If your ancestors are long-lived, you may want to aim for 100."

If everyone agrees that it's hell to be old and poor, then why do so many NeXters deny the need to take action? The reason is longevity risk is a personal economic "slo-mo." You know that you have to do something. You fully intend to do something. And you will do something. Some day. In a *USA TODAY* survey, more than 80 percent of Gen NeXt workers say they intend to support themselves in retirement with savings they'll put away later. F'sure this works... for awhile. But, like quicksand and pythons, the danger slowly envelopes you.

BRAIN SNACK: Missile to the Moon *is a 1958 b&w science fiction film directed by Richard Cunha. Escaped convicts Gary and Lon are caught hiding in a rocket by scientist Dirk Green, who forces them to pilot the ship to the moon. By accident, Greene's partner Steve Dayton and his fiancée June stow away on the ship. Once on the Moon, they fortuitously find a cave with oxygen (how convenient!) and encounter an underground civilization of scantily-clad, telepathic women (how nice!). The crew manages to escape Ledo, the sinister female ruler, and elude being crushed by lumbering granitic velocipedes (the "slo-mos"). Stepping into the sun to avoid a slo-mo, the jerk among them gets barbequed for his un-American greed. The rest return safely to terra firma.*[274]

In *Missile*, the rock men are slow moving but they are an omnipresent risk to complacent crewmembers. Similarly, NeXters are at risk of being financially crushed if they are not mindful of the long-term impact of their current lifestyle. The Center for Retirement Research at Boston College warns that young persons must consider complex choices regarding consumption vs. saving, work vs. leisure, and saving vs. investment throughout their extended life cycles. In addition to early planning for retirement, you need to consider the possibility that you may unexpectedly lose a job or become disabled *(optimism-2 trap)*. These can be Dream killers.

"I am young. Why should I care?" you snarkily quip *(inertia-1 trap)*. Here's why: past government and pension plan forecasts, independent of the technique they used, have consistently underestimated improvements in future life expectancy. On average, by three years. In other words, it is likely they will be two slices short of a full sandwich when it comes time to pay your benefits. According to an International Monetary Fund report, if everyone in 2050 lived just three years longer than now expected—in line with the average underestimation of longevity in the past—the longevity risk potentially adds *one-half* to the costs of aging up to the year 2050. And, warns finance professor Michael Kisser, this tsunami "constitutes a likely event."

Wake up dude. The slo-mos are in motion. If they catch up to you, they're gonna BBQ your hiney. The only reliable source of support in your old age looks back at you in the glass.

---

274 *Missile to the Moon* (1958) was a remake of the cheesy movie *Cat-Women of the Moon* (1953). According to film critics Michael and Harry Medved, *Missile* was runner up for their "coveted" *Golden Turkey* award, signifying one of the worst films of all time. It was aced out by *Plan 9 from Outer Space* (1959) by Edward D. Wood, Jr. *Plan 9* starred actor Bella Lugosi, aka Count Dracula, who was dead and buried (for real) before the film was released. *Young persons alert*: Watch these turkeys only with a cheese pizza and something else to do!

Reali-tude:
Don't let the "slo-mos" catch you napping!

The bottom line:

- What you see on television is not representative of the wealthy.
- Most wealthy people live quietly under the radar.
- Advertisers control the vertical and the horizontal—learn to immunize yourself.
- Longevity risk means your old-age safety net may be full of holes.

Cognitive Flaw: Ineptitude

> *I'm watching TV, but I find it hard to stay conscious. I'm totally bored, but I can't switch off...*
>
> ~ Porcupine Tree, British rock group, from *Fear of a Blank Planet*

Careless about the implications of your lifestyle? A healthy lifestyle is one that helps you maintain and improve your health and well-being. Although a healthy lifestyle is usually thought of as eating right and exercising, other factors affect your quality of life and longevity. A materialistic lifestyle, for example, influences your choice of vocation, use of credit, and level of stress. Risky behaviors that lead to an unplanned pregnancy, an automobile accident, or a criminal record can irrevocably change the direction of your life. Let's look at how failing to think seriously when making this important life-choice can put your future happiness at risk.

☞ *Lifebomb #4: "Oh, the wild joys of living!"*

Experts agree that the greatest threats to the well-being of young persons come from preventable and often self-inflicted causes. "We have a problem managing desire in a landscape rich with temptation," says essayist Daniel Akst, author of *We Have Met the Enemy*. Akst likens American life to "a giant all-you-can-eat buffet" that offers calories, credit, sex, intoxicants, and other invitations to excess. And while engaging in lifestyles you see as desirable or exciting, the choices you make may put you at risk for loss, death, or destroyed potential. For example, smoking puts you at risk for cancer, casual sex may result in you contracting a sexually transmitted disease, not completing postsecondary education may gamble your personal economic future, and so on.

"With greater freedom and independence, adolescents face new choices and risks," says psychologist Valerie Reyna, Director of Cornell University's Center for Behavioral Economics and Decision Research. "And while the statistics are frightening, they are not unknown to young people," she relates. For decades young persons have been bombarded by facts about the risks they face. Unfortunately, although these warnings typically improve their knowledge about the risks, they seldom alter their actual behavior. In one study of "risky" driving behaviors, young adults believed they would be likely to resist negative outcomes regardless of their behavior *(superiority-2 trap)*. These dim bulbs also intend to put on their seat belt if they see an accident coming...

As a general rule, adolescents and young adults are more likely than adults over 25 to binge drink, smoke cigarettes, have casual sex partners, engage in violent and other criminal behavior, and have fatal or serious automobile accidents, the majority of which are caused by risky driving or driving under the influence of alcohol.
~ Laurence Steinberg, psychologist

If memory problems are a hallmark of aging, problems with risk-taking are characteristic of youth. And not unlike the generations before them, there is a host of risky behaviors that have important implications for both their current and future well-being. The fact is many young persons engage in these practices as part of their everyday lives—frequently in combination—and for them, negotiating risks is far more complicated than simply "Just say no." Rounding up the usual suspects:

- *Smoking.* Smoked regularly over the past month? Do your kisses taste like an ashtray? If you smoke, your risk of developing lung cancer is approximately 23x higher (among men) and 13x higher (among women) compared with those who have never smoked. Nearly 450,000 Americans die from tobacco-related illnesses each year, wheezing their way from the here-to-the-hereafter. And for every person who dies from tobacco use, another 20 suffer from at least one serious tobacco-related illness. Yes, we know that you can stop anytime—you've done it a dozen times *(self-control-2 trap)*.
- *Accidents.* Accidents account for nearly half of all fatalities among American youth and traffic accidents are the leading cause of death. With more than half admitting they do it, an estimated 3,000 teen deaths and 300,000 injuries result from texting and driving each year. Labeling this an "epidemic," the industry has united behind a national "It Can Wait" ad campaign. According to the National Safety Council, cell phone use on its own was a factor in one quarter of *all* crashes (2010).
- *Unplanned pregnancy.* Got the urge to merge? Eighty-six percent of pregnancies among unmarried women in their twenties are unintended. Sadly, the new moms and kids are disproportionately likely to experience a range of negative outcomes. Women in their twenties account for 57 percent of abortions in the U.S., the highest abortion rate of any age group.
- *Unprotected sex.* Beware the gift that keeps on giving! Largely preventable, STDs cause harmful and often irreversible health problems. According to the Center for Disease Control, there are an estimated 19 million new STD infections each year, almost half of them among young people ages 15 to 24. Many more cases go undiagnosed. "Honey, there's something I need to tell you..."
- *Drinking.* Swilled five or more drinks in a row over the past month? College presidents say binge drinking is their most serious problem on campus. Forty-four percent of students attending 4-year colleges drank alcohol at the binge level or greater, with 48 percent reporting that "drinking to get drunk" is an important reason for drinking. Almost one-third said they were intoxicated 3 or more times per month.

- *Reefer madness.* Smoked marijuana over the past month? Thirty-three percent of college students have. Regardless of state law, the Feds still consider pot an illegal substance, although this stance is softening (Mr. Obama was in the "Choom Gang" and still managed to get a heady government job.) Pop positive and you still risk being fired, denied a promotion or hire, or losing a security clearance.
- *Plastic.* Young adults are confronted by a clash of lifestyle versus means. Overwhelmingly they have chosen lifestyle, paid for with plastic rather than from savings. In 2008–09, half of all college students had four or more credit cards and universities lost more students to credit card debt than to academic failure. Half of all college-age adults agreed with this statement: "I have experienced repeated, unsuccessful attempts to control, cut back, or stop excessive money use *(self-control-1 trap).*"

Why are young persons disproportionately responsible for the initiation of poor lifestyle choices and other risky behaviors? According to behavioral scientist Valerie Reyna, "Young persons are aware of the potential dangers of their actions, but they make calculated choices to 'play the odds.' They believe it's worth the risk for the perceived rewards, and although that calculation may be technically correct, it ignores the categorical possibility of disaster," says Reyna. In contrast, more mature deciders tend to "go with their gut" by assessing the gist—a general sense or impression of the situation along with its emotional meaning. In looking at the larger picture, they avoid a trade off of serious risks (say, dying in a car accident) against immediate rewards (the approval of friends).

Psychologist Laurence Steinberg sees risky decisions arising from physical and chemical changes within the maturing brain. Logic and reasoning capabilities appear to be more or less fully developed by age 15, but the ability to control one's impulses and resist peer influence continues to develop gradually into the early to mid-20s. As a result, beliefs about what peers are doing can influence decisions and resulting behaviors, even if those beliefs are incorrect *(inertia-2 trap).* Fortunately, resistance to peer influence increases with age, notes Steinberg. "The presence of peers increases risk taking substantially among teenagers, moderately among college-age individuals, and not at all among adults," he says. Tribal elders know this.

Reali-tude:
Don't let peers hijack your common sense.

☞ *Lifebomb #5: "The bare necessities: food, water, Facebook."*

Nowadays, much of our lifestyle experience plays out on-line. Social networking services facilitate the building of social relations among people who, for example, share interests, activities, backgrounds, or real-life connections. Users represent themselves on-line, often by a profile, along with their social links. There are hundreds of social-networking sites, the most popular being Facebook, MySpace, Google+, Twitter, and LinkedIn.

Facebook, or "FB," was launched in 2004 and is the largest social-networking service, by far. More than a billion people now log into it each month, double the

500 million it hit in July 2010 (think about that number for a second: it means that 1 out of every 7 people on the planet is active on FB, a staggering number by any account).[275] Who are these users? Most of them—about 80 percent—live outside of the U.S. and Canada. Many log in on mobile devices rather than personal computers and the company now has 600 million mobile users.

Why do we use Facebook? Facebook provides us with a sense of belonging. We use it to find people "like me," and exchange social and lifestyle experiences that make us feel connected. We do this in two ways, explains psychologist Deborah Serani. One is *bonding*, that is, reconnecting us with old friends and family, or exploring new relationships. Roughly two-thirds of social media users cite this as their main reason for using social media. The other is *bridging* as a means of strengthening ourselves. Bridging links us to people and organizations that share our political, social and community interests, or our career or professional pursuits.[276] In presenting preferred or positive information about ourselves, we can configure and adjust who sees what, and thus enhance our "optimal self." Many psychologists see Facebook activity as a reflection of a healthy social life.

BRAIN SNACK: *A study by recruitment-technology firm Jobvite reveals that 92 percent of recruiters do on-line research about candidates, and more than 75 percent of college students may be using Facebook in a way that will damage their job prospects after they graduate. Party pics and racists remarks aren't the only problem, says Larry Chiagouris, author of* The Secret to Getting a Job after College: *"A major cause for concern is people telling others about the organizations they belong to or the events they attend," he cautions. More than 70 percent of human resource professionals have denied an applicant a job offer based on what they found on-line, many of whom never learned why they were rejected.*

Interestingly, *Forbes* reports that not having a Facebook account may actually tag you as "suspicious" by hiring managers. Did you deactivate it because it was full of red flags? Are you hiding something? "It's increasingly clear that recruiters have a set of expectations about a would-be employee's social-media presence," observes financial writer Martha White. "It's worth keeping that in mind as you go about shaping your on-line identity," she advises *(projection-1 trap).*

Although we may stretch the truth, for the most part people are expressing their real personalities on FB rather than inflated takes on themselves, writes psychologist Sam Gosling in *Snoop: What your stuff says about you*. "It is very, very hard to fake differences in perception," he says. Pavica Sheldon, a communications professor, concurs. She finds that how people present themselves face-to-face seems

275 Not all of these are legit. According to Consumer Reports (May 2011) there were 7.5 million children under 13 with accounts, violating the site's terms of service. Five million of those were under 10.

276 England's Queen Elizabeth II added a Facebook page in 2010 to complement her YouTube channel, Flickr and Twitter accounts, and website.

to actually happen on Facebook, even if they are shy or socially awkward. In other words, what you see is what you (usually) get.[277]

But there are some downsides. In her book, *Alone Together*, sociologist Sherry Turkle is much more skeptical about the effects of the on-line community. "These days," she writes, "the ties we form through the Internet are not, in the end, the ties that bind. But they are the ties that preoccupy." Worse yet, says culture columnist Stephen Marche, "Curating the exhibition of the self has become a 24/7 occupation" *(superiority-1 trap)*. Preoccupation with monitoring the digital footprints of others has also become much more common. Whether captured by the desire to compare, curiosity, or jealousy, Facebook is not only being used to keep up with the Joneses, it's a way to keep track of the Joneses *(inertia-2 trap)*. The belief that others are doing better than you are may elicit feelings of low self-esteem, insecurity, narcissism, and envy, as well as replacing important offline ties with your family and friends. Regrettably, the Joneses seem to be winning.

> *Facebook certainly has its benefits, but at times it seems like a constant rat-race up a mountain of self-indulgence. Everyone is racing to post the "best" pictures of themselves doing the "best" things with the "best" people, posting the "best" status updates, checking in at the "best" places, and the like. I think the effect simply makes everyone else jealous and lonely that they did not reach the "finish line" first. Except the "finish-line" is not really a finish line, because the race never stops.*
>
> ~ scooterj2003, Internet blogger

"Like cell phones, nobody seems to notice the vast amount of time and energy—at work, at home, and now while on the move—people are devoting to Facebook," says psychologist Michael Fenichel, who has closely studied addictive behaviors. Facebook usage can "overtake" daily activities like waking up, getting dressed, using the telephone, or checking e-mail. In a 2011 study by etextbook seller CourseSmart, 48 percent of 18–34 year-olds check FB when they wake up; 28 percent before they get out of bed. The scary thing is they can't seem to shut it off.

How do you know when your Facebook use has become a compulsion? One exasperated mom puts it, "I can go a whole day without Facebook. But I've never made it through an entire weekend." Marriage and family therapist Paula Pile offers some tip-offs that you may be addicted to FB:

- The first thing you do after waking is "Check Facebook." And it's the last thing you do at night.
- You check it many times during the day (FOMO = Fear Of Missing Out).
- You stay up late on Facebook and are tired the next day.

277 Perhaps this is due to the familiarity of most FB friends. In a 2011 survey of 2,255 adults, Pew Research Center found that only a small fraction of Facebook friends are people that users have never met or met only once. The study also found that FB users are more trusting than similar Americans, and this can create problems for young persons. Popularized by the MTV show of the same name, *catfishing* refers to pranksters who create a fictitious online character and go fishing for a vulnerable and lonely person to humiliate and shame. Catfishing is often emotionally devastating for those affected.

- Nostalgia has you obsessing over old flames and reliving the past.
- You neglect your work, school, or family obligations in order to spend time on Facebook.
- Going for more than a day without using Facebook causes you stress and anxiety.

Why do *you* use Facebook? Next time, pause to question what you're doing on Facebook and consciously determine what you're really getting out of it. Do you balance your FB experience with other enjoyable pursuits in your life? Do you feel obliged to respond to some people on FB even though you'd prefer not to? Which parts of Facebook are truly constructive to your personal and professional life? Psychologist John Grohol, founder of *Psych Central* admonishes, "You cannot engage in 'deep introspection' into your life while constantly checking to ensure your cows are fed in Farmville or to play your next word in Words with Friends." "Facebook is merely a tool," says social psychologist John Cacioppo. "And like any tool, its effectiveness will depend on its user."

Reali-tude:
Facebook is only a tool—face-to-face is reality!

The bottom line:

- Generally, young persons are more likely than adults over 25 to engage in risky behaviors.
- To make better lifestyle decisions, understand the gist of the situation.
- Most threats to your well-being are self-inflicted.
- Facebook friends should be supplements, not surrogates to your social lives.

The Reality

Of course you are, my bright little star. I've miles and miles of files, pretty files, of your forefather's fruit. And now to suit, our great computer... your magnetic ink.
~ Moody Blues, British rock group, from *In the Beginning*

The expansion in mobile connectivity is astonishing. According to Cisco's 2012 "Visual Networking Index," there will be an estimated 10 billion mobile Internet devices in use globally by 2016 and Smartphone traffic will grow to 50 times the size it is today. The Boston Consulting Group estimates that around 3 billion people will be on-line by then, almost double the 1.6 billion on-line in 2010. Google's Android users are downloading apps at a rate of 1 billion a month. The future is arriving faster than we can process it.

Rewiring brain central

Technology is pervasive within Generation NeXt, many of whom say their use of modern, mobile technology is what distinguishes them from other generations. According to findings from the Pew Research Center, 96 percent of American 18–29 year olds own a cell phone of some kind and 70 percent own a laptop. Not too long ago, young persons walked with their heads up, looking at one another while talking. Now they walk with their heads down, sending a text while "conversing." No matter where you go—to a restaurant, a movie, a public restroom, and yes, even a funeral—you see young, obsessed zombies clutching and using wireless mobile devices (WMDs—how ironic is that?). Gripped by technology, they fondle their device like a rosary or Arabic worry bead.[278]

In a *New York Times/CBS News* poll, young persons admit that although WMDs make their lives better and their jobs easier, they are intrusive, increase their levels of stress, and make it difficult to concentrate. But these detractions are not enough to change their behavior: 73 percent of college students can't study without some form of technology and 38 percent cannot go more than 10 minutes without checking their e-device. Laments communications professor Clifford Nass, "We've got a large and growing group of people who think the slightest hint that something interesting might be going on is like catnip. They can't ignore it."

> **BRAIN SNACK:** *Millions bring their phones, tablets, e-readers, and laptops to bed each night. Based on mounting evidence in the medical community, the type of light produced by our portable electronic screens can make it harder to get good night's sleep. "While nighttime exposure to light of any kind interferes with sleep," says sleep researcher Steven Lockley, "blue light preferentially alters the brain. Your brain thinks it's daytime because we have evolved to only see bright light during the day." Gadgets high in blue light include computer monitors, digital phones, electronic gadgets, LED televisions, and digital clocks. Are you waking up feeling blue? Consider using dim, orange lamps if you must use a night light, experts say.*

No group compares to Generation NeXt, who, when given a choice, overwhelmingly prefer text messaging versus voice call. Fully 95 percent of 18–29 year olds use the text messaging feature on their phones, sending or receiving an average of 88 text messages on a normal day.[279] More alarming is nearly two-thirds of NeXters

278 *Nomophobia* is the fear of losing one's mobile phone. In a survey by Credant Technologies, travelers left behind more than 8,000 mobile devices at seven of the largest airports in the country in one year (2012). The most common place where mobile devices are left behind is at the Transportation Security Administration's (TSA) checkpoints and in restrooms.

279 Texting promotes "ambient awareness," which allows us to be more aware, if only subconsciously, of the rhythm of our friend's lives. In comparison, the median for Baby Boomers is 11 text messages sent or received per day.

say they've texted while driving. "We have sacrificed conversation for mere connection," says psychologist Sherry Turkle. "We are tempted to think that our little "sips" of online connection add up to a big gulp of real conversation. They don't," she says.

> *I don't communicate much with older people. So much of my life is set up over text. It's not about anything important—just a way to stay in touch with each other.*
> ~ Lisa A-G, college student, who sends and receives an average of about 6,000 text messages a month

Scientists say our ability to focus is being undermined by these bursts of information. "The technology is rewiring our brains," say Nora Volkow and Gary Small, two of the world's leading brain scientists. Young minds, shaped by the era of microprocessors, access to limitless information, and 24-hour news and communication, are remapping, retooling, and evolving. This constant exposure to info bites is causing them to become more impatient and impulsive, leaving little time for empathy and compassion. How can you resist the catnip? If you are to make meaning of the world around you, advises human development psychologist Mary Helen Immordino-Yang, you need to balance the high attention demands of fast-paced urban and digital environments with opportunities to focus inward and reflect. In other words, give your thumbs a break. Look in the glass and ask, "Why do I do what I do?"

Privacy has never been so public

> *You have no privacy. Get over it.*
> ~ Scott McNealey, co-founder, Sun Microsystems

Privacy is the ability of an individual or group to seclude themselves, or information about themselves, and thereby reveal them selectively. As new technologies blend our on-line and offline lives, "the lesson is a rather gloomy one," predicts information technology scientist Alessandro Acquisti, who specializes in the economics of privacy and how people conduct themselves on social networks. "We have to face the reality that our very notion of privacy is being eroded," he says.

One major reason personal privacy is increasingly at risk is that paper records have been mostly replaced by computerized records. Vast amounts of information, stored on computers, can be easily shared at the click of a button. Types of data routinely collected on us by various means include our credit history, our health history, our educational history, our employment history, how much we earn, what we eat, what we do in our spare time, what magazines and books we read, what calls we make, what we buy, what Websites we use, our sexual preference, blah, blah, blah. We swim in a sea of data ...and the sea level is rising rapidly.

Much of this digital tide is a product of our lifestyle choices. For example, we surrender personal data for the privilege of e-paying our bills and using our supermarket rewards cards. But that is only the tip of the proverbial iceberg. Our magnetic ink is blotted whenever we subscribe to a magazine, sign up for a book or music club, join a professional association, fill out a warranty card, give money to charities, tithe to our church or synagogue, invest in mutual funds, or make a telephone call. All of these transactions, and many, many more, leave a data trail that is stored in a computer. An equivalent amount of data is generated by what the McKinsey Global Institute calls "digital exhaust"—data given off as a byproduct of other activities such as Internet browsing and simply moving around with our Smartphone on.

The ubiquitous use of WMDs has opened a new front for the assault on your privacy. Every time you visit a Website, you leave an electronic footprint, or signal, that is communicated to the host site. Most of the major conduits through which you see the world on-line, including Google Search and Facebook, track these for later analysis. According to *Moveon.org* president Eli Pariser, author of the book *The Filter Bubble: What the Internet Is Hiding From You*, Google uses hundreds of "signals"—even when you're not logged in to Google—that track where you are sitting, your Internet address, the type of browser and device you use, who your friends are, Web pages you visited, how long you visit each one, search terms you entered, whether or not you responded to unsolicited banner ads, and many, many other data points. Facebook doesn't have to capture data. Users provide it voluminously.

What happens to these footprints? In a process called data mining, your on-line activities are electronically "hoovered" and then digitized, formatted, standardized, analyzed, and modeled to disclose your preferences, desires, and thoughts. Demographic data, combined with an extensive profile of your interests (such as preferences for magazines, travel, dining, hobbies, entertainment, etc.), create a growing historical profile of personal information that is sold or traded between companies, often without your knowledge or consent. "It's the power of individual targeting," says Eric Schmidt, Google's executive chairman, "The technology will be so good, it will be very hard for people to watch or consume something that has not in some sense been tailored for them."

Internet digital pioneer Jaron Lanier is neither happy nor upbeat about this. He accuses Facebook and Google of being "spy agencies" and "siren servers" for their irresistible attraction and suggests we are outsourcing ourselves into insignificant advertising-fodder. "Free services in exchange for personal information—that's the privacy bargain we all strike on the Web," he says. Like a sci-fi "B" movie... we have become part of the machine.[280]

---

280 You may be more exposed than you realize. One prominent study reveals that the vast majority of Americans (87 percent) can be identified with only three pieces of information: gender, zip code, and date of birth. These are easily gleaned from many online profiles created for popular social network sites. More ominously, researchers have demonstrated how Facebook and freely available personal information can be used to match faces in the street to detailed online profiles. Privacy expert Alessandro Acquisti asks, "What will privacy even mean in a world where a stranger on the street could guess your name, interests, or... credit score?"

Reali-tude:
Google never forgets.

They know what you want (even if you don't)

> *Advertising that connects the right customer at the right time. And let them invite their friends.*
> ~ Sheryl Sandberg, COO of Facebook

We have come to understand more and more of our lives through the logic of digital connection. "Social media is more than something we log into; it is something we carry within us," says social media theorist Nathan Jurgenson. With social media now an integral part of the Gen NeXt lifestyle, it is important to think about how this technology may increasingly be using you, rather than the other way around.

Beginning in 2009, Google began customizing its search results for each user. This means that what you've clicked on in the past increasingly determines what you see next. Author Eli Pariser calls this process an endless "you-loop," whereby the network functions like a one-way mirror. Partially transparent, it reflects your own interests while algorithms anticipate your behaviors, questions, and moods. Jeff Chester of the Center for Digital Democracy describes the innovation as a "stunning commercial surveillance system," triggering a personal information gold rush. Facebook, Amazon, Netflix, Pandora, Yahoo News, and hundreds of other companies are now increasingly personalized and present you with customized "recommendations" they think you're interested in.[281]

BRAIN SNACK: *When you visit a Website, a file called a "cookie" is copied to your device. Cookies are inherently harmless. They are simple text files that allow you to navigate the site, take advantage of hassle-free sign-ons, use the shopping cart, and so on. Although they don't identify you by name, cookies do store personal information when you register for services such as free e-mail accounts, news alerts, or personalized homepages. Cookies are also used by online advertisers to send you ads based on your browser preferences.*[282]

Since cookies track your browsing behavior without your consent, the practice has attracted a lot of controversy. Jonathan Mayer, a graduate student, unearthed that Google was secretly planting cookies on iPhone browsers for purposes of targeting their users with advertising. For this indiscretion (one of many), Google was fined $22.5 million by the U.S. Federal Trade Commission (FTC) in 2012. In 2013, the company paid $7M (about an hour's revenue) to settle lawsuits brought by Attorneys General from 38 states for violation of wiretapping laws in connection with data collection for its Street View program.

---

281 Try this experiment: search for something on Google. Then have a friend or two do the same search. Although many of the links are the same, they're in a different order and subtly "skewed." The important lesson is the Internet you see is not the Internet they see.

282 In a *Wall Street Journal* study, the top 50 Internet sites installed an average of 64 cookies and tracking beacons each so that other sites can target you. Why? They want to sell you something.

"Personalization is becoming big business," says investigative reporter Peter Maass. According to on-line privacy experts at PrivacyChoice, 140 different tracking entities routinely collect information about users of the top Facebook apps. In a recent investigation, the FTC found that kids are data magnets; more than half of the 200 most popular games and other apps for children from Apple and Google app stores were transmitting info to advertisers. Sites like Loopt and Foursquare broadcast a user's location from their mobile phone, providing an opportunity for targeted ads and special offers.[283] Advertisers love user personalization because it's the shortest line between the consumer (you and your kid) and the point of sale (them). Reverse your thinking about large social networking firms and see them as advertising companies whose customers are advertisers, not users. Now you understand.

Facebook is not your friend

> *I share, therefore I am.*
> ~ Sherry Turkle, psychologist

Facebook determines what appears in your *News Feed* by tracking every action you take on the network, such as clicking "Like," commenting, sharing, etc., according to secret weighting criteria. As with Google (and others), FB serves you what they think you want. "What you need to know," warns tech guru Mike Elgan of *Computerworld*, "is that Facebook will cut your ties to people—actually end the relationships you think you have—and block content that doesn't meet their criteria. Most people have no idea that their friends' activities are determining what content they see and don't see on Facebook," he says. And that's not all. Choose your Facebook friends wisely; they could help you get approved—or rejected—for a loan, as some lenders are beginning to scour your Facebook friends to assess your creditworthiness.

A *Consumer Reports* cover story (2012) reveals how little we know about the enormous amounts of highly sensitive information that Facebook collects and distributes, quickly and widely, to third parties. It reveals many causes for concern regarding Facebook and personal privacy:

- *Some people are sharing too much.* Projections suggest that 4.8 million people have used Facebook to say where they planned to go on a certain day (a potential tip-off for burglars) and that 4.7 million "Liked" a Facebook page about health conditions or treatments (details an insurer might use against you).
- *Some don't use privacy controls.* Almost 13 million users said they had never set, or didn't know about, Facebook's privacy tools. And 28 percent shared all, or almost all, of their wall posts with an audience wider than just their friends.
- *Facebook collects more data than you may imagine.* Did you know that Facebook gets a report every time you visit a site with a Facebook "Like" button, even if you

283 Many don't realize that a cell phone, Blackberry, or wireless laptop broadcasts its location whenever the power is on, whether or not a call is in progress.

never click the button, are not a Facebook user, or are not logged in? Much of this activity occurs below the user's radar.

- *Your data is shared more widely than you may wish.* Even if you have restricted your information to be seen by friends only, a friend who is using a Facebook app could allow your data to be transferred to a third party without your knowledge.
- *Facebook is "leaky."* Even when you don't explicitly state facts about your life, data brokers "infer" more information because of social network analysis. These inferences have the potential to jeopardize your career, insurance coverage, job advancement, and relationships.

In 2011, Max Schrems, a 24-year-old Austrian law student, sued Facebook's Dublin office for a complete record of his personal data. He was surprised to discover, among the 1,222 pages of information covering three years of Facebook activity, not only deleted wall posts and messages, some with sensitive personal information, but e-mail addresses he'd deleted and names he'd removed from his friends list. "It is very likely that no government or corporation has ever managed to gather such a huge amount of personal and often highly sensitive data," wrote Schrems in his complaint. His action spurred more than 40,000 requests for Facebook data in Europe.

Reali-tude:
On-line privacy control is *your* responsibility.

The enemy in the glass

The distribution of your personal information is spelled out in the various Internet privacy policies that you never read.[284] No wonder: a survey conducted by global branding firm Siegel+Gale found that Google and Facebook privacy policies can be more confusing to users than credit card agreements and government notices. Here's an instructive example to get the gist: "By clicking that you have read this agreement, you give *Young Person's Guide* and its partners the unlimited right to intercept and examine your on-line choices from this day forward, to sell the insights gleaned thereby, to retain that information in perpetuity, and to supply it to any third party without limitation. Click to approve and download." Oh btw, the statement "This agreement is subject to change at any time, and supersedes all prior agreements" is hidden in the margin of one of the back pages of the book.[285]

When asked, people say that privacy is important to them. When observed, their actions seem to suggest otherwise. A 2010 study by *Lawyers.com* revealed a clear disconnect—users are worried about the dangers of disclosing personal infor-

284 While most Websites' user agreements say they do not sell personal information or share it externally, they maintain the right to change the rules at any time. Don't think it will happen? You've been set up like a bowling pin dude. What you originally "Liked" on Facebook was once private. Later, the company decided to make that information public in order to facilitate advertising. Sorry—it's business.
285 Grateful acknowledgement to journalist Cory Doctorow for the kernel.

mation on social media sites, but they do it anyway. The study found that more than two-thirds of respondents admitted to posting their first and last names and/or their photograph. Half of them included an email address. One university study found that 94 percent of students surveyed were sharing personal information on Facebook that they had not intended to make public. Another study revealed that only 5 percent of people thought to change their friend's list to private. "The data" says Carol Eversen, VP of marketing at LexisNexis, "suggests that Americans are not taking the necessary steps to protect themselves."

I make everything public on my Facebook account and I'm not worried about privacy because the more I share about who I am and what interests me, the more Facebook can bring me content that I care about.
~ Robert Scoble, startup liaison officer for Rackspace, a Web-hosting company

People post too much information for the public to view. Everything now that they have posted will be there forever and there is no taking any of it back. It is there for good. I don't trust any of these social medias.
~ John Crowley, Information Science professor

Recently, social network users are becoming more active in pruning and managing their accounts, observes digital media expert Mary Madden of the Pew Research Center. Almost two-thirds of them have deleted people from their "friends" lists, 44 percent have deleted comments made by others on their profile, and more than a third have removed their names from photos that were tagged to identify them. A majority of respondents—58 percent—now restrict access to their profiles, and about a fourth are choosing to "alter personally identifiable information" such as their dates of birth "to protect their privacy," she adds. *Consumer Reports* cites this as "evidence that people are treating Facebook more warily." That's a good thing!

"I have nothing to hide," you say. Yes Grasshopper, but you are not your profile. Databases can contain errors, and data compiled from disparate sources and differing contexts can lead the user of your data to misjudge your tastes, preferences, and character. "Data brokers buy, compile and sell a wealth of highly personal information about you, but there's no way to find out what they have or if it's correct," says John M. Simpson, the head of Consumer Watchdog, which advocates for digital privacy. Have you thought about how lenders, credit agencies, insurance companies, and yes, prospective employers, might react if the information they gather about you via keyword searches is erroneous? How about being dropped for health insurance coverage, or not having your life insurance policy renewed, or losing out on a prospective job because you were deemed "too risky?" Fair or not, there's not much you can do about it—Google says it will remove results only for legal or copyright reasons.[286] *Young person's alert:* your on-line reputation isn't their problem. It's yours.

> *Maximize your privacy settings, but even then, assume anything you do on Facebook can be seen by all of your friends, your mom, your great-great-grandchildren, your employer, health insurer, and the government.*
> ~ Ed Skoudis, security instructor at the SANS Institute

Many social media giants have come under fire for not being upfront about how they use information on users' on-line activities. In settling federal investigations, Facebook and Google have paid fines and agreed to 20 years of privacy audits (Lexis Nexis and Choicepoint are also under 20 year orders). The FTC has proposed legislation that would give consumers access to information collected about them, allow them to correct and update the data, and opt-out of having their on-line behavior monitored and shared. But this has gone as far as a one-legged dog. In 2012, the Obama administration published *Consumer Data Privacy in a Networked World: A Framework for Protecting Privacy and Promoting Innovation in the Global Digital Economy.* Called an on-line privacy "Bill of Rights," it outlines seven basic protections that give consumers clear guidance on what they should expect from those who handle their personal information. It also sets expectations for companies that use personal data. But the compliance is voluntary, which translates into "fat chance."[287]

"Facebook was not originally created to be a company," declares co-founder Mark Zuckerberg. "It was built to accomplish a social mission—to make the world more open and connected." So, here is a novel thought. Now that Facebook is a huge, publically-owned, profit-maximizing behemoth, who really benefits from you being "more open and connected?"

Reali-tude:
Reputation matters.

Age to perfection

> *People are living longer than ever before, a phenomenon undoubtedly made necessary by the 30-year mortgage.*
> ~ Doug Larson, cartoonist

286 While Facebook does not technically own its members' content, it has the right to use anything that is not protected with its privacy and applications settings. For instance, photos, videos, and status updates set to public are fair game.

287 Were you a campaign supporter for President Obama? Investigative journalist Michael Isikoff reports that personal data you voluntarily shared with the campaign has been transferred to an advocacy group created to advance the White House agenda on legislative issues. The database contains info on millions of Obama donors, voters, and supporters. Did you contact the campaign through Facebook? Guess what—your friends and "Likes" were downloaded. Did you contact their Website through a mobile app? Your cell phone numbers and address books were downloaded. Via a Web browser? Computer cookies captured your browsing and online spending habits. Welcome to the machine.

Returning to what psychologist Nathan Jurgenson calls IRL ("in real life"), how can you ensure that you will age respectably to three-digits? Gerontologists tell us longevity is based on two main factors: genetics and lifestyle choices. Research involving twins reveals that how we take care of ourselves dominates longevity gains until we reach age 80; after that, almost everything is due to genetic factors. "Having Mercedes-Benz genes helps," says geriatric doctor Bradley Willcox, "but lifestyle choices are absolutely critical, especially if you're stuck with Ford Escort genes like most of us are." For example, not smoking ups the odds of reaching 100 by seven times. Other lifestyle choices that affect how long we live include marital status, geographical location, exercise, nutrition, amount of sleep, hygiene, driving habits, environment, and stress level. If you are an aspiring centenarian, "the only proven way to live longer is to live healthy," says longevity expert Mark Stibich. Carrot anyone?

***BRAIN SNACK:** According to the U.S. Centers for Disease Control and Prevention (CDC), the leading causes of death in the United States in 2010 were, in order of frequency, heart disease, cancer, and stroke. Yet alternative physician Joseph Mercola highlights that iatrogenesis, meaning "brought forth by a healer" (from the Greek iatros for healer) is one of the leading causes of death and injury in the United States. Iatrogenesis is an inadvertent adverse effect or complication resulting from medical treatment or advice. Mercola cites inadequate patient evaluation, lack of monitoring and follow-up, and failure to perform necessary tests as examples, along with the adverse effects associated with exposure to prescription drugs and medications. According to Mercola, an estimated 2 million people come down with hospital-acquired infections of any type in every year, and approximately 100,000 die from those infections.*

Increasingly death seems less of a worry for NeXters than the possibility of spending decades alive and sick. In the long run, being physically disabled is sad payback for youthful indifference and neglect. The extra life span you will "enjoy" will likely require long-term care and completely wipe out your savings (despite gains in longevity, on average 10 years is now spent with chronic disability, and rising). To avoid this, look in the glass and examine your own lifestyle choices and behaviors. Here are a few to consider.

- *Are you what you eat?* Absolutely…and these days, it's super-size. Two-thirds of U.S. adults are overweight (weighing 170 pounds or more for a man 5'9" tall). Over one-third of adults are obese (202 pounds or more at the same height).[288] The culprits: too many carbohydrates, too much food, too little exercise. The average American's intake is 3,700 calories per day and this exacts a steep cost. A wide girth is closely linked with high blood pressure, high blood sugar levels, and an excess of cholesterol and fats in the blood. Obesity significantly raises the risk of more than 20 chronic diseases and health conditions such as diabetes, heart

288 Severe obesity is projected to double by 2030, when 11 percent of adults will be nearly 100 pounds overweight or more.

disease, stroke, and some cancers. It also adversely affects joint wear, fertility, and mental health by fostering low self-esteem and depression. More than half of adults went on a diet in 2010.[289]

- *Are you a lounge lizard?* According to an article in *The Lancet*, one of the world's leading general medical journals, slothful activity has nearly the same deleterious effect on life expectancy as smoking. Sitting down for more than three hours a day can shave your life expectancy by two years. Watching TV for more than two hours a day can shave another 1.4 years, medical experts say. Researchers at the Longevity Project find that those who work the hardest live the longest.[290]
- *Are you stressed out?* These days, who isn't? Stress is frequently misunderstood as a longevity factor because there are two types. Bad stress ("distress") is described as a feeling of being overwhelmed, worried, or run-down. This stress reduces our quality and length of life. Good stress ("eustress") is the healthy tension associated with hard work, social challenges, or demanding careers. This stress pays off handsomely.

Finally, while good genes can help boost the odds in your favor, this kicks in much later in life. Thomas Perls, a medical professor who manages a study of nearly 1,600 centenarians, has shown that among those with centenarian siblings, men have nearly a 17 times greater chance than other men of living to 100 and women have a 9 times greater chance. In a study of people who lived to 95 or older, medical doctor Nir Barzilai and colleagues found that "centenarians may possess additional longevity genes that help to buffer them against the harmful effects of an unhealthy lifestyle." The only glitch is you first need to reach 95 to find out if your genes qualify. So, what can you do in the meantime? For the vast majority of the population, prescribes Barzilai, good lifestyle choices remain the critical element to a longer and healthier lifespan.[291]

Reali-tude:
Don't count on genes to compensate for poor lifestyle habits.

You control the horizontal. You control the vertical.

Excellence is not a singular act, but a habit. You are what you repeatedly do.
~ Shaquille O'Neal, basketball player

289 A Rockstar energy drink, popular with young persons, has 60 grams of sugar in a can, equivalent to putting 15 sugar cubes into a single cup of coffee. In 2010, First Lady Michelle Obama launched *Let's Move!*, an initiative to encourage youth to eat healthier foods and exercise more.

290 The Longevity Project is an eight-decade research project examining the longevity of more than 1,500 children. Begun in 1921 by psychologist Lewis Terman, it attempts to answer the question of who lives longest—and why—based on personality traits, relationships, experiences, and career paths.

291 Microbiologist Leonard Hayflick discovered that cells tend to divide a set number of times and then stop. Known as the *Hayflick limit*, this happens because protective endcaps on our chromosomes (called telomeres) shorten with each cell division. Once a telomere erodes too much, the cell becomes inactive or dies. Gene researchers find that healthy lifestyle experiences can slow down the telomere degradation, helping to defy genetic destiny.

Psychologist William James said, "All our life . . . is but a mass of habits." Habits govern our lives more than we might acknowledge, raising questions about how many of our daily lifestyle actions are the result of actual decision-making. Psychologist and habit researcher Wendy Wood suggests that about 40 percent of a young person's actions are habits, not real decisions. Reporting on Wood's findings in his book, *Making Habits, Breaking Habits*, PsyBlog creator Jeremy Dean says forming a habit takes surprisingly longer than most of us believe. If the habit is simple, say drinking a glass of water after breakfast each day, 21 days is about right. But for something hard, say running for 15 minutes after dinner, the time to make a habit concrete is much longer. On average, says Dean, it takes 66 days until a habit is formed. In one case, a habit was still not formed after 84 days of trying.

How do we go about forming a habit? In *The Power of Habit*, author Charles Duhigg explains what he calls the "habit loop" of habit formation: choose a trigger, associate it with a behavior, and reward yourself for doing the behavior. For example, place your sneakers by the front door to remind you to go for a run before breakfast. Then, after your run, reward yourself with your favorite coffee, he says.

But health psychologist Kelly McGonigal, who teaches a course called *The Science of Willpower*, sees this as a simplistic solution. Many of us do a poor job of controlling our habits, especially when it comes to what she calls "really freakin' hard changes" like addiction, weight loss, or overcoming anxiety-based procrastination. McGonigal stresses that we won't reach whatever goals we seek—from happiness to good health to financial security—without first learning to harness self-control. And that can be very challenging.[292] To succeed, she says, you need skills for tolerating distress, cravings, anxiety, and discomfort. You need social support or role models, as well as self-compassion for the inevitable setbacks. You also need to be mindful when you might be acting in ways counter to your goals and recognize new, unplanned opportunities that will move you forward. Finally, you need willpower for when you are most overwhelmed by desire, stress, anxiety, boredom, or self-doubt, McGonigal says.

Where to turn when you want to make a really freakin' hard change to your lifestyle? One smart choice: ask a tribal elder. Having (hopefully) learned something from their mistakes, tribal elders are reservoirs of wisdom. Their more experienced eye recognizes when a decision is important and deserves your attention, and they can be an important resource for improving your self-control.

In the final analysis, education may be the most powerful factor associated with living better and longer. The findings from a study by 15 leading academic experts in aging and longevity at the Population Health Institute found that "Education exerts its direct beneficial effects on health through the adoption of healthier lifestyles, better ability to cope with stress, and more effective management of chronic diseases." The impact of education on lifespan is so powerful, the authors

292 Chapter 10 discusses why, of all cognitive traps, *self-control* is the most important to appreciate and the most difficult to avoid.

conclude, that improving people's health and lifestyle behaviors alone "are not likely to have a major impact on disparities in longevity." In other words, the more education you have, the more likely that you will make healthier lifestyle choices and live a longer, happier, and more fulfilling life.

Reali-tude:
Early investments in healthy life-choices will have a large payoff as you age.

The bottom line:

- While our tools change quickly, basic human nature adjusts at a slower pace.
- What happens in Vegas doesn't stay in Vegas; not if you go posting, tweeting, and blogging about it.
- 70–80 percent of your lifespan depends upon your lifestyle choices.
- Education and good habits may be the most powerful factors in living a longer and healthier life.

Doctor's Prescription (Rx)

To err is human, but to really foul things up you need a computer.
~ William E. Vaughan, columnist

For some of us, social media use offers feelings of greater connectivity, increased self-esteem, decreased loneliness, and even warm feelings of nostalgia. For others, on-line socializing elicits feelings of low self-esteem, insecurity, narcissism, and envy—as well as replacing important offline ties with family and friends. Which describes you? Here are some tips to help you use Facebook in a positive way:

- Ask why you're on Facebook. Is it to connect ("bond") or to network ("bridge")?
- Reflect on how you use Facebook. Do you spend too much time reading the news feeds of others? Do you only cue into your own profile to look for connections or do you venture beyond to connect with others? Are your conversations creating support, or are they provocative, challenging, or taunting?
- Ask yourself what your activities on Facebook do for you socially and emotionally.[293]
- Adjust your social media experience to help you feel good about yourself and the others you're choosing to share your on-line time with. If you discover that using Facebook isn't as valuable a tool for you, bow out.

293 A United Kingdom study suggests that loneliness is more prevalent among the social-networking younger generation than in older people. Nearly 60 percent of those aged 18 to 34 speak of feeling lonely often or sometimes, compared to 35 percent of those aged over 55. Young persons say talking to hundreds of people on social networks is not like having a real relationship and when they are using these sites they are often alone in their bedrooms. More women than men report loneliness and are more likely to feel depressed as a result.

- Whether you are an extrovert or an introvert, find your comfort "self-disclosing" zone. Facebook should be a place that you design for your social needs.
- Interface beyond the virtual world by spending quality time socializing in real time with real people.

Young persons want to have a sense of control over their Facebook information. Facebook offers many privacy controls, but good luck understanding them. *Consumer Reports* offers these tips:

- *Think before you type.* Even if you delete an account (which takes Facebook about a month), some info can remain in Facebook's computers for up to 90 days.
- *Regularly check your exposure.* Each month, check out how your page looks to others and review individual privacy settings if necessary.
- *Protect basic information.* Set the audience for profile items, such as your town or employer. Resist the temptation to add people you don't really know or don't want to engage with. Sharing info with "friends of friends" could expose it to tens of thousands.
- *Know what you can't protect.* Your name and profile picture are public. To protect your identity, don't use a photo, or use one that doesn't show your face.
- *"UnPublic" your wall.* Set the audience for all previous wall posts to just friends.
- *Turn off Tag Suggest.* If you'd rather not have Facebook automatically recognize your face in photos, disable that feature in your privacy settings.
- *Block apps and sites that snoop.* Unless you intercede, friends can share personal information about you with apps. To block that, use controls to limit the info apps can see.
- *Keep wall posts from friends.* You don't have to share every wall post with every friend. You can also keep certain people from viewing specific items in your profile.
- *When all else fails, deactivate.* When you deactivate your account, Facebook retains your profile data, but the account is made temporarily inaccessible. Deleting an account makes it inaccessible to you forever.

Talking Points

> *I think fitness is important. I think a healthy lifestyle is important. I think putting positive energy out there is important and just staying connected with the people.*
>
> ~ LL Cool J, rapper, actor

Lots of young persons identify with a desired lifestyle, yet refuse to devote the necessary mental effort to define how they will achieve it. Many engage in risky and addictive behaviors as part of their everyday lifestyle, discounting the inevitable adverse effects they will have on their later quality of life. Others simply do not care. They live their version of the American Dream, to quote Sir Elton John, "Like a candle in the wind." Don't be one of them!

Reali-tude:
Instead of looking to others to change your mind, why not change it yourself?

Chapter 17 describes some tools to help you acquire wisdom by interviewing others. To benefit from these techniques, you need only have access to a parent, educator, or other trusted adult (tribal elder) and a desire to listen and learn. Based on the ideas in this chapter, here are some starters:

1. "I am trying to improve myself. Some say the American Dream—that anyone can rise from humble beginnings and succeed—may be failing. Reflecting on your experience, or that of someone you know, do you recall a situation where lifestyle choices either significantly benefited or hindered their long-term well-being?" If they say "Yes" then ask:

    - "Would you tell me the gist about what happened please?"
    - "How did you (they) feel about this at the time?"
    - "What two things did you learn from this that you can share with me?"

2. "I am trying to improve myself. Today, many young persons feel that sharing who they are on-line is more important than any concerns for privacy. Reflecting on your experience, or that of someone you know, do you recall a situation where being "open and connected" either significantly benefited or hindered their long-term well-being?" If they say "Yes" then ask:

    - "Would you tell me the gist about what happened please?"
    - "How did you (they) feel about this at the time?"
    - "What two things did you learn from this that you can share with me?"

    In either case, if they say "No," simply say "Thank you."

3. Making good lifestyle choices that promote a longer life often means sacrificing short-term pleasures. Reflecting on your experience, or that of someone you know, what two suggestions would you have for a young person that is contemplating these choices?

4. "I want to make wise life-choices. Reflecting on your experience, would you have two ideas that I can implement to improve my judgment and decision-making skills? Be sure to thank them for their response.

Knowledge Nuggets

My lifestyle has made me a walking time bomb.
~ Jack Wild, actor (millionaire at age 18, alcoholic at 21, dead at 53)

1. *What do quiz developers know about you?* Facebook quizzes are fun little distractions. But those seemingly harmless tests also gather personal information about you and your Facebook friends. When you open an application to take a quiz, you grant its developer access to almost everything in your profile, including pictures, wall posts, and the groups you've joined. You also grant access to most of the information on your friends' profiles. Find out what developers collect about you and your friends every time you take a Facebook quiz at: https://www.facebook.com/login.php?api_key=973dda444fe96621fc30f2bbf212937a&v=1.0&next=http%3A%2F%2Fdotrights.org%2Fapps%2Faclunc_privacy_quiz.php&canvas=1&_fb_q=1.

2. *What does Facebook have about me?* You can ask Facebook to send you "your data" using a link that appears under Account Settings. If you don't see it, Google "download my information from Facebook" and follow the instructions in the first search result from facebook.com. What you get from Facebook is an email with a link that downloads a zip file. Extract the file. Not included are comments you have left on other people's walls. The set of data called "Ads" is a list of search terms used to target you with ads. Some of them might surprise you!

3. *Are you an innie or an outie?* Psychologists find that intrinsically motivated people are much happier than those who are extrinsically motivated. Intrinsically-motivated people are driven by their own values and are represented by self-acceptance, affiliation, and community feeling. Extrinsically-motivated people focus on financial gain, their appearance, and social popularity and generally seek acceptance by something or someone outside themselves. People who are the most extrinsically-motivated, and stay that way for a long time, begin to lose touch with the things in life that bring them the most joy. See what motivates your lifestyle at: http://www.getrichslowly.org/blog/2011/06/08/the-psychology-of-consumerism.

4. *Her life helps your health.* Her name was Henrietta Lacks, but scientists know her as HeLa. She was a poor Southern tobacco farmer who worked the same land as her slave ancestors, yet her cells—taken without her knowledge—became one of the most important tools in medicine. Grown in culture, her cells are still alive today, though she has been dead for more than 60 years. HeLa cells were vital for developing the polio vaccine, and uncovering secrets of cancer, viruses, and nuclear bomb effects. They also helped lead to important advances in vitro fertilization, cloning, and gene mapping. Read Henrietta's story at: http://rebeccaskloot.com/the-immortal-life.

5. *Where to go for info?* See Appendix F for additional information relating to this chapter.

Part 5: Making Smart Choices

(Develop the Power)

Chapter 16

How To Make Better Decisions

Nothing is more difficult, and therefore more precious, than to be able to decide.

~ Napoleon Bonaparte, Emperor of the French

The Gist

The Good:

- Good decisions come from having a good decision-making process
- Rational decision-makers use logic, objectivity, and facts

The Bad:

- Most decisions have time, information, and cognitive constraints
- Heuristics can introduce risky beliefs and errors in judgment
- Young persons readily recognize bias, except when it is their own

The Reality:

- Intuition is an impression, a hunch, or a sense of something not evident
- Intuitive decision-making is the default mode of thinking
- Lack of experience is the Achilles' heel for intuitive decisions
- Gist-based thinking is a skill; tap tribal elders to master it

Introduction

It is our choices, Harry, that show what we truly are, far more than our abilities.

~ Dumbledore, in *Phoenix* by J. K. Rowling

When ancient Greeks (and later, the Romans) had to make everyday decisions, they consulted the gods by drawing lots, casting dice, and interpreting dreams. For matters of the utmost importance, however, they sought to hear the words of the gods directly from the mouth of an oracle. An oracle was a person who was considered to be a source of great knowledge, wisdom, or prophecy. The most famous of these was the Oracle of Delphi.

In the eighth century B.C.E., the city of Delphi was considered to be the center of the known world. Located about 75 miles west of Athens in ancient Greece, people flocked there by the thousands to worship the god Apollo. Son of Zeus, Apollo was considered by the Greeks to be the embodiment of moral discipline and spiritual clarity. The splendid temple they built and dedicated to him was perched on the south slope of Mount Parnassus, high in the mountains. The site was surrounded by steep cliffs, so getting there was a major hassle. One either had a long trek across the mountains or a sea voyage to the north shore of the Gulf of Corinth. To the ancients, however, the pilgrimage was worth it to hear what they believed was truth.

For nearly a thousand years the ancient peoples of the Mediterranean had faith in the Oracle's ability to divine the future. Greek and foreign dignitaries, heads of state, even troubled common folk made the arduous journey. They paid great sums for the Oracle to petition Apollo's spirit for advice and offer prognostications on critical matters. No major decision was made without first consulting the Oracle. In time, Delphi flourished as an international center and became one of the wealthiest sanctuary cities in the ancient world.

Although classical Greece was male dominated, paradoxically the Oracle at Delphi was a woman! Called the *Pythia*, or "one who spoke on behalf of the gods," it was the job of the high priestess to "channel" the spirit of Apollo.[294] Roman historian Plutarch (ca. 46–120 A.D.), who had served as a priest at Delphi, related details about how she managed to pull this off and enrich a city. According to his description, the Pythia sat on a tripod over a rock fissure in the temple's inner sanctuary.[295] Inhaling deeply, she would lapse into a trance and then deliver her

294 Pythias were virgins who dedicated their lives to prophesying on behalf of the god Apollo. Today we have Dr. Laura.

295 The Greeks called the inner chamber of the temple *omphalos*, or "navel of the world."

sometimes incomprehensible prophecies. The priests of the sanctuary duly interpreted her messages and delivered them to the people who had made the request (for a tidy fee). Notwithstanding their notoriety, the oracles were quite fickle in their prescriptions. Often their incantations signified dual and opposing meanings, leaving much to the imagination of the client. One prescription not left to the imagination was "Will that be cash, check, or Capital One?"

BRAIN SNACK: *In 1996, modern investigators excavated the sanctuary at Delphi. Geologists found active faults in the rock of Mount Parnassus and identified the limestone under the temple as bituminous (oil bearing). It is likely that the rock fissure over which the Pythia sat was a small fracture extending up from these faults. In his writings, Plutarch described an intoxicating gas that emanated from the cleft, with a sweet smell like expensive perfume. Of the hydrocarbon gases, only ethylene has a sweet smell, leading researchers to suspect that ethylene was likely inhaled by the Pythia. Could it be the Oracle at Delphi received her divine inspiration while being stoned? What a gas!*

In practice, the Pythia dealt less in visions of the future than in making smart choices. For example, where to locate a new colony, when to attack an enemy, how to lift a curse, who to choose as leader, what offering to make to which god, who to marry, should the baby's room be pink or blue, and so on. No kingdom, city, or ordinary citizen could afford to make these important decisions without first consulting her. Fortunately, we no longer need to rely on the Pythia to divine our choices!

Reali-tude:
Ultimately, the choices you make are your responsibility.

The Good

Did you ever have to make up your mind?
~ The Lovin' Spoonful, American pop rock group

Whether simple or complex, private or public, decisions are an essential part of our life. Since everything we do in life requires a decision of some kind, the ability to make smart choices is a particularly vital skill to master. The decisions we make often affect not only our own life, but also the lives of our friends, our family, and our community. It is also worth noting that the global economy is increasingly putting a premium on sound judgment and strong decision-making skills.

Decision-making is the process of identifying alternatives and sufficiently reducing uncertainty and doubt to allow a reasonable choice to be made from among them. Most all young persons will face a number of strategic inflections, or major turning points in their life. Should I go on to college? What kind of career is right for me? Am I ready to get married? Should I have a baby? Where should I live?

What kind of lifestyle do I want to have? What are my expectations for the long-term? When you think about it, how we respond to these essential questions of life largely defines who we are. These decisions are too important to leave to chance.

> *People of our generation have so many more factors and choices to consider in answering these questions than any previous generation—even our parents'. Just compare the choices available to us for careers, spending money, and traveling with those available to people our age thirty years ago. So while we're asking the same questions as say, the ancient Egyptians, our list of potential answers is much, much longer.*
>
> ~ Comment at a workshop on adolescent decision making

"Making a good decision and avoiding a horrible one is not a chance act," says management professor Michael Roberto. "It's a skill," he advises, "one that can be learned, honed, and perfected." But determining which decisions are wise and which are foolish or imprudent is not always clear. Even when we can distinguish between a sensible and a not-so-sensible choice, we don't always have the discipline to follow our heads. Being aware of the underlying psychological, social, and emotional components that influence decision making—whether they are your own decisions or the decisions of others—can provide a greater sense of control over the process and outcomes.

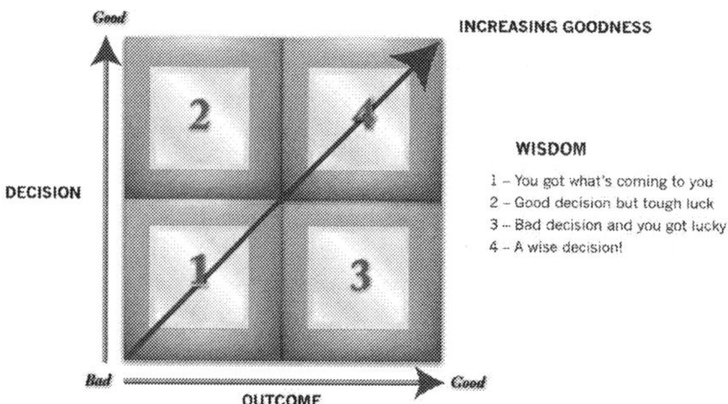

Figure 16.1 Decision-making outcomes.

What constitutes making a "wise" decision? As shown in Figure 16.1, the quality of a decision is not the same as the quality of the outcome. A good decision can be good (adds positive value), neutral (adds no value), or poor (adds negative value).[296] For example, say that you did extensive analysis and decided to purchase a particular company stock. Unfortunately, the day after you bought the stock, a tsunami leveled the headquarters building. Your decision was still a good one, even though you lost your shirt on that investment. A bad decision is one that was based on inadequate or unreliable information, or one that did not reflect what you really wanted. A bad decision is usually a result of a poorly thought-out decision-making process, but it can still have a good outcome. This means you got lucky. For example, if you throw a dart at the stock pages and buy the one it hits, your decision is a bad one, even if the stock price rises. Although you scored

296 Adapted from March, J.G. and Simon, H.A. (1958), *Organizations*. Wiley: New York.

a good outcome purely by accident, the wise decision-maker doesn't rely solely on dumb luck in order to succeed. Understanding the "choosing" process can enable you to examine mistakes that you (or others) may have made in the past so you can more adeptly avoid them in your future.

It is important to realize that each of us has a highly individualized approach to decision making. What works for your friend may not be what works for you. And that's okay. Despite personal preferences, however, researchers say all of us have two basic decision styles. Some of us prefer to gather information, objectively weigh different options, and analytically determine which choice is best. Psychologists refer to this style as the *rational choice mode.* Others prefer to rely on experience, values, and perceptions (commonly referred to as "gut feel") to make up their mind on the spot. This style is called the *intuitive choice mode.* Most of our decisions are made using this intuitive style, in large part because it is faster, more convenient, and less stressful. Regardless of your preferred style, the best approach depends on the significance of the decision, the challenges involved, and the time available for analysis.

A good controllable decision is never an accident. It is always the result of logical intention, sincere effort, intelligent direction, and skillful execution. A good decision represents the wise choice of many alternatives and the outcome is one that adds positive value to your long-term success.

Reali-tude:
Be suitably prepared when an important decision is required.

Rational choice

The very essence of being decision literate is asking yourself the question, "I wonder what the cost is?" when something attracts you.
~ Helen Meyers, President, SC Council on Economic Education

Since the rational choice mode consumes considerable time and effort, we tend to use it only when we are faced with an important or complicated decision. If we rationally decide everything, we would never get anything else done! Rational decision-making does not mean making the one "right choice" in some larger ethical, social, or human sense. It simply means that you are motivated by self-interest to better yourself with the least effort and resources possible. By this definition, a person who disciplines himself to move toward bettering himself is rational. Someone who consciously seeks to make himself worse off is irrational and self-destructive. Unless you are more than a little weird (or truly altruistic), most all of us are driven by our own self-interest.[297]

297 Economists refer to an ideal but fictitious person called *Homo economicus*, or "economic human." Homo economicus is endowed with complete rationality, total self-interest, and perfect information. The problem, of course, is humans are not perfect. We tend to be driven by emotions not logic, and emotions are often irrational. Thus, we procrastinate, are overconfident in our judgment and abilities, underestimate the long-term consequences of our actions, and lack adequate self-control. In fact, we

The rational decision maker scopes out his best economic interests and then acts accordingly—not on habit or custom—but on a deliberate and knowledgeable reasoning about the possible results of his actions. He presupposes that there is one best outcome and his final choice is what he expects will bring him the maximum gain. This "optimizing strategy" sprang from the philosophy of hedonism,[298] which held that individuals calculate the actions that will maximize their self-interest and behave accordingly. This is a natural response. Most of us want to get the largest slice of the pizza for our self, all the while trying to avoid any surprises (such as getting thrown out of the kitchen). As a rational decision-maker, we tend to follow a decision process that typically includes the following steps, not necessarily listed in the order in which they occur:

- Identify the decision to be made (it may be a problem or an opportunity).
- List all of the relevant choices.
- Identify the potential consequences of each choice.
- Assess the likelihood of each consequence actually occurring.
- Determine the important effects of these consequences.
- Combine all this information to decide which choice is the most appealing.

This "balance sheet" calculation approach has some distinct advantages. First, it defines the problem and establishes clear preferences. It also helps ensure that we include all relevant decision alternatives and explicitly consider how they contribute or detract from our goals (i.e., we identify the costs and benefits). Finally, it allows us to carefully review our logic, facts, and assumptions so that we can submit it to others for review and comment. Of course, the downside is someone might nab the pizza while we are doing our analysis… Below are four easy-to-use methods for making rational decisions (see Appendix C for some nifty decision templates):

Making a rational choice where you have only one alternative ("Go/No-Go"):

- *Pros-Cons & Interesting Implications:* In using this approach, write the proposed decision down. Below it, construct a table with three headings, "Pluses," "Minuses," and "Interesting implications." List all of the characteristics you can think of. Intuitively we make simplified analyses like this every day, such as when we ask ourselves, "Shall I ride the bus or won't it save me enough time to be worth my while?"
- *Weighted Pros and Cons:* Benjamin Franklin proposed this method in a 1772 letter to Joseph Priestly.[299] Faced with making a difficult decision, Franklin

are not really 100 percent self-interested—we sometimes perform altruistic acts such as volunteering, parenting, or giving one's life for one's country.

298 A philosophical doctrine that holds that pleasure is the highest good or the source of moral values. The name derives from the Greek word *hĕdonismos* meaning "delight."

299 Joseph Priestley (1733–1804) was probably the greatest English scientist since Newton and the discoverer of oxygen. He was also an important social philosopher and a founder of what was then

suggested that you list the pros and cons as they come to mind over a period of time, not just at a single sitting. Then weight the items to establish their level of importance and ascertain the balance of the pro/con scores. Franklin's cost-benefit analysis is useful to assess heady decisions such as, "Should the parentals subsidize my car insurance?"

Making a rational choice where you have a number of good alternatives and many factors:

- *Grid analysis:* This is a great technique to use in almost any important decision where there isn't a clear and obvious preferred option. For example, a windsurfing enthusiast is about to replace her car and has always loved open-topped sports cars. While she needs it to carry her board and sails, it also needs to be good for business travel. She has narrowed her choice down to four models, but none is good for all three things. If six factors are important to her (e.g., cost, fuel efficiency, etc.), which car is her best choice?

Making a rational choice when you have a number of equally attractive but different options:

- *Paired Comparison:* Agonizing over several choices that seem equally attractive? This method is perhaps the most straightforward way to compare "apples with oranges," that is, completely different options. Wondering whether you should invest your hard earned money in a college education, a new Internet business, or in an index stock fund? This nifty technique can help you prioritize those gut busters!

Some people dismiss these processes as robot-like and reject the notion that important decisions in our lives can be made analytically. A cartoon in the *New Yorker* magazine shows a man sitting at a computer and saying to a woman: "I've done the numbers, and I will marry you." Granted, some decisions should not be based solely on comparing soulless numbers, but the rational decision making process can still be a very useful framework to help clarify your thinking.

Thinking like an economist doesn't mean you have well-defined, memorized rules and answers to any question that can arise. You have a framework that can provide you with the questions necessary to think your way through, analyze, and reason your way to an important decision. It's all about seeing the world in a particular way, and perhaps sometimes improving the rationality of the decisions you make in that world.

~ Randall Bartlett, economist

---

called the *Rational Dissenters.* Rational Dissenters believed that reason and necessity, coupled with liberty and freedom, were the guide to all human progress and social reform.

Reali-tude:
A reasoning mind is the key to achievement.

The bottom line:

- Your life is the sum of all your choices.
- Good decision-making is a skill that can be learned and improved.
- The quality of a decision is not the same as the quality of the outcome.
- The decision-making style that works for your friends may not work for you.

The Bad

> *Wisdom comes from good judgment, and good judgment comes from experience. Experience comes from a series of times when you used bad judgment.*
> ~ Anonymous

Ideally, when we make a decision we would want to have all possible information, all of it accurate, along with every possible alternative. In real life, however, constraints on identifying and defining alternatives always limit the quality of our decision outcomes. How thorough we can afford to be in making our choice is dependent on the importance of the problem, the time we have available to solve it, and what it takes for us to research solutions. As a result, this introduces a certain amount of uncertainty into most of our decisions. If there is no uncertainty, there is no decision. Rather, what we have is an algorithm—a series of steps that we follow to achieve a static result.[300] Let's look at some ways that risk can enter the picture.

Time and information constraints

> *If you see ten troubles coming down the road, you can be sure that nine will run into the ditch before they reach you.*
> ~ Calvin Coolidge, 30th President

Many decisions must be made by a certain time, such as, "Marry me this year or move out, worm!" Decide too quickly and you risk not giving the problem (your mate) adequate consideration. Wait too long, and some choices may no longer be available (your ex-mate). As new information and alternatives become available, hindsight is always more accurate than foresight. We can look back and possibly see there was a better choice than the one we actually selected (your ex-mate's, ex-friend).

We have the same conundrum regarding the complexity and reliability of information. Too little information and we risk not comprehending the extent of the problem. Too much complexity and we may delay the decision or avoid it

300 An algorithm is a logical, step-by-step procedure for solving a problem in a finite number of steps. In computers, these steps are typically written out as a flow chart. In cooking, the algorithms are our recipes!

altogether. Too much information, especially in a short period of time, and we can experience information overload. When this happens, we remember only some of what we received, often that which we received early on. Have you ever gone shopping for something where you looked at many alternatives—cell phones, cameras, shoes, greeting cards—only to decide that you actually liked the first one best?

There are some benefits to delaying a decision:

- *More careful analysis.* We can gather more information, verify its reliability, and do a more thoughtful analysis ("Honey, do you really think we can afford to have a child?").
- *Glad I waited.* We might see new alternatives (say, the release of version 2.0).
- *On second thought.* Our preferences might change ("With the longer commute, I really need to have a gas sipper instead of a gas guzzler").

Delaying a decision, however, can also generate risks:

- *Paralysis by analysis.* We avoid a decision for fear of making the wrong choice. The benefit of making some decision, even a random choice, is usually more beneficial in the long-run.[301]
- *Up the creek without a paddle.* Hesitate on that bargain of a lifetime and you may find it is no longer available when you come back to buy it.
- *More likely to change.* Delaying makes it much less likely that you will stay with the status quo (i.e., you are much more likely to select the new choice).

How much time, energy, and processing power we devote to a decision depends upon how important we perceive it to be. For situations that involve high stakes, such as strategic inflections, we may do a rigorous analysis over a period of weeks or months. For decisions that are difficult but not worth a major effort, we may take hours weighing the pros and cons before choosing an alternative. For easy, everyday, or reversible decisions, we simply apply a dollop of common sense and make up our minds in seconds or minutes.

BRAIN SNACK: ***In making a decision, all of us are constrained by the available time and information, along with our individual information-processing ability. It is impossible for anyone to consider all of the potential options and then compute the single alternative that will maximize the gains and minimize the losses. We simply cannot keep that many ideas in our mind at one time. Nor can we***

301 In *The Paradox of Choice, Why More is Less*, psychologist Barry Schwartz shows how the dramatic explosion in choice—from the mundane to the profound challenges of balancing career, family, and individual needs—has paradoxically become a problem instead of a solution. Often we don't know or are unsure what to decide and we resort to informal decision support techniques such as tossing a coin or asking an astrologer. Schwartz makes the counterintuitive case that eliminating choices can greatly reduce the stress, anxiety, and busyness of our lives.

anticipate the effects of unexpected influences. In the real world human decision-making is rational, but only within limits. Nobel laureate Herbert Simon (Economics, 1978) coined the phrase "bounded rationality" to describe this reality.

It never pays to search endlessly for the one best alternative. Typically we consider our options one by one and then select the first one that is adequate to meet our minimum level of acceptability. For instance, if you are very hungry, you might decide to stop at the first decent looking restaurant in town rather than select the best restaurant from among all of them. This process, called "satisficing," was coined by Simon as a combination of the words "satisfactory" and "sufficient." Satisficers try to find a solution that is "good enough." In other words, they go with the first acceptable choice (Whopper with cheese, please). By contrast, *maximizers* spend three hours and a half-tank of gas trying to find the very best parking place at the mall.[302] For small decisions, such as where to park, what to drink, which pen to use, which tie or dress to wear, and so on, the satisficing strategy is the way to go.

Reali-tude:
The "optimum" is the enemy of the "good."

Cognitive constraints

Life is lived forward but understood backwards.
~ Soren Kierkegaard, Danish philosopher

Rational decision-makers must look dispassionately at all of the facts before choosing. Like dieting, however, this is easier said than done. This is because there's a fly in the soup—the brain isn't a flawless piece of machinery. It is powerful and comes in an easy to carry container, but there's a growing view among economists that psychological factors other than pure reasoning often drive people's decisions. We use heuristics, or hardwired mental shortcuts, to help lighten our cranial load so we don't have to break a mental sweat. But rules of thumb can get us into trouble if the going gets complicated.

At every stage of the decision-making process, our needs, motives, desires, expectations, and the context of the situation influence our rational judgment. Misperceptions, biases, habits, and other tricks of the mind in the form of questionable beliefs distort our perception of ourselves, our circumstances, and those surrounding us. Even with perfect information we are not highly competent in knowing what to do with it, and what happens is we end up making bad choices. Like a werewolf, some of the outcomes may haunt us down the road. Table 16.1 summarizes the psychological traps we looked at in earlier chapters.

Young persons recognize the existence of these (and other) biases and the impact they have on the decision-making process. But they fail to recognize the

302 Research shows that "maximizers," who tend to take longer making decisions, more often regret their decisions.

	Cognitive Traps	Questionable Beliefs
Confidence	**Optimism Trap** (overconfident in our judgment)	1. Overestimate the likelihood that the outcomes we want will occur 2. Underestimate the impact of random chance and uncontrollable events
	Superiority Trap (overconfident in our capabilities)	1. Exaggerate the extent of our knowledge, ability, or memory 2. Overemphasize our sense of self-control over events
Change	**Framing Trap** (misunderstand the context of change)	1. Underappreciate how others shape our opinion and desires 2. Tunnel vision regarding other possible outcomes and contingencies
	Inertia Trap (unwilling to change the status quo)	1. Procrastinate or deny the need to take action 2. Overly influenced by our peers (the "herd instinct")
Maturity	**Projection Trap** (underestimate the long-term consequences)	1. Underappreciate how different tomorrow's preferences will be from today's 2. Focus our attention solely on the immediate situation at hand
	Self-Control Trap (inability to control our emotional impulses)	1. Sacrifice our long-term interests for short-term rewards and pleasures 2. Fail to follow through on our intentions

Table 16.1 Cognitive Traps.

role these same biases have in shaping their own judgment and inference. This tendency to recognize (and even overestimate) the operation of bias in human judgment—except when that bias is their own—has been called the *bias blind spot*. The term was created by social psychologist Emily Pronin, and is named after the visual blind spot. Research shows that in many instances, smarter people are more vulnerable to these thinking errors, have larger bias blind spots, and when aware of their own biases, are not better able to overcome them.

The degree to which people are aware of their level of self-control varies, however. Behavioral economists Ted O'Donoghue and Matthew Rabin describe the behavior of what they call *naïfs* (a naive or inexperienced person) as simple and straightforward. Naïfs are fully unaware that they harbor any bias whatsoever. Thus, they fall prey to a panoply of questionable beliefs and risky behaviors. They procrastinate on unpleasant tasks, believe people get ahead in life because they are lucky, overindulge in the present, and fail to follow through on their good intentions. In a nutshell, when a naïf makes a controllable decision, he is totally oblivious that he may be wrong.

Sophisticates are fully aware they harbor biases and attempt to minimize the extent to which bias may influence their judgment and decision making. They tend to be critical thinkers, understand the value of taking the long-view, and actively seek advice from tribal elders (trusted adults). In between the extremes are the *partially naïve*. While they are aware they may have some biases, they underestimate their magnitude. For example, a college student who repeatedly does not have the will power to forgo tempting foods or quit smoking always predicts that she will have this willpower tomorrow. Are you a naïf? A sophisticate? Look in the glass—which describes you?

> *If you were in a canoe, you'd probably want to know about any holes in the boat before you start paddling. Biases can be holes in your reasoning abilities and they can impair your decision making. Simply noticing these holes isn't enough; a canoe will fill with water whether you are aware of a hole or not. But by being aware of the holes you can devise methods to patch them up. The entire domain of the scientific method has largely been an effort to overcome the natural inclination towards bias in reasoning.*
> ~ Mad Mike (The Bruiser), psychologist

All of the traps in Table 16.1 can work in isolation. But even more dangerous is they can also work in concert and amplify each other.[303] The best protection against all psychological traps—in isolation or in combination—is being aware of their ubiquitous existence. Forewarned is forearmed.

Reali-tude:
Minor sustained biases can generate large cumulative losses.

Luck

> *Don't be deceived by life's outcomes. Life's outcomes, while not entirely random, have a huge amount of luck baked into them. Above all, recognize that if you have had success, you have also had luck.*
> ~ Michael Lewis, financial journalist

The other factor that might affect a decision outcome is luck, also called fortuity. Luck is a belief in good or bad fortune in life, caused by accident or by chance, and believers feel it is beyond a person's control. This belief is pervasive in common speech. For example, we have all heard the phrases "Good Luck!" to wish a blessing on someone or "It was just his luck" to describe a misfortune. Unlike chance or probability, luck is distinct in that it is always either good or bad.

Rationalist decision-makers discount luck. They prefer to make decisions "by the book" and feel that a belief in luck is a result of poor reasoning or wishful thinking. Many rationalists—especially those who are successful—feel their success was somehow inevitable and don't want to acknowledge any role played by accident in their lives.[304] Some barriers that rationalists commonly cite for people relying on luck include:

---

303 The use of pesticides is a good example of this phenomenon. When two pesticides are used together, the toxicity does not double; it is 35 times greater than a single pesticide. When three pesticides are used, the toxicity goes up 100 times greater. Problem-solving errors tend to act in the same manner. The thorniest problems occur when a number of errors come into play.

304 The *illusion of control* bias can cause you to overestimate the amount that your actions will influence results. Advises author Anna Quindlen, "The illusion of control is the besetting addiction, and

- Fear of failure (others will disapprove of the decision);
- Fear of success (others will thereafter expect perfection);
- An inability to set priorities and a feeling of being overwhelmed;
- A hope that someone else will decide.[305]

Today, many young persons are in a fog about how to produce the success they feel they deserve. Their mental focus is limited to uttering "I wish" and the rest is left to faith and luck. Rhonda Byrne's motivational best-seller *The Secret*, for example, basically says that you get what you wish for. According to Byrne and motivational guru James Ray, you are a field of vibrating energy. Their universal "law of attraction" says that when you're in a certain vibration, you will attract to you that which you're in harmonic vibration with. They claim this works for personal finance, relationships, intellectual pursuits, physical and spiritual development, fill-in-the-blank. If you don't have the things you want, you simply don't have enough faith, they claim. Your wish... is the universe's command.[306]

From a physicist's point of view, this is so much codswallop. Psychological research has shown that wishful thinking may indeed lead to poor decisions. While positive fantasies allow us to anticipate success in the here and now, they don't alert us to the problems we are likely to face along the way. Although a man has faith that he will be rich, he must discover what means, actions, or conditions are required to achieve wealth. While a woman may pine for luck in love, she needs to think about what love is, what values it requires, and whether she possesses any virtues to be loved. Success requires that you be more than a backseat driver, which can quickly depress motivation.

On the other hand, some researchers have found that luck induces positive thinking, thereby altering one's responses for the better. Psychologist Richard Wiseman, author of *The Luck Factor*, has extensively studied the concept of luck. He demonstrates that lucky people do have more good things happen to them than the unlucky ones, but not because of chance or luck. According to Wiseman, luck is determined by your state of mind and the way you engage the world. When compared to "unlucky" people, the "lucky" subjects were found to be significantly more extroverted and open. They were twice as likely to smile and engage in eye contact. They were also half as anxious. Wiseman concludes that maximizing chance opportunities, listening to gut-feelings, expecting good fortune, and seeing the bright side of bad luck all enhanced one's "luckiness." Thus, a belief in good luck can be self-reinforcing and may possibly be an adaptive meme.

---

delusion, of the modern age. Life is haphazard. We plan, and then we deal when the plans go awry. Control is an illusion; best intentions are the best we can do. Life is full of close calls."

305 The word *decidophobia*, or fear of making serious decisions, was coined by philosopher Walter Kaufmann (1973).

306 Since Norman Vincent Peale's book *The Power of Positive Thinking* was first published in the 1950s, belief in the clout of excessive optimism has almost become a modern religion. If only people believe in themselves, their abilities, and how great their future is going to be, everything will work out just fine.

The key lesson: empowering yourself so as to generate your own luck is better than simply waiting to get lucky. Success is not inevitable. Make luck work in your favor by climbing into the driver's seat and accepting responsibility for your own choices in life. Some of you will make this transition relatively easily; others will get into serious troubles before eventually bringing yourselves under control; some will never overcome a belief that success comes only to those who are lucky. Part of growing up is acknowledging that timing and luck have a role in fulfilling your aspirations, and that there is much that a young person, aware of her own limitations, can do to improve her situation. Reading the *Young Person's Guide* is one of them!

Reali-tude:
Luck is the intersection of preparation and opportunity.

The bottom line:

- Most people are much poorer at decision-making than they think.
- Bad life-choices are not fixed by hitting the "undo" button.
- Young persons are quick to recognize bias in others but not themselves.
- Luck is not always the residue of design.

The Reality

Most decisions are seat-of-the-pants judgments. You can create a rationale for anything. In the end, most decisions are based on intuition and faith.
~ Nathan Myhrvold, former CTO at Microsoft

Academics describe the rational approach to making controllable decisions as "sequentially linear." This is a fancy way of saying it is a step-by-step, straightforward analytical process. Suppose, for example, that you want to decide whether to get married. The rational approach would be to weigh the benefits and drawbacks. You identify the criteria for the lucky woman (outgoing, good listener, athletic, etc.) and then list the available choices likely to have these criteria (Janeen, Mia, Erica, etc.). You evaluate each friend and choose the one who best meets the criteria. The process for this decision is straightforward: decision whether, select criteria, identify alternatives, match criteria to alternatives, make your choice... Miller time.

The problem is this is not the way that people, especially young persons, usually act. In real life, we often make important choices without going through the decision-making steps systematically. We find ourselves going back and forth, cycling between defining the criteria we want our choice to meet and identifying the alternatives. A decision whether to get married is almost certainly a contingent decision, which is to say, "It all depends." If we frame the decision as, "I'll get married if I can find the right person," it is highly likely that your criteria will be influenced by the choices you have available. For example, Erica is a real hottie. But you suddenly discover that Janeen loves to travel, a desirable characteristic that you had not thought of before. So you immediately add "travel" to your criteria list and cycle through the evaluation process again. Since Erica is a lounge lizard, she drops down the list. Instead of a linear process, complex decision-making in the real world tends to be highly recursive, that is, we go back and forth before we decide.[307]

> *Human behavior... is not under the constant and detailed guidance of careful and accurate hedonic calculations, but is the product of an unstable and irrational complex of reflex actions, impulses, instincts, habits, customs, fashions, and mob hysteria. In light of modern psychology, 'let reason be your guide' is apparently a counsel of unapproachable perfection.*
> ~ Jacob Viner, economist

A young person's nous[308] is far from fool proof. Attitudes and feelings may unduly affect their judgment, along with pressure from friends and family. Researchers tell us that adolescent brains may not yet be equipped to adequately think through situations and understand the risks and consequences. This is especially true when facing emotionally-laced decisions. In contrast to experienced adults, young persons may:

- See only either-or choices rather than a variety of options;[309]
- Lack the knowledge or feeling of control over their lives to come up with alternative choices;
- Have a hard time interpreting the meaning or credibility of information;
- Not be able to accurately estimate the probability of negative consequences.

What is intuition?

> *Everyone has an opinion on intuition but no one does much about it.*
> ~ Mark Twain, humorist, author

Many young persons compensate for their lack of experience by relying on intuition rather than rational thinking. Intuition is commonly thought of as an impression, a hunch, or a sense of something not evident. Some speculate that intuition might actually be a form of intelligence at a level we simply cannot access with rational thought. Viewed as more holistic and "big picture" oriented, the intuitive approach provides us with fast, automatic, and effortless decisions.

---

307 A recursive process is when one of the steps of the procedure involves rerunning the procedure. A joke among lexicographers (a.k.a. wordniks) is defining recursion as "See: recursion." For computer programmers, it is getting caught in an infinite loop.

308 Nous is reason and knowledge, as opposed to sense perception. From the Greek word *noos*, meaning "mind."

309 The simplest decision model with only two alternatives is known as *Manichaeism*. Manichaeism is the duality concept, which divides everything in the world into discrete either/or polar opposites. Examples include good and evil, black and white, night and day, mind and body, etc. In ancient times this duality concept was a sufficient model of reality to make their world manageable and calculable.

BRAIN SNACK: *According to psychologist Carl Jung, intuition is not a magical sixth sense or some sort of paranormal process. He also didn't see it as something contrary to rationality or a random process of guessing. Rather, Jung described intuition as something outside the province of reason, "accessing the internal reservoir of cumulative experience and expertise developed over a period of years, and distilling out of that a response, or an urge to do or not to do something, or choose from some alternatives, without being able to understand consciously how we get the answers."*

We often use the terms intuition and gut-feel interchangeably, but they are not the same. Everyone has heard the expressions "go with your gut," "trust your gut feeling" and "gut instinct." These are physical manifestation of intuitive thinking, that is, a subtle sense that we get about whether something is right or wrong. According to team coach Chris Baxter, new situations often awaken memories of previous experiences. The emotions our memory associates with those earlier experiences are manifest as our gut-feel. If our previous experience was positive, our gut-feel is reassuring; if the converse is true, we feel uneasiness. We may even feel positive (or negative) feelings toward both alternatives, with an anxiety caused by our inability to see a clearly preferable option.

Psychologists tell us that intuition is inseparable from effective decision-making but the circumstances in which we can successfully apply intuition vary considerably. Situations that favor the use of intuitive thinking are those that involve:

- *Uncertainty.* When there is a high level of uncertainty or there is little precedent to draw on. For example, when starting a new job you might want to "play things by ear" until you better understand the policies, personalities, and the bathroom location.
- *Fuzziness.* When the facts are limited or don't clearly point the way. Gals will usually stop to ask someone for directions; guys always seem to equate this with defeat at Waterloo.
- *Time crunch.* When time is limited and you are under pressure to come up with the right decision. If a collision is imminent, it matters less whether you turn right or left—the important thing is turn!

Psychologists Keith Stanovich and Richard West describe intuition in terms of cognitive systems. *System 1*, or intuitive reasoning, is shared with other animals and is old in evolutionary terms. It is quick, automatic, effortless, and influenced by emotion. When you act on intuition in the present moment—say, where to get a burger—you are using System 1 thinking. In comparison, *System 2*, or rational reasoning, is evolutionarily recent and distinctively human. It is slower, more conscious, logical, and requires more effort. You are using System 2 logic when you are carefully weighing options to buy a new notebook computer. Psychologists tell us System 2 reasoning seems to be in charge of making decisions that concern the future.[310]

Reali-tude:
Practical experience cultivates the kernel of intuition.

Advantages of using intuition

> *Trust your hunches. They're usually based on facts filed away just below the conscious level.*
> ~ Joyce Brothers, psychologist

Mathematician Blaise Pascal (1623–1662) wrote: "We know the truth not only by the reason, but by the heart." Pascal's observation was, and is, controversial because it contrasts with what we have traditionally been told: listen to your reason and ignore your intuitions. But calculation-based decision-making of the sort recommended by wonky economists has some serious pitfalls, and this is where intuition can help. Here are some of the advantages offered by the intuitive approach:

- *Efficiency:* Intuition allows us to perform complex tasks rapidly and with minimal attentional resources. We can often compress years of experience into split seconds, short-circuiting a lengthy rational decision process. In everyday life, we often do a quick "pros and cons" assessment and get on with business.
- *Focuses on what matters most:* Intuitive decisions help us take into account the things that we really care about and excludes things we don't. If we are motivated about the outcome, we can be sure that the decision was significant to us.
- *Includes "soft" data:* Unlike fact-based analytical thinking, intuition brings creative information and insights into the judgment process. It is sensitive to the circumstances of the decision and the inherent complexities of human relationships. Falling in love by the numbers just isn't the same!
- *Rational analysis can mislead:* Simply because an approach is quantitative doesn't mean that it is necessarily accurate or correct. In truth, rational analysis is not immune from the same misleading perceptions, assumptions, and biases as is intuition. Remember Fukushima? The Titanic?
- *Handles complexity.* Intuition can accommodate more complexity than our conscious minds. Choices in complex matters (such as which car to buy) may best be left to steep in unconscious thought. Scientists say this is a survival tactic that allows us to overcome some of the limits of our rationality.

"We may actually know more than we think we know in everyday situations," say psychologists David Myers and Ken Paller. "Unconscious memory may come

310 In one key respect, researchers do not see Systems 1 and 2 as completely distinct processes. The automatic integration of information in the brain plays a crucial role in decision making, independent of whether people decide intuitively or deliberately. Chapter 10 describes the physiology of these two cognitive systems.

into play, for example, in recognizing the face of a perpetrator of a crime or the correct answer on a test," says Paller. "Intuition may have an important role in finding answers to all sorts of problems in everyday life," he suggests, and recommends that we not rely solely on our conscious memory. Developing our intuitive nature and creative capabilities are often the deciding factors between failure and success. As a minimum, it can spare us countless headaches.

Social scientist Ap Dijksterhuis goes one step further in suggesting that subconscious thoughts are actually superior for complex decisions. Our consciousness is good at following precise rules—arithmetic, solving anagrams, etc.—but has only limited capacity for handling more complex problems. "It is much better to follow your gut," suggests Dijksterhuis. "When you have to make a decision, the first step should be to get all the information necessary for the decision. Once you have the information, you have to decide, and this is best done with conscious thought for simple decisions, but left to unconscious thought—to 'sleep on it'—when the decision is complex," he says.

> *Despite their misgivings about the idea of some sort of romantic intuition, many twenty-somethings told us there is something to be said for the idea of acting on gut instinct. Whether they are trying to decide on a job, a location, or a living arrangement, sometimes, they say, you really just do know.*
>
> ~ from *Quarterlife Crisis: The Unique Challenges of Life in Your Twenties*

What if we have no conscious knowledge? Can gut-feel still guide our decisions? Neurologist Antonio Damasio thinks so. Before you apply any kind of rational analysis to an important decision, do you feel any negative vibes associated with a given response option (even for the briefest moment)? If so, what Damasio calls a *somatic marker*[311] may be generating an unpleasant gut-feeling as a warning signal. But don't stop thinking about complex decisions in the belief that you can rely totally on unconscious thought. You won't learn nuclear physics by simply putting the book under your pillow.

Reali-tude:
Trust your gut. You will make better decisions consistently.

The bottom line:

- Good intuitive decision-making is learned through an accumulation of experience.
- Gut-feel is a subtle physical sense that something is right or wrong.
- Our intuition can handle more complexity than our conscious minds.
- Most everyday decisions are intuitive.

---

311 From *soma*, the Greek word for body, and marker, because attention is focused (marked) on the potential negative outcome.

Disadvantages of using intuition

Decide promptly, but never give any reasons. Your decision may be right, but your reasons are sure to be wrong.
~ Lord Mansfield, British Chief Justice

A Chinese proverb states "Two-thirds of what we see is behind our eyes." In other words, we have a habit of seeing relationships where none exist. We often place our fortunes, our relationships, and sometimes our very lives at the mercy of a hunch. After the facts are known, we intuitively feel that we knew something all along, which leads us to believe we know more than we do.

To see why, consider the following. Many of us believe that we are capable of distinguishing between situations in which we can safely rely on intuition from those that require more careful thought. But we are often wrong. Educator Max Bazerman has extensively researched decision-making. In his book *When Not to Trust Your Gut*, he explicitly warns "most of us trust our intuition more than evidence suggests that we should." Psychologist Stuart Sutherland (*Irrationality: the Enemy Within*) goes so far as to state that "intuition is in fact remarkably bad."

A simple example of this tendency was made famous by psychologist Roger Shepard.[312] How do the two tables on the next page compare in size and shape? If you're like most people, the table on the right appears to be more of a square than the one on the left, which looks longer and skinnier. The difference is obvious. Or is it? If this is what you think, you are wrong—your intuition has failed you. Trace the top of either table on a piece of paper and then line up your tracing over the other table. The two surfaces are identical in size and shape!

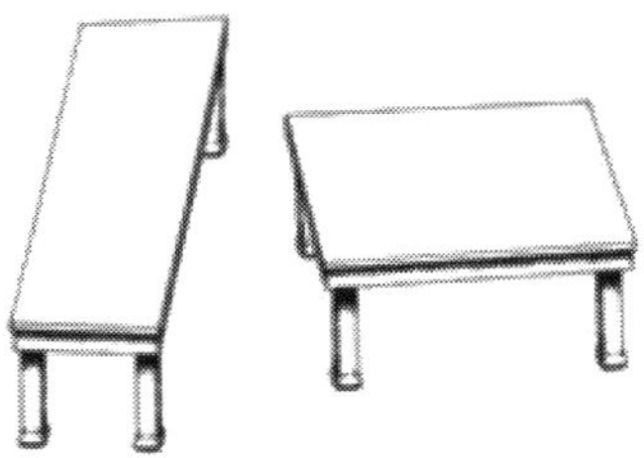

Illustration of two tables

Just as intuition biases your vision, it can sabotage your judgment. Remember, at one time intuitive common sense told us that the Earth was flat and the center of the universe, that disease resulted from demons and could be healed by bleeding, and praying to the fertility gods made your crops grow. Commonsense intuitions are not accurate forecasts—rather, they are right after the fact. Just because we've seen something occur one way several times, doesn't mean it will always occur that way. We are good at deceiving ourselves into thinking that we know more than we do, or knew more than we did.

---

312 From: Roger Shepard, *Mind Sights: Original Visual Illusions, Ambiguities, and Other Anomalies*, W. H. Freeman & Co. New York (1990).

Out of more than a hundred studies comparing the accuracy of actuarial (i.e., rational) and intuitive prediction, in not one instance have people done better, though occasionally there has been no difference between the two methods. In the great majority of cases, the actuarial method has been more successful by a considerable margin.
~ *Martin Poulter*, philosopher

As rational choosers, we should rely on intuition only where it is likely to be beneficial. The problem is we don't. Why not? Today's frantic pace of life means we are busier and face more time constraints. Having more on our minds pushes our ability to process information to the limit. To cope, we fly by the seat of our pants, default to simple strategies, and let gut-level attitudes guide our actions.[313] Our rational mind is convinced that we will get the outcomes we want, but in practice much of the time our reliance on intuitive thinking makes us prone to costly errors. Here are some disadvantages to this approach:

- *Selective perception.* An option may seem emotionally appealing simply because you failed to consider other available choices or you made incorrect assumptions. It is amazing how the look of the ugliest babe (derp) in the bar improves if (s)he's the only one available at closing time!
- *Beware of Jonesing.* Intuitions vary from day-to-day and they are subject to intense craving. Thinking, "I just gotta have some Doritos" can emotionally swamp other desires (such as losing weight).
- *Garbage in, garbage out.* Since intuition is a product of memory, your interpretation of an event can differ from what really happened. The accuracy and usefulness of your memories are only as good as the accuracy of your interpretation. Judges testify that eyewitness evidence can be very unreliable.
- *No factual basis.* Despite your narcissistic feelings of grandeur, if other people disagree with your choice, you cannot simply contend that your intuitions are stronger or better than the intuitions of others.
- *Open mouth, insert foot.* Intuitions tend to occur automatically and unconsciously so they can be difficult to adjust or prevent if they are inappropriate. This has caused many a first date to become a last date.
- *Lack of control.* When it matters most, people find it hardest to recognize their own cognitive traps and keep their emotions in check. Shopping malls thrive on your weakness for immediate gratification.

People put great trust in their intuition, but professionals tell us the past 50 years of decision-making research challenges this trust.[314] Wise deciders learn to sift reality from illusion, sensible predictions from easy hindsight, and true insights from false intuitions.

---

313 Scientists call this auto-pilot decision-making process *deliberation-without-attention*.

314 From his experience with 3,000 patients, clinical psychologist Daniel Cappon says his observations do not support the belief that women are more intuitive than men. "Western societies, dominated by males and dominated by science, came to distrust this false belief," he says.

Reali-tude:
If you lack experience, always test your hunches.

Putting intuition to work

> *Most people make decisions without thinking very much. The secret to making wise decisions and using power as a path to enrichment is to become more aware of what we are doing and to enlarge our capacity for awareness.*
> ~ M. Scott Peck, from *The Road Less Traveled*

Some people seem to possess an abundance of intuition. Warren Buffet is an investment guru because he has better "market sense." Gary Kasparov is acknowledged as the greatest chess player because he has better "chess sense." Wayne Gretzky is the greatest hockey player because of his legendary "hockey sense." These, and other intuitives are generally successful because they can see things more clearly and find the best solutions to problems more quickly than others, says psychologist Paul T. P. Wong. There is no doubt that all of these individuals have a very high level of intelligence, are keen observers, and have quick minds. But, does having more market sense make Mr. Buffet a more intuitive duck hunter than say, Dick Cheney? Or, does having more chess sense make Mr. Kasparov more intuitively adroit at promoting pointy bras than Madonna?

Clearly the answer is no. The primary reason that people like Warren Buffet are intuitively successful is they have a huge store of knowledge and experience in their area of expertise. Social scientists call these areas *domains*. Within their domain, intuitive judgments may be more effective for them than their more systematic, deliberative ones. Once out of their domain (or if the problem is taken out of its normal context), things get dicey. Who do you want selecting your matching bathroom linens? Mr. Gretzky or Martha Stewart? You get the picture.

In reality, most hunches do not operate in a vacuum. Intuition processes are implicitly learned through a distillation of years of cumulative experience and a "seasoned" judgment process. They originate from the mass of facts, patterns, concepts, techniques, abstractions, formal knowledge, and beliefs that are impressed on our minds. These impressions, called *schemas*, reflect what we believe will work in a particular situation. Schemas are tucked away in our brain, to be automatically activated in the future by certain situational clues and habits. And they are constantly updated as a result of our exposure to new experiences and knowledge. Over time, we learn to recognize and manage the cognitive traps that interfere with intuition. This is a part of growing up.

But young persons have a problem—they don't have any experience. Experience is an active participation in events or activities, leading to the accumulation of knowledge or skill. Although years of experience do not automatically make you an expert, by definition having no experience guarantees it. And even if you get the facts right, you may still not derive the proper meaning that is key to good decision-making. So, how does a nubile NeXter overcome her lack of experience? Learn to use gists.

What is a gist? A gist is "the overall meaning and sense of what is the best course of action," say psychologists Valerie Reyna and Charles Brainerd of Cornell University. Gist-based thinking is not simply the retrieval of instances experienced in the past. The experience per se is not what is important. Rather it is the distillation of the meaning of past experiences—what is *understood or learned* from those experiences and emotions—that can be applied to recognizing similar future instances. "Gists can lead us to make better choices," says Reyna, "by answering the question, 'What does (or should) the information mean to me?'" Reyna and Brainerd's research illuminates several characteristics of gist-based versus rational thinking:

- Paradoxically, young persons are more rational (more deliberative and detail-oriented) than adults, yet they are notoriously poor decision makers.
- Gist-based thinking is the more advanced of the two reasoning processes and is our default mode of thinking. It typically leads to better judgments even when precise details such as numerical data are easy to understand and can be remembered.
- Judgments, decisions, and consequent behaviors are affected by the gist that a person understands, rather than the verbatim facts that he or she is presented with.
- As we grow older and more experienced, we shift from a rational to an intuitive perspective. This "seeing the forest more than the trees" (i.e., System 1) thinking enables adults to make quicker decisions.

Gist-based thinking is not a gift but a skill. And like any skill, it's something you can learn. When your gut feeling is telling you something, don't ignore it, but don't unquestionably trust it—it isn't always right. Find out why you have a gut-feel by examining your existing beliefs and attitudes. Figure out whether you missed something by purely objective analysis; perhaps this situation differs in some critical aspect from those that your gut-feel is based on? If you are still unsure, tap the wisdom of tribal elders around you. They have the life-experience to help you generate accurate and meaningful gists. When speaking with them, the operative words are: ask, listen, and think. *Young person's alert:* be honest whether your reservoir of experience is deep enough to validate your gut-feel. In the case of controllable life-choices, many times it will not be.

> *Making decisions is a tough thing to do. Personally, I seek advice from friends and family. Sometimes we are too blinded with our problems we often miss certain details about the issue we are trying to deal with, so seeking advice from people who may see a clearer picture of the problem will be of great help.*
>
> ~ JOIEMARVIC, Internet blogger

Intuition complements rational analysis and if done right, is generally a good thing. To make wise life-choices, be aware of your own cognitive traps, think rationally about the facts, and understand the gists. It is likely that you will forget all of the boring details anyway. For many of us, this is probably the best that we can hope for.

Reali-tude:
Experience is inevitable, learning is not.

The bottom line:

- Separate the vital few decisions from the trivial many decisions.
- Learn to distinguish situations in which you can rely on intuition.
- The more complex the decision, the more we benefit from using gists.
- Gists rely on past experiences and manifest themselves as gut-feelings.

Doctor's Prescription (Rx)

The decision itself is the culmination of the decision-making process. What is ignored is the lengthy, complex process of alerting, exploring, and analyzing that precede the final moment.
~ Frank Harrison, professor of management

Developing power over an unpredictable future takes more than just talent, ability, or heartfelt dreams. The secret to achieving personal economic success is to be an effective decider. Appendix C has some templates designed to help improve your decision-making skills. Below are some additional tips that can be constructively applied to both rational and intuitive decision styles:

- *Decide to decide.* Do you really need to make a decision? At decision time, think about its:
  - § *Importance*: What priority is this decision? Is there a downside to not deciding?
  - § *Urgency*: How quickly must you act? Is there a deadline? Can actions to address the situation be done gradually?
  - § *Credibility*: Do you have sufficient information to make a good decision? Is the information reliable?

- *What is the problem?* Define the decision that needs to be made and write it down (it may be a threat to be avoided or an opportunity to take advantage of). Subtle causes are often underestimated—what seems like one problem may actually be a *Gordian Knot*[315] of different problems all interconnected. Pinpoint each problem and tackle them separately.
- *Do your homework.* Gather as much information as you can to assess your options and consider priorities. Do not act on your first thought without looking for alternatives and don't simply hope something is true or assume it exists as it first

315 The story of the Gordian Knot is associated with Alexander the Great. In 333 B.C.E., while wintering at Gordium, Alexander attempted to untie a large knot. Legend had it that anyone who could untie the Knot would be King of Asia. When he could find no end to the knot to unbind it, he sliced it in half with a stroke of his sword. This is often used as a metaphor for solving a very difficult problem by a bold stroke.

appears. Research shows that adding just one more option to the decision process significantly boosts the chances for success. When you are ready to decide ask yourself, "Have I omitted anything?"

- *What is the worst case?* Think about what could go wrong with each decision. Look beyond the obvious by asking "what if" type questions to assess the worst consequences of various courses of action. Could you live with the consequences? Do you need a "back up" contingency plan? What are the counter-arguments? Is this a long-term solution or simply a band-aid fix?
- *Don't be a lemming.*[316] Opinions of friends can help you to gain perspective and sooth emotions. Consider their feedback but avoid blindly accepting what others suggest. Events described by a trustworthy source may have originated with someone less credible. Give special attention to those who do not agree with you.
- *Control your emotions.* Focus on facts and gists, not on emotions (this is very difficult to do). Don't make any serious decisions if you are angry, hurt, depressed, desperate, or frightened. Wait a day before deciding (to avoid a knee-jerk reaction). Never decide just to get revenge.
- *Ban the bias.* Selfish biases are detrimental to intuitive functioning. Be less certain in your views—your understanding is far from perfect. Let go your ego, be open-minded, and suspect that you may be wrong on a great many things. Examine evidence with a cold eye and force yourself to weigh both sides fairly. Ask yourself, "How do I know this to be true?"
- *Tune in to your gut-feel.* Listen to what your gut-feel has to say without an agenda of your own. Seek evidence that tests your intuitive beliefs. Your gut-feeling can often give you good decision-making guidance. If you have no gut-feeling inside, it could be that you lack the experience to assess the gist. For complex decisions, tap the wisdom of tribal elders.
- *Be true to yourself.* Follow the values you inherited from your family and friends. If you make a decision that is in line with your values, you will be more likely to feel at peace with what you decide. If you don't feel good when you make a decision, you will likely regret it later.

Finally, the world is not simple—it is infinitely complex—and you will not be able to make sound decisions without a true understanding of reality. Coming to grips with the complexity of the world is a sign of maturity. Here are three universal tips that can make a big difference in making quality life-choices:

- *Broaden your experiences.* This is the single most helpful tip for young persons. Making a deliberate effort to expose yourself to a variety of different experiences helps you look at things from different perspectives. Developing extra *mind-eyes* that compare seemingly unrelated situations will reveal opportunities.
- *Be prepared.* Prepare yourself in advance mentally, emotionally, and psychologically to deal with possible opportunities, issues, and temptations that may come

316 An epithet for one who blindly follows another on a course of action that will lead to the destruction of all. It is also the name of a small rodent that lives in the arctic region.

your way. This is especially important when the situation is accompanied by intense emotions, needs, or cravings.

- *Acquire wisdom.* Formulate gists to help you avoid the cognitive traps. Tap the wisdom of trusted adults. Ask yourself: "If someone I cared about asked me for my opinion in a situation such as this, what advice would I give?"

Reali-tude:
Always ask the question, "What is the cost?"

Talking Points

It has been said that man is a rational animal. All my life I have been searching for evidence which could support this.
~ Bertrand Russell, philosopher

Chapter 17 describes some tools to help you acquire wisdom by interviewing others. To benefit from these techniques, you need only have access to a parent, educator, or other trusted adult (tribal elder) and a desire to listen and learn. Based on the ideas in this chapter, here are some starters:

1. "I am trying to improve myself. Sometimes young persons fail to comprehend that a seemingly rational decision today can be seen as irrational later in life. Reflecting on your experience, or that of someone you know, do you recall a situation where immature judgment resulted in a young person jeopardizing his long-term well-being?" If they say "Yes" then ask:

    - "Would you tell me the gist of what happened please?"
    - "How did you (they) feel about this at the time?"
    - "What two things did you learn from this that you can share with me?"

2. "I am trying to improve myself. Sometimes young persons fail to comprehend that using one's intuition can be a curse as well as a blessing when deciding on a course of action. Reflecting on your experience, or that of someone you know, do you recall a decision situation where a young person's intuition jeopardized her long-term well-being? If they say "Yes" then ask:

    - "Would you tell me the gist of what happened please?"
    - "How did you (they) feel about this at the time?"
    - "What two things did you learn from this that you can share with me?"

    In either case, if they say "No," simply say "Thank you."

3. "I want to make wise life-choices. Reflecting on your experience, would you have two ideas that I can implement to improve my judgment and decision-making skills? Be sure to thank them for their response.

Knowledge Nuggets

The only real valuable thing is intuition.
~ Albert Einstein, physicist

1. *Is your decision-making rational?* "Reality exists and is what it is, regardless of whether we want it to be or not," wrote philosopher Ayn Rand (1905–1982). Her philosophy, called *Objectivism*, says each person has within him the ability to live a rich, fulfilling, independent life. According to Rand, the most important tool for us to achieve success is reason, or the power of rational thinking. In a world of increasingly subtle manipulation, her lesson for young persons endures: check your premises. You must understand what is behind the choices that you make. Rand's storylines of human achievement are controversial, but her books remain best sellers among young persons. For a revealing (albeit heady) 3-part interview with her, see: http://www.vision.org/visionmedia/printerfriendly.aspx?id=15467.

2. *Can you read tea leaves?* Intuition, according to psychologist Daniel Cappon, is the archetypal jewel in the crown of human intelligence. "Intuition is like a very old whore who has been revitalized and rejuvenated and is on her way to becoming a very respectable lady," he says. Cappon's *Intuition Quotient Test* or "IQ2" is a non-scientific psychological self-assessment inventory on intuitive ability. It is a cluster of 20 intuitive skills that generally estimate a person's ability to use their intuition. Cappon is convinced that everyone has some capacity for intuition. But not everyone uses it and not all those who apply it use it equally well. Are you intuitively inclined? Discover your divining proclivities at: http://www.selfgrowth.com/articles/are_you_intuitive_0.html.

3. *Speed dating anyone?* In his book *Blink: The Power of Thinking Without Thinking*, social scientist Malcolm Gladwell describes the phenomenon of *blink*, the ability to make a snap judgment based one decisive glance. Gladwell concludes that we can make better instant judgments by training ourselves to focus on the most relevant facts, and that less input (as long as it's the right input) is better than more. For example, lots of couples get married after only a couple of months yet remain compatible. These intuitive judgments, what Gladwell calls *thin slicing*, seem to straddle between conscious reasoning and unconscious gut feeling. For more insights and a grunch of examples, see: http://www.wikisummaries.org/Blink:_The_Power_of_Thinking_Without_Thinking.

4. *The power of hunches.* In *Gut Feelings*, psychologist Gerd Gigerenzer offers convincing evidence for the power of hunches over laborious data crunching. Hunches, gut feelings, and intuition are colloquial descriptions for heuristics, those efficient cognitive shortcuts we use to make quick decisions. Gigerenzer and colleagues have run tests on dozens of real-world problems in fields as diverse as economics, biology, and health care. In every case, they found that one good reason proved

superior to data-greedy mathematical equations in making the best choices. Learn more at: http://www.nytimes.com/2007/08/28/science/28conv.html.

5. *Out with the old.* Delaying a decision makes it much less likely that you will stay with the current situation. In a series of experiments, participants were asked to choose between their current selection and an alternative. When they made their choice straight away, 82 percent opted to stay with the current option. When they delayed their decision, however, this dropped to 56 percent. If you delay, you'll move away from the default. That fact needs to be built into your decision, whatever you are trying to decide about. Lovebirds pay attention at: http://www.spring.org.uk/2010/04/does-delaying-decisions-lead-to-better-outcomes.php.

6. *Where to go for info?* See Appendix F for additional information relating to this chapter.

Chapter 17

Tapping Tribal Elders

Learn from the mistakes of others; you don't have time to make all of those mistakes yourself.

~ Admiral Hyman G. Rickover, father of the U.S. nuclear submarine

The Gist

The Good:

- Wisdom is the exercise of sound judgment
- Tribal elders are valuable well-springs of wisdom, but only if you use them

The Bad:

- Knowledge does not guarantee wisdom
- *Truthiness* describes things people "know" regardless of the evidence
- Our beliefs are like possessions that we vigorously defend
- Often the hardest people to convince are the ones most misinformed

The Reality:

- Tribal elders are parents, educators, and other trusted adults who care
- *Feedforward* allows you to learn from the mistakes of others
- Mentors are wise and trusted counselors and teachers
- Think critically about any advice you receive
- You don't mind hearing the advice—you just hate to take it

Introduction

He who knows and knows that he knows,
He is wise, follow him.
He who knows and knows not that he knows,
He is asleep, awaken him.
He who knows not and knows not that he knows not,
He is a fool, shun him.
He who knows not and knows that he knows not,
He is a child, teach him.
~ Arabian proverb

In his ten volume work *Nicomachean Ethics,* the Greek philosopher Aristotle (384–322 B.C.E.) distinguishes between two intellectual virtues, or beneficial qualities: *sophia* and *phronesis* (pronounced fron'-ay-sis). According to Aristotle, sophia is the ability to discern why the world is the way it is. Phronesis, on the other hand, is concerned with how to act in particular situations. It is often translated as "practical wisdom" or "prudence." In a nutshell, phronesis says that one can learn the principles of what to do, but applying them in the real world, in situations one could not have foreseen, requires experience of the world. Unlike factual knowledge, gaining phronesis requires time and maturity. It comes from having ridden tall in the saddle, walked the talk, been there, and done that.[318]

> *Whereas young people become accomplished in geometry and mathematics, and wise within these limits, prudent young people do not seem to be found. The reason is that prudence is concerned with particulars as well as universals, and particulars become known from experience. But a young person lacks experience, since some length of time is needed to produce it.*
> ~ Aristotle, in *Nichomachean Ethics*

Although experience is an effective way to learn, it can be a painful way to go about it. As a certified smart person, you quickly realize that learning from the mistakes of others is preferable to making those same mistakes yourself! For those of you who ignore the warnings of others—thinking you know better, or that this time is different—try sticking a finger in the lamp socket to see if it's energized. Think of it this way: your driver's ed. class showed you gory photos of mangled cars and dried blood expressly so that you would not have to learn by experience.

318 Why should we heed the ideas of some ancient "philoso-dude" who was completely ignorant of the modern world? Science and technology change. What makes us human doesn't.

To be "world-wise" involves more than straightforward reasoning. Historian Barbara Tuchman defines wisdom as "the exercise of judgment acting on experience, common sense, and available information." Wisdom often requires new thinking about old problems and in some cases, these new ideas might not be acceptable at first. Author John Catherwood outlines some characteristics of wisdom as follows:

- Wisdom is usually practical.
- Wisdom is not the same as knowing facts.
- Being wise is not the same as being clever (you can be too clever for your own good).
- Knowledge does not guarantee wisdom.
- It is through learning from our mistakes (and the mistakes of others) that we gain wisdom.

Wisdom gained by experience is always won at a psychological price. It may, for instance, be the loss of one's naivety or the end of innocence. It could be the embarrassment of realizing you are not as unique as you thought. Or, that maybe your parents were right after all. The wise young person knows her limitations and recognizes that being embarrassed is preferable to being dead. By proactively learning from the mistakes of others, she might be able to avoid going down the same blind alleys they did, thank you very much.

Reali-tude:
Smart people do dumb-ass things too.

The Good

Listening to parents' advice is sort of like watching commercials. You know What's coming, you've heard it all before, it's a big bore, but you listen anyway.
~ Anonymous

Due to various circumstances—most of which have to do with money—many young adults have returned home to the nest. This practice is so prevalent that your generation has also been labeled the *Boomerang Generation.* Factor flashback: In an interesting twist, the situation was reversed with your parents' generation, the Baby Boomers. Most of them could not wait to escape the home scene regardless of personal finances. Many opted for communal living, tie-dyed shirts, long hair, and the mantra of counterculture psychologist Timothy Leary to "Turn on, tune in, and drop out." NeXters, the fact that your parents were able to make it this far should give you some cause for hope!

The majority of young persons remain very close to their parents (or other trusted adult with whom they might share a close personal relationship, such as a grandparent, step-parent, educator, etc.). These trusted adults care about you—they want you to succeed in life. These are your "tribal elders" and each one represents a potential mother lode of wisdom if you will take the initiative to stimulate conversation. Have them reflect on their experiences. Ask them what skills, attitudes, and behaviors they wish they had learned when they were your age. If they screwed up, this is a golden opportunity to learn what *not* to do.[319] You will be amazed what can be applied to your own life. In reality, most people are happy to provide advice if asked. The key is you have to ask!

> Keyes: *How come people don't learn from the experience of others? If divorce is so prevalent in our society, why don't people look around and say all these folks are getting divorced; maybe I should take marriage more seriously and realize that it's a commitment and it's not based on emotion.*
>
> Noe: *That's something I hear a lot... the friends and the peers that I have whose parents were divorced, they feel strongly that they never want to get divorced. They have sort of learned the negative lesson from what their parents did incorrectly.*
>
> ~ from an interview by Alan Keyes, diplomat, political activist

If your parents are not available (or do not care), seek out another experienced and responsible adult that you trust, preferably someone more than 30 years old. If this is not an option, snag an older friend or colleague. Chances are they know you better than you know yourself. Ask questions and draw on the collective wisdom of those who have already walked the journey. Most older people, and the older the better, know important things. They are experts in some things, deeply experienced in others, insightful in all. Nota Bene[320]—when it comes to *your* personal economic future, you cannot afford to be an Army of One!

Reali-tude:
Acquire nuggets of wisdom from others.

The Bad

> *When I was a boy of fourteen, my father was so ignorant I could hardly stand to have the old man around. But when I got to be twenty-one, I was astonished at how much he had learned in seven years.*
>
> ~ Mark Twain, humorist, author

Beliefs are things that we have confidence or faith in and we accept as true. Psychologist Robert Abelson compares our beliefs to possessions. People "adopt"

319 When the Athenians were alarmed at the internal stagnation of the Greek Republic, they asked the great statesman Demosthenes (384–322 B.C.E.) what they should do. Sipping a demitasse, Demosthenes calmly advised, "Do not do what you are doing now."

320 Latin phrase used to direct attention to something particularly important. Basically, it means "Note well" and is often abbreviated as "NB."

(hold or cling to) a belief from the time it is "obtained" to the time it is "discarded" (given up or abandoned). When someone challenges our beliefs, it is if someone criticizes our possessions. We protect those beliefs by ignoring or resisting information that threatens them.

The fly in the ointment is our beliefs can be false. Many of us use the words "believe" and "know" interchangeably, but in a strict sense they are very different. Belief typically applies to something we are either unsure about or for which we have insufficient proof. For instance, saying "I believe that *Death Note* is the most popular anime series," may in fact be false if *Fruits Basket* is shown to have sold more copies. Slightly less extreme than beliefs are opinions (or feelings). These are strongly affected by our attitudes and perceptions. Everyone has a right to his/her opinion, but no one has a right to be wrong in the facts. Knowledge, in its strict sense, only applies to things that are true.

So the question is, "What is the difference between genuinely knowing something as opposed to merely believing or having an opinion?" We already know the answer: evidence. When we believe something, we should take a moment to ask ourselves, "What evidence is there to support this belief?" Typically there is a lot less evidence than we want to admit. The failure to understand this difference is significant and can easily disconnect us from reality.

BRAIN SNACK: *"Truthiness" was first used in its recent satirical sense by television comedian Stephen Colbert of the* Colbert Report.[321] *Truthiness depicts things that are spoken as true, repeated as if true, that might even sound true, but in fact are not true. It is what we intuitively know from our gut without regard to evidence, logic, intellectual examination, or facts. "It used to be, everyone was entitled to their own opinion, but not their own facts," said Colbert in a 2006 interview in* The Onion's A.V. Club. *"But that's not the case anymore. Facts matter not at all. Perception is everything. It's certainty. Truthiness is 'What I say is right, and [nothing] anyone else says could possibly be true.' There's not only an emotional quality, but there's a selfish quality," he said.*[322]

In following what we believe rather than what we know, we tend to look for evidence that confirms our preconceptions. This is called confirmation bias, a psychology term that describes when people not only see differently, but reason differently, as a result of their unique perspective. As a result, they become one-sided in their thinking and opinions. Educator David Perkins labels this tendency as *myside bias*, with "myside" referring to "my side" of the issue under consideration. Psychologist Jonathan Baron notes a disturbing trend where "people consider one-sided thinking to be better than two-sided thinking, even for forming one's own opinion on an issue." This leads to several troublesome consequences:

321 Truthiness was selected as its 2006 Merriam-Webster Dictionary *Word of the Year* by a 5-1 margin over the second-place word google.

322 *The Onion* is an American "fake news" organization that features satirical news reporting.

- Greater confidence does not mean higher accuracy. Paradoxically, those who express the least accurate beliefs often have the highest degree of confidence in their beliefs.
- When we look for relevant evidence, we tend to search our own memories rather than asking questions of another person. When we do ask, we often judiciously choose the "right" people to consult, thus increasing the chances we will hear what we want to hear.
- When the initial evidence supports our preferences, we are generally satisfied and terminate our search. When the initial evidence is hostile, we often dig deeper, hoping to find more comforting information. It is very important to ask, "Is my reality based on facts or perceptions?"

Reali-tude:
Our beliefs are our reality.

The bottom line:

- Emotionally biased thinking ("truthiness") overpowers logic.
- Confirmation bias causes us to seek evidence that we are right not wrong.
- The hardest to convince they are wrong are often the ones who are the most misinformed.
- Tribal elders can be a valuable source of wisdom, but only if you tap them.

The Reality

> *None of us got where we are solely by pulling ourselves up by our bootstraps. We got here because somebody—a parent, a teacher, an Ivy League crony or a few nuns—bent down and helped us pick up our boots.*
> ~ Thurgood Marshall, U.S. Supreme Court Justice

Three techniques can help young persons acquire nuggets of wisdom and make smarter choices. *Feedforward* is active listening to the experiences of others. *Mentoring* is a commitment to a long-term relationship with another person. *Perspective-taking* imagines what a tribal elder would do in a similar situation. All are pithy and easy to do. Depending on how faithfully they are applied, they can be powerfully effective in changing attitudes and behavior.

Technique #1: Feedforward

> *Feedforward is my "special sauce" methodology for eliciting advice from people on what you can do to get better in the future.*
> ~ Marshall Goldsmith, executive coach

Psychologist Marshall Goldsmith is one of corporate America's preeminent executive coaches and has helped more than eighty CEOs attain a higher level of success. In collaboration with economist Jon Katzenbach, Goldsmith developed a simple but very effective technique called "feedforward," which he outlines in his book *What Got You Here, Won't Get You There*. Goldsmith has repeatedly demonstrated the value of feedforward in getting senior executives to recognize their delusions, change their behaviors, and improve their lives.[323]

If the feedforward technique works for the rich and powerful, might it also help those on the other end of the wealth spectrum? The answer in a New York second is, "Soitainly!" Of course, there are two differences between you and Goldsmith's typical client: you are not CEO of a huge corporation and your wallet is two figures thick (sometimes one), not seven. With respect to the first difference, who cares? Like you, they put on their trow one leg at a time. Regarding the second, your impecuniosity simply means that you get the same benefit as the "suits" without having to pay more than the cost of this book. Such a deal!

Let's get started. Most of us agree with the adage "forewarned is forearmed." For example, isn't it better to get some helpful tips about purchasing a new car *before* you find yourself in the sales manager's office? Well, the same is true about our behavior. In his *Poor Richard's Almanac*, American statesman Ben Franklin said, "Experience keeps a dear school, but fools will learn at no other." Note that Franklin did not say, "Experience is the best teacher" as is commonly quoted. Rather, he meant that experience can be a painful and costly way to find out what not to do. Young persons are perennially inclined to learn Dr. Franklin's advice the hard way. Don't be one of them!

Feedforward can help. Feedforward is a neat way to solicit practical suggestions from others, and involves nothing more than asking a few open-ended questions. If you will, think of feedforward as a mini-interview, where they do the talking and you do the listening. Sure, you might not be able to verify all of the inputs you receive but that's okay—there is always a nugget of wisdom in any honest conversation. And, in a sort of backward logic, from their answers you will almost always learn some questions and insights that you had not considered.

Using feedforward with someone you know

> *If you have not the experience, ask. There is no shame in asking, but do not pretend you know when you don't.*
>
> ~ Mother Teresa, Albanian Catholic nun

Feedforward is a deceptively simple process. Yet some of the simplest ideas are also the most effective! And since the steps are so easy to do, you have no excuses not to try them. Feedforward enables you to better understand yourself by soliciting positive suggestions for your future from others. It is done without criticism of their past (or yours) as a means of encouraging them to share some personal experiences with you. Armed with these inputs, you can better identify your own ignorance and ineptitude, and adjust your personal economic behaviors in a beneficial way.

323 This section draws on Goldsmith's feedforward process, whose contribution is gratefully acknowledged.

Does it work? If the obstacle to achieving long-term success is behavioral, and if you are motivated to improve yourself and will give the process a fair chance, feedforward will almost always prove beneficial. Ready? Let's give it a shot. Feedforward asks you to do four simple steps:

1. Pick one questionable belief from Figure 16.1 (page 377) that you would like to change in order to make a significant, positive difference in your life. This is your objective. If you think you don't need any changes, ask your family or friends and they'll be happy to suggest several!
2. Begin with an introductory statement such as, "I want to improve myself." Then describe your objective in a one-on-one dialog with a tribal elder. For example, you might say, "I am trying to resist the temptation of immediate gratification so I can..." Or, "I am trying to avoid being adversely pressured by my friends when it comes to deciding about..."
3. Ask that person for two suggestions for the future that might help you achieve a positive change in your selected belief or habit. The only ground rule is if you are speaking with someone who knows you or has worked with you in the past, there can be no mention of the past. Everything is about the future.
4. Listen attentively to the suggestions. Some may explain why, others won't. You are not allowed to judge, rate, or critique the suggestions in any way. You can't even say something positive such as "That sounds like a good idea." The only responses you are permitted are "I see," "I appreciate your suggestions," "Thank you," and no more. Remember, the purpose of the interview is simply to learn, not to discuss or debate.

State your objective to the tribal elder. Ask for two ideas. Listen. Say thank you. That's it! Here is an example of the feedforward process in action:

You: *You say, "I want to improve myself. I would like to become a better saver and I am trying to resist the temptation to spend all that I earn. Would you suggest two ideas that I can implement in the future that will help me resist my impulsive desire for more stuff?"*

Other: *The other person suggests, "If I were you, I would first cut up all of my credit cards except for one and firmly resolve not to use that card to pay for anything under $25. This forces you to pay cash for most all of your purchases. Second, if the purchase is more than $100, wait one night before you buy it. This allows you time to mull over whether you truly need that item or you simply want it."*

You: *You say, "I appreciate your suggestions, thank you."*

These two ideas, shared by another party without judgmental bias, represent feedforward. Do not limit yourself to asking one person. To do so would dramatically reduce the number of suggestions for improvement that you receive. Also, consider not limiting yourself to only people you know. They will anticipate what they think you want to hear rather than provide unvarnished advice. Soliciting independent inputs from people in all walks of life takes advantage of the wisdom of crowds and provides you with a rich trove of possibilities for affecting positive change in your life. The art is in asking the right questions. Don't believe this? Ask an attorney!

Reali-tude:
People are often in error but never in doubt.

Using feedforward with someone you don't know

> *I wish I knew then what I know now.*
> ~ Baby Boomer's lament on lost youth

The purpose of feedforward is to solicit suggestions to help you improve a particular behavior or habit. But what if you are soliciting advice from a stranger or someone on the Internet? Understandably, you might not want to reveal your shortcomings to the universe. Or, it could simply be that you do not want to admit that you are less than perfect. No problemo. The generic version of feedforward works by invoking a neutral "third party" approach. News reporters use this trick to avoid pissing off their interviewees. The generic feedforward process asks you to do four simple steps:

1. Pick one risky belief or risky behavior from Figure 16.1 (page 377) that you would like to change in order to make a significant, positive difference in your life. This is your objective. Again, if you think you do not need any changes, your family or friends will be happy to suggest several.
2. Begin with an introductory statement such as, "I want to improve myself. Then describe your objective in the third person as a question. For example, you might say "Sometimes young persons... (describe the belief). Do you recall a situation..." Or, "Reflecting on your experience, or that of someone you know, do you recall a situation...?"
3. If they say yes, ask that person, "Would you tell me the gist of what happened please?" After listening (reading) attentively, ask "Would you share two "lessons learned" from this experience that might be helpful to a young person?"
4. Again, you are not allowed to judge, rate, or critique the suggestions in any way. Not even "That sounds like a good idea." The only responses you are permitted are "I see," "I appreciate your suggestions," "Thank you," and no more. Remember, the purpose of the interview is to learn, not to discuss or debate.

State your objective in a third party context as a question. Ask for the gist and two ideas. Listen. Say thank you. That's it! Here is an example of the generic feedforward process in action:

You: *You say, "I want to improve myself. Sometimes young persons misjudge their ability to control events. Reflecting on your experience, or that of someone you know, do you recall a situation where overconfidence jeopardized a young person's long-term well-being?"*

If they reply "Yes" ask, "Would you tell me the gist of what happened please?"

Other: *The other person relates, "Sure. I worked with someone who dropped out of college and bet big against the dot.coms. When the bubble collapsed, he was millionaire at age 21. As he is 27 now, I asked why he was running network cabling for a living. He told me he was so confident in his ability to "feel" the market that he bet his entire wad on oil price futures. He figured he could fast trick his nest egg into $10 million. He called it wrong and lost everything."*

You: *After listening, you ask ask "Would you share two "lessons learned" from this experience that might be helpful to a young person?"*

Other: *The other person relates, "First, if you think that you alone know how to beat the market, you will lose your shirt. Second, watch the greed. If you do get lucky, stash half the cash and play with the remaining half."*

The generic feedforward technique allows the interviewee to talk about someone he knows rather than about himself. This avoids a situation where he or she might feel embarrassed or fearful. By the same centavo, you avoid any uneasiness about sharing your problems with others. Sort of like those Elizabethan-era balls where everybody wore a mask (but you knew who they were anyway).[324]

These templates demonstrate the technique to get you started. If you prefer your questions to be less formal, that's fine. If you need to clarify what they are saying, that's okay too. The key is to focus on the future and ask open-ended questions. These encourage a full, meaningful answer using the subject's own knowledge and/or feelings. It is the opposite of a closed-ended question, very popular with parents, which encourages a short or single-word answer (almost always, "No"). If you are honest in your attempt to learn, respectful in your demeanor (i.e., don't cop an attitude), and you understand that the other person is probably talking about *himself*, you will succeed in increasing your stock of wisdom.

The entire process only takes 5 minutes, so why not ask as many tribal elders as you can? The more you ask, the more you will learn. As long as people are providing you with good ideas that you can use, and you are not churlish about it, feedforward will provide an ongoing benefit. Take notes if you like and consider keeping a personal journal. (Btw, if you tap your parents, be sure to approach them at their convenience so you'll get their full attention. Don't ask Mom while she is practicing her presentation to the company's Board of Advisors or badger step-Dad while he's dissecting the Thanksgiving turkey.)

***BRAIN SNACK:** In the sci-fi cult classic,* Forbidden Planet *(1956), Earth interplanetary cruiser C57D travels to the planet Altair IV, located 16 light years from*

324 Most people are much better at giving advice than taking it. All of us like to think we know best what will make us happy. Research suggests that when it comes to spending our money, however, we are better off to ask and heed the advice of others. They may well have a better insight into what we'll enjoy than we do ourselves, especially if they've already experienced it themselves.

Earth. Its mission is to check on a research team that was sent earlier to explore the planet. After landing, Captain Adams and his crew discover that philologist[325] Dr. Edward Morbius and his beautiful daughter Altaira are the only survivors of the exploration team. Morbius shows the crew of C57D the marvels of the Krell, the race that once inhabited the planet. Although the Krell possessed an extraordinary intelligence, one that was 1 million years ahead of the human mind, they self-destructed some 2,000 centuries earlier. Using their brain-boosting "plastic educator" machine, Dr. Morbius taps the Krell's vast knowledge and experience. Trekkies use a similar process of one-on-one knowledge transfer that they call "mind meld."

Here on Earth, tap the collective knowledge and experience of the great minds that exist in your own civilization. Through the magic of feedforward, you can significantly enhance your common sense quotient (CSQ) by acquiring wisdom from parents, educators, trusted adults, and even strangers. This will put you light-years ahead of your peers and make you the envy of the universe. May the force be with you, live long and prosper, to infinity and beyond, and all that. Just try it dude.

Why feedforward works

The trouble with our times is that the future is not what it used to be.
~ Paul Valery, French poet

The great thing about feedforward is that the *Young Person's Guide* does not establish what you personally need to do to change for the better. You don't establish it either. They do. Who are they? Tribal elders. Everyone with a few gray hairs who knows you, cares about you, and thinks about you. Although we don't want to admit it, we are all surrounded by smart, well-meaning people who understand us better than we understand ourselves. This also includes people you do not know that will gladly share some heartfelt advice if you ask them. It is a great way to learn without having to step in the same doo-doo they did.

Feedforward works because it forces us to ask for perspectives and suggestions. In doing so, we enlarge our universe of useful ideas for improving ourselves. We might expect that most of our adverse beliefs, behaviors, or habits would be corrected by others, but corrective feedback is not as common as one might think. Consider how often we hold back when the roles are reversed and we see someone with his fly open or with a sprig of broccoli between her teeth. When a co-worker confides that she is underappreciated and underpaid, we remain silent or nod in apparent approval even if we consider her complaint groundless. This is because we are reluctant to openly disagree with others. We prefer to avoid the unpleasant emotions produced by discordant interactions. As poet Heinrich Heine phrased it, "God has given us speech in order that we may say pleasant things to our friends."

---

325 A *philologist* is a linguistics scientist who studies and analyzes ancient texts and languages, especially with regard to the cultural history.

Psychologists tell us the reason feedforward works is because people do not take it as personally as they do feedback. Feedforward is not seen as an insult or a put down, but is received in the spirit in which it is offered—as a helpful hand up. Most of us enjoy helping others but we hold back because we think it is rude or intrusive to try to help someone who has not asked for our assistance. Asking solves this by giving the other person a license to answer. The value of this license cannot be overestimated. They respect your efforts in trying to improve yourself—it is the feeling that when we help another person, we help ourselves. And in the end, isn't this what it is all about?

Reali-tude:
Focus on the future. You cannot change the past.

Technique #2: Mentoring

The first principle is that you must not fool yourself—and you are the easiest person to fool.

~ Richard Feynman, physicist

In the epic poem, the *Iliad*, Menelaus, king of Sparta, was married to Helen. Fairest of the fair, Homer described her as the most beautiful woman in the world. Unfortunately for her hubbie, she caught the roving eye of Paris, the Trojan king. Never one to pass up a pretty smile and some fringe bennies, Paris abducted Helen from Sparta and beat feet back to Troy. Enraged, Menelaus tapped the great warrior Odysseus, king of Ithaca, to bust Paris' chops and bring Helen home.

Upon cruising off to wage war on the Trojans, Odysseus instructed his wife Penelope (no slouch in the looks department either) to keep her mouth shut, her legs crossed, and the coffee warm. He placed his wise and trusted counselor Mentor in charge of tutoring his infant son Telemachus, and asked him to keep an eye on the joint. Over the next 20 years, Mentor was largely responsible not only for Telemachus' education, but for the shaping of his character, the wisdom of his decisions, and the clarity and steadfastness of his purpose. Twenty years later, having cleaned Paris' clock, Odysseus triumphantly returned to reclaim the palace.[326] Today, Mentor's name—spelled with a lower-case "m"—is a widely used term for a wise, trusted, and caring teacher.

What is mentoring?

We need to start a conversation.

~ Hillary Clinton, U.S. Senator

326 In a fascinating feat of archaeological sleuthing, scientists used clues in Homer's text regarding an eclipse, along with astronomical data, to pinpoint the date of April 16th, 1178 B.C.E. as the most likely date of Odysseus' return from his journey after the Trojan War. How cool is that?

To mentor is to serve as a wise and trusted counselor to someone less experienced. A mentor is an individual, always more experienced, who guides another individual's development and serves without regard for personal gain. Athletes, politicians, and religious leaders benefit from mentor relationships, as do craftsman and artists. In many occupational settings, mentoring has become the "hot tool" du jour to help employees grow, advance their careers, and build their networks. With Boomers approaching retirement age, corporations are creating mentoring programs to impart older workers' knowledge and expertise to younger ones.

- *The mentor*: Ordinarily several years older, the mentor has greater knowledge and experience in the area of personal or professional life that the mentee is entering. He or she may be a parent, teacher, sponsor, adviser, supporter, older friend or co-worker, confidant, and/or a role model.
- *The mentee*: Also called the *protégé*, the mentee is the student of a mentor. As a novice in the ways of the mentor's world, the mentee stands to benefit from the mentor's guidance and advice.
- *The Mento*: A scrumptious candy that is fun to drop in your friend's Coke (har-har).

Besides their obvious value in professional development, mentors have a measurable impact on youth, especially in educational settings. Big Brothers Big Sisters of America, for example, helps "at risk" students reach their potential through professionally supported, one-to-one relationships with mentors. In her book *Big Questions, Worthy Dreams*, leadership professor Sharon Daloz Parks charters mentors with supporting young college students and challenging them to take the more difficult steps of evaluating and re-evaluating their thought processes. A mentor offers a long-view perspective that encourages a student when he needs a gentle shove, and lends an ear when he needs to talk with someone.

Some potential benefits for the mentee include:

- Greater knowledge and enhanced life skills;
- Development of wisdom and improved judgment;
- Access to a role model with regular and constructive feedback;
- Encouragement, increased confidence, and greater self-esteem;
- Personal and professional network referrals and opportunities;
- Improved satisfaction with his or her life.

Some potential benefits for the mentor include:

- Sharing one's skills, experience, and wisdom;
- Providing a young person with advice, moral support, and direction;
- Serving as an exemplar that the mentee can seek to emulate;
- Enhanced personal satisfaction and feelings of self worth;
- Challenging discussions with others who have a fresh perspective;
- Learning new things and developing new networks.

Not all mentoring occurs through face-to-face interaction. The mentoring process is flexible and can also take place through other media such as the telephone and email. If honestly pursued, the magic of mentoring can make a big difference in the lives of both mentor and mentee.

Reali-tude:
To be successful requires effort and commitment.

Misconceptions about mentoring

We are all pawns in a game whose forces we largely fail to comprehend.
~ Daniel Ariely, behavioral economist

In his book, *Mentoring: How to Find a Mentor and How to Become One*, executive mentor Bobb Biehl discusses some misconceptions about the mentoring process. Five of these misconceptions, adapted to the unique perspectives of Generation NeXt, include:

- *Mentors are at least 83 years old.* Many young persons assume that you have to be very old to be wise and mature enough to be a mentor. This is simply not the case! Some young persons are wise beyond their years. Similarly, some older people are every bit as ditsy as when they were 16. When selecting a mentor, concentrate on finding a person that has had the requisite life experiences and temperament for you. As a rule of thumb, try to find someone 30 years of age or older. The relationship you want is adult-to-adult, not adult-to-child, or child-to-child.
- *Mentors have all the answers.* Overall, Gen NeXters tend to be very skeptical. They question the veracity of information and have a tendency to de-legitimize traditional sources of knowledge. Mentors are not perfect, and they don't need to be. But NeXters do expect him or her to be honest and they can smell a dilettante a mile away.
- *Mentors have a script.* The mentoring process is unique to each mentee. Learning is based on the mentee's agenda, priorities, questions, and needs, not on some "pre-packaged" program. The common denominator is being dedicated to the relationship. As trust evolves over time, mentees find they are able to ask questions they would never feel comfortable asking others. No canned actions can replace a mentor's compassion in helping the mentee to shape his or her future.

- *Mentees are held to account.* Mentoring is not a power game and accountability is not the principal focus of the mentoring relationship. Rather, the focus is on supporting, strengthening, and encouraging the mentee. The mentor is in a unique position to demonstrate the importance of being accountable and can help the young person to develop this notion into a force of habit.
- *Mentoring is the same as coaching.* No, it isn't. Mentoring is the process of using a specially selected individual to provide broad guidance, support, and advice. The mentee sets the agenda and since mentoring relationships are ongoing, good ones can last for a long time. In contrast, coaching generally has a short-term duration, such as a sports season or a college course. It tends to be impartial, with the emphasis on performance in a specific area in need of improvement. Achieving a goal for reducing weight or getting a high SAT score would be good tasks where a coach might be helpful.

There you have it. Two techniques, feedforward and mentoring, that can add to your stock of wisdom and help you overcome your lack of experience. They can help you change your beliefs, your behaviors, your habits, indeed your life. The first technique is structured, quick to implement, and provides you with nuggets of wisdom on how to improve yourself. The second is unstructured, requires a substantial commitment of time and effort, and provides a "guiding angel" to help you solve problems that do not have simple answers. Select your technique of choice, or better still, try them both!

Technique #3: Perspective-taking

To know the road ahead, ask those coming back.
~ Chinese proverb

Most of us are pretty bad at taking advice from others. We don't mind hearing the advice; we just hate to take it. Most of the time we think we know better and thus we underweight the opinions of others relative to our own. In large part this is why young persons seem almost pre-destined to make their own mistakes—they have a tendency not to listen until after it's too late. Of course this is a shame because often tribal elders have important insights on life's experiences that NeXters don't have themselves.

How can we force ourselves to properly weigh tribal elders' advice and exploit their wisdom? Research by psychologists Ilan Yaniv and Shoham Choshen-Hillel shows that thinking from an imaginary person's perspective has the desired effect of encouraging us to take other people's advice. Using a technique called *perspective-taking*, we simply imagine a tribal elder who is faced with the same situation and then ask our self what they would do. Think of it as the secular equivalent of the Christian question, "What would Jesus do?"

The procedure is straightforward and easy to apply. Rather than accept the best choice from your own point of view, distance yourself from your perspective and ask yourself what a tribal elder would say or do in similar circumstances. When we adopt a tribal elder's perspective, we tend to more readily engage as an impartial spectator and become less prone to default to our own pre-conceived opinion. Applying this technique is likely to help you improve your decision-making.

Reali-tude:
To acquire wisdom, listen and try to understand all that you hear.

The bottom line:

- "Feedforward" solicits positive suggestions for future improvement.
- Unlike feedback, feedforward is viewed as a helpful hand up.
- Mentors are wise and trusted counselors and teachers, not coaches.
- Taking a tribal elder's perspective can help you more impartially accept their advice.

Doctor's Prescription (Rx)

There are no stupid questions, but there are a LOT of inquisitive idiots.
~ Larry Kersten, sociologist

What to look for in a mentor?

First and foremost, clearly define the kind of person for whom you would like to be a mentee. Fundamentally, you want to find a person that you naturally enjoy being with, has more experience than you have, and who is willing to help encourage you to win in life. Once you have identified this person, you have located a potential mentor. Before you approach him or her, however, mentally review the following ideal qualities to be sure your selection is appropriate. Your ideal mentor should be:

- *Completely honest.* This is a critical attribute. Like an umpire, a mentor must be able to "call 'em as he sees 'em." It is a little like having a loving uncle or aunt who will occasionally take you aside and tell you things you need to hear but frankly don't necessarily want to hear.
- *A good model.* A part of a mentor's role is teaching by example. She must be competent and let you watch what she does as part of the learning process. You must see qualities in her that you admire and that you would like to have one day.
- *Deeply committed.* Both of you must approach the relationship as a serious commitment. Your mentor must be dedicated to your growth development and be willing to stay primarily on your agenda, not his own. Benefits from mentoring often take considerable time, in some cases, years.
- *Open and transparent.* Every mentor had experienced struggles that the mentee never sees. Ask your mentor to share his struggles and failures as well as his

stories of success. Keep in mind there is much that can be learned from what went wrong as well as from what went right.

- *A skilled teacher.* Many people do things well, but don't know how to tell another person how they did it. A mentor must be able to share her knowledge and wisdom in ways that a mentee can understand. It is important that she have strong interpersonal skills, be an excellent communicator, and be patient.
- *A believer in you.* A mentor must be realistic in assessing your capabilities. He needs to look at you and be able to say, "Yes, I think this person has tremendous potential. If I invest some of my life in this person, I think he has what it takes to make a real difference."
- *Worldly wise.* A good mentor has personal strength and is an enthusiastic, lifelong learner. If each member is receptive to learning from the other, an atmosphere of mutual respect is established.

Implementing a mentor relationship

> *Knowledge without self-reflection does not lead to wisdom. The reflective element is the most crucial step for wisdom to develop.*
> ~ Monika Ardelt, sociologist

At its core, mentoring is a learning partnership. Mentees observe, question, and explore—mentors demonstrate, explain, and model. This collaboration provides both mentor and mentee with ongoing opportunities to challenge assumptions and self-reflect. The problems best suited for mentoring tend to be the thornier ones and done correctly, the payoff is a win-win. The following steps will get you off on the right foot.

- *Think about what you'd like your mentor to do for you.* Mentoring applies to the professional as well as the personal realm so give some thought to your needs. Possibly you want your mentor to offer advice on continuing education and advancing your career. Or maybe you are looking for professional connections in your chosen field of study. It could be that you need help in managing your money or rebuilding your self-esteem after being in an unhealthy relationship. Perhaps all you want is for your mentor to simply listen and offer advice when you need to visit with someone neutral. A good mentor can help you make sense of your situation and clarify the problem(s) that need to be solved.
- *Think about possible mentors.* Your circle of family and older friends represents a good starting point. From there, you can expand your search to include teachers, someone from your community or your church, people you work with, and others who are significant in your life. Keep an open mind in matching your needs to a prospective mentor—they can often help you in ways you hadn't planned for or didn't expect. Be sure to evaluate each individual to convince yourself that he or she is a good candidate. To start, limit your universe of possibilities to people you know. Approaching strangers, particularly in matters that involve personal finance or identity data, needs to be done with caution.

- *Approach a potential mentor.* Spend some time learning about the people that you intend to ask. Just because a person is busy does not automatically disqualify him from consideration (if this is the case, you might want to first bounce the idea off someone who knows the candidate well). If you have an established relationship with a tribal elder, ring her up for a chat. For others, consider sending an email to request a convenient time for a telephone conversation or meeting where the two of you can discuss your proposal. If properly timed, sometimes just dropping by may work.
- *Ask for the commitment.* Before you actually ask someone to be a mentor, be sure to explain why you selected the person as a potential mentor and how you would like the person to help you. While it is preferable to make your request in person, if this is not possible then ask by phone. You should also give some thought to the benefits that the relationship will bring to the potential mentor. Always be prepared that your prospect may turn you down. If this happens, do not take it personally. It is likely that the person has other responsibilities that would stand in the way of being a quality mentor and is simply being honest with you. If you do get turned down, be sure to thank the person and always ask for a referral to someone they think might be a good mentor for your needs.

The four 'C's of a successful mentoring relationship:

- *Commitment* of both mentor and mentee;
- *Clarity* of purpose and desired outcomes;
- *Communication*: raw honesty and a willingness to be vulnerable;
- *Confidentiality*: what happened in Vegas stays in Vegas.

Like all worthwhile pursuits, finding a mentor takes work and involves some risk. Nevertheless, the benefits you can reap from a relationship with a quality mentor are substantial and are well worth the effort you will put into your search. A mentor will give you the gift of time and talent, but keep in mind that you are not owed anything by someone who volunteers to help you. Conversely, you are not bound to do everything that they suggest you do. If either of you reach a point where you see the mentoring process as no longer productive or needed, tidy up the loose ends and end the relationship as responsibly and respectfully as possible.

Good luck and happy hunting!

Knowledge Nuggets

> *Young people are becoming overly satisfied with too little information and are too impatient to work their way through.*
>
> ~ Henry Kissinger, former U.S. Secretary of State

1. *How about a mentor?* Mentors provide wisdom and expertise to less experienced individuals to help them advance their careers, enhance their education, and guide their personal lives. Many of the world's most successful people have

benefited from having a mentor. Securing a quality mentor is unlikely to happen unless you do your homework, make the case, and ask. What to look for in a mentor? See: http://www.family.org/marriage/A000001040.cfm.

2. *Are strong relationships better than weak?* A famous 1973 experiment concluded that weak ties (contacts), not close friends, are most likely to bring us new information and job opportunities. This has been refuted in a study of executive recruiters by researchers Aral and Van Alstyne. Their findings show recruiters who relied on close peeps, or "high-bandwidth" relationships, made out better (more money) than those who relied on a wider circle of casual acquaintances. This implies that a small circle of trusted tribal elders can provide you with more valuable wisdom than a gaggle of unknowns. You can get the gist at: http://www.wired.com/magazine/2011/04/st_thompson_homophily.

3. *Where to go for info?* See Appendix F for additional information relating to this chapter.

Chapter 18

Yes You Will!

My life isn't theories and formulas. It's part instinct, part common sense. Logic is as good a word as any, and I've absorbed what logic I have from everything and everyone.

~ Audrey Hepburn, actress

The Gist

The Good:

- Your impartial spectator keeps you grounded in reality
- Know when to hold 'em and when to fold 'em
- Wisdom is anticipating the consequences

The Bad:

- Many people elect to remain ignorant of the world they live in
- Young persons spend little time thinking about how they think
- Common sense is not common
- Failure is a real option

The Reality:

- Seeing the world in shades of gray is a sign of maturity
- Critical thinking is the prudent response to change and complexity
- The lesson: understand reality, know yourself, make smart choices
- Learn about success, failure, and "wrinkle wisdom" from tribal elders
- Who cuts your slice of the pie? YOU DO!™

Introduction

Who are you going to believe? Me or your own lying eyes?
~ Richard Pryor, comedian, social critic

Adam Smith (1723–1790) was a brilliant, if not eccentric, Scottish university professor who was known to talk in rapt conversation with invisible companions. Economist, philosopher, and psychologist all rolled into one, Smith authored *The Theory of Moral Sentiments* (1759) and *An Inquiry into the Nature and Causes of the Wealth of Nations* (1776). The latter, usually abbreviated as *The Wealth of Nations*, is considered his *magnum opus*[326] and the first modern work of economics. It earned him an enormous reputation and would become one of the most influential works on economics ever published. Smith is widely cited as the father of modern economics and capitalism.

Moral Sentiments[327] presents a commonsense theory of psychological factors that underlie human decision making, motivation, and interaction. In publishing the book, Smith's goal was to explain the source of mankind's ability to form moral judgments in spite of man's natural inclinations toward self-interest. Smith felt that the act of observing others makes us sympathetically aware of ourselves. In other words, we imagine how we would feel if we were in the place of the other person and this "feeling with" affects our own behavior.

Smith contends that much of human behavior is under the influence of the "passions"—emotions such as fear and anger, the drives of hunger and sex, and other motivational factors such as pain. Our passions are moderated by an internal voice of reason, an imagined "man within the breast" that allows us to see our own feelings from the perspective of an external observer rather than simply being blinded by our own needs. It is the approbation, or disapproval, of what Smith calls our *impartial spectator* that makes us aware of the nature of our own conduct. For example, how do you feel when you discover that the previous "reliever" peed on the toilet seat? Pissed off? You bet! When you squirt your lizard, however, it is the impartial spectator that reminds you to aim carefully.

> *When we are about to act, the eagerness of passion will seldom allow us to consider what we are doing with the candour of an indifferent person. This self-deceit, this fatal weakness of mankind, is the source of half the disorders of human life.*
> ~ Adam Smith, from *The Theory of Moral Sentiments*

---

326 From the Latin meaning "great work," this refers to the largest, and perhaps the best, greatest, most popular, or most renowned achievement of a writer, artist, or composer. Although *The Wealth of Nations* is widely regarded as Smith's most influential work, it is believed that Smith himself considered *The Theory of Moral Sentiments* to be a superior work.

327 Moral sentiments are feelings or emotions of approval, disapproval, gratitude, resentment, and so on.

The internal struggle between our impulsive, fickle, and indispensable passions and our impartial spectator is the most fascinating part of Smith's thinking. Although our passions are in the driver's seat, Smith believed that the impartial spectator can help override our compelling behavior, describing it as a "moral hector who, looking over the shoulder of the economic man, scrutinizes every move he makes." Like a "higher conscience," the impartial spectator is our internal voice of reason and dispassionately reminds us to pause and consider the long-view. It is what helps us resist having unprotected sex, one for the road, or that third slice of pizza.[328]

In this respect, Smith's work anticipated much of the modern view of behavioral economics. As the driver of our actions, Smith's idea of an impartial spectator neatly explains our concurrent use of reason and emotion. So, how does this affect us? In surveying our own questionable beliefs, we need to examine our thinking as we imagine any other fair and impartial spectator would examine it. And to do this, we need to acquire wisdom.

Reali-tude:
Passions say "Indulge!" Impartial spectator says, "Not so fast!"

The Good

Information is not knowledge,
Knowledge is not wisdom,
Wisdom is not truth,
Truth is not beauty,
Beauty is not love,
Love is not music,
and Music is THE BEST.

~ Frank Zappa, American composer, from *Packard Goose*

The field of information science describes wisdom as the end product of a hierarchical continuum. At the other end of the spectrum is data. Data is simply symbols, signals, or facts that have no meaning or value. A continuous string of hundreds of thousands of numbers, for example, is data. Organize and process that same string of numbers so it is useful for a specific purpose or context—say, a city phone directory—and it becomes information (for scoring a hot pizza at two am). Lawrence Prusak, founder of IBM's Institute for Knowledge, describes information to be "a message, one-dimensional and bounded by its form: a document, an image, a speech, a genome, a recipe, a symphony score. You can package it and instantly distribute it to anyone, anywhere." Pepperoni anyone?

But having information does not mean you are knowledgeable.

328 If passions are sufficiently intense, the impartial spectator can be stifled or even rendered impotent. Hell hath no fury like a woman scorned...

"Society is drowning in information, yet starved for knowledge" says global strategic communications expert Judith Strother. Knowledge differs from information because it originates and is applied in the minds of knowers. It is a fruit salad mix of framed experience, values, perspectives, contextual information, expert insight, know-how, and grounded intuition.[329] Knowledge is more useful to us because it helps us evaluate and incorporate new experiences and information. Over time, we accumulate, integrate, and apply knowledge to help us interpret information and decide how to handle a specific situation.

But having knowledge does not mean you are wise.

In ancient Greek mythology, the goddess Metis ("the Wise One") symbolized divine wisdom. One of the lesser Titans, she was the personification of prudence, good counsel, and advice. In the lower case, Greeks used the term *metis* to describe a person with good judgment, that is, someone who has practical knowledge, a feel for the landscape of reality, and the ability to adapt to changing circumstances. A person that today, we call wise.

What is wisdom?

Psychologists pretty much agree that wisdom involves an integration of knowledge, experience, and deep understanding with a tolerance for the uncertainties of life. There's also an awareness of how things play out over time that confers a sense of balance, optimism, and calm. British social philosopher Isaiah Berlin describes the art of being wise as "a special sensitiveness to the contours of the circumstances in which we happen to be placed... the 'sense of reality,' the 'knowledge' of how to live."[330] Wisdom isn't knowing specific facts or possessing knowledge of a field, points out cultural commentator David Brooks in his book, *The Social Animal: The Hidden Sources of Love, Character, and Achievement*. It consists of knowing how to treat knowledge. "Wisdom," says Brooks, is "being confident but not too confident; adventurous but grounded. It is a willingness to confront counterevidence and to have a feel for the vast spaces beyond what's known." Like speech, wisdom is an accumulated skill," remarks Brooks, and is acquired slowly and through experience.

That a tomato is a fruit is knowledge; not to use it in fruit salad is wisdom.
~ S. M. Sapatnekar, epidemiologist

People generally recognize wisdom when they encounter it. In as much as it is possible to quantify wisdom, we do in fact get wiser with age, observes social psychologist Igor Grossmann. Two critical aspects of wise reasoning, recognition of the limits of personal knowledge and awareness that more than one perspective

329 In organizations, knowledge often becomes embedded not only in documents and repositories but also in organizational routines, processes, practices and norms.

330 Isaiah Berlin (1909–1997) wrote extensively on the concepts of political philosophy and liberty. He has been described as having one of the finest minds of his time.

on a problem can exist, increase as we get older, he says.[331] In a study of wisdom in the elderly, sociologist Monica Ardelt found that being "reflective," or the ability to develop insights by looking at events from many different perspectives, was the most crucial element for wisdom to develop.

NeXters, do not assume that your prejudices are correct. Hindsight is always wise. *Young person's alert*: tribal elders may not be sharp as you, but the substance of their judgment is superior to your cleverness. Tapping their wisdom will give you a huge advantage over your friends!

Reali-tude:
Wisdom is anticipating the consequences.

The Bad

Thinking sucks.
~ Beavis

There is nothing we do as humans that does not involve thinking. Our thinking tells us what to believe, what to reject, what is important, what is unimportant, what is true, and what is false. Thinking is the key factor that determines the outcomes of our life-choices: who we marry, how many kids we have, where we live, what our level of education is, and our choice of lifestyle. In short, our thinking guides everything we know, believe, want, fear, and hope for. It follows, then, that the quality of our thinking is the primary determinant of the quality of our lives. You are what you think!

But thinking is volitional. Thinking requires focus, something many young people fail to apply when it comes to evaluating and judging life's situations. With minimal awareness, they fill their gaps in knowledge with emotion and the opinions of friends. If they do focus, they tend to do so selectively, ignoring the situational context and the long-term ramifications. Why is this? Focus requires effort—it is easier to accept something as true (or not knowable) than it is to ask questions and test it against the facts of reality. Better to simply "go with the flow" and react later if something goes awry. Objectivist philosopher Barbara Branden cites this as the #1 source of ineffective thinking.

Like a backseat driver, he passively ends up where the car does. Mentally, he is carried along passively. He merely observes whatever intellectual scenery his subconscious feeds him by chance association. He doesn't direct the progression of his thoughts; and his conclusions and decisions, if any, are determined not by facts

331 In extending his research on wise reasoning to the Japanese culture, Grossman found, in contrast to the West, that students are viewed as their masters' equals almost from the beginning.

and logic, but by the random ideas, memories, emotions, and images which lead his mental processes.
~ Barbara Branden, author of *The Passion of Ayn Rand*

Considering that cognitive skills are critical to personal economic success, young persons seem to spend remarkably little time thinking about how they think. Indeed many Gen NeXters take umbrage when the teaching of cognitive skills is even mentioned. Such an affront to your self-image is not generally well received. After all, any derp can see that you already think.

Or, do you? Hmkay... stand by for Reality 101: far too many of you have certain and complete knowledge that your knowledge is certain and complete. You are confident that a few key strokes into an electronic search engine will make you an instant expert. You choose to remain ignorant because reality may demand a change in your beliefs, require you to take undesired actions, or cause unpleasant emotions. Far from solving problems, these actions create a false sense of security, self-importance, or self-righteousness.

NeXters, to truly appreciate the complexities of the world and the intricacies of human experience, it is essential that you THINK. Look in the glass and get in touch with your impartial spectator. Become more aware of your own questionable beliefs, remind yourself to examine your assumptions, and make an effort to challenge what you think you know.

Reali-tude:
Any desire for the ends must include the means.

There ain't no way to hide your lying eyes

All of us need to concede that perhaps we are not as good, honest, effective, and well-intentioned as we believe. In a classic experiment, social psychologists George Quattrone and Amos Tversky found that if given a reason, we will happily lie to ourselves and look for evidence that confirms our comforting self-deception. Our fuzzy thinking—not ignorance, but the refusal to know; not blindness, but the refusal to see; not emotions, but the refusal to examine them—induces an inner fog that spawns erroneous beliefs and hyper-sensitive emotions and puts them squarely in the driver's seat. We set out on the road of life, confident that our conjectures represent reality. Most often, they don't. There is wisdom in realizing how much we deceive ourselves, and that in the end, even we are not to be trusted.

BRAIN SNACK: *In a national survey of 2,250 adults by Pew Research Center, Americans believe their fellow Americans have gotten fat and consider this to be a serious national problem. But when they think about weight, they appear to use different scales for different people. Nine-in-ten American adults say most of their fellow Americans are overweight. But just seven-in-ten say this about the*

people they know. And less than four-in-ten (39 percent) say they themselves are overweight. Got Cheetos?

Most of us are trapped in our beliefs, many of which are questionable, say psychologist Linda Elder and strategist Richard Paul in their book *25 Days to Better Thinking and Better Living.* Lacking the sense to question our naiveté, we are unaware that we have never examined the beliefs, concepts, assumptions, and world-views in our thinking for veracity or quality. Trapped in an egocentric narrow-mindedness, we are stool pigeons for being overly confident, we misunderstand the need for change, and we sacrifice our long-term happiness for short-term gains. In other words, we are victims of our own cognitive traps.[332] This leads to the stark revelation that the single greatest threat to your long-term personal economic success is the person staring back in the glass: YOU.

Reali-tude:
Stop believing your own lies.

The bottom line:

- The impartial spectator provides a realistic view of your own ability and prospects.
- Wisdom is the application of common sense and good judgment to things that matter.
- Questionable beliefs and risky behaviors arise from fuzzy thinking.
- Nothing is so firmly believed as that which least is known.

The Reality

I know it's true, oh so true, 'cause I saw it on TV.
~ John Fogerty, Credence Clearwater Revival

The underlying causes of faulty reasoning and questionable beliefs will never simply disappear. Without the wisdom that comes from age and direct experience, attempts by young persons to cope with the complexities of modern life too often lay bare their shortcomings. "We tend to see the world as black and white," says psychologist Jeff Larsen, "whereas thinking in shades of gray is a sign of maturity." Young persons will always prefer black-and-white over shades of gray and are tempted by the idea that everything that happens to them is controllable. What can be done to compensate for deficiencies in your everyday thinking and spare you from the kinds of lifebombs described in the *Young Person's Guide?* Three life-skills can help improve the quality of your reasoning: common sense, critical thinking, and personal responsibility.

332 For a complete lineup of the cognitive traps, see Chapter 16.

Life-skill #1: Develop common sense!

Common sense is the collection of prejudices acquired by age eighteen.
~ Albert Einstein, physicist

Sociologist Duncan Watts, principal research scientist at Yahoo! Research and author of *Everything is Obvious (Once You Know the Answer)* finds the idea of common sense surprisingly hard to pin down. "Roughly speaking," he notes, "it is the loosely organized set of facts, observations, experiences, insights, and pieces of received wisdom that each of us accumulates over a lifetime." Merriam Webster dictionary describes common sense as exercising "sound and prudent judgment based on a simple perception of the situation or facts."

Street smart: a person who has a lot of common sense and knows what's going on in the world. This person knows what every type of person has to deal with daily and understands all groups of people and how to act around them. This person also knows all the current shit going on everywhere... and knows how to make his own right decisions, knows how to deal with different situations, and has his own independent state of mind. A street smart person isn't stubborn and actually listens to shit and understands shit.
~ from *Urban Dictionary*

The idea that common sense represents the basic level of practical knowledge and judgment that we all need to help us live in a reasonable and safe way implies two related but different things. First is *common sense knowledge*, which are basic things that everyone "in common" needs to know to successfully function in today's fast paced society. These go to the heart of personal survival, self-knowledge, and long-term health and safety. For example, common sense tells you to always back up your important computer files! A few common sense knowledge basics that everyone should know include:

- *Your money.* Budgeting and self-restraint in spending are common sense in action, along with having all of your important financial decisions, loans, and agreements in writing.
- *Your body.* Knowing your nutritional, sleep, and exercise needs and limitations is important. Common sense tells you it is not healthy to be significantly under/over weight or to ignore a medical condition.
- *Your outlook.* Resourcefulness is a key part of using common sense. "Doing more with less" can help you to thrive under difficult conditions, not feel deprived, and keep an upbeat self-image.

Then there is *common sense reasoning*, what management consultant Karl Albrech calls "the mental ability to cope with the challenges and opportunities of life." It is how we reason about cause and effect, explain the things we observe, and judge how we respond. In other words, common sense is the ability to see the dots where none seems to exist. Some common sense reasoning skills that can help you make smarter life-choices are:

- *Plan ahead Fred.* Is what you are trying to accomplish practical and have you accounted for everything? If things go wrong, can you fix them? If not, what will be the consequences? Are your own emotions, beliefs, and practices overriding your common sense?
- *Pause and reflect.* Periodically observe "the forest" around you. Reflecting over past experiences enables you to continually refine your understanding of the world and how it works. This will enable you to set goals that are realistic so you can take sensible actions toward meeting them.
- *Do less, think more!* Siimon Reynolds (*Why People Fail*) says that many of us suffer from "obsessive do-itis." This simply means we're obsessed with "doing" instead of "thinking." Approach everything with an open mind and try to allocate thinking time every single day, even if it's only 20 minutes.
- *Question sources.* Often we are so used to nodding our head that we forget its okay to ask someone why they presume something to be so. Ask yourself if what you hear from others or in the news passes the smell test. Just because other people do or use something isn't a sign that it will suit you too.
- *Consult with others.* Your understanding can almost always be improved upon. Ask yourself "Is it possible I may be wrong?" This is especially important if you are linked emotionally to a decision. Discuss situations with tribal elders to widen your appreciation of their perspectives and ideas.

Don't confuse common sense with intelligence or experience. Although these might enhance one's common sense, they are not the same thing. There are kids in elementary school who demonstrate more common sense than some very intelligent adults. In his book *What Intelligence Tests Miss*, psychologist Keith Stanovich explains that individuals with high IQs are as likely as others to go for quick, easy answers, adopt beliefs that preclude rational thinking, or be unaware of the rules of chance and probability. Sure, brainiacs are good at logical, linear, and computational tasks, he says. But excelling in the real world requires other characteristics such as setting realistic goals and possessing moral virtues such as honesty, rigor, and fair-mindedness. And these capabilities are not measured by standard intelligence tests.

BRAIN SNACK: *Intelligence quotient, or "IQ," is a measure of relative intelligence. In 1905 French psychologist Alfred Binet developed the first IQ test to determine which school children were "too slow" to benefit from regular instruction. While most children reach the same level of complexity, or mental age, at about the same time, some are slower to learn difficult concepts and perform challenging tasks. A 6-year-old, for example, who can do no more than a 3 year-old has a mental age of 3. Dividing the mental age by the chronological age (3 divided by 6) gives a mental quotient, or MQ, of .5. Binet then determined IQ by*

multiplying MQ times 100 (in this case, the child has an IQ of 50). Binet's test provided the basis for the modern IQ tests used today.[333]

If simply being intelligent does not determine the maturity of your judgment, what does? According to Stanovich, what really matters to your real world performance is collecting information before making up your mind, seeking various points of view before you come to a conclusion, and thinking about future consequences before taking action.

Common sense ain't common

> *For every hard question, there's a common sense answer that's simple, seductive, and spectacularly wrong.*
> ~ Eric Klinenberg, sociologist

Who has not heard a parent or teacher scold, "How could you have done that? What were you thinking? Didn't you have any common sense?" This begs the question, "Can common sense be taught?" To some extent the answer is "Yes," claims psychologist Daniel Willingham. "With sufficient practice, people can come to recognize the types of errors the reflective mind makes, and learn to avoid them," he advises. Recognizing that—horror of horrors, our beliefs might actually be wrong—is 80 percent of the battle. In the *Young Person's Guide* we have looked at three types of cognitive errors that are capable of overriding our common sense:

1. *Confidence traps:* Each of us creates a reality out of our own experiences. We make sense of our world through this personal lens, and for the most part, we understand that our sense of reality is fallible. For some of us, however, perception of reality represents truth. On the slippery slope of self-confirmation, we are overconfident in our judgment and capabilities. Disallowing for doubt, we neglect to apply common sense in our life-choices.
2. *Change traps:* Seeing ourselves as rational "choosers," most of us believe that we always strive to make the most rational choices possible. The problem is we don't, and this overrides our common sense. We prefer not to "rock the boat" from the status quo. As mental lounge-lizards, we fail to take into account the "spin" in what we read and hear. We are also unduly influenced by friends and easily swayed by current popular fads and social opinion.
3. *Maturity traps:* People are wired to focus on the near- versus the long-term. Acting on impulse or emotion, we overlook key connections between today's decisions and tomorrow's consequences. We fail to project our current emotional or physical state into the future. And we heavily value instant gratification, even when it is clearly in our own interest not to do so. Maturity traps "stealthily" skirt our common sense and are the most risky of all cognitive traps.

333 The majority of us have an IQ between 85 and 115.

When we rely on common sense, we forego a more thorough effort to solve a problem. In this respect, common sense is actually a very useful method for resolving everyday situations. For example, why waste time analyzing the menu when you could already be enjoying the meal? But wisdom consists of using common sense about when to use common sense. Things go wrong when common sense seems so obvious to us that we are tempted to use it to simplify assumptions in complex situations that we haven't really thought through. Resist this temptation. It can lead to poor judgment, dumb choices, and a boatload of regret.

> *Throughout my 30+ years in business, I have always found that those individuals that possessed a high degree of "common sense," that could actually think, had intuition, had initiative, gained wisdom based on their experiences, were highly motivated, were and are by far much more creative, contributed more, interacted well with others, and were more interesting people in general. Degrees are nice, but only up to a point. I think an individual needs a certain amount of common sense to know how to put their schooled knowledge to work.*
> ~ anonymous Internet blogger

Whatever your age, background, training, IQ, or experience, common sense can be learned and applied to everyday situations. "Valuing doubt, learning from failure, and being aware of one's limitations are increasingly important skills to coping with the white water world of change and uncertainty," advises psychologist Peter Standen. The *Young Person's Guide* is but one source of common sense. Feel free to cherry pick, discard, or adopt those things that suit you. After all, doing so is just common sense!

Reali-tude:
Belief + Doubt = Common sense.[334]

The bottom line:

- Common sense helps prevent you from making irrational mistakes.
- Developing good common sense requires life-long discipline and practice.
- Cognitive traps (biases) can override your common sense.
- Maturity is the ability not to see the world as absolutes, but shades of gray.

Life-skill #2: Think critically!

> *All the problems of the world could be settled if people were only willing to think. The trouble is that people very often resort to all sorts of devices not to think, because thinking is such hard work.*
> ~ Thomas J. Watson, former president, IBM

334 A variation of artist Barbara Kruger's conceptualization of power and control in Washington, D.C. "Adding doubt to belief actually subtracts something from belief: blind uncertainty," says Kruger.

We have all been lectured on the importance of critical thinking. But what does it really mean? Adult learning educator Steven Brookfield, author of *Developing Critical Thinkers*, identifies the first step in critical thinking as recognizing and then scrutinizing the assumptions that guide us through life. Critical thinking is only possible when "people probe their habitual ways of thinking for their underlying assumptions—those taken-for-granted values, common-sense ideas, and stereotypical notions about human nature . . . that underlie our actions," relates Brookfield. Critical thinkers don't automatically accept a particular idea, statement, lifestyle, or solution. Rather, they reflect on the alternatives, reach a well-justified conclusion or answer, and accept the consequences.

Thinking critically ensures that we use the best thinking we are capable of by basing our decisions on facts, not emotions. It guards against our falling prey to trap thinking and uncritically accepting social rules and taboos. *Young person's alert:* critical thinking is our only guarantee against delusion, deception, and superstition.

No matter how skilled we are as thinkers, we can always improve our reasoning abilities. Too often we make bad decisions because we do not prepare ourselves in advance how to deal with possible opportunities, issues, and temptations likely to come our way. Of course, this is not to say that we must be a critical thinker all the time, but we should have those skills available to be employed when needed. The best preparation for unforeseen contingencies is to develop the habit of systematically cultivating critical thinking in our everyday life. To do this, we need to think about how we think.

We become a critical thinker by developing specific attitudes, traits, and skills. These techniques will serve as our impartial spectator, enabling us to evaluate arguments and question the quality of our reasoning and conclusions. Here are some insights on being an effective critical thinker:

- Reality does not care what you think:
    - § Just because you (or a group of people) believe that something is (is not) true doesn't mean it is.
    - § Objective truth exists. Facts do not cease to exist because they are ignored.
    - § Logic is not absolute. How we interpret facts may vary.

- Critical thinking does not assure that one will reach either the truth or correct conclusions:
    - § You may not have all the relevant information. Important information may remain undiscovered or may not even be knowable.
    - § Your bias(es) may prevent effective gathering/evaluation of the available information.
    - § The degree of effort needs to be proportional to the importance of the outcome.

- Most information you receive is "packaged" by persuaders:
    - § They hope their info will affect your thinking in some designed way.

§ They will almost always present their position in the strongest possible light.
§ Be sensitive to the importance of what is *not* said.

- Without an open-mind, you will never know the truth:
  § Nix the ego. Weigh alternative interpretations, viewpoints, and perspectives fairly. Do not reject unpopular views out of hand.
  § Recognize your own cognitive traps, emotional impulses, and selfish motives.[335]
  § Change your mind if warranted by new evidence or a reassessment of your real interests.

- Think outside the bun!
  § *Focus your thinking.* It is human nature to think, but it is not natural to think well. Formulate your thoughts in words instead of images to clarify questions and identify key assumptions. Few important life questions can be answered with a simple "yes" or "no." Most situations have more than one alternative.
  § *Consider the consequences.* Ask a series of "if-then" statements to help you think about possible unintended consequences. For example, "If I join the Navy, then I will…" Asking, "What will I lose?"; "What will I gain?"; and "How could my choice affect my family, friends, and self?" can help you trace significant implications. Be sure to learn from your near-misses!
  § *Turn over the rock.* Avoid considering only those possibilities that are already strong and/or appealing as you may seek evidence in their favor, ignore contrarian evidence, and be overly confident in your initial choice. Be open to subtle possibilities. Ask "Why?"; "How?"; and "What about this?" and let the opinion you form be your own.
  § *Save face.* Decide whether the situation calls for a new response, a modification of the old way of doing things, or the usual same-o, same-o. Allow time before responding so your intuition can steep. Resisting pressure to make an instant judgment often saves embarrassment or regret down the road.

According to Richard Paul, Research Director at the Center for Critical Thinking, critical thinking is the only prudent response to the accelerating change and increasing complexity of our world. "No gimmick, no crafty substitute, can be found for the cultivation of quality thinking," says Paul. "The quality of our lives can only become more and more obviously the product of the quality of the thinking we use to create them," he advises. Unfortunately, all too often we accept what we see and hear, becoming passive absorbers of information rather than critical listeners or readers. Like wildebeests, we simply moooove along with the herd.

---

335 The Classical Greek philosopher Plato (429–347 B.C.E.) desperately wanted man to grasp and never let go of the "sacred golden cord of reason." Ultimately he had to acknowledge that his fellow-beings were anchored in the life of feelings, "jerked about like puppets by the strings of desires and fears that made them dance." Plus ça change, plus c'est la même chose!

No one can deny that a (world) network of economic and psychic affiliations is being woven at ever increasing speed, which envelops and constantly penetrates more deeply within each of us. With every day that passes it becomes a little more impossible for us to act or think otherwise than collectively.
~ Pierre Teilhard de Chardin, Jesuit priest, transhumanist

Each of us must each take it upon ourselves to become lifelong learners, searching for ways to continuously upgrade our reasoning and critical thinking skills. Complex problems have many facets, and we must uncover meaning to understand linkages, complexities, and long-term implications before we make a decision. Many young persons are still under the sway that thinking more or less "takes care of itself." By and large, we treat knowledge as something that can be given to us and inserted into our minds by memory alone. But this is a flawed conception—knowing the entire human DNA sequence still does not explain why we fall in (or out of) love!

"To prepare us for the real world," says philosopher Richard Paul, "we must concentrate on teaching ourselves how to think, thus freeing us to think for ourselves, critically, fair-mindedly, and deeply. In the future, notes *The Economist*, "learning to think for oneself could well be more important than simply learning to read and write." *Young person's alert:* excellence in thinking cannot be produced with simplistic procedures and slogans. Real life isn't the classroom.

Reali-tude:
Critical thinking focuses on judgment and interpretation.

The bottom line:

- Be skeptical regarding what you hear and read.
- Move toward a questioning approach to knowledge and self-reflection.
- Investigate competing evidence and challenge your beliefs.
- Critical thinking must be systematically cultivated as a life-long endeavor.

Life-skill #3: Take responsibility!

I don't think of myself as a poor deprived ghetto girl who made good. I think of myself as somebody who from an early age knew I was responsible for myself, and I had to make good.
~ Oprah Winfrey, humanitarian, talk show host

For some NeXters, life can be a challenge just to survive. You struggle to maintain your sanity while working two jobs plus going to school. You are to be admired for your courage and tenacity—although the path is difficult, you will succeed. Others of you have yet to bear the full brunt of independent personal economics and thus are not proximate to any significant degree of discomfort or responsibility. You are content to kick the can down the road, slumming with your friends, until hunger or boredom forces you to do something about it.[336] Even then, your parents will have to hound you to take action. You think that you will take action, you fully intend to get around to it, but in the end you won't do anything. Success will be yours...someday. You know it, they know it, hell we all know it.

Reality check: success is not due to a fortuitous concourse of stars at our birth. Rather, it is due to a steady trail of sparks from the grindstones of hard work, determination, good planning, and perseverance. It's what YOU DO that defines you and creates success. You are responsible for the choices you make in life, and for better or worse, you inherit the long-term consequences. What does taking real responsibility for your actions mean? It means consciously taking control and causing the results that you want in life. Psychotherapist Nathaniel Branden has extensively researched self-responsibility,[337] and based on his principles, here are some suggestions to help you reach your full potential:

- *Clear your inner fog.* You have a choice: you can pay attention and be fully present when you are making a controllable decision, or you can be physically present but mentally absent. You are responsible for the level of consciousness you bring at life's inflection points and you are responsible for the results.
- *Be captain of your fate.* Other people don't make you talk or act in certain ways. Once you recognize that you are the source of your own decisions and actions, you are far more likely to proceed wisely and to act in ways that will not cause regret down the road.
- *Still waiting for Zorro?* Stop imagining that someone will come along to "rescue" you—to solve your problems and fulfill your wishes. A self-responsible person recognizes that no one is coming to make life right or to "fix" things. Nothing will improve unless you do something to make it happen.
- *Know thyself.* Many people are happy to reflect passively on what others believe and value. Or they assume that their ideas arise naturally out of their feelings, by instinct. Self-responsible people work to become aware of their beliefs and values before making up their own minds.
- *You can't do it all.* The way we spend time and energy is either in sync with our values or out of sync with what we claim is important. The way you prioritize your time is your own choice. If you are overwhelmed, re-examine your values and set priorities that make more sense.
- *Self-discipline.* Overcome your natural urge to do what is fun, easy, and quick. Self-discipline takes time to develop and requires you to motivate yourself intellectually. Keep in mind you are competing for success against others who are mainly lazy, greedy, and think only of short-term gain.

---

336 Lions have this strategy down to a science. On average, lions laze in the shade for about 20 hours each day. The reason they are successful is they make very effective use of the remaining four hours. You don't.

337 Nathaniel Branden was a former associate of Objectivism philosopher Ayn Rand and is widely referred to as the father of the self-esteem movement in psychology. His book, *The Six Pillars of Self-Esteem*, is considered the definitive work in the discipline.

- *Pick your friends, not your nose.* You can resent others when they repeatedly hurt or disappoint you. You can feel sorry for yourself for getting involved. Or, you can recognize your responsibility for choosing with whom you spend time and make different choices.
- *Harness the power within.* Believe your happiness is primarily in your own hands and you give yourself enormous power. Don't wait for events or other people to make you happy. If something is wrong, don't respond, "Someone's got to do something!" Instead, say "What can I do?"
- *Look in the glass.* In taking responsibility for your life, you'll recognize other people's rights to do the same. Other people do not exist as means to your ends, any more than you live in service to their goals. This is true in your personal relationships as well.

In his book *Taking Responsibility*, Branden tells us we can become more aware of whether we are acting responsibly in any situation by asking our self "If I wanted to be fully self-responsible right now, what would I be doing?" In addition, suggests Branden, cultivate your own self-responsibility by beginning each day looking in the glass and asking two questions:

1. What's good in my life (school, home, job, etc.)?
2. What do I need to do to get what I want?

"The first question keeps us focused on the positives," advises Branden. "The second reminds us that our life and well-being are our own responsibility and keeps us proactive." This technique is so easy to do, why not make it a daily habit?

Reali-tude:
Some let it happen; others make it happen; some wonder what happened.

The bottom line:

- It is more empowering if you think of responsibility as the "ability to respond."
- The world arrives where logic resides (after taking a few detours).
- The only mind you control is your own.
- Don't cheat the person in the glass.

Failure IS an option

There are three basic kinds of failure: failure to learn, failure to anticipate,and failure to adapt.

~ Eliot Cohen and John Gooch, *Military Misfortunes*

Have you ever wondered why life is so hard? Or rather, why is life never what you envisioned it would be? This is a very modern lament, says ultra-smart person Marilyn vos Savant. For just the past few decades, parents have reared and educated their children to believe that they can be anything they want to be, if they only try hard enough. Yet, tribal elders know this is not true. M.I.T. Dean of Admissions Marilee Jones explains that it is the adults, not their children, who are causing the problems. "When you say (young persons) have unrealistic expectations," says Jones, "that's because those are expectations that have been set for them by the adults in their world."

NeXters, parents have spent a lot of time coaching you on what to do to achieve success. Yes, they want to believe that you are great. Yes, they want to preserve your egos. But in so doing they shy away from something equally as important: the value of exposing you to, and preparing you for, failure. "The truth is life is about producing failure," observes author David Brooks. "We progress through a series of regulated errors where every move is a potential failure to be corrected by the next one. Like walking, you shift your weight off balance with every step, and then you throw your other leg forward to compensate," says Brooks. Some failures are spectacular and public. For others, it's simply falling short of expectations—in their careers or personal lives.

Educators say failure is something Gen NeXt wants to hear more about. "They are very concerned with failure," says generational cultures expert Rich Honack. Current 20-somethings "have always succeeded," he notes. "They've always gotten trophies when they go out for a sports team. They've always gotten 'A's. Their parents have told them be the best and protected them from failure." And this can be devastating later when they experience their first real failure in life.

> *One area where it is impossible to hide from failure—success inevitably comes, on average, just half the time—is college sports. In his 2006 book* Excellence Without a Soul, *former Harvard University dean Harry Lewis recounted being asked by a dean if it was true that the university planned to admit fewer athletes. 'That would be terrible," the dean told Lewis. "They are the only people here who know how to lose."*
> ~ Justin Pope, education reporter

Hearing about failure is far more instructive, and interesting, than hearing about success. "People typically have a much easier time recounting, in often vivid detail, where they screwed up in life than they do explaining what they did right," say education reporters Justin Pope and Timothy Noah. Yale law professor Anthony Kronman finds that high-achieving freshman are often most riveted by the flawed characters in his *Great Books* class. In Thucydides' *History of the Peloponnesian War,* for example, Kronman says students are most drawn not to the heroes, but to Alcibiades, a 5th-century B.C.E. Athenian politician. Alcibiades screwed up by making too many enemies and squandering his talents.

Look in the glass dude(tte). You are a smart and talented young person. Have you considered the possibility of failure? Do you know how to lose?

Why you need tribal elders

> *Ninety percent of everything is crap.*
> ~ Theodore Sturgeon, science fiction author

Like Lady Godiva, knowledge is all about exposure and NeXters have this in abundance. "Electronic media of one sort or another now seems to occupy every spare moment" says English professor Mark Bauerlein, author of *The Dumbest Generation*.[338] This absorption with technology is creating "a world of ubiquitous connectivity and pervasive proximity," says strategist Mark Federman, and this influences how young persons make sense of the world surrounding them. Increasingly they are putting greater faith in the wisdom of crowds (such as Google) and prize the confidence of their peers above that of trusted sources of wisdom.

But is this wise? Maybe not Mabel. What young persons lack—and what tribal elders have by definition—is tread wear on the road of life. Tribal elders are helpful because they can shock you out of your cognitive box.[339] If you really want to know how your attitudes and behaviors come across, let a tribal elder hold the mirror and tell you what *they* see. Why, your blind spots are perfectly obvious to them! These are the people in you life who are most likely to be agenda-free and who truly want you to succeed.

Explaining your thoughts to a tribal elder forces you to be self-skeptical, i.e., an impartial spectator, if only for a moment. In doing so, you sometimes hear your thoughts more clearly yourself. Listen to what they say. Learn from the bad; assimilate the good; discard the rest. We all claim to want truth. This is a guaranteed delivery system!

The bottom line:

- Young persons are very concerned with the prospect of failure.
- We learn wisdom from failure much more than from success.
- Explaining a situation to another person can help you clarify it in your own mind.
- Save yourself some painful scars by learning from the mistakes of others.

The ways of the wise

> *You can't connect the dots looking forward; you can only connect them looking backwards. So you have to trust that the dots will somehow connect in your future. You have to trust in something: your gut, destiny, life, karma, whatever. Because believing that the dots will connect down the road will*

---

338 In 2012, Ofcom, Britain's telecommunications regulator, said that a startling 60 percent of teenagers who use smart phones describe themselves as highly addicted to their devices. So do 37 percent of adults.

339 Psychologists tell us that we develop internal maps of our personalities. Then we use these schemas to understand and explain our current and future behavior to ourselves. For example, "I'm always on time for meetings so I'm a conscientious person."

give you the confidence to follow your heart, even when it leads you off the well worn path.
~ Steve Jobs, Apple founder

When young persons leave the shelter of their families and the structured environment of schools, they may experience a hard clash of reality with their expectations. This has contributed to a growing sense of gloom about achieving the American Dream. A 2010 poll of 18–29 year olds by Harvard's Institute of Politics found that eight out of 10 said they expect difficulty finding a job after graduation. Fewer than half said they believe they will be better off than their parents when they reach their parents' age. Why the pervasive gloominess? Part of the reason is their narrow perspective due to limited life-experience. Or, when it comes to the future it's simply safer—and lazier—to be a pessimist.

NeXters, guard against irrational pessimism. Doom and gloom is a growth industry and twenty-four seven news coverage has paralyzed many of you to future possibilities. You have become so afraid of worst-case scenarios that you have all but forgotten present realities. Ask a tribal elder to share his or her perspectives. They lived through the threat of nuclear annihilation and their parents fought and won a world war. They will tell you that life in this country is less hard than it has ever been. Soothsayer Warren Buffet sums it up: America's best days lie ahead.

Now we can sit in our study by the fireplace and watch 20+ years of Charlie Rose interviews, jump on a plane for $99 and be anywhere in the country in hours, carry 20,000+ songs, movies, and books on a tiny device in my car, get far more miles per gallon, have major surgery through an opening the size of a pinhole, video chat with friends and family around the world, cure certain types of blindness with stem cells, and twenty year old kids become multi-millionaires in a year from Internet businesses.
~ Joshua McKennon, financial investor

Young persons who are emotionally positive about their chances for achieving personal economics stability have a history of succeeding. You are doers, not dreamers. You make your own luck rather than wait to get lucky. You are "situationally aware" of the gists of what is happening in the real world and are not misled by the apparent evidence of everyday experience. You are attuned to who you are, why you feel the way you do, and what your limitations are. You exercise mature judgment in making smart life-choices. You are tomorrow's success stories.

Does every generation have to learn the hard way? No! There is a good deal that a young person can do as a mature decider to improve his or her quality of life. To develop power over an unpredictable future, follow the ways of the wise:

- Know the gist of the terrain to discern what really matters.
- Understand your cognitive limitations and question your beliefs.
- Think critically, develop your intuition, and make common sense a habit.
- Exercise prudent judgment that is adaptive to the long-view.

- Seek counsel from others and learn from their triumphs and failures.
- Be guided by your impartial spectator and your ethical beliefs.
- Take 100 percent responsibility for what happens in your life.

There you have it. Stop whining and start winning by working toward the future that you want to achieve. Young persons, you too can succeed! Yes, you can! Yes, you will!

Graduation

Attention Generation NeXt! In the end, it's all about freedom—the freedom to choose your path. Many different ways of life are fulfilling and will bring you great happiness if you invest in making smart life-choices. "Hard work and perseverance matter more than genius," advises management guru James Collins. After decades of close observation, he argues that everybody can be successful, so long as they stick to a set of demanding but not impossible rules. By good fortune, you hold in your hands a compendium of life-success rules, guidelines, and lessons. Read them, absorb them, and most importantly, apply them. And to those who have read the entire *Young Person's Guide*, you are commended for your good judgment.

Ahem. Attention NeXters! In recognition of your fulfillment of the requirements for a degree in "Advanced Life-Lessons," will the candidates please step forward? Audience, please hum a few bars of *Pomp and Circumstance*...

YPG Wizard: *"Therefore, by virtue of the authority vested in me by the Universitartus Committiartum E Pluribus Unum, I hereby confer upon you the honorary degree of Th.D. That's... Doctor of Thinkology."*

Camera: *Zoom in on the Wizard's hand as he passes the coveted sheepskin to you, dear graduate.*

Fade to black: *You respond, "Baaa."*

Congratulations Doctor! You are hereby granted all rights and privileges associated with your degree. When opportunities arise, you will find yourself much better prepared to succeed. Why not start today using your ThD. to take charge of your future, adjust your attitude, and begin your new life? As they say in the Air Force, AIM HIGH! That's all (for now) folks. Good thinking, good luck, and may the curb rise to meet your feet.

Reali-tude:
Keep calm. Carry on. Get 'er done.

The bottom, bottom line:

- Today is already the tomorrow, which was shaped by your decisions of yesterday.
- Poor decisions can be costly, both in money and in quality of life.
- You alone are responsible for your long-term success.
- It is later than you think. Just do it.

Doctor's Prescription (Rx)

Attitude is more important than the past, than education, than money, than circumstances, than what people do or say.
~ W. C. Fields, film producer, actor

Your attitude, that is your general outlook on life, largely determines how you perceive and react to the realities of life. Having the right attitude helps motivate you to adapt your thinking, take control of your personal economic choices, and accept responsibility for fulfilling your life's dreams. "Get real, with an attitude!" Based on the wisdom presented in the *Young Person's Guide,* here are some universal Reali-tudes^{TM} that are key to your personal economic success:

1. *Be aware within!* Although you feel that you know everything (or can get it online), you have very limited life experience. This affects the way you think and react. A hallmark of growing up is the realization that you are but one butterfly in a rabble of millions. The world did not begin when you were born.
2. *Be aware without!* Wake up and smell the hot breath of reality. If you screw up, it is your responsibility, not your parents, or the school, or the government. Bad decisions have consequences. Fear is a powerful motivator. Ask questions and listen to the wisdom of elder tribesmen.
3. *Be engaged!* Life is complicated. Simple solutions are useful only for fast food meal deals. Look beyond texting updates and consider the complexities of your controllable decisions. If you want to set realistic expectations, do something unusual for your species: THINK.
4. *Be humble!* It is not all about you. You do not exist to be entertained. To soar with the eagles, you must first trot with the turkeys. Wisdom is about exercising mature judgment and taking prudent action. Learn from the mistakes of others—you don't have the time, energy, and money to make them all yourself.
5. *Be worried!* Yes, it is different this time—the stakes are much higher. Many of you don't understand the personal risks you face and lack any urgency to do something about it. Get your rear in gear and take steps to improve your knowledge, get a quality education, and be a competent decision-maker.
6. *Be honest!* You see the world, not as it exists but as you want to see it. Most of you see only black & white, but reality is almost always shades of gray. Often success comes down to timing and circumstance. You are the primary source of decision risk. No one can protect you from yourself!

7. *Be authentic!* Your attitudes are influenced by your emotion-laden perceptions, which—guess what?—may be wrong at any time. When it comes to exercising mature judgment, what you know that just ain't so (lack of care) can be more damaging than what you don't know (lack of knowledge).
8. *Be realistic!* Many NeXters see overly rosy futures that won't come to pass. Many consider themselves to be above average, but by definition half of you aren't. Not recognizing your own susceptibility to cognitive traps is a major problem for young persons. The world is not fair. Success is not inevitable. Deal with it.
9. *Be open-minded!* Life is change. The world will not wait until you are ready. Just because your friends believe something is true does not make it so. Procrastination makes you feel better, but only temporarily. Not understanding reality sets you up to be fleeced. Unwilling to change? You will not grow.
10. *Be mature!* Immature decision-makers look to satisfy short-tem needs and wants. Mature choosers think about the long-term consequences of their decisions. Lack of self-control over impulsive desires can lead to bad life-choices. Be careful what you wish for because you just might get it.
11. *Be sincere!* Many young persons marry for the wrong reasons. If you or your partner lacks commitment and responsibility, you made a mistake. Money is behind most breakups and the longer the marriage, the harder it is to untangle the knot. Divorce is often a traumatic and scarring experience.
12. *Be prepared!* A kid is the biggest game changer—once you have a child, your life will never be the same. If you are not emotionally ready, you cannot walk away from your "inconvenient" obligations. Never do three things mindlessly: get married, have kids, or get divorced.
13. *Be smart!* Some form of higher education is a must. College is the best route for most, but not for all. Education is what you make of it and doesn't determine intelligence or guarantee you a job. Follow your heart—most of you will end up in a career not directly related to your major anyway.
14. *Be adventurous!* Stop whining if you still live with your parents. They are doing you a favor—living on your own costs far more than you think. When you can afford it, step out of the comfort zone and find a place that's right for you. Later you will appreciate having experienced different places.
15. *Be healthy!* Live long and well by making sound, healthy lifestyle choices. Education, good habits, and self-control are your best allies to achieve the American dream. Facebook is not your friend. Your on-line profile is not you. Live within your means—everybody is trying to sell you something.
16. *Be decisive!* Base your decisions on facts, not emotions or luck. Match the complexity of the solution to the problem. Understand situational gists and trust your intuition and gut. Always consider your motivations. Ultimately, you are the one who makes the call and takes the fall.
17. *Be wise!* Wisdom comes from reflecting on experience, which you do not have. Don't let emotions overpower your logic. Tribal elders are well-springs of wisdom—use them! Be receptive, ask questions, and listen closely. Try to find a mentor who cares about you and will commit.

18. *Be empowered!* Use common sense, think critically, and take responsibility to improve your everyday reasoning. Failure IS an option. Consistently cultivate the art of personal economics success: understand reality as it exists, know your limitations, and form the conscious habit of making smart life-choices.

Reali-tudes™ for tribal elders:

1. *Be encouraging!* You forget the fear of an unpredictable future that you had when you were your kids' age. The world you grew up in has changed but life-skills are universal. Stimulate conversation, share stories, and communicate meaning to them through gists. Be an ally in your children's success!

The Guy in the Glass

I have been to the top of the mountain, and it was cool.
~ Butthead

Dale Wimbrow (1895–1954) was an American composer, radio artist, and writer. He is best known for the poem, *The Guy in the Glass*, which he wrote for publication in *The American Magazine* (1934). Although written in the masculine gender, it applies equally well to everyone. Read this poem to yourself in front of the glass when you are faced with a controllable decision. Better still, post it on your refrigerator.

When you get what you want in your struggle for pelf,[340]
And the world makes you King for a day,
Then go to the mirror and look at yourself,
And see what that guy has to say.

For it isn't your Father, or Mother, or Wife,
Who judgment upon you must pass.
The feller whose verdict counts most in your life
Is the guy staring back from the glass.

He's the feller to please, never mind all the rest,
For he's with you clear up to the end,
And you've passed your most dangerous, difficult test
If the guy in the glass is your friend.

You may be like Jack Horner and "chisel" a plum,
And think you're a wonderful guy,
But the man in the glass says you're only a bum
If you can't look him straight in the eye.

You can fool the whole world down the pathway of years,
And get pats on the back as you pass,
But your final reward will be heartaches and tears
If you've cheated the guy in the glass.

340 Money, especially when gained in a dishonest or dishonorable way.

The Last Word

We got a date with destiny, and it looks like she ordered the lobster.
~ The Shoveler, from *Mystery Men*

These days, knowledge is like air. All you ever needed to know is at your fingertips, along with multiple apps for just about everything. Push a button on your mobile device and success is all but assured.

But wait... something is missing! That something is wisdom.

Young person, what apps do you use to acquire wisdom without having any life-experience? Which ones will help you better understand yourself? Or get you to think beyond this weekend, or this year? Which apps will help you develop power over an unpredictable future so you can make smart choices and succeed in life? Where do you find a clever avatar for those things?

That's precisely the point. The *Young Person's Guide* is your app.

— Q.E.D. —

Who cuts your slice of the pie?
You do!™

Each of us cuts our own slice of the pie in life. Whatever the goals and aspirations we want to fulfill, our ability to reach those goals is largely in our own hands. We are all born with a remarkable potential for achievement, with numerous natural talents and aptitudes. It is up to us to become aware of our innate resources and capabilities, and to fine tune and develop them into practical skills that we can utilize daily to achieve our goals. Individually, each of us cuts our own slice of the pie.

~ Thomas Crescenzo, economist (1987)

Appendix A

What Trusted Adults Need to Know

I am not young enough to know everything.
~ J. M. Barrie, creator of *Peter Pan*

The Gist

The Good:

- Overwhelmingly, your kids trust you as parents
- Tribal elders are their kids' most trusted source of financial advice

The Bad:

- NeXters move back in with parents primarily for economic reasons
- Many young persons have been insulated from financial reality
- The dirty little secret: Boomers and NeXters face a retirement crisis
- If you don't get it, they won't get it

The Reality:

- The world that tribal elders knew, understood, and controlled is changing
- Young persons are "mad as hell" and don't want to take it anymore
- Boomers have belatedly discovered their financial vulnerability
- Parents, don't sacrifice your retirement to support your adult children

Introduction

And these children that you spit on
As they try to change their worlds
Are immune to your consultations
They're quite aware of what they're going through.
~ David Bowie, English musician, from *Changes*

This appendix is for parents and other trusted adults. A trusted adult is an older person with life experience who is close to a member of Generation NeXt (16 to 30 years old). Trusted adults may be a grandparent or other close relative, an educator, or maybe just a good friend. Collectively, we call these people who closely connect with young persons their "tribal elders."

About half of Gen NeXters will live to be more than 80 years old. Yet many of them will spend some or all of their golden years in poverty. This need not be preordained! The problem is many NeXters simply do not have the interest, patience, or maturity to think about their long-term personal economics. Chances are you acted the same way when you were this age. The difference is you now have the benefit of hindsight. Your task is to discuss the long-term implications of poor life-choices with young persons you care about. Share your knowledge, experiences, and wisdom with them. If you fail to comprehend the big picture, they will too.

The Good

To me, life is like the back nine in golf. Sometimes you play better on the back nine. You may not be stronger, but hopefully you're wiser. And if you keep most of your marbles intact, you can add a note of wisdom to the coming generation.
~ Clint Eastwood, actor, director

Overwhelmingly, your kids trust you as parents. Numerous studies show parents having a very significant positive influence in the lives of their children. When asked about their degree of contentment, 73 percent of 1,280 young persons ages 13–24 said their relationship with their parents made them very or somewhat happy. Roughly eight-in-ten Gen NeXters said they talked with their parents in the past day; nearly three-in-four saw their parents at least once a week; and half said they saw their parents daily. Seventy percent of 9,000 college students surveyed said they communicated "very often" with a parent or guardian, with electronic means being the most common and expect to retain close parental bonds after leaving home. In their study *Avoiding the Workforce Crisis*, The Concours Group confirmed that Generation NeXt is strikingly family-centric:

- 86 percent trust their parents;
- 90 percent of teens report being *very* close to their parents (in 1974, more than 40 percent of Boomers said they'd be better off *without* their parents);
- Parents are often cited as their heroes.

Independent in most everything else, the one area where young persons respect and listen to their tribal elders' views is money and finance. According to the NOP Research Group, the overwhelming majority of 18–24 year olds (88 percent) say their parents are an important influence on decisions regarding money. In a study by the American Savings Education Council of 1,000 students ages 16 to 22, 94 percent said they turn to their parents for financial advice on major decisions. About three-quarters of Gen NeXters say their parents have helped them financially in the past year and parent-child co-purchase decisions are common. Regardless of background or living circumstances, parents and grandparents continue to have a major impact on the finances and financial attitudes of this generation.

Reali-tude:
NeXters turn first to tribal elders for financial advice.

The Bad

I'm not a girl, not yet a woman.
~ Britney Spears, entertainer

Researchers tell us that most 18- to 25-year-old individuals do not consider themselves to be adults. A *TIME Magazine* cover story let America "Meet the Twixters," young adults who live off their parents and personal networks, try one career and then another, and fall in and out of love. According to the report, "They're not lazy... THEY JUST WON'T GROW UP" (emphasis theirs). This period, referred to by psychologist Jeffrey Arnett as "emerging adulthood," is a time of protracted adolescence and delayed entry into adulthood. It is a time of ongoing exploration of, and experimentation with, possible life directions.

That is much different from the Baby Boom generation, writes political commentator David Brooks. "People who were born before 1964 tend to define adulthood by certain accomplishments—moving away from home, becoming financially independent, getting married, and starting a family," he says. "In 1960, roughly 70 percent of 30-year-olds had achieved these things. By 2000, fewer than 40 percent of 30-year-olds had done the same."

Lacking a clear sense of direction, many NeXters return home to the nest, where the rules are murky. Often to the distress of their parents, this has allowed them to stay younger and responsibility free for longer. Old success recipes don't apply, new norms have not been established, and everything seems to give way to a less permanent version of itself. The job market is fluid. Social life is fluid. Life is fluid. This is now so common that NeXters are snarkily referred to as the *Boomerang Generation* by Boomer parents.

But the prime mover behind this mass migration of young persons is not R&R. It is lack of moolah. Experience Inc., a Boston firm that recruits at universities across the country, found more than half of the students surveyed moved in with their parents after college, and 48 percent of these said they did so to save money.

> *Contrary to popular stereotypes, the reason kids are moving back in with their parents, can't land career-path jobs, and take longer to graduate from college and settle down isn't just a widespread generational laziness or some other pervasive psychological flaw. The reason is overwhelmingly economic.*
>
> ~ Anya Kamenetz, author of *Generation Debt: The New Economics of Being Young*

Social researchers confirm this. The Pew Research Center found that almost seven-in-ten Baby Boomers with kids are supporting an adult child financially. Investigators at the University of Michigan found that parents—regardless of how much money they have—give an astoundingly large average of 10 percent of their income to their adult children. "Children are still our largest expense, well after they leave home," says economist Barry Bosworth at the Brookings Institution. Taking care of your adult children is one of those things that you don't expense for and many parents do not see how bankrolling their adult children could be hurting their own financial future.

Today's problems, yesterday's solutions?

> *In times of change, the learner will inherit the earth while the learned are beautifully equipped for a world that no longer exists.*
>
> ~ Eric Hoffer, philosopher

Okay Boomers, so your children are Klingons. This would seem to be an excellent learning opportunity to set a good example of fiscal responsibility. Are you measuring up?

In a word, no. Boomers candidly admit that they have not succeeded in their efforts to transmit their traditional values of thrift and self-discipline to their children. And the stats are not encouraging. Despite young persons' hunger for guidance, only three-in-ten American parents talk to their children regularly about personal finance and even fewer (26 percent) of 13 to 21 year olds report their parents actively teaching them how to manage money. Financial planner Mike Condrey finds that only two-in-ten young adults age 16–22 have ever had a personal finance class. This means that a lot of young persons are not getting the coaching they need to adequately prepare them for the economic realities of adulthood.

I'm a 25 year-old recent graduate and I am attempting to become financially literate—which includes learning about and contributing to my retirement, investing, and the like. I agree that our generation exhibits extremely immature behavior when it comes to saving and consuming. However, I do not place the entire blame on simply making excuses and laziness. There is a lack of awareness that should be addressed by not only students but also parents, colleges, and employers. Learning how to properly manage your money has to be taught and practiced—things our generation has gone without (at least, that was the case with me).
~ Nina S., "Downside of Youth"

Boomers, think back to 1968. That was the year that civil rights leader Martin Luther King, Jr. and former U.S. attorney general Robert F. Kennedy were assassinated. LBJ surprised the nation by choosing not to run for reelection. Richard Nixon was elected President with his sidecar, Spiro Agnew. But none of these was the most important event that year. What was significant to you then was turning eighteen! Somewhere, you have the birthday photo (complete with red eyes) that Mom took of you with her Instamatic and pop-on Flashcube to prove it.

Fast-forward to your big "SIX-OH" celebration. Today your camera might better be described as a sophisticated computer that happens to do a decent job of recording images. Consider how Alan Cooper (called the father of Visual Basic) described his latest camera:

My newest camera... is a third generation digital camera and the smartest yet. In fact, it has a full-blown computer that displays a Windows-like hourglass while it "boots up." Like some mutant fish with extra heads, its On/Off switch has now grown to have four settings: Off/ARec/MRec/Play. "ARec" means "automatic record" and "MRec" means "manual record." As far as I can tell, there is no difference. There is no "On" setting, and none of my friends can figure out how to turn it on...
~ Alan Cooper, from *The Inmates Are Running the Asylum*

What's the big deal Neil? Attention white-haired shoppers—this is not the world that you grew up in![342] The parable of the Instamatic versus the digital camera illustrates that yesterday's simplistic solutions may not be appropriate for today's complicated situations. Young persons face far more complexity today than their tribal elders did. And the better prepared young persons are to adapt and change, the better they can assert themselves and succeed.[343] Of course, this requires that they think farther than one weekend ahead and more deeply than

342 For students now entering college, phones never had cords and the computers they played with as kids are now in museums. Few incoming freshman have ever worn a wristwatch or know how to write in cursive. These are among the 75 items on the Class of 2014 Beloit College Mindset list. The list is meant to remind teachers that cultural references familiar to them might draw blank stares from college freshman.

343 The KISS principle, or *Keep It Simple Stupid*, has been attributed to 14th-century English logician and Franciscan friar, William of Ockham. Called *Ockham's (Occam's) razor*, it states that the best explanation of an event is one that "shaves away" assumptions until it is the simplest possible. Or, as Aristotle put it, "Nature operates in the shortest way possible."

140 characters. Tribal elders, your job is to help expand their minds. Timothy Leary is not dead—he is in the Ethernet.

Reali-tude:
The 4th "R" in education: reading, 'riting, 'rithmetic, and real world.

Tribal elders: helpful or hindrance?

What a drag it is getting old.
~ Mick Jagger, from *Mother's Little Helper*

Unwittingly, many tribal elders have reduced their children's ability to compete in the global marketplace. The term *helicopter parent* is a pejorative expression for Baby Boomer parents that pay extremely close attention to their child's experiences and problems. They see kids as less mature, less capable of self-management, and thus in need of more supervision. These parents, like helicopters, hover closely overhead, rarely out of reach, whether their children need them or not. The label gained popularity when American college administrators began using it in the early 2000s as Generation NeXt began reaching college age. This hyper-concern now extends into the job market with some Human Resources departments reporting that parents are beginning to intrude on salary negotiations. If you need a villain, blame it on the world's longest umbilical cord, the cell phone.

Social historian Barbara Dafoe Whitehead sees a distinction between *over-parenting* and helicopter parenting. "Over-parenting is swooping down to rescue them and not letting your kids take the consequences of their actions," she says. Social psychologist Susan Newman maintains that "when parents are making decisions for their children all the time, when they get out on their own they don't know a thing about disappointment." Adds Newman, "I've seen a lot of these children who are parented in the helicopter manner who can't make a decision. They are calling home constantly: 'I don't get along with my roommate, what should I do?' 'My roommate ate my food, what should I do?'" Psychologist Meg Jay advises parents not to rush to the rescue. Rather, they should emphasize that they believe in their child's ability to solve the problem on his or her own.

We're in a generation that was kind of shielded from a lot of financial responsibilities. The financial landscape is dramatically different today—and yet financial education has not caught up.
~ Carmen Wong, from *Gener@tion Debt: Take Control of Your Money*

Futurist Richard Watson calls this a *cotton-wool* world. Isolated by a global media that exports fear from around the world, family anxieties have been magnified and realistic perspectives banished. "This is odd because most data supports the view that the world is actually a much safer place than it was twenty, fifty, or even one hundred years ago," says Watson. Today, people tend to look at the world through the eyes of the unluckiest and view worst-case scenarios as the most likely outcomes. "In the interest of safety, helicopter parents have provided a false sense of security, or cotton-wool, to their children and this has fostered an inability to cope with uncertainty and discomfort," he says.

John Bell, co-founder of YouthBuild USA, blames "adultism," or behaviors and attitudes based on the assumption that adults are better than young people. According to Bell, adults have enormous importance in the lives of almost every young person, yet as a society we largely consider young people to be less important than and inferior to adults. Reinforced by social institutions, laws, and customs, adultism can lead to feelings of anger, insecurity, and lack of self-confidence among youth. "It is useful to reflect on our interactions with young people for signs of unintended disrespect in tone, content, or unspoken assumptions," says Bell. "Young people are often mistreated and disrespected simply because they are young."

> ***BRAIN SNACK:*** *It crawls...it creeps...it eats you alive! In the schlock sci-fi/horror cult classic,* The Blob *(1958), a shooting star falls to Earth. An elderly gentleman finds the meteorite and curiously prods it with a stick. The rock cracks open, and like a Tootsie Pop, it has a chewy center. The goop that emerges suddenly lunges up the stick, dissolves the geezer's flesh, and then moves on in search of other victims. As it absorbs more people, it gets bigger, turning red with their blood. The Blob is a monster of appetite, an absolute and voracious consumer. It cannot be killed!*[344]

Ignoring the special effects (the Blob looks like a silicone breast implant on steroids), the main plot of the movie is the failure of the establishment to trust the younger generation. Despite repeated warnings of the danger from young persons, few parents take them seriously. Later, on the brink of disaster, the community unifies to fight the monster, validating the views of the younger generation. The lesson we take from *The Blob* is that parents need to listen to their upstart but honest kids. The world that Boomers understood and controlled is over. Trust in "the way we've always done it" is eroding.[345]

Feel free to substitute your own Blob: the environment; Wall Street; health care; corporate America; Republicrats; technology; government bureaucracy; social trends. All are amorphous monsters of appetite that cannot be killed. Baby Boomers, you need to take young persons seriously, help them get a grip on reality, and convey wisdom. This is not 1968. Your time is almost over.

---

344 Film star Steve McQueen finally stops the creature by freezing it with CO_2 fire extinguishers and the military transports it to the North Pole for safekeeping. With global warming, watch for a gooey comeback.

345 According to Pew Research Center, almost eight- in-ten people believe there is a major difference in the point of view of younger people and older people today. This is the highest spread since 1969, when about three-quarters reported major generational differences in conflicts over the Vietnam War and civil and women's rights. Asked to identify where older and younger people differ most nowadays, NeXters were more likely to report disagreements over lifestyle, views on family, relationships, and dating. Older people cited differences in a sense of entitlement and in manners.

Reali-tude:
If you don't get it, they won't either.

Do NeXters lack motivation?

The reason people blame things on the previous generation is that there's only one other choice.
~ Doug Larson, humorist

With good intentions, many parents seek to insulate their children from financial pressures at an early age. In the process, however, they often fail to adequately prepare them for the economic realities of adulthood.[346] As a result, many NeXters lack a sufficient degree of personal economic maturity. Even when they realize the importance, they fail to take action. In a study of 19 to 27 year old university students, the overwhelming majority (more than 90 percent) responded that saving was "Very important" or "Important," at this stage in their life. Yet, at the behavioral level, only one-tenth reported that were responsible enough to have a monthly budget.

The root problem? They lack motivation. Let's face it—there is an abundance of quality information relating to personal finance. Private industry, government agencies, schools, periodical columns, Internet blogs, "how to" books, rich uncles, and so on provide practical information and useful guidance. But the importance of acting on this information is not registering with Generation NeXt! Their continued lack of engagement in financial matters clearly demonstrates that the challenge is more than simply obtaining the right information to make a good decision. The harder problem is behavioral—that is, actually *doing* something about it.

Why is this? The sad fact is many young persons are intellectually disengaged, preferring to blithely avoid dealing with the nettlesome complexities of real life. They lack motivation and the discipline to ask questions, extend their horizons, and gain a clearer assessment of their limitations.[347] Worse yet, some do not respond *at all*. Faced with what they perceive as an overload of information, they apathetically react only as events compel them. Nile crocodiles exist in a similarly torpid state of mind, but they only need to eat twice a year. NeXters have neither the patience nor the endurance.

School students understand freedom much better than they do responsibility. The only limits they recognize are red lights when they begin to drive, otherwise everything is an 'old folks' attempt to limit what they think is their 'freedom.' It is hard to

346 Michael Ungar, author of *Too Safe for Their Own Good*, sees risk as very much a part of our lives. His research has shown that the more we try to protect ourselves from risk, the worse we deal with it and the less resilient we are.

347 In his bestseller *The World Is Flat*, Pulitzer Prize winning journalist Thomas Friedman concludes that many American college students, when compared with their counterparts in other countries, lack the drive and intellectual competencies to be competitive.

tell teenagers anything because they already know everything. When they become parents they will be outraged with their children's actions.

~ Reardon (responding to a story about hundreds of high school teenagers boycotting a Hawaiian-themed party in their high school gymnasium after a newly imposed ban on sexually suggestive dance moves)

Generation NeXt is fending for itself to figure out how to make good decisions and succeed. Ironically, this requires a considerable degree of sophistication at a time when most young persons prefer their news quantized into clever phrases, which (in their minds) is sufficient for them to become instant experts. This narrow mentality can lead them to underappreciate the complexity and seriousness of the economic issues stacked against them today. In *The Dumbest Generation*, author Mark Bauerlein contends that cyber-culture is turning young people into know-nothings. "It's the dependence factor, the unimaginability of life without new technology, that is making kids less entrepreneurial, less initiative-oriented, less independent," he says. We tribal elders are in large part responsible for not having motivated our children.

Not everyone sees the sky falling. Sociologist William Galston predicts that when the Gen NeXters do eventually settle down, they might actually "turn out to be more capable" adults than their predecessors were. Jeffrey Jensen Arnett, editor of *Emerging Adults in America*, agrees. "Thirty is the new 20," he writes. "The transition to adulthood is longer than it used to be, but it's still a temporary stage." Commenting on those who have served in the U.S. Armed Forces, former Joint Chiefs Chairman General David Petraeus refers to today's young veterans as the "next greatest generation of leaders."

Reali-tude:
They often know what to do; they just don't do it.

The bottom line:

- Tribal elders are the most trusted source of financial advice for Gen NeXters.
- Many young persons have been insulated from financial reality by their parents.
- The world that tribal elders knew, understood, and controlled is changing.
- Many NeXters are intellectually disengaged regarding personal economics.

The Reality

You're old... groaning like a geezer. Where you once had muscle, you've got jelly rolls, buddy, you're as ancient as the Dead Sea Scrolls. 'Cause you're old... man, you're old.

~ SpongeBob SquarePants, from *The Yellow Album*

Tribal elders, look in the glass (mirror). If you are not a white-haired dude(tte),[348] you soon will be. Baby Boomers, those born from 1946 to 1964, number about 78 million; the first turned 65 in 2011. There are presently more than 37 million Americans who are 65 and older and the U.S. Census Bureau estimates that this number is expected to nearly double by 2030. "The problem," says Mark Iwry, senior fellow at the Brookings Institution, "is that people often underestimate their life expectancy." Thus, many don't plan financially to live until they're 90 because they don't think they'll ever get to be 90. Adds Iwry, "They never focus on or plan for the 50 percent chance that they'll outlive the average life expectancy, the 25 percent chance that they'll outlive it by a lot and the 15 percent chance that they'll outlive it by a lot more." Indeed, many Boomers pay more attention to their sagging boobs and waistlines than their sagging financial condition.

BRAIN SNACK: *Originally suggested by psychiatrist Carl Jung, the "midlife crisis" generally hits people in their forties, give or take a decade. A midlife crisis is a sense of worry regarding our life's direction and purpose. It can be brought on when we become bored or discontent with our lives, incur debt, or lose a loved one. Author Catherine Mayer coined the word "amortality" to describe the desire by Baby Boomers to look as young as possible and reject age-appropriate behavior. Examples include Simon Cowell (American Idol), Madonna, and Nicholas Sarkozy (former president of France). Midlife crisis can also be triggered when we become conscious of our aging body. Advances in cosmetic surgery helps Boomers lose weight, tuck a tummy, re-inflate a boob, implant a pec, remove hair or spider veins, and "youthenize" a face. Results vary from freak to fantastic.*[349]

While a sagging face can be fixed in an hour, a sagging investment portfolio cannot. And the 800 pound gorilla that no one wants to acknowledge is this country faces a retirement crisis. The American Association of Retired Persons (AARP) describes Americans as "dangerously unprepared for retirement." A 2011 survey of U.S. workers age 25 and older conducted by the nonpartisan Employee Benefit Research Institute (EBRI) found only 13 percent very confident that they will have enough money to retire comfortably. In its 2013 survey, research director Jack VanDerhei says faith in retiring with enough money and on time is at all-time lows since the start of the survey 23 years ago. Although account balances in 401(k) plans have largely recovered, one in four Boomers still working say they will never retire, about the same number as those who say they have no retirement savings. "This is a lesson for workers today," says Mathew Greenwald, co-author of the EBRI study. "Do not put off saving," he warns.

---

348 Derision made famous by celebutante Paris Hilton during the 2008 Presidential campaign.

349 Explorer Juan Ponce de Leon sailed with Christopher Columbus on his second voyage to the Americas in 1493. False legend has it that de Leon tromped through the swamps of what today is Florida, searching for the verdant island of "Bimini" and its mythical water fountain that promised eternal youth. Today we have Visa or MasterCard. In 2008, Americans had 2.5m Botox injections, 355,671 breast implants, 341,144 liposuctions, 195,104 eyelid lifts and 147,392 tummy tucks.

You were planning to retire when?

> *I think very little about my retirement savings, because I know that thinking could make me poorer or more miserable or both.*
> ~ Daniel Kahneman, Nobel Laureate (Economics, 2002)

The money that Boomers will live on during their sunset years comes from two principal sources: what they socked away as personal saving and investments, and what the government provides. And each of these sources has some discomfiting problems.

1. *Traditional pensions.* Some 20 million workers (about one-third) still participate in traditional pension plans, according to Boston College's Center for Retirement Research. Pensions (also called *defined-benefit* plans) have some great advantages. First, most of the saving and investing was done by employers, who also bear the risk that retirement assets will fall short of promised benefits. When compared to self-funded retirement plans, pension plans have on average shown higher contributions, better informed investment choices, lower costs, and higher rates of investment returns. Best of all (at least in theory), you stand to collect that check for as long as you live. No worries. What a country!

Um, maybe not. Clearly those lucky people with traditional pensions are sitting a lot prettier than the more than half of U.S. families that aren't covered by any kind of pension at their current jobs. But clouds are on the horizon. The financial crisis shredded employers' ability to fund such plans for the long haul and a growing number of company pensions are winding up in the hands of the Pension Benefit Guaranty Corporation (PBGC). PBGC is a government agency and payer of last resort for bankrupt pensions, but—guess what?—the agency has been underfunded to the tune of $billions and billions.

Many public pensions are not secure either. The dirty little secret is funds that pay pension and health benefits to police officers, teachers, and millions of other public employees across the country are facing a shortfall that could run into trillions of dollars. This is because the accounting techniques used by state and local governments to balance their pension books disguise the extent of the crisis facing these retirees. Unfunded entitlements today are the invisible rabbit of American politics. Billionaire investor Warren Buffett has labeled their sunny projections "accounting nonsense" adding, "Because the fuse on this time bomb is long, politicians flinch from inflicting tax pain given that problems will only become apparent long after these officials have departed." It is a sign of the times that some public pension plans have begun asking employees to begin contributing to their pensions.

2. Accounts funded by contributions from workers. When it comes to funding retirement, the buck has passed from employers to employees. According to EBRI,

individual retirement accounts (also called defined-contribution plans) 350 have largely taken the place of traditional pensions. Sixty-seven percent of workers say they have a defined contribution plan (up from 26 percent in 1988). Um, Houston, we have a problem. Too few workers realize how much they need to contribute to guarantee a decent retirement and are often ill-equipped to make decisions about financial products that extend across long periods of time.

You have a very severely harmed, injured consumer in terms of income slow-down, job uncertainly, job loss, wealth loss, inadequate savings, and high debt levels.
~ Laura Tyson, head, Council of Economic Advisors (Clinton administration)

The average U.S. defined-contribution plan underperforms a defined-benefit plan by around a percentage point a year. One reason is mutual fund 401(k) fees are bleeding you to death. Economist Robert Hiltonsmith of the think tank Demos calculates that a median-income, two-earner family household will pay, on average, nearly $155,000 over the course of their lifetime in effective total 401(k) fees. To put this in perspective, this household could have bought a house with the amount they paid in fees. *The Economist* projects that an employee who pays into an individual retirement account for 40 years may get only half the retirement income he could have expected under a pension system. When the plan member eventually discovers how low her pension really is, by then it is too late to do anything about it.

3. *Home equity*. For most people, the house they live in is their biggest retirement asset. Upon retirement, many Boomers had planned to cash in on the value of their homes by selling and then buying less expensive houses, renting, or moving in with the kids. Reverse mortgages have also become a popular vehicle for extracting equity from their homes to finance their retirement. Um, Dallas, we have a problem. Before the financial meltdown, households were on a binge—they spent and borrowed—as if there was no tomorrow. Between 2000 and 2007 the average American increased his personal consumption by 44 percent, much of which was financed by debt in the form of home equity loans. In five years, American households extracted $2.3 trillion of equity from their homes. They blew 20 percent of this on consumption, 19 percent on sprucing up their homes, and 44 percent on assets such as stocks (just before the financial meltdown). The hangover from this party continues to be long and painful.

Soon-to-retire Boomers lost a whopping $2 trillion in home equity thanks to the stock market crash and the housing market meltdown. By the end of the first quarter 2009, 27 percent of American households owed more than their homes were worth. An AARP survey found that those who were having the most difficulty

350 A defined contribution plan is a retirement plan controlled by an employee, who decides how much to contribute and how to invest the funds. Examples are 401(k), 403(b), 457, Simplified Employee Pension (SEP), and Savings Incentive Match Plan for Employees (SIMPLE) plans.

adjusting to declining home values were 45 to 54 year-olds, followed by those 55 to 64. Moody's Investors Service warns it will take 10 years before housing prices regain their peak, a huge problem for those who are relying on their home as their primary retirement savings. Many Boomers find themselves wheezing "adiós por siempre" to their "champagne wishes and caviar dreams."

4. *Savings and investments.* Until the financial maelstrom, saving was not in the lexicon of many Boomers. The U.S. Commerce Department reported that in 2005 Americans' personal savings rate dipped into negative territory (minus 0.5 percent), something that had not happened since the Great Depression. This meant that they not only spent all of their after-tax income the year prior, but they had to dip into previous savings or increase borrowing to finance purchases of cars and other big-ticket items.

As paychecks evaporated and work hours shrank during the recession, Boomers began saving more.[351] But the dollars lost were not the most worrisome aspect of the financial crisis, says financial columnist Jim Jubak. "Market losses get recouped in market rallies," Jubak points out. "What we've lost that can't be replaced is time." From its peak in October, 2007 through March, 2009, the S&P 500 Index lost almost 49 percent. Shave that off a $100,000 investment, Jubak says, and you'll need a 96 percent gain just to get back to even. Younger savers can overcome such a huge hit with time, but it's much tougher for people close to retirement and nigh impossible for retirees forced to pull money out to live on.

For many white hairs, financing a relatively comfortable retirement, which never looked easy, looks increasingly impossible. In 2014, the value of the average 55-64-year-old household's retirement account was $120,000. The Boston College Center for Retirement Research estimates that the average worker will need $420,000 in addition to social security to retire comfortably at age 65.

5. *Uncle Sam.* In 2009, applications for retirement benefits were 23 percent higher than the previous year. What happened on the way to the Forum? The recession hit and many older workers suddenly found themselves laid off with no place to turn but Social Security. They decided that a small check from Uncle Sam was preferable to no check at all. Law professor Alan J. Auerbach comments that "A lot of people who in better times would have continued working are opting to retire. If they were younger, we would call them unemployed." And depressed employment places a significant strain on a system that depends on contributions from current workers (via payroll deductions) to pay the benefits of current retirees.

The bulk of government benefits, notably Social Security and Medicare, are bestowed on people who are retired. Social Security is a pay as you go program. When American workers pay into Social Security the money does not get invested

351 The personal savings rose to 6.2 percent in May, 2009 (and has since come down). Although saving is good for the individual, it is not for the greater economy. When 79 million people—nearly a third of Americans—started spending less and saving more, companies panicked and scrambled to adjust.

somewhere so that you can draw on it twenty or thirty years later, as it would in a private pension fund. Rather, that money is used to pay current retirees. Straight from young Peter to pay old Paul. The program is one big pyramid scheme, and like any good pyramid scheme, works fine as long as there are enough workers on the bottom to continue paying the retirees at the top.
~ Charles Wheelen, author, *Naked Economics*

Um, we have another problem, Galveston. Soon there will not be enough workers on the bottom. The Baby Boom generation is so much bigger than succeeding generations, the ratio of people in the retirement years, 65 and older, to those in the working years, 20 to 64, will rise sharply. According to the U.S. Census Bureau, the ratio will increase from 20.6 percent in 2005 to 35.5 percent in 2030. As a result of this demographic shift, fewer young persons will be footing the bill for an increasing number of white-hairs. What about those "lockbox" dollars you paid the government over a lifetime of working? They are now represented by government bonds, or IOUs, that will have to be repaid as Social Security draws down its trust fund. By then, Congress will face a Faustian bargain:[352] cut benefits to retirees, sell your kids into financial slavery, or reduce the overall standard of living. What's lost on young persons is the Social Security crisis is everyone's crisis.

Well, there you have it Boomers. For many of you, the Great Recession has been the sharpest trauma since the Second World War, wiping out jobs, wealth, and hope itself. Americans wealth shrank so much, reports the Federal Reserve, that 2010 median family net worth, inflation adjusted, was no more than it had been in 1992. Many of you have been pulling money from 401(k) accounts and other investments to support your accustomed lifestyles. People are working much harder for less pay, and being highly educated is no longer a guaranteed barrier to unemployment. Those best positioned (about 30 percent) are mostly there because you worked hard, developed a long-term pattern that increased savings and reduced spending, and avoided triggering a lifebomb along the way. But even you are not immune to a financially debilitating event such as periods of unemployment, hardships associated with divorce or separation, or an unexpected health problem.

"I think a very large number of people will never have the life they had at one time.
~ David B., IT manager

In the long-run, what does the crystal ball reveal? Well, the likely choices are limited. The government is faced with reneging on its promises, inflating the currency, or most likely both, in order to manage its debt. Everyone will feel the spoiling effects of an increased supply (and thus reduced value) of stocks and bonds as Baby Boomers sell their portfolios to pay for rising living and health care costs. Especially young persons.

Welcome to the new normal. Enjoy your weekend.

352 A pact with the devil.

Reali-tude:
Some Boomers choose to continue working. Many have no choice.

The bottom line:

- Many tribal elders did not plan for an extended retirement.
- Boomers and post-Boomers are facing a retirement crisis.
- The Social Security crisis is every person's crisis.
- The rules have changed.

Doctor's Prescription (Rx)

I'M AS MAD AS HELL AND I AM NOT GOING TO TAKE THIS ANYMORE!
~ Howard Beale, fictional TV news anchorman in the movie *Network*

Not long ago, Boomers thought that they were never going to die. Filled with a self-confidence that came from a period of unprecedented prosperity, they thought markets that stumbled would always rebound more strongly than ever. After all, had not they always done so in the past?

Sorry, but no cigar this time Cecilia. The naked truth is the Baby Boom generation has buried its mistakes under a mountain of cash that Generation NeXt hasn't even earned yet. If every penny of Boomer's savings—and every other American's savings—is put to the task, NeXters will still be paying for their parents' expenses all their life. On top of personal debt, the U.S. government has issued trillions more in IOUs every year, each one emblazoned with "In Gen NeXt We Trust" on it. NeXters are not even out in the real world yet and they are getting the bill for 50 cents of every dollar the Feds spend, almost none of it earmarked for them. They are inheriting the mess that we Boomers are leaving behind.

So, NeXters are turning to the bank of last resort—Mom and Dad—but a British report from Fidelity International reveals a collision of intentions. More than half of adults under 35 are relying on a big inheritance from their parents to fund their futures instead of putting away pension savings of their own. Yet two-thirds of Baby Boomers say they plan to enjoy their lives by spending their savings and cashing in the equity in their homes. Unlike *their* parents, helicopter parents say that they are not concerned about leaving a legacy. *Young person's alert*: beware the Ghost of Christmas Future.

Gen Y's anger towards the Baby Boomers is different from the past. Previous hostility between generations usually faded as the younger generation matured. Today, I see hostility toward the older Baby Boomers growing—it's not until young person's age that we start to see the damage to this country that they and their "good intentions" have done.
~ MeadsJN, Internet blogger

What do young persons have to say about the approaching tsunami? Many, if not most, are totally in the dark. Others see the light but don't care. That leaves a few who really understand what is going on and they are seething with anger. Like Howard Beale, they are fed up and MAD AS HELL... and they have every right to be.

Tribal elders, here's what you can do

> *It's my generation—the Woodstock generation, the Baby Boom generation—that's largely to blame for today's kids at risk.*
> ~ Bill O'Reilly, TV journalist, teacher

Young adulthood is a period of searching as young persons look for place and purpose amid a bewildering array of new experiences and complex choices. It is a time when most young persons find themselves re-examining their earlier beliefs and assumptions as they make formative life decisions. Rather than the traditional 18 or 21 that was recognized by their parents, thirty is now seen by many as the real point of transition to adulthood. It is this milestone that young persons worry about, the benchmark date by which they feel they should have made some important decisions about accepting responsibility, making independent decisions, and becoming financially independent. This is the time they finally need to cut the umbilical cord and leave home. And for many, this is not a comfortable feeling.

Leadership professor Sharon Daloz Parks urges thoughtful adults to provide responsible strategic mentorship during this important decade in life. Lacking the knowledge, experience, and maturity of their parents, many young persons have distorted perceptions of reality and risk. *Ignorance*, not having the right knowledge to accurately judge a situation, and *ineptitude*, carelessness in applying what they know, can "trap" their better judgment and lead to bad outcomes:

- *Ignorance.* Many young persons know little about the world and themselves. Most risky are the things they think they know are true, but in fact are not true. Ignorant young persons are tempted to hold overly simplified beliefs with excessive confidence and overestimate the likelihood that what they want to happen will in fact occur. They underappreciate the degree to which they may be unknowingly manipulated by others and underestimate the long-term consequences of their present decisions.
- *Ineptitude.* Peer pressure—the perception of what is prevalent or popular among their core group of 3 to 8 friends—most influences young persons, even if they recognize the potential for negative consequences. Inept young persons are tempted to be overly confident in their own abilities and believe everything that happens to them is controllable. This stubborn, "I've made up my mind, don't confuse me with the facts" mentality can lead to impatience, impulsiveness, and a strong penchant for immediate gratification.

Whether a result of laziness, a lack of wisdom, or simple stupidity, these mental weaknesses are part of our human psyche. Indeed, all of us suffer from them in varying degrees—they can never be eliminated. What can you do as a tribal elder to improve your children's awareness of themselves, increase their knowledge of world reality, and develop the skills for making smart choices? Look in the glass. What do you see? Life experience. You've got it. They don't. Your job is to impart wisdom.

> *Young people are educated in many ways, but they are given relatively little help in understanding how a life develops, how careers and families evolve, what are the common mistakes and the common blessings of modern adulthood.*
> ~ David Brooks, cultural commentator, author

How can you ensure their speedy development? You can't because acquiring wisdom from experience takes time. But you may be able to help them compensate so they can avoid some painful pitfalls.

Use gists to help them reduce risk

> *Our kids are not going to graduate and follow the safe path. Our role is to help them provide the right amount of risk and responsibility... and we will help to shape them into adults that will do much better in their lives.*
> ~ Alan Kearns, founder of CareerJoy

According to psychologists Valerie Reyna and Charles Brainerd of the Center for Behavioral Economics and Decision Research at Cornell, young persons use different decision rules and view consequences differently from older generations. As people grew older and more experienced, they become more intuitive. More of their decisions are based on what Reyna calls the *gist*, or an overall sense of what is the best course of action. This approach, in which "one sees the forest more than the trees," says Reyna, enables adults to reach the bottom line more quickly, and in the process, reduce their risky behaviors.[353] Young persons can improve their decision-making, they say, if they develop certain habits of mind.

That's where you come in. Tribal elders, the nature of your relationship plays a major role in encouraging young persons to make smart choices. In formulating a gist, answer the question, "What should this information mean to my kid?" It is not your experience per se that is important. Rather, it is what you understood or learned from your experience—not verbatim facts but the bottom-line interpretation of a situation—that will help a young person recognize and deal with similar future situations. It is important that you also include your gut emotions since young persons can get the facts right and still not derive the proper meaning. This is the "secret sauce" that will help them avoid the lifebombs.

Your job is to formulate the gist and help them assess what the information means to *them*. Remember: the gist is only as good as their level of understanding.

---

353 Consequences of risky behaviors may not evident until later in life (consider the California woman whose driver's license was suspended for failing to pay a $59 Illinois speeding ticket 27 years earlier).

Here are some suggestions how you can facilitate the development of mature, gist-based thinking in your children:

- Use brief and consistent messages, repeated over time.
- Get them to consider the worst-case scenario, as adults do.
- Simplify complexity and distill the emotional meaning of what you learned.
- Advise them to categorically avoid dangerous risks rather than weigh them in a rational, deliberative way.
- Get a sense of what they understand by asking them.
- Explain that some things may not make sense to them at this time.

Tribal elders, read the entire *Young Person's Guide*. What you learn may surprise you. As a minimum, read the gists at the beginning of each chapter. Each gist is a capsule of the important "take-aways." Also, read the *Bottom Lines* and *Reali-tudes* (see Appendix D for a compendium). These represent "wrinkle wisdom."

Reali-tude:
Your kids will forget everything but the gists.

Touch-points offer learning opportunities

> *The simple but critical premise... is that the key to getting people to improve their financial behavior is to first give them the information which they can use to confidently engage in the desired behavior.*
> ~ Steven. J. Devlin, financial gerontologist

In a study of attitudes on retirement, a majority of older workers said what they most needed was advice on how to teach their own children about money and finances. The challenge, they said, was not so much what to provide, but how best to provide it, since most young persons simply lack interest in finances almost irrespective of source. On occasion, however, they are acutely interested. These are *touch-points*; event driven opportunities where mainstream young adults seek financial information.[354] By understanding what today's youth most value, you can determine how to most effectively engage them. Some of these are listed below.

- Touch-points for 18–20 year olds (and older):
  - § Saving for college
  - § Opening a student account
  - § Getting their first credit card
  - § Opening a new account for their first wages

354 Sourced from a British study of 18–24 year olds (2004) conducted by the Financial Services Association. This study is described as "one of the most comprehensive studies performed on young people's information needs in relation to personal finance."

    - § Access to large amounts of money (e.g., student loans)
    - § Saving and/or loans for vacations or car purchases

- Touch-points for 21–24 year olds:
    - § Student overdrafts
    - § Juggling costs of living (often without budgeting)
    - § Short-term saving for bigger purchases
    - § Credit card debts
    - § Loan repayments

Most NeXters turn to parents to provide nearly all of their financial information requirements. If parents are unable to help, they will ask other family members or friends in their personal networks. Tribal elders should recognize that these touch-points represent opportunities to learn. By anticipating these events, NeXters can begin to seek information themselves and, perhaps more importantly, recognize the need in the first place. Engaging young persons while they are motivated by self-interest can help improve their judgment when the stakes are higher.

Reali-tude:
Hit 'em while they're hot.

Help them change their behavior

> *A clear resource needed by young people in the 21st century is for . . . enduring relationships with caring adults who can help them through the maze of information and options.*
>
> ~ Jeylan Mortimer and Reed Larson, social scientists

Tribal elders, help your children by encouraging them to be more mature in their decision behavior. Unlike most tribal elders, young persons are not set in their ways, but getting them to change the color of their stripes can be a challenge. Merely changing their attitude is not sufficient to guarantee a change in behavior (if you have ever strutted like a rooster at a Tony Robbins seminar but felt flat as a flounder three days later, you know the story . . .). Psychologists tell us *adult behavior modification* (ABM) can be a useful process to help change behavior, and it can be applied to everything from stopping a drug addiction to balancing a checkbook weekly. Using ABM principles, here are some things that you can do to help your kids adopt good personal economic behaviors:[355]

355 Adapted from *Understanding Adultism: A Key to Developing Positive Youth-Adult Relationships* (Bell, 1995), *Parenting Tips for Staying Close to Your Adult Child While Letting Them Go* (Burrell, 2009), and *Critical Thinking—How to Prepare Students for a Rapidly Changing World* (Paul, 1995).

- *Be an advisor.* Good advisors offer thoughtful expertise when asked, couch things diplomatically, and expect that at least half of what they say will be ignored. That's OK! Your input is just a part of what your now-grown child may be using to make a decision. Avoid hurt feelings by prefacing your advice with phrases such as "One possible solution might be..." or "One thing to consider is..."
- *Ask the right questions.* Step more into their points of view and help focus their attention on what is most important. Look for opportunities to teach personal economic lessons in the course of everyday life. Solicit their views by asking "What do you think about..." or "If you were faced with..." Listen attentively when they talk about their thoughts, experiences, and feelings.
- *Think critically.* Success comes from having a *realistic* outlook. Hold them responsible to think about and discover their own capacity to figure out life situations. Help them increase their self-awareness, identify their assumptions, and question their habitual inferences. Have them generate their own "what ifs." Tribal elders who do not themselves think critically cannot foster critical thinking in young persons.
- *It's OK to be unsure.* Many young persons feel they must always "save face" to protect their image and find it difficult or embarrassing to ask others for help. Reassure them it is alright for them to say things like, "I'm not sure;" "I don't know;" "I was wrong"; or "I have to think about that." Call attention to the extent of your own limitations and assure them that tribal elders do not have the answers to all their questions.
- *Be respectful.* Your child will probably hear implied criticism in just about everything you say. Shifting from "parental authoritarian" to "inquisitive tribal elder" creates a more positive emotional climate so you both can talk openly. Speak to the complexities in your life as well as in theirs.
- *Relax control.* Welcome their ideas and support their initiatives. By giving them more control over the gains they can make from their decisions, they will be more likely to pay attention to the consequences of the losses. Let them learn from their mistakes as long as they do not endanger their long-term success. Curb the inclination to take over—it is not your choice to make. If you truly think they are making a terrible mistake, be frank but tactful.
- *Walk the talk.* Parental behavior is a far more powerful influence on young persons than their efforts to convey the "right" information. Give them accurate information about the ways of the world. NeXters are quick to pick up on inconsistencies if what tribal elders say and what they do, do not match. If you are wealthy, motivate your kids not to coast on your affluence.
- *Be honest.* Make a conscious effort to help them welcome change and not be afraid to grow. Don't sell them short and never lie to them. In the end, character counts.

Reali-tude:
High expectations bring high results!

Young persons will always prefer black-and-white over shades of gray and hold overly simplified beliefs of a complex world. They will be overly confident in their judgment and capabilities, fail to appreciate the realities of change, and underestimate the degree to which their selfish actions today will affect their long-term happiness. They are tempted by the idea that they can control everything that happens to them. Think back to when you were their age, and then give 'em a break.

Unquestionably, as parents and tribal elders, you are in the best position to help your children acquire wisdom. Even a bad outcome from your life experience can be a great learning opportunity. If you were bone-headed and screwed up, tell 'em up front. If you have no idea what you are doing (or are not smarter than a 5th grader), admit it. If you simply do not want to talk about your past, be honest and say so. According to legendary basketball coach Bob Knight, negative thinking actually produces more positive results, in sports and in daily life. Coach Knight, the second-winningest coach in NCAA history with 902 victories, explains that victory is often attained by the team that makes the fewest mistakes. So, do whatever you have to do—lecture, encourage, or badger—to help them understand their vulnerabilities and learn how to avoid the lifebombs that can destabilize their future well-being.

Their receptivity to ask, listen, and reflect on the wisdom of tribal elders can help them secure personal economic success. Initiate conversation. Communicate to your children the gist of how the world operates, help them become aware of their own mental traps, and share wisdom so they can make life-choices in a purposeful manner rather than by default. Encourage them to ask questions big enough that will challenge them to grow and help develop their imagination and critical thinking skills. Instill in them the art of the long-view: a future into which they can project themselves with some sense that good things are indeed possible. These habits will shore up deficiencies in their everyday decision-making and help develop their confidence.

And so we come to the bottom, bottom line. Educating your children about sound personal economic behaviors is *your* responsibility. Be a catalyst, stimulate their interest, and like the Moken, warn them of the Laboon. In the final analysis, you are the app for your children. Yep. That's your job.

Reali-tude:
Be an ally in your children's success.

Postscript

Live long and prosper.
~ Mr. Spock, human-Vulcan in *Star Trek*

For Generation NeXt, the future is hopeful. In the long-run, business will regain its shine and the survivors will emerge leaner and stronger than before. The U.S. is still judged by the rest of the world as the best place to make money and pursue happiness. The American Dream—the idea that in this country anyone can rise from humble beginnings and succeed—still beckons this generation.

For you, the Baby Boomers, the sand has all but run out. It's now their turn at bat. As a final word of advice, if you find that you are working not by choice but simply to survive, if you see yourself getting older and poorer, if Fancy Feast is an entrée at your dinner table, then you need to watch out for number one. Remember the oxygen mask procedure: provide for your financial safety and well-being first, and then attend to your children's.

It's fiscally irresponsible to spend your retirement money on your children's education. It's heresy to some, but it's true: your retirement plans are more important than your children's college funds. Your kids can get through college somehow, and you will probably find a way to help them, but it's more important to plan for your retirement. Remember, your kids can get student loans, but there's no such thing as a retirement loan. It won't make you bad parents.

~ Sally Herigstad, financial advisor

Reali-tude:
The wisdom contained here is of permanent importance.

The bottom, bottom line:

- Read the guide. Let your kids read it. Start the conversation.
- Gists and touch-points represent great learning opportunities—use them.
- Have your kids formulate the habit of tapping the wisdom of tribal elders.
- Do not sacrifice your own financial plans to support your adult children.

Appendix B

Generation Next Traits

Trait	Description
Consumer orientation	Extreme consumerism. Seeks instant gratification and looks for the best deal. Everything is negotiable and expects to bargain.
Entertainment orientation	Lacks engagement unless something is entertaining, easy, and fun. This attitude is not compatible with serious and/or protracted efforts. Majority of time spent on the Internet is for entertainment purposes.
Entitlement	Striving for a quality of life only known by the rich and famous. Wanting the best and thinking they deserve it. Expectations and aspirations, both financial and in degree of personal fulfillment, might be regarded as unrealistic.
Value free	Consumerism competes with religion and modern science/reason. Freedom from guilt can be liberating, but might also make it difficult for young people to evaluate propriety or impact of their behavior to themselves and others.
Instant gratification	Not lazy or against hard work. Culture tends to place great importance on meeting personal needs and immediate gratification is expected due to a childhood of receiving it. There is very little perceived value in the traditional value of delay of gratification.
Short event horizon	Related to instant gratification, many have poor critical thinking, problem solving, and long term planning skills. Many have failed to be fully inculcated into the modern values of reason, logic, and planning.
Self-interested	"Generation Me"—intrusively taken care of by parents, many see themselves as special stars. This can lead to a high level of self-interest and self importance. May face culture shock when faced with expectations that reward results rather than effort.
Skepticism	Tendency to de-legitimize authority and traditional sources of knowledge. Questions veracity of information, and places greater importance on subjective and personal experience.
Cynicism	Many view social institutions of government, the media, religion, and business/economy as corrupt and untrustworthy.
Stressed	Pressures of work, money, and debt issues, along with personal and social stressors can be overwhelming. May lack adequate skills or sufficient links to traditional sources of refuge (peers, family, neighborhood, church) to handle stressful expectations placed on them.
Civility/caring	Blunt and expressive. Self expression favored over self control. Making their point is most important. Incivility is frequently rewarded while civility is not. Aggressively unsentimental and simply hope the situation will go away.

Intellectually disengaged	Possibly least studious generation ever, with high measures for boredom and tardiness. Knowledge is not a major goal, except for information that directly relates to earning goals. Limited ability to separate meaningful from meaningless.
Reduced self-efficacy	In a complex, information rich, and demanding world, many opt for willful naiveté, accepting they can not know all they need to know, or meaningfully control their lives. Many believe fate or coincidence have more impact on their lives than their own efforts.
Relationships	Considerable relationship experimentation. Some resort to more manageable on-line and virtual relationships. Some may have difficulty with long term intimacy development.
Parents	Trusting and close contact with parents and family. High parental involvement ('helicopter parent'). Nearly three-quarters have received financial help from parents during the past 12 months. Parents are principal financial advisors.
Diversity	More diverse group than any other generation. More comfortable with cultural, racial, and sexual orientation diversity.
Techno-literate	Wired since birth, very comfortable with technology. Impatient with a lack of technological sophistication in others.

Dr. Mark Taylor, former Director of Guidance Services, Arkansas State University-Beebe, has researched the characteristics of Generation NeXt and presented suggestions for helping them be successful in postsecondary education (www.taylorprograms.org). His contribution to the material used in this appendix is substantial and gratefully acknowledged.

Appendix C

Decision-Making Tools

Appendix C.1

Aristotle's Debias Method

Useful in situations where bias may be driving the decision.

Socrates (469–399 B.C.E.) was a Classical Greek Athenian philosopher, credited as one of the founders of Western philosophy. His method of inquiry, known as the *Socratic Method* of questioning, allows for a tribal elder to quickly evaluate what a young person does and does not know.

As coaches and mentors, tribal elders can ask questions that will help a young person examine his attitudes, beliefs, knowledge, and logic. These questions are not intended to create an environment of judgment, but rather to lead to a collaborative and open-minded discussion. The key to achieving a solid, tenable conclusion is to ask *open-ended* questions that stimulate the young person's critical thinking and reasoning. Do not ask yes/no type questions that assume they already have the answer.

The Socratic Method is particularly useful for ferreting out biases. Using the Socratic Method, a tribal elder evaluates a young person's argument by asking open-ended questions such as the following:

What do you mean by_________________?

How did you come to that conclusion?

Why do you believe that you are right?

What is the source of your information?

What assumption has led you to that conclusion?

What happens if you are wrong?

Can you give me two sources who disagree with you and explain why?

Why is this significant?

How do I know you are telling me the truth?

What is an alternate explanation for this phenomenon?

Appendix C.2

Pros & Cons Method

Useful in situations where there is only one alternative and many factors to consider.

Selection of an appropriate decision technology depends mostly on the type of information available and the technical working knowledge of the decision-maker. The Pros & Cons method is intended for decisions that can be framed as simply a "yes-no" or "go-no go" regarding a specific course of action. For example, Should I look for a new job? Is it prudent to shift more of my 401(k) portfolio to higher-return, higher-risk investments? Shall I pop the question? Is the timing right to take that dream cruise? Blah, blah.

Confidence in decision-making abilities comes from having made successful decisions in the past. Think about the positive decisions you have made already. How did you make those decisions? What resources helped guide you through the decision-making process? If you lack direct experience, you may need to connect with objective and trusted sources. Support from tribal elders can have a big influence on your important decisions and help ease the anxiety of making a good choice.

Pros & Cons method

The Pros & Cons method is a handy tool to assess a single alternative ("yes-no") outcome. Intuitively we make simplified analyses like this every day. One useful variant of this method is PMI, invented by creative thinking author Edward de Bono.[356] PMI helps you identify the good points (P = Plus), the bad points (M = Minus) and the interesting points (I = Interesting) about a decision. For example, you may be deciding if you should get a pet, or whether a part-time job while in school makes sense. Interesting points are factors that are neither good nor bad but are worth noticing. Here is how to do it:

1. Define, as specifically as possible, the decision that needs to be made. Ask yourself "Do I really need to make a decision?" and "When does the decision need to be made?"

356 Edward de Bono was the originator of the term *lateral thinking*, which is about reasoning and the development of ideas that are not immediately obvious using only traditional step-by-step logic. De Bono authored *Six Thinking Hats*, a tool for group discussion and individual thinking and has been a vigorous proponent of teaching thinking as a subject in schools.

2. On a piece of paper, write down the proposed decision as a question. Frame your decision as a simple "yes-no" (or "go-no go") type question.

3. Divide the paper into three columns and label the headings "Plus," "Minus," and "Implications."

4. In the "Plus" column write down all the positive points of taking the action that you can think of.

5. In the "Minus" column, write down all of the outcomes of the decision that are negative or less desirable. Sometimes the same points are both an advantage and a negative influence.

6. Under "Implications," write down the interesting implications of the action, whether positive or negative. This will help you avoid a cognitive trap, such as short-term thinking.

7. In the course of writing down your pros and cons, you may identify some outcomes that are uncertain or are too hard to predict. Write these outcomes down on a separate piece of paper.

8. Conduct research to clarify the outcomes that you are unsure about and then add those to the appropriate column.

9. For outcomes that are simply too hard to predict, you might want to talk with tribal elders to get their inputs and opinions. Then add them to your list.

10. As you complete the table, it should become clearer whether the decision you are considering is advisable.

The main weakness of this approach is that it does not consider the degree to which a particular factor is good or bad. As a result, the number of pros and cons in each column is not necessarily indicative of whether or not you should move forward with the decision. Nevertheless, this process forces you to see both sides of an argument and think more broadly about an issue before making a decision.

Pros & Cons template

Decision question:		
Plus	**Minus**	**Implications**

Pros & Cons example

Decision question: Drake asks, "Should we buy our first home in today's real estate market?"

Pros:

- Historically low interest rates.
- Plentiful supply of homes from which to choose and most sellers are negotiable.
- Housing affordability index (relative indicator of affordability) is higher, creating a wider margin of disposable income above mortgage payments.
- Overall, median home values are stable in the local market.
- Federal tax credits for qualified first time home buyers.
- Virtually impossible to pick the top or the bottom of any market...close is good enough.

Cons:

- Loans rates might decline even further.
- Supply may continue to increase and sellers become even more negotiable.
- Disposable income, home prices, and interest rates may collectively create a more favorable purchasing scenario.
- Government stimulus for home ownership may grow larger.
- Best to wait and ensure we get the best possible deal.
- This will put us in hock up to our eyeballs.
- Hubbie hates home repairs.

Implications:

- We need a place to live and put our junk anyway.
- Pride of ownership will ensure that we outdo the Joneses.
- No more competing with our dorky neighbors for a parking space.
- Won't have to move again when rug rats come on scene.

Decision question: "Should we buy our first home now?"		
Plus	**Minus**	**Implications**
Low interest rate	*Rates may decline*	*Need a place to live anyway*
Plentiful supply	*Supply may increase*	*Want to outdo the Joneses*
High HAI	*More favorable scenario*	*No competition for parking*
Values have stabilized	*Gov't may increase stimulus*	*Don't have to move for kids*
Tax credits	*Wait for better deal*	
Timing is close enough	*Put us in big debt*	
	Hubbie hates repair work	

Deciding is the easiest part of decision-making. As far as that goes, all you need is a coin to decide whether to move from Chicago to Tucson. In reality, the hard part comes on either side; executing sound judgment before the decision is made and committing to a course of action afterward. Once you have made a decision, get moving on it! Worrying or second-guessing yourself will only cause grief. Remember, no decision is set in stone; you always have the option of changing your mind in the future. For Drake, thinking about the competing influences and reflecting on the "big picture" led him to decide that the time was right to purchase a home for his family.

Appendix C.3

Ben Franklin's Method

Useful in situations where there is only one alternative and many factors to consider.

An extension of the Pros & Cons method is called *Ben Franklin's method* (also known as Weighted Pros & Cons method). It is for decisions that can be framed as a "yes-no" (or "go-no go") type question. The method was described by Benjamin Franklin in a letter dated September 19, 1772 to English scientist Joseph Priestly. Priestly had been wrestling with a perplexing decision and had asked Dr. Franklin for his advice. Franklin wrote to his chemist friend that the problem of deciding inexplicable situations is "all reasons pro and con are not present to the mind at the same time..." Our minds are like a pendulum swinging back and forth, swayed by cognitive traps that cloud our judgment and lead to bad decisions.

> *My way is to divide half a sheet of paper by a line into two columns; writing over the one Pro and over the other Con. Then during three or four days' consideration, I put down under the different heads short hints of the different motives, that at different time occur to me, for or against the measure. When I have thus got them altogether in one view, I endeavor to estimate their respective weights; and where I find two, one on each side, that seem equal, I strike them both out. If I judge some two reasons con equal to some three reasons pro, I strike out five; and thus proceeding, I find where the balance lies; and if after a day or two of further consideration, nothing new that is of importance occurs on either side, I come to a determination accordingly.*
>
> ~ Benjamin Franklin, printer, scientist, statesman

Franklin admitted that his decision-making method was purely procedural. It could not advise him what to do, only how, and he hinted that this comparatively simple idea has complicated ramifications. For example, the pluses and minuses are not all immediately obvious and their weighting is subjective. How, for instance, do you quantify an increase in self-esteem? Moreover, our decisions are not made in isolation; there are usually several competing options. For example, if you do not invest in a new Xbox One, you can replace the worn tires on the car or simply leave the money in the bank.

Nevertheless, the real value, related Franklin to Priestly, is that "though the weight of reasons (pro and con) cannot be taken with the precision of algebraic quantities, yet when each is thus considered, separately and comparatively, and the whole lies before me, I think I can judge better, and am less liable to take a rash step."

Making decisions like Ben Franklin

Franklin's decision-making format is the same as the Pros & Cons model with three refinements:

1. List the factors (pros, cons, implications) as they come to mind *over a period of time*—not at a single sitting;
2. Assign a weight to each factor to indicate its degree of importance or influence;
3. Ascertain the overall balance before deciding accordingly.

Expanding on the PMI method previously described, here is how to apply these refinements:

List the factors.
Define, as specifically as possible, the decision that needs to be made. Ask yourself "Do I really need to make a decision?" As Dr. Franklin noted, not all our thoughts occur to us at a particular point in time or even necessarily when we consciously try to list them. Initially, it is wise to reflect on the decision that faces us and over time add to (or subtract from) our pros and cons lists. It is also useful is to ask, "When do I have to decide?"

Weight the pros and cons.
Franklin's letter did not specify how to weight the factors. One way to assess the importance of a factor is to assign it a number that ranges from 1 (not all at important) to 10 (extremely high importance). The weights in the Plus column are assigned a plus (+) sign and those in the Minus column are assigned a minus (-) sign. Weights for implications can be either plus or a minus, depending on whether you feel that they positively or negatively influence the decision question.

Balance and review.
As Franklin suggested, you may wish to simplify matters by striking out any offsetting pros and cons. Add the weights in each column and write the totals at the bottom. Mindful of signs, add the column totals and write in the final decision total score. Then scan the pros, cons, and implications you have listed, being especially attuned to your subjective weightings. Finally, take stock of what the totals tell you about the decision facing you and try to get a "gut feel" for the overall balance. Here is some guidance in that regard:

- A set of pros and cons clearly skewed in favor of the pluses might indicate that you should go ahead with the decision. Likewise, a set that is clearly skewed in favor of the minuses might suggest that you should avoid taking this action.

- A roughly balanced set of pluses and minuses suggests a difficult decision, one with no clear basis for committing to or foregoing the course of action. You might need to give more thought to the factors and their weightings or check with a tribal elder. Alternatively, you may conclude that now is not the time to decide.

Ben Franklin's template

Decision Question:					
Plus	Weight	Minus	Weight	Implica-tions	Weight
Total (1)		Total (2)		Total (3)	
				Decision total (1+2+3)	

Ben Franklin's example

Decision question: Tracy asks, "Should I move to the big city?"

Pros:

- The amenities and the night life! (+4)
- One-hour drive from Auntie's house. (+3)
- Public transportation makes it easier to get to places I want to go. (+5)
- Great community college system. (+6)
- Growing region for jobs in my field. (+8)
- Open and diverse culture. (+3)

Total Pro = +29

Cons:

- Where did all the grass go? (-5)
- Winters are cold and clammy. (-3)
- Cost of moving from home will be substantial. (-7)
- Will miss my family and friends. (-9)
- Very expensive—may have to live in low-rent district to afford. (-10)
- More pollution and stress. (-2)
- Will have to give up my horse. (-7)

Total Con = -43

Implications:

- Freedom to start my own life! (+3)
- The prospect of moving out on my own is a little scary. (-2)
- Meet more people. (+1)

Total Implications = +2

Decision Total = (+29) + (-43) + (+2) = -12

Decision Question: Should I move to the big city?					
Plus	**Weight**	**Minus**	**Weight**	**Implications**	**Weight**
Amenities/ nightlife	+4	*Too much concrete*	-5	*Freedom to be me*	+3
Close to Auntie's	+3	*Cold winters*	-3	*Scary moving out*	-2
Easy trans-portation	+5	*Moving costs*	-7	*Meet new people*	+1
Good col-leges	+6	*Miss family/ friends*	-9		
Growing jobs	+8	*Very expen-sive to live*	-10		
Diverse cul-ture	+3	*Pollution and stress*	-2		
		Nix the horse	-7		
Total (1)	**+29**	**Total (2)**	**-43**	**Total (3)**	**+2**
				Decision total (1+2+3)	**-12**

A strongly positive score shows that an action should be taken; a strongly negative score that it should be avoided. A moderate score would suggest a compromise or taking no action at this time. For Tracy, the security and comforts of a settled rural existence seem to outweigh the call of the "bright lights." After conferring with two tribal elders (her mom and her aunt), she decided that it would be much better for her to live outside the city near her Aunt, but close enough to travel in if necessary.

Appendix C.4

Grid Analysis Method

Useful in situations where there are a number of good alternatives and many factors to consider.

Every decision has its advantages and disadvantages. The trick is to figure out which choice will give you more of the former and less of the latter. The problem with using the Pros & Cons methods is they deal with only one option. You do it or you don't; all or none; guilty or not guilty. But what about situations where you have several good choices, say, Tom, Jordan, and Nate? Great guys, but who should you pick as your main squeeze? This calls for a more sophisticated approach! Grid Analysis (also known as *Pugh Matrix Analysis*)[357] is a useful technique for making these types of decisions.

Grid Analysis method

Grid Analysis is frequently used in engineering for making design decisions but it can be applied wherever you have a number of good alternatives to choose from and many different factors to take into account. Grid Analysis is a great technique to use in almost any important decision where there isn't a clear and obvious preferred option. This includes everything from investments options, to vacation possibilities, to possible husbands! While the directions make it seem more complicated that it really is, the examples will show you it is actually quite simple. Here is how to do it:

1. Define, as specifically as possible, the decision that needs to be made. Ask yourself "Do I really need to make a decision?" and "When does the decision need to be made?"

2. Print (or draw) the template on a piece of paper. Write down the proposed decision as a question.

3. Label the first column "Criteria" and the second column "Importance Factor." To the right of those two columns, create as many columns as you have possible choices (options). Label these columns with the names of your choices.

357 Stuart Pugh (1929–1993) was a design engineer in industry and later an academic. He authored *Total Design: Integrated Methods for Successful Product Engineering* (1990), which described the systematic activities necessary, from the identification of the market/user need, to the selling of the successful product to satisfy that need.

For example, say you have recently been offered a job in Seattle and another in Phoenix.

4. In the "Criteria" column, list all the major elements that influence your decision. Thus, if you are trying to decide between these two job opportunities, you would list things like location, pay, benefits, job security, work hours, enjoyment, etc.

5. In the "Importance Factor" column, assign each criterion a number from 1 to 10 according to how important that element is to you. Put down the first number that comes to you; don't over think it. For example, if the time the job will allow you to spend with your family is very important to you, you would give that criterion an 8 or a 9. If being close to your family isn't as important, you might give it something like a 4. And if you can't stand their guts, maybe a 1 or a 2.

6. In the "Option 1" column, assign a "grade" from 1 to 10 indicating how that option measures up to the first criterion. Again, don't think too much about it; just put down the first number that comes to your mind. For example, if the job in Seattle offers an excellent health insurance plan, you might give it a 9 for "benefits." If the job in Phoenix would sometimes have you working 60 hour weeks, then you might give it something like a 5 for "work hours." Write the number for each criterion in the blank to the right of the multiplication (x) sign.

7. Multiply the importance factor times the grade for the first criterion in Option 1. For example, if you rated the importance of the pay element as an 8, and you graded the Seattle job a 7 for its salary potential, calculate 7x8 and write "56" after the equals (=) sign. Do the same for all of the other elements in that column.

8. Once you have multiplied all of your importance factors by your grades, add all of those numbers to get a total for that choice. Write that sum in the blank at the bottom of the column.

9. Repeat steps 5 – 8 for the other choice columns. The option that has the highest number of points is probably the best choice for you.

The advantage of this approach is that subjective opinions about one alternative versus another can be made more objective. Also, by not weighting the criteria elements, you can perform a quicker selection process. Grid Analysis can be a great tool to help you make more informed, rational, and confident decisions!

Grid Analysis template

Decision question:					
Criteria	Importance factor	Option 1	Option 2	Option 3	Option 4
		x___=___	x___=___	x___=___	x___=___
		x___=___	x___=___	x___=___	x___=___
		x___=___	x___=___	x___=___	x___=___
Option totals		____	____	____	____

Grid Analysis example 1[358]

Decision question: You ask, "Should I take the job in Seattle or the one in Phoenix?"

Decision question: "Should I take the job in Seattle or the one in Phoenix?"			
Criteria	**Importance Factor**	**Seattle**	**Phoenix**
Work hours	9	x 7 = 63	x 5 = 45
Commute	5	x 6 = 30	x 4 = 20
Cost of living	7	x 4 = 28	x 9 = 63
Salary	8	x 7 = 56	x 7 = 56
Health insurance	9	x 9 = 81	x 7 = 63
Retirement benefits	5	x 3 = 15	x 8 = 40
Weather	4	x 5 = 20	x 3 = 12
Closeness to family	4	x 2 = 08	x 8 = 32
Opportunity to advance	8	x 6 = 42	x 6 = 48
Recreation possibilities	8	x 8 = 64	x 5 = 40
Job stability	7	x 3 = 21	x 7 = 49
Option totals		428	468

The Seattle job scored 428 and the Phoenix Job scored 468. Looks like you are moving to sunny Phoenix! Be wary of the tendency to give the choice that you really want higher scores, even if it doesn't warrant them. One way to counter this is by sharing your findings with a trusted adult. This process is beneficial because it forces you to consider all of the factors that go into your decision.

358 Example sourced from Brett and Kate McKay, *How to Make a Decision Like Ben Franklin* (2009).

Grid Analysis example 2[359]

Decision question: Jackie asks, "Which vehicle should I buy?"

Jackie's car is on its last legs and she needs to replace it. She is a windsurfing enthusiast and needs a vehicle that not only carries a board and sails, but will also be good for business travel. She has always loved open-topped sports cars. Unfortunately for Jackie, no car is good for all three things. Here is her analysis:

Decision question: "Which vehicle should I buy?"					
Criteria	**Importance Factor**	**Sports Car**	**SUV/ 4x4**	**Family Car**	**Wagon**
Cost	8	x 2 = 16	x 0 = 0	x 4 = 32	x 4 = 32
Ability to carry board	10	x 0 = 0	x 6 = 60	x 4 = 40	x 6 = 60
Store sails/equipment	2	x 0 = 0	x 4 = 8	x 2 = 4	x 6 = 12
Long distance comfort	4	x 2 = 8	x 4 = 16	x 6 = 24	x 6 = 24
Fun!	6	x 6 = 36	x 2 = 12	x 0 = 0	x 0 = 0
Stylish look	8	x 6 = 48	x 2 = 16	x 0 = 0	x 1 = 8
Option totals		**108**	**112**	**100**	**136**

This gives an interesting result. Despite its lack of fun, at 136 a station wagon may be Jackie's best choice. If she still feels unhappy with the decision (this is her gut feel talking), maybe she has underestimated the importance of one of the factors. Perhaps she should give "fun" a weight of 7 and buy an old beater station wagon to carry her board!

359 Example sourced from MindTools' *Grid Analysis* (2010).

Appendix C.5

Paired Comparison Method

Useful for weighing the relative importance of decision alternatives.

If you have ever had your eyes tested, you have seen (pun intended) this technique in action. The optometrist has you look at an eye chart through a number of different lenses and asks, "Which of these lenses enables you to see the eye chart better? This one...or this one?" She flips the lenses back and forth until you tell her which one is clearer. The optometrist then selects another set of lenses and repeats the process until the best lenses have been identified to correct your vision. The exam is a systematic process of presenting pairs of different lenses and eliminating lens options until the best lens is found.[360]

Paired Comparison method

Paired Comparison Analysis is a decision-making tool that is simpler and less rigorous than the Grid Analysis method. Like the optometrist, we determine the most attractive of a set of alternatives by comparing them against each other one at a time. In general, paired comparisons can be used any time you have a set of options, issues, or criteria that you would like to rank or prioritize. It is ideal for comparing "apples with oranges" and can be applied to completely different situations, from the trivial (where to dine out with the family) to the complex (allocating resources for an investment portfolio). This technique is also useful if you are having trouble estimating the "Importance Factors" for Grid Analysis. Follow these steps to use the technique:

1. Define, as specifically as possible, the decision that needs to be made. Ask yourself "Do I really need to make a decision?" and "When does the decision need to be made?"

2. Print (or draw) the template on a piece of paper. Write down the proposed decision as a question.

3. Jot down a list of all the options (elements, etc.) that you will compare. Assign a letter to each.

360 A sommelier (pronounced "sem-mel-yay"), or wine expert, follows a similar process in comparing wines.

4. On the template, label your options as both row and column headers. You will be comparing each option with each other option, one-by-one.

5. Cells where you will be comparing an option with itself are blanked out—there will never be a difference in these cells! Cells where you will be duplicating a comparison are also blanked out.

6. Within the remaining cells, compare the option in the row with the option in the column. Write the letter of the option that is most important in the cell.

7. Within that cell, score the difference in importance between the two options on a scale of 0 (no difference in importance) to 3 (much more important). Write this score next to the letter.

8. Add the scores for each letter throughout the table and enter the total score (you may want to convert these values into a percentage of the total score). This gives you a relative feel for what are the most important criteria in this decision.

Use of Paired Comparison Analysis makes choosing easy where priorities are not clear or are competing in importance. One drawback to this technique, as with other self-evaluations, is that it is subjective. Little or no objective information is exposed that identifies why you support each option.

Paired Comparison template

Decision question:							
Criteria	**A**	**B**	**C**	**D**	**E**	**F**	**Total Score**
A	—						
B	—	—					
C	—	—	—				
D	—	—	—	—			
E	—	—	—	—	—		
F	—	—	—	—	—	—	

Paired Comparison example

Janeen was disappointed that her love life sucked. Frustrated, she realized that root problem was within her. She had never taken time to rate the most important qualities in a man. If she knew her priorities, she felt that she could make better decisions before her mind fell victim to her heart. Her first step was to list all of the criteria she could think of and assign a letter to each one:

A = Good personality
B = Intelligent and witty
C = Communicates well
D = Emotionally inclined
E = Physically attractive
F = Financially independent

Next, she created a Paired Comparison table. She compared the importance of criterion (A) to the other criteria along the row. Janeen felt that personality was more important than either intelligence or physical attractiveness, so she scored those a "1." Personality was much more important to her than being emotionally inclined or financially independent, so she scored those a "3." She did not see any difference in importance between personality and communicating well, so she scored that criterion a "0," and so on. Janeen's completed table is shown below.

Decision question: What is the relative importance of my relationship criteria?							
Criteria	**A**	**B**	**C**	**D**	**E**	**F**	**Total Score**
A	—	**A,1**	**A, 0**	**A,3**	**A, 1**	**A, 3**	**8**
B	—	—	**C, 1**	**B, 2**	**B, 1**	**B, 1**	**4**
C	—	—	—	**C, 3**	**C, 2**	**C, 0**	**6**
D	—	—	—	—	**E, 3**	**D, 2**	**2**
E	—	—	—	—	—	**F, 2**	**3**
F	—	—	—	—	—	—	**2**

Paired Comparison Analysis revealed that her primary criterion for a healthy relationship was to find someone who has a great personality and is a good communicator. It is much less important to Janeen that he is emotionally inclined or financially independent (she comes from a wealthy family). Here is the nifty part—rather than rely on gut feel, Janeen can use these weightings as her "Importance Factors" on her Grid Analysis scorecard! Converting to percentages, Janeen ranks her preferences for a beau as follows:

Good personality = 32%
Communicates well = 24%
Intelligent and witty = 16%
Physically attractive = 12%
Emotionally inclined = 8%
Financially independent = 8%

Watch out guys!

Appendix C.6

Hail Mary Method

Useful in situations where you simply cannot make up your mind.

Here are the steps:

1. Pose your decision as a choice between two alternatives.
2. If you have more than two alternatives, compare two first, then compare the winner of that pair against the next alternative, and so on.
3. Assign one alternative as heads, and the other as tails.
4. Flip a coin. See how you feel about the result.
5. If you feel relieved, this is the right alternative.
6. If you feel disappointed, pick the other choice

That's it! Accept your decision and act on it accordingly.

Appendix C.7

Why Don't You Act on Your Decisions?

Useful in situations where you don't know why you cannot decide.

Some young persons feel overwhelmed when they are faced with making a decision. If you are having difficulty making a decision, look at the statements below.[361] Mark the ones that best explain why you might be having difficulty. You may want to write a brief description explaining how the statement pertains to you directly. Think about the three questions listed below the statements. Then review this assignment with a tribal elder or other trusted adult to determine what action steps should be taken next.

___ I have made very few important decisions on my own, so I do not know how to take action.

___ I feel that it makes no difference whether I do it or not, it is out of my control.

___ I am concerned about what others will think; maybe they will disapprove.

___ I don't know what action steps need to be taken, so I don't know where to begin.

___ I have not set priorities, so I do not know what to do first.

___ I am overwhelmed by all that needs to be done so I do not take action on any of it.

___ I tend to procrastinate. I put making decisions off until someone or some event forces me to take action.

___ I am afraid of failing. What if I make the wrong decision or take the wrong action?

___ I am afraid of succeeding. If I succeed I will have to deal with what comes next.

___ I am not willing to give up immediate gratification for long term gain.

361 Adapted from Virginia Gordan, *Academic Advising: The Pivotal Point in Assisting Students to Attain Educational and Career Goals* (2007).

Ask yourself the following questions:

1. Have you checked any of these reasons? Many people have these thoughts when faced with a decision. How do the ones you have identified relate to your personal economic future?

2. What can you do to counter these thoughts and behaviors?

3. Which of these do you want to discuss with a tribal elder?

Appendix D

"Wrinkle Wisdom" Cheat Sheets

Appendix D.1

Reali-tudes™

The Lesson:

- The present casts its shadow far into the future.

Chapter 1: Who You Are

- Always drink upstream of the herd.
- Remember those who care about you. There are very few of them.
- You are not entitled to anything.

Chapter 2: Defining the Problem

- Heed warnings by tribal elders.
- Watch your back—no one else will.
- Wake up and smell the hot breath of reality.

Chapter 3: How This Guide Can Help

- The best place to find a helping hand is at the end of your arm.
- God forgives, but capitalism does not.
- Your mind, like a parachute, works best when it is open.

Chapter 4: The Path to Success

- In our youth, time seems endless (from 17 on, it's all downhill).
- Waste your time, waste your life.
- Pigs get fed, hogs get slaughtered.
- Learn from the mistakes of others.
- Little things matter.

Chapter 5: The Stakes are High

- Beware the phrase, "It's different this time."
- Credit services companies make money from your stupidity.
- Do not rely on the government to help you.

- What you don't know can hurt you.
- What you don't do (right) can hurt you.
- Gen NeXt, you got screwed.

Chapter 6: How Risk Develops

- Risk is a four-letter word.
- You don't see things as they are. You see them as you are.
- There is no substitute for sound judgment.
- You cut your own slice of the pie.
- Risk exists, independent of your (mis)perceptions.
- The ultimate risk is regret for what might have been.
- The rich are different.
- Don't get left behind.
- To control risk, control yourself.

Chapter 7: Where Mistakes Originate

- Reality is an objective absolute.
- Always consider the sources of your information.
- Believing something is true does not make it so.
- If you think education is expensive, try ignorance.
- Lack of care is as big a risk as lack of knowledge.
- Absence of evidence is not evidence of absence.
- Make good judgment a habit.
- To know a person's attitude, read his bumper sticker.
- Attitudes are influenced by our perceptions.
- People are often unaware they have an attitude.

Chapter 8: Confidence Traps

- Overconfidence breeds carelessness.
- Optimism and confidence are good in moderation.
- Failing to recognize confidence traps prevents you from working to correct them.
- "I don't know" is an acceptable admission.
- Believing you are above average does not mean you are.
- Life is not fair; get used to it.
- Handle routine matters in a routine manner.

Chapter 9: Change Traps

- Today is the tomorrow you worried about yesterday.
- Life is change, growth is optional. Learn to adapt.
- Failing to recognize change traps prevents you from working to correct them.

- Watch what they do, not what they say.
- Understand reality as it exists, not as you want it to be.
- Tomorrow is another day. But what about the day after tomorrow?
- Manage delay like you manage everything else.
- You can't roller skate in a buffalo herd.
- Change comes at a cost.

Chapter 10: Maturity Traps

- Maturity is the art of the long-view.
- To curb impulsiveness—think twice, act once.
- Failing to recognize maturity traps prevents you from working to correct them.
- Be careful what you wish for because you just might get it.
- Self-discipline is doing what you have to do, whether you feel like it or not.
- The ability to delay gratification is a key factor for success.
- Don't get bitter, get busy.
- If you do not control events, events will control you.

Chapter 11: Who You Marry

- Marriage is a financial as well as a romantic union.
- Make sure that your best man is not the tax man.
- If you cohabitate, avoid joint ownership of assets.
- Divorce has significant short-term and long-term consequences.
- Don't get married because you want to get out of a bad situation.
- Objectively discuss money management before matrimony.
- Don't waste your time, energy, and reputation marrying for money.
- Try to marry within one academic degree.
- Marriage is not for the fickle.
- Cohabitating works if you are serious about marriage.
- If you are not compatible, fold your tent as early as possible.
- For better or for worse, your spouse is your financial partner.

Chapter 12: Number of Children

- Pregnancy is like an omelet: the chicken is involved but the ham is committed.
- Kids are bad investments with big returns.
- You cannot walk away from your obligations because they are now inconvenient.
- Each child costs the equivalent of a house to raise.
- Children don't come with a manual.
- Loving one's children and loving parenting are not the same thing.
- Don't trade a few hours of fun for a lifetime of regret.

- What is the point of having kids if you cannot engage them?
- Fertility is a joint decision. Copulate carefully.
- Kids are imperfect choices with uncertain outcomes.
- Never do three things mindlessly: get married, have children, get divorced.

Chapter 13: Level of Education

- Education is your passport to opportunity.
- Yes, it still pays to get a college degree.
- Some form of postsecondary education is a must.
- A four-year college degree is not for everyone.
- Don't let college be where your dreams are put on hold!
- Intelligence is not determined by level of education.
- Payment of tuition does not guarantee you a job.
- Follow your heart, not the money.
- If we are all Super Heroes, then no one is super.
- If you think education is expensive, try ignorance.
- Heavy debt and no degree = disaster.
- Make sure your degree is worth the cost.
- A university degree no longer confers financial security.

Chapter 14: Where You Live

- While you were sleeping, the world has changed.
- Place affects all aspects of your life.
- Living on your own costs more than you think.
- Check the selection criteria behind those "Top 10" rankings.
- Places, like people, have personalities.
- Find a place that is the right fit for you.
- The death of distance has been greatly exaggerated.
- You are where you live.
- High paying jobs are clustering.
- Experience the world while you are young.
- Live where you want to, not where you have to.
- If you don't like the neighbors (or the job), move!

Chapter 15: Choice of Lifestyle

- Keep your dreams lubricated.
- If you are young, in time you will be old. Those who are old were once young.
- Keys to success: become educated and work hard.
- Want to be less materialistic? Turn off the TV.
- Don't let the "slo-mos" catch you napping!
- Don't let peers hijack your common sense.
- Facebook is only a tool—face-to-face is reality!

- Google never forgets.
- On-line privacy control is your responsibility.
- Reputation matters.
- Early investments in healthy life-choices will have a large payoff as you age.
- Don't count on genes to compensate for poor lifestyle habits.
- Instead of looking to others to change your mind, why not change it yourself?

Chapter 16: Improving Our Decisions

- Ultimately, the choices you make are your responsibility.
- Be suitably prepared when an important decision is required.
- A reasoning mind is the key to achievement.
- The "optimum" is the enemy of the "good."
- Minor sustained biases can generate large cumulative losses.
- Luck is the intersection of preparation and opportunity.
- Practical experience cultivates the kernel of intuition.
- Trust your gut. You will make better decisions consistently.
- If you lack experience, always test your hunches.
- Experience is inevitable, learning is not.
- Always ask the question, "What is the cost?"

Chapter 17: Tapping Tribal Elders

- Smart people do dumb-ass things too.
- Acquire nuggets of wisdom from others.
- Our beliefs are our reality.
- People are often in error but never in doubt.
- Focus on the future. You cannot change the past.
- To be successful requires effort and commitment.
- To acquire wisdom, listen and try to understand all that you hear.

Chapter 18: Yes You Will!

- Passions say "Indulge!" Impartial spectator says, "Not so fast!"
- Wisdom is anticipating the consequences.
- Any desire for the ends must include the means.
- Stop believing your own lies.
- Developing common sense requires discipline.
- Critical thinking focuses on judgment and interpretation.
- Some let it happen; some make it happen; others wonder what happened.
- Keep calm. Carry on. Get 'er done.

Appendix A: What Tribal Elders Need to Know

- NeXters turn first to tribal elders for financial advice.
- The 4th "R" in education: reading, 'riting, 'rithmetic, and real world.
- If you don't get it, they won't either.
- They often know what to do; they just don't do it.
- Some Boomers choose to continue working. Many have no choice.
- Your kids will forget everything but the gists.
- Hit 'em while they're hot.
- High expectations bring high results!
- Be an ally in your children's success.
- The wisdom contained here is of permanent importance.

Appendix D.2

Bottom Lines

Chapter 1: Who You Are

The bottom line:

- Generation NeXt is the largest U.S. consumer group ever.
- Gen NeXt is the smartest generation yet.
- The world-view of NeXters was shaped more by events than by parents.
- NeXters are close to their parents and value their advice on major decisions.

The bottom line:

- NeXters are often naïve—what you don't know you don't know can hurt you.
- Fear and anxiety about the unknown can lead to isolation and inaction.
- Virtually none of you will become rich and famous.
- Limited life-experiences can skew your thinking, usually in an adverse way.

Chapter 2: Defining the Problem

The bottom line:

- Your standard of living is projected to be less than that of your parents.
- Look in the glass: YOU are the problem (and the solution).
- You must take responsibility for your future success.
- Heed the warnings of others—no one will save you.

Chapter 3: How This Guide Can Help

The bottom line:

- Economics is the choice of allocating limited resources to unlimited wants.
- Personal behavioral economics looks at how our thinking influences our economic behavior.
- Preventing a problem is usually much less painful than fixing it.
- Develop the habit of thinking long-term versus short-term.

The bottom line:

- Many of your expectations will ultimately prove unrealistic.
- You cannot solve complex problems using simplistic solutions.
- Fear is a powerful motivator.
- Do something different today: THINK!

Chapter 4: The Path to Success

The bottom line:

- There are significant economic advantages to being young.
- Time is a young person's greatest advantage.
- Wisdom is the exercise of good judgment and prudence.
- Affluenza and narcissism are unhealthy, "me centered" values.

The bottom line:

- Personal economic servitude (Level 0): Gain control and become self-sufficient.
- Personal economic stability (Level 1): Make smart choices and avoid the lifebombs.
- Personal economic security (Level 2): Spend less than you earn and manage the difference.
- Personal economic success (Level 3): Know what's important and achieve your dreams.

Chapter 5: The Stakes are High

The bottom line:

- You will likely experience several speculative bubbles in your lifetime.
- Once everyone else is "doing it," resist the temptation to join.
- The 2008 financial system meltdown was a valuable life-lesson.
- The stakes are high for Generation NeXt.

The bottom line:

- Thanks to AARP, today is the "golden age" of benefits for retirees.
- Companies have shifted responsibility for retirement funding to you.
- There is a fiscal train wreck headed straight for Generation NeXt.
- You need to be worried—it is hell being old and poor.

The bottom line:

- Americans and their government are drowning in debt.
- Generation NeXt faces serious personal economics challenges.
- Young persons do not understand the impending risk to their future.
- There is a disturbing lack of urgency to act on the problem.

The bottom line:

- To be ignorant is to lack knowledge or education (clueless).
- To be inept is to lack competence or motivation (careless).
- Young women and minorities are at particular risk.
- The future is out there . . . somewhere.

Chapter 6: How Risk Develops

The bottom line:

- Risk varies from person to person.
- The use of heuristics simplifies decision-making.
- Bias increases the risk of an adverse outcome.
- Rules of thumb do not always work.

The bottom line:

- A bad Type 1 or Type 2 decision is an irritant.
- A bad Type 3 decision gambles your future.
- A bad Type 4 decision can ruin your life.
- Risk rises with increasing probability and consequence.

The bottom line:

- Ignorance and ineptitude are mental weaknesses that set cognitive traps.
- Cognitive traps are questionable beliefs (mental fallibilities).
- Immature judgment leads to bad decisions, risky behaviors, and unintended consequences.
- Lifebombs are trap thinking, put into action.

The bottom line:

- People often have only a vague idea of the risks they face.
- Emotions and rules of thumb are frequently used to assess risk.
- Your perception of risk does not necessarily represent reality.
- No one can protect you from yourself.

The bottom line:

- Social class depends largely on your education, personal income, and job role.
- Statistics answers the question, "How likely is it that I will . . . ?"
- Possibility does not mean not probability.
- The rich are governed by a different set of rules from most Americans.

The bottom line:

- There is a 97–99 percent probability you will be middle class or below.
- Growth in middle class family income came from adding a second earner.
- The middle class is getting squeezed.
- Education is the single most important factor to improving earnings.

Chapter 7: Where Mistakes Originate

The bottom line:

- We often hold questionable beliefs despite clear evidence they might be harmful.
- A meme is cultural information that replicates in the mind like genes in the body.
- Technology vastly multiplies the reach and potency of memes.
- Memes influence what we know and how we behave.

The bottom line:

- Mistakes originate from ignorance and ineptitude (our mental weaknesses).
- "Knows-that" represents specific information about something.
- "Knows-how" represents practical expertise and skills.
- All of us might, at any time, be wrong.

The bottom line

- *Ignorance* is not knowing things we should know (lack of knowledge).
- *Ineptitude* is misapplying things we know (lack of wisdom).
- Cognitive flaws are destructive because they lead to self-deceptions.
- Things we know that just ain't so are the most troublesome unknowns.

The bottom line

- An attitude is a like or a dislike directed toward a specific thing.
- Attitudes are influenced by memes, other people, and direct life experiences.
- People often fail to realize that their attitude has changed.
- Young persons resemble their times more than they resemble their parents.

Chapter 8: Overconfidence Traps

The bottom line:

- The way you think influences your level of confidence.
- Positive thinking eliminates negative thoughts and emotions.
- Optimism is a positive attitude that hopes for the best.
- Confidence is how much you value yourself.

The bottom line:

- *Confidence traps*: ways of thinking that reflect a cocksure attitude.
- *Optimism trap:* a tendency to see overly rosy futures (they aren't).
- *Superiority trap:* a tendency to see yourself as better than average (half of you aren't).
- People rarely recognize their susceptibility to these traps.

The bottom line:

- You are not as unique as you (or your parents) think you are.
- Make sure your level of confidence is based on objective evidence.
- Many Gen NeXters are worried about their future (but don't want to admit it).
- Generation NeXt is really, really stressed out.

Chapter 9: Change Traps

The bottom line:

- Change is the product of instability and is ubiquitous.
- "Changeability" is how different and complex the future is from today.
- "Predictability" is the speed of change and how clear the future is.
- Globalization and technology advancement are the primary drivers of change.

The bottom line:

- *Change traps:* ways of thinking that reflect our preference to not "rock the boat."
- *Framing trap:* a failure to correctly interpret the context of a situation.
- Our preceptions are our realities.
- The rate of change is accelerating.

The bottom line:

- *Inertia trap:* an unwillingness to change.
- Mental inertia avoids having to change one's way of doing things.
- Procrastination is a common delaying tactic that makes us feel better.
- Herd instinct alleges, "If many believe it is so, then it is so."

Chapter 10: Maturity Traps

The bottom line:

- Mature decision-makers are prone to long-range thinking.
- To master the art of the long-view, supplant emotions with facts and reason.
- Impulsive behavior might not be your fault (but you still own the consequences).
- Reasoning and judgment capabilities are "works-in-progress" through age 25.

The bottom line:

- *Maturity traps:* ways of thinking about time that can adversely influence choice.
- *Projection trap:* a failure to accurately predict one's future preferences.
- Youth are more susceptible to the projection trap than adults.
- Compartmentalizing isolates decisions, blinding us to key interdependencies.

The bottom line:

- *Self-control trap:* a failure to control one's impatience and impulsiveness.
- "Discounting" means things in front of us now are worth more than things far away in time.
- We buy more, eat more, and save less tomorrow than we wish our tomorrow selves to do.
- Use commitment devices to resist immediate gratification.

The bottom line:

- Two worrisome megatrends are an aging population and the impending Baby Boomer retirement.
- The federal government will need to renegotiate the social promises it has made.
- Many Boomers are worried about outliving their money in retirement.
- You may have to provide for your parents in their golden years.

Chapter 11: Who You Marry

The bottom line:

- A civil marriage is one performed by an official (mayor, judge, peace officer, etc.).
- States allow religious marriage ceremonies to double as civil marriages.
- The national divorce rate has declined slightly but is still unacceptably high.
- Those in good marriages tend to have a better quality of life.

The bottom line:

- The #1 reason cited for a failed marriage is problems with money.
- Getting married may have significant tax implications.
- There may be legal ramifications if you cohabitate and break up.
- Many young persons fail to appreciate the trauma of divorce.

The bottom line:

- Women are becoming less dependent upon men or the institution of marriage.
- For blue collar men, the pool of available women for marriage is shrinking.
- Starter marriages encourage a lack of commitment and responsibility to the relationship.
- Cohabitation works for women who cohabited only with their eventual husbands.

Chapter 12: Number of Children

The bottom line:

- Once you have a child, your life will never be the same.
- Children bring many positive intangible benefits.
- Smart companies are increasingly accommodating working mothers.
- Society derives significant benefits from parents' investments in their children.

The bottom line:

- The best determining factor for having children is whether you are emotionally ready.
- Having too many children too soon is the #1 reason most people will never have any money.
- There are huge direct, personal, and opportunity costs to having children.
- No matter how hard you try, your children may disappoint you.

The bottom line:

- Couples are waiting longer to have children and more women are opting out.
- The number of single-parent, one child, and childless families is increasing.
- The main purpose of marriage is now seen as happiness and fulfillment, not child raising.
- No matter how strong your marriage, you *must* be prepared to raise the child by yourself.

Chapter 13: Level of Education

The bottom line:

- Higher education is a wise investment for most young persons.
- Yesterday's high school diploma is today's bachelor's degree.
- College can help you find yourself, earn more, and live better.
- Having a degree can lower you car insurance premiums.

The bottom line:

- Four years in high school, followed by four-years full-time in college, is your best bet.
- "Do you have a degree or not?" does not measure if you have the skills required.
- CTE offers rewarding careers, good-paying jobs, and college opportunities.
- Only one-quarter of young persons between 25 and 34 have a bachelor's degree.

The bottom line:
- A college education is what you make of it.
- In the school of hard knocks they give the test first, then the lesson.
- Overall, the bar has been lowered regarding academic rigor.
- Women and veterans are changing the college landscape.

The bottom line:
- Many young persons are not academically prepared for college.
- Since 1982, the cost of attending college has risen 3X faster than average family income.
- More than half of all students don't end up in a career directly related to their major.
- Employers are looking for experience as well as education.

Chapter 14: Where You Live

The bottom line:
- Where you live matters.
- Areas with large numbers of singles attract other singles.
- NeXters want to live where they can best "be themselves."
- Urban areas offer the best opportunities for young persons.

The bottom line:
- Where you live makes a big difference on the bottom line.
- Areas that pay high salaries often have lower quality of life.
- High paying industries are clustering worldwide.
- People are happier when their personality matches that of the region they live.

The bottom line:
- Don't be afraid to move where the opportunities are.
- Balance competing factors before deciding which city is the best fit.
- There is much more to telecommuting than just being connected.
- Where you choose to live can have adverse long-term health effects.

The bottom line:
- Americans are increasingly divided by income and the kind of work they do.
- Creative class jobs are clustering geographically.
- Youth have greater mobility than any other age group.
- Happiness comes from having relative wealth and meaningful relationships.

Chapter 15: Choice of Lifestyle

The bottom line:

- For many, the American Dream has shifted toward material happiness.
- Life expectancy is a group statistical average; half of you will live longer.
- Longevity—how long you will actually live—is what counts.
- The number of centenarians in the U.S. is dramatically increasing.

The bottom line:

- What you see on television is not representative of the wealthy.
- Wealthy people take responsibility for their own success.
- Advertisers control the vertical and the horizontal—learn to immunize yourself.
- Longevity risk means your old-age safety net may be full of holes.

The bottom line:

- Generally, young persons are more likely than adults over 25 to engage in risky behaviors.
- To make better lifestyle decisions, understand the gist of the situation.
- Most threats to your well-being are self-inflicted.
- Facebook friends should be supplements, not surrogates to your social lives.

The bottom line:

- While our tools change quickly, basic human nature adjusts at a slower pace.
- What happens in Vegas doesn't stay in Vegas; not if you go posting, tweeting, and blogging about it.
- 70–80 percent of your lifespan depends upon your lifestyle choices.
- Education and good habits may be the most powerful factors in living a longer and healthier life.

Chapter 16: Improving Our Decisions

The bottom line:

- Your life is the sum of all your choices.
- Good decision-making is a skill that can be learned and improved.
- The quality of a decision is not the same as the quality of the outcome.
- The decision-making style that works for your friends may not work for you.

The bottom line:

- Most people are much poorer at decision-making than they think.
- Bad life-choices are not fixed by hitting the "undo" button.
- Young persons are quick to recognize bias in others but not themselves.
- Luck is not always the residue of design.

The bottom line:

- Good intuitive decision-making is learned through an accumulation of experience.
- Gut-feel is a subtle physical sense that something is right or wrong.
- Our intuition can handle more complexity than our conscious minds.
- Most everyday decisions are intuitive.

The bottom line:

- Separate the vital few decisions from the trivial many decisions.
- Learn to distinguish situations in which you can rely on intuition.
- The more complex the decision, the more we benefit from using gists.
- Gists rely on past experiences and manifest themselves as gut-feelings.

Chapter 17: Tapping Tribal Elders

The bottom line:

- Emotionally biased thinking ("truthiness") overpowers logic.
- Confirmation bias causes us to seek evidence that we are right not wrong.
- The hardest to convince they are wrong are often the ones who are the most misinformed.
- Tribal elders can be a valuable source of wisdom, but only if you tap them.

The bottom line:

- "Feedforward" solicits positive suggestions for future improvement.
- Unlike feedback, feedforward is viewed as a helpful hand up.
- Mentors are wise and trusted counselors and teachers, not coaches.
- Taking a tribal elder's perspective can help you more impartially accept their advice.

Chapter 18: Yes You Can

The bottom line:

- The impartial spectator provides a realistic view of your own ability and prospects.
- Wisdom is the application of common sense and good judgment to things that matter.
- Questionable beliefs and risky behaviors arise from fuzzy thinking.
- Nothing is so firmly believed as that which least is known.

The bottom line:

- Common sense helps prevent you from making irrational mistakes.
- Developing good common sense requires life-long discipline and practice.
- Our cognitive traps (biases) can override your common sense.
- Maturity is the ability not to see the world as absolutes, but shades of gray.

The bottom line:

- Be skeptical regarding what you hear and read.
- Move toward a questioning approach to knowledge and self-reflection.
- Investigate competing evidence and challenge your beliefs.
- Critical thinking must be systematically cultivated as a life-long endeavor.

The bottom line:

- It is more empowering if you think of responsibility as the "ability to respond."
- The world arrives where logic resides (after taking a few detours).
- The only mind you control is your own.
- Don't cheat the person in the glass.

The bottom line:

- Young persons are very concerned with the prospect of failure.
- We learn wisdom from failure much more than from success.
- Explaining a situation to another person can help you clarify it in your own mind.
- Save yourself some painful scars by learning from the mistakes of others.

The bottom, bottom line:

- Today is already the tomorrow, which was shaped by your decisions of yesterday.
- Poor decisions can be costly, both in money and in quality of life.
- You alone are responsible for your long-term success.
- It's later than you think. Just do it.

Appendix A – What Tribal Elders Need to Know

The bottom line:

- Tribal elders are the most trusted source of financial advice for Gen NeXters.
- Many young persons have been insulated from financial reality by their parents.
- The world that tribal elders knew, understood, and controlled is changing.
- Many NeXters are intellectually disengaged regarding personal economics.

The bottom line:

- Many tribal elders did not plan for an extended retirement.
- Boomers and post-Boomers are facing a retirement crisis.
- The Social Security crisis is every person's crisis.
- The rules have changed.

The bottom, bottom line:

- Read the guide. Let your kids read it. Start the conversation.
- Gists and touch-points represent great learning opportunities—use them.
- Have your kids formulate the habit of tapping the wisdom of tribal elders.
- Do not sacrifice your own financial plans to support your adult children.

Appendix E

Epistemological Underpinnings

He who loves practice without theory is like the sailor who boards ship without a rudder and compass and never knows where he may cast.
~ Leonardo da Vinci, artist, inventor, scientist

The Gist

The Good:

- Theory allows us to make sense of our world
- Understanding theory is not necessary to benefit from the *Guide*

The Bad:

- NeXters underestimate the influence of today's decisions on their future
- Clueless: not knowing reality and risk as they exist before deciding
- Careless: not understanding one's limitations before deciding

The Reality:

- Mature judgment is important for personal economics success
- Knowledge and awareness help compensate for lack of experience
- A "world-wise" education is important to making smart choices
- Tribal elders must pro-actively coach, motivate, and communicate
- Who cuts their slice of the pie? THEY DO!

Introduction

We all agree that your theory is crazy. The question which divides us is whether it is crazy enough.

~ Niels Bohr, Danish physicist to Wolfgang Pauli

YOUNG PERSON'S ALERT: THIS SECTION IS BORING!
PROCEED AT YOUR OWN RISK!

In common usage, people often use the word *theory* to signify a conjecture, an opinion, or a speculation about the world. Not necessarily based on facts, our theories represent what we think, not necessarily what we know. We use them to make choices in life.

In science, most fields are based on a foundation of knowledge that originates from practical experience and experiment. *Deterministic* sciences are fields such as math, chemistry, and many branches of physics. These "hard" sciences typically deal with tidy and predictable phenomena, with definitive outcomes. For example, 1+1=2, the double-helix of a DNA molecule, $E=MC^2$, and if you grill a hot dog, it always gets warmer not cooler. There is much to admire about the progress made in the hard sciences, where theories provide the basis for predictable results.

Probabilistic sciences, on the other hand, deal mainly with the messy, complex, and uncertain phenomena characteristic of the social sciences. Referred to as "soft" sciences, these include fields like psychology, economics, and medicine. Social scientists are generally more familiar than their deterministic cousins with how easy it is to be misled by the evidence of everyday experience. If psychology, for example, was an exact science, theories of human behavior would be obvious. And that would make poker players and Don Juans very unhappy!

A theory is also used to model reality. In this respect, it may be a pattern, plan, representation, or description. Picture a model of the atom, a highway map, a photograph, our Constitution, or even a love poem. All are models (that is, "theories") of reality. Here the word theory emphasizes a logically unified framework, generalization, or explanation of what is observed, and its meaning varies depending on the field. To construct a decision model for personal behavioral economics, we need not re-invent the wheel. We'll tap some theories of other smart cookies (besides us) and apply what is relevant to suit our purposes. Figure E.1 (page 513) shows a comparison of decision models.

The 'What'

In making theories, always keep a window open so that you can throw one out if necessary.

~ Bela Lugosi, horror film actor (*Dracula*)

1. Hsee, Christopher and Hastie, Reid (2006). *Decision and Experience: Why Don't We Choose What Makes Us Happy?*, Trends in Cognitive Sciences, Vol. 10, No. 1, pp. 31–37.

People systematically fail to choose optimally and maximize their happiness because of two factors: (i) the failure to accurately predict their future experience; and (ii) the failure to follow their predictions:

- *Failure to accurately predict the future experience.* Behavioral-decision researchers have identified a number of systematic biases that account for the failure to predict the future experience. They arise because prediction and experience occur in different states, but the predictor fails to appreciate the difference.
- *Failure to follow predictions.* A major cause of sub-optimal decisions is impulsivity—the choice of an immediately gratifying option at the cost of long-term happiness. When situations involve a short-term/long-term tradeoff, people do not choose what they predict will generate the greatest overall happiness.

2. O'Donoghue, Ted and Rabin, Matthew (2000). *Risky Behavior Among Youths: Some Issues from Behavioral Economics*, Institute of Business and Economic Research, Department of Economics, University of California, Berkeley.

Youths fail to behave in their best interests and for the most part remain agnostic about what those interests are. By and large, risky behaviors involve a trade-off between short-term benefits and long-term costs:

- Adolescents are similar to adults in terms of their ability to carry out the decision-making process. Youths, however, do not react optimally to intrinsic costs and benefits they face.
- Youths are more impatient than adults and have a time-inconsistent preference for immediate gratification. Such preferences imply a self-control problem where they are unable on a moment-by-moment basis to behave in their own long-term best interest.
- Young adults suffer from projection bias, which predicts that youths will under estimate how much their preferences will change as they age.
- Youths do not feel a greater sense of invulnerability than adults. In some ways they are overly pessimistic about their future.

3. Cauffman, Elizabeth (1999). *Adolescence Decision Making: Implications for Prevention Programs; The Decision-Making Framework*, from Summary of a Workshop,

Baruch Fischhoff, Nancy A. Crowell, and Michele Kipke, Ed., National Academy Press, Washington, D.C.

Level of maturity of judgment is a factor that may influence the decisions adolescents make. The less mature a young person is, the more likely that he or she will choose a less 'responsible' option (such as shoplifting, smoking marijuana, etc). Maturity of judgment encompasses three dimensions:

1. Responsibility—being self-reliant and having a healthy sense of autonomy
2. Perspective—taking the long-term view and concern for others
3. Temperance—being able to limit impulsivity and exercise self-control.

4. Hazlitt, Henry (1979). *Economics in One Lesson*, Crown Publishers, New York.

Today is already the tomorrow, which the bad economist yesterday urged us to ignore. The art of economics consists in looking not merely at the immediate but the longer effects of any act or policy. It consists in tracing the consequences of that policy not merely for one group but for all groups. A fallacy is something that is believed to be truth but is erroneous. Nine-tenths of harmful economic policies stem from two central fallacies:

1. Looking only at the immediate consequences of an act or proposal
2. Looking at the consequences only for a particular group to the neglect of other groups.

The 'How'

There goes another beautiful theory about to be murdered by a brutal gang of facts.

~ Duc de La Rochefoucauld, 17th century author

1. Reyna, Valerie F. and Farley, Frank (2006). *Risk and Rationality in Adolescent Decision Making*, Psychological Science in the Public Interest, Vol. 7, No. 1, pp. 1–44.

Fuzzy-trace theory (FTT) focuses on decision making, why adolescents make the (some-times bad) decisions they make, and how interventions may be better designed to steer young people toward better choices:

- Compared to adults, adolescents lack relevant experience to adequately recognize the risk of long-term consequences.
- Adolescents behave more impulsively than adults, reacting to immediate temptations without rational deliberation. They discount future rewards more heavily than do adults.

- Rather than deliberative and analytical, FTT is unconscious and intuitive. The goal is to make gist-based decisions automatic and non-deliberative and discourage risk tradeoffs.

2. Levin, Irwin, Schneider, Sandra, and Gaeth, Gary (1998). *All Frames Are Not Created Equal: A Typology and Critical Analysis of Framing Effects,* Organizational Behavior and Human Decision Processes, Vol. 76, No. 2, November, pp. 149–188.

The framing of a goal affects the persuasiveness of the communication. Which is more effective in influencing people's behavior—manipulating (framing) a situation to accentuate the positive or the negative?

- The impact of a persuasive message depends on whether the message stresses either the positive or the negative consequences of performing an act.
- In goal framing, a negatively framed message that emphasizes losses tends to have a greater impact on a given behavior than a comparable positively framed message that emphasizes gains.
- The effect may disappear or reverse for situations in which it is relatively easy to discount the negative frame in order to avoid facing adverse possibilities. This may happen with low involvement or low cognitive effort expended by participants.

3. Gahran, Brian (2003). *Expertise in Using Experts–A Study of Manager-Expert Strategic Decision Behavior,* doctoral dissertation, Alliant International University, ProQuest, http://www.proquest.com/en-US/products/dissertations.

How does a lay person manager evaluate the value and contribution of a technical expert, without being able to understand the contribution in detail? Key elements:

- Individual capability is comprised of one's success mentality, knowledge, talents, interpersonal skills, and capacity to perform the task.
- The expert's contribution ranges from simply a source of information to co-managing the firm's strategy formulation and implementation.
- Experts need to be calibrated in order to evaluate their credibility.

Application to Young Person's Guide

An ounce of action is worth a ton of theory.
~ Friedrich Engels, social scientist

Personal economics

Today is the product of all of your previous decisions. Young persons are prone to two principal flaws or "mental weaknesses," which can lead to questionable beliefs ("cognitive traps") and immature judgment:

- Not understanding reality as it exists before acting ("ignorance traps").
- Not knowing one's limitations in exercising care ("ineptitude traps").
- The art of achieving personal economics stability consists in understanding reality and risk as absolutes, knowing one's limitations, and developing the skills to make smart choices.

Young persons

Young persons think they know their own preferences and that what they choose is in their best interests. Unfortunately, they often lack the experience and wisdom to make good personal economics decisions. Key factors:

- *Naïve perspective.* Young persons underestimate the influence that today's choices will have on their long-term well-being.
- *Education is critical.* Many NeXters do not know what they do not know (but should) and fail to appreciate the risk inherent in what they know (that just ain't so).
- *The enemy within.* Young persons need to be aware of their own questionable beliefs and be receptive to other points of view.
- *The value of gists.* The use of gists can help reduce risk until a young person is developmentally better prepared.
- *The wisdom of tribal elders.* Counsel by trusted adults and advisors can help young persons make sense of the complexities of modern society.

Tribal elders

Young persons need to develop power over an unpredictable future. This power comes from understanding the reality of their world, being aware of their own limitations, and choosing wisely. Most young persons will make the controllable life-choices described in this book; if not made wisely, the consequences can be costly. What can you do?

- *Get their attention.* Young persons lack appreciation of the need to know. This shows up as a lack of desire to engage. Raise perceptions about linkages between their thinking and bad outcomes. Help them to be accountable for their future.
- *Provide a trusted "voice of experience."* Help young persons improve their perception of reality, successfully manage personal inflection points, and anticipate and avoid lifebombs (bad outcomes).
- *Be a coach.* Communicate the essence (gist) of the message, motivate young persons to improve their decision-making skills, and develop a sense of urgency.
- *Educate young persons.* Develop reasoned, facts-based arguments to educate young persons on the past, present, and future economic environment.
- *Develop and share gists:*

§ Emphasize personal economic risks associated with cognitive traps.

§ Provide an intuitive understanding of the potential long-term consequences of making bad life-choices.

§ Reinforce the long-term consequences of healthy behaviors (via positive images), and unhealthy behaviors (via negative images) through emotionally evocative testimonials.

Perspective	Macro	Micro			
Author	Hazlitt (1946)	Cauffman (1999)	O'Donoghue & Rabin (2000)	Hsee & Hastie (2006)	Gahran (2012)
Decision Factor #1	Looking at the consequences only for one particular group to the neglect of other groups	Take the long-term view and have concern for others (*perspective bias*)	Underappreciate how much preferences will change over time (*projection bias*)	Failing to accurately predict the future experience (*prediction biases*)	Not understanding reality as it exists (*ignorance traps*)
Decision Factor #2	Looking only at the immediate versus the long-term consequences	Limit impulsivity and exercise self-control (*temperance*)	Time inconsistent preference for immediate gratification (*self-control problem*)	Focusing on the greatest immediate appeal (*not following predictions*)	Not knowing one's limitations (*ineptitude traps*)
Decision 'Good'	Greater community economic benefit	Judgment maturity	Long-run well-being	Overall personal happiness	Overall personal economic success

Figure E.1 Comparison of decision models.

Postscript

Never worry about theory as long as the machinery does what it's supposed to do.
~ Robert A. Heinlein, science fiction writer

Theory, like the law, provides us with a framework to guide how we respond to our environment. No new captain would dare set sail without first getting the scuttlebutt[362] from another who had previously made the voyage. But a young person does not need to understand how the ride at Disneyland works or how sausage is made in order to benefit from the experience. Ultimately, it is common sense, critical thinking, and sound reasoning—the skills that our nation's judges use every day—that will best equip Generation NeXt to succeed in a complicated and changing world.

362 A nautical term for unverified information that is passed informally.

Appendix F

Where to Go for More Info

Online at: www.YPGBlog.com

Acknowledgements

The author gratefully acknowledges the contribution of Mr. Thomas A. Crescenzo, former economics professor, Southwestern College, whose original concepts provided inspiration for this book. Some of the proceeds from this book will be donated to the Thomas A. Crescenzo Memorial Scholarship Fund to help young persons better understand how to succeed in life.

I am especially indebted to mentors ADM Hyman G. Rickover, the father of the nuclear submarine, Dr. H. Igor Ansoff, the father of strategic management, and Dr. Patrick Sullivan, Professor Emeritus, for their demanding standards and disciplined approach. The overriding life-lesson I learned is details matter.

Special thanks to my editor, Dr. Robert Goodman of Silvercat Written and Printed Communication Services, my brother Chris of Chris Gahran and Associates Photography, and Karl Meimer of Utterly Creative Web Design for their sage wisdom and selfless contributions. I could not have done it without you.

To Dan (Dad) DeCarlo, teacher and inspiration to more than two generations of young minds to achieve their best, thank you for keeping the faith. To the many other family and friends who provided encouragement along the journey—you know who you are—thank you.

From the Author

Thank you for buying my book.

I am a writer, teacher, and mentor to young persons. I have worked in a variety of "career-enhancing" positions including software entrepreneur, nuclear submariner, information security consultant, grille man, geek professor, physicist, ski bum, librarian, chief flour engineer, and all around nuisance at home. I have a doctorate in Strategic Management from United States International University and an undergraduate degree in Physics from Florida Institute of Technology. I am proud to be a Chi Phi and an Eagle Scout.

My passion, discovered later in life, is observing human behavior at the crossroads of psychology and personal economics. My goal is to help you, ordinary Joe or Jane Youngperson, develop power over an unpredictable future. This requires that I be part economist, psychologist, strategist, and futurist. I don't claim to be an expert but that isn't what matters. What matters is opening your minds, exposing you to things you might not have yet considered, and stimulating you to think. None of us can predict the future—my aim is to prevent you from getting the future seriously wrong.

Many young persons acknowledge the importance of life-choices and the seriousness of their consequences—and then put them out of their mind. It's simply easier to put on blinders and believe everything will work out than to confront the complexities of modern life. I suggest it is better to be aware of potential problems than not. Search engines find the dots; this book connects them so you can apply it to your life. Think of it as the connective tissue between problems and answers. Sure, there are always exceptions and other points of view, so don't take anything as an insult because you happen to agree or disagree with what I say. Find a path that works for you.

Happiness, to paraphrase the Samuel Johnson adage, is the victory of hope over experience. But experience is a "lantern on the stern," which shines only on the waves behind us. Today, young persons are looking for a navigator, not a street directory to help them succeed—specific guidance from someone who knows them, their situation, and has traveled that way himself. Tribal elders have what I call "wrinkle wisdom," and can provide you with a sense of the real-world agenda. Learning life's lessons the hard way, need not be the only way!

The bottom line: success in life requires a realistic outlook. Understanding reality as it exists, recognizing how and why we form questionable beliefs, and being aware of how and when to question—these are among the most important elements that constitute personal power over an unpredictable future. Like the flower to the seed, the unintended consequences of tomorrow can be traced back to the decisions you make today. This compels us to look in the glass and ask, "In what ways are the seeds of my future success (failure) already with me?"

Making smart life-choices. Yep, that's what it's all about. Get 'er done.

Brian Gahran
www.YPGBlog.com

38670407R00291

Made in the USA
San Bernardino, CA
10 September 2016